TRADIVOX

VOLUME XIII

TRADIVOX

CATHOLIC CATECHISM INDEX

VOLUME XIII

Jean-Joseph Gaume

Edited by
Aaron Seng

SOPHIA INSTITUTE PRESS
MANCHESTER, NEW HAMPSHIRE

South Bend, Indiana
www.Tradivox.com

This book is an original derivative work comprised of newly typeset and reformatted editions of the following Catholic catechisms, once issued with ecclesiastical approval and now found in the public domain:

Gaume, Jean-Joseph. *The Catechism of Perseverance.* 2nd English ed., translated from the 10th French ed. Vol. 4. Dublin: M. H. Gill & Son, 1884.

Scripture references follow the Douay-Rheims Bible, per the imprint of John Murphy Company (Baltimore, 1899).

Cover and interior design by Perceptions Design Studio.

Sophia Institute Press
Box 5284, Manchester, NH 03108
1-800-888-9344

www.SophiaInstitute.com

ISBN 978-1-64413-374-3

LCCN: 2022949642

Dedicated with love and deepest respect
to all the English Martyrs and Confessors.
Orate pro nobis.

CONTENTS

ACKNOWLEDGMENTS

THE publication of this series is due primarily to the generosity of countless volunteers and donors from several countries. Special thanks are owed to Mr. and Mrs. Phil Seng, Mr. and Mrs. Michael Over, Mr. and Mrs. Jim McElwee, Mr. and Mrs. John Brouillette, Mr. and Mrs. Thomas Scheibelhut, Mr. and Mrs. Kyle Barriger, as well the visionary priests and faithful of St. Stanislaus Bishop and Martyr parish in South Bend, Indiana, and St. Patrick's Oratory in Green Bay, Wisconsin. May God richly reward their commitment to handing on the Catholic faith.

FOREWORD

The Catholic faith remains always the same throughout the centuries and millennia until the coming of our Lord at the end of the time, likewise "Jesus Christ is the same yesterday, today and forever" (Heb 13:8). The Catholic faith is "the faith, which was once delivered unto the saints" (Jude 1:3). The Magisterium of the Church teaches us solemnly the same truth in the following words of the First Vatican Council: "The doctrine of the faith which God has revealed, is put forward not as some philosophical discovery capable of being perfected by human intelligence, but as a divine deposit committed to the spouse of Christ to be faithfully protected and infallibly promulgated. Hence, too, that meaning of the sacred dogmas is ever to be maintained, which has once been declared by holy mother Church, and there must never be any abandonment of this sense under the pretext or in the name of a more profound understanding. May understanding, knowledge and wisdom increase as ages and centuries roll along, and greatly and vigorously flourish, in each and all, in the individual and the whole Church: but this only in its own proper kind, that is to say, in the same doctrine, the same sense, and the same understanding (cf. Vincentius Lerinensis, *Commonitorium*, 28)."[1]

An authentically Catholic catechism has the function of learning and teaching the unchanging Catholic faith throughout all generations. The Roman Pontiffs indeed, taught: "There is nothing more effective than catechetical instruction to spread the glory of God and to secure the salvation of souls."[2] Saint Pius X said, that "the great loss of souls is due to ignorance of divine things."[3] Therefore, the traditional catechisms have enduring value in our own day and age, which is marked by an enormous doctrinal confusion, which reigns in the life of the Church in the past six decades, and which reaches its peak in our days.

I welcome and bless the great project of the "Tradivox" in cataloguing and preserving the hundreds of long-lost Catholic catechisms issued with episcopal approval over the last millennium. This project will convincingly show the essentially unchanging nature of the apostolic doctrine across time and space, and so I invite the faithful of the entire world to support this historic effort, as we seek to restore the perennial catechism of the Church. The project of a catechism restoration on behalf of "Tradivox" will surely be of great benefit not only to many confused and disoriented Catholic faithful, but also to all people who are sincerely seeking the ultimate and authentic truth about God and man, which one can find only in the Catholic and apostolic faith, and which is the only religion and faith willed by God and to which God calls all men.

+Athanasius Schneider, O.R.C.,
Titular Bishop of Celerina
Auxiliary Bishop of the Archdiocese of Saint Mary in Astana

SERIES EDITOR'S PREFACE

SOME are surprised to find that when a given Catholic is asked to "look something up in the catechism," he may well respond: "Which one?" The history of the Catholic Church across the last millennium is in fact filled with the publication of numerous catechisms, issued in every major language on earth; and for centuries, these concise "guidebooks" to Catholic doctrine have served countless men and women seeking a clear and concise presentation of that faith forever entrusted by Jesus Christ to his one, holy, Catholic, and apostolic Church.

Taken together, the many catechisms issued with episcopal approval can offer a kind of "window" on to the universal ordinary magisterium—a glimpse of those truths which have been held and taught in the Church *everywhere, always, and by all*. For, as St. Paul reminds us, the tenets of this Faith do not change from age to age: "Jesus Christ yesterday and today and the same for ever. Be not led away with various and strange doctrines" (Heb 13:8-9).

The catechisms included in our *Tradivox Catholic Catechism Index* are selected for their orthodoxy and historical significance, in the interest of demonstrating to contemporary readers the remarkable continuity of Catholic doctrine across time and space. Long regarded as reliable summaries of Church teaching on matters of faith and morals, we are proud to reproduce these works of centuries past, composed and endorsed by countless priests, bishops, and popes devoted to "giving voice to tradition."

In This Volume

This volume contains the final installment of Abbé Gaume's monumental *Catechism of Perseverance*, which concerns itself with Catholic worship: its feasts and fasts, bells and blessings, vessels and vesture, signs and symbols, and all the many rites and ceremonies that are generally referred to today as "liturgy."

In our own pluralistic age that declares "freedom of worship" for all religions (or at least for those that civil authorities find agreeable), it is bracing to learn from Monsignor Gaume that "God did not wish that those pertaining to his worship should be left to caprice, to ignorance, to the passions of peoples and individuals," but rather "how necessary it was that God should regulate the external forms of religion." The remainder of his catechism springs from this central conviction.

> It is not true, therefore, as worldly levity would make out, that the external manner of honoring God is a thing indifferent and optional. Ceremonies, in order to be pleasing to God, must be introduced according to the prescriptions of God himself or his ministers. Hence, the rite.

One necessary conclusion of such divine influence regarding the establishment of the proper ceremonies for worship—those that are both "right and just," as the ancient Canon of the Roman Mass proclaims—is that every aspect of the Church's traditional worship must needs be imbued with profound meaning. From the rich ceremonies of the Roman Mass to the significance of various altar furnishings and other blessed objects, Gaume spends a great deal of time expounding upon precisely these meanings; for, indeed, "ceremonies are mysterious acts...like a thin veil that lets one have a glimpse of things purely spiritual."

Perhaps the most compelling aspect of this volume of the monsignor's catechism is its constant representation of the age-old axiom: *lex orandi, lex credendi*—"the law of prayer is the law of belief." As the author explains, external worship both contains and expresses the Catholic faith in its entirety, making the Christian's creed and his moral code manifest to the senses: "By external worship, the dogmas of faith and the precepts of morality are made sensible and even palpable to us: the fall of man, his redemption, his hopes of immortality, his duties, his dignity." For this same reason, Catholic rites are a constant pledge of right faith and a sure safeguard of orthodoxy:

> Hereby, our religion is secured from the caprice of innovators and the arbitrary interpretations of heretics. At all times, external worship has been brought forward to show to heretics the true doctrine of our Lord and the apostles.

Our only notable change to the current volume has been the addition of further descriptive text in the heading of each Lesson; otherwise, the current volume offers the *Catechism of Perseverance* body text from the second English edition of 1884 without change, in gratitude and intercession for its venerable author and his pupils across the years.

Editorial Note

Our *Catholic Catechism Index* series generally retains only the doctrinal content of those catechisms it seeks to reproduce, as well as that front matter most essential to establishing the credibility of each work as an authentic expression of the Church's common doctrine, e.g., any episcopal endorsement, *nihil obstat*, or *imprimatur*. However, it should be noted that especially prior to the eighteenth century, a number of catechisms were so immediately and universally received as reliably orthodox texts (often simply by the reputation of the author or publisher), that they received no such "official" approval; or if they did, it was often years later and in subsequent editions. We therefore include both the original printing date in our Table of Contents, and further edition information in the Preface above.

Our primary goal has been to bring these historical texts back into publication in readable English copy. Due to the wide range of time periods, cultures, and unique author styles represented in this series, we have made a number of editorial adjustments to allow for a less fatiguing read, more rapid cross-reference throughout the series, and greater research potential for the future. While not affecting the original content, these adjustments

Woodcut depicting an early method used in the production of Catholic catechisms, circa 1568.

have included adopting a cleaner typesetting and simpler standard for capitalization and annotation, as well as remedying certain anachronisms in spelling or grammar.

At the same time, in deepest respect for the venerable age and subject matter of these works, we have been at pains to adhere as closely as possible to the original text: retaining archaisms such as "doth" and "hallowed," and avoiding any alterations that might affect the doctrinal content or authorial voice. We have painstakingly restored original artwork wherever possible, and where the rare explanatory note has been deemed necessary, it is not made in the text itself, but only in a marginal note. In some cases, our editorial refusal to "modernize" the content of these classical works may require a higher degree of attention from today's reader, who we trust will be richly rewarded by the effort.

We pray that our work continues to yield highly readable, faithful reproductions of these time-honored monuments to Catholic religious instruction: catechisms once penned, promulgated, and praised by bishops across the globe. May these texts that once served to guide and shape the faith and lives of millions now do so again; and may the scholars and saints once involved in their first publication now intercede for all who take them up anew. *Tolle lege!*

Sincerely in Christ,
Aaron Seng

TRADIVOX

VOLUME XIII

THE

CATECHISM OF PERSEVERANCE;

OR,

AN HISTORICAL, DOGMATICAL, MORAL, LITURGICAL, APOLOGETICAL, PHILOSOPHICAL, AND SOCIAL EXPOSITION OF RELIGION,

FROM THE

BEGINNING OF THE WORLD DOWN TO OUR OWN DAYS.

BY MONSIGNOR GAUME,

APOSTOLIC PROTHONOTARY, DOCTOR IN THEOLOGY, VICAR-GENERAL OF MONTAUBAN AND AQUILA, KNIGHT OF THE ORDER OF ST. SYLVESTER, MEMBER OF THE ACADEMY OF THE CATHOLIC RELIGION (ROME), &c.

Jesus Christ, yesterday, and to-day; and the same for ever.—*Heb.* xiii. 8.
God is charity.—1 *John*, iv. 8.

Translated from the Tenth French Edition.

IN FOUR VOLUMES.

VOL. IV.

Second Edition.

DUBLIN:
M. H. GILL & SON, 50 UPPER SACKVILLE STREET.
1884.

THE

CATECHISM OF PERSEVERANCE;

OR,

AN HISTORICAL, DOGMATICAL, MORAL, LITURGICAL, APOLOGETICAL, PHILOSOPHICAL, AND SOCIAL EXPOSITION OF RELIGION.

FROM THE

BEGINNING OF THE WORLD DOWN TO OUR OWN DAYS.

BY MONSIGNOR GAUME,

APOSTOLIC PROTHONOTARY, DOCTOR IN THEOLOGY, VICAR-GENERAL OF MONTAUBAN AND AQUILA, KNIGHT OF THE ORDER OF ST. SYLVESTER, MEMBER OF THE ACADEMY OF THE CATHOLIC RELIGION (ROME), &c.

Jesus Christ, yesterday, and to-day; and the same for ever.—Heb. xiii. 8.
God is charity.—1 John, iv. 8.

Translated from the Tenth French Edition.

IN FOUR VOLUMES.

VOL. IV.

Second Edition.

DUBLIN

M. H. GILL & SON, 50 UPPER SACKVILLE STREET

1884

Nihil Obstat:
P. J. TYNAN, S.T.D.

Imprimatur:
+ EDUARDUS CARD. MAC CABE,
Archiepiscopus Dubliniensis
Hiberniae Primas.

Catechism of Perseverance

Lesson 1: External Worship; or, Christianity Brought before the Senses

The lawyer and the mathematician.—"You are therefore an angel, you are therefore a pure spirit!" Such were the words that, though not addressed to me, fell on my ears when, one day last September, I was taking my seat in a public coach on its way to the capital. These words, which passed from mouth to mouth, were accompanied with a sarcastic smile that quite puzzled me. I ventured to ask the meaning of the affair. One of my new traveling companions answered me thus:

"You noticed those two gentlemen who got down where we last stopped. The elder is a lawyer from Paris; the other is one of the greatest mathematicians of our day. Their superiority, their command of language, made them masters in our conversation: around them all was silence. The sight of a church that we passed gave occasion to some remarks on religion.

"'What is the use of churches?' asked the lawyer, 'the only temple worthy of the supreme being is, in my opinion, the universe. And then what is the meaning of all that outward show which Catholics make in their religious exercises? It simply materializes religion.'

"'Up to this,' answered the mathematician gravely, 'I took you for a man; I now see that you are an angel.'

"'If there is any angel here, it is you, sir,' replied the lawyer, politely.

"'Do you then consent,' said the former, 'to be numbered among the individuals of the human species? If you do, I must find very great levity in your words. I would lay a wager that your religious are not to your other studies in the ratio of one-to-a-thousand. Unless, I repeat, you are an angel, one of those pure spirits who, having nothing whatever material about them, behold truth face-to-face, you cannot dispense yourself from replying in the affirmative to each of the following questions:

"'Is it not true that we must take man as we find him, composed of a body and a soul?

"'Is it not true that our senses are the organs of our perceptions?

"'Is it not true that our soul is so dependent on our senses that it is scarcely affected by anything but what strikes them?

"'Is it not true that man owes to God the homage of his whole being?

"'Is it not true that, at the bar, you daily clothe your eloquent words with sensible images, and accompany them with a beautiful variety of inflections and gestures; or, what is the same thing, adopt every means of speaking to the senses of your hearers, so as to convey your own convictions into their souls?

"'Is it not true that you wear a peculiar costume in court, that you observe certain solemn and sacred formalities there, so as to inspire a greater respect for judges and their judgments?

"'Is it not true that, instead of administering justice in the open air, you meet in large, magnificent courts, either that the voices of the authorities may be better heard, or that the parties amenable to the law may be as well sheltered as yourselves from the inclemencies of the weather?

"'Now, tell me, what is all this but the external worship of human justice? And why all this but because you treat, not with angels, but with men, that is to say, with corporeal creatures, with creatures that can hardly be led in any other way than by the senses?

"'If then, sir, you would condemn the external worship of the Church, be consistent with yourself, and begin by removing from your speeches everything addressed to the senses; from the bar, all its consecrated rites and usages; from the administration of justice, all the external forms intended to secure respect for the judges and the laws; and from their foundations, those courts which defend you from heat, cold, rain, snow, and hail. Or rather let man be an angel, and then you may put away external worship. But as long as man is a being served and too often enslaved by organs, to try to reduce religion to something purely spiritual would be to banish it to the moon!'

"While an approving laugh welcomed the sallies of the old mathematician, the lawyer, perplexed, hastened to beat a retreat, and to take up a conversation on new ground. We were at this point when the guard sounded the bugle for a stoppage. The two gentlemen got down, and we trust that the hotelkeeper's table will make peace between them."

At the risk of disturbing the digestion of the "angelic" adversary of our ceremonies, we are going to call him back to the combat. It is not our intention to confound him, nor those who share his prejudices, but to instruct them all, by showing them the necessity, the beauty, the sanctity, and the advantages of the external worship of the Catholic Church.

Definition and origin of worship.—And, first, what is the meaning of the words, *external worship, ceremonies, rites, liturgy?*

In all languages the word *worship* means "honor," "respect," "veneration," "reverence," "service." In religious language we call "internal worship" those sentiments of faith, admiration, respect, gratitude, confidence, love, and submission which we owe to God, because we find all perfections in him. We call "external worship" the sensible signs by which we manifest those sentiments, such as genuflections, prostrations, prayers, vows, and oblations. We teach that when these testimonies are not accompanied by the sentiments of the heart, there is not true sincere worship, but mere hypocrisy—a vice with which our Lord Jesus Christ and the prophets often reproached the Jews.

We recognize a supreme worship which consists in sentiments and testimonies due to God alone; and an inferior or subordinate worship, which we render to the angels and saints, and by which we respect and honor in the angels and saints the supernatural graces that God has bestowed on them, the dignity that he has raised them to, and the power that he grants them. This inferior worship was already commanded and practiced among the Jews. God said to them, "Respect my angel, because my name is in him."[4] We see the woman of Samaria falling down at the feet of Eliseus, who has just restored her child to life, in order to honor in him the character of a holy prophet, a man of God, and the power of working miracles.[5] It is thus that in the civil order that is called "supreme worship" which is rendered to the king, and that "inferior" or "subordinate" which is rendered to his ministers.

It must also be remembered that in civil society the same external demonstrations are often employed to render inferior and supreme worship: on these occasions, the intention alone determines the meaning of the signs. People bow, take off their hats, go on their knees, prostrate themselves before the great as well as before kings, without intending all the while to render them equal honor. It is the same in religion as regards God and the angels and saints: nearly all the difference is found in the form of petition. We ask of God to grant us his graces by himself, and we ask of the angels and saints to obtain them for us by their intercession: two very different things.

Lastly, we distinguish an absolute and a relative worship. This distinction is also admitted in the civil order. The honors that are rendered to the king are absolute civil worship, because they terminate in him. The respect that is entertained for his image, his minister, and his ambassador is relative: they are not honored on their own account, but on account of the king. It is the same in the religious order.

This relative worship was also commanded and practiced among the Jews: "Adore the footstool of the Lord, for it is holy; adore the holy mountain."[6] When therefore the Jews prostrated themselves before the ark of the covenant, before the Temple, before Mount Sion—when they turned to pray in a particular direction—they did not mean to offer their worship to the ark, to the Temple, to Mount Sion, but to God, who vouchsafed to manifest his presence there. When we do the same before an image of our Savior or before his cross, it is not in these symbols that our worship terminates, but in Jesus Christ himself. Has he not said that the worship that is rendered to his saints is reflected on himself? "He that hears you hears me, he that despises you despises me, he that receives you receives me."[7] As you see, worship, internal and external, supreme or subordinate, absolute or relative, is a law of humanity, practiced everywhere in the civil as well as in the religious order. In prescribing it, the Church displays no absence of wisdom or reason.

Ceremonies.—External worship is not practiced without ceremonies. By *religious ceremonies* are understood mysterious, external acts, appointed to accompany divine worship, and to render it more august and expressive.

Ceremonies are mysterious acts, that is to say, they contain and express a hidden meaning. They are like a thin veil that lets one have a glimpse of things purely spiritual. I see a man falling prostrate: I require no other lesson to know that there is in his heart a sentiment of respect and submission; his ceremony lets me see it. He raises his eyes and hands toward heaven: I understand that he is invoking it. He strikes his breast: I see that he repents. In a word, there is no sentiment but appears outwardly by some particular gesture. So true is it that ceremonies are natural to man, and that we have an idea of their appropriateness within us. Hence, the word *ceremony* means "a manifestation of the heart."[8]

Founded on the nature of man, ceremonies have been in use among all peoples, in civil society as well as in religion. They are necessary, as the impious themselves admit; for, if external marks of benevolence sweeten manners, demonstrations of respect toward the deity render man religious.

Though ceremonies are natural to man, God did not wish that those pertaining to his worship should be left to caprice, to ignorance, to the passions of peoples and individuals. We ought to return him many thanks for this. Cast a glance over ancient and modern nations, and tell us if the ceremonies, sometimes infamous, sometimes cruel, often ridiculous, always superstitious, of pagan religions and heretical sects, do not prove how necessary it was that God should regulate the external forms of religion.[9] Besides, does it not belong to God alone and the delegates of his authority to prescribe the manner in which he wishes to be served, as it belongs to the kings of the earth to regulate the ceremonials of their courts?

From the beginning, the Lord has shown himself jealous of this sacred right: he has been pleased to exercise it in Person. When he gave his law to Moses, it was he himself that regulated the least details of worship. Later on, his divine Son prescribed the chief ceremonies of the Catholic Church, leaving to his apostles and their successors, guided by his Spirit, the exclusive right of establishing others. It is not true, therefore, as worldly levity would make out, that the external manner of honoring God is a thing indifferent and optional. Ceremonies, in order to be pleasing to God, must be introduced according to the prescriptions of God himself or his ministers. Hence, the rite.

Rites.—We call a "rite" a usage or a ceremony in accordance with the prescribed order. The word *rite* comes from the Latin *rite* or *recte*, which means "anything well done," "anything conformable to order." Hence, Catholic rites are religious ceremonies as they are prescribed by the Catholic Church. The Roman Rite means ceremonies such as they are prescribed at Rome; the Milanese Rite, at Milan,[10] etc.

Liturgy.—External worship, ceremonies, rites refer directly or indirectly to the greatest act of religion, the august Sacrifice of the Mass; because in Christianity, considered internally or externally, the Word incarnate is the final term toward which all things tend; hence the name *liturgy*, given to the whole collection of ceremonies and prayers that make up the external worship of the Catholic Church.

Liturgy is a Greek word, meaning "a public work," "a splendid work": this is what we call the divine service. The Mass, or the consecration of the Eucharist, is properly called the liturgy, because it is the most august act of the divine service. This is the reason why books, explaining the mode of celebrating the holy mysteries, are called liturgies.[11]

External worship necessary to man and to society.—According to the idea of the apostle St. Paul, the visible world is a mirror in which the invisible world is reflected. The wonders that surround us and that we see reveal to us truths that we do not see: God, his unity, his power, his wisdom, his goodness, his providence.[12]

Now, external worship is to the truths and precepts of religion what the visible is to the invisible world. It is a mirror in which we see truths of a supernatural order, as we see truths of a natural order in the visible world. By external worship, the dogmas of faith and the precepts of morality are made sensible and even palpable to us: the fall of man, his redemption, his hopes of immortality, his duties, his dignity.

What more shall I say? External worship is to religion what the word is to the thought: it is a true expression thereof, that is to say, it is in turn sweet, joyous, or awful, according to the nature of the truths that it expresses. In short, external Catholic worship is Christianity brought before the senses: and hence the general title of our lessons in this fourth part of the catechism. So much having been settled, we say that external worship is necessary to man and to society.

External worship is necessary to man, because he is not a pure spirit. Consisting of a body and a soul, he should necessarily have external signs to manifest his sentiments and make them known to others. It is even impossible for us to feel deep sentiments of love, joy, fear, hope, or admiration, without having recourse immediately to the external signs proper to exhibit them outwardly. Still more, the sentiments that we ought to have for God would spring up very slowly in the hearts of most men, and vanish very quickly, if there were no external signs employed to excite them, maintain them, and manifest them. What does not strike our senses never makes on us any very deep or lasting impression.

Here we find one of the fundamental reasons for external worship.

"Man being such," says the Council of Trent, "that, without the help of sensible signs, he can only with difficulty rise to the consideration of divine things, the Church, like a tender mother, has established certain rites, has ordered that certain parts of the Mass should be said in a low and others in a loud voice. She has also instituted ceremonies: such are mysterious blessings, lights, incense, vestments, and many other things, in accordance with discipline and apostolic tradition."[13] The end of all this is to add to the majesty of the adorable sacrifice, and to lead the minds of the faithful, by means of these visible signs of piety and religion, to the contemplation of the great mysteries hidden in Christianity.

On this point, the impious agree perfectly in their words and deeds with us. Religion reduced to pure spirituality, says one of them, is very soon banished to the regions of the moon. Another adds that dogmas disappeared with the external signs bearing witness to them. When, at the close of the last century, the disciples of these men, who could argue so well, were pleased to destroy religion among us, with what did they begin? With external worship. They first turned ceremonies into ridicule. They then pulled down temples, crosses, and altars.

But in vain does man wage war against nature. These pitiless enemies of external worship had scarcely taken the reins of government into their own hands when they felt all the necessity for public and solemn rites. In order to convert people to their ideas of morality, they hastened to practice what they had condemned by calling to their aid external worship. They only changed its immortal object, and referred it altogether to human virtues, which are but pompous nonentities when separated from their author.

They scoffed in their writings and in their lyceums at the worship of the saints, and substituted for it the worship of heroes, after the manner of the pagans, who rendered the honors of apotheosis only to persons remarkable for extraordinary feats, most generally the ravagers of nations. They jeered at the piety of Catholics toward the precious remains of the just man, and they rendered honors almost divine to their own great men. In fine, is there a single part of Catholic worship that they did not employ to win favor and credit for their lessons with the multitude? Hymns, canticles, altars, the tables of the law, the ark of the constitution, candelabra, sacred fire, holidays, statues of liberty and equality, tutelary genii, and other emblems of the revolution: Did they not offer us a collection of religious ceremonies as extensive as that of any other worship?

External worship is necessary to man, because man, composed of a twofold substance, owes to God the homage of his whole being, that is to say, of his body and his soul. The soul honors God by internal worship, and the body honors him in its way by external worship. It is not only his body that man submits and offers to God when he kneels or prostrates before him, but the material world altogether, of which the human body is a mysterious abridgment. In this manner, by internal and external worship, all creation returns to God, purified, ennobled, sanctified, deified so to speak: God enjoys through man the fullness of his works.

External worship is necessary to man in order to maintain internal worship: one cannot exist without the other. When associating matter to spirit, God associated matter in so admirable a manner to religion, that, when the soul is not at liberty to satisfy its zeal by making use of speech, of the hands, of prostrations, etc., it feels as if deprived of a part of the worship that it would wish to render, and even of that which would give it most consolation.

But if it is free, and under the influence of any strong sentiment, then eyes turned up toward heaven, hands stretched out, canticles, prostrations, adorations diversified in a hundred ways, tears that penance and love unite in producing, relieve the heart by supplying for its weakness. It seems henceforth that it is less the soul which associates the body to its piety and its religion, than the body itself which hastens to aid it, and to supply for what the spirit cannot do. Hence, in the action, not only the most spiritual, but also the most divine—Communion—it is the body that holds the place of a public minister and priest: as, in martyrdom, it is the body that is the visible witness and defender of truth against whatever attacks it.[14]

For the rest, does not daily experience teach us that the neglect of external worship brings on the decay of internal worship? Tell me, I pray, if you can, what is the internal worship rendered to God by all those men indifferent to our external worship. To what is their religion reduced? If we are to judge by their conduct, it is very evident that it is reduced to nothing at all.

Summing up, external worship is necessary to man in order to manifest, to complete, and to maintain internal worship. From all this, we have the following argument: no God without religion; no religion without internal worship; no internal worship without external worship; therefore, man, being what he is, consisting of a twofold nature, no God without external worship. The necessity of external worship is therefore founded on the nature of man and on the nature of God.

We have added that external worship is necessary to society. It is God who has made peoples and societies, as he has made individuals: he has a right to their homage. Moral persons, public persons, they can pay their tribute to God only by public adoration. A people without public worship would be an atheistic people; and, as an atheistic people never existed, therefore, from the origin of the world, public worship!

Add that public worship among all nations is wholly for their advantage. They require it in order to live. A simple argument will prove this. No society without religion; no religion without internal worship; no internal worship without external worship; therefore, without external worship no society. Society is so much the more enlightened, prosperous, tranquil, and powerful, as its external worship is more perfect and better observed.

Advantages of worship.—From the necessity of external worship, as well for man as for society, let us pass on to its advantages.

First advantage of worship: It brings before our senses all the truths of religion under the patriarchs, under the law of Moses, and under the gospel.—External worship, and we speak of Catholic worship alone, recalls all truths, which are the basis of conduct and the safeguard of society. Let us follow it rapidly from its origin to our own days. Under the patriarchs, in the early ages of the world, when idolatry was gaining ground everywhere, the object of external worship was to impress on men the essential dogma of one only God, the Creator and preserver of the universe, the absolute master of nature, the supreme dispenser of goods and evils, the protector of families, the avenger of crimes, and the rewarder of virtues—to make them remember that man is a sinner and has need of pardon. All ceremonies, even the least in appearance, tended to draw closer among them the ties of cordial friendship. It would be easy to show this by considering them in detail. External worship preserved the first men from idolatry, and from all the crimes that would have been its consequence. Since man requires external rites, he cannot be preserved from superstitious ceremonies but by holy and rational practices.

Under the law of Moses, when men, coming forth from the domestic state, entered the national state, religious rites were intended to remind the Jews that God is not only the sole master of nature, but the supreme legislator, the founder and Father of civil society, and the arbiter of nations, of which he disposes as he pleases, rewarding them by prosperity and punishing them by adversity. Most of the Jewish ceremonies were so many monuments of those miraculous events which proved the mission of Moses, the special protection of God over his people, and the certainty of the promises that God had made to them. They should therefore keep the Jews on their guard against the general errors of other peoples—against the local or national gods to which the Gentiles offered incense. God himself declares by his prophets that he prescribed this multitude of ceremonies to the Jews only to check their inclination to idolatry.[15]

And see! while the Philistines, the Chaldeans, the Persians, the Greeks, the Egyptians, the Carthaginians, the Gauls, the Romans, all those peoples so highly lauded, were falling prostrate before infamous and cruel deities, whose feasts they celebrated with human sacrifices and abominable ceremonies, the Jewish people alone adored one only God, thanks in a great measure to their external worship, which raised between them and pagans an insurmountable barrier!

Under Christianity, when all peoples are called to make but one family, united by the bonds of the one faith and the same charity, ceremonies have a still more august object and more sublime meaning. They continually set before our eyes a God sanctifying men; who, through Jesus Christ, his Son, has redeemed us from sin and damnation; who, by endless graces, provides for all the wants of our souls; who has established between all mankind a universal religious society, which we term the "communion of saints."[16]

Thus, under Christianity, as under the patriarchs and under the law, that is to say, from the beginning of the world down to our own days, external worship has been an uninterrupted preaching and a solemn profession of the dogmas most essential to man and to society: the creation, the unity of God, providence, the original fall, the coming of the Redeemer, the spirituality, liberty, and immortality of the soul, the resurrection, the future life. This preaching is necessary; for any people not faithful in practicing the ceremonial that God has prescribed is not slow to despise these very truths. External worship has also been an intelligible lesson on morals to the ignorant as well as to the wise, continually reminding them of their duties toward God, toward their neighbor, and toward themselves—duties that flow naturally from the dogmas of which we have been speaking. The ceremonial of the sacraments, for example, is a picture of the obligations of the Christian in all the circumstances of life. The true faithful understand these mysterious lessons: spoken in a figurative language that makes on their hearts the sweetest, the liveliest, and the most salutary impressions. Woe to those who have eyes not to see and ears not to hear! This insensibility, which renders them like senseless beasts, or idols of wood and stone, is the first punishment of their unbelief.

PRAYER

O my God! who art all love, I thank thee for having established external worship in order to preserve religion. Grant us the grace to understand well the meaning of the ceremonies of the Church.

I am resolved to love God above all things, and my neighbor as myself for the love of God; and, in testimony of this love, I will study with much care this fourth part of the catechism.

Lesson 2: Christianity Brought before the Senses (Continued)—Advantages of Worship, Ceremonies

Second advantage of worship: It settles all the truths of religion.—Not only does external worship continually repeat for the mind, the heart, and the senses, the dogmas of faith and the precepts of morality, but it has moreover the inestimable advantage of settling them.

Our ceremonies, our prayers, are so many incorruptible witnesses to the belief of ancient times. They are like an immense picture gallery, which begins with the origin of the world, is continued past Moses, and stretches out to the threshold of eternity. All the pictures, sometimes terrible, sometimes beautiful, always truthful, painted at times so far apart and by hands so different, show us religion ever the same, though unequally developed, ever proportioned to the comprehension, the needs, and the social condition of the human family, for whom it was made.

This external worship, so magnificent in its entirety and so varied in its details, renders to religion an authentic, living, and perpetual testimony, while it settles every matter of importance, as monuments of bronze or marble fix and perpetuate the remembrance of human events. Hereby, our religion is secured from the caprice of innovators and the arbitrary interpretations of heretics. At all times, external worship has been brought forward to show to heretics the true doctrine of our Lord and the apostles, and to throw a flood of light on disputed words of holy scripture.

To the Arians, the fathers of the fourth and fifth centuries opposed the hymns of the primitive Church which attributed divinity to Jesus Christ; and to the Pelagians, the prayers by which the Church continually implored the help of divine grace. In modern times, the same means have been employed against protestants. From old liturgies, preserved by Eastern sects, separated from Catholic unity since the fourth century, there have been drawn unanswerable proofs of the real presence, auricular confession, prayers for the dead, etc. Having nothing sound to say in reply to this argument, what have our innovators done? They have suppressed among them all display of that external worship which would condemn them. This was the shortest way[17] to get rid of difficulties.

Third advantage of worship: It is the chief social bond.—The third advantage of external worship is that it is a social bond. History teaches us that the first meeting-grounds of nations, the first monuments of peoples, and the first asylums of social virtue were places consecrated to the deity, altars, and tombs. The patriarch, a traveler in the desert, gathers his children and his grandchildren around an altar of stones and green sods, in order to offer sacrifice to the Lord, of whose miracles and promises he speaks to them. Three times a year the great solemnities of the Pasch, Pentecost, and Tabernacles, call all the Israelites to Jerusalem. They pray, adore, sing, weep, eat, and rejoice together. Behold the bonds of charity, formed or drawn closer!

It was to the catacombs that Christians, dismayed and dispersed by persecution, went to learn how to live as saints and to die as heroes. Here, in their generous blood, is modern society cemented. Later on, monasteries and mother churches were in Europe the first places of reunion.[18] It was hither that the inhabitants of vast districts flocked to assist at the divine service. Near the old church were established inns, to feed the crowds of pious pilgrims who came to hear Mass. To the inns were soon added shops, in which articles most wanted were sold.

Hence the name *Mass*, which in the German language still means "a fair" or "a market." People say the "mass of Strasburg" and the "mass of Frankfort" to denote the fairs held in these cities. Often even the humble cell of the solitary has given birth to towns and cities. It was around the wooden cross planted by the missionary that the vast cities of the New World sprang up. Today still, the true point of reunion is the parish church. Destroy it, and the inhabitants of country districts, that is to say, three-fourths of mankind, will live forever isolated, like the savage tribes of America.

The commune, you say, will bring them together. I should be glad of it; but it will not civilize them. To civilize men, it is not enough to bring them together; it is necessary to make them better. Now, Catholic worship alone has this advantage: our churches are true schools of morality. Here, all the inhabitants of a district, met in the house of their heavenly Father, listen to the word that is everlastingly social, because it is all charity. Here, they listen to the voice of their pastor, of their bishop, and they understand that they have friendly relations with the other inhabitants of an immense region.

Here, they perceive that the name of the sovereign pontiff is mentioned with respect, and they pray for him, while they understand that they are the members of a great society, to be found at all points of the globe. For them there are no more seas or mountains, Greeks or barbarians. They behold in all Catholics their dearest friends. They know that, when praying, they pray with them; that, when assembled at the foot of the altar, millions of voices, united with theirs, rise from the East and the West, and all bear together to the throne of God the petitions, the homage, and the affections of the great human family.

And then how many souvenirs calculated to make people better! This church, in which one has been baptized and married, and into which one will be carried for the last time at death; this old white-haired pastor, who instructed children and gave them their first Communion; this cemetery in which one's ancestors sleep, and through which one must pass to enter the church: all these souvenirs, and many others besides, contribute far more than is generally supposed to make people more detached from the earth, less selfish, more moral, in a word, more social. If you have any doubts on this point, see what becomes of the inhabitants of towns and villages who do not frequent the church.

Here again, in these reunions, people are reminded of that equality which is necessary for the welfare of society, because it humbles the pride of some and raises the courage of others. In the church, titles and dignities are no longer known: the priest beholds only children and brethren. When announcing future marriages; when naming husbands and wives, or godfathers and godmothers; when addressing his sermon to the faithful, he does not say, "Gentlemen and ladies," but "my brethren and my sisters." Here, in fine, at the sacred table, at the table of God, the common Father of kings and subjects, all take their places without distinction: this is the only table in the world at which there is no upper end.

The true type of civilization is therefore the parish and not the commune, the church and not the mayor's office. In the parish, we hear of God, of mutual charity, of heaven, of virtues; in the commune, we hear of private interests, of sales, of purchases, of contracts, of rentals, of fields, of vineyards, of beasts. In the parish, I see a priest, who teaches in the name of God, who consoles, who encourages, who calls to duty, who restores peace to the soul, who reconciles enemies; in the commune, I see a mayor who reads the decisions of the prefect, an inspector of the rural districts who makes his reports, a collector who requires taxes, a justice of the peace who inflicts fines, and police who lead off to prison. What do you think: which of the two, the parish or the commune, is more proper to make people better? If it is the parish, return thanks to Catholic worship, without which the parish would not exist.

When speaking of the sacraments, we showed how they give man a high idea of his dignity, how they consecrate the most solemn periods of life, and how they supply all the means of living holily, that is to say, of being on earth a citizen useful to temporal society and after death a glorious inhabitant of the heavenly Jerusalem. We shall soon see how consoling and useful are the Catholic festivals to man and to society. Let us say a word on the influence of Catholic worship on art: this will be, if you like, its fourth advantage.

Fourth advantage of worship: It has an admirable influence on art.—Art is the daughter of religion. The artist who does not believe in another life, who does not behold above his head a world more perfect than ours, to which his soul may take flight for models and inspirations, is dead even in this life. For him there is no poetry, no future, no glory: it is at the altar of faith that the lamp of genius is lighted. O arts and artists! fall on your knees before Catholic worship: to it you owe your honor. The Virgins of the Blessed Angelico, the Gothic cathedrals, the chant of the preface, the *Te Deum*, the *Stabat Mater*, the *Lauda Sion*, the *Dies Irae*, all these masterpieces and a thousand others are the offspring of Catholic worship. That worship, therefore, is most beautiful, majestic, divine, which inspired so many geniuses and created so many masterpieces. Where are the masterpieces of poetry, architecture, painting, or music, inspired by protestantism, Mahometanism, or any other society separated from the true Church?

It is also to Catholic worship that we owe the noblest instruments of music—the organ and the bell: the organ, which seems a combination of all instruments—the organ, which, by the variety of its tones, touches every chord of the soul, speaks every language, employs every voice, the voice of sorrow, the voice of anger, the voice of hope and joy, the voice of death, the voice of heaven; the bell, which fills our towns and villages with indescribable harmonies—the bell, which in a moment makes a thousand hearts beat with the same sentiments.

"Considered in regard to harmony, bells have unquestionably a beauty of the first order: that which artists term 'grand.' The roar of thunder is sublime, and it is so only by its grandeur. It is the same with the winds and the waves, volcanoes and cataracts, the voice of a whole people. With what pleasure would Pythagoras, who lent an ear to the hammer of the blacksmith, have listened to the sounds of our bells on the eve of a solemnity of the Church! The soul may be softened by the accents of a lyre, but it will not be seized with enthusiasm as when the thunder of battle bursts upon it, or when a mighty pealing in the clouds proclaims the victory of the God of hosts."[19]

To perpetuate the truths of religion, to settle them and place them beyond the reach of the attacks of impiety and heresy, to be a social bond, to elevate and to console man, to inspire the arts and to lead to the production of inimitable masterpieces: these are some of the advantages of Catholic worship. Is anything more needed to entitle it to our respect and love? Ah! we ought to be proud, we Catholics, to profess a worship, the fruitful source of so many beauties, the principle of so many virtues.

Origin and varieties of ceremonies. Let us now speak of the origin of the ceremonies that belong to this worship, of the respect that is due to them, of the fruits that they produce, and of the necessity of knowing them. It was God who placed in man the need of manifesting by external signs the sentiments that spring up in his soul: he is therefore the first author of ceremonies. He made their necessity be felt. He himself inspired the first religious acts, and regulated their manifestation among the Jews. Later on, his Son, having come down among men, revealed certain essential ceremonies, and invested his Church with power to regulate the worship that men owe to God.

Such is, as we have already said, the high origin of ecclesiastical ceremonies. They come from God, whether he instituted them himself through Jesus Christ his Son, or they were established by the apostles or their successors, whom he filled with his Spirit and invested with his authority.[20]

Hence, ceremonies of divine institution, apostolical institution, and ecclesiastical institution. The first are those which our Lord himself instituted, as the blessing and consecration of the chalice, the formulas of the sacraments; the second are those which the apostles established, as the custom of men to pray with uncovered heads and turned toward the East, and certain prayers of the divine office; the third are those which the Church has instituted in the course of time, as a great many blessings, genuflections, prayers, processions, etc.

Considered in their nature, the ceremonies of the Church are divided into essential and accessory ceremonies. The former belong to the very essence of sacrifice and sacraments. For this reason, they cannot be changed: such are the words of the consecration of the Eucharist, and of the forms of the sacraments. The latter, which regard the decency, convenience, or majesty of the divine service, may differ according to places. They may even be changed according to times and circumstances; because the Church received from our Lord the power to institute and to modify them for the glory of God and the salvation of mankind.

This power she has used at all times. In effect, the progress of ages, the customs of nations, the habits of peoples require in accidental forms some modifications, which a wise and considerate authority has always the right to make.[21] Accordingly, we find a great difference, for example, between the Greek Rite and the Latin. Yet Greek and Roman Catholics profess the same religion, have the same faith, observe the same precepts.

This diversity of rites, when approved by the Church, does not therefore affect in the least the unity of the Church. What do I say? It helps to display more fully her enchanting beauty. "The unity of the faith," says St. Augustine, "which is the same throughout the whole Church, is what makes the beauty of the spouse of Jesus Christ, according to the words of the prophet: 'All the beauty of the king's daughter is within.'[22] If, in the worship that produces this unity of faith, there are found different practices, this diversity of ceremonies is only the variety in the robe of the heavenly spouse, according to what is said in the same place:[23] 'The spouse wears a robe of various colors, embroidered with gold.'"[24]

Philosophers and protestants have pretended that our ceremonies were copied from the pagans. I do not know a more stupid reproach. It is certain that all ancient peoples had some religious ceremonies. In this heap of superstitious practices, there remained, as in their creeds and morals, some shreds of a primitive revelation. What did the Church do? The heiress of all truth, she made a sorting of the true and the false, the good and the bad. Adopting what she found good and true, she drove off the usurpers, and said to them, "I was before you. I was the first. I go back to the early days of the world. I received the truth as a trust and an inheritance. I take back what belongs to me. Everything true, good, or laudable that you have preserved is mine." Then she purified, she sanctified these usages, as she sanctified the temples of idols, and turned them to the glory of their true master.

Such is the meaning of St. Augustine's answer to Faustus the Manichee.[25] "The employment of ceremonies in the worship of the true God," says Bergier, "is not a loan: it is a restitution for a theft made by the pagans. The true religion is more ancient than false ones: it is entitled to recover the rites that its rivals have profaned. Are we to abstain from praying to God because the pagans prayed to Jupiter, or cease to place ourselves on our knees because they prostrated themselves before idols?"

Not to repeat what we have already said on the necessity of external worship, let us tell in a few words the use of ceremonies. Some are a profession of our faith: for example, when we accompany the Blessed Sacrament, or honor the images and relics of the saints, we show boldly that we are Christians and Catholics. Others render sensible to us the invisible effects of grace: for example, the pouring of water on the child's head in baptism. Others warn us of our duties: such is the tonsure, which reminds ecclesiastics of their renunciation of the vanities of the world; such also is the black garb of ecclesiastics and religious, which is a continual preacher of the spirit of sacrifice. Others inspire us with a profound respect for sacred things: such are the chants of the Church, the sound of bells, the richness of sacerdotal vestments, the order of the ministers who serve at the altar. In fine, nearly all, observed in a becoming manner, produce spiritual graces: as the sacramentals, exorcisms, and many others besides.

Respect due to them.—Let us conclude that there is nothing more proper to fill us with admiration for our ceremonies than their noble origin, their antiquity, their beauty, their utility. They came from heaven. They have lived through century after century. They place religion beyond the reach of novelties. They help us to rise to the most spiritual things. They captivate our senses. They rejoice our hearts. They impart to worship such grandeur and dignity that impiety itself cannot refuse, without becoming guilty in the eyes of science and reason, to venerate rites so replete with wisdom, and productive of so many happy results for man and society. Hence, St. Teresa, that most loving, inspired soul, used to say, "I would give my head for the least ceremony of the Church."

Do you require other motives for your veneration of our holy ceremonies? You will find these motives both in the great importance that the Church attaches to them, and in the deplorable consequences that arise from a contempt of them. The Church commands her ministers to know them, and, having studied their spirit, to act carefully in accordance therewith. A priest cannot without a crime and without detriment to the integrity of the sacrifice or the validity of a sacrament omit any one of its essential ceremonies. If he should neglect, through levity or ignorance, some ceremonies not essential, he would sin in a manner more or less grave, according to the greater or less importance of his voluntary omission.

It is only in case of extreme necessity that the ceremonies not essential to the integrity of the sacrifice and the validity of the sacraments can be omitted: for example, when the priest that celebrates Mass is threatened with death by the destruction of the building, or by the approach of the enemies of religion, thirsting for his blood. In pressing danger of death, the ceremonies of baptism are suppressed, with the obligation, however, of supplying them if the child survive.

Eagerness to study them.—The Church goes still further: she orders her ministers to explain ceremonies to the faithful.[26] Wherefore, it is a duty of the latter to study them. You easily understand this. Ceremonies have been established to edify us, to instruct us, to rouse our attention; particular graces are attached to them; they are a book, a set of pictures, presented to us by religion. But this book, beautiful as it is, will be a closed book for us, will say nothing to our faith, if we are not acquainted with the language in which it is written. Expressive as you imagine these pictures, they will be only vain images for us, if we are not acquainted with their subject, or their meaning, or their object.

External worship will then be almost useless to us. The sight of our holy ceremonies, instead of reanimating our faith, exciting our love, satisfying a holy curiosity, will only inspire us with disgust and weariness, perhaps contempt; for it is the character of the ignorant to scoff at what they do not understand. These people are nowadays to be met with everywhere. Would it not be a shame for Christians to be unable to defend their worship, and to be taking part in ceremonies of which they could not render an account?

Yet how many of the faithful are there who have long assisted at Mass, have appeared in the church as godfathers or godmothers, and have seen confirmation, extreme unction, all the sacraments administered, without understanding anything of what was occurring before their eyes! We behold at the present day an extraordinary eagerness to discover the meaning of old manuscripts, and of inscriptions on profane columns and tombs: ought we not to be ashamed, we Christians, to have less anxiety to understand the meaning of our ceremonies, a thousand times more instructive than all the monuments of pagan antiquity?

PRAYER

O my God! who art all love, I thank thee for having made plain before my eyes all the truths of religion. I ask thy pardon for not having sufficiently respected the ceremonies of thy Church.

I am resolved to love God above all things, and my neighbor as myself for the love of God; and, in testimony of this love, I will study with much care the ceremonies of the Church.

Lesson 3: Christianity Brought before the Senses (Continued)—Architecture and Ornament

Since we are going to explain Catholic worship in detail, it is natural to begin with the church, where it is practiced.

Churches: Their necessity and their ornamentation.—Though God is everywhere, though the universe is a magnificent temple, yet there must be churches. At all times and among all peoples, there have been places specially consecrated to the honor of the deity. The tops of mountains and the depths of forests were chosen in preference: the former, because they seemed to bring man nearer to heaven; the latter, because they were found more favorable to recollection.[27] These places became among the pagans so many scenes of crime. The worship of the stars, which were better seen from the tops of mountains, was the first idolatry. It is very probable that one of the reasons why God wished that a tabernacle should be constructed was to convince the

Jewish people that it was not necessary to ascend mountains in order to draw near to God, and that he himself vouchsafed to draw near to his people, by rendering his presence sensible in the portable temple erected to his honor. The tabernacle was therefore a preservative against idolatry.[28]

It was also a means of maintaining the piety of the Israelites, by inspiring them with greater respect and fear of the Lord, and by enabling them to acquit themselves conveniently of the duty of divine worship. As a matter of fact, the tabernacle was placed in the midst of their camp. There were to be seen, brought together within a narrow enclosure, the symbols of the presence of God and the marks of his omnipotence. The ark of the covenant, the tables of the law, the two cherubim with outstretched wings, the vessel full of manna, the rod of Aaron, all spoke eloquently to them of the benefits and the power of God, the master of the elements, the supreme legislator, the monarch of the angels, the avenger of crimes, the Father of his children—alone holy, alone worthy of respect, love, praise, and adoration.

All these things, and others still more admirable, the poorest village church repeats to Christians. It is not true, therefore, as some impious people pretend, that there is no other temple needed than the universe. No; the universe is not enough. Three-fourths of the human race, accustomed to the sight of the universe, behold it without emotion; whereas they are struck with admiration at the sight of a temple richly or neatly adorned. How can anyone enter our somber cathedrals without being seized with a religious awe? Besides, the universe, with all its magnificence, does not say to the heart near so much as a modest village church. On the tops of hills, in the face of the sky, you do not find a cross, nor an altar, nor a tabernacle, nor a holy table, nor a tribunal of mercy, nor a sacred font, nor the tombs of ancestors, nor any of those symbols so rich in memories and so powerful over the heart and the senses.

And then the church is a social place. How, I ask, would you assemble men, women, and children, young and old, in the open air, on the tops of hills, when the ground is covered with snow and ice, or the rain falls in torrents? To destroy churches is therefore to destroy external worship; to destroy external worship is to destroy internal worship; and to destroy internal worship is to destroy religion, is to destroy society. Ah! instead of destroying churches or lessening their number, we ought to build new ones: the more you build, the fewer prisons shall you need.

Those silly censors, therefore, do not deserve to be heard, who oppose what common sense dictates to all mankind. Let them go and adore God in the face of heaven, on the summits of mountains, after adoring him in the temple: Who will prevent them? But they do not adore him in any manner, and they would wish to put a stop to every public exercise of religion, because they know that, without external worship, it could no longer exist.

Churches must be suitably adorned. The impious say again, "What is the good of so much luxury in churches? Was not Jesus Christ born in a crib, and did he not institute the Eucharist in a room?"

What is the good of so much luxury in churches? According to them, whatever is done to honor God is so much lost. This language is not new: it was that of Judas, murmuring against Magdalen, who had poured out a precious ointment on the feet of the Savior. Truly, our modern Judases can with a good grace complain of the magnificence of Catholic worship! See, they call themselves the friends of the people, and they take it well that riches should be lavished on the most unworthy creatures, on theatres that corrupt morals, on amusements of every kind; but they bewail the expenses incurred in the demonstrations of religion, because such demonstrations instruct men, excite them to virtue, and console them with the hope of future happiness! They pretend pity for the miseries of the people, and not only are they unwilling to retrench anything from their own comforts in order to relieve them, but they even wish to deprive them of the only means left of cheering and encouraging them: which is done in the temple of the Lord by motives of religion.

It would doubtless be better, in their opinion, that the people should go and enjoy themselves in places of debauchery and schools of vice. Hence, such attractions have been multiplied. But where shall they go who fear the infection of these dens, and who do not wish to be perverted? Ah! let us leave fools to rave, and, for ourselves, consult the simple light of reason and the experience of all nations.

Yes, there must be a certain luxury in our churches, because it is necessary to give men a high idea of the Divine Majesty, and to make worship deserving of respect. The only way to succeed herein is by the help of external pomp. Man cannot be taken but by his senses: this is the principle from which we must set out. It will be impossible to captivate his imagination, if we do not place before his eyes some objects to which he attaches great value.

Unless the people find in religion the same magnificence that they find in civil ceremonies—unless they see as pompous a homage rendered to God as is rendered to earthly powers—what idea will they form of the greatness of the master whom they adore? This is the reflection of St. Thomas. Protestants feel today the sad consequences of that nudity to which they have reduced divine worship. Even an infidel admits that the retrenchments made on divine worship in England have banished piety and encouraged atheism and irreligion there. Hence, our separated brethren reestablish gradually in their temples those ancient symbols which their forefathers pulled down, burned, and profaned with so much fury and blindness.[29]

If, therefore, we adorn churches, it is not because God has any need of this magnificence, but because we have need of it in order to raise ourselves toward him. We ought to offer him our gold, our riches, our masterpieces of art, because it is a duty to render the homage of all these things to him from whom wealth and talents come. This tribute of gratitude and adoration is a title to new benefits, while ingratitude is like a scorching wind, which dries up the source of graces. From this new point of view, the pomp of worship is also entirely for our own interest.

Our Lord, it is true, was born in a crib, and instituted the Blessed Eucharist in a room. By this simplicity and poverty, he wished to show us his immense love, which, to be shown, did not need the grandeur of edifices or the pomp of ceremonies. Ye poor of all generations! he wished to teach you that you also might participate in the mysteries of his love, and that he would vouchsafe to dwell even in your thatched chapels.

He also wished to teach Christians that true worship is a worship of the mind and the heart, and thereby to preserve us from the illusions of carnal people, strongly inclined to imagine that a display of ceremonies and a multitude of victims are all that the Lord requires of them. But he did not wish to forbid the magnificence of external worship. Otherwise, he would have abandoned the Church his spouse to the spirit of deceit, he would have ignored human nature, he would have sought the annihilation of religion. Let us remark, moreover, that he himself set an example of the luxury which he required in his churches. If he was born in a stable, he wished to have for the institution of the Eucharist a large and well-furnished apartment—*grande, stratum!*

Suitable garments for festivals.—External pomp should pass from the material to the living temple, that is to say, to man. One ought to be better dressed on festivals, in order to show more respect for God; in order to acknowledge that all goods come from him, and that all ought to be consecrated to his service. This sentiment is so natural that it is in the hearts of all men.[30] The poor man himself, the simple rustic, understands it so well that, to join religious assemblies on feast days, he attires himself in his very best style.

It ought to be so, that outward apparel may remind one of purity of soul; that the disparity placed by fortune between the rich and the poor may vanish somewhat before the sovereign master, in whose eyes all men are equal. It was already the same in the old law. Jacob, about to offer a sacrifice as the head of his house, ordered his people to wash themselves and to change their clothes.[31] God commanded the same thing to the Hebrews, when he was going to give them his law on Mount Sinai.[32] This external mark of respect is found among all nations. All, without exception, blend with the homage that they render to the deity the utmost pomp in their power.[33]

Do not think that this outward apparel, this festive look is without influence on the mind and the heart. Oh, no; for it excites and indicates the internal dispositions with which one ought to go to church. Above all it awakens that sentiment which ought to predominate above every other, the sentiment of joy. In point of fact, to visit the church is to visit our Father's house, the house where he waits for us with open arms and a burning heart, to welcome and embrace us, to feed us with his heavenly bread, and to inebriate us with his delicious wine.

To visit the church is to visit the house where we were born; where we tasted our first joys; where our mind was opened to truth and our heart to innocence; where our steps were strengthened in the paths of happiness, which are always near those of innocence; where we meet again the friends of our childhood and all our dear relations, and where we pray with and for them, as they themselves pray with and for us; where we eat together the same blessed food, reminding us that we are all members of one family; where all our voices mingle with those of the angels in their everlasting canticle to the praise of our Father: "Holy, holy, holy, Lord God of hosts," of angels and men!

To visit the church, near which is the cemetery, is perhaps to visit the grave of our mother, our sister, or our brother, on which it will be permitted us to lay, as we pass, a tear, a prayer, or a flower. To visit the church is to visit the place where the rich shall be told to give alms to the poor; the great, to be protectors of the little and the weak; masters, to treat their servants kindly; all, to love, to help, and to forgive one another as children of the same family, and to have but one heart and one soul. Why should we not be filled with gladness, like the Israelites invited to the Temple of Jerusalem: "We rejoiced, at the news that we should soon go to the house of the Lord"?[34] Full of these sentiments, let us set out for the church. That we may respect and love it still more, let us be sure to know it well. A history and description of it will here be useful.

Description of ancient churches.—From the beginning, our ancestors had places set apart for the assemblies of religion and the offering of the holy mysteries.[35] But it is in the catacombs that we must look for the first elements and models of our churches.[36] All that we behold herein reminds us of those ever-venerable places: we make the remark when speaking of each part of the church. When it was permitted Christians to celebrate their worship in the broad daylight, they hastened to build churches, and to arrange them in the manner most convenient for the observance of the ceremonies used in those days of holy memory. The Church was divided into seven parts,[37] as shown on the plan below:

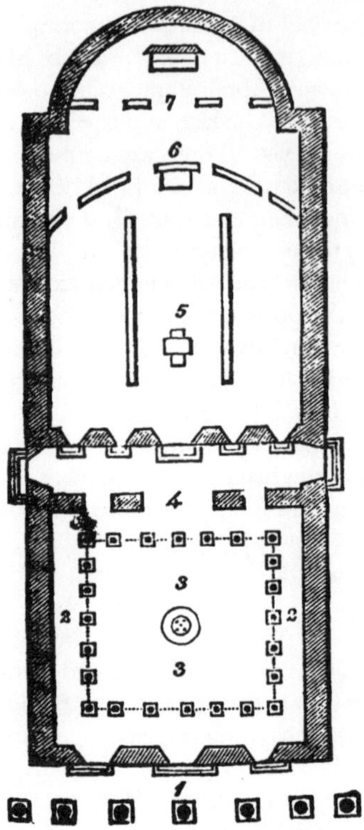

1. *The porch or outer vestibule.*[38] This was an oblong space at the entrance of the church. It was covered, and the covering was supported by pillars, placed along at intervals. Emperors looked forward to it as an honor to be buried under the vestibule of a church. This made St. Chrysostom say that emperors were in the house of the fishermen, that is to say, in temples dedicated to the apostle, what porters were in the house of the emperors.

2. *The cloister.*[39] From the vestibule, one passed into the cloister. This was a kind of alley, supported by pillars, and surrounding the third part of the church, called the "parvise." It was here that penitents of the first class remained. They were termed *flentes* or "weepers," because they wept for their sins, and implored the pity of the faithful who entered the church.

3. *The parvise.*[40] The parvise was a square court. It had no other covering than the sky, and no other lamps than the sun, moon, and stars, that all those who entered it might contemplate at leisure the beauty of the heavens, and prepare themselves by the adoration of the God of nature for the adoration of the God of redemption. In the middle of the parvise was a fountain, a symbol of purification: all washed their hands and faces here before going farther. On the basin of the fountain were engraven these words: "Wash your sins and not merely your faces."[41]

This fountain was blessed by the priest on the eve or the day of the Epiphany. Suppressed in the course of time, it was replaced by holy water fonts. The custom of purifying oneself with water before appearing in the presence of God is as old as the world. The patriarchs and the Jews observed it.[42] We find it among the pagans, though incredulous guardians of revelation. Thus, at the first step we make in the church, we meet with a souvenir of the most venerable antiquity. Would that, when taking holy water, we were animated with the same sentiments of respect and compunction as our virtuous ancestors! For this purpose, let us remember that holy water, taken with respect and compunction, effaces venial sins.[43]

4. *The inner vestibule.*[44] Going forward, one passed from the parvise into the inner vestibule. In large churches, this inner vestibule was separated from the nave by a wall. Here were placed the catechumens, the energumens, and the penitents called *audientes* or "hearers," because it was permitted them to hear the hymns and psalms that were sung in the church, as well as the word of God. They remained in this place till the deacon, raising his voice, said, "Outside, hearers and unbelievers!" Admission to the inner vestibule was likewise granted to pagans, Jews, heretics, and schismatics, so that they might listen to the instructions of the ministers of the gospel, and be converted, if God should vouchsafe to touch their hearts.

5. *The nave.*[45] Several large doors opened between the inner vestibule and the nave. This principal part of the church was called as at present the "nave," from the Latin word *navis*, "a ship." It received this name for two reasons: the first, because it was much longer than broad; the second, to remind Christians that the Church is a ship.

Nothing more common in the fathers than to compare the Church to a ship. Our Lord is the invisible pilot; Peter, its visible pilot; the sacred ministers, its crew; the faithful, its happy passengers. Ever beaten about by the storm, the Church is never sunk beneath the waves nor dashed against the rocks. One must be on board of it to cross the sea of life, to escape the deluge of iniquities that covers the earth, and to arrive safe and sound at the heavenly shore. What admirable meaning in this simple word of our religious language! It is the whole history of man here below: Have we ever thought of this?

At the entrance of the nave, near the wall that separates it from the inner vestibule, were the third class of penitents, called *prostrati*, or "the prostrate." After spending three years in the cloister bewailing their sins, and three years in the inner vestibule listening to the word of God, they had still six years of penance to do before being admitted to the public communion. They remained prostrate at the end of the nave, so as to receive the imposition of the bishop's hands when he passed.

A little way up the nave was the *ambo* or *jubé*, from the summit of which the holy scripture was read to the people and the word of God preached. Placed in the middle or on one side of the nave, it was large enough to accommodate several readers. Bishops usually preached from the steps of the altar; but St. Chrysostom preferred the ambo. Beyond the ambo were the fourth class of penitents, called *consistentes*, because they stood upright, or *competentes*, because they resembled children, says St. Augustine, who press the womb of their mother to be born to the light.[46]

From this spot the nave was divided lengthwise by two partitions, which prevented men and women from seeing each other. Between the partitions was a large space for the movements of the sacred ministers. The men were on the left and the women on the right. By considering our Lord seated in the tabernacle, which faces the faithful, the men are then found really on his right. This place, in keeping with their dignity, is still assigned them in a great many churches.[47]

All, both men and women, remained standing, or on their knees, or seated on the ground with legs across after the manner of the Easterns: there were no benches or chairs for the faithful. Later on, the religious, who spent a great part of the day in the church, supported themselves, each with a staff, having a crossbar at the top, and called a "crutch." Afterward, they had seats fastened to the walls. These are now represented by the stalls of canons, who neither sit nor stand, but simply lean. From this, there was only one step to introduce into churches benches and chairs for the faithful. Yet Spain has kept to the early custom:[48] it has no chairs in its churches.

6. *The choir.*[49] This part of the church was so called because it was reserved for the holy ministers leading the chant and prayer. It was separated from the nave by a semicircular railing.[50] Around it were ranged seats of greater or less height according to the dignity of the ecclesiastics: the highest was for the bishop, so that he might warn, overlook, and guard the flock.

7. *The sanctuary.*[51] The sanctuary was separated from the choir by a railing or balustrade, which had three doors: the one in the middle, larger than the other two, was called the "holy door". As the sanctuary terminated in a semicircle, this part of the church was called the *apse,*[52] that is to say, "a rounded end." The curtain at the entrance hid the altar and prevented the holy mysteries from being seen at the time of consecration: it was not drawn aside till afterward. This was what made St. Chrysostom say, "When you are at the sacrifice, wherein Jesus Christ, the Lamb of God, is offered up, and you hear the signal given, join together in prayer. When you see the curtain drawn aside, think that heaven is opened and the angels descend there."[53]

In the sanctuary was the altar. Beside the large altar there was a small one, on which were laid the bread and wine offered by the faithful for the holy sacrifice. This altar has been replaced in our churches by a credence table: it is here that the cruets are still left. Clerics alone could enter the sanctuary: hence it came to be called the sacred and inaccessible place.

The altar was usually at the east.[54] Our ancestors in the faith, regarding our Lord as the true sun of the world, as the "orient from on high," placed their altars on the East side, and turned in that direction to pray, so as to manifest their faith and their hope.

Under the altar was a subterranean grotto called a "crypt,"[55] in which lay one or more bodies of martyrs; on the altar were lights; along the sides of the church were mural paintings, pictures, and chapels; finally, the part of the church behind the altar was rounded, so that the shape of our churches is that of a niche: all so many souvenirs of the catacombs! Sacred souvenirs, if ever there were any! We have them still daily before our eyes, and perhaps they never say a word to our hearts. May it be so no longer! Ignorance, at all events, will no longer serve us as an excuse.

Our present churches full of souvenirs of the catacombs: Crypt, altar, balustrade.—A word on each of these venerable souvenirs. Let us begin with the crypt. In a great many old churches, there is still to be seen under the principal altar a crypt or subterranean chapel: this is a souvenir of the catacombs. As a matter of fact, it was in the subterranean chambers of those vast cemeteries that our ancestors in the faith offered up the holy mysteries. When they were allowed to build churches, they preserved as many souvenirs as possible of those times of trial and virtue. To see what our superb basilicas have borrowed from the catacombs, let us cast a rapid glance at the multitude of little churches now sunk in the bowels of Rome. Hollowed out of the tufa, they are generally of greater length than breadth: at the end, which is rounded and has an arched roof,[56] is the tomb of a martyr.

This tomb was called an "altar," because it was on the table of marble or stone covering it and projecting forward that the holy sacrifice was offered. It was also called a "confession,"[57] because the martyr, by dying, had confessed his faith: his bones were here to confess it still, and to bear witness to it. In some of these little churches, we still find a marble slab bored through, and placed like a kind of railing before the martyr's tomb: the first model of the balustrades raised in Christian temples before the principal altar, and whose original object becomes evident after seeing the catacombs. It is clear, as a matter of fact, that this slab was intended to secure the sacred remains gathered in the tomb from the injuries likely to be caused by an over-ardent and inconsiderate zeal, and also to inspire more veneration for the place in which they rested.

At Rome, churches have been built over these subterranean churches: the altar of the grotto corresponds to the central point of the intersection of the nave and the cross-aisle. The entrance of the grotto, to which steps lead down, is closed by a grating. Above this grotto and on a level with the floor of the church, there is a second altar, serving for the celebration of Mass. It reminds us by its shape, and even by its position, directly over the subterranean altar or tomb, of its sepulchral origin and its first use. Nearly all the ancient basilicas of Rome, though rebuilt in modern times with more or less splendor and magnificence, present this essential trait of the monuments of primitive worship.

We will here cite but one example. Among the churches of the most ancient period, one of the most remarkable in the eyes of all is the church dedicated to St. Prisca, daughter of a Roman senator, baptized by St. Peter himself. Having been put to death for the faith, her body was laid in a coffin that has the shape of an old altar. This tomb of Prisca was placed in the middle of her own room, in her father's palace, the remains of which are still to be seen on the Aventin Hill. The room, with the tomb that it contained, became thus a kind of little mortuary temple; and when, later on, the church that still exists was built over it, it formed the subterranean confession thereof.[58]

Thus, this interesting edifice presents all that was to be found in the catacombs: a tomb serving as an altar, a subterranean chapel, and a church above—monuments born one of another, and in which the worship of the dead is linked, by a close relationship, to that of the deity, in the same manner as Christianity is united materially to antiquity by the very erection of this church on the foundations of a Roman palace.[59]

Religion has so much respect for the customs of days gone by that all her altars are shaped like a tomb, and in these altars we find one or more cavities called "tombs," which contain the relics of some saint: there is no altar without relics. The tomb is generally placed in the middle of the altar: here rests, after consecration, Jesus Christ, immolated for the glory of his Father.

Thus, within the space of a square foot, the Church, our mother, brings together all that is most powerful to touch the heart of God—our Lord and the martyrs immolated for his glory! She is like a widow, who, in order to obtain a favor, goes to the prince, and, offering him on one side the bones of her sons and on the other the body of her husband, killed in the service of the state, says to him, "Behold my titles to your favor!" Is there a prince in the world that would refuse the petition of this widow? God would therefore do less than men if he did not hear the Church when she offers him in our holy mysteries the blood of her spouse and the remains of her children.

PRAYER

O my God! who art all love, I thank thee for having been pleased to choose an abode among men. Grant me the grace always to go to church with a deep sentiment of love, like that of a child going to its father's house.

I am resolved to love God above all things, and my neighbor as myself for the love of God; and, in testimony of this love, I will take holy water with great respect.

Lesson 4: Christianity Brought before the Senses (Continued)—Lights, Paintings, Bells

Further description of our churches.—Let us continue to explain the souvenirs of the catacombs still to be seen in our churches. Not to understand them would be both a pity and a shame. A pity, since things the most capable of filling our souls with a religious respect, and of strengthening our faith, by setting before our eyes the customs, virtues, and trials of our ancestors, would be for us as if they were not. Instead of being seized with a religious awe on crossing the sacred threshold, we should enter our churches as if they were some ordinary buildings. A shame: yes, shame on the child that knows neither the shape nor the divisions of the parental house—that can neither justify the wisdom of its ancestors in the arrangement of the edifice which they bequeathed to it nor give an account of the customs which they established and which itself observes without knowing why! But it will not observe them for a long time. When a book is written in an unknown tongue, it is left to others, or rather it is thrown into some neglected corner, to go to moths and dust. Is this not one of the reasons why we see our churches deserted by a great many persons, and our ceremonies regarded as a dumb and meaningless show, even by some of our "faithful"?

Having spoken in the last lesson of the crypt, the altar, and the balustrade, it remains for us to give an account of the lights, the side chapels, and the paintings that adorn our churches—new souvenirs of the catacombs!

Lights. Obliged to shun the light of the sun, our ancestors supplied for it by lamps and torches in the subterranean places that so long served them as a retreat and a temple. Their lamps are found by thousands in the catacombs. They are met in two very different positions, which certainly bespeak two distinct intentions. The first are inserted in little niches, or fixed on little brackets projecting along the corridors, or yet oftener suspended by chains from the roofs of chapels. Everything proves that they were to guide the steps of the faithful, and to throw light on the religious ceremonies that were practiced here. The second are fastened outside to the tombs on which the holy mysteries were celebrated. Sometimes they are even laid inside sepulchres, as a symbol of immortality. This intention cannot be doubted, since it is derived from a custom followed in Christian funerals.[60] The custom of having lamps is retained among us under another form, by means of lighted candles at the ceremony of the obsequies.

The lamps of both classes are, for the most part, of burnt clay; some are of bronze, silver, and even amber. They have generally the shape of a boat, because, among our ancestors, a boat was one of the most popular symbols of the Church. We will only mention as an example one beautiful lamp, found lately in the catacombs. It is shaped like a boat, and carries two persons, St. Peter seated at the helm, and St. Paul standing at the prow as if preaching the gospel. Most of these lamps are ornamented with symbolical figures: palm branches, crowns, lambs, doves, fishes, candlesticks. We very often meet with the monogram or figure of our Lord. Hence is derived the usage of representing at the foot of our altar-candlesticks some of the attributes of our Lord or the Blessed Trinity.

The sight of our candles takes us back, therefore, eighteen hundred years to the times of persecution, to the very cradle of Christianity. Will this sight not affect our hearts? It takes us back even much farther, for the use of lights in the divine worship is traceable to the times of the Mosaic law. Inheriting all the immortal ceremonies of the synagogue, as well as the revelations made on dogmas and morals from the beginning of the world, the Catholic Church has preserved for all generations an ever-present history of the past.[61]

Lamps were employed not only to banish darkness, but also to manifest joy and gratitude on account of the benefits of God. They were also a figure of our Lord, the true light of the world. "We never celebrate the holy mysteries," says an ancient, "without using tapers. It is not to banish the darkness of the night, since we say Mass in broad day, but to represent him who is the uncreated light, without whom we grope at noon."[62]

Side chapels. We now come to another souvenir of the catacombs. We have seen that at the bottom or nearly at the bottom of the grottoes or vaults there was a martyr's tomb, serving as an altar for the holy sacrifice. The walls of the vaults are full of niches,[63] containing the remains of one or more martyrs. Behold the certain origin and the primitive form of the side chapels of our Christian churches: they are like so many little niches, each with its arched roof, and the relics of its martyr.

It is, in fact, clear that the idea of these chapels, foreign to the plan of ancient temples, was borrowed from nothing but the catacombs at a time when the Church, already sure of victory, was removing into her temples the monuments of her persecutions, and placing them there in such a way as to recall the memory, always so useful to piety, of those times of trial and misery when cemeteries served as churches, when tombs served as altars, and when the blood of martyrs, according to the happy expression of Tertullian, became the seed of new Christians.[64]

It is also for the same reason that ancient churches are so dimly lighted. While their faint rays encourage recollection, they also recall the mysterious gloom of the catacombs. And now, when we are in our churches, will all these tombs, all these martyrs that surround us say nothing to our hearts? Can the church be still for us a dull, profane, unimportant place?

Paintings. Pictures and images are eloquent books. Whatever we see with our eyes makes a deeper impression on us than words. Such is the experience of all ages and of all countries. Hence, the early Christians were fond of painting subjects in keeping with their sad position. The old and the new testament afforded a rich mine, from which they drew everything that could be expected of poor people, buried in dark chambers underground. But when we think on the hands which traced them, on the places and circumstances in which they were executed, how venerable are those first rough botches of Christian art!

Let us mention the chief subjects that still find expression on the partitions of our subterranean churches. From the old testament: the history of Jonas; Moses touching the rock of Horeb with his rod, or, as a legislator, receiving the tables of the law; Noe in the ark; the sacrifice of Abraham; Adam and Eve; the three children in the furnace; Daniel in the lions' den; Elias carried up to heaven; David with his sling; Job seated on the ground; Tobias with a fish. Of all these subjects, that of Jonas is the most frequently repeated. He therefore seems to have been the most interesting study for our ancestors—doubtless because he was an image of the resurrection, in which the marvelous appears to the highest degree.

From the new testament: our Savior on the Blessed Virgin's knees; receiving the presents of the three Magi; seated amid the doctors, or amid his disciples, or with his twelve apostles, or between St. Peter and St. Paul; multiplying the loaves; curing the paralytic; restoring sight to the blind; raising Lazarus to life; as the good shepherd. The subjects of these paintings lead us to a conclusion certainly very remarkable.

The catacombs, intended for the burial of the early Christians, peopled for a long time with martyrs, ornamented during periods of persecution and by persons under the influence of sad thoughts and painful duties, present nevertheless only heroic traits in all that forms the historical part of these paintings. It is the patriarchs and the prophets—Abraham, Moses, Jonas, David—that are their heroes, serving as an example to the martyrs, as a consolation to the oppressed. Not a trait or a personage taken from the stern realities of the hour went to distract the faithful from the accomplishment of their pious duties; and, on the eve as on the morrow of persecutions continually recurring, they encouraged themselves to persevere in the faith only by the sight of Daniel thrown to the lions, or the three children in the furnace, and not by that of Christians delivered like themselves to the flames of the pile or the beasts of the circus.

The decorative part of these paintings is no less remarkable. Nothing therein but what is pleasing and graceful: representations of the good shepherd, vine branches, pastoral scenes, *agapae*, Christians in prayer, palm branches, crowns, lambs, stags, doves; in a word, nought but motives of joy, innocence, and charity.[65]

Such are the paintings of the catacombs, paintings as a whole so pure and pleasing in their object; paintings from which it would seem that the gospel should never meet with enemies or opponents, since it shows itself so indulgent and humane; paintings in which the martyr is to be found only at prayer; paintings in which Christianity is revealed only by symbols of gentleness and peace.

In succeeding ages, when the martyrs belonged to history, their combats and triumphs became the ordinary subjects of our sacred paintings. It was the same with the memorable deeds of all those martyrs of peace, that is to say, of all those saints whose lives, consecrated to penance, to the welfare of their kind, to the propagation of the gospel, were a long crucifixion of the flesh and its concupiscences. Such are the models that the Church holds up today for the respect and imitation of her children: this usage goes back to the most remote antiquity.[66]

If we have admired the genius of Christianity in the paintings of the catacombs, the paintings of our churches offer us another subject of admiration. By placing pictures of the saints within the sacred enclosure, the Catholic Church reminds her children of the communion that exists between them and the blessed inhabitants of the heavenly Jerusalem. She shows us the saints as present at prayers on earth; she makes them the chief protectors of the peoples whom they have edified by their virtues; she regards them as always interested in the spread of justice and peace among mankind.

Until the time of the gospel, every people reserved its homage for its patriotic heroes. In Catholic worship, the true just man is honored at the same time by all nations. On our altars, virtue has no longer any country but one: it is independent of laws, manners, and customs. All the distinctions of land, wealth, birth, and talent are forgotten. The anchoret of Thebaid, the Roman pontiff, the emperor, the simple shepherd, the old man of a hundred years, and the young virgin scarce blooming into womanhood are found in the same rank. All ages, all climes, all states are here represented; and, in this family gallery, virtue is what it ought to be, the patrimony of the world; and the example of the virtuous becomes profitable to the whole human race.

It is not only by the assemblage of all these saints that the Church says to us, "I am Catholic; to me belong the true virtues of all ages, for it was I that inspired them," but also by the efforts that she makes for the decoration of her temples.

"I am Catholic." This is what she says to us by all inanimate creatures: these branches, these vine leaves, these stalks of wheat, these fruits, these trees, these flowers of every kind, which adorn the walls of the holy temple. All parts of creation find space here to praise God in their manner, and it is the powerful hand of the Catholic Church that brings them together.

"I am Catholic." This is what the Church continues to repeat to us by the variety of strange figures that she introduces into our ancient basilicas. The devils appear everywhere conquered. Here, they uphold tremendous masses on their crushed shoulders; there, in the shape of hideous animals, they serve as spouts for the rain. Vices themselves have their place here, and, by their horrible appearance, excite the smile or the disgust of the spectator. Christianity resembles a conqueror, who drags his vanquished enemies after his chariot, and perpetuates from generation to generation the memory of his triumphs. Diocletian and Maximian, after deluging the earth with Christian blood fifteen hundred years ago, raised two marble columns to immortalize the pretended victory of paganism over Christianity. Diocletian and Maximian are no more, and their columns are fallen. Christianity stands erect. The pagan gods serve it as a footstool, and its temples, so many monuments of its victories, have already lasted longer than the empire of the Caesars.

"I am Catholic." I am immortal; mine is the empire of all ages, mine the monopoly of true virtues, mine the victory over paganism: this is what the Church says to us by the paintings and the decorations of her temples. These admirable things, to which must be added all those stones so delicately cut; all those pieces of marble lace; all those exquisite carvings; all those windows, wherein the perfection of art is disputed by their variety, their richness, their solidity, and their mellow colors; all those slender, graceful pillars; all those little spires, shooting up to heaven; all those numberless masterpieces, wherein faith, adoration, prayer, and love seem to say to God, "I have done all that I could to honor thee; if I have not done better, it is not my fault."—Tell me, do not all these things awake in your mind a thought of faith, in your heart a feeling of love and admiration? Ah! if they do not, I have no more to say to you. It will be enough for me to pity you, as we pity one that is blind, or deaf, or paralyzed, or dead.

Let us leave the church for a few moments—its august ceremonies will soon recall us—and speak of the bells.

Bells.—The use of bells is very ancient in the Church: it certainly goes back beyond the eighth century. Who was the introducer of bells? Many assert that it was Pope Sabinian, the successor of St. Gregory the Great.[67] It is believed that the first of our bells were cast in Campagna, a province of Italy: hence the name *campanae*, which was given them in order to distinguish them from those large bells called *sonnettes*, known for a long time.[68]

During the first three centuries, the Christians, obliged to hide from persecution, had no public signal for calling to the holy offices. It is probable that they gave notice to one another privately, or that in their meetings the day and the hour of their next meeting were announced publicly. When peace was given to the Church, under Constantine, and vast basilicas were constructed, there was undoubtedly a public signal for summoning the faithful together. The general opinion is that it was the sound of thin boards struck with mallets, or else of large wooden rattles, stronger than those which are still used on the last three days of Holy Week.

In some monasteries, trumpets were used; in others, the invitation was given by singing, "Alleluia." At length, the use of bells became general throughout the West, and gradually passed over to the East. When bells were invented, it was necessary to build high towers for them, that their sound might be heard afar off. On most of these towers there was placed a little pyramid, surmounted by a globe, over which flourished a cross. On the cross was put a cock, a popular emblem of the use of bells in the Church. To the pastors, it recalled vigilance; to the faithful, zeal for prayer and readiness for labor:[69] in the same manner as the cross, placed on the globe of the pyramid, announced to heaven and earth the victory of Jesus Christ over the world.

Its baptism. Like everything else used in her worship, the Church blesses the bell. This blessing is called its baptism. Not that she imagines the bell susceptible of any inward virtue or true sanctity; but her intention is to withdraw it from the order of common things, and to announce that, having been once consecrated to the service of the Lord, it can no longer be employed for other purposes without a kind of profanation. She wishes also to render mysterious and holy both the instrument and the sound which shall summon the faithful to all that is most sacred under heaven—the word of God, the offices, assistance at and participation in our holy mysteries.

The bell is the trumpet of the Church militant:[70] it should sound on all the great occasions of life. Hence, the variety of prayers and ceremonies with which it is blessed. It should sound at baptism, and it is purified with holy water. It should sound the combats of our life, from the day on which we enter the sacred arena by confirmation till that on which our deathbed receives us: accordingly, it is repeatedly anointed with holy chrism and the oil of the sick. It should sound for the adorable sacrifice: accordingly, it is perfumed with incense. It should continually remind us of Jesus crucified, the author and the finisher of our faith:

accordingly, the sacred sign of the cross is often repeated over it. The name of some saint is given to the bell. A most charming idea! our ancestors thought that piety would be more active, more joyous, more faithful, if we imagined that a saint was calling us to church.[71]

When the bell is blessed, the priest or the bishop, the godfather, and the godmother sound it gently three times, as if to give it its mission. The bell is covered with a white linen cloth until it is raised up to the steeple, on account of the respect due to the holy chrism; and the officiating clergyman, having made over it the sign of the cross, retires to the sacristy.

Reason why it is rung in storms. In one of the prayers used at the blessing, the priest says, "O God! who, by Moses thy servant, didst command silver trumpets to be made, in order that, by the sweetness of their sound, the people might be warned to come to the sacrifice and to make ready to pray to thee, grant that this instrument, which is intended for thy Church, may be sanctified by thy Holy Spirit, so that, having been struck, and yielding a melodious and agreeable sound in the ears of thy people, their faith and fervor may increase from day to day; that the snares of their enemies, hail and rain, storms, whirlwinds, and tempests may be scattered; and that the dreadful effects of lightning may be prevented. Hold back by thy almighty hand the enemies of our salvation, and grant that, on hearing this bell, they may tremble at the sight of the cross of Jesus Christ, at whose name every knee bends in heaven, on earth, and in hell."[72]

Our learned and spiritual philosophers have laughed heartily at the simplicity of our ancestors, who rang bells to turn away storms. To ring a bell, they say with a wise look, is to shake a column of air, is to call down a thunderbolt. Yes, perhaps you argue well,[73] you who find in the sound of a bell only a material sound; but if you saw therein what our ancestors saw, what the Catholic Church, which knows a good deal more than you, sees—a prayer, a cry of alarm, an earnest supplication to the master of the elements—you would probably be more reserved. Now, the sound of the bell is a vocal prayer: as the blessing of the Church, mentioned above, informs you. If you ridicule it, will you not also ridicule God himself? Does he not say in express terms that the noise of instruments, the sound of loud voices, the peal of trumpets, will excite his mercy? "You shall blow the trumpet, you shall shout aloud, and a remembrance of you shall come before the Lord your God, and you shall be delivered out of the hands of your enemies."[74]

If the progress of science lets you turn away the thunderbolt without having recourse to prayer, give the glory thereof to the God of science, who enables you to recover a part of the first man's empire over creatures; but do not despise your ancestors, who had recourse to prayer for the attainment of the same end.

Harmony of bells with our sentiments. What shall we say of all the impressions that the sound of the bell makes on the man and on the Christian? This sound has ever so many secret relations with us. How often, in the stillness of the night, have the tinklings of an agony, like the faint beats of an expiring heart, terrified the guilty who were on the watch for crime! The sweetest feelings are associated with the sounds of bells. When, before the song of the lark, we hear, at break of day, the little bells of our hamlets, one would be inclined to say that the angel of the harvest was telling on some instrument of the Hebrews the history of Sephora or of Noemi. The chimes of bells in the midst of our festivals seem to increase the public gladness. In calamities, on the contrary, these same sounds become terrible. Our hair still stands on end at the remembrance of days of murder and fire, filled with the clamor of the tocsin.

All the feelings that the bells of our temples excite are so much the more beautiful as there is mingled with them a thought of heaven, a thought of charity and religion. From the hand bell that a man rings in the streets of our cities during the night before one of our festivals, repeating the words, "Awake, ye who sleep, and pray for the departed!" to the bell of the lonely hamlet that sounds the curfew as a signal for the wandering traveler in the neighboring forests or mountains, and to the drone that is sounded at night in some seaports as a notice to the mariner to beware of rocks and shoals—all bells are associated with our present condition, and bring into our souls, one after another, a religious sadness, joy, hope, and fear. How comes this mystery to pass? It is because bells are essentially religious. If they had been attached to any other monuments than our churches, they would have lost their moral sympathy with our hearts.[75]

PRAYER

O my God! who art all love, I thank thee for having preserved in our churches so many souvenirs, no less proper to excite our piety than to confirm our faith. Grant us the grace never more to be deaf to so many voices, preaching thy love.

I am resolved to love God above all things, and my neighbor as myself for the love of God; and, in testimony of this love, I will enter the church with the greatest respect.

Lesson 5: Christianity Brought before the Senses (Continued)—Blessings, Cemeteries

Since we have just spoken of the blessing of the bell, and shall soon come to that of the cemetery, this is a good place to say a few words on blessings in general.

Blessings in general: Principles on which they rest.—To understand something of the blessings of the Church, we must recall several most certain truths. a) Creatures, being the work of a good God, came forth good from his hands, that is to say, perfectly adapted to the twofold end of their existence, the glory of God and the welfare, physical and moral, of man. b) Creatures were vitiated by the devil, when, defiling man, he defiled all things depending on man. As a consequence, creatures, under the influence of the wicked spirit, no longer serve to the glory of God and the welfare of man. All have become instruments of sin and death. They lament this sad slavery, this cruel tyranny, which lays hold on their homage, and prevents them from corresponding with their vocation. Hence the apostle St. Paul tells us that they sigh for their deliverance.[76] c) God does not wholly abandon man or any creature to the sway of the devil. From the day of the fall, all his thoughts have tended to the deliverance of creation. If we ask our Lord why he came on earth, he reveals to us his Father's thought and his own, saying, "I came to turn out the prince of this world, to destroy his works and to take away sin or evil."[77] d) God can effectually banish the devil and withdraw creatures from his malign influence. He can also entrust this power to his messengers.

On these great principles, admitted by all people, rest the power and the usage of blessing in the Catholic Church. It is therefore to bring back man and the creature to their primitive sanctity that she blesses them. This blessing sets creation free gradually, until the supreme moment when, the prince of this world having been utterly defeated, and his influence destroyed, God will become "all in all."[78] Then shall man be changed into a new being; then shall there be a new heaven and a new earth; then shall all creatures sing, because they shall be worthy to sing, the immortal canticle of the angels: "Holy, holy, holy is the God of hosts; all things are full of his glory!"

Thus you see, in a simple blessing, the Church relates for us the whole history of the world, the fall and the redemption, the terrestrial paradise and Mount Calvary, time and eternity! Have we ever reflected on this?

What they teach us. The blessings of the Catholic Church also remind us of a truth the forgetfulness of which is a fruitful source of iniquities: it is the greatness of man. We do not esteem ourselves enough; we have not a right idea of what we are worth. Images of God, who is sanctity itself, we are created to be holy, that is to say, to be consecrated to God, disengaged from evil, free from the slavery of the wicked one. Our mind, our heart, our imagination, our senses are so many sacred vessels that should admit only holy thoughts, holy affections, holy images, holy things: sacred vessels that should touch nothing defiled.

There is not one of her blessings by which the Church does not recall this noble idea to man, and say to him, "My son, the earth is too small for thy heart. Thou art holy, consecrated to God, made for God: aspire to that good alone which can satisfy thee. Thou art holy, see!—I bless the elements that are at thy command, water, fire, earth; I bless thy meats, thy meadows, thy fields, thy vineyards; I bless the animals that serve thee, because they are to come near thee, to be in contact with thee; I bless thy last abode—what do I say?—I consecrate it by the hands of a pontiff, because its clay is to mix with thy dust. Holy, thou shouldst, after thy death, rest in something holy, as thou wast born and as thou didst grow and live amid holy things." All this being so, it is easy for you to understand what is the meaning of blessings in the Catholic Church.

In the language of the Church, "to bless a thing" means to draw it from its natural state, to separate it from common and ordinary purposes, to change it from profane to holy, to devote it to God and to the ceremonies of religion, to communicate to it a special virtue; in a word, to apply it to pious and sacred uses.

We said before that God, after creating the universe, blessed it. Hence, all creatures are good, and were applied to the glory of God or sanctified by a general blessing or approbation. "God," says the scripture, "saw all the things that he had made, and they were very good."[79] But sin, having entered the world, spoiled and vitiated all creatures.[80] Hence, the indispensable necessity of purifying them "by the word of God and by prayer,"[81] so as to put to flight the devil and to counteract his influence. Such is the profoundly philosophical reason for blessings.

Their antiquity. Accordingly, we see them in use from the beginning of the world. In the old testament, Moses, by a blessing that heaven reveals to him, sweetens the waters of Mara.[82] Eliseus purifies the springs of Jericho by casting salt into them, while he pronounces these words: "Thus saith the Lord: I have made these waters wholesome, and they shall no more give death."[83] Tobias, by prayer, blesses the nuptial chamber, and drives out the devils.[84] We know the solemn and mysterious blessing that was given every year to the new sheaf and the new fruits. Before victims were sacrificed, hands were imposed on them, and oil, wheat, etc., were prayed over, in order to be sanctified and made worthy of God.[85]

Our Lord confirmed by his example what was done under the old law. He blesses five loaves and two fishes, with which he feeds an immense multitude;[86] he imposes hands on the sick in order to heal them; he blesses little children; he blesses and offers to his Father, at the last supper, the bread and wine which he is going to change into his body and blood.

Inheriting the doctrine and the power of Jesus Christ, the Church has made a constant use of blessings. At the period when she appeared, the devil reigned as a sovereign over the world, the empire of which he had usurped: he infected every part of it. Hence that belief of the pagans, unfortunately so true, though ill understood, that all parts of nature were animated by spirits or genii. It should rather be said that they were degraded, tyrannized over by devils. What was most deplorable was that the devils, regarded as the masters of all creatures, received on this account the homage due only to God. The philosophers themselves maintained that food and other common things were presents from these demons or genii. Later on, the Marcionites and the Manichees pretended that all bodies had been formed by an evil principle, the enemy of God.

To scatter all these errors and to banish the devil from his empire, the Church hastened to make use of blessings. Hence, among the early Christians, the prayers and the sign of the cross repeated every moment, before making use of any creature; hence, all those admirable formulas of blessings which the Church has drawn up and which we trace to her cradle. Most of those which we still avail ourselves of are to be found in the sacramentary of Pope St. Gelasius, who lived in the fifth century; and this pope was not their author. They are much used among the different sects of Eastern Christians, separated from the Roman Church since the first ages of Christianity. St Paul himself speaks of blessings when he says, "Every creature of God is good…; it is sanctified by the word of God and by prayer."[87] Now, blessings are prayers intended to sanctify: here, therefore, it is an apostolic custom.

As is plain, the Church, sent to sanctify the world and to drive out the devil, has therefore the power to bless, since it is by a blessing that the world is sanctified and restored to its primitive state. When she blesses, she gives a proof of her profound wisdom, and at the same time continues a practice as old as the world.

Their effects. The effects attached to her blessings are general and particular.

The general effects are: to withdraw the object blessed from the sway of the devil, and to free it from his malign influence; to separate it from common and profane things; and to communicate to it the virtue of exciting sentiments of faith, love of God, and religion, and thereby obtaining supernatural effects and the remission of slight faults.

The particular effects correspond to the intentions of the Church, and are different according to the thing that she consecrates and the end that she has in view. Sometimes it is to strengthen a soul against the temptations and attacks of the enemy of salvation. Sometimes it is to place the body out of the reach of inconveniences that might befall it. She blesses fire, that it may not injure man, but become for him an emblem of charity and truth. She blesses water, that it may serve to purify him. She blesses temples, altars, and vessels of sacrifice, because nothing can be too holy for the worship of the Lord. She blesses the abode of man and his food, that he may enjoy peace, and take gratefully and without fear what he requires for the support of his body. She blesses cattle, meadows, and fields, so as to preserve them from scourges that might render them worthless, and deprive the poor laborer of the fruits of his toil.

In large cities, where the externals of religion are as much as possible laid aside, where the most laudable practices are treated as "popular devotions," the touching usages of which we speak have been lost. What need, indeed, of the blessing of God has the rich usurer or the reckless libertine, who perhaps does not believe in him? But country people, who feel themselves more immediately under the hand of God, who often see their crops and their prospects destroyed by a flood, who think that nothing can succeed if God does not take care of it, have recourse more frequently to the prayers of the Church, and add thereto some good works, alms, or services to the poor. The desire of rendering more efficacious the blessings that they ask, nourishes sentiments of humanity in them. Before ridiculing them, heretics and infidels should begin by showing in what these blessings are opposed to true philosophy, to true piety, to confidence in God, to gratitude, to obedience, to the word of God, to the general belief of the human race.[88]

Those who have the power to bless. As for those who have the power to bless, they are bishops and priests. Bishops, invested with the plenitude of the priesthood, can consecrate and bless all the objects that are under their jurisdiction. To them alone belong the blessings that are accompanied with unctions, such as the consecration of churches, altars, the chalice, and the paten; the coronation of kings and queens; the blessing of holy oils, abbots, abbesses, and knights. There are other blessings reserved to them besides, such as those of altar linens, ornaments, bells, and cemeteries.

The blessings that are within the sphere of priests are those of marriages, the fruits of the earth, water mixed with salt, ashes, branches, candles, etc.

The effect of a blessing does not depend on the dispositions of him who gives it; for he does not act in his own name, but in the name of Jesus Christ, whose instrument only he is. However, to remind him of the sanctity with which he should be adorned in this sublime function, he must be clothed with a surplice, the emblem of innocence, and a stole, the symbol of his power. A young clerk, the image of an angel, accompanies him, holding in one hand a holy water vessel, and in the other a lighted candle, figurative of charity and faith.

When repeating the formula of blessing, the sacred minister holds his hands joined, or raised toward heaven, in order to express the fervor of prayer and his ardent desire to be heard. He makes several times with his hand the sign of the cross on the object that he blesses, in order to denote that every grace comes from the cross, and that it is only in virtue of the merits of our crucified Lord that we have a share in his mercies. He sprinkles it with holy water, in order to signify that, by the prayer of the Church, it is taken out of the rank of profane things, and obtains all the purity of which it is susceptible. Holy water, sprinkled on an object, is also an external sign that a blessing is applied to it. If incense is used in any blessing, it is to ask of God that the accompanying prayer may be as a sweet perfume to him, and may rise even to his throne.[89]

Now that we know the reason, the origin, and the meaning of blessings, let us pass on to the cemetery. We have only one step to make; for, in the intention of the Catholic religion, the cemetery borders on the church.

Cemeteries.—The word *cemetery* means "a dormitory." It was Christianity that first gave this name to the place where the deceased rest: it is full of philosophy. In the eyes of the Catholic Church, death is only a sleep, since the place in which they who have lived rest is a dormitory. Now, sleep necessarily supposes an awaking. Henceforth, it will be impossible to pronounce the name *cemetery*—and who does not sometimes pronounce it?—without expressing the most consoling dogma for the good and the most terrible for the wicked, the dogma of the resurrection.[90]

From the beginning, the Church showed the greatest respect for the mortal remains of her children. This respect for the dead is a lesson that teaches the living to respect themselves; but the Church, ever wise, avoided two excesses into which the pagans fell. The Egyptians embalmed their dead, shut them up in coffins, and preserved them in their houses as a precious deposit. The Church did not think fit to adopt this useless delicacy, this superstitious curiosity. The Romans, on the contrary, burned their dead and kept only the ashes. This manner of doing away with the remains of a person whose memory deserves to be preserved has something inhuman in it. Yet the Romans acted thus only toward their friends. As for the hosts of slaves that they owned, they treated them with the same brutality after death as during life. In Rome, the bodies of slaves were thrown pell-mell into deep trenches called *puticuli*, or burned in the public *ustrines*. In the country, they were often left to dogs or to birds of prey.

This is not all. The general custom among the ancients, with the exception of the Egyptians, was to place tombs in the country by the side of highways, in lonely eaves, or in gardens. The Catholic Church introduced practices much more conformable to reason, and much more likely to maintain a tender remembrance of the deceased. She began by abolishing the custom of burning the dead. It is far better to bury them, and thus realize the prediction made to sinful man: "Thou art dust, and thou shalt return into the dust from which thou wast taken."[91] She then desired that the dead should be assembled in one place near her temple, so that she might watch over bygone generations, as a mother watches over the cradle of her sleeping child.

What do I say? The first temples of the Catholic Church were actually cemeteries: the catacombs were nothing else. It was amid the dead that the living met to pray, and to offer up the sacred mysteries. Later on, when peace came, and it was lawful to build Christian temples, the Church hastened to consecrate a place for the burial of her children. She wished that this place should be near her temple, in order to preserve the memory of her cradle, and to teach men that a mother does not forget her children, even when they are no more. This ancient and holy custom, which seeks to have the cemetery inseparable from the church, is preserved even to our own days in nearly every parish of the Catholic world, but nowhere, perhaps, with more fidelity than in the north of Switzerland.

We shall never forget the touching sights that hourly presented themselves to us, when traveling through the cantons of Soleure, Lucerne, and Schwytz. At the entrance of a village, sometimes most beautiful, always most neat, you see a church, whose whiteness and gracefulness, with its slender steeple, you admire before resting your eyes on the rich decorations of its interior. The cemetery encloses the church like a fortification: the principal entrance leads to the large door of the church. After opening the gilt iron gate that secures it, you ascend a few stone steps. On your right hand and also on your left is placed a large holy water font: in each there is a sprinkling-brush, to cast, when entering, some holy water on the dead.

All the graves, covered with grass, are arranged in lines perfectly regular, and separated by paths strewn with sand, so as to render more easily approachable to everyone the grave that holds what he regards as most dear. Not one of these modest graves but is surmounted by an iron cross about two feet high! The three visible ends of the cross are of copper, gilt. To the center is attached a plate of the same metal, on which are inscribed the name of the deceased, the dates of birth and death, and a prayer or a text of scripture.

When, by the last rays of the setting sun, you see "God's Acre" from afar, shining with an elegant simplicity, all its crosses of equal height running in symmetrical lines, their black and yellow colors contrasting so well with the green grass of the graves, I cannot describe the sweet melancholy that seizes on your heart: tears of tenderness rush to your eyes, and prayers mount to your lips; memories of antiquity crowd on your soul.

Situation near our churches. You imagine yourself borne back eighteen centuries to the catacombs of Rome: before you there is a perfect image of them. Here, as in subterranean Rome, you see in the center the altar of the principal martyr: it is the church. Before the altar, Christians on their knees preparing for the combat by the reception of the bread of the strong. Around the living, a circle of the dead, who, from their tombs, encourage them by telling them of detachment, crowns, rest, and immortality. You are delighted to find the Catholic Church ever the same, and you regret that a decay of faith, much more than anxiety for the public health, has separated the cemetery from the temple among us, and removed the dead from the sight of the living.

It is said that the custom of burying in or near churches has become dangerous in large cities. This supposition is more or less gratuitous. Until it is proved, it would be well to let us hold it as doubtful. We are so much the more authorized in asking this, as it tends to impeach the Catholic Church, and comes from persons whose levity, to say nothing else, is clear to a demonstration. It would also be well to let us bear in mind that at Rome burials take place in churches,[92] and that, notwithstanding the heat of the climate, no inconveniences are found to arise therefrom.

We will next ask if a single instance can be cited from history of an epidemic brought about by the practice of burying in cities. Lastly, we say that it is an excellent thing to remove from cities all the sources of disease; but, to be consistent, we should not leave there, build there, endow there certain places of assembly a hundred times more destructive to life than the burial of the dead. Among those who nowadays push cemeteries aside and blame so severely the ancient custom of the Catholic Church, how many, perhaps, only seek to banish every sad idea, so that they may taste their pleasures without the least mixture of bitterness or remorse, while they try to palliate their epicurism by pretended zeal for the public good!

Sentiments which they inspire. Be it as it may in cities, we maintain that in the country, where the air has free play and there is no danger, the established custom should not be changed. It is most proper that, before entering the temple of the Lord, the faithful should have an opportunity of resting their eyes on something that will awake in their minds a thought of the shortness of this life, a hope of a happier future, a tender recollection of their relations and friends.[93]

To separate the cemetery from the church is to destroy one of the most beautiful harmonies that the Church has been able to establish. This harmony well deserves to be considered something; for society gains much more thereby than is generally supposed. In a small space, we meet with three Churches—the Church of heaven, the Church of earth, and the Church of purgatory: Is not this a great lesson on brotherhood? The Church of heaven, consisting of angels and blessed souls, whose pictures, hanging from the walls, recall their victories and their invisible presence, is gathered around this altar—the tomb of a martyr or a saint—on which is immolated the God whom it contemplates face-to-face, and whom we adore under the Eucharistic veils. The Church of earth appears to our eyes in a multitude of men, women, and children praying together. The Church of purgatory has also its place—consisting of our friends and relations, whose voices seem to come up from those graves on which we pray, saying to us with Job, "Have pity on us, have pity on us, at least you our friends!"[94]

Believe me, it is good in this age of cold selfishness and indifference to leave Christianity the means of recalling to the minds of her children the memory of her cradle. It is good that the place of prayer should be a catacomb. Prayer made in the midst of graves is more recollected. The resemblance between the mysteries of religion and those of the grave; the immediate contact in some manner between time and eternity, between the ashes of ancestors and man on his knees, in presence of the immortal King of ages, on the wreck of generations that are no more: all this gives rise to wholesome thoughts, and inspires more than one noble sentiment, more than one virtuous resolution.

Blessing of a cemetery. All cemeteries are blessed. This usage goes back to the very birth of Christianity. Religion, which so often blesses man, which blesses his fields, his meadows, his food, his cattle, his house, to teach him that he is holy, since everything around him must be holy in order to come in contact with him—religion also blesses and consecrates the place of his burial, so as to remind him that death does not divest him of his holiness, and that he continues worthy of respect in the dust of the grave.

This blessing of our last abode is a source of many useful lessons to the living. Let us consider them. First, to make the cemetery more venerable, the blessing of it is reserved to the bishop: only that he can delegate the power to a priest. The more man becomes in some manner contemptible, and the nearer he approaches to nothingness, the more religion surrounds him with respect. On the eve of the ceremony, there are five wooden crosses, the height of a man, set up: the first in the middle, higher than the others; the others before, behind, to the right, and to the left, at the ends of the cemetery. In front of each cross rises a wooden stake, two feet high, with three wooden sconces at the end.

What is the meaning of this ceremony, apparently so nonsensical? Far from your lips be the impious smile of contempt! Everything in religion is grand; everything full of mystery. These wooden crosses, placed at the four cardinal points, represent the Savior of the world, him who is "the resurrection and the life" of the whole human race.[95] These stakes of whitish color, which one would mistake for fleshless tibias,[96] are an image of man, who becomes by death like dry and useless wood. The night following the erection of the cross recalls the darkness of the tomb, as the ceremony of the next day is a bright picture of the resurrection. This cross, standing before these stakes, declares aloud that Jesus Christ protects in the tomb even the remains of man, that he keeps them under his hand, and that he will restore them to life at the appointed time.[97]

The next day, the bishop, wearing a surplice, stole, and white cope, goes to the cemetery. White is used, because the ceremony is to be a joyful one, and to proclaim a consoling mystery. Preceded by the clergy, the bishop advances and takes up his place before the cross in the middle. Fifteen candles are lighted, three on each of the stakes before the crosses.

Placed on this sapless, lifeless wood, too faithful an image of man in the tomb, these lighted candles announce the resurrection. Their number indicates and proclaims to the four corners of the world the Blessed Trinity, in whose name and by whose power the resurrection shall be effected. The prayer that the bishop immediately recites reveals to us the spirit of these beautiful ceremonies. Here it is: "O Almighty and merciful God, who art the guardian of souls, the anchor of salvation, and the hope of the faithful, graciously hear our humble prayer, and vouchsafe to purify this place by thy heavenly blessing, and to make it holy, so that the bodies which will rest here may, after the course of this life, deserve, on the great day of judgment, a blessed immortality, and a share in eternal happiness with the just souls, through Jesus Christ," etc.

After this prayer, the clergy and faithful kneel down before the cross, and beseech all our brethren in heaven to join their supplications with ours: the Litany of the Saints is sung. When this is over, the celebrant walks round the cemetery, which he bedews with holy water, pronouncing these words: "Sprinkle me, O Lord, with hyssop and I shall be cleansed." During this ceremony, the choir sings the psalm *Miserere*. It is a long lamentation, which takes from the place and the occasion something sad and solemn, capable of touching the heart of God.

The bishop returns to his place before the cross: it is here, indeed, that it becomes him to pray. He addresses to the God of life and death the following prayer: "O God, who art the Creator of the universe, the Redeemer of the human race, and the disposer of all creatures visible and invisible, we ask thee with a suppliant voice and a devout heart to vouchsafe to purify, bless, and sanctify this cemetery, wherein, after this life, the bodies of thy faithful are to rest. O thou who, of thine infinite mercy, hast forgiven all the sins of those that placed their trust in thee, deign, of thy goodness, to give eternal comfort to their bodies, which will rest here, awaiting the sound of the trumpet of thine archangel, through Jesus Christ, our Lord," etc.

These last words, by which the bishop proclaims the resurrection to come, are immediately followed by a ceremony that is a striking image of it. He takes from the stake the lighted candles, and places them on the three ends of the cross, beginning with that in the middle. This act says to man, "The hope of a resurrection, which goes down with thee into the grave, will be realized by Jesus Christ. Thou art his member; he is thy head. He is risen. Lo! his body already shines with immortality." The stake is then removed. But the cross remains erect. It is here to say to all generations, "You shall rise again. Your Redeemer lives. He watches over you. He rears the standard of his victory on the very spot where death conquered you." The bishop, no longer beholding aught in the cross save the God whom it represents, salutes it respectfully and incenses it three times; after which he retires.[98]

O men! be no more afraid of death; you shall not be long its prey. Behold the emblem of the resurrection and immortality awaiting you, in the very place of your burial. If such usages were found among a few antiquated peoples, our modern savants would be at a loss for eloquence enough to praise them: from our youth we should be telling them over and over again in prose and verse. Why, therefore, so much indifference? Why that ignorance in which we are left regarding these usages, so full of instruction and poetry?

Are they, because they belong to the Catholic Church, less venerable? O men! how long will you keep two weights and two measures?

PRAYER

O my God! who art all love, I thank thee for having taken so much care to sanctify me and all creatures. Grant me the grace to understand well the salutary lessons that thou dost give me by all thy blessings.

I am resolved to love God above all things, and my neighbor as myself for the love of God; and, in testimony of this love, I will have a great respect for myself.

Lesson 6: Christianity Brought before the Senses (Continued)—Time, Festivals

We are acquainted with the church and the cemetery, this double dwelling, in which all the mysteries of life and death are accomplished. What does religion do in temples? What festivals does she celebrate there? These are the questions which we have now to answer. But our answer, to be understood, requires a few preliminary explanations. The meaning of time and its division, together with the name *festival*, must be known.

Definition of time.—First, what is time? If we wanted to define time in itself, we should say with a celebrated poet that "time is a movable image of an immovable eternity."[99] But this is not our object. We shall look at time as it is in its relation to man, and man fallen.

Man, like the angel, was created free and destined for a magnificent reward. This reward he should merit by making of his liberty a use conformable to the will of God. The angel abused his liberty, and was punished without mercy. Man also abused his liberty. After original sin, God could have treated him as he had treated the angel: he could have taken time away from him, and cast him, with the speed of lightning, into an eternity of woe. Thanks be to God! he did not treat him thus. He was pleased to grant time to man. But why? That man might do penance. If man would not do it, he should be treated like the rebellious angel, and, at the end of time, hear from the mouth of the supreme judge this irrevocable sentence: "Depart from me, ye cursed, into everlasting fire, which was prepared for the devil and his angels."[100] We may now ask what is time in the eyes of faith, that is to say, of truth. Time is the period of the trial of the human race. It is the delay granted by the divine justice to fallen man in order to do penance. Yes, time or life is to be a continual penance: an infallible oracle, at one with reason, proclaims it.[101]

How many errors dissipated, how many systems overthrown, how many ideas corrected, perhaps how many regrets excited in more than one soul by this single definition! How many grey-haired old men learn here that one may die at the age of a hundred years without having lived a single day! When we reflect on this definition and cast a look over the face of the earth—when we see the use that kings and peoples, learned and ignorant, rich and poor, old and young, make of time—we may well hide our faces in our hands, and sit down, like Jeremias, to weep for the wreck of intelligence. O man! son of a culprit and a culprit thyself, thou hast only a day to wash off the stain that sullies thy soul, and this day thou dost employ in sullying it more. O fallen king! thou hast only a day to regain thy throne, and this day thou dost employ in running after phantoms. O slave of the devil! thou hast only a day to break thy yoke, and this day thou dost employ in riveting thy chains. Behold the night cometh, the deep dark night of eternity, when no one can work anymore, and thou thinkest not of it!

Division of time.—To recall man continually to himself, the Church has divided time. Like everything else that comes from the Catholic Church, this division of time bears the grand seal of wisdom and utility. The ecclesiastical year is divided into three parts. The first, which comprises the time of Advent until Christmas, retraces for us the four thousand years of preparation, the sighs and hopes of the ancient world, until the moment when the heavens, opening, let the just one, the Desired of Nations, come down. The second, which extends from Christmas to the Ascension, includes the whole mortal life of the Redeemer. The third, which begins at Pentecost and ends at All Saints, recalls the life of the Church.

Thus, this division of time, which retraces for us the whole history of the world, and the whole history of Christianity, past, present, and future, terminates with the festival of heaven. In effect, all things lead thither: heaven is the end of all things.

This division, which has passed into the ideas and even the language of man, inspires him without his perceiving it with holy thoughts, and gives him an understanding of himself and of life. It exercises on the morals of peoples an influence far more salutary than is generally imagined. If you doubt this, the impious of the last century, more intelligent than you, did not doubt it. In their fury to abolish Christianity, see what eagerness they displayed to sweep away this division of the year, that they might be rid of the memories attached to it, and might substitute for it their own republican calendars. Time and reason did quick justice to this foolish attempt. The ideas of eighteen centuries are not to be effaced in a day, especially when these ideas recall events that embrace the whole history of the human race. Man and Christianity are so bound together that, in order to abolish the latter, it would be necessary to annihilate and then create anew the former.

Among the events that make up our history, there are some glorious, some sad, some consoling: the Church consecrates the memory of all. But—how admirable!—amongst the saddest events that religion presents to our consideration, there is always room left for hope, consequently for joy. This is the reason why she calls by the name of *festivals* the days on which she celebrates their anniversaries.[102]

Festivals.—The word *festival* means "a happy day," "a pleasant day," "a day of solemn assembly." Among all ancient peoples there were days of festivity or assembly, whether civil or religious. As they used to be followed, so they are still generally followed, by repasts in common: hence the name *feast*, which means "a banquet," "a repast of joy and ceremony." We may, therefore, say either that *festival* comes from *feast* or that *feast* comes from *festival*. The reason is because there is no festival without a feast. The Church herself forbids fasts on Sundays, and, as a general rule, on holidays. The most holy personages have always felt that ordinary mortifications should cease on festivals, and that it is becoming to make a feast then, that is to say, a better repast than usual. Their views are confirmed even by the conduct of the anchorets of Thebaid. On festivals, these wonderful men used to depart a little from their accustomed frugality and austerity.

Why did they act in this manner? Because all festivals here below are an image of, or a prelude to, the everlasting festival. Now, in the everlasting festival, soul and body shall have their own separate joys. Such is the reason why innocent feasts have at all times, among Christian peoples, accompanied their religious solemnities.

With the material feast, conformable to the spirit of Christianity, our Lord, the Blessed Virgin, and the saints prepare for us on our festive days a spiritual feast. They set before us, like so many exquisite dishes, their instructions and their virtues. Then, doing the honors of the table, they say to us, "Will you have some humility? Here it is. Take and eat: *accipite et manducate*. Some meekness? Here it is. Take and eat: *accipite et manducate*. Some patience, some prudence, some charity. Here they are. Take and eat: *accipite et manducate*." So of the other virtues. The soul makes its repast from them by studying them, admiring them, and imitating them.

Here we understand by *festivals* those days on which we assemble to praise God. In this sense, festivals are as necessary as the assemblies of religion. Never had any people public worship without festivals forming part thereof: hence, we find them established from the beginning of the world.

The patriarchs had their festivals. They assemble their family, sometimes on an eminence, under the shade of a cedar or a palm tree, sometimes before a stone of the desert:[103] they wash themselves, change their clothes, purify themselves, offer sacrifices in acknowledgment of the benefits that they have received from God. Noe saved from the deluge, Abraham laden with the blessings and promises of God, Isaac assured of God's favor, Jacob returned from Mesopotamia and protected from his brother's anger, celebrate these happy events by raising altars and offering sacrifices. Having become a nation, the descendants of the patriarchs had also their festivals, whose object, number, and pomp God himself vouchsafed to regulate.

Christianity continues the long chain of sacred traditions: it also has its festivals. We shall soon speak of them in detail.

Their object under the patriarchs, under Moses, under the gospel.—The chief object of festivals varied according to times. Under the patriarchs, in the primitive religion, the chief object of festivals was to impress on mankind the idea of one only God, the Creator and ruler of the universe, the Father and benefactor of his creatures. In the Jewish religion, festivals were intended to awaken the remembrance of one only God, the legislator, supreme master, and special protector of his people. In Christianity, they show us a God the Savior and Sanctifier of men, all whose designs tend to their eternal salvation. Thus, nothing serves better than festivals to point out for us the direct object of religious worship during the three great epochs of revelation. One would be inclined to call them magnificent lamps placed along the high road of ages, to show the generations that follow the exact point reached in the development of truth among the generations that went before.

Another object of festivals is to fix, by recalling them every year, the memorable events of religion. And what great events were those recalled to the Jews by the festivals of the Pasch, Pentecost, and Tabernacles! What events do not these same days repeat to Christians! Then the Ascension, the Assumption, Christmas, and so many others! The whole history of the human race is broadly sketched, as it were, in religious festivals. The Jews also perpetuated events of minor importance by festivals. The deliverance of the inhabitants of Bethulia by Judith and the deliverance of all the Jews by Esther were objects of perpetual festivals with them.

Festivals of the martyrs and saints.—It has been the same in Christianity. From the beginning, the festivals of martyrs were celebrated. According to our ancestors' way of thinking, the death of a martyr was a victory for him, an example for his brethren, and a triumph for religion. The blood of this victim was cement to the edifice of the Church. The day of his death was solemnized; an assembly met at his tomb, and the holy mysteries were celebrated there. The courage of the faithful was hereby roused. This custom appears in the Acts of the martyrdom of St. Ignatius and St. Polycarp—the second century—and we cannot doubt but that it was followed in Rome immediately after the martyrdom of Sts. Peter and Paul.

The testimony of the apostles and their disciples, sealed by their blood, was too precious not to be brought continually before the eyes of the faithful. The same motives that led to the establishment of the festivals of the martyrs gave rise to festivals of confessors, that is to say, of saints who, without having suffered death, had edified the Church by the heroism of their virtues. Their life was a glorious testimony to the holiness of Christianity, and a proof that the morals of the gospel are impracticable to none. What more useful lesson to consecrate by a perpetual festival?

Superiority of Christian festivals.—The foregoing remarks let us see the superiority of Christian over Jewish and patriarchal festivals. In the latter, there were great events honored, no doubt; but, great as they were, they were only a shadow of far greater events. What conclusion have we to draw unless that our dispositions for celebrating them ought to be far more perfect than those of the Jews and the patriarchs?

Their beauty and harmony. What shall we say of the beauty of festivals, that is, of their harmony with the seasons in which they occur, with the mysteries which they recall, and with the wants of our heart? He is much to be pitied who is insensible to the admirable succession of our solemnities. Take away our festivals, and see what a dull monotony reigns throughout the course of the year! Try to change the order in which they are celebrated, and you will see how profound was the wisdom that arranged their dates!

To take a few examples. Place the festival of Easter in autumn, when all nature presents an image of death, and the days shorten, and the trees grow bare, and the dry leaves are blown about by the wind like the dust of the tomb, and the sky is overcast with gloomy clouds: What do you think of the change? Is there not a striking contrast, an extreme difficulty of entering into the spirit of the solemnity? In like manner, celebrate Corpus Christi in January, and tell me whether you experience the sentiments of gladness that the triumph of the man-God ought to inspire.

On the contrary, suppose that instead of celebrating Christmas in winter, we should celebrate it in the beautiful days of summer: Would you not immediately feel a weakening of your compassionate piety toward the newborn babe of Bethlehem? How difficult to excite in our hearts, under a broiling heat, the tender sentiments that we should have for this little infant perishing with cold! Place Christmas again on the 25th of December, and you will feel, as if in spite of yourself, a loving pity for the divine child, born in the middle of a long winter's night, in a damp cave, open on all sides to the piercing winds. You need not be surprised: in the one case, there is a discord between the festival and the season; in the other, there is a harmony. Order being restored, obstacles disappear, and, without an effort, the heart feels all that it ought to feel.[104]

Go down still deeper into these mysterious harmonies, and you will see that, in the course of the year, there is not a want of our heart but the succession of our festivals satisfies. The heart of man is so made that it cannot, it will not always have the same sentiments. Variety is its life; monotony, its death. It is like a lute, which sounds well only when the strings are touched by an experienced hand. We require, in point of fact, one after another, sentiments of hope, faith, a holy sadness, joy, gladness, and love—a few smiles and a great many tears. We require, above all, a great variety of motives to excite us to the love and practice of virtue.

Now, study well the linking of the three parts of the ecclesiastical year, and tell us if—thanks to the arrangement of our festivals!—there is a single virtue that, in a year, is not proposed for our imitation, or a single fiber of our heart that is not stirred. Woe, woe to those who have no other way of distinguishing the seasons than by sensations of heat or cold, and for whom all our religious harmonies are as if they were not! This moral insensibility, this spiritual paralysis, is more than a misfortune: it is a punishment. It is the punishment of those who, having become like beasts by their appetites, have deserved to know life no longer but by gross sensations.[105]

Their social advantages. Our Christian festivals have yet other advantages. They concern in the highest degree the material well-being of man and the peace of society. So true is it, as infidels themselves acknowledge, that religion, whose only object seems to be the happiness of the next life, is also the best means to render us happy in this life!

"What is to be thought," asks John James Rousseau, "of those who want to deprive the people of their festivals, as if they were so many distractions, turning them aside from their labors? This maxim is false and barbarous; and so much the worse if the people have only time to earn their bread. They are necessary, to eat it with joy: without which, it will not long be earned. The just and beneficent God who wills that they should be occupied wills also that they should refresh themselves. Nature imposes on them exercise and rest, pleasure and pain alike. The disgust of labor oppresses the miserable more than labor itself. Do you wish to have the people active and laborious? Give them festivals… The days thus lost will be worth much more than the others."

For the people, therefore, festivals are necessary, and by *the people* I mean great and little, rich and poor, learned and ignorant, kings and subjects; for all are human beings, consisting of a twofold nature, and controlled by the senses. But what festivals will you give the people in order to render them more active and laborious? Civil festivals? But they are only for the inhabitants of large cities. The expenses that they involve and the preparations that they require make it impossible to have them in the country. If you have only civil festivals, you condemn never to see festivals those for whom a long continuance of toil and privation renders them most necessary. Civil festivals? But nowadays, divided as we are with political enmities, civil festivals wound and humble one party or another: the triumph of the conquerors exasperates the conquered.

Will you leave to the people the task of providing festivals for themselves? But the people, and by *the people* I mean, as I said before, the rich as well as the poor, those who dwell in palaces as well as those who sleep under thatch, will seek them in debauchery. You will see some, hurrying from the table to the theatre and from the theatre to the table, squander away their property in folly. You will see others bury themselves in taverns, degrade themselves, brutalize themselves, and, wasting in a few hours the support of their families for a whole week, condemn their wives and children to hunger and tears.

This unwise principle, once set on foot, will every day make new progress. Playhouses, coffee rooms, schools of vice, all sorts of places of debauchery will increase. A false policy, a sordid interest, a wild recklessness will say that these pestilential establishments have become necessary. Good citizens, honest employers will complain of it: they can no longer keep in their workshops either their men or their apprentices. Useless lamentations! The people must have their festivals.

You deprived the people of those which suited them, because they alone could render them more active and laborious, consequently more moral. You turned the people into ridicule when they assisted at them, you disgusted the people with them: they sought others. Now, these immoral, discontented people disturb your sleep, and mar your enjoyments, until such times as they can pay you with pillage and violence for your impious lessons. The longer the delay, so much the worse for you!

And what, then, were those festivals which suited the people, because they suited society altogether? They were religious festivals. First, all may take part in them. The inhabitants of the country are no more excluded than those of the city. They are not burdensome either to rich or poor: it is often regarded as an honor and a pleasure to contribute to their splendor. Here no one is crushed. It is not a triumph over others that is celebrated: there are no parties in our temples. Children have no dislikes when they are gathered together round their mother's knee: if there are any tears, they are tears of joy or repentance. Profane concerts, the immodest dances of theatres, the shouts of revelry, the transports of rage, the excesses of debauchery are replaced by holy canticles, by magnificent and impressive ceremonies. The passions are lulled to rest. The soul recovers its vigor. Man, sweetly refreshed, becomes more active and more disposed to labor, because he becomes better.

Yes, to make man better, that is to say, more moral, is the great advantage, the special advantage of religious festivals. They assemble men at the feet of their common master, increase peace and affection among them, and recall the memory of those events on which religion is grounded, and which are so many benefits of God. They lead us to virtue, by setting before us splendid models, saints of every age, rank, and profession, who, having been what we are, weak and tempted, say to us from the heights of heaven that it only remains for us to be one day what they are now. Do not tell us that these beautiful lessons, given amid the display of our ceremonies, in turn majestic, graceful, and terrible, are altogether useless: lest we should despair of humanity. If they are so, what becomes of your high-sounding maxims and your fine theories about the indefinite perfectibility of the human species?

The Church, therefore, by instituting festivals, provided for the good of society as well as of individuals. In a well-ordered state, religion, morals, social virtues are no less necessary than money, labor, business: men are wanted, not beasts or automatons. Now, do you know any better means of having men and citizens than religion? And on what occasions does religion exercise more sway than on our solemnities?

Sanctification of festivals.—In days not long gone by, there was a complaint of the multitude of festivals, and lo, they were nearly all suppressed, at least in France. What have we gained thereby? The laborer, the tradesman has worked a few days more; but has he become happier? Alas, no! he has gained nothing, even by his work. He now spends more days in debauchery than he used to spend in the church, when all our festivals existed. The difference is even to his loss: the days of our festivals used to cost him nothing, while the days of his libertinism now cost him his money and his health.

The Church therefore showed herself truly wise and truly motherly in multiplying her solemnities. Never did she make a better use of her power. Happy shall we be if we profit at least of the festivals left to us! For this purpose, we must sanctify them, we must enter into the spirit of each solemnity. But what, then, is the spirit of a solemnity? It is the intention that the Church proposed to herself in instituting the solemnity. This intention we must know well in order to penetrate our souls with dispositions conformable to it. Sometimes, it is a virtue that is commanded us; sometimes, it is a sentiment that we must renew: there is always something to believe and to imitate.

Let us yield to grace, and the Holy Spirit will tell us all that we should do to celebrate our festivals in such a manner that they may become for us a pledge of admission to that everlasting festival of which they are a faint image. A preparatory novena and the Holy Communion are the true means of profiting of the graces which God pours out on these holy days with more than ordinary abundance. May they prove days of such blessings for all who read these lines![106]

PRAYER

O my God! who art all love, I thank thee for having established festivals in order to remind me of thy benefits and the more effectually to lead me to virtue.

I am resolved to love God above all things, and my neighbor as myself for the love of God; and, in testimony of this love, I will prepare for festivals by a novena.

Lesson 7: Christianity Brought before the Senses (Continued)—Sundays, Divine Office

Sunday: Its history, its object, and its observance among the early Christians.—The first of all Christian festivals is Sunday. Its history is this: God, having created the world in six days, rested on the seventh. He sanctified it, and commanded men also to sanctify it. "Remember," he said, "to keep holy the sabbath day. You shall do no work on that day, you nor your children, nor your menservants, nor your maidservants, nor your cattle, nor the stranger that is staying with you, that they may all rest as well as you. Remember that you yourselves served in Egypt, and that God brought you out thence by his power: therefore does he command you the day of rest."[107]

Thus the rest of the sabbath or the seventh day was commanded to the Jews, not only from a motive of religion, but also from a principle of humanity. The same causes exist in the institution of the Sunday. The repose of soul and body, the welfare of the whole man, is the object of the institution of the Lord's day, which may also be justly termed "man's day." Impiety showed itself cruelly unreasonable when, suppressing the Sunday, it tried to calculate the strength of workmen as if they were beasts of burden. Man, however robust, needs rest. All nations have felt it, and have appointed days to provide for this necessity.[108] The seventh is the most suitable.

"It is now known by experience that the fifth is a day too near and the tenth a day too remote, for rest. Terror, which could do everything in France, could never make the peasant keep the decade, because there is a weakness in human strength, and it has been remarked in animal strength. The ox cannot work nine days successively: at the end of the sixth, its moans seem to ask the hours fixed by the Creator for the general repose of nature. The peasants used to say, 'Our oxen know the Sunday and will not work on it.'"[109]

We have said that the rest of the seventh day recalled the existence of God, the Creator of the universe. Now, after the extinction of paganism and idolatry, it was no longer necessary to continue to celebrate the sabbath, or the rest of the seventh day, in memory of the creation. The belief of one only God, the Creator, could no longer be lost; but it was most important to consecrate by an everlasting monument the memory of that great miracle which serves as a foundation to Christianity—the resurrection of our Lord.

The establishment of Sunday renders this fact incontestable, and keeps it ever present to the eyes of the generations that come and go on the earth. It was the very witnesses of the event who established the festival intended to perpetuate the memory of it. They caused it to be commemorated, in the very place where it had occurred, by thousands of men able to prove of themselves the truth or the falsehood of their assertions, and to obtain from others all the information desirable. Unless those people were all seized with the most extraordinary madness, how could they agree to render testimony, by a public ceremony repeated every eight days, to an imaginary event, or to one of which they were not perfectly convinced? Add that, in order to practice this ceremony or to assist at it, it was necessary during the space of three hundred years to run the risk of tortures and death.

Sunday is therefore an ever-living proof of the resurrection of our Lord.[110] Consider how our ancestors in the faith celebrated this great day. Let us go back in imagination eighteen centuries, and enter one of those catacombs lighted up by a multitude of little lamps hanging from the roof or fastened to the walls. Around these tombs of martyrs, what are we going to see, what are we going to hear? Let us be attentive: St. Justin will explain for us all the ceremonies of the primitive Sunday.

"On the day of the sun, that is, Sunday,[111] all those who dwell in town and country meet in one place. The first thing to be done is to read the writings of the apostles or the prophets, as long as time permits. The reading over, he who presides delivers a discourse to the assembly in order to instruct them, and to exhort them to practice the sublime maxims of virtue and religion which they have just heard. We then all rise[112] to make our prayer in common. We pray for ourselves, and for those who are baptized at the time, and for all mankind, of whatsoever nation, that all may come to a knowledge of the truth, may lead a holy life, full of good works, may keep the commandments of the Lord, and may at length attain to eternal glory. The prayers ended, we salute one another with the kiss of peace.

"Then some bread and a cup of wine and water are presented to him who presides. Having taken them, he renders glory to the Father in the name of the Son and the Holy Ghost, and makes him a long thanksgiving for those same gifts, which it has pleased him to grant to us. The prayers and thanksgiving concluded, all the people present say in a loud voice, 'Amen'—a Hebrew word, meaning 'So be it!' Then those whom we call deacons distribute to each of the persons present some bread, and wine and water, consecrated with thanksgiving, and carry thereof to the absent.

"We call this food the Eucharist, and no one is permitted to partake of it if he does not believe the truth of our doctrine, if he has not received the remission of his sins and a new life, and if he does not live according to the precepts of Jesus Christ. For we do not take it as common bread or ordinary drink, but as the flesh and blood of our Savior. He has taught us that, by the efficacy of the Eucharistic prayer, which contains the very words of the Savior, this bread and wine become the flesh and blood of this same Jesus who was made flesh for our salvation. In effect, the apostles teach us in the memoirs which they have left us and which are called gospels that Jesus Christ commanded them to act thus, when, having taken bread and returned thanks, he said, 'Do this in commemoration of me: this is my body'; and having taken the cup in like manner and returned thanks, said, 'This is my blood.'

"We then recall these things in memory of our brethren. Those who have means relieve the poor, and we are always of one heart with one another. In all these offerings, we bless the Creator of all things, through his Son Jesus Christ and the Holy Ghost. The alms which each one gives with the greatest freedom are placed in the hands of him who presides, and who is charged to assist widows, orphans, strangers, the sick, in a word, all who are in sorrow from any cause whatsoever.[113]

"We are accustomed to assemble on the day of the sun, because it is the day on which God began the creation of the world. It is also the day on which Jesus Christ our Savior rose from the dead, and appeared to his apostles and taught them what we have just set before you."[114]

Is it a history of the Sunday of the second century that we have just heard, or rather a history of the Sunday as we still see it in the nineteenth century? Is it a picture of a catacomb or of a Catholic temple that has just passed before our eyes? It is both. Admire, ye children of the holy Roman Church! the vigor with which your mother lays the seal of immortality on all that she touches. What your ancestors did, do not you still do? Are not all the memories of the primitive Sunday preserved among us?

At our High Masses, do we not find these readings from the holy books of the old and the new testament, these prayers in common, these instructions to exhort us to virtue, this bread distributed to the faithful, these gifts made to the poor and to captives? If proud minds despise a High Mass, it is because they are unacquainted with the old and holy usages that it recalls. A wonderful thing! there is not in all Christendom a village that does not every eight days present souvenirs of antiquity to the most learned, souvenirs of the Caesars, the circus, the catacombs, and the martyrs![115]

Prayer in common: The divine office.—The prayers in common of our ancestors in the faith afford us here an opportunity of speaking of the divine office, that is to say, of the true prayer in common, or rather the public prayer of Christianity. Though the faithful say the office no longer, yet they assist at it at least once on Sundays. They even recite a part of it, vespers for example, and sometimes compline. Their piety, their respect for the prayers and usages of the Church cannot but gain much if they know the meaning of the office in its entirety.

Origin of the divine office.—All men have prayed, and prayed in common. The early Christians were particularly fond of assembling to offer up to God the sacrifice of their lips. Their ears still rang with the words of their divine master: "Where two or three are gathered together in my name, there am I in the midst of them."[116] Pursued like innocent sheep by cruel wolves, they endeavored to find the strength and constancy necessary for them by placing their hearts, their desires, and their prayers in common with those of their brethren, whose fortunes and dangers they also shared.

By night as well as by day, the hours were regulated for prayer. The *Apostolic Constitutions* tell the faithful to pray in the morning, at the third hour, at the sixth hour, at the ninth hour, in the evening, and at midnight.[117] St. Jerome, writing to an illustrious Roman lady on the education of her daughter, says: "Place near her a virgin of mature years, a model of faith and modesty, who may teach and train her by example to rise at night to pray and to sing psalms; in the morning, to sing sacred hymns; from terce to sext and none, to continue the combat, like a heroine of Jesus Christ; about sunset, to light her lamp, like a wise virgin, and offer the evening sacrifice."[118] The same saint assures us, in his letters, that the Christian reaper used to accompany his labors with the singing of psalms, and that the vinedresser, cutting his vine, would repeat the canticles of David.[119]

The monks of Egypt and Thebaid, and the solitaries of Palestine and Mesopotamia, used to meet several times a day to recite psalms and to sing hymns to the glory of the Lord. It was not religious alone that prayed thus at different hours of the day and night: the generality of the faithful followed this holy custom. St. Augustine, addressing his people, says, "My dear brethren, rise, I beseech you, at a better hour to assist at the watches. Come especially to the offices of terce, sext, and none. Let no person dispense himself from this holy work, unless he is prevented by some sickness, by some service that he renders to the public, or by a great necessity."[120]

The collection of all these prayers is called the "divine office," because it is a duty that we fulfill toward God, in order to adore him, to appease him, to thank him, and to ask his graces. We see from what has been said that the office, almost the same as it still exists, reaches back to the most remote antiquity. The Church, inheriting old traditions, established it to perpetuate the sacred canticles that had resounded through the Temple of Jerusalem, and had found an echo along the slopes of Mount Sinai and the shores of the Red Sea. She wished thus to make easy for Christians the exercise of prayer.

Different hours of the office.—Here again, a tradition of three thousand years. David said to the Lord, "I sing thy praises seven times a day";[121] and the divine office is divided into seven parts, which are called "hours," because they are recited at seven different hours of the night and day. The names of these hours are matins, prime, terce, sext, none, vespers, and compline. This division comes from the most remote antiquity.[122] Lauds, which are sometimes reckoned an eighth hour, form part of matins or the office of night. It is therefore on the venerable authority of a tradition of three thousand years that the division of the office into seven hours, adopted by the Church, has been established. But on what does this tradition itself rest? On the admirable harmonies of the number *seven* with God, man, and the world.

a) The number *seven* is that of the gifts of the Holy Ghost. "The old serpent," says St. Jerome, "driven out of the human heart, returns with seven devils more wicked than himself. It is impossible for us to resist him if we are not strengthened by the seven gifts of the Holy Ghost. It is in order to obtain them that we pray seven times a day."[123] b) The number *seven* is that of the capital sins. It is in order to avoid them, or to raise ourselves out of them if we have fallen into them, that we pray seven times a day. c) All the spiritual and temporal wants of the human race are seven in number, expressed in the seven petitions of the Our Father. It is in order to obtain the objects of these petitions that we pray seven times a day. d) The number *seven* is that of the days of creation and God's rest. It is in order to recall this great week, which saw the world come forth from nothingness, and to excite ourselves to thank God for every part of creation, which we must use well, if we would reach the holy rest of eternity, that we pray seven times a day. The reasons for this sevenfold division already existed three thousand years ago. Behold the foundations of a venerable tradition, and the proof of the profound wisdom of the Church!

"What dreams!" will perhaps be the exclamation of some shallow-minded men, unaccustomed to reflect. Ah, well! let them be dreams as much as you please; but we would rather dream with St. Jerome, St. Basil, and St. Augustine than argue with you.[124]

Beauty of the office.—To have an idea of the excellence of the divine office, it will be enough for you to know of what it consists. It is an abridgment[125] of all that is most beautiful in the most beautiful of all books, the Bible; of all that is most affecting and most sublime in the *Lives of the Saints*; of all the prayers that have issued from the inflamed hearts of the noblest geniuses that the world has ever seen; of all the sacred canticles that faith has suggested to Christian piety. It contains, in their entirety, those inimitable songs, those immortal poems of the royal prophet, in which the heart, the mind, and the imagination find an ocean, as it were, of unrivaled beauties, of the purest thoughts, of the most divine sentiments. Was there ever a more beautiful collection of more beautiful things? Was there ever a more powerful prayer?

A monarch wishes to load his dear spouse with favors; but he wishes that she should ask him for them. And lo! he himself draws up the petition, states the manner in which it is to be presented, and then places it in her hands, swearing by his heart to grant all that he has promised, as soon as she presents it to him from her hand, her lips, and her heart. Behold God, the Church, and the breviary!

Oh, what power over the heart of God must not those three or four hundred thousand priests have, who daily present themselves seven times before his throne, in order to ask him, as he wishes, for the favors which he himself has promised to his beloved spouse the Church, and of which she has need! And when we think that, every hour of the day and night, there are thousands of priests engaged in this sublime function, that the East prays when the West rests, so that the voice of prayer is never interrupted, do we not seem to be in the heavenly Jerusalem, where the blessed repeat unceasingly the canticle of eternity, "Holy, holy, holy, Lord God of hosts"?[126] What a flood of blessings does not this powerful supplication bring down on the earth! O guilty world, to it thou owest thy preservation, and thou forgettest it!

What more shall I say? All ages, all countries, all languages sing with us when we sing the psalms of David. While these immortal canticles are resounding through the vaults of our churches, they are repeated at Rome, Jerusalem, Pekin, Mexico, Petersburg, Cairo, Constantinople, Paris, London. The Temple of Solomon, the plains of Babylon and Memphis, the banks of the Jordan, the deserts of Egypt, the catacombs of Rome, and the basilicas of Nice, Corinth, and Antioch have heard them.

Through how many mouths purer than mine have they passed! Tobias on his bed of sorrow, Judith in the camp of Holofernes, Esther at the court of Assuerus, and Judas Machabeus at the head of the warriors of Israel, repeated them. Antony breathed them in the desert, Chrysostom at Antioch, Athanasius at Alexandria, Augustine at Hippo, Gregory at Nazianzen, Bernard at Clairvaux, and Xavier in Japan; and, after so many centuries, after expressing such a variety of sentiments, these immortal canticles are still as new as when, for the first time, David sang them on his harp. And does this not touch your heart? Does this not raise up your ideas? Does this not enable you to understand all the power of the incommunicable name of the Church your mother—*Catholic*?

Matins.—The first hour of the office is called "matins," "watches," or "nocturns," because it was formerly recited at night, as is still done at Christmas, and because it is now said in chapters at a very early hour of the morning. On Sundays and holidays, matins are divided into three nocturns—or parts consisting of three psalms,[127] three antiphons, and three lessons preceded by a blessing and followed by a response. The holy scripture furnishes the first lessons. The second are taken from the works of the fathers, or the *Lives of the Saints* whose festivals are celebrated. The third comment on the gospel of the day, a few verses of which are quoted.

In the first place, matins of Sunday are divided into three nocturns. The word *nocturn* means "an office of the night." The ancients divided the night into four parts, each of three hours: the first from six o'clock in the evening till nine; the second, from nine till midnight; the third, from midnight till three o'clock in the morning; and the fourth, from three till six. Each part was called a "watch" or a "duty." People spoke of the "first watch," the "second watch," and so on. These terms were taken from military speech. Soldiers "watched" or "did duty" every three hours.[128]

Like the armies of the Caesars, the army of Jesus Christ, the Church, always in the field, commands ecclesiastics to keep guard in turn throughout the camp, especially during the night; for this is an evil time, say the fathers, a time when the tempter comes, a time of sin.[129]

Hence, in the early ages, the nocturns were recited separately: the first during the first watch, the second during the second, the third during the third, and lauds during the fourth. The faithful assisted at them; but, after each nocturn, they were free to go and take their rest until the next. Even the most delicate persons would not be absent from them. We have seen that St. Jerome, writing to a lady, a descendant of the Paul Aemiliuses and the Scipios, told her to conform to this custom, and to train her daughter from childhood to rise at night, in order to sing hymns and psalms.[130]

In the course of time, the Church, having regard to human weakness, permitted the three nocturns together with lauds to be recited at one watch of the night, but her intentions did not change. She wishes to honor, by the various hours of the office, the principal mysteries of the Savior's passion, to give us the most useful lessons, and to procure for us the graces appropriate to each of our wants. We shall develop all these things when explaining the different hours of the office.

It may be asked why matins, which are the first part of the office, begin in the evening. It is because the ecclesiastical day begins in the evening: a venerable usage, which reminds us of antiquity, for among the Jews also the day began in the evening. Heiress to the synagogue, the Catholic Church continued this usage—full, moreover, of mysteries. In effect, matins are recited during the night: because it was during the night that the firstborn of the Egyptians were put to death by the destroying angel—an ever-memorable event, which led to the deliverance of the Israelite nation, an ancient figure of the Church; and because it was during the night that the liberator of the world was born, and that he accomplished a part of the mysteries of his sorrowful passion.

In memory of these events, the greatest recorded in the annals of the world, in thanksgiving for these benefits, and also in expiation of the crimes of the Jews and so many others committed during the night, the Church wished that priests and religious, all the angels of prayer, should be engaged in adoration and should pay the debt of the universe. Was it not, think you, a beautiful idea?

As soon as the bell tolled, how grand it was to see those priests, those religious, those white-haired old men go to the church! One would have said that it was a great battalion rushing to arms at the sound of the trumpet. "Having reached the church," says one of these old soldiers of Jesus Christ, "we prostrate ourselves before the altar, and salute our general, protesting that we shall always be obedient to him, and acknowledging that we cannot conquer without him."[131]

The office begins; but in what manner? As every supernatural work ought to begin, with an avowal of our own weakness. The priest makes the sign of the cross on his lips, saying, "O Lord, thou wilt open my lips, that my mouth may sing thy praise!" But, while the priest asks of God permission and grace to sing his praise, the devil redoubles his efforts to render this prayer useless. It is on this account that the priest, arming himself with the omnipotent sign of the cross, immediately adds, "O God, come to my aid!" The whole choir, each individual penetrated with a sense of his own weakness, answers in a loud voice, "O Lord, make haste to help me!" Instantly, the priest says, "Glory be to the Father, and to the Son, and to the Holy Ghost." And the choir answers, "As it was in the beginning, is now, and ever shall be, world without end!" That is to say, eternal glory to the God of eternity!

Why this hymn of glory and gratitude so soon after a cry of distress? Here is the reason. The Lord said, "You have not ended invoking me, when lo! I am with you."[132] Full of confidence in the promise of her divine spouse, the Church, understanding that she is heard, hastens to render glory to the Blessed Trinity. The *Gloria Patri* was composed by St. Jerome, who sent it to Pope Damasus. Through the petition of the holy anchoret of Bethlehem, the sovereign pontiff directed that this doxology should be sung at the end of the psalms.[133]

From Easter to Septuagesima Sunday, the *Gloria Patri* is followed by the *Alleluia*, a Hebrew word, which means joy or gladness. The Church places it at the head of her offices, to excite us to joy in serving God, according to the recommendation of the prophet: "Serve the Lord in joy."[134] And when will a child be happy if not when it sings the praises of its father?

After the *Alleluia* comes the invitatory or invitation. The priest is not content to praise God alone. A prophet of the new law, an ambassador of the Most High, he invites all his brethren to praise him also. The invitatory is an expression that gives in brief terms the special reason why we should praise God on the festival that is being celebrated. It is usually followed by these words, "Come, let us adore," which the choir repeats six or seven times in all. For, after setting before his brethren the particular motive that they have to praise God on the festival, the officiating clergyman gives them the general and unchangeable reasons for so doing, contained in the psalm *Venite exultemus*. He says, "Come, let us praise the Lord: he is our salvation."

The choir: "Come let us adore."

"He is the God of gods, the master of the universe; and, notwithstanding his greatness, he does not despise the prayers of his children."

The choir: "Come, let us adore."

"The sea belongs to him, the earth is the work of his hands. He made us ourselves, and we have not been afraid to offend him. Let us fall on our knees, let us pour out tears of love and repentance before him: we are his people, and the cherished flock that eat out of his hand."

The choir: "Come let us adore."

"He invites us to do so. Let us not be deaf to his voice, for fear the same should happen to us as happened to the Israelites of the desert."

The choir: "Come, let us adore."

"They were forty years in the wilderness, and were condemned never to see the promised land."

The choir: "Come, let us adore."

Search all ancient and modern poets, and tell us if you can find anything to compare with this magnificent dialogue. This sweetly measured converse, so proper to form in the heart the spirit of prayer, ends with a burst of love toward the Holy Trinity: *Gloria Patri*, etc.

PRAYER

O my God! who art all love, I thank thee for having instituted the Sunday. It is much more for my advantage than for thine that this holy day should be consecrated to prayer. Grant me the grace to sanctify it well.

I am resolved to love God above all things, and my neighbor as myself for the love of God; and, in testimony of this love, I will endeavor to become thoroughly acquainted with the ceremonies of the Church.

Lesson 8: Christianity Brought before the Senses (Continued)—Matins, Lauds

The hymn.—After the *Gloria Patri*, a burst of love toward the Holy Trinity, and after the invitatory, a song of joy or sadness according to the mystery that is celebrated, comes the hymn, the hymn intended to praise God, to raise our thoughts and affections on high, to form or to strengthen within us those sentiments and virtues which the festival of the day ought to inspire. Hence, all present are standing, all hearts are stirred, and all voices unite to sing the hymn.

Three things, says St. Augustine, constitute our hymns: 1) praise; 2) the praise of God; 3) singing.[135] The use of them reaches back to the cradle of Christianity. Our ancestors in the faith used to sing hymns in their houses and in the catacombs: they followed herein the counsel of St. Paul himself.[136] St. Chrysostom was the first to establish the singing of hymns during the office of the night. The occasion of his doing so was this: during the night, the Arians used to wander up and down the streets of Constantinople, singing hymns full of their impious doctrines. The Christians, when going home from the office, used to meet these heretics and be exposed to the pain of hearing them. To prolong the office until the Arians had returned to their houses, and also to strengthen the piety of the faithful by orthodox chants, the holy patriarch added hymns to matins and lauds.[137]

At matins, the hymn precedes the psalms; at lauds, vespers, and compline it follows them. It precedes them at matins, because the morning is for the just, who have the joy of a good conscience, while the evening is for penitents, whose conscience is stung with remorse. Joy leads the former to labor, figured by the psalms, as we shall show later on. It is by labor that the latter are to attain to joy. The hymns are sung standing, to show by this attitude of the body that the heart ought to be lifted up toward God while the mouth declares his praise. Thus, everything in external worship reminds us of the necessity of internal worship. Everything seems to repeat to us the saying of our divine master, "The Father seeks adorers in spirit and in truth."[138]

The antiphon.—The hymn ended, the officiating clergyman intones the antiphon. What is an antiphon? An antiphon is an alternate chant, a chant executed by two choirs that answer each other. The antiphon denotes the love of God; and the psalm, the labor of good works. The clergyman intones the first word of the antiphon, in order to animate the psalm, that is to say, labor, with the spirit of charity, without which labor is worth nothing. The psalm sung, the whole choir takes up the antiphon again, in order to continually blend charity with faith, whose works are efficacious only through charity. Thus, these two great virtues of Christianity are here like two sisters occupied in the same work, and cheerfully helping each other. The priest who alone intones the antiphon reminds you of Jesus Christ, the only source of charity. The whole choir singing it at the end of the psalm shows you the effusion of the charity of Jesus Christ among all his members.

The singing of antiphons dates from the most remote antiquity. St. Ignatius the Martyr, the glory of the East and the hero of the second century, having heard the blessed spirits sing antiphons in choir in the celestial Jerusalem, made known his revelation, and usage established the same in the terrestrial Jerusalem.[139]

The psalms.—After the antiphon comes the singing of the psalms: so Pope Gelasius ordained. These divine canticles recall the sufferings, the labors, the struggles of a persecuted king, and the joy that he finds in the protection of heaven, while they are an enthusiastic expression of the liveliest gratitude. Prophetic songs, they relate the trials, the fatigues, the battles, the triumph, and the glory of the true David, of the Church his spouse, and of the faithful soul, his beloved child, his living image. Thus, four voices are heard in the psalms: the voice of David, the voice of Jesus Christ, the voice of the Church, and the voice of the Christian.

It is therefore evident that the psalms represent the labor of life, the labor of good works. The word *psalm* means "a song that is executed on the psaltery." The psaltery was a musical instrument: "I will sing thy praise, O Lord, on my psaltery of ten strings!"[140]—mysterious words! which point out that we ought to praise God by keeping his ten commandments; for he alone praises God worthily who observes his law.

Pope Damasus ordered that the psalms should be sung in two choirs: an admirable arrangement! Do you not seem to see the saints on earth exciting one another to the labor of good works, while sharing with one another their joys and their hopes, their tears and their sighs, their gratitude and their love—continually acquainting one another with the inflamed words that they address to God, the protector of the weak, the support of the orphan, the Father of the poor, the Comforter of the afflicted, and the rewarder of the just? Do you not also seem to behold the accomplishment of the precept of the great apostle, "Help one another, hear one another's burdens"?[141] Lastly, do you not seem to behold those cherubim of whom Isaias had a glimpse, and who, standing before the throne of God, their faces veiled with their wings, cried out to one another, "Holy holy, holy, is the Lord God of hosts; the earth is full of the splendor of his glory"?[142]

Like the antiphons, the psalms are sung standing, in order to denote ardor for labor, zeal for good. You see the canons merely leaning against their stalls, while they are sung at all the hours of the office, except compline. We shall soon tell the reason for this exception.

Each psalm is followed by a *Gloria Patri*, to render glory to God for the good that he has just wrought; to remind us of the adorable Trinity, from whom all things come, and to whom all should return; to assure us that faith in the Blessed Trinity is the foundation of the Christian life, and to show that in all circumstances, in sorrow as well as in joy, in labor as well as in rest, we wish to praise and bless the Lord.

Versicles.—After each nocturn come three lessons. The lessons themselves are preceded by versicles and blessings, which we must explain first. The versicle is a short maxim, a striking remark, a warning given to rouse attention. It may, in effect, happen that, during the recital or singing of the psalms, which occasionally takes a long time, we yield to distraction or weariness. The versicle is therefore sung by one voice, that this variety may lay hold on the minds of the hearers, and keep them attentive to what is going to follow. What do you think of this idea? Did the Church your mother, who made this admirable arrangement, show that she understood human weakness well? Could you have found a better means to maintain attention of mind and devotion of heart?

To the versicle sung by a childlike voice succeeds the *Pater*, intoned by the grave voice of the officiant. The *Pater* is said because a lesson is going to follow. And should not man, who requires understanding and wisdom to grasp and relish holy truths, ask them of him who gives in abundance and without repentance? The *Pater* is said in a low voice to excite recollection, and to denote that we speak all alone with God, and that he hears, without the help of words, the prayer of our heart. Having come to the words, *Et ne nos inducas*—"And let us not yield to temptation," the priest raises his voice that he may teach all why the *Pater* is said, and prevent reader and hearer from yielding to the temptations of the devil during the lesson: a temptation of vanity for the one, and a temptation of negligence for the other.

Blessings.—The *Pater* is followed by a short prayer, called a blessing. It is intended to obtain what has just been asked for in the Our Father. In this new prayer, the three Persons of the adorable Trinity are addressed one after another.

The only question now is: Who shall be worthy to read the word of God? One of the assistants rises, and, turning toward the officiating clergyman, who represents Jesus Christ, says to him in a loud voice, *Jube, Domne, benedicere*—"Command, sir, to bless"; that is to say, "Order someone to announce your word of benediction."[143]

These little details contain a lesson of the highest importance: they teach us that in the Church no one must act as a minister unless he has been called to do so by legitimate authority. It is not for the ecclesiastical state alone that divine vocations and missions are necessary: they are also necessary, though in a different degree, for the other states of society. Whence come so many of the evils that afflict us, if not from the fact that there is hardly any person in his place or willing to remain in it? But let us return to our subject.

To this request for a blessing, which is repeated before every lesson, the officiant answers by prayers proper to interest all the citizens of the heavenly Jerusalem in the success of the holy lecture. Sometimes he asks that the Lord may vouchsafe to open our hearts to his law, lest the holy word that we are going to hear should be like a seed that is carried away by the birds of the air, or choked by briars, or trampled underfoot by the passersby. Sometimes he asks that we may be admitted to the happiness of the saints, of whose virtues we are going to read. The priest desires all things for us in the name of God: he shows us hereby that it does not belong to him, a sinful man, to bless, but to him who alone is good, that is to say, the author of every good.

The lessons.—Minds attentive, a blessing obtained, the graces of understanding and wisdom asked—the lessons begin. They consist of passages from the old or the new testament, the commentaries of the fathers or doctors, and the Life of the saint whose festival is celebrated. The scripture is the law; the writings of the fathers or doctors, its explanation; the Life of the saint, its application. What more complete instruction? The better to hear it, everyone sits and keeps a profound silence. Are there any words in the world that better deserve this attitude of recollection and respect?

The responses.—The lessons end thus: *Tu autem, Domine, miserere nostri*—"But do thou, O Lord, have mercy on us." An affecting acknowledgment of our misery! Yes, my God! the reader seems to say, "Forgive us the faults that may have accompanied this reading: in me, the sentiments of vanity or negligence of which I have been guilty; in my brethren, the distractions or little fervor with which they may have listened to thy divine oracles."

All the assistants answer: *Deo gratias*—"Thanks be to the Lord!" They refer to the lessons. Their meaning is this: if it is a duty of man to thank God for the corporal food which he daily receives from him, how much more sacred is the obligation of thanking him for the manna of his word, with which he nourishes our souls! Children of God, let us return thanks to our heavenly Father for the spiritual food which he has just given us!

We are now instructed by, and also grateful for, the doctrine which we have just received. But what means have we of showing our gratitude unless by putting the holy word into practice and imitating the admirable examples just set before us? It is to this that all the assistants oblige themselves by the responses, which are recited immediately after the lessons, and alternately by the two choirs. The responses of the third lesson end with a *Gloria Patri*, so as to remind us that all our prayers and all our works ought to be referred to the last end of all things, the Blessed Trinity.

Thus is recited or chanted the first nocturn, that is to say, the first part of matins. In the early ages, it was said about nine o'clock in the evening, the time when men are accustomed to go to rest. It had no invitatory in some churches, because the sacred ministers recited it alone, the people not being called. This first nocturn was properly termed a watch or vigil, in memory of the shepherds who were keeping watch over their flocks in the neighborhood of Bethlehem when the Savior of the world was born. What mysteries does this sacred hour recall to us: the watch of the shepherds, the Savior's tender farewell to his apostles, and his agony in the Garden of Gethsemani! If we have faith, what generous sentiments of the heart and fervent prayers shall we unite, during this first nocturn, with the pledges of the great victim's love!

In churches where the people did not assist at the beginning of the office, the second nocturn began with the invitatory, because all the faithful, men and women, were called to it. Here again a beautiful tradition, a touching harmony! Ecclesiastics, the angels of the earth, invited to the adoration of the Savior the faithful entrusted to their care, as the angels of heaven had invited the shepherds of Bethlehem. The second nocturn was sung at midnight. How many mysteries does this sacred hour also recall to us: the birth of the Savior, the summons of the angels, the adoration of the shepherds, the sufferings of Jesus before the tribunals of Annas and Caiphas!

The third nocturn was recited about three o'clock in the morning. This for three great reasons: first, to honor the Savior in the humiliations that he suffered during the dreadful night that he spent at the mercy of servants and soldiers; second, to ask pardon for the sentence of death pronounced against him about this hour by Caiphas; third, to expiate St. Peter's denial.

"Here is the reason," say the fathers, "for this mysterious distribution of our solemn matins. The three nocturns recall the three great epochs of humanity: the patriarchal epoch, the Mosaic epoch, and the Christian epoch. Each of these epochs is divided into three periods. Hence, in each nocturn, three psalms, three anthems, three lessons. They are like a poem divided into nine cantos.

"The patriarchal epoch has its first period from Adam to Noe; its second, from Noe to Abraham; and its third, from Abraham to Moses.

"The Mosaic epoch has its first period from Moses to David; its second, from David to the captivity of Babylon; and its third, from the captivity of Babylon to the Messias.

"The Christian epoch is likewise divided into three periods. The first, which comprises the foundation of the Church by our Lord, and its establishment by the apostles, is the period of martyrs. The second, which comprises the time of great heresies, and of the great lights of the East and West, is the period of the fathers of the Church. The third, which comprises the time of peace that followed the extinction of the great heresies, is the period of the Church victorious."[144]

The number *three*, so often repeated, is a hymn to the three adorable Persons of the Trinity, as the nine psalms are a memorial of the nine choirs of angels, and of all the harmonies of the celestial Jerusalem, in whose canticles the terrestrial Jerusalem, a younger sister, invites all her children to join. Hence, on our solemn days, the voice of heaven and the voice of earth blend into one sweet loud voice, saying, "Holy, holy, holy is the God of hosts; the heavens and the earth are full of the splendor of his majesty." What a source of holy and affecting thoughts for the enlightened and pious believer! What a source of purest inspiration for the Christian poet!

The Te Deum.—The third nocturn ends with the *Te Deum*. A hymn, a prayer, an epic poem, the *Te Deum* is all that can be desired, all that can be found most beautiful in any language. Immortal honor to you, Ambrose and Augustine! sublime geniuses, illustrious saints, who could express the thoughts of your minds and the affections of your hearts as seraphs would express theirs, if seraphs spoke the language of mortals! The *Te Deum* is so exceedingly beautiful that protestants, cold as they are in their prayers, frozen as is their worship, enemies as they are of the Roman Church, have carefully retained it.

But why is it said at the end of the third nocturn? Behold the answer. All the children of God, the priests and the faithful, have just praised the Lord, have encouraged one another to fervor and charity. They have just heard the reading of the law which dilates their hearts, and the history of their brethren already glorified in the bosom of their common Father. They have seen the palm branches and the crowns, a never-ending reward for labor of short duration. How do you think that all together, full of these thoughts, should not burst forth into thanksgiving? Be no longer surprised that they sing the *Te Deum*. The sounds of bells, which formerly joined with their voices, were a new expression of the general gladness and ardor, and a solemn summons to all creatures to praise with them a Father so great and so good.

Lauds.—The three nocturns form the first three parts of matins; lauds form the fourth. This division was established, as we have already said, to sanctify the four watches of the night. Lauds were recited in olden times, and, properly speaking, should still be recited at break of day. The reasons are these: a) it was at break of day that our Lord rose triumphant from the tomb; and b) it was at break of day that he walked on the waves, and made St. Peter walk thereon.

The word *lauds* means "praises." As a matter of fact, it is in this part of the night office that we particularly celebrate the praises of God, and that we thank him a) for the resurrection of our Savior, the fundamental miracle of Christianity, wrought at this time; b) for the grace that he grants us to walk, like St. Peter, during the night of this life, on the stormy sea of the world; c) for the creation of the universe, of which the gradual appearance of light presents us an image; and d) for the paternal care with which he has watched over us during the night, and the goodness with which he gives us a new day.

Like the nocturns, lauds begin with the invocation *Deus in adjutorium*, accompanied with the sign of the cross, and followed by the *Gloria Patri*, the *Alleluia*, and the announcement of the antiphon. At the end of each psalm, the *Gloria Patri* is repeated. Gratitude desires that it should be so. Have we not seen that the psalms express good works, Christian labors? What then can be more just than to return thanks to God, from whom every good work comes, and who consequently deserves to be praised and thanked "as it was in the beginning," when he created heaven and earth; "is now," when he preserves material and spiritual works, both of which exist only by him; and "ever shall be," when there shall be a new heaven and a new earth, and God shall be all in all?

At lauds there are five psalms, or rather four psalms and a canticle, said.[145] The renovation of our five senses, that is to say, the repairing of our whole being by Christianity, the principal mysteries of which have just been celebrated during the night, the mysterious reason for the number *five*, and the important lesson which the Church gives us at the beginning of a new day.

After the first three psalms, the canticle of the three children in the furnace is sung. The Church wished to remind us of the tribulations of the just at all times and of their joy in the midst of trials, as well as of that providence which watches over them. Her voice seems to say to us, "In the beginning of this day, remember that you have been regenerated by Jesus Christ. Live, therefore, holily. Watch over your senses: take care not to profane them. Painful trials await you; but do not fear—they will turn to your glory. The Lord, who delivered your forefathers, will watch over you: the canticle which you now recite is a proof of it."

The canticle is followed by the fifth psalm. Here is the meaning of this psalm, as well as the reason for the place which it occupies: the children of the Church make answer to the promises of victory which she has just given them. "We know it," they say; "we shall be conquerors, and we bless the Lord for it, and we invite all creatures in heaven and on earth to bless him with us." It is on this account that the fifth psalm of lauds always begins with the word *Laudate*—"Praise." This invitation is addressed in turn to angels, to saints, to all inanimate creatures, to the Church, to the nations, to men of every tribe and tongue. Grateful man desires that all other creatures in existence should unite with him to bless the universal benefactor.

The canticle of the three children in the furnace is not followed by the *Gloria*, because the adorable Persons of the Trinity are praised from one end of it to the other.[146]

The little chapter.—After the last antiphon comes the little chapter or lesson. It consists of some verses of scripture, corresponding to the office of the day. If this lesson is shorter in the offices of the day than in those of the night, it is because the occupations of the day call for our presence. As the little chapter is usually recited by the officiating clergyman, it is not preceded by the *Jube Domne*, or asking of a blessing. Besides the instruction that the little chapter gives us, it is intended to revive fervor in the souls of the assistants. The Church wishes thus to preserve them from the punishment of the Jews, who, disgusted with the manna, were exposed to the bites of serpents.

At lauds in particular, the little chapter is admirably adapted to rouse our courage, whether to perform good works or to encounter the devil. Sometimes we are exhorted to remain steadfast in the faith; again, to run to works of mercy; again, to clothe ourselves as warriors with the armor of light. Then the choir, like an army which has just been electrified by the harangue of its general, hastens to answer with one voice, *Deo Gratias!*—"Thanks be to God, we are ready!" And, like an army of who ask for nothing more than to be let march against the enemy, it intones a hymn, a hymn expressive of its ardor, its gratitude, and its boundless confidence in God, who never summons to battle but to lead to victory.

The hymn over, the versicle follows. It is like a refrain intended to carry the enthusiasm of the Christian soldier to the highest pitch. It is sung by a single voice, to which all the others answer. This is done the better to fix attention and to show the unanimity of all present.

After the versicle comes the antiphon. How well placed is this expression of love after the hymn, in which we have just sung of the victory obtained by the saints, our elder brethren, and of that for which we hope ourselves! Love, which makes union, also makes strength.

The canticle.—But weak man is so much inclined to diffidence that the Church wishes again to reassure him. This is the reason why she places here the canticle *Benedictus*—"Blessed be the Lord God of Israel!" It shows the literal fulfillment of all the promises that God made to the patriarchs and the prophets. "Men of little faith," the Church seems to say to us, when making us sing this canticle, "why do you doubt? Has the Lord, for whom you are going to fight during the day, ever failed in a single one of his promises? Ask the ages gone by. Do you not see him always the same, with one hand helping his soldiers, with the other crowning the conquerors?"

The *Benedictus* sung, and the Christian's hope in God having become like a strong anchor that holds a ship amid the storm, thanks are returned to the Blessed Trinity in the words *Gloria Patri*, etc. A new protestation of boundless love is made by a repetition of the antiphon. Lastly, the fulfillment of all the promises of God is asked by the prayer that concludes the office.

Go now, soldiers of Jesus Christ, of the house of God, of the camp of Israel, go to the combat: there is nothing to prevent you from reaping a harvest of laurels! Oh, if we were to recite these admirable prayers of the office with understanding, and in that spirit of faith which put them together, should we not, on going forth from them, be—to use the saying of St. Chrysostom—like so many lions breathing fire, and make the infernal legions tremble by a single look? And why should it not be so? On whom does it depend? On us; on us alone!

PRAYER

O my God! who art all love, I thank thee for having established so many beautiful prayers by which we may assuredly obtain all the graces that we require. I ask pardon for the little faith with which I have prayed heretofore.

I am resolved to love God above all things, and my neighbor as myself for the love of God; and, in testimony of this love, I will often say with the apostles, "Lord, teach us to pray!"

Lesson 9: Christianity Brought before the Senses (Continued)—Day Office

Day office.—To the guilty nights of the world, the Church has just opposed holy watches. Her angels have been in adoration before God. They have asked mercy for worldlings. They have driven away from the sleeping flock the roaring lions, more terrible in the darkness than in the light. In turn they have mingled their voices and their tears with those of the angels to honor the birth and the agony of the God of Bethlehem and Gethsemani. What will they do now?

The night is past. Behold the dawn, which gilds with its bright hues the sharp ridges of the mountains! Behold the birds, which celebrate by their joyous songs the arrival of the sun! Behold the flowers, which, opening their cups, exhale a sweet perfume, to be borne up on the morning breeze to heaven: one would say that they were thousands of golden pearly thuribles kindled before God! Nature is a temple. Here are the musicians and the incense of the sacrifice! All creatures seem moved, seem born again. Once more, what will the children of God, the angels of prayer, do? With the voice of nature, they will blend theirs: the office of the day begins. Prime, terce, sext, none, vespers, and compline are the parts composing it.

All the hours of the day, as well as those of the night, the Savior marked with benefits: he must be blessed for them. The hours of the day, as well as those of the night, bring new duties to man: he must beg grace to perform them. Such, in general, are the objects of the day office. Its existence and division may be traced to the most remote antiquity.[147] Let us enter into details.

Prime.—Prime is the first hour of the day office. It bears the name *prime*, because it is recited at the first hour of day, that is, about six o'clock in the morning, according to the manner of reckoning among the ancients. This hour was established a) to honor our Lord covered with ignominy by the Jews and led before Pilate; b) to honor his apparition to the disciples on the shore, after his resurrection; and c) to offer to God the firstfruits of the day, as the Jews offered him their firstfruits, that they might thus consecrate all to him.

Prime consists of the invocation *Deus in adjutorium*, the *Gloria Patri* followed by *Alleluia*, a hymn, three psalms, an antiphon, a little chapter, a response, and a few other prayers. The hymn which we sing at prime, and which was already sung in the thirteenth century,[148] expresses well the sentiments that faith ought to awake in the mind of a Christian at the birth of a new day. On beholding the material sun, which enlightens the physical world, we beseech the sun of justice and truth to rise for us, that, walking by his light, we may avoid both the darkness of error and the snares of the devil. We pray this divine sun to be himself our guide.

"Do you see these sheep," says one of our fathers in the faith, "which, sheltered during the night in the fold, ask at morn to be let out into the broad fields? They call for a shepherd to lead them to pasture, and to defend them from the attacks of the wolves. We also, when dawn summons us to holy labor, hasten to ask a master who may instruct us, and a protector who may guard us. Both are needed. Otherwise, the infernal wolf would drag the sheep into hidden nooks and there tear them to pieces."[149]

The Church reminds us beautifully in the psalms of prime and in the Symbol of St. Athanasius[150] that, in order to escape the arrows of the devil, we must clothe ourselves with the same armor as all Christian heroes have borne: the shield of faith, the helmet of hope, and the sword of charity. It is the more earnestly to encourage us to do so that this thoughtful mother sets before our eyes the struggles and the victories of the saints. At prime, the martyrology is read—a bloody but glorious history of our brethren, who, once soldiers like us, now repose in heaven, on the rich couches of their immortal honors.

After the reading of the martyrology, the officiating clergyman says, "Precious before God." "Is the death of his saints," answers the choir. Then, in the name of all his brethren, the celebrant expresses this wish, so worthy of a Christian: "May the Blessed Virgin and all the saints help us by their prayers with the Lord, that we may deserve to be protected and saved by him!" After this prayer, the celebrant says thrice, "O Lord, come to my aid"; and the choir adds, "O Lord, make haste to help me!" This triple repetition is intended to obtain protection against our three great enemies: the devil, the world, and the flesh. It is followed by the *Gloria Patri*, to return thanks, in the name of all our brethren, to the adorable Trinity, from whom the precious death of the saints came, and from whom ours will come.

But alas! falls are to be feared, so great is human weakness. Beforehand we ask mercy, saying three times, *Kyrie* or *Christe eleison*—"Lord" or "Christ have mercy on us!" To make sure of obtaining this mercy, we recite the Lord's Prayer. We conclude by beseeching our heavenly Father to guide his children, and *his children* are ourselves; and to help us to guide our children, and *our children* are our thoughts and works.

Terce.—Terce is the second hour of the day office. It received this name because it was recited at the third hour of the day, according to the manner of reckoning among the ancients. With us, terce corresponds to nine o'clock in the morning. Prime and terce consist of the same parts, with the exception of the concluding prayers. The Church, our mother, who, by her sacraments, imprints sanctity as it were on all our senses, also writes her sacred mysteries on all the hours of the day. Her office recalls them one after another to our adoration and our love. The Savior pursued by the sanguinary shouts of the Jews, bound to the pillar, and cruelly scourged, and the Holy Ghost descending on the apostles and giving birth to the Church, are the memorable events which we celebrate in the prayers of terce. Like the other hours, this one may be traced to the apostolic times.[151]

In memory of the new law, written in flaming characters on the hearts of the apostles, there is sung at the little hours that psalm in which David so magnificently celebrates the sweetness and perfection of the law of grace and love. The hymn also recalls the descent of the Holy Ghost, who is besought to renew in our favor the wonders of the upper chamber.

Sext.—Sext is the third hour of the day office. It corresponds to noon. The same composition, the same antiquity as the preceding one.[152] Great thoughts are awakened in it, for great events consecrated this memorable hour. At terce, the Church led us to the praetorium, and, in presence of its bloodstained pillar, opened our lips in prayer. At sext, taking us by the hand, she guides us to Calvary, and stops us before a huge instrument of torture. Jesus raised on the cross is the first object of our prayers and meditations at the hour of sext.

Here is revealed a beautiful harmony, which did not escape the sagacity of our ancestors in the faith. Instructed by tradition, they tell us that it was at the sixth hour of the day that Adam became guilty and perished by the fruit of a tree. To make the reparation coincide with the fall, Jesus would be lifted up at the same hour on a life-giving tree.[153] Another event is also the object of our gratitude. It was at the hour of sext that Peter had a clear revelation of the vocation of the Gentiles, and that he received a command to carry the gospel to the nations: an inestimable benefit, of which you and I feel to this day the effects. Thus we have the Son of God nailed to a cross, and Peter giving the gospel to the nations: Could there be need of anything more to excite our fervor and gratitude during this new hour?

None.—None, which continues these admirable reminiscences, is the fourth hour of the day office. It comes to us at three o'clock in the evening, which was the ninth hour of the day among the ancients: hence, its name. It contains the same parts as the preceding ones, and offers us the same antiquity.[154] It is still at the great scene of sorrow that the Church detains us. The sun darkened, the earth trembling, the veil of the Temple rent; the man-God or new Adam expiring, and from his side, opened by the lance of a soldier, giving birth to the new Eve, the Catholic Church, our tender mother: such are the events that this hour recalls to us. Could there be any more proper to make us pour out prayers and tears before God?

The psalms of the little hours of Sunday offer us a harmony so beautiful that we cannot deny ourselves the pleasure of drawing your attention to it. It will show that everything, to the least iota, in the offices of the Church, is arranged with a wisdom and a breadth of view that can never be sufficiently admired. All the little hours of this day consist of two psalms, the second of which is divided between prime, terce, sext, and none. Each division of the psalms contains sixteen verses. Why these two psalms only? Why these sixteen verses? These two psalms recall the two covenants of God with mankind, the old and the new. These sixteen verses denote the interpreters of this twofold covenant. For the old, the twelve minor and the four major prophets; for the new, the twelve apostles and the four evangelists.[155]

The psalms and hymns of the little hours are likewise in harmony with the various hours of the day at which we recite them. At sunrise the beginning, at terce the continuation, at sext the perfection, at none the end of charity and life; for alas! life is but a day.

Vespers.—Vespers are the fifth hour of the day office. Their antiquity is the same as that of the Church.[156] Oh, how justly did the Church consecrate this hour to prayer! What recollections does it awaken! First, the sacrifice offered every evening in the Temple of Jerusalem; then, the institution of the Blessed Eucharist; lastly, the taking down from the cross and the burial of our Lord. Such are the reasons for which the Church so earnestly desires that we should be in prayer at this memorable hour.

Do those Christians of all ages and conditions who disdain to assist at vespers know the value of prayer? Do their hearts beat with gratitude? "Vespers," they say with impious levity, "are for priests." Was it not then for you that the Holy Eucharist was instituted? Do you then owe nothing to God for this benefit? Was it not then for you that Jesus Christ was sacrificed? Does the hour then at which these great miracles were wrought make no impression on you? And what do you do at this sacred hour, when burning tears should flow from your eyes and mix with your burning prayers? If I want to know, I have only to ask the public promenades, or houses of profane amusement and pleasure: they will answer me.

Ah, will you never be ashamed at thus wounding Christian propriety? What would our ancestors in the faith have thought if someone had told them that their children would profane an hour so holy, an hour laden with so many benefits? Shame on those for whom gratitude is too heavy a burden! Their ungrateful hearts were never good hearts. They resemble those fruits which the sun cannot ripen, and which have neither taste nor perfume. Shame on the servile souls that go to the church only in the morning through fear, and dispense themselves from going at all in the evening, when there is no anathema, no threat of mortal sin to alarm them!

As for us, docile Christians, the more vespers are neglected by others, the more we ought to make it a duty to assist at them: our obligations seem to become greater with their indifference. Let us come to the foot of the altar that we may pray, lament, adore, and return thanks for our ungrateful brethren, too happy if we can indemnify their Savior and ours!

The beauty of the evening office would alone suffice to make us assist at it. Vespers consist of five psalms, five antiphons, a little chapter, the *Magnificat*, and only one prayer, if there is not a commemoration of some festival. The number *five* was established to honor the five wounds of our Lord, and to expiate the sins that we have committed during the day by our five senses.

The trumpet of the Church militant—the bell—has sounded three times: the first, to announce the office; the second, to tell us that it is time to set out; and the third, to say that the office is beginning. Having arrived at the church, the clergy and laity recollect themselves for a few moments. They prepare their souls by reciting a *Pater* and *Ave*: these two prayers they say on their knees and in silence. The office opens with the sign of the cross, to invoke the aid of the Blessed Trinity, and to confess the mysteries of the incarnation and redemption. The hand, which, in making it, turns to four sides, reminds you that the Son of God came to call together his elect, scattered toward the four winds. When, therefore, you see the officiating clergyman, from his raised seat, making this adorable sign, imagine that you behold Jesus Christ on the cross of Calvary, with arms stretched out to embrace the children of Adam who have become his, and calling all to his heart in these words of ineffable love: "I thirst, I thirst for you."[157]

When making the sign of the cross, the priest turns toward the altar and says, *Deus, in adjutorium meum intende*—"O God, come to my aid!" The faithful, also standing and turned toward the altar—to show that all their confidence is in the merits of Jesus Christ—answer earnestly, *Domine, ad adjuvandum me festina*—"O Lord, make haste to help me!" Then, to manifest beforehand the gratitude with which this heavenly protection inspires them, they sing in a transport of love, *Gloria Patri*, etc.—"Glory be to the Father," etc. Their delight and eagerness to proclaim the praises of their Father who is in heaven are expressed by the word *Alleluia*. During Lent, a time of fasting and penance, the *Alleluia* is replaced by other words, which have the same meaning: *Laus tibi Domine, Rex aeternae gloriae*—"Praise be to thee, O Lord, King of eternal glory!"

After the announcement of the antiphon, intended to kindle our charity,[158] a chorister intones the first psalm: *Dixit Dominus Domino meo*—"The Lord, the eternal Father, the Almighty God, said to Jesus Christ, his Son, my Lord, on the day of his glorious ascension, 'Sit at my right hand.'" In this magnificent psalm the Church sings the eternal generation of the Son of God, and his priesthood, likewise eternal, as well as his eternal, absolute sway over the world, become the conquest of the cross. But what! are not vespers intended to honor the burial of Jesus Christ? How then is it that the Church, with all her tenderness, kneeling, so to speak, on the grave of her divine spouse, utters only songs of joy and hymns of triumph? Ah, it is because she sees life coming forth from the womb of death, and victory from sufferings: a grand lesson for you and me!

The second psalm of vespers on Sunday is the *Confitebor*—"I will praise thee, O Lord!" It is like a continuation of the first. By the mouth of David, the Church sings the benefits of the reign of her divine spouse. She celebrates in particular the institution of the divine banquet, to which all the generations of men that come into this world are invited.

What remains now but to describe the happiness of those who submit to the rule of Jesus Christ. This is what the Church does in the third psalm: *Beatus vir qui timet Dominum*—"Happy is the man that fears the Lord!" Beside the simple and touching description of the happiness of the just man, who fears God and keeps his commandments, the Church places a picture of the sinner. During his life, he is miserable; at the moment of death, he gnashes his teeth and withers away with fear. After his death, he enters the place of torments, at whose gate he bids an everlasting farewell to hope.

The Church has reminded the just that the Lord makes them happy, if they carry his sweet yoke: What more natural than that she should now exhort them to sing of their happiness? Accordingly, this intelligent mother, taking up the words of the royal prophet, exhorts them in the fourth psalm to praise and bless the greatness, the power, and above all the admirable goodness of their heavenly Father: *Laudate, pueri, Dominum, laudate nomen Domini*—"My children, praise the Lord, praise the name of the Lord!" This invitation excites a burst of love, and all mouths and hearts unite to answer, "Yes, let the name of the Lord be blessed now and forevermore"—*Sit nomen Domini benedictum ex hoc nunc et usque in saeculum!* In the course of this admirable psalm, all vie with one another in proclaiming the special reasons that they have to bless the good God, the God who watches over the poor and the weak as the apple of his eye.

From the personal motives that urge each of us individually and all mankind generally to love and bless God, the Church passes on to the special motives of the great Catholic family. Unless our hearts are made of brass, these benefits are such that we ought to melt away in love on thinking of them. This is the object of the fifth psalm: *In exitu Israel de Aegypto, domus Jacob de populo barbaro*—"When Israel came forth from Egypt, the house of Jacob from the midst of a barbarous people." Here, the Church, taking us back more than 3,500 years to the shores of the Red Sea and the deserts of Sinai, unveils before our eyes a magnificent picture of the wonders that God wrought in order to draw the Israelites out of Egypt, and to bring them into the promised land.

Under the miracles of Egypt, the Red Sea, the desert, and Sinai, she enables us to see more glorious and consoling ones wrought in our own favor: our deliverance from the devil, sin, death, and hell by baptism; faith, which leads us through the desert of life, as the pillar led Israel; the law of grace coming down from Calvary, as the old law came down from Sinai; the bread of angels nourishing our souls, as the manna nourished the Hebrews.

And these miracles of the new law are presented as a pledge of still greater miracles, by which the Lord will lead us from the desert of this life to the heavenly Jerusalem. Such are the benefits that the Church recalls to our minds.

Then, like David, comparing the mighty and strong God with the weak and powerless idols of the nations, this tender mother urges us with all the force of her charity to renounce the worship of strange gods, in order to attach ourselves irrevocably to the Lord, who has given us such splendid proofs of his greatness, power, and goodness.

This psalm, with which there is no profane poetry to compare, is followed by an antiphon and a little chapter. The little chapter is taken from some book of the old or the new testament, that breathes the spirit of the festival and teaches the same lessons. The celebrant reads the little chapter standing, and addresses himself to the faithful, who have just sung the praises of God, that he may encourage their zeal and give new strength to their piety. A standing position becomes the holy words that he utters, and shows the respect that he entertains for the members of Jesus Christ who are listening to him. The assembly receives this short exhortation gratefully, and answers, *Deo gratias*—"We return thanks to God!"

A hymn is then intoned: a hymn expressive of love, ardor, courage to do what has just been said. It is the song of an army marching to battle. The hymn varies with the festival, so as to express sentiments in keeping with the occasion.

The Church has just sung the benefits of the Lord. She has beheld in the past her deliverance from the devil, her establishment on earth, numberless favors of which she has been the object. She has beheld in the future the gates of heaven open to admit her to everlasting happiness. How shall she express all her gratitude? She sinks under the weight of it. She looks round for an interpreter of her feelings. She finds one.

Instead of her voice, another is raised, at the sound of which heaven and earth must be silent: a voice so sweet, so pure, so melodious, and withal so powerful, that it will undoubtedly delight the heart of God. It is the voice of the Blessed Mary. Behold, then, the fair maid of Juda, the Mother of God, the Virgin of virgins, the Queen of heaven going to tell in the most harmonious accents the gratitude of the virgin of the earth, the chaste spouse of the man-God, the Catholic Church! The *Magnificat* is intoned, a sublime canticle, a transport of ineffable love, a poem of ten cantos, a magnificent prophecy, which merited for Mary the glorious title of Queen of prophets: "My soul doth magnify the Lord," etc.

Everyone stands during the *Magnificat*, through respect for the inspired words of Mary, and because this noble attitude corresponds with the joy of a heart laden with favors, and disposed to undertake anything that may assure its benefactor of its gratitude. In solemn vespers, the celebrant leaves his place at the moment of the *Magnificat*, and, preceded by a clerk carrying a censer, ascends to the altar, and blesses the incense with these words: *Ab illo benedicaris in cujus honore cremaberis*—"Mayest thou be blessed by him in whose honor thou art about to be burned!" When pronouncing the formula of the blessing, he makes the sign of the cross, in order to show that it is only through the merits of Jesus Christ that any blessings are poured down on the earth. He then takes the censer from the hands of the clerk, and incenses the cross placed over the tabernacle; afterward, the altar on the right and left sides; lastly, all the upper and front parts, as if to surround the altar, a figure of Jesus Christ, with the perfume of incense, symbolic of the belief of the faithful and the fervor of their prayers.

This ceremony ended, the clerk incenses the celebrant in order to do him honor as the representative of Jesus Christ. After the incensing, the priest sings, *Dominus vobiscum*—"May the Lord be with you!" The faithful answer, *Et cum spiritu tuo*—"And may he be with you!" Then follows the prayer of the Mass called the "collect," because it brings together, as it were, the prayers and desires of all present, in order to offer them to God. The priest says again, *Dominus vobiscum*, and, after this sigh of peace and charity, the clerks invite the faithful to praise and bless the Lord, *Benedicamus Domino*—"Let us bless the Lord!" All the assistants answer, *Deo gratias*—"Thanks be to God!" Thus ends this part of the evening office. Do you know anything more beautiful, or more perfect?

PRAYER

O my God! who art all love, I thank thee for having instructed me in the holy ceremonies of thy worship. Grant that they may renew in me the spirit of faith and prayer.

I am resolved to love God above all things, and my neighbor as myself for the love of God; and, in testimony of this love, I will attend regularly at vespers.

Lesson 10: Christianity Brought before the Senses (Continued)—Compline, Latin, Chant

Compline.—This is the last hour of the office. It is intended to honor the burial of our Lord and his sleep in the tomb. Compline consists of preparatory prayers, four psalms, an antiphon, a hymn, a response, the canticle of Simeon, a prayer, and a hymn to the Blessed Virgin.

During vespers, man, laden with benefits, has just expressed his gratitude to God. He is animated with the best dispositions: the earth appears a gloomy place to him and life a burden; he sighs for heaven. But he has not yet reached the term of his exile: more than one trial remains for him. Already the declining day announces the approach of night, an evil time from whatever point of view we consider it. Man, a weary soldier, is going to sleep; but the devil will not sleep. On the contrary, he will lay new snares for his prey. A roaring lion, he will attempt with greater violence to carry off some of the sheep. Such is the condition of man at the close of day. What should he do to avoid the ambushes of the enemy, and to remain faithful to God until the return of light? Before you offer your advice, I will explain for you that which the Church gives, and you can then tell me whether you know anything better.

"My son," she says to him, "throw yourself into the arms of your heavenly Father. Be sober and cautious. Ask the angel who guards you and the saints who love you to protect you. Above all, ask Mary to watch over you as a mother watches over her sleeping child, that you may obtain the tranquil rest of night and the perfect rest of eternity. Under her powerful protection, you may sleep in peace: the devil cannot hurt you."

And to strengthen in the Christian these lively sentiments of childlike confidence, the Church makes him recite compline.[159] The proof of what we have just said is to be found in the explanation of this last hour of the office. A voice rises to invoke the divine blessing. The celebrant, who represents God and the Church, makes answer by wishing the faithful a quiet night and a holy death. To obtain both, he recommends sobriety, watchfulness, all that can offer a vigorous resistance to the enemy. For this end, there are two infallible means: prayer and humility. Prayer—and the *Pater* is said; humility—and priest and people acknowledge their faults by saying the *confiteor*.

Yes, the humble acknowledgment of our faults, joined with prayer, is the true way to go securely to rest. Woe to the guilty man who falls asleep without repentance! If he die, he will awake in hell. The confession made, these sentiments of repentance and confidence shine out brightly in compline, preceded by the invocation, "Convert us, O God, who art our Savior, and turn away thine anger from us!" The only thing that can separate us from God, and prevent him from taking that paternal care of our rest which we ask, is sin. This is the reason why we begin by entreating him to convert us. We lay before him the most powerful motive for granting us this grace, by reminding him that he is our Savior.

In the first psalm, the royal prophet manifests his gratitude to the Lord for the evidences of protection that he has received from him, and implores the divine aid against all his enemies. His trust is in God, on whose paternal bosom he calmly rests. What canticle could better be placed in the mouth of a Christian, this new royal prophet, who, having fought his enemies and ended the day with the help of God, is going to acquire in needful rest the new strength and vigor necessary to carry on the war against the opponents of his salvation? Such is the meaning of the psalm, *Cum invocarem*—"When I invoked this God, the author of my justice, he heard me."

"My children," the Church says in this first canticle, "do you therefore invoke the Lord: your hopes shall not be deceived." Full of confidence in the infallible words of his mother, the Christian answers by singing the second psalm: *In te Domine, speravi*—"In thee, O Lord, I have hoped; I shall never be confounded." Would you know how God protects the man that hopes in him? The third psalm will inform you. It shows us such a man resting confidently on the protection of the God of heaven. It shows us the devil and his ambushes, the wicked and their machinations, driven far from the abode of the just: *Qui habitat in adjutorio Altissimi, in protectione Dei caeli commorabitur*—"Whosover relies on the arm of the Almighty, shall live in peace under the protection of the God of heaven."

What now remains? An advice to give, a very wholesome advice: it is to be on our guard, and, if we awake during the night, to turn our heart immediately to God. Such is the object of the fourth psalm: *Ecce nunc benedicite Dominum*—"Now therefore bless the Lord." The hearts and voices of all unite to sing the antiphon, that is, to declare that they will be faithful to this wise recommendation. The hymn that follows is a sigh to the heavenly Father, beseeching him to be himself the keeper of his children, the protector of their souls and bodies, during the evil time of night.

The celebrant, on his side, sums up all these desires, and, reading the little chapter, presses God to grant the favor so earnestly sought: "Thou art with us, O Lord, and thy name is invoked upon us; do not forsake us!" The faithful, full of confidence, thank the priest and bless the Lord in these words: *Deo gratias*—"Thanks be to God!"

Here begins, between all these children of the same family, now assembled at the feet of their common Father, and soon to be scattered to their different abodes, a kind of farewell, a Christian goodbye, whose simplicity and tenderness cannot be expressed: the heart must only feel it.

A child of the choir sings with a voice pure as that of an angel: *In manus tuas, Domine, commendo spiritum meum*—"Into thy hands, O Lord, I commend my spirit."

The faithful answer: *In manus tuas, Domine, commendo spiritum meum*—"Into thy hands, O Lord, I commend my spirit."

The choir child: *Redemisti me, Domine, Deus veritatis*—"Thou hast redeemed me, O Lord, the God of truth." An angel of the earth has laid before God the most powerful motives to protect us. We belong to him; he has bought us at a great price; and he is the God of truth, a God faithful to his promises. And he has promised to protect us.

The faithful: *Commendo spiritum meum*—"I commend my spirit."

The choir child: *Gloria Patri, et Filio, et Spiritui Sancto*—"Glory be to the Father, and to the Son, and to the Holy Ghost."

The faithful: *In manus tuas, Domine, commendo spiritum meum*—"Into thy hands, O Lord, I commend my spirit." The thought of banishment from home and of the approach of the dangers of the night casts over this answer a melancholy which prevents the completion of the *Gloria Patri*. The words "as it was in the beginning, is now, and ever shall be" are reserved for heaven. The Church on earth never utters them but in moments of joy.

The choir child: *Custodi nos, Domine, ut pupillam oculi*—"Keep us, O Lord, as the apple of thine eye."

The faithful: *Sub umbra alarum tuarum protege nos*—"Protect us under the shadow of thy wings."

Tell me. Do you know any words of address more beautiful than these? Do you know anything that better represents the candor of a child in the arms of its father? This dear child, sure that God who reigns in heaven loves it with the utmost tenderness, has only one desire: to quit this land of exile, this valley of tears, and go and rest peacefully in the bosom of the Lord. And lo! its mother, the Catholic Church, always inspired, puts into its mouth the words of the old man Simeon, who, having seen the salvation of Israel, asked only to die: *Nunc dimittis*, etc.—"Now, O God, let thy servant depart in peace." A prayer then follows, which admirably sums up all the petitions made to God in compline.

The Christian family is therefore going to separate. But he who is its head, its father on earth, cannot leave his children without wishing them the richest blessings. The priest is not satisfied with the ordinary salutation: *Dominus vobiscum*—"The Lord be with you!" He wants more touching language, words more expressive of his affection for them and his desire to see them happy. He says, "May the Almighty Lord, Father, Son, and Holy Ghost, bless and keep you. Amen!"

Before departing, all together salute for the last time their tender Mother in heaven, beseeching her to cast a look of mercy on her children, and to open her maternal arms to them. Is there, I ask, any asylum more secure than a mother's bosom? You then hear the vaults of the temple resounding with the *Alma Redemptoris*, the *Ave Regina*, the *Regina Caeli*, or the *Salve Regina*, to which the angels listen with delight, and which they hasten to repeat on their golden harps, in the heavenly Jerusalem, at the feet of the Virgin full of grace, our Mother and their Queen.

Go now, beloved children, and sleep in peace: remorse will not disturb you. "Thus, the Sunday passes pleasantly for those who know how to sanctify it. Prayer, charity, innocent joys, meetings of families, and refreshing leisure fill it up. And when this day draws to a close—when, like all other days, it prepares to sink into the abyss of the past—it departs radiant with the glory of the good works that it has produced, and perfumed with the incense that it has burned on altars."[160]

Let us conclude our remarks on compline by saying that this last hour of the office is indicated by the ancient fathers of the Church.[161] The custom of prayer before retiring to rest seems to have been established by nature itself: the Church consecrated it. When telling us to thank God at the close of day, she proposes for our adoration the Savior laid in the sepulchre. Thus, in her daily office, she honors her divine spouse from his birth to his burial. What an excellent subject of meditation for her children! What an admirable means of making them all that they ought to be, every one of them a new Jesus Christ![162]

The use of the Latin language in the liturgy: Wisdom of the Church.—All the hours of the office the Church offers to God in a language nowadays unknown to most of the faithful. She also addresses them to him in a chant. It is proper that you should admire in these practices the deep wisdom of your mother. And first, why use the Latin language in public prayers?

1. *To preserve the unity of the faith.* At the birth of Christianity, the divine service was performed in the common language of the people in most churches. But, like all other human things, languages are subject to change. The French language, for example, is not the same now as it was two hundred years ago: a great many words have become obsolete; others have changed their meaning. Our phrases differ as much as our fashions from those of our ancestors. But one thing should be unchangeable, namely, faith. To secure it from the instability of living languages, the Catholic Church employs a settled language—a language that, being no longer spoken, is no longer subject to change.

Experience proves that in this, as in everything else, the Church is guided by a divine wisdom. See what occurs among protestants. They would have living languages in their liturgies, and they have been obliged over and over again to renew their formulas, to retouch their versions of the Bible. Hence, endless alterations. If the Catholic Church had chosen to act in this manner, it would have been necessary to assemble a general council every fifty years or so, in order to draw up new formulas for the administration of the sacraments.

2. *To preserve the catholicity of the faith.* Unity of language is required to maintain a close bond of affection and an easy communication of doctrine between the different churches of the world, and to connect all better with the center of Catholic unity. Take away the Latin language, and an Italian priest traveling in France or a French one in Italy may no longer be able to celebrate the holy mysteries or to administer the sacraments. This is what happens to the protestant clergyman. Out of his own country, he can hardly ever take part in public worship. A Catholic is at home in any of the countries of the Latin Church.

Honor therefore to the sovereign pontiffs, who neglected no means of introducing everywhere the Roman liturgy! The impartial man finds herein a new proof of their enlightened zeal for catholicity—that sublime characteristic of the true Church. Alas, if the Greeks and Latins had only had one language, it would not have been so easy for Photius and his followers to draw away the whole Greek Church into schism, while attributing to the Roman Church errors and abuses of which she was never guilty!

3. *To preserve that majesty which becomes religion.* A learned language, confined to educated men, inspires more respect than a living language. Would not the holiest mysteries seem ridiculous as if expressed in language too familiar? Every person understands this. Protestants themselves, the sworn enemies of the Roman Church, felt it as well as others; but, rather than give up their anti-Catholic prejudices, they chose to become inconsistent with themselves. They translated the divine office into French. Very well. But had not the inhabitants of Lower Brittany, Picardy, Auvergne, and Gascony as much right to it in their peculiar dialects as the Calvinists of Paris had to it in pure French? Why did not the reformers, so zealous for the instruction of the common people, translate the liturgy and the scriptures into all these jargons? Would it not have helped very much to entitle religion to respect?[163]

On the contrary, the Greek language in the East and the Latin in the West preserve, by their very antiquity, a majesty that most admirably befits the much greater majesty of the Catholic Church. For a religion the mistress of the world, there ought to be the language of the rulers of the world, as for an immortal doctrine there ought to be an immutable language. If religion and reason ought to return thanks to the Catholic Church for having adopted the Greek and Latin languages, science ought to be no less grateful to her. By immortalizing the languages of the Greeks and Romans, the Church immortalized their literature, in the same manner as the popes, by sanctifying the monuments of the Caesars, saved them. Without the cross that rules above it, the Trajan Column would long since have ceased to stand.

For the rest, it is not true that, owing to the use of a dead language, the faithful are deprived of a knowledge of what is contained in the liturgy. Far from prohibiting this knowledge to them, the Church recommends her ministers to explain to the people the different parts of the holy sacrifice and the meaning of her public prayers.[164] Still more, she has not absolutely forbidden translations of the prayers of the liturgy, by which the people may see in their own language what priests say at the altar.[165] Therefore, it is not true that she wished, as protestants accuse her, to hide her mysteries. No, she only wished to put them beyond the reach of change, an inevitable consequence of changes in language.[166]

The use of the chant or singing: Its origin.—From the language of the Catholic Church, let us pass on to the chant. Let us speak of its origin and beauty. Singing is natural to man: we find it everywhere over the world. Singing is essentially religious: in the beginning it was constantly employed in the divine worship. This general accord proves that singing is agreeable to the Lord, and that it is a lawful means of rendering him the worship that we owe him. But what is singing? Singing, answers a pious old author, is the language of angels; perhaps it is the language spoken by man before his fall.[167]

On this hypothesis, our present speech would only be a ruin of the primitive.[168] Man having been wholly degraded by original sin, it is conceivable that his speech underwent a like degradation. At least it seems that singing will be the language of heaven, or of man perfectly regenerated, for there is no mention of aught but songs and harmonies among the blessed inhabitants of the heavenly Jerusalem. Whatever there may be in these conjectures, singing is a lively and regular expression of the sentiments of the soul. Its power is magical: this is another mystery.

To bring man back to his primitive language, or to teach him that which he is to speak in heaven, religion has consecrated the use of singing in her divine exercises. She does not wish that men should meet at the foot of the altar without speaking the language of innocence or the language of angels. An exile, it is in our temples that man hears again the idioms of his native land. A fallen king, it is here, too, that he stammers over the language which he will speak on the day of his happiness. Do you know any lesson more useful, any idea more admirable?

Singing has other advantages. It touches the heart and leads to devotion.[169] It banishes tepidity, and gives us a holy gladness in going through the divine office, which might otherwise seem long and tedious.[170] It is a solemn profession of faith and love, by which we declare that we glory in invoking our Lord and in celebrating his praises, notwithstanding the blasphemous sneers of the wicked.[171] Finally, it drives away the clouds raised by the devil, and obtains many special favors from God, as we see in the scripture.[172] Man sings, therefore, and the Church sings with him. Hereby she shows herself a worthy heiress of all that is true, good, and beautiful in the traditions of the world. For all peoples have sung.

We shall not speak of the pagans. They had perverted the use of singing: instead of honoring the God of nature, they sang the scandalous crimes and adventures of their false deities.

The Hebrews were no sooner formed into a nation than they knew how to vary the tones of their voice in publishing the praises of the Lord. Who did not learn the sublime canticles of Moses, Debbora, David, Judith, the prophets? David did not confine himself to the composition of psalms: he established choirs of singers and musicians to praise God in the tabernacle. Solomon observed the same practice in the Temple. Esdras reestablished it after the captivity of Babylon.

From the origin of Christianity, singing was admitted into the divine office, especially when the Church had obtained liberty to give suitable pomp and circumstance to her worship. She had full authority on this point from the lessons of Jesus Christ and his apostles. The birth of our divine Savior had been announced to the shepherds of Bethlehem by the canticles of angels. Those of Zachary, the Blessed Virgin, and the old man Simeon are well known. The Savior himself, during the time of his preaching thought well that crowds of people should accompany him, at his entrance into Jerusalem, singing, "Hosanna, blessed is he that cometh in the name of the Lord; long life and prosperity to the Son of David!"[173] And they continued this as far as the Temple. St. Paul exhorts the faithful to excite one another to piety by hymns and spiritual canticles.[174] He himself sang with Silas at midnight in his prison.

Our ancestors in the faith put in practice the lessons of the great apostle. Pliny the Younger[175] having questioned them to know what took place in their assemblies, they told him that they met on Sundays to sing hymns to Jesus Christ, as to a God. It has been the same all through the course of ages. The greatest men that the Church has produced and the earth admired attached so much importance to singing that they did not disdain to lay down rules for it themselves, and to teach it to others. Witness St. Athanasius, St. Chrysostom, St. Augustine, St. Ambrose, and Pope St. Gregory!

After the example of David, Pepin, king of France, and, above all, Charlemagne, his son, took great care of religious singing. Having remarked that the Gallican chant was less pleasing than the Roman, they sent intelligent clerics to the capital of the Christian world in order to learn the chant of St. Gregory, and soon introduced it into Gaul. Yet all the Churches of Gaul did not adopt it uniformly. Many only took a part, and mixed it with that previously in use. Such is the cause of the differences noticed between the chants of various dioceses.[176]

Beauty of the chant.—Nevertheless, this chant, such as it exists at the present day, and though it has suffered heavily in passing through the hands of modern barbarians, still retains some beauties of the first order, and remains, by the use to which it is applied, far above ordinary music. It presents to unprejudiced judges an undoubted character of grandeur, a most noble melody, a rich variety of inflections.

Is there anything, for example, more sublime than the solemn chant of the preface, or the *Te Deum*? What more sadly affecting than the lamentations of Jeremias, or more gloriously joyful than the hymns of Easter? Where shall we find anything more majestic than the *Lauda Sion*, or more heartrending than the *Dies Irae*? The office of the dead is a masterpiece: one would imagine that it was the dull echoes of the tomb. In the office of Holy Week, we remark the passion of St. Matthew: the recitative of the historian, the cries of the Jewish mob, and the noble answers of Jesus make up a pathetic drama.

Pergolesi displayed in his *Stabat Mater* the splendor of his art; but did he surpass the simple chant of the Church? He varied the music on every stanza; and yet the essential characteristic of sadness consists in a repetition of the same sentiment, and, so to speak, in a monotony of sorrow. Different reasons may cause tears to flow, but tears have always a like bitterness. Besides, we seldom weep at once over a multitude of evils; and, when wounds become numerous, there is always one that, by its acute pain, seems to absorb all the others. That chant which returns again and again on different words imitates nature perfectly. The afflicted man expresses his thoughts on a variety of images, but the depth of his grief remains ever the same.

Pergolesi therefore ignored this truth, which is inseparable from a right theory of the passions, when he was unwilling that any sigh of the soul should resemble a preceding sigh. Wherever there is variety, there is distraction, and wherever there is distraction, there is no more sadness.[177]

What shall we say of the psalms? Most of them are sublime in their gravity, especially the *Dixit Dominus*, the *Confitebor Tibi*, and the *Laudate Pueri*. The *In Exitu* presents an indescribable mixture of joy and sadness, hope and melancholy. The *Kyrie*, the *Gloria*, and the *Credo* of great festivals raise the soul on high; and the *Veni Creator* expresses in admirable tones the earnest supplications of a heart that desires to be heard.

Example: St. Augustine.—Need we be surprised, after this, that our sacred singing should make a deep impression on men with ears and hearts? "I could not, O my God!" cries out St. Augustine, "help considering the depth of thy counsels in what thou hast done for the salvation of mankind, and the sight of these wonders filled my heart with incredible sweetness. How many tears did the hymns and psalms that were sung in thy church make me shed: how deeply moved was I to hear thy praises resounding from the lips of the faithful! For, as their divine words struck on my ears, the truths that they expressed sank into my heart, and the warm feelings of piety that they excited there brought to my eyes an abundance of tears, but delicious tears, tears that were the greatest joys of my life."[178]

Example: John James Rousseau.—And, to bring forward a very different man, we shall say that people still remember to have more than once seen John James Rousseau present at the vespers of Saint-Sulpice, in order to feel there that divine enthusiasm from which a sensitive soul cannot defend itself, when it takes part recollectedly in our simple but sublime melodies. The mere recitative of our prayers made such an impression on this man that he could not listen to it without being moved even to tears. "One day," says Bernardine de Saint-Pierre, "having taken a walk with Rousseau to Mont-Valérien, we made up our minds, when we reached the top of the mountain, to ask a dinner from the hermits that live there. We arrived among them a little before their time of going to table; and while they were in the church, J. J. Rousseau proposed to me that we should enter and make our prayer. The hermits were just then reciting the Litany of Providence, which is very beautiful. After we had made our prayer in a little chapel, and the hermits had set out for the refectory, John James said to me with much emotion, 'I now feel the truth of what is said in the gospel, "When several of you come together in my name, there shall I be in the midst of you." The soul is here filled with peace and happiness.'"[179]

Such is the chant of the Church, with the effects that it produces. We so call "plain chant," and not that pretended religious music which has too long made its way into our churches: a worldly, profane, sensual music, which interprets no Christian idea, which tires the people, who cannot understand it, and which is intended far less to praise God than to win admiration for the man who can overcome so many difficulties and give such a display of vocal gymnastics. May our Lord return to the earth, and drive the singers out of the temple!

PRAYER

O my God! who art all love, I thank thee for having established so many means of speaking to my heart. Do not permit me to be insensible to thy voice.

I am resolved to love God above all things, and my neighbor as myself for the love of God; and, in testimony of this love, I will sing with my heart as well as with my mouth the praises of God.

Lesson 11: Christianity Brought before the Senses (Continued)—Sacrifice, Calvary, and the Mass

If it is useful to explain the canonical office, of which the faithful recite only a part and that only once a week, it is necessary to enter into a detailed account of that sublime act which is performed daily on our altars, and at which all Christians are strictly bound to be present on Sundays and holidays. This divine act is the Mass, is Catholic sacrifice.

Nature and necessity of sacrifice.—What is sacrifice in general? Is sacrifice indispensable to religion? Is the Mass a true sacrifice? Is the Mass necessary? Such are the preliminary questions that we have to answer.

And, first, what is sacrifice? "Sacrifice, properly so called, is an offering, made by a lawful minister, of a sensible thing, which is immolated, either by being destroyed or changed, in honor of God, to acknowledge his supreme dominion over us and our total dependence on him."[180]

Sacrifice is more than a mere offering. What essentially constitutes it is the change or destruction of the thing offered: an indispensable condition, which is found even in the unbloody sacrifice, as we shall soon see.

The definition of sacrifice gives an answer to our second question: Is sacrifice indispensable to religion? When you admit a God, the Creator and preserver of all things, the source of all the natural and supernatural goods that the creature enjoys, you are bound to admit that the creature owes him homage for all that it is and has. Yet more: God himself cannot dispense the creature from this duty, because he cannot dispense himself from the necessity of doing everything for his own glory, being the end of all his works as well as their beginning. To assert the contrary would be to admit that God can act for some other end than himself, that is to say, for an end unworthy of him. This would be to rob him of his wisdom, to overturn all ideas of his being; to deny him.

Now, the true means of acknowledging and honoring the supreme dominion of God, not only over life and death, but over being itself, is sacrifice. In point of fact, God is the author of every being. To honor his supreme dominion over a created being requires nothing less than the total destruction and consumption of this being. If in a sacrifice all is not destroyed and consumed by the death of the victim, this arises from the imperfection of human worship and the inability of man to do more. Here, therefore, death is only a representation of the total destruction of the being, which ought to take place in sacrifice, as a homage to the divine being and to his dominion over every created being.

It follows hence that every sacrifice demands the destruction, yet not always the death of the victim, death being only one of the ways in which things can lose their proper existence, or by which the destruction of things can be represented; for the destruction of things offered to God in sacrifice under the law of Moses was effected in various ways. For example, the loaves of proposition were destroyed by manducation and consumed by the natural heat of the stomach; the paschal lamb, by death; other victims, by fire.

Sacrifice is therefore the essential, indispensable act of religion. We can no more imagine a religion without sacrifice than a God without dominion over his creatures, or creatures without an obligation of rendering homage to their God. If the state of innocence had continued, there would have been sacrifices, since there would have been a religion; but there would not have been bloody sacrifices, since death entered the world only by sin, according to the language of the apostle St. Paul.[181]

Ancient sacrifices.—From the time of sin, sacrifice became bloody, and should do so. The remembrance of the original fault was deeply engraven on the mind of man: he felt that he had need of expiation. God was careful to reveal to him its nature and merit, together with all the circumstances that should accompany it.

"The gods are good, and we hold from them all the property that we enjoy: we owe them praise and thanksgiving. But the gods are just, and we are guilty: we must appease them, we must atone for our crimes, and the best way to do so is by sacrifice." Such was the belief of antiquity, and such is still, under a variety of forms, that of the whole world. The first men, from whom the great body of the human race received their knowledge, believed themselves guilty: all general institutions were founded on this dogma. So that all men in all ages have continually acknowledged a primitive and universal degradation, and said, like us, though in a manner less explicit, "our mothers conceived us in sin";[182] for there is not a Christian dogma but has its root in the inmost nature of man, and in a tradition as old as the human race.

Convinced that he was guilty, that he had deserved death, that he needed expiation, man slaughtered victims. God himself taught him the merit of bloody sacrifices. In point of fact, how could man imagine that an animal immolated in his stead should exempt him from death, and that God would permit this substitution? If the idea had not been revealed to him, it would have been the strangest, nay, the most absurd that could be conceived. But, when teaching man of the bloody sacrifice, God said to him, "Thou art guilty, thou deservest death: I wish thee to acknowledge it. Thou shalt therefore immolate victims, and thou shalt own thereby that thou thyself shouldst be immolated. Instead of thy blood, I will accept theirs; I will exempt thee from the death that thou deservest, and will forgive thee the crimes that have made thee worthy of it."

To keep man from forgetting that it was he who should be the victim, God wished that the animals chosen for the sacrifice should be the most valuable, the most gentle, the most innocent, and the most closely connected with man by their instincts and habits. Finally, unable to immolate man in order to save man, the most human victims in the animal species were chosen, if we may be allowed so to speak. The victim was always burned either in whole or in part, in order to show that the natural punishment of crime is fire, and that the substituted flesh was burned instead of the guilty flesh.[183]

The pagans did not stop here. They concluded that the more important a victim was, the more efficacious would be the sacrifice. This belief, all right at its root, but corrupted by the devil, gave rise everywhere to the frightful superstition of human sacrifices. Men came to such a pass as to believe that they could no longer supplicate for a head but at the price of a head.[184] Behold the universal state of affairs under ancient paganism! When we arrived in America at the close of the fifteenth century, we found this belief still existing there, but grown much more ferocious. It was necessary to bring to the Mexican priests as many as twenty thousand victims a year; and in order to procure them, it was necessary to declare war on some people; but, lacking a sufficiency, the Mexicans sacrificed their own children. The sacrificator opened the breast of his victim, and hastened to snatch out the living heart. The high priest squeezed out its blood, which he poured into the mouth of an idol, and all the priests ate the flesh of the victims.[185]

Far from pleasing God, these pagan sacrifices were horrible crimes, which justly provoked his anger. The sacrifices of the Jews were, indeed, innocent, but of themselves were absolutely inefficacious. And what proportion, may I ask, could there be between the anger of a God and the blood of a goat? An insult offered to an infinitely perfect being is infinite. To make the reparation equal to the offense, an expiation of infinite value is needed. Now, this expiation you shall in vain look for among the ancient sacrifices. If God vouchsafed to accept them, it was not on account of their intrinsic value, but as images of a sacrifice worthy of him, that is to say, of infinite merit. But a sacrifice of infinite merit supposes a victim of infinite value. God alone is infinite. The only victim worthy of God, capable of making an expiation proportionate to the offense, is therefore God himself.

Yes, a God, the victim of a God, immolated for man, is the profound mystery at which human reason is staggered, and of which it sought the accomplishment and figured the omnipotent efficacy by a multitude of weak sacrifices. God did not leave the human race unaware that this multitude of sacrifices could not satisfy his justice, and that they should one day be replaced by a sacrifice alone worthy of him. Here is what he said to the Jews by the mouth of Malachias, five hundred years before the immolation of the great victim: "I am tired of you, and I will no more receive a gift from your hands. For, from the rising of the sun even to the going down thereof, my name is great among the nations. In every place there is a pure victim offered and sacrificed to the glory of my name, because my name is great among the nations."[186]

The Lord chose rather to dissemble and to wait for four thousand years; but at length the clock of eternity struck the hour of the great expiation. In the fullness of time, the Lamb of God, the august and holy victim, so impatiently expected, came down on earth. Immolations, hosts, holocausts, sacrifices of every kind, vain shadows, begone! The reality is come! The human race has no more need of you: one single sacrifice is going to take your place. It alone will meet all the requirements of the Creator and the creature.

Let us hear the Son of God, the Father's Catholic priest,[187] who, on entering the world, announces the end of all figurative sacrifices. "O my Father!" he says, "thou wouldst not have victims or oblations; but a body thou hast fitted for me. Holocausts and sacrifices for sin did not please thee. Then said I, Behold I come to do thy will; thy will is a law written at the head of the book of my life and engraven on my inmost heart."[188]

And the holy victim was immolated, and we know the place, the day, the hour, and the efficacy of his sacrifice. "The altar was at Jerusalem, but the whole world was bathed in the victim's blood."[189] At the sight of this blood, God and man, heaven and earth, angels and all other creatures fall, as it were, into transports both of grief and joy. This blood was useful to all. To God, it gave glory; to man, peace. "For it pleased God to reconcile all things by him who is the source of life and the firstborn among the dead, having made peace by the blood which he shed on the cross, both as to what is on earth and what is in heaven."[190]

The sacrifice of Calvary, a bloody sacrifice, is the end and sum of all the ancient sacrifices.—From the words which the Son of God addresses to his Father it is clear that the sacrifice of the Savior was substituted for all the ancient sacrifices, and that it includes all their properties. These sacrifices were of four kinds.

1. The holocaustic sacrifice, in which the victim was wholly burned. The chief end of this sacrifice was to honor God in his infinite sanctity, in his supreme dominion, and in the plenitude of all his perfections.

2. The pacific sacrifice. It was offered to God in thanksgiving for his benefits and to render him homage for his gifts.

3. The propitiatory sacrifice. It was offered to render to the justice of God the satisfaction due thereto, on account of our sins, and to make him propitious toward us.

4. The impetratory sacrifice. It was offered to obtain from the liberality of God the graces and goods necessary for spiritual and corporal, temporal and eternal life. Though this sacrifice seems to regard only the interests of the creature, yet it is a homage which we render to God, an acknowledgment of our dependence on him, by recognizing him as the source and the cause of all blessings.

We must not forget that, in all these sacrifices, the priests and people should have part in the victim, by eating some of it. This eating was so essential that in the holocaust, which wholly consumed the victim, the people did not cease to participate: they ate of another host that was offered with the holocaust. Such was the great law and indispensable condition of sacrifice, a law revealed from the origin of time and a condition imposed by God himself, since, what is very remarkable, this custom of partaking of the victim existed among all peoples.

"Throughout the whole earth," says Pelisson, "the flesh of victims was eaten. In all nations, the sacrifice that ended thus was regarded as a solemn feast of man with God. Whence it comes that we meet so often in the old pagan poets with the banquet of Jupiter and the viands of Neptune, denoting the victims that were eaten after being sacrificed to these false deities. And if among the Jews there were holocausts, that is to say, sacrifices in which the victim was wholly burned in honor of God, they were accompanied with the offering of a cake, so that even in these sacrifices there should be something for man to eat."[191]

The deity is communicated with by means of the substances that are immolated to it: this was the law of the whole world before the birth of the Savior. We repeat it: communion formed part of the sacrifice, was the complement of the sacrifice and the bond of religious unity. This universal idea was true and prophetical. True, it came from a primitive revelation; prophetical, it announced another communion, as the ancient sacrifices announced another sacrifice.

This sacrifice was that of Calvary, which, as it is time to show, corresponds perfectly with the ancient sacrifices and fulfills them all. 1) The sacrifice of Calvary was holocaustic or latrial, since it was wholly consecrated and offered to God, for whom the victim was wholly immolated. 2) It was pacific, since it was offered to thank God for his benefits and to render him homage for his gifts. 3) It was propitiatory, since it was offered to expiate the sins of the world and to satisfy the divine justice. 4) It was impetratory, since it was offered to obtain for all mankind the goods necessary for the life of soul and body in time and eternity. It fulfilled and replaced all the ancient sacrifices, since it was of infinite value. Such is the doctrine of the Catholic Church.[192]

Like all the ancient sacrifices, the sacrifice of the new covenant should be accompanied with communion in the holy victim. This sacrifice being that of all time, and of all lands to the end of time, communion in its victim should be possible to all the generations appearing on the earth to the consummation of ages. And behold how it entered into the incomprehensible designs of omnipotent love to perpetuate even to the end of the world, and by means far above the grasp of our weak minds, this same sacrifice of Calvary, offered materially but once for the salvation of the human race! Out of immense goodness, regardless of an extraordinary degradation, the deified and continually immolated flesh of the victim of Calvary is presented to man under the outward form of his choicest food; "and whosoever refuses to eat thereof shall not live."[193]

As a word, which in the material order is only a series of circular undulations set going in the air, like those which we perceive on the surface of water into which something has been thrown; as a word, I say, comes in its mysterious integrity, no matter what standpoint we take, to every ear touched by the agitated fluid—so the corporal essence of him who is called the Word, radiating from the center of omnipotence, which is everywhere, enters whole and entire into every mouth, and is multiplied to infinity without being divided.

Quicker than lightning, more searching than the thunderbolt, the blood of the man-God "penetrates the bowels of the guilty" to wash away their stains.[194] By a real, divine affinity, it takes possession of the elements of man, and changes without destroying them.[195] It is thus that, since the coming of the Redeemer, man has communicated with God, no longer in a figurative, but in a real and substantial manner. It will be always thus, as long as there are men to sanctify.

The Mass is a true sacrifice, the same as that of Calvary, and is necessary.—Now, the continuation of the sacrifice of the cross, which enables man to have part by manducation in the great victim of Calvary, is the Sacrifice of the Altar. Here then is the answer to our third question: Is the Mass a true sacrifice?

Yes, the Mass is a true sacrifice. In point of fact, the Mass or the Sacrifice of the Altar is the same as that of the cross. On the altar and on Calvary, I behold the same victim, the same priest, the same motives. The only difference is in the manner of offering: on Calvary it was bloody; on the altar it is unbloody.[196] There, guilt; here, innocence. There, executioners; here, a priest.

First, on the altar and on Calvary, it is the same victim, our Lord Jesus Christ, who is offered and immolated under the appearances of bread and wine.

It is the same priest. On Calvary, our Lord immolated himself. "I lay down my life of myself," he tells us, "no one takes it from me. I sacrifice it of my own free will."[197]

The same on the altar. The mortal priest is only a minister of the immortal priest. It is only by his command and delegation that he acts, according to the words, "Do this in commemoration of me." To show still better that it is only in the name of Jesus Christ that the priest acts, he does not say, "This is the body of Jesus Christ," but, "This is my body." The secondary priest disappears to let the principal priest change the substance of the bread and wine into the substance of his body and blood.

On the altar and on Calvary the object of the sacrifice is the same. God is the only being to whom it is offered. It was for the glory of God, to acknowledge worthily his supreme dominion, by laying before him a victim equal to himself, that the sacrifice of Calvary took place. It is the same with the Sacrifice of the Altar. The Catholic Church never offers the Mass to a saint or an angel—not even to the august Mary. Sacrifice being an act of supreme worship, it cannot without idolatry be offered to any creature. Heretics who dare to accuse the Church of this offense calumniate her.

Fifteen hundred years ago they received an answer from St. Augustine:

"We do not build temples, ordain priests, institute sacrifices, for the martyrs; for they are not our gods. It is their God that is our God. True: we honor their tombs, as those of faithful servants of God, who fought for the truth till death, and shed their blood to propagate the true religion and to defeat error. But who ever heard a Catholic priest, standing before an altar consecrated to God over the body of a martyr, say in his prayers, 'O Peter, Paul, or Cyprian! I offer this sacrifice to thee'?

"When we offer at their monuments, we offer to God, who made them men and martyrs, and who associated them to his angels. And if these solemnities were instituted at their sepulchres, it was to return thanks to the true God for the victory that they had won, and to urge us to make ourselves worthy by imitating their courage, of having part in their reward. All the acts of religion and piety performed at the tombs of the holy martyrs are therefore honors rendered to their memory, and not sacrifices offered to them as if they were gods. In a word, whosoever knows the one great sacrifice of Christians, which is offered to God at these tombs, knows also that we do not offer sacrifice to the martyrs."[198]

The sacrifice of the altar is offered for the same motives or the same ends as that of Calvary, namely, to adore God, to thank him, to beg his graces, and to expiate our sins. Such is the faith of the Universal Church. Such is also the word of our Lord: "Do this in commemoration of me"; that is, "Offer, as I have just offered, the same victim to the same God, and for the same ends."[199] The Sacrifice of the Mass is therefore the same as that of Calvary: the manner only of offering is different.[200] What do I say? In the Sacrifice of the Mass, the Savior renews not only the mysteries of his death, but also those of his resurrection and his glorious life.

1. He renews the mysteries of his death. Changing bread into his body, our Lord offers this adorable body as he offered it on the cross. The Eucharist includes his passion.[201] We announce his death by eating thereof, according to the expression of St. Paul, and because he offers on our altars his precious death;[202] and it is true to say, with St. Cyprian, that the sacrifice which we offer is the very passion of the Savior.[203] All the external display of Calvary, which is wanting on the altar, had nothing in common with the sacrificator. The essential part of the sacrifice of the cross consisted in the oblation which our Lord made of his body. The same oblation takes place on the altar.

2. He renews the mysteries of his resurrection and his glorious life. On the altar, the Savior offers himself as at his resurrection, since he there offers his glorious and immortal body. He offers himself as at his ascension, since he still ascends from the altar of earth to that of heaven, according to the words of the Canon, in order to dwell there and to intercede on our behalf, thus offering always one and the same victim. This is the reason why we say at Mass that we offer the sacrifice to renew the memory of the passion,

resurrection, and ascension of our Lord Jesus Christ. Behold, therefore, on the altar the assemblage of all the mysteries that were the various parts, or the continuation, or the fruit of the sacrifice of the Savior, and the literal fulfillment of the prophecy of David: "By giving food to those who fear him, he renewed the memory of all his wonders!"[204]

These explanations are an answer beforehand to our fourth question: Is the Mass necessary?

Yes, the Mass is necessary in the Christian plan of our sanctification. True, the sacrifice of Calvary fully satisfied God for all our sins, fully discharged all our debts, because it was of infinite value. It was enough, and more than enough, to sanctify a thousand worlds, were they a thousand times more guilty than ours. All this is true, and yet the Mass is necessary; for the sacrifice of Calvary must be consummated in us, must be applied to us by communion with the great victim.

Now, this divine victim could not be eaten by the faithful on Calvary. Behold what was wanting at the altar of the cross! It is at the altar of the Church that this manducation is accomplished by Communion. The same victim is offered on Calvary and on our altars; but there it is only offered, here it is offered and distributed, according to the expression of St. Augustine.[205] "It is at the altar," adds St. Ambrose, "that the perfection of the sacrifice of the cross is attained; for Jesus Christ here nourishes us daily with the sacrament of his passion."[206]

Thus by the sacrifice of the cross, our Lord paid our ransom; and by that of the altar, he applies the fruit of this payment to us. It follows hence that the sacrifice of the great victim, begun on Calvary, did not end then, but began to last forever.[207] It was necessary that all the generations of men coming into the world should find the divine banquet ready, and should be able to sanctify, Christianize, and, if we may so speak, deify themselves, by incorporating themselves with the flesh and blood of Christ, the only, the eternal victim of heaven and earth. The Mass is therefore absolutely necessary in the Christian plan of our sanctification.

PRAYER

O my God! who art all love, I thank thee for having instituted the sacrifice of our altars, in order to perpetuate the sacrifice of Calvary, and to apply its fruit to us. Grant me the grace always to assist at Holy Mass with the dispositions necessary to profit by it.

I am resolved to love God above all things, and my neighbor as myself for the love of God; and, in testimony of this love, I will assist at the Sacrifice of the Altar as I should have done at that of Calvary.

Lesson 12: Christianity Brought before the Senses (Continued)—Vestments

Excellence of the Holy Sacrifice of the Mass.—Place together the merits of the ever Blessed Mary, the adorations of the angels, the labors of the apostles, the sufferings of the martyrs, the austerities of anchorets, the purity of virgins, the virtues of confessors, in a word, the good works of all the saints from the beginning to the end of the world; add thereto in imagination the merits of the saints of a thousand worlds more perfect than ours: it is of faith that you will not have the value of a single Mass. The reason is easily understood. All the honors that creatures can render to God are finite honors, while the honor that accrues to God from the sacrifice of our altars, being rendered to him by a divine Person, is an infinite honor.[208] Such is therefore the excellence of the adorable sacrifice of our altars, considered in itself.

It has no less excellence if you consider it in its effects. This is a consequence of what we have just said. Of all works, there is none dearer to God than the Holy Mass; none that is so effectual in disarming his wrath, none that strikes such a terrible blow at the powers of hell, none that procures such an abundance of graces for wayfaring man, none that obtains such great relief for the souls in purgatory.

Hence those splendid, but just remarks of the fathers and doctors of the Church. "The Mass," says St. Odo, abbot of Cluny, "is a work to which the salvation of the world is attached."[209] "It is to the Mass," adds Timothy of Jerusalem, "that the earth owes its preservation."[210] "Every time that our Lord is immolated on the altar," continues St. Bonaventure, "he does the human race no less a favor than when he became man."[211] "The Sacrifice of the Altar," says St. Thomas, "being only the renewal and application of the sacrifice of the cross, one Mass is as efficacious for the welfare and salvation of mankind as the sacrifice of Calvary."[212] Hence, the conclusion drawn by St. Chrysostom, "One Mass is worth as much as the sacrifice of the cross."[213]

Let us now suppose that a savage, coming forth from the heart of a forest, is suddenly transported to one of our Christian cities, and someone says to him, "Among us there is a sacrifice in which, at the voice of a priest, the heavens are opened, and the Son of the great Spirit descends on an altar, is immolated in the hands of the sacrificator, and gives us his flesh to eat and his blood to drink, that he may make us live by his life and transform us into gods." What do you think would be the thoughts of this poor savage? What his respect for so great a sacrifice? What his desire to take part in it? Can you describe his religious awe before, his emotion during, his joyous gratitude after its celebration?

Well, all these feelings we, yes we ought to experience. What do I say? They ought to be so much the more perfect in us as we are richer in knowledge and grace. Nevertheless, let each one of us here lay his hand on his breast, and say whether he does not envy the dispositions of the ignorant savage whom we have just mentioned. Let us hasten to change our conduct. Otherwise, what excuse shall we have to offer to the supreme judge? What answer shall we make to the reproach, too well deserved, "Woe to thee, Bethsaida, woe to thee, Corozain! For if the miracles that I have wrought before your eyes had been wrought in Tyre and Sidon," that is to say, among the most corrupt and savage people, "they would long ago have done penance in sackcloth and ashes"?[214]

To avert this anathema, we have two duties to fulfill. The first is to assist faithfully at Mass, remembering the proverb, which experience has a thousand times confirmed: "The Mass is no more a loss of time than an alms is a loss of money." On this subject, we read in the *Life of St. John the Almoner* the following story:

Two men of the same trade dwelt in the same town. One had a large family. The other had nobody but his wife. The former made it a duty every morning to hear Mass, at which he earnestly recommended to the adorable victim both his spiritual and temporal wants. The latter, on the contrary, not to be absent a moment from his work, never appeared at the church during the course of the week: he often failed to be present at Mass even on Sunday, under the pretense that he was too busy.

Nevertheless, while the former prospered, the latter remained as needy as ever. "How is it," said he one day to his acquaintance, "that you succeed in everything, and the more I toil, the less progress I make?" "You have only to come with me tomorrow morning, and I will take you to the place where I find the means of gaining so much." The next morning he was at his neighbor's door, saying, "Here I am!" "Well, let us set out!" His neighbor took him to the church, and, after hearing Mass, told him to go to his work. The next day he did the same thing. At length, on the third day, the man said to his pious neighbor, "It is useless to be taking me anymore to the church: I know the way there myself. What I want you to do is to show me the place where you gain so much, that I may profit from your information."

"My friend! that place is the church. I know no better for laying up spiritual and temporal treasures. It is not I that say so, but Jesus Christ himself. Do you not know the words of the gospel, 'Seek first the kingdom of God and his justice, and all things else shall be given to you besides'? And is it not at Mass that our Lord, the master of all things, opens his treasures?" At this reply, the poor workman was astounded. However, faith reviving in his heart, he followed the example of his friend. Every morning he went to Mass, and, after laying his wants before his heavenly Father, went to his work. God blessed it; and he soon saw his affairs prospering beyond all his expectations.

Our second duty is to bring to the adorable sacrifice the dispositions required by the priest who offers it, and the victim which is offered, and of which we ought to partake.[215] With this view, let us carefully call to mind the excellent instructions and pious sentiments of which the Church offers us an abundant supply in all that precedes and accompanies the celebration of our august mysteries.

Preparation of the priest.—Take first the priest who is its minister, and see with what care he is prepared for this wholly divine employment. Consider this man, become superior in power to the angels themselves. The Church drew him away from the common multitude in order to raise him to functions that make the heavenly spirits tremble. She kept him in retirement; she proved him for a long time; she made him ascend by many steps before he was able to reach the sanctuary. It was necessary to mold his heart, to furnish his mind, to be assured that his lips would be faithful dispensers of knowledge and his conduct a pattern for the flock. A pontiff of the new covenant, after consulting heaven and earth, after repeated fasts and supplications, poured on him the divine unction, the oil of a royal priesthood. The word of Jesus Christ is pledged: his promise is express. The Holy Ghost descended on this man, and communicated to him gifts most excellent and powers superhuman.

So many preparations were not enough. The sacred minister rises before dawn to have leisure for long prayers. When at length the bell tolls the hour of the sacrifice, the priest, recollected, trembling at the thought of his sublime functions, advances to offer up the victim that reconciles the creature with God. Silence in heaven! silence on earth! he is going to negotiate on the most important interests of the human race.

Arrived at the sacristy, the priest washes his hands, saying, "O Lord, purify my hands, that I may be able, without stain of soul or body, to accomplish thy holy ministry!" The usage of washing the hands before prayer reaches back to the apostolic ages; the early Christians never failed to do it. Thus does the Church, in her least practices, preserve venerable traditions.

Ornaments of the priest.—Let us now pause to consider the sacred vestments with which the priest is about to clothe himself. They are like a book full of instruction and piety, perhaps often opened before our eyes and never understood by us. The vestments of the priest who celebrates the holy mysteries are the amice, the alb, the girdle, the maniple, the stole, and the chasuble. If the celebrant is a bishop, he adds others, which we shall explain hereafter.

In the old law, God wished that the priests and Levites should wear special consecrated vestments when immolating victims. The Church, inheriting ancient traditions, wished that her ministers should also wear a peculiar and sacred dress in the exercise of their sublime functions. The respect due to holy things both by priests and the faithful called for it. Besides, have not men always need of outward and sensible signs, which remind them of the invisible greatness of mysteries? Hence, the use of sacerdotal garments reaches back to the apostles.[216]

"Ecclesiastical vestments, of which priests and other ministers make use in order to offer divine worship to God with all the respect that it deserves, ought to be decent and blessed, and, as such, none should make use of them but priests and others devoted to the holy ministry."[217] You have now heard the words of St. Stephen, pope and martyr, who lived in 250. "A divine religion," adds St. Jerome, "has one dress for the ministry of the altar, and another for common use."

In times of persecution, the sacred vestments were necessarily less rich; but, when the Church enjoyed peace, and counted among her children the mighty of the world, she was not afraid to celebrate her worship with magnificence. Whatever is excellent in the world comes from God, and should be dedicated to his glory. "Gold and silver are mine, saith the Lord."[218] And what nobler use can be made of them than to employ them in the worship of him who formed them from nothing and gave them as a present to us?

Originally, the greatest respect was entertained for sacred vestments. Women were not allowed to touch them. They were kept in consecrated places with religious care. The priest Rogatian made such account of a tunic with which he had been clad when offering the holy sacrifice that he bequeathed it to St. Jerome, for whom he entertained a special veneration.[219] Let us now study the origin of these various ornaments, the changes that time has made in them, the intention of the Church in ordering her ministers to wear them, and the reason why they are of different colors according to festivals.

1. *Amice.* The amice[220] is a white veil, which the priest first places on his head and then lowers to his neck and shoulders. He fastens it with two strings, which cross each other on his breast. The word *amice* comes from a Latin verb meaning "to cover."[221] This article of dress was introduced more than a thousand years ago in order to cover the neck, which ecclesiastics and laics had previously left bare.

The length of the offices and the continuity of the chant in the large and cold basilicas of the Middle Ages required this precaution. Its natural object is therefore to preserve the voices of those who have to sing the praises of God, and to remind the priest of the modesty with which he should use his voice and the care he should take to retrench during the sacrifice every word foreign to this divine action. Hence the bishop, when giving the amice to a young candidate for ordination, warns him that it is a sign of restraint and modesty in the use of his voice.

The faithful who assist at Mass are, so to speak, co-sacrificators with the priest, and, to some extent, bound to bring thereto the same dispositions. They should accordingly apply this notice to themselves, and remember that, once in presence of the holy altar, all discourse with earth is forbidden.

As everything connected with the priest should recall Jesus Christ, the sovereign sacrificator, the amice figures the Son of God, who, having come down from heaven to save the world, concealed his divinity under his humanity.[222] It is also a sign of that ignominious veil with which his adorable face was covered when a reckless mob, ridiculing the idea of his being a prophet, bandaged his eyes, and said, "Prophesy to us, O Christ, who it was that struck thee!"[223]

Placed on the head, the amice figures the helmet of a warrior, and reminds the priest that he is a soldier. In point of fact, the priest who prepares to offer up the holy mysteries is going to engage in a great combat. This last signification of the amice is expressed in the prayer that the priest recites when taking it: "O Lord, place on my head the helmet of salvation, that I may be able to bear up against the blows of the devil!"

2. *Alb.* The alb,[224] so called by reason of its whiteness, is traceable to the most remote antiquity. The high priest of the law was clothed with it for the sacrifice. The pagans themselves made use of this garment, when immolating victims to their deities: it was a theft from the true religion. Everywhere people understood that, in order to approach the deity, other garments were required than the skins of beasts, with which God had covered guilty man.

It is a remarkable fact that priests, not only among Christians, but also among Jews and pagans, have always employed linen tunics in religious functions. The custom has been universal.[225] What may be its reason? "Because," answers a pagan philosopher, "garments made from the coverings of animals are not pure enough."[226]

That which Pythagoras had a glimpse of, our Christian authors have explained to us clearly. Man had always a consciousness of his fall. He knew that garments made from the substance of animals were a disgraceful livery, a shame, a punishment. He laid them aside when approaching to God, and showed by taking others his desire to recover his purity when returning to God. In effect, he would have used garments of white wool for his religious functions if he had only wished to indicate his disposition of purity. But no: there was therein a remembrance of his primitive defilement, and he took garments of linen.[227] These new garments were therefore an emblem of the new life of innocence and sanctity which was sought in sacrifices.[228]

The alb was also a garment peculiar to the Roman nobility. It was by this toga, this gown with a train, that persons of distinguished rank were known. As there is no dignity on earth equal to that of the priesthood, it was proper that the garment to which custom attached the noblest ideas should be consecrated thereto. The alb, by its length and its whiteness, reminds the priest of perseverance in good works, of the gravity that should accompany his functions, and above all of the great purity that he should bring to the celebration of the divine mysteries. The prayer that he recites when taking it leaves him no room to doubt of the Church's intention. "O Lord," he says, "wash me, purify my heart, that, having been made white in the blood of the Lamb, I may forever rejoice in the joy of those who have worthily performed their functions!"

Adorned with their albs, the ministers of altars resemble the crowd of faithful servants whom St. John shows us in the Apocalypse, clad in white robes, standing continually before the altar of the Lamb, engaged in serving him in his temple—which is heaven. Here we have the same altar, the same victim, the same sacrifice: Why should not the sacrificators of the Lamb have robes whitened in his blood? It is therefore an image, not only of the most beautiful antiquity, but of the heavenly Jerusalem, that the alb sets before our eyes.

At the sight of this habit of the priest, the faithful call to mind the holiness of the sacrifice at which they assist, and the dispositions of innocence or at least of repentance which they should bring to it. In the course of his passion, our Lord, the Son of God, was also clad, by command of Herod, in a white robe, figured by the alb, which thus became a memorial of this circumstance in his ignominies.

3. *Girdle.*[229] After taking the alb, the priest girds himself, like a warrior making ready for the fray. The girdle and the alb have the same antiquity. Ancient peoples, who wore long and loose habits, always used a girdle, that they might be more at their ease in walking and working. Nowadays, the girdle answers the same purpose: it is intended to hold up the alb, which might otherwise prove inconvenient. Moreover, it warns the priest that his virtue should be strong and energetic, and that, in order to ascend the altar and to drink the blood of the immaculate Lamb, he should renounce the least sentiment of a worldly or sensual life. The Church wishes that, when thus girding himself, he should beg of God to encircle his reins with a girdle of innocence and purity, so as to preserve the fairest of the virtues.

The girdle, which is a kind of cord, may help to remind us of the manner in which our Savior was bound in the Garden of Olives, before his judges, at the pillar, and when ascending Calvary. The faithful, when going to Mass, should also gird themselves with the cords of the Savior, that is to say, should rid themselves of all vain and dangerous superfluities, and confine themselves within the limits of Christian mortification, so as to walk without embarrassment in the footsteps of their divine master, and fight valiantly with him.[230]

4. *Maniple.* The maniple,[231] which the priest wears on his left arm, was formerly a kind of handkerchief, intended to wipe the face during the holy offices. Viewed in this light, the maniple is of the highest antiquity. About the tenth century, it was usual to

beautify this handkerchief with fringes and gold, so that it became an ornament, whose mysterious meaning was both a history of our miseries and a consolation amid them.[232]

It served to wipe away tears and sweat. This ancient use of the maniple reminds us that we are here condemned to labor; that heaven suffers violence; that we must earn the bread of immortality in the sweat of our brow; that we have a thousand reasons to bewail the night of our exile, but that the day of eternity will soon dawn, when the Lord will wipe away all tears from our eyes: the happy day, when, walking joyfully, we shall appear before the Father of the family as industrious reapers, laden with the sheafs that we have gathered amid toils and tears.

Such is the meaning of the prayer that the priest addresses to God, when hanging the maniple on his arm: "O Lord, may I deserve to carry the maniple of grief and pain, that I may receive in joy the reward promised to labor!" The Savior has sweetened this labor, by joining to his own the whips and scourges of which the maniple is a figure, and which he sets before our eyes in the holy sacrifice.

The bishop takes the maniple only when he is at the altar, after reciting the *confiteor*. Would you wish to know the reason? Formerly the chasuble, of a round shape, enclosed the whole body, and the maniple, which served as a handkerchief, was last of all laid on the arm that remained free. This custom, then common to all priests, is no longer followed except by bishops. The subdeacon gives the bishop the maniple after the confession, because in old times it was usual to raise the chasuble at this moment, so that the priest might not be inconvenienced when ascending the altar.[233]

5. *Stole*. The stole,[234] which goes round the priest's neck and falls to his knees, is an ornament of dignity and authority. It is used in the administration of the sacraments, and as often as there is any function having for its immediate object the adorable body of our Lord; also, on a few other prescribed occasions.

You know that, alas! the prevarication of our first father stripped us all of the noble raiment of our immortality, of which the stole is a figure. On seeing the stole, we ought, both priests and people, to lament our misfortunes like fallen kings, to thank our Lord for the remedies that he has given us, and to lift up our minds and hearts toward that blessed abode where, all sharing in sacerdotal functions before the eternal altar of the august victim, we shall be arrayed in stoles of glory and the bright ornaments of a royalty worthy of God.

But, to attain this end, we must share in the ignominies of Jesus Christ, and lay on ourselves the bonds with which he burst ours. Such is the lesson that the stole of our ceremonies teaches us. Hence, when taking it, the priest is careful to say to God, "Restore to me, O Lord, the garment of immortality which I lost by the prevarication of my first father, and, though unworthy I approach thy sacred mysteries, grant that I may arrive at eternal felicity!"

The stole, at first called *orarium*, because it served to wipe the face, was a very fine, clean, linen cloth, which persons of distinction wore round their neck. We trace it to the early ages of the Church. The Council of Laodicea, reserving this honorable article of dress to bishops, priests, and deacons, forbade it to other ministers.[235]

6. *Chasuble*. The chasuble[236] is the last ornament of the priest who is going to celebrate. It was formerly a very large, round cloak, without any opening in the sides. It was common both to lay and ecclesiastical people. But the former ceased wearing it, and the Church, which knows how to sanctify the commonest things, retained it, and gave it solely to priests when offering up the holy sacrifice: this was eleven hundred years ago. The Greeks have preserved the chasuble without any change. The Latins have gradually removed from it, within the last three centuries or so, whatever interfered with the freedom of the arms. In its early shape, it should be lifted up when the priest had to use incense or to elevate the sacred host and chalice. Notwithstanding its present shape, the

custom of holding up the chasuble on these occasions is still retained, as a memorial of bygone days. Fidelity in maintaining her least ceremonies is a great service rendered by the Church to historical studies. How many manners and customs, telling so much of olden times, would have been lost if the Church had not, by adopting them, immortalized them!

The same motive preserves another custom, of which few persons know the origin or meaning. In Lent and on other fast days, the deacon and subdeacon serve at the altar without a dalmatic. As in the early Church, their functions were more numerous at such times on account of the crowds of the faithful: they laid aside their ornaments or drew them up higher, so as to be more free. *Diaconi levant planetas in scapulas*, says the Roman Ordo. Nowadays, therefore, the putting away of the dalmatic is a remnant of an old usage.

The bishop, when giving the chasuble to a priest at ordination, warns him that it is a sign of that charity with which we should be wholly clothed; of that charity which should be extended over all our works, and which should give merit to all other virtues, as this vestment covers all other vestments; of that charity which should make us pity the miseries of others and teach us to cover them with a mantle of mercy, hiding them from the sight of men, and a mantle of forgiveness, blotting them out of the sight of God.

The chasuble is also a figure of the yoke of our Lord, which priests and the faithful should daily carry: that sweet, delightful yoke which is our glory and our happiness. When taking it, the priest expresses himself thus: "O Lord, who hast said, 'My yoke is sweet and my burden light,' grant that I may carry it in such a manner as to obtain thy grace!"

A large cross is drawn on the chasuble; and others, smaller, on various things serving for the sacrifice. The object of this is that we may have continually before our eyes our obligation to carry the cross after the Savior, and may remember that we can do nothing but by the cross, that the cross is our only hope, and that the altar is a true Calvary, where the sacrifice of the cross is renewed and perpetuated, and where we ourselves should be immolated on the cross of Jesus Christ.

Ornaments of the deacon and subdeacon.—From the ornaments of the priest, let us pass on to those of the deacon and subdeacon, who assist him at the altar. Besides the amice, alb, girdle, and maniple, deacons wear a dalmatic and stole peculiar to them. The special habit of the subdeacon is the tunic.

Deacon's stole. The deacon's stole is placed on the left shoulder. This custom was borrowed from the Romans. In the solemn feasts of this kingly people, the principal ministers of tables carried a towel of honor on the left shoulder. The Church gave this mark of distinction to those who should serve at the divine banquet, and at tables round which the faithful assembled to celebrate their innocent *agapae*. But this white linen cloth, fastened on the left shoulder of deacons, fluttered about when they were walking here and there, and going to fulfill their ministry in the church. As it might inconvenience them, especially when it had assumed a very long shape, the two ends were brought down to the right side and secured there. The same thing is still done at the present day.

No matter what our state is, we are all deacons, that is to say, servants of Jesus Christ. Let us take care to cut off whatever might trip us in the way of the commandments, or fetter us in the practice of good works. Such are the lessons given us by the deacon arrayed in his stole.

Dalmatic. The dalmatic[237] is so called because it was a garment peculiar to the inhabitants of Dalmatia. Pope St. Sylvester ordered that deacons should use it in church: they had worn a tunic[238] previously. The dalmatic, in its early shape, had short wide sleeves, very convenient for those who had a great deal to do. It became common to bishops and deacons. It was made of white silk, ornamented with gold and two purple bands. This is the reason why it has become a dress of solemn occasions, one that should inspire both the deacon who wears it and the faithful who see it with a holy joy. Such is the meaning of the prayer that the bishop addresses to the deacon when clothing him with it at ordination, and that the deacon himself recites when taking it to serve at the altar.[239]

Tunic. The special ornament of the subdeacon is the tunic.[240] In the early ages of the Church, the subdeacons served at the altar with merely an alb. Later on, they received a tunic, which is also a garment of honor and joy.[241] Among the Romans, the tunic was the ordinary dress of common servants. It is now, like the dalmatic, an exceedingly rich ornament, made of the same stuff as the priest's chasuble, with short wide sleeves, incapable of hampering.

Surplice. The inferior ministers wear a surplice.[242] This garment was formerly longer than now; but its color has remained the same. In the time of St. Jerome, ecclesiastics were already ordered to assist at the holy offices only in white garments: a useful order, by which the Church wished to remind her children both of the innocence required by the august mysteries, and the nuptials of the Lamb, at which the saints assist with garments whose dazzling whiteness is an image of purity.[243]

Cope. The cope[244] is another sacred garment, common to ministers of various ranks. It was formerly a large cloak, like those used at present, only that instead of a collar it had a hood, which might be drawn over the head during rain; hence the name *pluvial* given to the cope. It was used in the ceremonies of the Church before the eighth century.[245] Its richness and bright colors figure the robe of glory and immortality with which we shall be clothed after the resurrection.[246]

As you see, the sacerdotal garments are a mysterious book in which the simple faithful may find great lessons on purity, charity, virtue in general, and the learned a record of the manners and customs of the most venerable antiquity. From every one of these ornaments, as from every one of the ceremonies of Catholic worship, there issues a voice, which says to men, whether Christians or not, "Out of the depths of all these things, fifteen, eighteen, thirty, sometimes sixty centuries contemplate you!" All human generations live again before your eyes, represented by some of their rites or some memorable events in their history. Is it possible to have knowledge and faith without being seized, on beholding them, with a profound respect, and a truly religious veneration? He for whom all this is mere dumb show leaves room to doubt whether there still remains in him any vestige of an intelligent being.[247]

Richness of ornaments.—Assuredly, garments wrought in gold and beautified with embroidery do not add to the value of a sacrifice. The Lord prefers pure morals to the most gorgeous ornaments. But is it not the duty of man to render as much honor to God as possible, and to turn to the majesty of his worship whatever is most fair and rich on earth? The ministers of a king never appear before him without being arrayed in costly attire. They would insult their master, would seem wanting in deference to his majesty, if they entered his presence without ornaments—testimonies of his favors, or symbols of the powers delegated to them. The Church wishes that the priests of Jesus Christ should act in the same manner. To give more glory to her spouse and inspire her children with more piety and respect, she requires that the ornaments of her clerics should be not only decent and becoming, but always rich in proportion to the state and wealth of the faithful.[248]

PRAYER

O my God! who art all love, I thank thee for having made the sacred vestments of thy ministers so numerous. Grant that I may henceforth be instructed on beholding them and excited to practice the virtues which they represent.

I am resolved to love God above all things, and my neighbor as myself for the love of God; and, in testimony of this love, I will carefully study the ceremonies of the Church.

Lesson 13: Christianity Brought before the Senses (Continued)—Vestments, Vesture, Furniture

Ornaments of bishops.—The ornaments of which we spoke in the last lesson are common to all priests. There are others reserved for bishops, who put them on when they have to officiate solemnly: such are the slippers and stockings, pectoral cross, small tunic and dalmatic, gloves, ring, miter, crosier, pallium (if the pontiff has a right to wear it), and gremial. These ornaments, like the others, abound in souvenirs of the most remote antiquity, and give enlightened Catholics the most beautiful lessons on Christian wisdom and sanctity.

1. *The slippers and stockings.*[249] The foot-covering of the ancients, especially the Romans, consisted of a sole held fast by leather strings, which crossed on the upper part of the foot and passed round the leg. Under the emperors this covering was replaced, for people of rank, especially princes and senators, by another of a richer description called *compagia*, adorned with gold and purple, and hiding the foot much better.[250]

To show by every means possible her veneration for holy things, the Church hastened to give her pontiffs the senatorial foot-covering, the most distinguished then known; it was her aim to have the august mysteries celebrated with such outward splendor as would command respect and excite sentiments of piety.

When not engaged in their functions, the bishops wore the ordinary foot-covering. This is the reason why, even to this day, the bishop, having reached the church and ascended his throne, assumes the ancient foot-covering, and lays it aside again after the holy sacrifice. The prayer that the bishop recites when taking this noble gear calls to mind that he is a successor of the apostles, sent like them to announce the gospel: "O Lord, put shoes on my feet, that I may go and announce the gospel of peace, and protect me under the shadow of thy wings!"

The prohibition of the Church to all her ministers, priests, deacons, and subdeacons, not to approach the altar without having their feet covered, lasted as long as Roman sandals lasted, which left the feet almost bare. Hence all wore some kinds of *compagia*, but different from those of the bishops.[251]

2. *The pectoral cross.* In the early ages of the Church, the faithful, both men and women, wore a little cross hanging from the neck: a venerable usage, of which we cannot too much lament the decline. To perpetuate it as far as lay in her power, the Church wished that her pontiffs should carry a cross on their breast, especially when celebrating the holy mysteries. This cross, set before the bishop, reminds him both of that God who died for him and of the martyrs who sealed with their blood the faith that he professes. For the pectoral cross is full of the relics of martyrs, as the prayer that the bishop says when taking it shows.

3. *The small tunic and the dalmatic.* The small tunic and the dalmatic,[252] which are the ornaments of the subdeacon and deacon, remind us that the bishop is invested with the plenitude of the priesthood, as they tell himself that he should have all virtues in a superior degree.

4. *The gloves.*[253] Before the eighth century, gloves already formed part of the episcopal garb.[254] They call to mind a celebrated event in the history of the patriarchs, and give the bishop a great lesson on sanctity. Jacob, wishing to obtain his father's blessing, came to him, his hands covered with kidskin. This stratagem, which led the holy old man into a mysterious error, obtained the most abundant blessings for Jacob. Like Jacob, the pontiff asks God the Father for true goods. In order to obtain them, he tries to be confounded with his elder brother, our Lord Jesus Christ, as Jacob concealed himself under the garb of Esau, so as to obtain the paternal blessing.

Such is the meaning of the prayer that the bishop makes when he takes his gloves. "O Lord," he says, "surround my hands with the purity of the new man, descended from heaven, that, according to the example of Jacob, thy well-beloved, who, having covered his hands with the skin of a kid, obtained his father's blessing, after offering him excellent meat and drink, I may obtain, in consideration of the choice victim offered by my hands, the blessing of thy grace!" It is not that God can be deceived; but he wishes that, when we appear before him in order to receive his favors, we should be new Jacobs, that is to say, new Jesus Christs.

5. *The ring.* The ring[255] is the sign of the spiritual alliance that exists between the bishop and his Church. It is like the seal of their contract. Among the ancients, as well as among moderns, a seal was put to contracts, so as to confirm and authenticate them. Hence the custom that still exists of giving a ring in the celebration of marriage. The episcopal ring is not only a sign of the alliance of the bishop with his Church, but also a mark of the authority of the Holy Ghost, in virtue of which the bishop has a right to distribute employments. He wears it on the forefinger of the right hand, according to the custom of the Hebrews, because this is the finger that indicates silence. The bishop is thus reminded of the inviolable secrecy of mysteries, and the perfect discretion with which he should announce them, lest he should throw pearls to swine.[256]

All these lessons, useful to priests and to the faithful, as well as to pontiffs, are contained in the words addressed to the bishop, when the consecrating pontiff gives him the ring: "a mark of discretion and dignity, a sign of fidelity, that you may know how to be silent regarding what ought to be kept silent, to manifest what ought to be manifested, to bind what ought to be bound, and to loose what ought to be loosed."[257]

6. *The miter.* The miter[258] takes us back to the most remote antiquity. The high priest and the sacrificators of the Mosaic law had their heads adorned with it.[259] The history of the Church makes mention of the miters of St. John the Evangelist and the apostle St. James.[260] True, the miter, such as bishops wear it nowadays, differs from the ancient in its material, and in the ornaments that increase its splendor; but in the main it is the same.

A covering of glory and dignity, the miter reminds the bishop of his sacerdotal supremacy, the consecration of all his senses, and the perfect knowledge that he should have of the old and the new testament, figured by the two bands that fall on his shoulders.[261]

Penetrated with these thoughts, the bishop asks of God, when taking it, the strength and discretion necessary to avoid all the snares that the devil may lay for him.

7. *The crosier.* The crosier[262] is an emblem of the pastoral power. It is the shepherd's crook: a touching figure, which shows us the Church as a fold, of which the faithful are the flock and the bishops the pastors. It is not blind or brute force that governs, but charity, a solicitude enlightened and maintained by faith. When giving the crosier to the bishop on the day of his consecration, the following words are addressed to him: "Receive this staff, a sign of thy sacred government, and remember to strengthen the weak, to steady those who totter, to correct the perverse, to guide the good in the way of everlasting salvation; receive also the power to raise up those who are worthy, and to put down those who are unworthy, with the help of Jesus Christ our Lord."

Thus, what a scepter is to a king, that the crosier is to the bishop. It has been in use since the early ages of Christianity.[263] When the bishop ascends the altar, he lays the miter and crosier aside: his power vanishes before that of Jesus Christ. For a contrary reason, he resumes its ensigns when he turns toward the people.[264]

8. *The pallium.*[265] If the pontiff is an archbishop or a patriarch, he takes the pallium after being clothed with all his other ornaments. The pallium is an ornament that is worn on the shoulders. It is formed of two little bands of white wool, about two inches wide, which hang on the shoulders and breast, and are studded with dark crosses. Metropolitans wear it as a mark of their jurisdiction over the churches of their province. It is also regarded as an emblem of humility, innocence, and charity. It serves to remind

the prelate who is adorned with it that he ought, after the example of Jesus Christ, the prince of pastors, to seek the lost sheep, and to bring it home on his shoulders. The very material of the pallium acquaints us with this affecting signification.

It is made of the wool of lambs perfectly white. On St. Agnes's day, and in the church of her name, built at Rome on the Nomentan Way, there are some lambs blessed every year, whose wool is to be employed in making palliums. They are then kept by a community of nuns till the time of shearing them arrives. The palliums made of their wool are laid on the tomb of St. Peter, and remain there all the night before his festival. Next day, they are blessed on the altar of the church dedicated to him; after which, they are sent to the prelates who have a right to wear them. This right is limited to certain days, and does not extend beyond the church. On the contrary, the sovereign pontiff carries the pallium always and everywhere, as being invested with supreme power and universal jurisdiction over all the churches.[266]

The pallium is of the highest antiquity. St. Isidore of Pelusium,[267] who lived in the middle of the fifth century, and St. Gregory the Great speak of the pallium and explain its various significations.[268] Its origin is referred to St. Linus, the second successor of St. Peter.[269] It recalls the ephod worn by the high priest among the Jews.

9. *The gremial.*[270] When the bishop sits during Pontifical Mass, there is a piece of silk or other precious stuff, called a gremial, from the Latin word *gremium*, "the lap," placed on his knees. It lets the pontiff rest his hands, and preserves his ornaments, which might otherwise be injured by perspiration.[271]

Such are the ornaments peculiar to bishops. If we reflect on all this mysterious apparel with which religion surrounds her ministers, when they have to offer the holy victim, behold the thoughts that come naturally to our minds: "Very august therefore is this victim; very holy therefore is Catholic sacrifice; very awful therefore are the functions of the priesthood! We ourselves, who assist at these divine mysteries, ought therefore to be very pure!" And this was assuredly one of the ends that the Church proposed to herself when establishing her numerous ceremonies and giving to her priests so many vestments, doubly venerable by their antiquity and their signification.

Colors of ornaments.—The variety of their colors is not less instructive. White, a figure of the innocence of the Lamb of God, and red, a figure of his blood shed for us, go back to the apostolic times. The other colors are also of high antiquity.[272] The Church, the divine spouse of Jesus Christ, likes to appear before him in dress of pleasing and mysterious variety. True, her essential glory and beauty are within; but this outward display is an expression thereof. According to the circumstances in which she finds herself, she lets her dispositions appear outwardly, that she may inspire similar ones.

White. White, a symbol of purity and sanctity, is used on festivals of our Lord and the Blessed Virgin, the angels, pontiffs, confessors, virgins, in a word, the just who have not shed their blood for the faith. White, by reminding us of the Lamb of God, says to us, "Love purity: holy things are for the holy. Offer to God a spotless soul, worthy to be one day received into the heavenly Jerusalem, where nothing defiled can ever enter."

Red. Red, which at once suggests the idea of blood and fire, is employed to celebrate the festivals of the martyrs. As it is the work of the Holy Ghost to enlighten minds and inflame hearts, and as he descended on the apostles in the form of tongues of fire, red is used to honor him. Could it be that this image of blood and fire would leave us cold and cowardly? Do the memories of the amphitheatres and the upper chamber touch no chords in our hearts? Have we not received the same Spirit? Are we not the children of the martyrs, or has their blood ceased to flow in our veins? Can we complain of the little sacrifices that are asked of us, when we behold this host of witnesses, who won the victory by an immolation of themselves?

Green. Green is employed for ordinary Sundays and ferias. Is it not, in point of fact, proper to consecrate by more frequent use that color which we have continually before our eyes? Is it not becoming that the inhabitant of the country, who goes every morning to receive the blessing of the Father of the family before he visits his farm, or who comes on Sunday to rest himself in the presence of the Lord after the toils of the week, should find in our temples an image of his fields, his trees, his fruits? Is there not in all this a beautiful and touching harmony? And then, all you that delight in contemplating the wonders of nature, are you not happy to meet at the altar something that reminds you of the benefits of the Creator, and a new motive to bless him who gives verdure to our meadows and fertility to our plains, who clothes the lilies of the valley, and feeds, not only the little birds, the cottage musicians, but all creatures that breathe?

Purple. Purple, which is partly dark and partly bright, recalls both the labors and the advantages of penance. It is employed at times when sorrow and hope are the motives of divine worship. Thus, in Advent, we weep and sigh. We weep, but we weep only on account of delay. We sigh, but these sighs call down the just one. Purple is therefore used. In Lent we weep over our faults, but we behold pardon at the end of the holy quarantine. We weep over the sufferings of Jesus Christ, but we behold the glorious day of his resurrection appearing. We weep in calamities, in public or private afflictions, but we expect that our tears shall soon cease to flow. This ineffable mixture of sadness and comfort, of sorrow and hope, is expressed by purple.

At the death of kings, as power does not die,[273] and the same stroke that makes the crown drop from one head makes it fall on another, purple is taken. This color should therefore always remind us of our misery, but rouse our courage by a consideration of the infinite mercies of the Lord. It should always tell us that the way to glory is through tribulations; that our only hope is in the cross, and our only happiness here below in hope, because there is no joy on earth without suffering.

Black. But when the Church bewails her children who are wholly dead to the present life—beholding only the pains of purgatory from which they have to be delivered, hearing only their pitiable supplications, considering only with alarm the dreadful passage from time to eternity, feeling always the unfortunate wound that brought death into the world, uncertain always as to the last dispositions of those for whom she prays—then this tender mother, overwhelmed with grief, clothes herself in black, and thus appears before her divine spouse.

By this gloomy color she tells him eloquently how great is her affliction, and what sad thoughts are awakened in her mind by the punishment of sin that has been taking place in the world for the last six thousand years. I may be mistaken, but it seems to me that the priest, arrayed in his black ornaments, is, without saying a single word, a very eloquent preacher. I fancy that I can hear a voice from that chasuble, all covered with tears, saying, "Remember, man, that thou art dust, and into dust thou shalt return. Thou knowest not the day nor the hour: be ready. Yesterday for thy brother; tomorrow, perhaps today, for thee."

In conclusion, the faithful who assist at our sublime mysteries should remember that it is to them, much more than to the Israelites, that these words are addressed: "You are the priests of the living God, a royal race, a people of saints";[274] and that the preparation which God prescribes to the sacrificator of the new covenant in order to ascend the altar, he requires of them in order to approach thereto. As he formerly sent Moses to the people, to sanctify them for two days and to command them to wash their garments, because they should be witnesses of the presence of the Lord on the mountain, so he wishes that his priests should warn the faithful never to approach the holy mountain of the true Sinai without that collection of inward and outward virtues figured by the sacerdotal vestments.

Altar furniture.—The altar furniture and the sacred vessels will continue to repeat the same warning. Let us open our minds and hearts to receive it.

Altar. The altar represents a tomb. We know why: the tombs of the martyrs were the first altars of Christianity. Such is also the reason why the relics of saints and martyrs are enclosed in our altars. In the early ages, altars were of wood, stone, or marble, as was found most convenient. They were solid, or supported on pillars and pedestals. Before offering the holy sacrifice, they were covered with a large cloth of linen or silk, which was called a pall. In the time of St. Augustine, altars were already adorned with flowers.[275] Even the walls of churches were often decorated with garlands of lilies and roses.[276] Nowadays three cloths are laid on the altar; the uppermost one is enriched with lace and embroidery, and must descend to the ground. The Church prescribed the use of these three linen cloths, easily washed, to guard against the serious inconveniences that might result from a fall of the chalice. The altar must be consecrated by a bishop. Before this consecration, which is derived from the highest antiquity, it is not permitted to celebrate the holy mysteries thereat.[277]

Canons. On the altar you see three cards called canons, because they help to direct the priest, by setting before his eyes the prayers that he could not read with so much ease from the missal. The largest is placed in the middle before the tabernacle, the second to the left, and the third to the right. The altar, according to an ancient usage, is placed at the east end, so that the faithful in their prayers may look toward the rising sun, an image of him who is the true sun, and whose light, having scattered the darkness of paganism, enlightens every man coming into the world.[278]

Tabernacle. In the middle of the altar is the tabernacle, wherein the Holy Eucharist is reserved. It is furnished inside with white silk, and covered outside with a veil. When speaking of Communion, in the second part[279] of the catechism, we explained the shape of ancient tabernacles. The custom of keeping the Blessed Sacrament in a tabernacle, placed in the middle of the altar, at the very foot of the cross, is of very high antiquity.[280] Do you remark all the beautiful traditions recalled by the word *tabernacle*? The desert, Mount Sinai, the manna, Aaron and his Levites, all the prodigies wrought in favor of the ancient Church more than three thousand years ago, are brought together in this single word. In our own epoch, this same word reminds you of still greater prodigies: the last supper, Mount Calvary, the Redeemer's life on earth, and his continual presence among the children of men. Tell me: Do you know any other word with richer or sweeter recollections?

Cross and candles. The tabernacle is surmounted by a large cross. Many ages have already seen it there; many generations have already adored it there. It is there to remind us that the Sacrifice of the Altar is a continuation of the sacrifice of Calvary, and to show that this supreme act of religion is referred to God alone, not to saints or martyrs. Three candles (or at least one) on each side burn during the Mass to honor the sign of the redemption and to recall the catacombs. Religion, history, antiquity, all that is most proper to elevate the soul, to touch the heart, to captivate the senses, is found on a Catholic altar. If the altar is only a stone to the sensual or the indifferent, it is the most eloquent of books to the instructed and the virtuous. Volumes of commentaries would hardly suffice to explain it. O children of men! how long will you have eyes and see not?

PRAYER

O my God! who art all love, I thank thee for having taken so much care to instruct me, by multiplying the ornaments and insignia of religion. Open my mind and heart to such holy lessons.

I am resolved to love God above all things, and my neighbor as myself for the love of God; and, in testimony of this love, I will be grateful to God for having established the sacred ceremonies of religion.

Lesson 14: Christianity Brought before the Senses (Continued)—Sacred Vessels, Holy Water

Sacred vessels.—If the ornaments of ministers and the furniture of the altar abound in reminiscences and instructions, the sacred vessels afford no less interest to the pious curiosity of the learned and the simple. And first, their consecration and splendor remind us of our consecration to the Lord and the sanctity that he requires of us; for we are also sacred vessels. It is our duty to be much holier and purer than the vessels intended for the altar, since a thrice holy God, whose adorable body merely touches chalices and ciboriums, is incorporated with us. The principal of these vessels are the chalice, paten, ciborium, and monstrance.

1. *Chalice.* The chalice is as old as Christianity. It was in a cup that our Lord consecrated his divine blood, and gave it to his apostles to drink. The chalice was a vessel used by the Jews at their meals. All drank of the same cup, which was handed from one to another as a mark of friendship. The same custom still exists among many people of the old and the new world.

In the early ages, when our forefathers were rich only in their poverty and virtue, chalices were sometimes made of glass, copper, or other like material; but, as soon as their means permitted it, chalices and other sacred vessels were made of gold or silver. Pope Zephyrinus, who was elected in 203, forbade their being thenceforth made of any other metal.[281] The Church requires at present that chalices should be made of silver[282]—at least the cup, the inside of which must be gilt. Out of respect for the body and blood of our Lord, vessels intended for the service of the altar are consecrated: this consecration is of the highest antiquity.[283]

When all the people used to communicate under the species of wine, chalices were much larger than they are nowadays. There is mention made of one whose weight was eighteen pounds, given by Charlemagne to the Church of Aix-la-Chapelle. These chalices had generally two handles, so as to be more easily carried. It would seem nevertheless that it was not from the principal chalice that the people took the precious blood, but rather from smaller chalices, in which there was placed part of the Savior's blood, consecrated at the altar in the principal chalice.[284]

It was also in private chalices that the people offered the wine and water that were to be consecrated:[285] they have been replaced by cruets. However holy all these vessels intended for the altar were, the most pious and enlightened bishops, such as St. Ambrose of Milan, St. Augustine of Hippo, and St. Deogratias of Carthage, did not hesitate to sell them for the relief of the poor and the redemption of captives: they gave less for more.[286]

2. *Paten.* The paten is a little plate of gold or gilt silver, on which the bread to be consecrated rests. When, in the beautiful days of the Church, all those present at Mass had the happiness of receiving the Holy Eucharist, each of the faithful presented at the offertory the bread that was to be changed into the body of our Lord. These offerings were placed on the paten and laid on the altar. Patens were then very large: it is not even doubted that there were many of them. The priest also made use of them for breaking the bread, and distributing it more conveniently. Nowadays the paten is useful only to the priest, for holding the host which he has to consecrate at the holy sacrifice. The custom of offerings has been abolished. The number of communicants is unfortunately less considerable, and ciboriums, in which the consecrated particles of the Eucharist are reserved, are used for their distribution.

3. *Ciborium.* The ciborium, made in the shape of a covered chalice, must be of silver, with the inside of the cup gilt. This precious vessel was formerly kept in a silver tower or dove hanging above the altar: it is now placed in the tabernacle, where it is covered

with a veil. The ciborium naturally recalls the ark of the covenant, which contained the manna, a figure of the Eucharist. But as far as the reality excels the figure, so far does the ark of the covenant in the new law excel that among the people of Israel. This is enough to show what ought to be our respect for it. In front of the tabernacle is suspended a lamp which burns day and night. It is put here to tell us that Jesus Christ, the eternal light of the world, is present on our altars, that he awaits our adoration, and that our life ought to shine like a lamp before him by the sanctity of our works.

4. *Monstrance.* Within the tabernacle, which must be furnished on the inside with white silk, and covered on the outside with a veil, is also placed the monstrance. The monstrance, shaped to resemble glory or the sun, reminds us of the true sun, whose glory enlightened the world. When, prostrate at the foot of the altar, we behold the monstrance appearing, what sentiments should burst on our soul at the recollection of the people on whom this divine sun has not yet risen, and of the whole world before this sun had risen on it!

The monstrance is not as old as the other sacred vessels: its origin is traced to the time when impiety and error attacked the fundamental dogma of the real presence. Ever attentive to the wants of her children, the Church protested against the blasphemy and heresy. By establishing the solemn festival of the Blessed Sacrament, she furnished Christian souls with an opportunity of showing their faith, and rendering to her divine spouse, a prisoner of love in our tabernacles, the adoration and homage which he deserves.

Previously, it was considered enough to raise a little before the eyes of the faithful, after the Canon at Mass, the body and blood of our Lord, saying, *Omnis honor et gloria*—"All honor and glory to him!" From the time of the heresy of Berengarius, an elevation of the holy species was made immediately after the words of consecration. In the body of the church, those present bowed down to adore, and the bell announced, as it still does, to those who could not be present at the sacrifice, that the Son of God was descending on the altar, and that they should offer him their respects and their desires.

About the same time, processions of the adorable sacrament were made with much pomp. In the church, and at resting places prepared outside, the people were blessed with the sacred host. It was at first carried in a kind of purse, as is still done when administering it to the sick far from the church. Shortly, in order to exhibit the Savior with more splendor to the adoration of the faithful, portable tabernacles were introduced. They were called "Melchisedechs" or "monstrances." They are now sometimes called "ostensoriums."

We see them of every shape and size. Many represent a turret bored through. This emblem is rich in Christian ideas and venerable recollections, as we explained when speaking of Communion. Monstrances used to be of gold or gilt silver, sometimes enriched with precious stones. Nowadays, at least the glory should be of silver, and the crescent or circle, holding the sacred host, gilt![287]

Blessing of holy water.—We have just explained all the preparations for the tremendous sacrifice. The priest with his ornaments, and the altar with its furniture and sacred vessels are known to us. If it were an ordinary day, we should immediately accompany the holy minister to the altar; but we must not forget that we are explaining the ceremonies of Sunday. Now, the Mass of this first of days is preceded by a blessing of holy water and a procession.[288] The blessing of water enters into the general blessings of the Church: the same principle established it. Like the others, it contains the whole history of the human race. It tells us of the creation of man and the world in a state of perfection; the degradation of man; the victory and wicked influence of the devil; and the rehabilitation or sanctification of all things by our Lord.

The blessing of water comes, like the rest, from the apostolic times.[289] St. Paul gave an absolute precept regarding it in these words: "Every creature must be purified and sanctified by the word of God and by prayer."[290] Speaking of water in particular, St. Cyprian says, "Water must be purified and sanctified by the priest."[291] The custom of blessing water every Sunday before Mass is of the highest antiquity: it is evidently connected with the custom that the early Christians had of washing their hands and faces in blessed water, to purify themselves before entering the church.[292]

What, then, does the Church mean by blessing water and pouring it on the faithful? A tender mother, full of solicitude, she wishes to remind her children of their fall and their redemption; she wishes to purify them, and to give them all the sanctity that they require to assist worthily at the stupendous mysteries; she wishes, lastly, to preserve them from whatever might sully or injure them. With this view, she joins to her prayers the signs most appropriate to denote her object.

The property of water is to wash. Salt preserves it from corruption. And water and salt mixed are an emblem of purity and innocence. Here we have the matter of holy water. Invested with the power of her divine spouse, to whom all power was given in heaven and on earth, the Church orders her ministers to withdraw these two creatures, water and salt, from the power of the devil, and to render them useful to man, not only by recalling them through sanctification to their original destiny, but by communicating to them a peculiar virtue. And the priest exorcises the water and the salt.

To exorcise means "to conjure and to command": it is a term that befits only those who speak with supreme authority. In the language of the Church, to exorcise is to conjure the devil, to drive him away, to forbid him to injure. To exorcise water and salt means that the priest commands the devil, on the part of God and through the merits of the cross of Jesus Christ, to leave these two creatures free, to avail himself of them no more for injuring men, so that they may thenceforth be useful to our salvation. Such is the meaning of the exorcisms that are made on inanimate creatures.

They are addressed, but it is to the devil that the commands go, in the same manner as it was on the devil that the divine anathema recoiled after the fall of our first parents, though God spoke only to the serpent. That creatures are vitiated, that the devil has great sway over them, and that they require to be sanctified, are truths of the Catholic faith in regard to which we supplied proofs when speaking of blessings in general.

Therefore, on Sunday, before Mass, the priest—representing him who created the elements, who during his mortal life commanded inanimate creatures, the sea, winds, and storms, and who so often drove out the devil from possessed persons—dresses himself in amice, alb, girdle, and stole turned crosswise, and proceeds to the blessing of the water.

He begins by asking the help of God: *Adjutorium nostrum*, etc.—"Our help is in the name of the Lord." The faithful, represented by the clerk, answer: *Qui fecit*, etc.—"Who made heaven and earth." Can the Church put her trust anywhere else? Then the priest, stretching out his hand as a sign of authority, and to show that he acts in the name of the Almighty, continues: "Salt, thou creature of God, I exorcise thee in the name of the living God +, the true God +, the holy God +, that God who by the prophet Eliseus cast thee into the waters to render them wholesome. I exorcise thee that thou mayst become a source of salvation for the faithful, and mayst procure health of soul and body for all those who taste thee. Let the unclean spirit depart; let his malice and cunning vanish from every place where thou shalt be scattered, and this in the name of him who will come to judge the living and the dead, and the world by fire."

The salt freed from the evil influences of the devil, what remains for the priest but to implore the Lord to come and take possession of his creature, to bless it anew, and to make it useful to the human race? He invites all the faithful to unite with him in begging this favor. "Let us pray," he says, and he continues: "O Almighty and eternal God, we humbly beseech thy sovereign clemency. Vouchsafe in thy mercy to bless + and to sanctify + this salt, which thou hast created for the use of the human race. May it serve all those who take it to the salvation of their souls and bodies, and may whatever is touched or sprinkled with it be preserved from all impurity and all the attacks of the wicked spirits. Through Jesus Christ our Lord, who liveth and reigneth with thee, in the unity of the Holy Ghost, world without end." All the faithful answer by the mouth of the clerk: So be it—"Amen!"

The salt is purified, that is to say, brought back to its original destiny, the use of man and the glory of the Creator; it is moreover enriched with special virtue against the artifices of the devil. Whatever impiety or worldly levity may say, this is really the case. To end all doubts on the matter, let us propose the following questions: Is it true that creatures are vitiated, and subjected to the devil, who employs them to tempt and to injure man? Is it true that God can purify them, and withdraw them from the influence of the devil? Is it true that he wishes to do so? Is it true that he can and will communicate his power to chosen men? Is it true that he has communicated his power to them? Has he said so?

To answer these questions in the affirmative is to be a Catholic. To answer them in the negative is to throw common sense to the winds, and to go to law with the human race. And who are you to arrogate to yourself such a right, and to say that you alone are wise, you alone are enlightened among mortals?

The priest, having sanctified the salt, assumes once more the attitude of command. He extends his hand, and, addressing the water, says: "Water, creature of God, I exorcise thee in the name of God + the Father Almighty, in the name of Jesus Christ + his Son our Lord, and by the virtue of the Holy Ghost +, that thou mayst be a pure and holy water, capable of destroying the power of our enemy and conquering both him and his apostate angels. Through our Lord Jesus Christ, who will come to judge the living and the dead, and the world by fire."

And the priest invites the faithful to ask with him that God may be pleased to do what he asks. "Let us pray," he says, and he continues: "O God! who, for the benefit of the human race, hast given wonderful properties to water, graciously hear our prayers and pour down the virtue of thy blessing + on this element, which has been prepared for various purifications. Grant that, serving thy mysteries, it may receive the effect of thy grace to banish the devils and to heal the sick; that everything sprinkled with this water, in houses and other places where the faithful assemble, may be preserved from all impurity and all evil. Let this water remove therefrom every breath of pestilence or corruption. Let it destroy the snares of the hidden enemy, and whatever might be an obstacle to the health or the repose of those who dwell there. In fine, let this well-being, which we ask through thy holy name, be secured against all kinds of attacks. Through Jesus Christ our Lord," etc.

During these exorcisms and prayers, the priest often makes the sign of the cross in order to call to mind that it is through the merits of our Lord that the devil loses his power and creatures cease to be hurtful to us.

The priest then takes the salt in his right hand, and lets it fall into the water in the shape of a cross, pronouncing these words: "May this mixture of salt and water take place in the name of the Father, and of the Son, and of the Holy Ghost!" The faithful answer by the mouth of the clerk: So be it—"Amen!" Then follows a magnificent and touching prayer, by which the priest conjures the Lord, in the name of the Church, to give the holy water all the virtue expressed in the previous prayers.

He says: "O God! whose power is invincible and empire immovable, who dost triumph gloriously over every opposite power and crush with a mighty hand the malice of thine enemies, we humbly beseech thee, O Lord, to look with a favorable eye on this creature of salt and water, to increase its virtue, and to sanctify it with the dew of thy grace, that, by the invocation of thy holy name, every corruption of the unclean spirit may be banished from those places where it shall be sprinkled; that the fear of the venomous serpent may be driven far from thence; and that, imploring thy mercy, we may everywhere be assisted by the presence of the Holy Ghost. Through our Lord Jesus Christ," etc.

These prayers teach us that there are five effects attained by holy water: a) to chase away the devil from those places which he has infested, and thus put an end to the evils which he has caused; b) to keep the devil far from us, the places where we dwell, and the things which we use; c) to serve for the cure of the sick; d) to bring us on every occasion the presence and help of the Holy Ghost, for the welfare of our souls and bodies; and e) to efface venial sins.

And all these effects are really produced by holy water. To call them in question, we must deny ecclesiastical history from its first to its last page. We must, like protestants, accuse the Church of superstition and error. We must regard as impostors or fools the greatest and most virtuous men that ever appeared on the earth: Tertullian, Origen, St. Augustine, St. Chrysostom, St. Epiphanius, St. Jerome, St. Gregory, St. Bernard, and many others.[293]

This is enough to justify the Church, our mother, who sprinkles holy water on men, on creatures, on the dead themselves, to excite within us sentiments of contrition, charity, and devotion; who every Sunday sprinkles with it the faithful and the temple in which they meet to assist at the holy offices; and who always keeps it at the door of the house of God. This is also enough to justify the faithful, who, following the advice of the Church, should not be content with merely taking holy water at the temple, but should carry it to their houses, keep it there carefully, and use it when going to rest, when rising, and at various other times during the day, in order to banish far from them the spirit of darkness, and to secure for them the help of God in a thousand unforeseen dangers of soul and body.[294]

Sprinkling of holy water.—The water having been blessed, the priest, clad in his alb and stole, makes an aspersion with it. The Church wishes to purify the faithful, so that they may assist at the holy sacrifice with more attention, innocence, and purity. What else is needed to make us take a firm resolution never to be absent from the aspersion? If we are distracted, tepid, weary during Mass, who is to blame? Have we adopted the means established by the Church to avoid these defects?

Arrived at the foot of the altar, the priest intones this verse of the fiftieth psalm: *Asperges me*—"Thou wilt sprinkle me, O Lord." And the choir continues: "With hyssop and I shall be cleansed; thou wilt wash me, and I shall be made whiter than snow." The Church chose this verse because it exactly describes the effects of holy water.

But why did the royal prophet say, "thou wilt sprinkle me with hyssop," and not with anything else? For three reasons. First, because hyssop is a small plant, whose leaves, pressed into a bunch, are well suited to hold drops of water for sprinkling. Secondly, because the medicinal property of hyssop is to dry up or set right the bad humors of the body, which makes it a very appropriate sign of the purification of soul and body by holy water. Thirdly, because the sprinkling of the blood of the paschal lamb on the doors of houses, the sprinkling of the blood of victims on the people at the foot of Mount Sinai, and the sprinkling of the water that cleansed lepers, were all made with a bunch of hyssop.

These sprinklings were figures of those of the blood of Jesus Christ. Now, it was proper that the reality should be accomplished by the same means as the figure. During the sprinkling, we should therefore regard ourselves as the people of Israel, whose tribes, passing before Moses at the foot of Mount Sinai, were sprinkled with the blood of victims, and beg for ourselves a sprinkling with the blood of our Lord, the great victim, that is to say, the application of the merits of his precious blood, which alone can wash away sins and preserve us from all evils.

In paschal time, namely, from Easter to Trinity Sunday, we hear sung: *Vidi aquam*—"I saw water issuing from the right side of the temple," etc. Wholly occupied with baptism, which was administered on Easter Eve, the Church chose these words to recall it to the minds of her children. This sacred temple, open on the right side, is the Savior, from whose pierced side there flowed blood and water, emblematic of the sacrament of regeneration. Let us enter therefore into the views of this good mother, and earnestly implore the preservation or the restoration of our baptismal innocence.

Having intoned the *Asperges*, the priest recites in a moderate tone of voice the psalm *Miserere*. If we desire to obtain the purification of our soul, let us endeavor to share the sentiments expressed in this canticle of the penitent king. On his knees at the first step, the priest sprinkles the altar with holy water three times—in the middle, on the gospel side, and on the epistle side. Then, being still on his knees, he sprinkles himself: for this purpose he raises the end of the sprinkler to his forehead. He next sprinkles the choir, which he walks round. The Church proposes hereby to drive far from this holy and terrible place the spirit of darkness, who, according to the fathers, makes every effort in his power to disturb priests and ministers during their holy and terrible functions. Finally, he sprinkles all the people by passing through the nave. On his return to the altar, he invokes the Lord, and beseeches him to grant to the congregation the effects attached to holy water. This is his prayer: "Hear us, O holy Lord, Father Almighty, eternal God, and vouchsafe to send down from heaven thy holy angel, who may keep, protect, visit, and defend all that are in this place. Through our Lord Jesus Christ."

And this prayer, which has lasted so many ages,[295] which has crossed the lips of so many holy priests and bishops, which has sounded in the ears of so many saints, our ancestors and our friends; this prayer, which reminds us of the power of protecting angels, their miracles of charity in regard to Abraham and Tobias, the services of him who guards us; this prayer, I say, has everything that it requires to fill our hearts with confidence, gladness, and piety. May it always produce in us these holy dispositions!

PRAYER

O my God! who art all love, I thank thee for having established blessings to sanctify all creatures. Grant me the grace never to use them but for thy glory.

I am resolved to love God above all things, and my neighbor as myself for the love of God; and, in testimony of this love, I will always endeavor to be present at the sprinkling of the holy water before Mass.

Lesson 15: Christianity Brought before the Senses (Continued)—Processions, First Part of Mass

Processions in general.—The aspersion ended, the procession begins. Before we go to it, let us know what we are doing. The procession is a solemn, religious march of clergy and people. It is also one of those rites of the Catholic Church whose existence sets before our eyes the most remote antiquity.[296] Jews, Christians, pagans, all peoples have made processions and still make them.

Antiquity of processions. Who has not read the account in the scripture of the magnificent procession which the holy king David made, and at which he was present with all his court, to remove the ark of the covenant from the house of Abinadab to that of Obededom?[297] Who is not aware of the still more magnificent procession in which Solomon, accompanied by all the people of Israel, removed the ark of the covenant to the Temple of Jerusalem?[298] Do we not annually figure on Palm Sunday that solemn procession which led the Son of God himself, amid the applause of the crowd, into Jerusalem and the Temple?[299]

All Christian ages offer us processions. We shall cite only a few, but they are memorable examples.

In the course of the third century, about the year 274, the bishop of the Church of Charres, in Mesopotamia, the ancient Haran, where Abraham had dwelt, was a holy and learned man named Archelaus. This bishop had a Christian friend named Marcellus, distinguished by his birth, his wealth, and his piety. Charres bordered on the Roman and Persian empires, and was therefore much exposed to the evils of war.

One day, the Roman garrison of the city and province brought 7,700 prisoners before the bishop. They had decided on selling or killing them. As they asked a large sum of money, Archelaus, uneasy, went away to his friend Marcellus, who immediately opened his treasury, and, without taking any note of the amount, began to distribute to the soldiers even more than they had asked. The soldiers were astonished at this charity. Some would only take a fourth of the price that they had proposed; others would take nothing but the expenses of their journey; others would even quit the service in order to become Christians.

Meanwhile, Marcellus learned from one of the captives the cause of their misfortune: they were all Christians. Accompanied by their wives and children, they had gone to a place of pilgrimage, according to the custom of their ancestors, in order to obtain rain in a time of drought. As they were spending the night in fasting and watching, sleep overcame them. The Roman army, finding them in this state, took them for enemies in ambush, killed three hundred and wounded five hundred of them during the night, and led off the rest, with the harshest treatment, to Charres, which was a journey of three days.

Marcellus burst into tears at this news. He immediately got seven hundred tables ready, at which he himself served like another Abraham. He treated the prisoners thus for fifteen days, after which they asked leave to return home. He kept none but the wounded, until they were healed. He then sent them back too, supplying them plentifully with all that they required for their journey. To these acts of charity, he added another: it was to go with a great many persons and bury those who had been killed at the place of pilgrimage, or who had died on the way.[300]

Thus do our least ceremonies give evidence to all generations of remarkable occurrences in the history of the human race. The Sunday procession has another souvenir: the first Christian processions took place in the catacombs.

What were the recollection and fervor of those processions of Christians, most of whom were destined for martyrdom, walking by the glare of their torches in subterranean galleries, under the guidance of a bishop still more venerable by his virtues than by his white hairs! It is easy to form an idea thereof. May this salutary idea ever accompany us, when we walk in the footsteps of our forefathers.

But what! the procession on Sunday within a church—is it not made in a catacomb by the glare of torches, amid the tombs of martyrs, whose sacred bones rest, on our right and left, in the side chapels of the basilica? And we ourselves—ought we not to be martyrs of peace, as St. Cyprian says,[301] always ready to immolate ourselves and always immolating our concupiscences to God, for whom our ancestors shed their blood? What do I say? Is not our faith, according to the expression of Tertullian, an engagement to a martyrdom of blood?[302]

In the sixth century, the plague was desolating Rome. Pope St. Gregory the Great ordered the celebrated procession which, by reason of the seven companies of the faithful who composed it, retained the name of the "septiform procession." It was scarcely over when the plague ceased; not a single new case of illness occurred, and all the sick recovered. We may travel on in the same course to the sixteenth century. At this period, Milan was attacked by the plague. The great archbishop of this city, St. Charles Borromeo, organized a solemn procession. He himself appeared therein, barefooted and with a rope round his neck, to obtain an end of the terrible plague. His prayer was heard.

A century afterward, in 1629, the plague ravages Salins, a town in Franche-Comté. Every day increases the number of victims, and no check can be put to the evil. The magistrates of the town have recourse to the Comfortress of the Afflicted. They come in a body to the principal church, and, in the name of the people, a vow is made to go in procession to Our Lady of Gray, about thirty-five miles distant. The vow has its effect; but it cannot be fulfilled for two years. On the 23rd of August, 1631, a thousand of the inhabitants of Salins, preceded by the clergy and magistrates of the town, set out for Gray, passing through Quingey, Toraise, and Marney. As they go on foot and at processional pace, it is three days before they arrive. All Gray comes forth to meet the pious pilgrims. Next day, a general Communion takes place in the chapel of the Blessed Virgin, and it is only on the 31st of August that the procession, eight days after its departure, reenters Salins, amid the ringing of all the bells and the singing of the *Te Deum*.

Who does not know of the Marseilles procession in the last century? Even today, in all parts of the Catholic world, processions are most numerous to Our Lady of Rocamadour, to Our Lady of Chartres, to Our Lady of Boulogne, to St. Anne of Auray, to Our Lady of Hermits in Switzerland, etc., without mentioning local processions. During the Rogation days, processions furrow the country; and on the Assumption, all France is in procession.

Universality of processions. To prove the universality of processions, it remains to show them in use among ancient and modern pagans. The devil, whom Tertullian rightly calls "a mimic of God"—*simia Dei,*[303] could not fail to adopt the mysterious rite of processions, and to turn it to his own worship. Through all antiquity, in East and West, at Delphi, at Rome, and in Gaul, we behold pagans marching in procession. One of these sacrilegious processions was remarkable among them all: we refer to that of Autun in honor of the goddess Cybele, which gave occasion to the martyrdom of St. Symphorian.[304]

Satan does not sleep: he continues to parody our august ceremonies. The people of the East—Hindus, Chinese, Buddhists, Brahmins—have monstrous processions. One of our Indian missionaries speaks thus of the pagan processions that took place at Mysore in 1866:

"During the cholera, the pagans invoked all their gods to banish the evil goddess. There was every day a hubbub impossible to describe. I saw one of their processions: it greatly resembled a masquerade of our own country. At the head of the procession there marched onwards and from side to side, like a drunken man, a huge pagan, having a sword, with which he slashed the air, so as to pursue the goddess. After him came some women, who were consecrated to all the debaucheries of the temples and were regarded as possessed. Their appearance would easily make one believe it. Their disheveled hair fell like serpents on their shoulders and breasts. They executed infernal dances all along the way, turning like tops and acting as if they were really possessed.

"Then appeared a god, borne on a palanquin, and surrounded with lighted torches, pans of incense, etc. Last of all came the crowds, howling and shouting in a manner that seemed enough to make all the devils laugh, and accompanying this madness with the noise of drums, fifes, trumpets, iron rods, and whatever else could yield a sound. When the procession was passing under our windows, I was horrified at the sight of the women that led it. One of them fell down on the ground before me; the spirit possessed her. She was beaten all over with coconuts, of a large size and very hard. It seemed enough to kill her a thousand times. At length, the daughter of Satan awoke, and the procession, which had been stopped, resumed its course. For more than a month, nothing was to be heard of anywhere but these processions.

"Our dear Christians, while their neighbors were invoking the devils, raised their hands to heaven and cried to the God of all mercy. Every evening for nine days, the church was crowded with the faithful. Prostrate on the ground, they besought the sovereign master to have pity on his people, and to turn away from them his just anger.

"On the last day of the novena, a great procession in honor of St. Sebastian closed these pious prayers.

"After this procession, the Christians were spared from the scourge, which still fell heavily for several weeks on those around them."

The antiquity and universality of processions demonstrate that they are of divine institution. Where could man have discovered the idea that a solemn march would honor and appease the deity? Heiress of all genuine traditions, the Church, when adopting processions, took possession of her own property wherever she found it, among Jews as well as among pagans. From the beginning, she did this. As we have said, her first processions took place in the catacombs, until such times as she could make them in the broad daylight.[305]

Source of their efficacy. But what is the meaning of this mysterious work? Why does the Church, in time of joy as well as of grief, command her children to go in procession? In other words, whence does the efficacy of processions come? Processions, as we have said, are ancient and universal only because divinely instituted. They are perpetual only because efficacious. Why efficacious? Because at once a public prayer and a wholesome instruction.

A public prayer. It is of faith that prayer has special efficacy. "Where two or three are gathered together in my name," says our Lord, "there am I in the midst of them."[306] Moreover, a procession is a prayer to the ringing of bells, to sweet singing, to the bursts of musical instruments: that is to say, with conditions of success indicated by God himself. "If you go to war," he said to the figurative people, "you shall blow the trumpets, and the Lord will remember you and will deliver you from your enemies. In your days of rejoicing, you shall take care to accompany your banquets and your sacrifices with the sound of instruments, and a remembrance of you shall rise to your God: I am the Lord."[307]

The imperishable signature that is read at the foot of this decree makes the decree itself imperishable. Hence it comes that all peoples, at all times, have accompanied their religious solemnities with vocal and instrumental music. By carrying out the divine prescription even in hamlets, the procession realizes one of the conditions of its efficacy. When we see multitudes of people bearing aloft in triumph the venerated images of the Savior, Mary, and some saint, walking along the streets of the city or the roads of the country, and at the same time praying, singing, or weeping, what do they say to God but that they are full of confidence in him, that they lovingly thank him as the source of everything good, or that they wish to move him as the avenger of crime and the moderator of all calamities? They desire that this homage rendered to all the perfections of God should be public, and that every kind of voice should join in interpreting their sentiments.[308]

A wholesome instruction. The procession is an image of life; it is the whole history of the human race: past, present, and future. What, in point of fact, is the life of man on earth but a march to eternity? Come from God, he returns to God. Let us see how eloquently the procession acquaints us with this fundamental truth.

The procession sets out from the Church, where the living God dwells, and returns to the point of departure. This is human life coming from God and returning to him.

The procession has scarcely begun to move, when the sound of bells is heard. These are the trumpets of the Church militant, which send the prayer of man to heaven, and which proclaim the march of the great King and his army: a march continually varied by battles with the infernal legions, the seductions of the world, and rebellious passions.

The procession is headed by the cross, which is accompanied with lights. This is Jesus Christ, the guide of human life. For he is the way, and the truth, and the life: the way, out of which there are only ambushes and precipices; the truth, out of which there is only the darkness of error; the life, out of which there is no life worthy of the name, either as regards the mind or the heart, time or eternity.[309]

The procession unfurls its banners, which glow with representations of the Blessed Virgin and the saints. Then come the shrines, like triumphal cars, bearing the sacred relics of the glorious conquerors of the world, the flesh, and the devil. All are here to direct the steps of man, to rouse his courage, and to assure him of their protection.

The procession is like the train of those blessed souls, and advances with prayers, or in turn singing its regrets, its hopes, its joys, and its sorrows. This is a most striking image of life, such as it really is and as Christianity regards it. Is it not amid prayers and tears and sighs and consolations that the exile of heaven makes his pilgrimage to the borders of his native land?

The procession takes various courses, pursues various routes, and, after a journey more or less checkered, returns to the place from which it set out. It is always human life. After a few years, which we call childhood, youth, manhood, and old age—years full of vicissitude, toil, sickness, misfortune, and persecution—it returns to God, from whom it came forth.

The procession enters the church again, and the cross is replaced at the foot of the altar. This is Jesus Christ reentering heaven, leading after him the elect, enlightened by his word, guided by his example, saved by his blood. The faithful have also returned to their starting point: Who are they? Children of God returned to their Father; exiles arrived safe at home.

The procession is over: life is ended. Man has received a most wholesome instruction. He knows whence he came and whither he is going. He knows the object and the conditions of his existence on earth. The procession, speaking to his senses, has engraved on his soul all the truths that should serve him as a compass or as a shield. It is thus that man, being brought back to his true relations with God, finds himself in a condition to obtain everything that he requires. Hence the efficacy of processions for those who take part in them with the proper dispositions, that is to say, with understanding, recollection, and piety.[310]

This efficacy becomes greater if we reflect on another mystery. Human life is a procession: the whole human race, whatever it may do, is in procession. But there are two processions: the Christian procession, headed by Jesus Christ, who, with the banner of his cross, is its guide to heaven; and the worldly or anti-Christian procession, with its standard borne by the devil, who leads it to hell. The last judgment will only make this truth more manifest. After the sentence of the supreme judge, two processions shall be seen filing off: one to the realms above, the other to the flames below. Which procession have I followed hitherto? Let my works speak.

The Sunday procession before Mass. We know the meaning of processions in general, their antiquity, their universality, and their efficacy. It is by them that we become familiar with great events, the memory of which they perpetuate from generation to generation. Such in particular is the Sunday procession before High Mass. It was established to recall a circumstance of our Lord's resurrection.

The gospel informs us that angels, addressing the holy women who came on the morning of Easter Sunday to the sepulchre, said to them: "Go, tell his disciples and Peter that the Lord will go before you into Galilee."[311] And the Lord himself, meeting them as they were leaving the sepulchre, said to them, after they had adored him: "Go, tell my brethren to go into Galilee: there they shall see me."[312] The Church, taking these words to herself, sets out on the march every Sunday before the adorable sacrifice, and goes like the holy women to announce in all parts to her children that her spouse is risen. It is on the same day and almost at the same hour when this order was given on Calvary to the holy women of Jerusalem, that the Church complies with it at every point of the globe. And she has done so for eighteen hundred years.[313]

Division of the Mass.—We have returned with the procession. Let us now recollect ourselves: the august sacrifice is about to begin. We shall divide the Mass into six parts.[314] The first is the preparation for the sacrifice: it is made at the foot of the altar. The second extends from the introit to the offertory; the third, from the offertory to the Canon; the fourth, from the Canon to the *Pater*; the fifth, from the *Pater* to the Communion; the sixth, from the Communion to the end of Mass.[315]

Meaning of the word "*Mass*." The word *Mass* means "dismissal." In the early ages of the Church, there were two dismissals of the attendants. The first took place after the gospel and sermon, when the deacon warned the catechumens, infidels, penitents, and all others who were not to participate in the holy mysteries, to leave the church: this dismissal was called the "mass" or the "dismissal of the catechumens." The second took place when, after the celebration of the holy sacrifice, the same deacon said to the faithful: "Go, the moment of departure is come!"[316] And this second dismissal was called the "mass" or the "dismissal of the faithful."[317]

Some great doctors, including St. Thomas, Hugh of St. Victor, Innocent III, St. Bonaventure, and Bellarmine, give the word *Mass* a higher meaning. It comes, they say, from the Latin verb *mitto*, "to send." As a matter of fact, in the Holy Sacrifice of the Mass, the eternal Father sends us his only Son, as a victim to offer to His Majesty. The Church, which receives him in this state, immolates him by the hands of the priest, and thus sends him back to the eternal Father.

The Sacrifice of the Altar, says St. Thomas, is called the Mass, because Jesus Christ is therein sent to us from God, in order to be offered to him as a pure host, pleasing in his sight. Whence it comes that, at the end of Mass, the deacon, turning toward the people, dismisses them, saying: *Ite, missa est*—"Go, the host is sent, sent to God, that it may be pleasing to him."[318]

According to these princes in theology, the word *Mass* signifies the mission of missions, the sending of the great victim to the human race by the eternal Father and that of this same victim to the eternal Father by the human race. It is on this account that at Mass the prayers of the Canon, during which the august sacrifice is accomplished, are termed the *action*—the action properly so called, before which all others fade away. A new proof of the deep philosophy in Christian language!

The name *Mass*, given to the holy mysteries, seems to have been born with the Church. We trace it to the origin of Christianity. About the year 166, Pope St. Pius, writing to Justus, bishop of Vienne, says, "Our sister Euprepia, as you well remember, gave her house to the poor, in which we are now residing and celebrating Masses."[319] In 254, Pope St. Cornelius, writing to Lupicinus, bishop of the same Church of Vienne, says, "It is not now permitted Christians to celebrate Mass publicly, even in the best known catacombs, such is the violence of the persecution."[320]

First part of the Mass: Preparation at the foot of the altar.—The first part of the Mass is the preparation that is made at the foot of the altar. The priest, charged with the most sublime and awful ministry, comes forth in his ornaments from the sacristy, and advances modestly and gravely to perform the great act that is to reconcile heaven with earth. Yet a moment and he will make heaven shower down on the world the most abundant blessings, or rather make it send down the just one, the source of every grace. Arrived at the foot of the altar, which he salutes with profound respect, he does not venture to ascend its steps, or if he does ascend them for a few indispensable arrangements, he soon descends them again, as if repelled by the majesty of that God who is going to appear.

He bows anew and says, *In nomine Patris*, etc. To sacrifice a victim, he must have a right over its life. Now, God alone has a right over the life of the Word incarnate, the victim of the Sacrifice of the Altar. To be able therefore to offer Jesus Christ to God the

Father, the priest requires the authority of God himself. This authority has been promised him: it is attached to the priesthood. He invokes it saying: "In the name of the Father."

In the name of the Father, who alone has a right to sacrifice his Son, over whose life he alone has a right; in the name of the Father, by whose authority, choice, and vocation, I am a priest.

In the name of the Son, that is to say, in his Person and in his place, as making part with this one eternal priest, associated to his ministry, and invested with his power, that he may do by me on earth what he did himself on the cross and what he still does in heaven.

In the name of the Holy Ghost, that is to say, in his power; for it was by him that the victim of this sacrifice was formed in the womb of the Blessed Mary, and it is only by him that I can have the sanctity necessary for my dreadful duties. Such therefore is the meaning of the sign of the cross which the priest makes on himself at the beginning of Mass.

In the name of the Father, of whom I am a priest;

In the name of the Son, in whom I am a priest;

In the name of the Holy Ghost, by whom I am a priest;

In the name of the Father, to whom I offer the sacrifice;

In the name of the Son, whom I offer in sacrifice;

In the name of the Holy Ghost, by whom I offer the sacrifice.

The priest must bring all these things to his mind before venturing to immolate the great victim. Co-sacrificators with the priest, the faithful should also bring them to mind. For this purpose, they should make with the utmost attention and respect the sign of the cross which begins the Mass.

Astonished at what he is now going to do, the priest exclaims: "What! I shall go to the holy mountain, I shall ascend to the altar of the living God!"—*Introibo ad altare Dei!* At this point there begins, between him and the assembled people, represented by the clerk who answers Mass, one of those beautiful dialogues which cannot be imitated in any human language. Afraid that the priest should desist in terror, the clerk seems to encourage him in the name of all the people, who earnestly desire to reap the fruits of the sacrifice. "Yes," he says, "you will go to the good and gracious God who rejoices our youth"—*Ad Deum*, etc. These words do not reassure him yet.

Then, in a direct address, he beseeches God to enter into judgment with him, before he crosses the sacred threshold. He conjures him not to have regard to his faults, but only to remember that he belongs to the holy nation, and that he wishes to be wholly separated from deceit and iniquity. He implores the divine light from on high, the Spirit of truth and faith which may guide his steps to the mountain of salvation, the august resting place of the majesty of the Almighty.

While he is thus occupied with the Lord, always trembling at his own unworthiness, the people, represented by the clerk, alarmed at his indecision and delay, interrupt him with several motives of encouragement. They remind him that the Lord is our strength and our support; that he knows how to heal our wounds and to restore the beauty of our souls. "Yes," they say to him again, "you shall go to the altar of God, who rejoices our youth." Yielding to so much pressure, the priest exclaims: "Yes, O my God! I will sing Your praises in the face of the world; and thou, my soul, why art thou sad and why dost thou disturb me?" The people continue: "Hope in the Lord; we will bless him with you: he is our Savior and our God." The priest answers: "Glory be to him"—*Gloria Patri*, etc. And the people, uniting their voices with his, complete the praises of the adorable Trinity: *Sicut erat*, etc.

But, as if he repented of the promise he has just made, the priest is again astonished: "What! I shall ascend to the altar of God!" Assuredly, the people answer him, the God of mercy calls you to it: once more, "It is the good God, the God who rejoices our youth." Very well, so be it, says the priest, "I put my trust in the name of the Lord"—*Adjutorium nostrum*, etc. It is well placed, answer the people, "For he made heaven and earth"—*Qui fecit*, etc. Then bowing low, and striking his breast, like the publican who durst not lift up his eyes, the priest declares himself guilty in the sight of heaven and earth. Placed between the heavenly and the earthly Jerusalem, he calls these two cities to hear the narrative of his faults, and entreats them to beg pardon for him—*Confiteor*, etc.

The people of earth, uniting with those of heaven, answer: "May the Lord God Almighty have mercy on you, and, after forgiving you your sins, bring you to life everlasting"—*Misereatur*, etc. While the whole Church asks pardon for its minister, he remains stooped in the attitude of a suppliant. Before raising his head, he gives expression to the only wish of his heart: "Amen!" May it be so, he says to the people; may the Lord hear your prayers and purify my soul!

Touched by the humility of the priest, the people understand that they also have need of pardon and mercy. And, in fact, do they not offer with the priest? Must they not be holy like him? Will the Lord look with complacency on the offering of his minister, if the people for whom he prays do nothing to purify themselves? Taking now in their turn a penitential attitude, the people humbly confess their faults, strike their breasts, and ask the priest, whom they call their father, to pray for them to Almighty God.

The priest answers: "May the Lord Almighty have mercy on you, and, after forgiving you your sins, bring you to life everlasting!" Then, joining his case with that of the people, he adds: "May the Almighty and merciful Lord grant us pardon, absolution, and remission of all our sins!" While saying this prayer, he makes the sign of the cross, to restore in himself and the people the image of Jesus crucified, an image of perfect innocence and holiness.

With what kind of eye, do you think, does the Church of heaven behold the Church of earth, her younger sister, thus humbling herself and repenting before their common Father? The sheep pray for the shepherd, and the shepherd for the sheep. Can there be a more touching spectacle, one more proper to draw down a flood of graces on the earth?

Full of confidence, the priest, addressing the Lord, says, "Now, O Lord, you will turn toward us, you will cast a favorable eye upon us, and this glance will give us life"—*Deus, tu conversus*, etc. The people add this affecting petition: "And your people will rejoice in you." Your people, the people whom you have so much loved, the people for whom you have wrought so many wonders, the people who are as dear to you as the apple of your eye—this people will rejoice in you, and the joy of the children will be the honor and happiness of the Father: *Et plebs tua*, etc.

This interchange of prayers, this communication of charity, this humiliation before God, all have brought back confidence and joy to hearts. Priest and people conclude their admirable dialogue by entreating the Lord to let the cry of their love ascend to him.

We have said that this dialogue is admirable. If we wished to examine it with the profane eyes of a literary critic, it would not be hard to show that the Church, who puts it into the mouths of her children at the moment of the most holy and awful act, understood perfectly the theory of the passions. In point of fact, a lively sentiment of grief, love, hatred, sadness, unworthiness, or anything else, falls back continually on itself. You may find various terms to express it, but it always returns. Now, see how the sentiment of unworthiness, misery, humility, that penetrates the priest and people in presence of the altar of a thrice holy God, is expressed again and again: not a word is uttered without being tinged with it.

The *Introibo* and the psalm *Judica* have been in use in the Roman Church for more than seven hundred years.[321] Before the ninth century, bishops and priests were at liberty to make this preparation either alone and silently or with ministers, according to their devotion. If sovereign pontiffs have changed the practice since, beware of imagining that they thought themselves wiser than their predecessors or the apostles. No, but circumstances have required it.

In Masses for the dead and at the time of the Passion, this psalm is suppressed, on account of the words: "O my soul, why art thou sad?"—*Quare tristis es*, etc. These words, which should banish all sadness, do not agree with the mournful ceremonies of the office for the dead and Passion time. Yet, even in the Masses referred to, the Church does not deprive the priest of the inward consolation which he hopes to find at the altar. This is the reason why he always says, "I will go to the altar of God, who rejoices my youth."[322]

Before quitting the people to ascend the holy mountain, the priest says to them: "May the Lord be with you"—*Dominus vobiscum!* And the people answer: "And also with your spirit"—*Et cum spiritu tuo!* These words, taken from scripture, have been employed by the Church from a very remote period to express the mutual salutations of priest and people: they contain a deep meaning.[323] Accustomed to hear them from the mouth of the priest, and perhaps to answer them out of habit, have we ever meditated on what he promises us on the part of God and what we desire in our turn?

"May the Lord be with you!" Could the priest make a better wish? It is at the moment of sacrifice that he addresses the faithful in these words, which mean: "During the sublime action in which heaven shall be opened, in which God will come down, and in which I shall treat of your most important interests, may the Spirit of God rest upon you! May he form in you the spirit of prayer; may he give you the holy dispositions of repentance and fervor necessary for the success of your petitions! May the Lord be with you at this moment, when he himself so ardently desires to be united to you."

Can there be a wish of greater tenderness? Let us place no obstacle to it, and it will be accomplished in our favor.

The answer that the people make to the priest is of the same nature: "And with your spirit." They do not say, "And with you," because, as an author of the ninth century remarks, "everything is mysterious and spiritual in the functions which he is going to fulfill, and his heart cannot be penetrated with a due sense of his sublime ministry unless his spirit applies itself to reflect on the great truths contained in the prayers which he has to recite." In a word, the people no longer regard the priest as a man but as a pure spirit, an angel of God, about to enter the terrible sanctuary for their sake, and to perform the noblest function with which a creature can be honored.

Thus the priest wishes that the Lord may be with the faithful, and the faithful make the same prayer for the priest, to the end that our Lord may be all in all; that he alone may pray, love, adore in all hearts, and that all hearts together may form but one heart in Jesus Christ. To maintain this union, the beautiful prayer that expresses it is repeated as often as eight times during the Mass: may we never forget it!

Relations between the ceremonies of the first part of the Mass and the passion. During a long course of ages,[324] Catholic piety has delighted to behold in the ceremonies of the holy sacrifice of our altars the various circumstances of the sacrifice of the cross. It has loved to follow step-by-step the great victim, walking slowly from the Garden of Gethsemani to the hill of Calvary. Along this sorrowful way, it experiences a touching variety of sentiments: compunction, gratitude, humility, confidence, love. Without giving these matters an exaggerated importance, we shall set them forth one after another. St. Francis de Sales will be our guide: it will readily be admitted that we could not choose a better.[325]

The Holy Mass is celebrated in memory of the passion of our Lord, as he commanded his apostles: "Do this in remembrance of me." As if he should say: "When you offer the august sacrifice, remember my passion and death." Let us enter into the views of the Savior, and, during the first part of Mass, regard the priest going to the altar as Jesus entering the garden, the priest reciting the first prayers of Mass as Jesus praying in the garden, the priest bowing at the *confiteor* as Jesus prostrate on the ground, the priest kissing the altar as Jesus receiving the kiss of Judas, the priest moving to the epistle side as Jesus led away a prisoner.[326]

Sentiments that ought to predominate our hearts. Whatever there may be in these comparisons, it is certain that compunction and humility are the two feelings which ought to predominate in our hearts during the first part of the Mass. This is plainly shown by the prayers and ceremonies of which it consists.

PRAYER

O my God! who art all love, I thank thee for having established the Holy Sacrifice of the Mass, in which thou dost apply to me the merits of thy passion and death. Grant me the grace to assist at it with more piety than I have hitherto done.

I am resolved to love God above all things, and my neighbor as myself for the love of God; and, in testimony of this love, I will say the *confiteor* at the beginning of Mass with much piety.

Lesson 16: Christianity Brought before the Senses (Continued)—Incense through Gloria

The priest and the people have just wished each other the true dispositions to profit well of the august sacrifice. May the Lord be with his people and his minister! May he pray, love, and adore in them and with them, and may the most abundant blessings be secured to them! After recommending the faithful to pray always, *Oremus*—"Let us pray," the priest sets out and advances slowly toward the altar, redoubling his entreaties that he may enter undefiled into the holy of holies. A new Moses, he does not forget, when ascending Sinai, the beloved people whom he leaves on the plain. For the faithful as well as for himself, he makes this prayer: "We beseech thee, O Lord, to take away from us our iniquities, that we may enter thy sanctuary with a pure heart. Through Jesus Christ our Savior. Amen."

Arrived before the tabernacle, he makes a low bow and kisses the altar in order to show his respect for Jesus Christ, who will soon descend there, and his veneration for the holy martyrs whose relics are deposited there. He accompanies his action with the following prayer: "We beseech thee, O Lord, through the merits of thy saints whose relics are here, and of all thy saints, that it may please thee to forgive me all my sins. Amen."

When placing the relics of martyrs under the table of the altar, the Church of earth wished to imitate what St. John had remarked in heaven: "I saw under the altar of the Lamb," he says, "the souls of them that had been slain for the name of Jesus."[327] It is with justice that the priest recommends himself to the saints in general and the martyrs in particular. The prayers of some and the blood of others, united to the merits and blood of our Lord, are of infinite value, and their powerful intercession is well calculated to obtain for him the forgiveness of all his sins. The priest makes these two prayers in a low voice, because they regard himself personally: they are of very ancient use in the Church.[328]

Incense.—In Solemn Masses, the deacon, after the priest has made the foregoing prayers and kissed the altar, begs him to bless the incense, saying: "Bless, reverend Father!" The word *father* is very touching, by reason of the venerable antiquity that it recalls. It is the name that the early Christians used to give to priests and bishops, as well as to relatives. Nothing could be more reasonable: Are not priests and bishops the fathers of our souls? The custom of using this term is preserved intact in religious communities, where the holy traditions of the primitive Church have taken refuge along with the true spirit of the gospel. The celebrant puts incense into the censer, saying: "Be blessed by him in whose honor thou shalt be burnt!" And he blesses it, making the sign of the cross. He then receives the censer from the hands of the deacon, and incenses the cross, the inner part of the altar toward the candlesticks, the front of the altar, and the two sides of the altar.

What is the origin of incensing? This is one of those questions for which your pious curiosity is anxious to obtain an answer. To trace the origin of incense in divine worship, we must go back 3,500 years, and, entering the desert of Sinai, hear God himself prescribing to Moses the manner of preparing the perfume that should be burnt in the tabernacle.[329]

When a usage rests on such antiquity and comes from a source so worthy of respect, it may assuredly be continued without a blush. One of the chief functions of the priests of the old law was to burn incense on the altar of perfumes. The pagans, unbelieving heirs of primitive tradition, retained the use of incense in their ceremonies.[330] The Catholic Church, in adopting it as her own, was not an imitator of the pagans: she only practiced under the gospel what had been commanded under the law.

The Savior himself taught her by his example that the offering of incense would still be pleasing to God. Among the presents that he inspired the Magi to lay at his feet, frankincense is expressly mentioned. Later on, the Son of Man, invited to dine at the house of a Pharisee, complained that no one had perfumed his head, as was done with persons whom it was intended to honor.[331] Mary, the sister of Lazarus, did not fail in this matter on a like occasion.[332] From the first ages, the Church used incense;[333] and we see Constantine scarcely mounted on the throne of the Caesars when he hastens to make presents of golden censers to churches, to be employed during the celebration of the august mysteries.[334]

What now is the meaning of this usage, so ancient and so general?

1. The incense burnt during the holy mysteries is like a holocaust offered to God. We testify hereby that all creatures should be engaged and consumed in his service and for his glory. The Eastern liturgy clearly expresses this intention, since it accompanies the act of incensing with the following prayer: "Glory be to the most holy, the consubstantial, and the life-giving Trinity, now and forevermore!"[335]

2. The incense burnt at the altar, from which the perfume spreads through the church, is a figure of the good odor of Jesus Christ, which is spread from the altar to the souls of the faithful. All Christian antiquity agrees in giving it this beautiful and mysterious signification.[336] The fathers tell us that the censer represents the humanity of Jesus Christ; the fire his divinity; and the smoke his grace. "The censer," says St. Augustine, "is like the body of the Lord, and the incense like the same body offered in sacrifice for the salvation of the world and received as a sweet perfume by the heavenly Father."[337]

Full of these mysterious and sublime ideas, the early Christians had so much veneration for the incense burnt in church that they strove to breathe its odor, saying what the priest still says at the present day: "May the Lord kindle in us the fire of his love and the flame of eternal charity!"[338]

3. Incense has always been taken for a lively expression of prayer, and of our ardent desire that it should rise in the sight of God as a sweet perfume. The prayer that accompanied the use of incense in ancient liturgies and still accompanies it at the present day leaves no room for doubt on this matter. "O Jesus Christ," says the Eastern Church, "who art God, we offer thee this incense as a spiritual perfume, that thou mayest vouchsafe to receive it on thy holy and sublime altar, from which we expect the effects of thy mercy!"[339] "Let my prayer, O Lord," says the Western Church, "ascend toward thee as sweet incense!" It was doubtless to conform to the spirit of the Church that, in the year 526, at Caesarea in Palestine, the holy priest Zozimus, bursting into tears on the occasion of the city of Antioch being swallowed up, brought the censer into the choir, lighted it, and, falling on the ground, joined to the smoke of incense his sighs and his supplications, that he might appease the wrath of the Lord.[340]

It is therefore certain that incense has always been regarded as a symbol of our prayers. Could there be any symbol more expressive? The incense rises on high only through the activity of the fire that sends it forth; and our prayers, which are really but the desires of our hearts, cannot ascend to God if they are not animated by the fire of divine love. What rises from the censer is of good odor: a touching lesson, which tells us so to prepare our souls that nothing may issue thence but what is pleasing to God. All the incense is consumed, all rises in smoke: so all our desires should tend to God, none should rest on the earth.

4. If incense represents the prayers of the saints here below, much more does it represent those of the saints above. This is the reason why the apostle St. John tells us: "The ancients fell down before the Lamb, all of them having...golden vials full of perfumes, which are the prayers of the saints."[341] Since incense is an emblem of prayer, the first incensing could nowhere enter better than after the petition *Oremus*, in which we ask of God to regard the supplications of the saints on our behalf.

Formerly, the altar was incensed all round. Nowadays, the arrangement of places no longer permitting this, it is incensed on the upper part and the three sides that appear. The celebrant, having incensed the altar, hands back the censer to the deacon. The deacon then incenses the priest: we must tell the reason. Among all people, especially in the East, incensing was a mark of honor. To do honor to a person, the room in which he was received was perfumed;[342] odoriferous oil was poured on his head; ceremonial garments were perfumed.[343] Among the presents that Jacob sent to Joseph in Egypt, he included perfumes, and the queen of Saba did homage to Solomon by offering him a large quantity of the most exquisite perfumes.[344]

Conformably to this usage, the altar is incensed, because it is a figure of our Lord Jesus Christ; the holy gospel, because it contains the words of Jesus Christ; the priests and Levites, because they are ministers of Jesus Christ; the relics of the saints, because they are the precious remains of the members of Jesus Christ; the choristers, that is to say, those who sing the praises of God, because they are in a manner the instruments of which the Church makes use to render the homage of prayer to the Eternal, through Jesus Christ; princes and superiors in the temporal order, because, all authority coming from God, it is honored in those who are here below the living images of the King of kings and the Lord of lords; the faithful themselves, because they are brethren of Jesus Christ, a royal priesthood, a people bought at a great price. We must be on our guard, therefore, against misunderstanding all these honors: they are relative, and return to him who alone is worthy of honor, empire, and glory.[345]

Second part of the Mass: From the introit to the offertory.—It comprises the introit, the *Kyrie*, the *Gloria in excelsis*, the collect, the epistle, the gradual or tract, the gospel, and the *Credo*. The Church joins to instruction the praises of God and prayer, because the minds of the faithful must be filled with holy thoughts and their hearts with holy emotions, in order to be disposed for participation in the tremendous mysteries. This practice, so full of wisdom, comes to us from the early ages. Great care was then taken not to introduce anything into this part of the Mass that had too marked a relation to the Sacrifice of the Eucharist, for fear of revealing the mysteries to catechumens, who could assist at prayers and readings up to the time of the oblation.[346]

Introit. When, therefore, the priest has been incensed, he moves to the epistle side and begins the introit. The word *introit* means "entrance," because the introit is sung at the moment when the priest goes to the altar. Some think that it used to be sung when the faithful were entering the church: this is said to be the reason why it consisted of a whole psalm, and occasionally of several.[347] The establishment of the introit is due to Pope Celestine. Before him, the Mass began with reading from the holy scripture, as is still done on the eves of Easter and Pentecost.[348] The introit, which originally extended to a whole psalm, has been reduced to a few verses; but the *Gloria Patri* has been retained, because every psalm is followed by this prayer in the office. Besides, could the Mass begin better than with the praises of the most Blessed Trinity to whom the holy sacrifice is to be offered?

Why did the Church prefer the songs of the royal prophet in the choice of the introit? An ancient author answers thus: "The approach of the priest to the altar figures the first coming of the Son of God on earth, and the introit is the cry by which the ancient world called for the Desired of Nations. The words of David are employed most frequently because he was of the number of those kings and prophets who so ardently desired to see what we see and to hear what we hear.[349] Happier than all these holy personages, the children of the Catholic Church give expression to their joy by hailing the advent of the Redeemer. They possess him for whom patriarchs, prophets, kings, priests, all the just of ancient times, called in these burning words: 'Send us, O Lord! the Lamb, the ruler of the world; come, O Lord! and do not delay!'"[350]

During the introit, at which we should consider it our duty to be present, let us unite our hearts, our desires, with those of the ancient just; let us enter into their dispositions. An ardent desire is an indispensable condition to profit well of the adorable sacrifice. Oh, what would have been the dispositions of Abraham, Isaac, and David, if they had had the happiness, like us, of assisting at Mass, at the immolation of that Lamb of God for whom they called with so much ardor!

The priest says the introit at the epistle side, and remains here a long time during the Mass. The reason is this: in ancient churches facing the east, the sacristy is at the south, on the right of those who enter, and the priest, standing at this side, finds himself nearer to all the ministers who come from the sacristy to the altar. It is for the same reason that the seat for the bishop or the celebrant in Solemn Masses is placed on this side.

The altar, which is the proper place of the sacrifice, is not the necessary place of the introit, nor of anything else that precedes the oblation. It is now more than a thousand years since the sovereign pontiff began, after kissing the altar, to remove to his seat, and to return only for the offertory. Bishops still do the same at Solemn Masses. There is another reason for this usage: the length of what is read or sung to the time of the offertory. It required one to leave the altar, so as to sit down,[351] especially on great festivals, when the introit was read twice, as is still done, for greater solemnity.

Kyrie eleison. After the introit, the priest, with his hands joined, as a sign of humility, of annihilation before the majesty of God, goes to the middle of the altar in order to say alternately with the people, represented by the clerk, *Kyrie, eleison* three times, *Christe, eleison* three times, and *Kyrie, eleison* three times again.

Kyrie and *eleison* are two Greek words, which mean: "Lord, have mercy!" The use of this prayer, begun in the Greek Church, is of the highest antiquity in the Latin Church. "Considering," says an ancient council, "that in the Church of Rome, as well as in all the provinces of the East and of Italy, there is established the holy and most wholesome custom of often repeating *Kyrie, eleison*, with deep sentiments of fervor and compunction, we wish that, with the help of God, it should be introduced into all our Churches, at matins, Mass, and vespers."[352]

How had it begun in the Greek Church itself? Nothing more touching than its origin. In the early ages, catechumens and penitents assisted at Mass till the offertory. Moved by the desires of the former and the tears of the latter, the faithful were careful to recommend them to the Lord. The catechumens and penitents went on their knees, and the deacon said, "Catechumens, pray!" Then, addressing the faithful: "Let the faithful pray for them, and especially the children!"[353] Oh, yes, the children! those angels of the earth, whose pure hearts and innocent hands, raised to heaven, are all-powerful with God! And the deacon made various petitions aloud for the catechumens. He said, "Let us all pray for the catechumens, that the Lord, full of goodness and mercy, may hear their prayers and grant them the petitions of their hearts." The faithful, and especially the children, answered, *Kyrie, eleison*—"Lord, have mercy!"

The deacon: "May he discover to them the gospel of Jesus Christ!"

The faithful, and especially the children: *Kyrie, eleison*—"Lord, have mercy!"

The deacon: "May he enlighten them and teach them his commandments!"

The faithful, and especially the children: "Lord, have mercy!"

The deacon: "May he inspire them with a chaste and wholesome fear; may he open the ears of their hearts, that they may occupy themselves with his law day and night!"

The faithful, and especially the children: "Lord, have mercy!"

The deacon: "May he bring them together and reckon them among his flock, making them worthy of regeneration and of the robe of immortality!"

The faithful, and especially the children: "Lord, have mercy!"

The deacon: "May he cleanse them from every stain of body and soul; may he dwell in them along with his Christ; may he bless their coming in and their going out; may he crown all their undertakings with success!"

The faithful, and especially the children: "Lord, have mercy!"

The deacon: "May they receive the forgiveness of their sins by baptism, that they may be made worthy of the holy mysteries and of the abode of the saints!"

The faithful, and especially the children: "Lord, have mercy!"

After these invocations for the catechumens, the deacon began others for the penitents. The faithful, and especially the children, replied as before: "Lord, have mercy!" The number of these invocations was not strictly determined. Hence it came to pass that, in the beginning, when the Church had applied these prayers to all the faithful, the *Kyrie, eleison* was recited more or less frequently according to circumstances. Nowadays, a pious custom, approved by the Church, causes the *Kyrie*, or *Christe, eleison* to be said nine times, in imitation of the songs of the angels, who are divided into nine choirs. The *Kyrie* is said three times in honor of the Father; the *Christe* three times in honor of the Son; and the *Kyrie* three times again in honor of the Holy Ghost. The three Persons of the Blessed Trinity are equally adored and invoked.

The Latin Church has preserved the Greek words in order to show that the Western Church was united to her sister, the Eastern Church, and that God was praised and blessed by her efforts in all languages.[354] Henceforth, when we hear *Kyrie, eleison*, let us go back in imagination to the ancient basilicas of Constantinople or Nice, and endeavor to repeat it with the same sentiments, above all with the same innocence, as the children of those happy ages; or rather, let us say it like the blind man of Jericho, who used no other prayer to obtain from the Son of God that cure which he so earnestly desired. Alas! this prayer suits us no less than him. May there be in our hearts the same feelings as in the hearts of so many saints who have said it before us!

Gloria in excelsis. After the *Kyrie*, the priest, still at the middle of the altar, extends his hands as a sign of prayer, and, raising them to the level of his shoulders, in order to show by this gesture his love for heavenly things and his desire to possess them, intones the *Gloria in excelsis Deo.* At this last word, he joins his hands and makes a bow out of respect for the name of God.

The *Gloria in excelsis* touches the very cradle of Christianity. The angels intoned this canticle of love over the crib of the babe of Bethlehem, and the Church continued it: such is the origin of the *Gloria in excelsis.* From the time of St. Athanasius, the faithful recited it at their morning prayers: poor simple women knew it by heart.[355] For more than the last thirteen hundred years at least, it has been the usage to say it at Mass.[356] The *Gloria* is sometimes omitted—as in Advent and Lent, and at Masses for the dead. The office then recalls penance or sadness, and we do not dare to rejoice or sing of heavenly glory when we bewail our own misery or the sufferings of the souls in purgatory.

A canticle of praise and love, the *Gloria* finds its place admirably after the *Kyrie*. The Church has just cried for mercy to her divine spouse. Fully confident that she has been heard, she intones the hymn of her gratitude, and, borrowing the very words of the angels, sings of the great mystery of the incarnation, which is the source of her joy, her hope, and her glory. She blesses the Lord for it, and thus solicits his all-powerful protection.

The priest, who intones it alone, and whom all the people answer, recalls very well the manner in which it was sung by the angels. One of these heavenly spirits appeared to the shepherds, and told them the great news. He had not done speaking when a multitude of angels, uniting their voices with his, sang: "Glory be to God on high, and peace on earth to men of good will!"[357]

The introit expresses the desires of the patriarchs; the *Gloria in excelsis* announces their fulfillment. Two great epochs of the human race, that before and that after the Messias, thus meet in the second part of our Catholic sacrifice. Is this thought not wonderful enough to move us? Will it fail to enlighten our mind, to steady our imagination, to inflame our heart?

PRAYER

O my God! who art all love, I thank thee for having perpetuated the sacrifice of Calvary. Grant me the grace to enter into those sentiments of compunction, gratitude, and joy, which are naturally suggested by the first prayers of Mass.

I am resolved to love God above all things, and my neighbor as myself for the love of God; and, in testimony of this love, I will endeavor to say the *Kyrie, eleison* like the early Christians.

Lesson 17: Christianity Brought before the Senses (Continued)—Collect through Prose

Second part of the Mass (continued).—When concluding the *Gloria in excelsis*, the priest makes the sign of the cross. This usage takes us back eighteen centuries. It sets before our eyes the early Christians, who, as we know, never failed to make the sign of the cross at the beginning and at the end of their principal actions. Could they, or can we, have recourse too often to this all-powerful sign, or be too often reminded that every blessing comes from the cross? Careful to preserve the holy practices of the early ages, the Church wished that, during the august mysteries, the sign of the cross should be made: at the end of the *Gloria in excelsis*; before the gospel; after the *Credo*, Lord's Prayer, *Sanctus*,[358] etc.

The canticle of the angels has just died away. Peace, brought to the world by Jesus Christ, has been announced: What more natural than that the priest, the angel of peace here below, should wish it to the faithful? But how is he going to do so? He kisses the altar, as if to draw this peace from the very bosom of the Savior. He kisses it in the middle, because there is the consecrated stone, the tomb of martyrs, the figure of the cornerstone of the Church—Jesus Christ. He joins his hands, and, with eyes cast down, turns toward the people, opens out his hands as if to denote his charity, and says, "May the Lord be with you!" In the East, priests, instead of saying, *Dominus vobiscum*—"the Lord be with you," have always said, *Pax vobis*—"Peace be to you!"

It was with these sweet words that the Savior, after his resurrection, saluted the apostles. The bishops of the West have preserved this usage. When they are done reciting the *Gloria in excelsis*, they say, *Pax vobis*—"Peace be to you!" As nearly everywhere till the eleventh century, bishops alone said the *Gloria in excelsis* at Mass, they alone also said, "Peace be to you," on account of the close relation between these words and the angelic hymn. The people answered: "And to your spirit!" Full of gratitude for the excellent wish that the priest had just made them, the faithful returned his salutation by praying for him.[359]

Enriched with the blessings of his brethren, the priest turns to the epistle side, and says, "Let us pray." This is the second time since the beginning of Mass that he has given himself and the people this necessary warning. Let us pray: our hearts have just been united by a wish of mutual charity. The Lord is with you; he is also with me. He prays in you; he prays in me. Let us have confidence: Is not the Son of God, who reigns in our hearts, always heard for the reverence that is due to him?

And the priest holds his hands open and raised: a souvenir of three thousand years, a tradition of eighteen centuries. A souvenir of three thousand years: it was with hands raised toward the Temple of Jerusalem that the Israelites prayed.[360] A tradition of eighteen centuries: it was with outstretched hands, to imitate Jesus Christ stretched on the cross, that our ancestors prayed, expressing thus their readiness for martyrdom, for the sacrifice of wealth, family, life itself, rather than deny the faith[361]—a touching usage, if ever there was such, and one that the Church has been careful to preserve. Henceforth, when we see a priest with his hands extended at the altar, on the mountain of sacrifice, can we forget our Lord on the cross, our ancestors in the catacombs? Can we forget that we are the children of Jesus Christ and the martyrs, and that we ought to be their imitators, at least in the dispositions of our hearts? And if we no longer lift up our hands in prayer, let us at least lift up our thoughts and affections.

Collect. Having warned all the people to pray with him, the priest begins the prayer.[362] It is also called the "blessing," because it is intended to draw down on the Church the blessing of God; and the "collect," for two reasons: first, because it is made for the assembled people—the word *collect* means "assembly"—and secondly, because it is a summary of all that the priest should ask of God for himself as well as for the faithful.

Most of the collects that are still in use were drawn up by the sovereign pontiffs St. Gregory and St. Gelasius, but in the main they came from apostolic tradition.[363] Nothing more venerable, and, we may add, nothing more complete: the collects of the Mass are a rare collection. However varied our wants, our desires, or our sufferings, there is not one but finds expression in these admirable prayers. There is besides in these collects a simplicity and unction that we look for in vain elsewhere. To the Catholic Church alone it belonged to compose them. The true spouse alone knew the way in which to speak to her Lord, the language that would touch his heart. As far as she excels the sects in the truth of her teaching, so far does she excel them in the beauty of her prayers.

On ordinary days, the priest says several of these collects. On great solemnities, he limits the number to one, in order to fix the minds of the faithful on the mystery of the day, the only object that should engage them on important festivals. On the festivals of the saints, the collects are petitions in keeping with the chief virtues that distinguished those friends of God, and an encouragement to us to imitate their example. But the Church has taken care to let us see the essential difference that she makes between the saint whom she honors and the God whom she invokes. Here the saint is mentioned under the name of *servant*, and God is supplicated under the names of *Lord* and *master*.

The collects are usually addressed to God the Father, because it is to him that the sacrifice is offered. They conclude thus: *Per Dominum nostrum Jesum Christum*—"Through Jesus Christ our Lord." This means that it is in Jesus Christ and by Jesus Christ every prayer is made; for there is no other mediator between God and man than the Savior Jesus. It means that Jesus Christ, who charged himself with all our debts, likewise charged himself with the presenting of all our supplications to his Father. Lastly, it means that every grace is given us in consideration of the merits of Jesus Christ. As this divine intercessor is immolated on the altar, and we give him to his Father in exchange for the benefits that we expect, there is nothing more proper than this formula to excite our confidence. When asking through Jesus Christ, we have a right to obtain everything. Would that we were well convinced of this when reciting the collect!

At the end of the collect, the assistants answer: "Amen!" This word is a short but energetic exclamation that means: "May it be so! May the wishes that you have just expressed to the Lord be heard! We desire it; we unite with you in asking it; and we promise to place no obstacle thereto, either in deed or in will." The meaning of the word sometimes varies, according to circumstances. Said after an exposition of the truths of faith—for example, after the Symbol—it means: "All this is true; I believe it." After asking a favor, *Amen* means: "I join in the petition"; after explaining a duty: "I agree to what has been said."

Amen! Behold again one of those words which we ought to utter with the most profound respect. And how could it be otherwise if we reflect that, from century to century, it has crossed the angelic lips of so many holy pontiffs, so many virgins, so many hermits, so many Christians, our ancestors in the faith and our models in virtue? Repeated by the martyrs in the catacombs, in prisons, and on scaffolds, it seems still covered with their blood and with their charity.[364]

What must be our feelings if we think that this *Amen*, pronounced by angels and saints, resounds, and will forever resound through the courts of the heavenly Jerusalem! Let us rouse our faith, and the Church of earth will give us a lively representation of the Church of heaven, if, when singing the same canticle, we sing it in the same spirit. If we can only say, "Amen," let us endeavor at least to say it like the angels, the saints, the elect. Let us beware: Have we never lied in repeating this beautiful word? We say, "Amen," to whatever the Church asks and promises in our name, and perhaps we follow no less the perversity of our wills. O my God! what is the *Amen* of the hypocritical and the covetous, the ambitious, the revengeful, and the voluptuous, but a cruel mockery? Woe to him that is thus guilty!

Epistle. After the prayer, the celebrant says the epistle in an intelligible voice, because it is an instruction for the people. At High Masses, it is sung by the subdeacon. In the early ages, this duty pertained to the lector: the epistle was not sung but read.[365] The usage of reading the scripture in religious assemblies comes from the highest antiquity. The Jews began their prayers in the synagogues by reading Moses and the prophets.[366] The early Christians imitated this practice at their Sunday meetings. "We assemble," says Tertullian, "to read the divine scriptures, and to see therein what suits various times."[367] To the reading of the old testament was joined that of the new. "In the assembly," says St. Justin, "we read the prophets and the apostles."[368] The Church took great care to continue this practice.

Not only was the holy scripture read in the early ages of the Church, but also the *Acts of Martyrs*,[369] and the letters of sovereign pontiffs and other bishops, which were called letters of peace or communion. This correspondence tended to keep alive charity and union between the head of the Church in Rome and all the other bishops throughout the world. It also served to distinguish Catholics from heretics: the letters were sent from one Church to another, so that the faithful might know those with whom they ought not to communicate.[370]

This reading was called the "epistle," because it was usually taken from the epistles of the apostles, particularly of St. Paul. Debtors to Greeks and barbarians, missionaries to the whole world, the apostles could not remain a long time in the churches that they had founded. To maintain in the faith those children whom they had lately begotten to Jesus Christ, they did not forget, amid their travels and labors, to write them letters full of useful advice. Never did a loving family experience more joy on hearing from a dear absent father than did these fervent Christians on receiving letters from their fathers in the faith. Evidences of apostolic solicitude and tenderness, these epistles were preserved with the utmost care: they were read in the holy assemblies. The bishops developed their meaning to the faithful: an excellent usage, to which we are indebted for so many of the beautiful works of the fathers of the Church.

We sit during the epistle. The early Christians did so too, in order to attend to the reading with more recollection. Let us always listen to it, as we should listen to St. Peter, St. Paul, or St. John, if he appeared before us. It is their words that sound in our ears, as they sounded in the ears of our ancestors. May they make the same impression on us as on them! We are indebted to St. Jerome for the arrangement of the gospels and epistles, so as to suit all the Sundays and principal festivals of the year. He sent his work to Pope Damasus. The Roman Church adopted it, and it was from this Church, the mother and mistress of all others, that that order came to us which we still follow at the present day.[371]

And now, why is the epistle read before the gospel? It is not without a deep reason. In the introit, we heard the voice of the prophets; in the epistle, we hear the voice of the apostles, the voice of inspired men, who prepare us to hear the voice of the master. Do you not seem to be present at the accomplishment of the words of St. Paul, writing to the Hebrews: "God spoke to men by many voices and in divers ways, and last of all… by his Son"?[372] Do you not seem to see our Lord himself renewing at Mass what he did during his mortal life, when he sent St. John the Baptist, or his apostles in twos, before him to prepare his ways? Do you not seem to see the faint streaks of the dawn and the golden beams of the morning preparing the way for the magnificent blaze of the broad sunlight? What sweet recollections in the order of our holy reading![373]

Gradual and tract. The word of life has fallen on hearts like a salutary dew, to refresh them, and to enable them to bring forth fruits worthy of an eternal reward: the epistle has been read. Full of gratitude, the faithful answer that they are disposed to do what they have been taught. Their answer is expressed in the gradual or response, the tract, the Alleluia, and the prose. The answer of the faithful is called the "gradual," because the choristers appointed to proclaim it stood on the lower steps of the ambo or jubé: the same thing is still done at the present day. On great festivals, we see those who have to sing the response or Alleluia go over and take up their place beside the choristers at the lectern, which represents the ambo.[374]

The responses, established or rather arranged by St. Gregory, are always in harmony with the truths or exhortations contained in the epistle.[375] The faithful declare by them their good will, and their readiness to conform themselves in all things to the apostolic precepts. On days of mourning and fasting, as in Lent, the answer of the people is called the "tract," because it is sung slowly and sadly: it is the exile's lament.[376] On the other hand, when the Church is in joy, as during paschal time and on Sundays consecrated to the memory of the resurrection of her spouse, the singing of the response is less grave: it is even preceded and followed by the Alleluia.

Alleluia. Alleluia is a Hebrew word that means "Praise God!" but at the same time expresses an emotion, a joyous transport, that no Greek or Latin word is found capable of conveying. Wherefore, it has been left unchanged. There is no use in saying anything else: *Alleluia* is a word of the language of heaven, a word that the blessed Jerusalem let fall on earth, and that the pilgrim Church hastened to pick up. It is the song of her great solemnities, those happy days when she endeavors to share beforehand the joys of her elder sister, by stammering over a part of the eternal canticle. "St. John," says Cardinal Bona, "heard the choirs of angels in heaven singing, 'Alleluia,' on their golden harps, to let us know that this ineffable word came down from heaven to the Church."[377]

The custom of singing, "Alleluia," is praised by St. Augustine as a tradition of the highest antiquity. "We do not say the Alleluia before Easter," remarks this great bishop, "because the time of the passion of Jesus Christ corresponds to the time of the afflictions of this life, and his resurrection announces the beatitude which we shall enjoy hereafter. It is in that blessed life that we shall praise God unceasingly; but, to do so, we must begin to praise him in this world. Wherefore we often sing, 'Alleluia,' thus exciting one another to praise God. But strive that everything in you should praise him—your tongue, your voice, your conscience, your life, your behavior!"[378]

The Alleluia is therefore reserved for times of joy. But are we not to praise God at all times? Undoubtedly. Hence, when the Church tells us to lay aside the Alleluia on Septuagesima Sunday, she tells us to say, *Laus tibi, Domine, Rex aeternae gloriae*—"Praise be to thee, O Lord, King of eternal glory!" "These words have much of the meaning of the Alleluia, but not that transport or effusion of joy which it inspires: a joy which shall never cease in heaven, but which, alas! is often interrupted in this valley of tears."[379] The Church lengthens as much as possible the singing of the Alleluia: she would wish never to be interrupted in it. Hence, the great number of notes that accompany it. "We are accustomed," says St. Bonaventure, "to dwell with many notes on the last letter of the Alleluia, because the joy of the saints in heaven is unspeakable and unending."[380] This long series of notes is called a "pneuma."

Pneuma. The word *pneuma* means "a breath." It is, as we have just said, a long series of notes without words, and sung at the end of the Alleluia. Pneumas are also sung in certain churches after the last antiphon of the evening office on days of great solemnity. By this succession of unarticulated sounds, the Church shows that words fail her to express the raptures of her admiration and the languors of her love when she thinks on the beauties and delights of the heavenly Jerusalem. How, in point of fact, could human language describe what the eye of man has not seen, what his ear has not heard, and what his heart, large as it is, cannot conceive?

On hearing the Church sing these pneumas, does it not seem to you that you behold the queen of Saba, beside herself at the consideration of the glory of Solomon, unable to express the sentiments of her soul?[381] And yet those riches did not belong to her, that palace was not intended for her. Children of the true Solomon, heirs of his throne, future companions of his happiness, ah, let us endeavor to excite within us at the sight of heaven, that heaven which is prepared for us, some of the sentiments of the foreign queen!

Prose. The pneuma gave rise to the prose. It happened in this manner. Under the long series of notes, there were first some words placed, and then some verses, expressive of joy, and like a continuation of the Alleluia. Gradually their number swelled, and at length there were hymns, that is to say, songs of joy made in keeping with the festival. This change occurred about the ninth century. Hence it came a) that the Roman Church, always faithful to ancient usages, has only a very small number of proses; b) that proses are sometimes called *sequentia*, or "sequences," for they are a continuation or prolongation of the Alleluia; and c) that proses are said at Masses only when the Alleluia is sung.

We must except Solemn Mass for the dead, when the prose *Dies Irae* is said. Though, according to general opinion, it is the work of Cardinal Malabranca, who died in 1294, it was not said at Mass till the beginning of the seventeenth century. This was out of respect for the ancient usage, which did not permit proses to be said when there was no Alleluia. In the course of time, the reasons for the institution of proses ceased to be regarded, in order that nothing more should be considered in them than a mark of solemnity. The consequence was that they were retained in Solemn Masses for the dead, where we often meet with them in large numbers.

The word *prose* means "free language," language that is not cramped by metrical laws as in pagan poetry. So as to be more easily chanted and remembered, proses were usually rhymed. Hence has come the poetry of moderns. There is, besides, in a severance from pagan meter a liberty that well becomes prayer. Here, as everywhere else, we see that tender, and sometimes amazing, familiarity with which the Church speaks to her divine spouse. I do not know, but I think that the strict meter of verses, the obligation of confining a thought within a certain number of syllables, invariably long or short, checks the outbursts of the heart, damps its enthusiasm, cools its ardor. To say all in a word: it seems to me that proses, especially old ones, pray, and that our modern hymns do not pray or hardly pray. It is generally believed that the first author of proses was a monk of St. Gall, in Switzerland, named Notker, who lived about the year 880.[382]

It is therefore true that, whatever may be her ceremonies, her prayers, or her chants, the Catholic Church always appears to us the same, always careful to trace out for us in her external worship the virtues that we ought to practice and the sentiments that ought to animate us, if we would be pleasing to God. The carnal man, who sees only the surface of sacred rites, and hears only the harmony that strikes on the outward ear, finds some of our solemnities dreary and some of our chants monotonous. What do I say? He dares to indemnify himself by sacrilegious witticisms for the weariness that he feels in the temple of God. You need not be surprised. He lacks one of the senses, the sense of faith: he is a blind man, giving judgment on colors.

But the Christian who lives by the spirit, attentive to everything in the house of the Lord, fathoms the depths of all our ceremonies. Not a word is said, not a step is made, but he discovers its motive, understands its meaning, and turns it to his advantage.

PRAYER

O my God, who art all love! I thank thee for having blended so many instructions and prayers in the second part of the Mass, so as to prepare me worthily for the holy mysteries. Grant me the grace to be attentive to the meaning of all the canticles and ceremonies.

I am resolved to love God above all things, and my neighbor as myself for the love of God; and, in testimony of this love, I will listen to the epistle with a great desire to profit by it.

Lesson 18: Christianity Brought before the Senses (Continued)—Gospel through Offertory

Second part of the Mass (continued): Gospel.—When answering the epistle by the gradual or tract, the Alleluia, and the prose, the whole assembly of the faithful showed themselves ready to put in practice the holy lessons that had been given them. The voices of prophets and apostles have just prepared them to hear a voice more holy, that of the Son of God, the master of prophets and apostles. Yet a little, and he will speak: the gospel will be read. Let us recollect ourselves to hear it, or rather let us study the ceremonies that accompany the reading of it. They will suffice to give us the dispositions required by faith.

The priest goes to the middle of the altar, raises his eyes to heaven, and then, bowing low, asks of God that purity of heart and lips by which he may worthily announce the holy gospel. During this time, the faithful should also ask of God that their hearts may become good soil, in which the sacred seed may take root and bear fruit a hundredfold.

The usage of reading the gospel at Mass goes back to the time when this divine book was written.[383] Is it not proper that those who assist at the sacrifice of Jesus Christ should know his doings and his precepts, and give public evidence of their admiration for them? The gospel is the preacher of the cross, since he triumphed by it. Here you see the reason why the priest, before reading it, marks it with this adorable sign, and then makes the same sign on his forehead, his lips, and his heart. All the assistants imitate him.

We make the sign of the cross on our forehead, to declare that we believe the truths of the gospel, that we glory in them, and that we shall never be ashamed of them;[384] on our lips, to denote that we are ready to profess them boldly before the world, or, like our ancestors, in the very face of tyrants; and on our heart, to show that they are engraven there, that we love them, and that they shall always be the rule of our thoughts and our affections. At the reading of the gospel, all the faithful stand, like so many soldiers ready for the fray, eager to march in the footsteps of Jesus Christ whithersoever he calls them. This usage is of the highest antiquity.[385]

At the close of the reading, the priest kisses the gospel, as a mark of love and respect. All the people, represented by the clerk, answer: "Praise be to thee, O Christ!" Was there ever praise better deserved? What are we? We are captives of the devil, exiles from heaven, travelers that wend their way through the desert of life, this valley of tears. What is the gospel? It is the good news. To captives, news of their deliverance; to exiles, news that the gates of their native land are again open to them; to travelers, news that a kind guide has come down from heaven to lead them safe to their journey's end. Oh! if we feel what we have been since the preaching of the gospel, what we were before the preaching of the gospel, what we should still be without the preaching of the gospel, with what deep gratitude shall we say: "Glory be to thee, O Christ! the Savior of the world!"

In High Masses, the reading of the gospel is accompanied by ceremonies full of mysteries, all proper to nourish piety and that profound respect which we ought to have for the word of God. The deacon lays the book of the gospels on the altar. The usage of putting the book of the gospels on the altar and taking it therefrom came from this: that formerly it was carried in ceremony to the altar at the beginning of Mass. The Church wished that the people should represent Jesus Christ to themselves on seeing the book that contains his divine words.[386]

The honor of singing the gospel is reserved to the deacon. The respect due to this holy book, and the grandeur of the ceremonies that accompany the reading of it, required that this duty should be fulfilled by the sacred minister coming nearest to the sacerdotal dignity.[387] Formerly, in the Church of Alexandria, this noble task was performed only by the archdeacon. Elsewhere, it was reserved to priests and even to bishops on great festivals, as at Constantinople on Easter Sunday.[388] We may remark, by the way, that at Rome, when the sovereign pontiff celebrates Solemn Mass, the epistle and gospel are sung both in Greek and Latin. It is a cardinal that sings the gospel. The divine word, announced in these two languages, recalls the ancient union of the East and West. May divine providence one day restore it!

The deacon ascends the altar, goes on his knees, and repeats the prayer already referred to: "O Almighty God! cleanse," etc. In this deacon who ascends the altar, does it not seem to you that you behold Moses, called by Jehovah to Mount Sinai, in order to receive the law amid thunder and lightning, and to carry it to the people of Israel? The deacon falls prostrate at the foot of the altar and in presence of the book of the law, because he knows that it does not belong to man to make himself the organ of eternal truths. He rises and takes from the altar the book that contains these adorable truths, showing thus that he receives them from the mouth of Jesus Christ himself, represented by the altar.

The deacon goes on his knees again; he asks the blessing of the priest or bishop, and kisses his hand. The deacon had asked of God the grace to announce the gospel worthily. He now asks the permission of the priest or bishop to announce it; for, in the Church, no one should exercise any ministry without being called thereto. Answering his request, the celebrant says, "May the Lord be in your heart and on your lips, that you may worthily and becomingly announce the gospel." *Becomingly*, that is to say, with piety and modesty, so that it may be useful to yourself and edifying to all who hear you. On receiving the celebrant's blessing, the deacon kisses his hand, as a mark of respect and gratitude.

Then, preceded by incense, symbolic both of prayer, which alone can render the word of God fruitful, and the good odor of virtue, which this word diffuses in hearts,[389] the deacon walks to a place where he may be conveniently heard by the people. The thurifer is preceded by three ministers, of whom two bear lighted tapers, and the third a cross. These lighted tapers, preceding the sacred book, are a sign of the joy given us by the gospel; and remind Christians that Jesus Christ, whose word they are going to hear, is the light that enlightens every man coming into this world. The flame of these tapers is a symbol of the charity that the gospel ought to kindle in our hearts. One of the ministers bears a cross: the standard of the Savior declares in eloquent terms that he himself is going to speak in his gospel, and that maxims of crucifixion will be proclaimed. He wishes that his disciples should have his image before their eyes, in order that they may have proper sentiments in their hearts.

At the sight of the sacred book, all those in the choir rise out of respect. Penetrated with the same feeling, the clergy also stand, not resting in any manner on the stalls.[390]

For a very mysterious reason, the deacon turns northward to sing the gospel. The north wind represents the breath of the evil spirit; and the scripture itself, says an ancient author,[391] teaches us this signification, since it addresses the devil thus: "O Lucifer, thou didst say in thy heart, 'I will establish myself on the side of the north!'"[392] Hence, the reader of the gospel turns toward the left side of the church, which is usually the north, to show that he purposes to destroy the evil influences of the devil's breath.

The deacon raises his voice to say to the people: *Dominus vobiscum*—"The Lord be with you"; and he has more need than ever of help at this solemn moment. All the people immediately rise, answering: *Et cum spiritu tuo*—"And with your spirit." In past ages, we should have seen the faithful respectfully laying aside their staffs, and the knights of different orders and the Polish nobility unsheathing their swords and holding them erect during the reading of the gospel, thus professing their readiness to follow the holy law of the Lord, and to shed their blood in defense of religion. History is at hand, shining with their exploits, to bear witness that this was no idle ceremony.[393]

The deacon makes the sign of the cross on the sacred book, and then on his forehead, lips, and heart. He next announces which of the evangelists has transmitted to us the truth that the Church is going to propose for our meditation. Though our Lord committed to four of his disciples the care of recording his precepts and doings, yet there reigns among them such a perfect harmony that it is always "a continuation of the holy gospel of Jesus Christ"—*Sequentia sancti evangelii.* Hence, we answer: "May the glory of it be rendered to thee, O God!" The book of the gospels being placed on a desk, or held by the subdeacon, the deacon incenses it three times: in the middle, on the right, and on the left. The faithful receive notice that here is found the source of the perfume of the divine word, which is to be diffused through their souls.

The gospel sung, the subdeacon carries the book open to the celebrant, who kisses it, and he is incensed as the principal minister, who, according to the expression of St. Paul, "must everywhere spread the good odor of the knowledge of Jesus Christ."[394] From all this display that the Church makes at the reading of the gospel, from all the prayers that precede it, from all the ceremonies that accompany and follow it, what are we to conclude but that we should always assist at it with a pure heart, or at least a penitent heart, and that fear, reverence, docility, confidence, and fidelity are so many dispositions required to profit by the divine word?

On Sundays and holidays, the reading of the gospel is followed by an instruction. This usage is as old as Christianity: we see it practiced since the times of the apostles.[395] Nothing more natural. The gospel is like the manna that fell in the desert and had need of preparation before being used as food by the Israelites. The gospel, to be the food of our spiritual life, has also need of preparation: it is a bread that must be broken to little ones, that is, to the faithful. Such is the important duty of which the priest is going to acquit himself.

The instruction at High Mass is called the "prone"; but perhaps many do not know the meaning of this word. *Prone* means "announcement."[396] The priest announces the festivals of the week, marriages about to be celebrated, and, lastly, the word of God, which is only a commentary on the gospel. In a great many dioceses, all these things are preceded by beautiful prayers, which are called the "prayers of the prone." The Catholic family, united at the foot of the altar, prays for its spiritual and temporal superiors, for the living and the dead, a usage which teaches us all that charity as well as faith is catholic, and that, to share in the same sacrifice, we must, like our ancestors, have only one heart and one soul. We see hereby how important it is to assist at the parish Mass.

Have we ever reflected on all that is social in the evangelical instruction of Sunday? We shall find nothing of the sort among all the renowned peoples of antiquity. Thanks be to our Lord, who prepared for us in his Church a course of instructions, previously unknown to all the sages of the earth! And what a moral tone in these instructions! Humility, whose name has no synonym in any pagan language, put instead of pride, one of the worst diseases of our nature; the love of God and man preached as the end and the sum of the law, all virtues recommended, all vices condemned, all good inclinations encouraged and supported by worthy motives: such is the evangelical instruction, of which the holy equality of Christians is one of the most touching maxims.

Philosophy still distinguished between the free and the enslaved, between patricians and plebeians, and called the emperors gods, when the Church gave to all men the name of brethren, most dearly beloved children of God, heirs to his glory; when she established among the inhabitants of the earth an image of the society of heaven, and taught them, as she still teaches them, to consecrate the seventh day by communion in the same rites and the same prayers.[397]

Credo. No sooner has the priest descended from the pulpit, than he repairs to the altar, where he intones the *Credo*. This is a solemn declaration that we believe all the truths just explained and will faithfully reduce them to practice. The Symbol sung at Mass is, with a few exceptions, that composed in 325 by the General Council of Nice. It is also called the Symbol of Constantinople, because a general council, held in this city, added some explanations opposed to the new errors of the Macedonians. The Church considered that this formula, more extensive than that which comes to us from the apostles, would better inspire Christians with respect for the dogmas contained in it, and with fidelity in observing them. It is always the same faith that we profess, whether we recite the formula transmitted by the apostles, or sing with the Church the Symbol of Nice or Constantinople.[398]

How proper is such a thought to give energy to our faith! If a miracle of the divine power were suddenly to bring all the Catholics of the world into one of our churches; if the same miracle, awaking those of the past eighteen centuries from the sleep of the grave, were to associate them with the living, we should hear this vast multitude repeating the same Symbol that we repeat, and that our descendants will repeat after us.

Let us suppose the same miracle to recall to life all the heretics, all the protestants of different ages and countries, and that they are asked for a profession of their faith: What shall we hear? A confused mingling of voices, something that will remind us forcibly of hell or the Tower of Babel; as many symbols as sects, nay, as individuals in each sect: symbols opposed one to another, and changeable according to circumstances. If truth is one, tell us on which side it may be found—with Catholics or with protestants?

Up to the fifth century, the Symbol was not recited at Mass. On Good Friday alone, the bishop said it aloud during the instruction that he addressed to the catechumens. But the errors of the Macedonians making some progress, Timotheus, bishop of Constantinople, had it sung as a protest against heresy:[399] this was in 510. The custom soon passed into the West.[400] Yet it was not said at Rome till the beginning of the eleventh century. On this point, let us cite the remarkable words of an ancient author,[401] an eyewitness of the fact that he records:

"In 1016, the emperor St. Henry, having come to Rome, was greatly surprised to find that the *Credo* was not sung at Mass. He asked the reason of the clerics, who answered in my presence, 'The Roman Church does not sing the *Credo*, because she has never been sullied by any heresy, but, according to the doctrine of Peter, remains unchangeable in the integrity of the Catholic faith: she has no need of singing it, like churches that may have fallen into error.' Nevertheless, the holy emperor made earnest entreaty with the sovereign pontiff that the Symbol might be sung at Rome as in the rest of Christendom. Pope Benedict VIII yielded to his petition, and the Symbol was sung: which has been continued to this day."[402]

When, in singing the *Credo*, we reach the words, *Et homo factus est*—"And he was made man," we prostrate or bow to honor the abasement of the incarnate Word. "It is by humiliation," says St. Augustine, "that we must approach a humble God—humiliation, not of our body, but of our heart, which must be penetrated with proper sentiments regarding a God made a slave to give us liberty; made man—a poor man, he who commands all nature; an unknown man, he who was descended from the kings of Juda, and who was established King of nations; a mortal man, he who had not deserved death by sin. Let every creature therefore abase itself at the remembrance of a mystery in which a God comes down from the height of glory to an abyss of humiliations and indignities, in order to save a guilty world."[403]

We say the Symbol on certain days for three principal reasons. First: to proclaim from generation to generation the triumphs that the Church won over ancient heresies. Second: to bring it before the minds of the people. Hence it is said on all Sundays—days when Christians meet. Third: because of the relation of the Symbol with the festival that is celebrated. Hence it is said on festivals of our Lord, because mention is made of him in it; on festivals of the apostles, who announced its truths to us; and on festivals of doctors, who preached and defended these truths. We have seen that in the early ages of the Church the *Credo* was not sung. When it was to be said, the catechumens were obliged to leave, and the Mass of the faithful then began. All the foregoing part—from the beginning till after the instruction—made up the Mass of the catechumens.

Relations between the ceremonies of the second part of the Mass and the circumstances of the passion.—This is the place to speak of the resemblance that may be found between the various ceremonies of the second part of the Mass and the circumstances of the passion. In the priest saying the introit, piety beholds Jesus entering the house of Annas and Caiphas, where he was buffeted; in the priest reciting the *Kyrie*, Jesus denied by Peter; in the priest turning to the people and saying, *Dominus vobiscum*, Jesus casting a look on Peter and converting him; in the priest going to say the epistle, Jesus led to Pilate; in the priest going to say at the middle of the altar the *Munda cor meum*, Jesus led to Herod; in the priest going to read the gospel, Jesus mocked and sent back to Pilate.

Sentiment that ought to prevail in our hearts.—As for the sentiment that ought to prevail in our souls during the second part of Mass, the prayers therein contained tell us enough: it is faith. How strong and lively ought our faith to be when we think that before our very eyes, on this altar, in the hands of the priest, the Desired of Nations is about to be immolated for us—he for whom four thousand years longed and sighed, and who is the object of all events before and after his coming; he whom the cherubim and the seraphim adore: he in whom those legions of martyrs and other saints, our ancestors, believed. He who changed the face of the world and who will judge it; he who will glorify forever with himself the faithful imitators of his divine example! What profound awe should keep our souls attentive to the ineffable miracle that is going to be wrought!

Third part of the Mass: Offertory, as in the early ages.—It comprises the beginning of the sacrifice or the offertory and the prayers following to the preface. In the early ages, when all the prayers, ceremonies, and instructions of which we have just spoken, and which made up the preparation for the tremendous sacrifice, had been concluded, the deacon gave orders to the catechumens, penitents, Jews, and heretics to retire. Those only were allowed to remain who had received the grace of baptism, and who were supposed to have preserved it intact or to have recovered it by penance.

This ancient usage shows us the profound respect of the Church for the divine mysteries; and, as a consequence, the perpetuity of her faith regarding the real presence of our Lord in the Eucharist. It also shows us what sanctity we should bring to Mass. If sinners are no longer excluded, as formerly, the Church wishes at least that they should assist at it with a desire or beginning of conversion—with those groans which, coming from a contrite and humble heart, call down the mercy of the Lord.

Before the offertory, the priest salutes anew the faithful in the usual manner: *Dominus vobiscum!* The people, on their side, seeing the awful moment draw near, and feeling more deeply than ever how important it is that their sacrificator should be endued with virtue from on high, answer by again wishing him the help of the Lord: *Et cum spiritu tuo!* The priest, as soon as he turns back to the altar, says, *Oremus*—"Let us pray," exhorting the assembly to keep themselves more and more united to God as they make ready for the great act. Forthwith he recites the prayer called the offertory, because it was at this time that, in the primitive Church, the faithful offered the bread and wine intended for the sacrifice.[404]

Here is the manner in which the offering took place. The faithful brought the bread and wine that they wished to present at the altar. The men first and then the women laid their offerings on white cloths. The bishop received these offerings, which were placed by a subdeacon in a cloth held by two acolytes. The archdeacon received the little chalice or cruet[405] which each of the faithful presented to him, and poured some wine from it into a large chalice held by a subdeacon. The archdeacon laid on the altar as much of the gifts offered[406] as was needed for the Communion of the people, or rather he presented this quantity to the bishop, who laid it there himself. He then poured the wine through a strainer into the chalice that should be used for consecration. A subdeacon went and received from the chief cantor a cruet of water,[407] and brought it to the archdeacon, who poured therefrom into the chalice; after which he placed it on the altar before the pontiff, at the right side of the oblations.[408]

The priests and other ministers of the Church made their offerings at the altar; whereas, the faithful made theirs outside the choir or the balustrade that separated the clergy from the people.[409] It was here that the bishop or officiating priest received them. Out of respect for the sovereign dignity with which the emperor was invested, he was excepted from the general rule regarding the laity. He carried his offering to the altar himself, namely, bread that he had prepared with his own hands. This custom gave occasion to one of the most remakable facts in our holy antiquity. It is thus related by St. Gregory Nazianzen.

"The emperor Valens, being at Caesarea, went to the church on the feast of the Epiphany, surrounded by his guards, and mixed, as a matter of form, among the Catholic people; for he was an Arian. When he heard the singing of the psalms; when he saw the immense crowd, the order reigning in the sanctuary and all round it, the sacred ministers more like angels than men, St. Basil before the altar, with motionless body, steadfast look, and mind united to God, as if nothing extraordinary had occurred, and all those near him full of fear and respect: when, I say, Valens saw all this, it was so new a spectacle for him that his head reeled and his eyes grew weak. His agitation was not perceived at first; but, when it was necessary to bring to the altar the offering prepared with his own hands, seeing that no person would receive it according to custom, because it was not known whether St. Basil would approve thereof, he trembled in such a manner that, if one of the ministers of the altar had not reached out a hand to help him, he would have shamefully fallen to the ground."[410]

During all the time of the oblation, there were psalms sung. This custom was already in full vigor in the fourth century;[411] but its origin is to be traced much further back. Let us go to the Temple of Jerusalem, and we shall behold the Jewish people offering their holocausts and firstfruits amid the singing of canticles and the sound of trumpets and cymbals, that they might thus declare their joy in presenting to the Lord some of the gifts that they had received from his munificence. No less grateful than the Jews, our ancestors also accompanied their offerings with the singing of sacred hymns. We have inherited their practice: Have we also inherited their piety? The offertory, which we still sing, is therefore a very valuable lesson and a very venerable memorial. It is sung slowly, so as to let the priest have time to make the offering of bread and wine, as well as to say the prayers that accompany it.

When the offering of the people was ended, the bishop resumed his seat, and there washed his hands. He then returned to the altar. Let us prepare to follow him.

PRAYER

O my God! who art all love, I thank thee for having surrounded the holy sacrifice with so many prayers and ceremonies, well calculated to revive my faith and piety. Grant me the grace to be deeply penetrated with their spirit.

I am resolved to love God above all things, and my neighbor as myself for the love of God; and, in testimony of this love, I will listen to the gospel as I should listen to our Lord himself.

Lesson 19: Christianity Brought before the Senses (Continued)—Offertory

Third part of the Mass (continued): Offertory as at present.—You know how the offertory was made till the ninth century: we are now going to speak of the way in which it is made at present. The priest uncovers the chalice: the usage of covering the chalice with a veil already existed in the first ages of Christianity.[412] It tells us of the respect that the Church has always had for the vessels intended for the altar. He stretches out the corporal, that is to say, the linen cloth on which the body of Jesus Christ is to rest. The corporal must be of linen, because the shroud that enclosed our Lord was of linen: it is fourteen hundred years since St. Jerome said so. The Church appointed the use of a corporal for greater cleanliness, and to prevent the inconveniences that might arise if a drop of the precious blood should happen to fall on the altar.

The corporal was formerly as long and broad as the top of the altar, and permitted of being folded as a covering over the chalice.[413] But as this was found inconvenient, especially after the elevation of the chalice had been introduced, when some wished to keep the chalice still covered at the moment of elevation, there were two smaller corporals made: one of which was stretched out on the altar, and the other folded so as to cover the chalice. In some countries, there was a card placed between the two folds of the latter: it thus became firmer and more easily handled. The name *pall*, which it has always received, means "cloak" or "covering."[414]

The chalice uncovered, the priest takes the paten, on which is laid the little round thin piece of bread which we call the host, that is to say, the victim. Holding up the paten with both hands to the height of his breast, the sacred minister raises his eyes to heaven, and then casts them down. He thus indicates that he offers to God, who is in heaven, a pure and holy victim, though he is only an unworthy sinner.

The priest completes the offering by making the sign of the cross, as if already to place the victim on the cross, where it is to be immolated.[415] He then puts the paten half under the corporal, and covers the other half with the purificator, so as to keep it more carefully till he requires it for the breaking of the host: he purifies the chalice with a small linen cloth, called on this account a "purificator." He puts some wine into the chalice, and then some water, but very little, because the matter of the sacrifice, that which the Savior used, is wine, and no other liquid whatsoever. This mixture of wine and water is as ancient as the institution of the Blessed Eucharist. Tradition teaches us that the Savior put some water into the cup of wine which he consecrated.[416] He thus conformed to the rite of the Jews, which required that the paschal cup should contain wine mixed with water.

This mixture is full of mystery. Here is what is most instructive for us. The water represents the people: this idea has been given us by St. John himself[417] and several holy fathers.[418] We should make only one body with our Lord, and consequently we should be consecrated with him. He became like us by taking our humanity; but that the union may be perfect, he wishes us to become like him by clothing ourselves with his divinity. Now, the mixture of wine and water is an image of the adorable union of God and man, which took place at the incarnation; of the union of man with Jesus Christ, which takes place in Communion; and of the consummation of man in God, which will take place by glory.[419] Such are the great ideas expressed by the prayer that the priest makes when blessing the water representing the faithful people: that water which will henceforth be one with the wine of the sacrifice—that people who, by transubstantiation, will be one with the Son of God.

In Masses for the dead, the priest does not bless the water by the sign of the cross. This is a consequence of the mysterious meaning of the water. The sign is not employed to bless the water, which represents the people, because the mind is wholly fixed on the souls in purgatory, who are no longer in a way to be blessed by the priest. There is only a small quantity of water put into the chalice, "so that," says a council, "the majesty of the blood of Jesus Christ may exceed the frailty of the people represented by the water."[420]

In Solemn Masses, it is the subdeacon who puts the water into the chalice. The deacon presents the bread and wine, so that we may be well aware that the priest does not offer alone, that he does not sacrifice for himself alone, that he does not fulfill a ministry foreign to the rest of the faithful. The deacon and subdeacon, who occupy a kind of middle ground between priest and people, here represent all the people. When placing in the hands of the priest the substances that are to be consecrated, they offer them as it were in the name of the people, by the hands of the priest. What a lesson for us!

Another lesson in the elements that the Savior chose for his sacrifice! Bread, which is made of many grains of wheat, and wine, which is made of the juice of many grapes, most admirably represent the Church, which consists of many members, drawn from a corrupt mass to be changed into Jesus Christ, to become his mystical body, as the bread and wine are really changed into his natural body and true blood. What an eloquent inculcation of that truth, the basis of all society, the source of every virtue and sacrifice: you must have but one heart and one soul!

Bread and wine, therefore, take the place of those who offer them, and thereby of the whole Church; for bread and wine being the food, the sustenance, and, as it were, the life of men, when they offer them at the altar, they offer in a manner their life and the whole world, which was made for their service. They offer themselves to God, to be sacrificed for his glory with Jesus Christ their head. Such, in effect, are the true dispositions for making the oblation of bread and wine with the priest. "When thou sittest at the table of a prince," says the scripture, "consider what is set before thee; put a knife to thy throat, and know the prince expects the like from thee."[421]

"What is this table," asks St. Augustine,[422] "but that on which we receive the body and blood of Jesus Christ? And what is the meaning of 'expecting the like' but that which St. John says, 'As Jesus Christ gave his life for us, so should we give our life for our brethren!'"[423] Hence to assist at Mass in the spirit of a victim, a victim immolated with Jesus Christ, and for the same ends as Jesus Christ, namely, the glory of God and the good of our neighbor, is the true way to take part in the holy sacrifice. This one disposition includes all others.

The chalice thus prepared, the priest returns to the middle of the altar, and offers it as he offered the bread, with this difference: that he speaks no longer alone but in the name of all the assembly, whom he raises up to heaven, if we may so speak, in the water mixed with the wine. A sublime ceremony, which, with its accompanying prayer, shows clearly that Jesus Christ, as Tertullian says, is "the Catholic priest of the Father,"[424] purifying earth and heaven by his blood; "for he is the victim of propitiation for our sins, and not for ours only, but for those of the whole world!"[425]

The priest makes with the chalice the sign of the cross on the altar, to show that he lays the oblation on the cross of Jesus Christ. But, alas! we have reason to fear that our unworthiness introduces something not agreeable to God. Hence the priest bows, with hands joined on the altar, as the sign of a suppliant, and says in the name of all the assistants what the young Hebrew captives at Babylon said, when they were offering themselves as holocausts to be thrown into the furnace: "Receive us, O Lord! who present ourselves to thee with humble minds and contrite hearts, and grant that our sacrifice may this day be accomplished before thee in a manner pleasing to thee."

Then the priest raises his eyes and hands to heaven, in order to call down the Holy Spirit, that Spirit of fire, that sanctifying Spirit who sometimes visibly consumed the ancient sacrifices, and who daily consumes the gifts that we offer, by changing them so admirably. At the same time, he makes the sign of the cross on the chalice and host, to denote that it is by virtue of the cross he expects from the Holy Spirit the sanctification of the gifts intended to become the body and blood of the Savior.

This is a most precious moment for an offering of ourselves. What a motive of confidence! We are not presented alone to God: Alas! who wants our unworthiness? But presented with Jesus Christ, we henceforth make but one with him. Our misery is hidden and, as it were, absorbed in the infinite dignity of the Person of our Lord, to whom God the Father never refuses anything.

Let us enter deeply into those sentiments of oblation to which the occasion invites us. Let us offer the good in us, that, united to the merits of the Savior, it may be purified from the imperfections with which it is mixed, and become worthy of God; let us offer the evil in us, that it may be hidden and consumed by the great charity of the victim; let us offer our body with all its senses, our soul with all its faculties: Jesus Christ, our firstborn, reserves nothing. When we come to his sacrifice, we cease to belong to ourselves. We agree to be victims with him; we agree to return all to God, from whom we have received all, and to whom all belongs.

When the prayers and ceremonies of the offertory are ended, the deacon at High Mass presents the little boat to the celebrant, who blesses the incense, and first incenses the bread and wine. As we have said, incense is a symbol of our prayers and of the oblation of ourselves. The priest incenses the bread and wine, to show that we join with these oblations our desires, our persons, and our goods. This is most clearly expressed in the prayers which the priest recites at the incensing of the oblations and of the altar.

In some churches, it is after the incensing that the offering of blessed bread takes place, as well as various quests or collections. It is important to revive our faith on these two usages, thrice venerable by their antiquity, their touching reminiscences, and their excellent lessons.

"You shall be known as my disciples," said the Savior, "if you love one another."[426] Faithful to this command, our ancestors had but one heart and one soul.[427] The Church was only a large family, spread over all parts of the world. But all these brethren, who loved without ever seeing one another, were anxious to offer to one another some sensible sign of the charity that united them. They chose the most striking of all—bread. As bread consists of many grains of wheat so blended together that they form but one mass, they declared, by sending it to one another, that they were one among themselves: one in some manner as the three divine Persons are one among themselves. This bread received the name of "eulogy," because, before being sent, it was blessed: this usage dates from the apostolic times.[428] Yet more, the Eucharist was also sent. Deacons bore it to the most distant churches.[429] Such is the venerable origin of blessed bread.

It was therefore used at first to indicate and to maintain union with distant Christians. It was next used as a sign of union among all those assisting at the same sacrifice. The most excellent sign of union is the Holy Eucharist. But, alas! every person does not communicate. The Church therefore instituted another sign, which recalls the reception of the body and blood of the Savior, so that Christians may still say, though in a different sense, what the Christians of the early days said: "We all partake of the same bread."[430] Tell us whether any means more proper could possibly be found to impress upon the minds of men the eminently religious and social truth that they are all equal before God, since they all eat the same bread; that, in a word, they ought all to love one another as the members of one large family. O my God! how strange it is that thy holy religion should be so little understood and its precepts so ill observed![431]

We are now acquainted with the sentiments of respect, joy, charity, and confidence that should animate us in receiving the blessed bread. a) We ought to respect it. The fathers of the Church warn the faithful to entertain the greatest respect for these gifts, because they have received the blessing of priests, and not to permit the least particle of them to be trampled underfoot, even through unintentional negligence. b) We ought to receive it with joy and charity. Is it not sweet for brethren to assemble round the table of their common Father, and to eat the same bread there, without distinction of rich or poor, learned or ignorant; to think that millions of hearts beat in unison with theirs, and that the bread of fraternity which they now eat is also eaten at the same time by other brethren in Asia, America, Africa, and the lately reclaimed islands of Oceania? Was this great lesson of charity ever more needed than in an age when selfishness tends to dry up all the springs of the soul? c) We ought to eat it with a holy confidence, because this bread, blessed for us, may remove from our bodies, and also from our souls, by the remission of venial sin, whatever might disturb their harmony.

Along with the blessed bread, a wax taper and a piece of money are also offered. This usage takes us back to the most remote antiquity, when the faithful themselves provided all that was necessary for the sacrifice and the support of the sacred ministers: wine, and lights, and alms.

In many churches, the distribution of blessed bread is followed by a collection. Nothing seems more natural or touching to us than this usage. As a matter of fact, the doctrines and ceremonies of the Church must be translated into good works; for charity is essentially active. The children of the great family have just eaten of the same bread. The Church wishes that they should give real proofs of the charity that unites them. She therefore comes to them, imploring their pity for those among their brethren who are in need.

There are orphans to maintain; the bashful poor to be helped; old people sinking under the weight of years and infirmities; the sick and dying, with none to give them spiritual or corporal aid; yea, and even the dead, for the dead are also our brethren. Lastly, it is our Lord himself who asks for his altar, which is not adorned so well as it ought to be, and for his temple, whose bareness excites the pity of the poor themselves.

These motives to collect already existed eighteen hundred years ago. The world saw the great apostle traveling through the provinces of Greece and Asia, and making collections in the assemblies of the faithful for their poor brethren in Jerusalem. "He appointed," says St. Chrysostom, "that they should take place every Sunday."[432] "Hence," say Tertullian and St. Justin, "each one of us brings to the assembly on Sunday our little offering according to our means: no one is taxed. These offerings are a pious fund, which we employ for the relief of the poor, the sick, orphans and exiles, and those who are condemned to the mines on account of the faith."[433]

Do you ask why St. Paul appointed collections to be made chiefly on Sunday? St. Chrysostom will answer you: "Because Sunday is the day on which hell was conquered, sin destroyed, mankind reconciled with God, our race restored to its ancient glory—what do I say?—to a greater glory, in which the sun shines on the amazing miracle of man suddenly become immortal. Paul, wishing to move our heart, chose this day for soliciting our charity, saying to us: 'Think, O man! from what evils thou hast been delivered and with what goods thou hast been laden on this day.' If, then, we celebrate our birthday by entertainments and presents which we provide for our friends, how much more should we honor by our liberality that day which may justly be termed the birthday of the whole human race!"[434]

The same Father then exhorts the faithful to give something every Sunday toward the relief of the poor; for St. Paul makes no exception when he says that everyone, *unusquisque*, should lay aside some alms.[435] The poor are not excepted, since they are not so poor as the widow in the gospel, who had only two little mites and yet gave them away.

The eloquent patriarch next explains the reason why the Church lets the poor beg at the doors of her temples: "It is that every one, before entering, may purify his hands and his conscience by alms. Undoubtedly that was a holy usage which erected fountains near the doors of churches and oratories, that people might wash their hands before entering to pray; but that is a more holy and necessary usage which places the poor at the doors of our temples, that we may wash away the stains of our souls before appearing in the presence of a thrice holy God. Now, our ancestors placed the poor at the doors of our churches like so many purifying fountains; for alms are much more powerful to purify our souls than water is to purify our hands."[436]

Let us be on our guard, therefore, against abolishing the collections at our High Masses: we should thereby destroy one of the most precious vestiges of our holy antiquity. That protestants, who hold fast to nothing in the past, and whose doctrines tend rather to divide than to unite, should have swept away collections in their assemblies can be readily understood. But the Catholic Church will preserve them as long as she continues the heiress of the past, as long as she bears in her heart a mother's love, as long as she keeps before her eyes that it is by works and not by vain words that charity must be practiced. And then, what better preparation for sacrifice and Communion than alms given for the love of him who is about to give himself to us, and in the presence of the faithful for their edification?

Let us now return to the altar. The priest moves to the epistle side and washes his fingers. This ceremony, of the highest antiquity, has two reasons for its existence—one natural and the other mysterious. The natural reason is that the two previous ceremonies, namely, the reception of the offerings of the faithful, as it took place in former ages, and the incensing, which is still practiced to the present day, might require him from a sense of propriety to wash his hands. The mysterious reason is to teach both clergy and laity that before offering sacrifice they ought to purify their souls from the least stains of sin.

"You have noticed," says St. Cyril of Jerusalem, "that a deacon gives water to the priest who officiates and the other priests who surround the altar, to wash their hands. Do you imagine that this is for the sake of corporal cleanliness? Not so at all. We are not accustomed, when entering the church, to be in such a state as to need washing in order to be clean. This washing of hands reminds us that we ought to be free from all our sins, because our hands mean our deeds. To wash our hands is nothing else than to purify our works."[437]

Conformably to this thought, the rubric prescribes to priests the ablution only of the ends of their fingers. "This ablution," says St. Denis, "is not made to remove bodily stains. They have been already removed. It is to show that the soul ought to be cleansed from its least stains. Wherefore, the priest washes only the ends of his fingers, and not his hands."[438] While washing his fingers, the priest says the psalm *Lavabo*. It suits the action so perfectly that in the early ages it was already recited on the same occasion.[439]

Does this spectacle suggest no ideas to the faithful? Should not they also be pure, if they would assist at the tremendous mysteries? Let them say, therefore, with all sincerity: "Wash me, O Lord! yet more and more from my iniquities; purify the thoughts of my mind and the desires of my heart, that I may join in the dispositions of the priest and share in the fruits of the sacrifice."

PRAYER

O my God! who art all love, I thank thee for having reminded me, by the offering of blessed bread, that we are all brethren. Grant us all the grace to love one another as children of the same family.

I am resolved to love God above all things, and my neighbor as myself for the love of God; and, in testimony of this love, I will give something at the Sunday collection as often as I can.

Lesson 20: Christianity Brought before the Senses (Continued)—Orate Fratres through Canon

Third part of the Mass (continued).—In the name of the Church the priest has made the offering of the bread and wine, and the faithful have offered themselves with him as victims. After purifying himself from the least stains by washing his hands, he returns to the middle of the altar, bows a little, and presents the oblation to the most Holy Trinity in memory of the mysteries of Jesus Christ, and in honor of the saints, that is, to thank God for the favors with which he has loaded them and to merit their protection.

This ancient prayer[440] includes all the parties that have a right to the sacrifice, though in very different ways: God, to whom the sacrifice is offered; Jesus Christ, who is its victim, not merely offered to God, but offered in memory of his own passion, resurrection, and ascension—consequently set up, as it were, before the throne of God to plead our cause unceasingly; the Churches of heaven and earth, which unite in offering this Catholic sacrifice. The Church militant communicates in it sacramentally and receives from it new fruits of life. The Church triumphant also communicates in it, but invisibly, and it is by this continual communion that the glorious life of our Lord is communicated to the saints in heaven.[441]

Orate, fratres. While reciting this prayer, the priest holds his hands joined on the altar and his head bowed down. He thus shows that he acknowledges himself unworthy to offer the great sacrifice to the supreme being, and that one should be very innocent indeed to appear before God on behalf of the human race. At length he kisses the altar, a figure of Jesus Christ, thence to draw those holy dispositions of which he feels more and more the necessity. To communicate them to the faithful, he turns toward them, and, opening out the arms of his charity, says, "Pray, brethren, that my sacrifice, which is also yours, may be favorably received by God the Father Almighty!"

The priest says, "Pray, brethren" in a somewhat elevated tone, so as to be heard at least by those around the altar, since his invitation is addressed to the assistants. The most ancient motive of this exhortation comes from the offering of the people, which lasted a long time, and which might have caused distractions,[442] but the chief motive is that the nearer we draw to the moment of sacrifice, the more necessary are prayer and recollection.

The priest, hitherto confounded with the people, has in a manner conversed with them by various wishes expressed for their welfare, by various instructions given them, and even by prayers made in their name. He is now going to quit the faithful, in order to bury himself in the secret of the sanctuary. A new Moses, he is going to ascend the terrible mountain, where he will converse alone with God. But he does not forget, before setting out on this great journey, that he carries with him the weakness inseparable from humanity, and that he requires on so important an occasion to be helped by the prayers of the people. He therefore says, "Pray, brethren"—*Orate, fratres!* "Pray for me," as priests used to say, more than eight hundred years ago,[443] at this part of the Mass! "Pray for me a poor sinner," as the Carthusians still say, who have retained an ancient usage![444]

By this prayer the priest takes leave of the people, whom he will see no more till he has consummated the sacrifice. During all this interval, he will no more turn toward them, not even when he says, *Dominus vobiscum.* Wholly occupied with the great mystery which he is going to work, and devoutly turned toward the altar, as if he were come into the holy of holies, far away from the people, he will raise his voice only at the conclusion of the secret prayers, in order to exhort the faithful to lift up their hearts on high.

At the *Orate, fratres* the priest, turning toward the faithful, says *brethren.* This touching word dates from eighteen centuries ago; it resounded through the catacombs; it was pronounced by legions of saints: it was the name that our forefathers in the faith gave to one another. And when the astonished pagans asked them, "How are you all brethren?" they answered, "Because we are of one father, Jesus Christ, and one mother, the Church."[445] How affecting does this name become at the moment of the Mass when the priest pronounces it! Brethren, he says, united by the ties of blood, be also united by the ties of charity. Let us not separate now that there is question of our common cause. We are all going to sit at the same table, and to break the same bread. This bread will maintain one and the same life in us all. The same divine blood will flow through our veins, and be a pledge of the same inheritance for us all, my brethren!

He says, "my sacrifice, which is also yours." It is mine: I am the minister. It is offered for me: the victim belongs to me. It is also yours: you offer it yourselves by my hands, and the victim is yours. He adds, "that it may be favorably received." But what! can it be rejected—the oblation of the blood of a God, the only Son of the Father? No; but I have another victim to offer. It is you, it is myself; and the thrice holy God may find fault with this second victim. He may see injustices in our hands, criminal desires in our hearts, stains in our consciences. It is to move you to new sentiments of sorrow for our common sins that I repeat the warning to pray: *Orate, fratres!*

To an invitation so just and useful, the people answer: "Yes, we will pray that the Lord may receive the sacrifice from your hands for the honor and glory of his name, and also for our benefit and that of the whole Church." What a beautiful lesson on charity is this prayer! It reminds us that we are all children of one family. For it is to God, our common Father, that the sacrifice is about to be offered; it is Jesus Christ, our brother, who is about to be offered, and it is by the hands of a minister chosen from among us that he is about to be offered; it is for the sanctification of all that the great mystery, renewed before our eyes, will be consummated. If we wish our prayers to be well received, let us beware of putting any restraint or reserve on our desires. The priest answers: *Amen*—"So be it!" And he recites the prayer called the "secret": it bears this name because it is said in a low voice.

Behold! the priest has entered into the secret of the sanctuary, there to treat alone with God. And what does the new Moses do in this mysterious interview? He asks the Lord that the oblations of the faithful may be pleasing to him, and may obtain for them all the graces that his infinite wisdom knows them to require. The assistants, to be united to the priest at this moment, should beg of God that he would vouchsafe to purify and sanctify them, so that they may be made worthy of being presented to him as a sacrifice of sweet odor. This disposition is so much the more important as the moment of consecration draws nearer.

Fourth part of the Mass.—The fourth part of the Mass is about to begin: it extends from the preface to the *Pater*. Before explaining it, let us pause a little to study the relations between the third part of the Mass and the circumstances of the sacrifice of the cross.

Relations between the ceremonies of the third part of the Mass and the circumstances of the passion.—To eyes full of piety, the priest uncovering the chalice is Jesus stripped; the priest making the offertory is Jesus scourged; the priest covering the chalice again is Jesus crowned with thorns; the priest washing his hands is Pilate washing his hands; the priest saying "Pray, brethren" is Pilate saying, as he shows Jesus to the Jews, "Behold the man!"

Sentiments that ought to prevail in our hearts.—To know what sentiments should prevail in our hearts during the third part of the stupendous sacrifice, let us call to mind that the incarnate Word is now offered to the Father. Adoration, annihilation: behold what the example of the great victim cries out to us! Adoration, annihilation: oh, yes! let our whole being vanish away, as it were, to give honor to the supreme dominion of the God of life and death. Let us unreservedly offer up, with the great victim, our souls, our bodies, our goods. Glory and happiness are in the holocaust that is to transform us into Jesus Christ. Thus shall we attain the first end of sacrifice, which is to acknowledge the supreme dominion of God over all things in existence.

Preface. The preface opens the fourth part of the Mass. The word *preface* means "prelude," "introduction," "an action or a discourse that precedes." It is, in point of fact, to prepare for the Canon that the Church causes the preface to be said immediately before beginning the prayers of which the Canon consists. When placing a preface before the action of actions, the Church wished to imitate our Lord, who began by returning thanks to his Father before raising Lazarus to life, and before changing bread into his body and wine into his blood.

The preface is a glorious song of triumph. It is an invitation to lift up our hearts to God, and to join with all the heavenly choirs in praising and blessing him. It is of very ancient use in the Church, coming probably from the apostles.[446] St. Cyprian is quite clear regarding the motive of its institution: "The priest, before beginning the prayer (the Canon is the prayer of prayers), prepares the minds of the brethren by this preface: *Sursum corda*—'Lift up your hearts,' so that the people may be warned by their own answer: *Habemus ad Dominum*—'We have lifted them up to the Lord,' of the obligation on all to be occupied with God alone."[447]

The Roman Church counts eleven prefaces, of greater or less antiquity: namely, the Common Preface for those days which have no proper one, and the Prefaces for Christmas, the Epiphany, Lent, Easter, the Ascension, Pentecost, Trinity, the Apostles, the Cross, and the Blessed Virgin.[448]

The priest has left the people; he has bidden them a solemn farewell, recommending himself to their prayers. To mark in a more sensible manner this mysterious separation, the curtains and doors that divided the sanctuary from the rest of the Church were formerly closed before the preface.[449] They were not opened again till the time of Communion.

It is from the depths of this dread solitude that the priest, after invoking the blessing of God on the offerings of the faithful, suddenly raises his voice to intone the hymn of eternity: *Per omnia saecula saeculorum*—"Forever and ever!" As if he should say: "The Lord accepteth your gifts. He is pleased with the sacrifice: the sacrifice which is about to become a source of blessings for you. How could he refuse me? I prayed to him in the name of his adorable Son, whom he always heareth, and who liveth and reigneth with him forever and ever."

The people, sharing the joy of the priest, hasten to answer: *Amen*—"So be it!" We approve of the oblation which you have just presented and in which we are victims; we are happy that the Lord vouchsafes to accept it: *Amen*—"So be it!" The vaults of the temple resound with this solemn declaration, and the echoes of the Jerusalem above repeat it to the attentive angels. A dialogue here begins between the priest and the faithful, the beauty of which is increased by the inimitable chant that accompanies it.[450]

"May the Lord be with you!" says the priest from the depths of the sanctuary: prepare yourselves; there are great things about to occur!

"May he also be with your spirit!" answer the people: his assistance is now more than ever necessary for you.

"Lift up your hearts," says the priest. O God! when we think that this admirable invitation has been uttered thousands of times by Chrysostoms, and Ambroses, and Basils, and Augustines, and that it has been heard by millions of saints and martyrs; when we think of all the impressions that it made on those loving hearts, with what respect should we receive it and with what fervor should we correspond to it!

"We have lifted them up to the Lord." Is this always true? Are our hearts really disengaged from all affections to earth? Do we, at this solemn moment, forget our pleasures, and our business, and the various trifles that amuse us? Is that heaven which is about to open, or that victim which is about to descend, everything to us? Alas! what do I say? Is it anything to us? The Church hopes that it is. The priest delights in believing it, and therefore says, "Let us return thanks to the Lord our God" for this happy disposition, as well as for the benefits with which he has heretofore laden us, and the signal favors which he is still ready to grant us.

The faithful, in a transport of gratitude and love, exclaim: "It is just and reasonable."

Assured of the dispositions of the assistants, whose suffrages he has in a manner taken, the priest finds himself laden with all their wishes. He becomes the interpreter of all hearts; and, repeating the people's answer, carries it to the foot of the throne of God. With the motives of justice that engage us to return thanks to God, he joins motives of interest. "Let us return thanks to the Lord," he says, "it is a thing truly meet and just, right and salutary at all times and in all places." To prove this, the priest recalls the infinite greatness, holiness, and goodness of God: *Pater omnipotens, aeterne Deus.* On each festival he makes mention of some of his benefits in keeping with the occasion, and then adds the unchanging, sublime conclusion of all Catholic prayers: *Per Jesum Christum.* As if he should say, "All these thanks we return through Jesus Christ. A mediator between the earthly and the heavenly Jerusalem, God by nature, man by obedience, King of heaven, Lord of the human race, *Dominum nostrum*, it was he who untied our tongues that they might be able to praise God. It is he who unites our voices with those of the blessed spirits. It is by him that all the heavenly choirs render homage to the Eternal, according to the rank assigned them: *Per quem majestatem tuam.*" And then, O solemn moment! the canticles of men and angels blend into one canticle, into one sweet mighty voice, which repeats and will forever repeat: "Holy, holy, holy is the Lord God of hosts"—*Sanctus, sanctus, sanctus!*

Sanctus. The *Sanctus* is a hymn for which earth is indebted to heaven. Isaias, wrapt in spirit, heard it sung alternately by the seraphim;[451] and St. John says that the saints will make the heavenly Jerusalem resound with it forever.[452] The *Sanctus* is therefore one of those sublime duets which the Church triumphant has sent down to her sister, the Church militant, that the latter may practice it in the land of her exile, consoling herself with the hope of being one day able to sing it to perfection. The *Sanctus* is to be found in the most ancient liturgies.[453]

While saying the *Sanctus*, the priest lowers his voice, both because this change is a relief and it attracts attention. Yet he pronounces the words so as to be understood, because the people were always invited to say this canticle.[454] Hence it comes that, in High Masses, it is still repeated by the choir. To show the most profound respect while saying the *Sanctus*, the priest joins his hands and bows his head. A little bell is rung to warn the assistants that the priest is about to begin the great prayer of the Canon, during which the consecration will be effected and the mystery of the incarnation renewed. The *Sanctus* concludes thus: *Hosanna in excelsis*—"Save us, we pray thee who dwellest in the highest heavens!" *Hosanna*, a shout of joy, an exclamation full of energy, is a Hebrew word, like *amen* and *alleluia*, which the Church has retained without translating. When pronouncing these last words, the priest stands erect again and makes on himself the sign of the cross; for it is by virtue of the cross that we share in the blessings which Jesus Christ came to bestow on the world. The Canon immediately follows.

Canon. The word *canon* means "a rule." This name was given to the prayer of the Mass that begins with the words *Te igitur* and extends to the *Pater*, because it contains all the prayers prescribed by the Church for offering the holy sacrifice, and which are never to be changed. The prayers of the Canon are from all antiquity,[455] and the Council of Trent rightly observes that "they are made up of the very words of our Lord, the traditions of the apostles, and the pious institutions of holy popes."[456] The fathers also call the Canon the "prayer," that is to say, the prayer of prayers, because the greatest of all gifts, which is Jesus Christ, is asked therein; and the "action," that is to say, the action of actions, because it is in this part of the Mass that the most sublime action imaginable takes place.[457] The action of actions is sacrifice. Hence, in ancient languages, *to act* and *to sacrifice*, *action* and *sacrifice*, are expressed by the same word.

The Canon is, of all Catholic prayers, the most excellent and ancient: we cannot mention a time when the holy sacrifice was offered with other prayers. Henceforth, what veneration will be due to those prayers which our ancestors in the faith so often pronounced before us—prayers which were their chief consolation, and which obtained for them the strength necessary to resist tyrants, to endure tortures, to shed their blood for religion!

When the priest has finished the *Sanctus*, he raises his eyes and hands to heaven: this is to imitate the Savior, who, before working miracles, addressed his Father above. But he soon casts down his eyes, joins his hands, and bows as a suppliant. He then kisses the altar, which represents Jesus Christ, in order to show his love and respect for him, and to ask that his prayer may have power over the heart of God. And how could he fail to be heard? He offers to the most merciful Father the infinite merits of our Lord, his Son, in favor of the holy Catholic Church and all her children.

During this prayer, the priest makes the sign of the cross three times over the chalice and host, in order to show that it is through the merits of the cross of Jesus Christ he asks God to bless the bread and wine and change them into the body and blood of the Savior, as "gifts" which come from him, as "presents" which we offer to him, and as "the matter of the pure and spotless sacrifice" which is about to be made to him. The priest keeps his hands spread out to the height of his shoulders. Do you not imagine that you behold Moses on the mountain, Jesus Christ on the cross, our forefathers in the catacombs? It was thus that they prayed. Does this scene, so rich in memories, touch no chord in our hearts?

The priest has prayed for all the Church. He has asked peace and union among her children. He has asked protection for the sovereign pontiff, the center of Catholic unity and the representative of Jesus Christ on earth; for the bishop of the place, because he is appointed to guide a portion of the flock; and for the king, who is "an outside bishop." Lastly, he has asked grace for all those who profess the Catholic and orthodox faith.

In a second prayer, he recommends to God all those present, and more particularly those for whom he is about to offer up the holy victim.

Let us here acknowledge that the Church has a most motherly heart. Health of soul and body, peace, union, charity, the eternal salvation of her children: behold what she asks of her divine spouse! Behold, too, what she wishes that we should ask for one another! But all this is not enough for her tenderness. After assembling all her children that still travel with her on earth, after telling them to have but one heart, one soul among themselves, after gathering them in a manner under her wings, as the hen gathereth her chickens, this tender mother invites us to lift up our eyes with her and to contemplate our brethren who reign in heaven and who stretch out their arms toward us, and the angels who make ready to put our prayers into their golden censers, that they may offer them to the Lord as a sweet perfume.

She reminds us, therefore, of the consoling dogma of the communion of saints, which makes of Christians on earth and in heaven but one family, with common interests. "My beloved ones," she says to us, "you whom I now bring forth to Jesus Christ, have confidence; you are in communion with your elder brethren: their prayer will support yours; your sacrifice is theirs." And straightway she begins to tell us the names of some of these illustrious inhabitants of heaven: Mary our Mother, and Mother of Jesus Christ, our eldest brother; the apostles; and a few of our most glorious martyrs. During this prayer, the priest holds his hands raised, and bows respectfully at the names of Jesus and Mary.

Diptychs. It would seem sufficient, without naming so many of the blessed, to say, "honoring the memory of thy saints, through whose merits and prayers we beseech thee to grant," etc.; but the Church wished to remind us of a usage most venerable by its antiquity. There were formerly three catalogues or *diptychs* in every church: the word *diptych* means "a tablet folded in two."

On the first diptych were written the names of the Blessed Virgin, saints, apostles, and especially martyrs; and, later on, the names of bishops who had died in the odor of sanctity. When it was proposed to declare a man holy, his name was placed on the diptych of the saints. Hence the word *canonize*, because the name was mentioned during the Canon.

On the second, the names of some of the faithful still living, and commendable by their dignity, or by the services that they had rendered to the Church. This list contained the names of the pope, the patriarch, the bishop, the clergy of the diocese, kings, princes, magistrates, etc.

On the third, the names of some of the faithful departed in the communion of the Church. These three lists were publicly read in the church, during the Holy Sacrifice of the Mass, by the priest, a deacon, or a subdeacon.

We have retained some vestiges of this ancient usage. In the beginning of the Canon, we recite the names of the pope, bishop, king, etc.; in the first *memento*, the names of the living; and in the second, the names of the dead; and before and after consecration, the names of the principal saints of the Church. At the prone, we still find remains of the same tradition. Prayers are then offered up for the living and the dead, both of whom are named. To our mind there can be nothing more touching or charitable.[458] Behold how everything in our liturgy breathes the great virtue of Christianity, that virtue which civilized the world, that virtue which still constitutes the strength of nations, the happiness of families, and the charm of life—the virtue of charity!

PRAYER

O my God! who art all love, I thank thee for the great lessons on fervor and charity which thou givest me in the prayers of the holy sacrifice. Help me to understand these prayers well, and to repeat them like the early Christians.

I am resolved to love God above all things, and my neighbor as myself for the love of God; and, in testimony of this love, I will hear Mass in the spirit of a victim.

Lesson 21: Christianity Brought before the Senses (Continued)—Consecration, Elevation

Fourth part of the Mass (continued).—In the last prayer, the Church of earth entered into communion with the Church of heaven. The two sisters have met to offer up the august sacrifice which rejoices both. The priest is their minister: he is going to take possession of the victim in their name. Lo! he extends his hands over the chalice and the host. This imposing ceremony takes you back three thousand years. You see Aaron and his successors, the ancient pontiffs, extending their hands over the heads of victims, while taking possession of them in the name of God, and expressing by this sign that the animal whose blood should soon flow was substituted in their place, in place of guilty man, man worthy of death.

Thus does the Catholic priest act. But it is no more over a figurative victim that he extends his hands: it is over the true victim, expected during four thousand years; and his extended hands, like Aaron's, say that it is he who is guilty, he who ought to be sacrificed instead of the innocent victim. Oh, with what sentiments should we all unite in this prayer! What a holy awe should seize us when we behold this terrible ceremony—when we consider that here, under the hands of the priest, we are also placed as victims with our Lord!

The priest asks God that he would vouchsafe to accept this offering of our "service" and of his "whole family." These words allude to priests, who are more closely connected with the service of God than the faithful.[459] Peace in this world, freedom from sin, eternal salvation; these are the things which we hope to receive from the sacrifice and which we express in this prayer. Let us ask them confidently: the blood of the second Abel is powerful enough to obtain them.

The sacred minister has taken possession of the victim. He draws back his hands, and joins them as a sign of humility; for he is going to beg the greatest of miracles. Hitherto, there have been only bread and wine on the altar—the elements of the sacrifice. There is now question of obtaining their transubstantiation into the body and blood of the man-God. The priest therefore, reanimating his faith, arms himself with the sublime power that has been given him. Addressing the Creator of all things, he tells him to pronounce over the bread and wine, according to his promise, that omnipotent *fiat* which may change them into the body and blood of his Son, as it called forth the universe from nothingness.

By the ministry of the priest, we ask that this oblation may be "in all respects" blessed, that is to say, wholly, perfectly blessed—in other words, changed into the body and blood of the Savior, which is the blessing of blessings; and that thus the divine victim, the victim essentially blessed, may communicate all his blessings to us. The Church mentions in general whatever she can desire regarding the oblation of the altar when asking "that it may be in all respects blessed"; but, the better to describe the great grace which she expects, she details in the four following words all that she hopes from God.

Approved. That he may be satisfied with it, and that the oblation which we make of ourselves with Jesus Christ may no longer be rejected, but admitted with that of Jesus Christ.

Ratified. That it may become a permanent sacrifice, not changing like those ancient sacrifices of animals which were revoked, and that the oblation of ourselves may also be irrevocable, so that we may never have the misfortune of being separated from God.

Rational. Hush, human reason! Adore in silence him who created the universe with a word, and who can, by speaking, work prodigies more easily than thou canst utter thy thought! We ask that the victim on the altar may become a human victim, a rational victim, nay, the only victim endowed with reason, reason itself, the only victim worthy of reconciling us with God;[460] for none of the victims whose blood flowed on the altars of the ancient world during four thousand years were rational, or worthy of God or man.

Pleasing. That the oblation of the altar may become the body and blood of the beloved Son, in whom the Lord places all his delights. We ask that the oblation may not only become all this, but that it may become such for our welfare.

And do you see what simple language the Church uses in begging these prodigies of power and goodness? With as much simplicity as the scripture expresses the greatest of miracles in the order of nature, the creation—"Let light be"—and the greatest in the order of religion, the incarnation—"Be it done unto me according to thy word"—the Church asks that prodigy which contains all others, the great miracle of the change of the bread and wine into the body and blood of Jesus Christ—"that this oblation may become for us the body and blood of thy most dear Son, our Lord Jesus Christ!"

Is it not sublime? Find anything to compare with it in profane authors! Nothing, therefore, O holy religion! can be more true than that thou dost unite in thyself all the titles that can recommend thee to the love of Christians and the admiration of intelligent beings. On every page of thy liturgy, as on every one of thy dogmas and precepts, there shines the seal of thy heavenly origin! The priest, while saying the prayers that we have just explained, makes the sign of the cross several times, in order to show that it is in the all-powerful name of Jesus Christ that he asks the miracle.

Consecration.—At length we have reached the supreme moment when the Son of God, the Eternal, the Strong, the Mighty, the Creator of worlds, prepares to obey the voice of a mortal. The priest wipes the thumb and forefinger of each of his hands on the corporal, so as to remove moisture or dust from them, and to have them in a more proper state to touch the body of the Lord. With the fingers which he has purified, and which have been consecrated by ordination, he takes the host, and, in a plain, simple tone of voice, like that observed by the Savior—whose place he holds—when working miracles, he pronounces the all-powerful words of consecration.

The miracle is wrought! The priest falls on his knees. The assistants prostrate. And the bell tells the faithful at a distance to adore. Of old, at the sound of the sacred tocsin, they were to be seen casting themselves on their knees in houses, in streets, and in fields, and saying the Lord's Prayer. Meanwhile, the priest elevates the adorable body of the Son of God, who has just become incarnate in his hands, and at this moment of elevation the ancient basilicas were moved: the holy doors were opened, and the curtains, which had hidden the sanctuary, were drawn aside. No wonder that St. Chrysostom used to say to his people: "Look now on the interior of the sanctuary as the interior of heaven, that with the eyes of faith you may there see Jesus Christ, and the choirs of angels prostrate round the Lamb."[461] "Consider the King's table; the angels are his servants; the King is present in Person. If your garments are clean, adore and communicate."[462]

After laying the body of the Lord on the corporal, the priest consecrates the chalice of his blood, which he calls "a mystery of faith."[463] He concludes by repeating the words of the divine master: "As often as you do these things, do them in remembrance of me."[464]

These last words are the title deeds of the power of the priest, and the eternal proof of the mystery which he has just accomplished. The Almighty, that is, he who does whatsoever he wishes by a word, said to him: "You shall do what I have done; you shall change bread into my body and wine into my blood." And the priest does so. And let no infidel or heretic set bounds to the power of the Almighty! It is therefore an article of faith that, after the words of consecration, there no longer remains either bread or wine, but only their appearances, in order to show the place occupied by the invisible God, and to say to our senses: "He is here!"

Does not reason itself lead us to confess that it ought to be so? As a matter of fact, the preservation of external worship, after the abolition of the gross sacrifices of the old law, required a sign, the symbol of a moral victim. Our Lord, before quitting the earth, provided for the grossness of our senses, which cannot do without a material sign: he instituted the Eucharist, in which, under the sensible species of bread and wine, he concealed the invisible offering of his body and blood.

The elevation of the host is followed by that of the chalice, which the priest, after adoring, lays on the altar. The elevation and adoration of the Eucharist have not always taken place in the same manner as at present. Up to the beginning of the twelfth century, priests elevated the chalice and host at the same time, with these words: *Omnis honor*—"All honor and glory forever and ever!" This little elevation is still observed; but the Church, in order to protest against the error of heretics who had dared to attack the dogma of the Eucharist, and also to give Catholics an opportunity of solemnly manifesting their faith, established the usage of elevating the body and blood of our Lord after the consecration, and offering them to the adoration of her children.

Elevation. The elevation, such as it is practiced now, comes therefore from the beginning of the twelfth century; and it was the heretic Berengarius who gave occasion to it by his blasphemies against the real presence of Jesus Christ in this sacrament of love. Later on, it was practiced with much more reason when Luther and Calvin, developing the heresy of the archdeacon of Angers, attacked with implacable fury the dogma of the Holy Eucharist. To ring the bell as a warning for everyone to fall prostrate was not thought enough: candles were also lighted to make the moment more solemn.[465] This last ceremony is still observed with pomp in our Solemn Masses. The Roman rite appoints it for all Masses.

Subsequent prayers. The consecration and elevation over, the priest extends his arms and continues the great action. Obedient to the express command of the Savior, who said to his apostles and their successors, "As often as ye do these things, do them in remembrance of me,"[466] the priest says that, "in memory of the most blessed passion of Jesus Christ our Lord, and his resurrection from hell, and his glorious ascension into heaven," he offers to the incomparable majesty of God "a pure, holy, spotless host, the bread of eternal life and the chalice of everlasting salvation."

Nothing better than this prayer to lift up the soul and to fill it with a sense of religion! Though the Sacrifice of the Mass was chiefly intended to renew the memory of the passion of our Lord, the Church, following the directions of her divine spouse, also makes mention of the mysteries of the resurrection and ascension, because they are essentially connected with the passion.

Hence, in the Sacrifice of the Altar, we communicate with Jesus Christ dead, who, by dying, destroyed the empire of death, that is to say, destroyed the death of the soul and made the death of the body a passage to endless life. We communicate with Jesus Christ risen, whose resurrection is the principle and the model of ours. We communicate with Jesus Christ ascending into heaven, and hereby ascend in a manner with him, so that we may already regard ourselves as citizens of the blessed Jerusalem. Is it possible to call to mind the different fruits of all these great mysteries, and yet adhere so obstinately to the love of sensible things?

The priest, when saying this prayer, makes the sign of the cross five times: thrice on the host and chalice together, once on the host alone, and once on the chalice alone.

How eloquent is this repetition of the adorable sign! The Church wishes our minds to be penetrated with the great thought that the victim of the altar is the victim of Calvary. And lo! she wearies herself, as it were, in setting this truth before our eyes, before our ears, before all our senses, that it may sink deep into our hearts.

By the five signs of which we speak, the priest seems therefore to say: "We offer to Thy Supreme Majesty a 'holy host,' which was offered on the cross; a 'pure host,' which was fastened to the cross; a 'spotless host,' which was immolated on the cross; the 'sacred bread,' that is to say, Jesus Christ, the living eternal bread come down from heaven, who died on the cross to give us life; lastly, the 'chalice of salvation,' the blood of Jesus Christ—the mediator of the new covenant—blood shed on the cross to wash away our sins."

The Church, we repeat, wishes that during these moments, at once so precious and so awful, the priest and the faithful should be occupied with the Savior immolated on the altar. Could she, I ask, employ any means more proper for the attainment of this end than these signs of the cross so often renewed? Could she better display her faith in the miraculous change which has just been wrought? Could she more clearly tell her children to comport themselves at the foot of the altar as they should have done at the foot of the cross?[467]

A God is on the altar. How could it be that a victim of infinite value, offered to a God, would not be pleasing? Why then the following prayer, by which the Lord is besought to receive favorably the host presented to him? Ah, it is because the august victim is offered by the hands of a mortal; it is because with the spotless host there are joined other hosts infinitely less pure, the hearts of the faithful. Hence the Church, reminding the eternal Father that the sacrifice of his Son is the Catholic sacrifice, the sacrifice of which all ancient sacrifices were only shadows, beseeches him to give his children those holy dispositions which animated the ancient sacrificators when they were immolating their figurative victims: the innocence of Abel, the faith of Abraham, the sanctity of Melchisedech.

Let us here enter into ourselves. Have we the innocence and generosity of Abel, who offered the choicest of his lambs? Have we the faith and courage of Abraham, who raised the sword to immolate Isaac? Have we the sanctity of Melchisedech, who appears before us without father, without mother, without genealogy, that is to say, detached from all human affections? If we have not these dispositions, let us earnestly ask them during this prayer. If they are wholly wanting to us, how can we profit of the sacrifice or share in the approaching Communion?

The next prayer should inspire us with other sentiments. I behold the priest suddenly assuming the attitude of a suppliant: he casts down his eyes, bows low, and, joining his hands like a poor vassal, lays them on the altar. Why all this? It is because he is going to ask of God that the victim which he has just immolated may be borne by the hands of that angel who is sanctity itself to the sublime altar of heaven.

How shall we express the deep meaning of this prayer? In the last, the priest besought the Lord to accept graciously the host offered to him. All of a sudden, as if seized by an inspiration from on high, he finds an infallible means of causing this victim to be received, and also our desires and hearts which accompany it. Addressing himself to God, he begs him to command that the victim may be borne to the foot of his throne by the victim itself. Out of respect for our Lord, the priest does not dare to name him to God the Father: he is satisfied to designate him by the words *thy angel*. Yes, the angel of angels, the angel of great counsel, the mediating angel of the covenant,[468] who, equal to God, is sure to make both his sacrifice and ours acceptable, and to draw down on us the dew of all kinds of blessings.

The signs of the cross with which the priest accompanies his prayer indicate the real presence of this holy victim, this heavenly victim, on the altar of earth. A profound humility and an ardent desire of sanctity, so that nothing on our part may prevent our petitions from being well received, ought to be our chief dispositions during this prayer.

Lo! we who live on the earth and assist at the sacrifice are now well recommended to the Lord: all his blessings have just been invoked on our heads. At so precious a moment, when the Church can obtain anything, will she forget her other children, her children that are no more? Ah, if you think so, you little know what a mother's heart is! Her heart holds all her children: the most needy have the largest place there. Accordingly, the Catholic Church prays for her deceased children. Her very prayer is a lesson for the living. She prays for "those who have gone before us with the sign of faith and who rest in the sleep of peace"; therefore, we shall follow them.[469]

At these words, the priest joins his hands on his breast, fixes his eyes affectionately on the holy host, and prays[470] in silence for the departed ones whom he has the intention of recommending to God. During this prayer, we ought also to recommend our departed ones to God, and to renew our faith in the great motives that we have to pray for them: the glory of God, charity, justice, and our own interest.

The Church now returns to us who are on earth. In the course of the august sacrifice, we see this tender mother, all anxiety, ascending to heaven, descending to purgatory, and returning to this valley of tears, everywhere, collecting petitions, examining wants, soliciting prayers, and encouraging recommendations, so as to profit fully of the rich treasure opened up in the merits of the victim.

Thus, before the consecration, she commemorated the communion of saints, in which it was necessary to offer the Catholic sacrifice of heaven and earth. She has just begged the admission of the souls in purgatory into the celestial Jerusalem. She now implores the same favor for her children still journeying on the road of life: the priest asks earnestly for himself and the faithful the happiness of heaven.

Conscious of his unworthiness, he strikes his breast, acknowledges himself a sinner, like the publican in the gospel, and, that the assistants may hear him and join with him in supplicating the divine mercy, raises his voice a little. He then invokes the principal martyrs, into whose company he beseeches God to receive us, not in consideration of our own merits, but by granting us mercy and pardon, through Jesus Christ our Lord.

In this prayer are named those saints who are honored with a special worship by the Church of Rome, the mother and mistress of all other churches. They are all martyrs, and belong to various states: prophets, apostles, popes, bishops, priests, clerics, wives, virgins. A consoling lesson for us: we may therefore be saved in any condition of life, and the saints who are in heaven offer to the just who suffer on earth an assurance of their eternal happiness.

The priest has just begged admission into heaven for the dead and the living through Jesus Christ. He is going to show, at the conclusion of the Canon, the reason why he makes all his petitions through this divine mediator. He says, "By whom thou dost create," etc. In point of fact, it was by our Lord that God the Father created these things, the bread and wine, become the body and blood of his Son, not only inasmuch as he drew them from nothingness in the early days of the world, but he renews them by a continual miracle, which makes the earth annually bring forth new grains and new grapes. "By whom thou dost sanctify." It is by our Lord that these gifts, offered on the altar, are separated from common use and become a source of sanctification. "By whom thou dost vivify." It is by our Lord that God vivifies them, changing them into the precious body and blood which are the true food and the life of the world. "Thou dost bless and grant them to us, through Jesus Christ," as the true mediator; "with Jesus Christ," as God equal to God; and "in Jesus Christ," as consubstantial with the Father, and by whom all honor and glory are rendered to God the Father Almighty. Is it not enough to deserve that God should hear us when we ask through Jesus Christ?

The priest, when reciting these prayers, makes the sign of the cross many times. He makes it three times at the words *sanctify*, *vivify*, *bless*, in order to show that it is through the merits of the cross of Jesus Christ that we have the Eucharist, and that the bread and wine are sanctified, vivified, and blessed. He does not make the sign of the cross when saying, "Thou dost create," because all things were created by our Lord as the Wisdom of the Father, as the eternal Word, and not as a God incarnate and immolated on the cross. The other signs of the cross which accompany this prayer denote that the host and the chalice contain indivisibly Jesus Christ who died on the cross, and that, by his sacrifice, the Father and the Holy Ghost are worthily honored.

Let us also be careful to unite ourselves with the holy victim in order to honor the Father and the Holy Ghost, to praise them, and to begin on earth that hymn which we are to sing forever in heaven. I may be mistaken, but it seems to me that, during this prayer, it is particularly necessary for us to keep our hearts in harmony with our lips, lest those beautiful words should be belied by our attachment to creatures. In uttering this prayer, our voices unite with those of the angels and saints. But if, on returning to our homes, our thoughts are as earthly as before leaving them, our desires as carnal, our inclinations as irregular, then we fall, as it were, from heaven to earth, we quit the abode of immortality to amuse ourselves in a land of exile, and, like fools, we prefer the language of men to that of God. May all this inconsistency cease!

Relations between the ceremonies of the fourth part of the Mass and the circumstances of the passion.—What shall we now say of the touching relations which piety has discovered between the ceremonies of this fourth part of the Mass and the circumstances of the passion? The priest recites the preface: Jesus is condemned to death. The priest makes the *memento* of the living, and lays at God's feet the wants of the earth: Jesus carries his cross. The priest continues the Canon, during which the consecration takes place: Jesus advances toward Calvary, and a holy woman wipes his adorable face with a linen cloth. The priest blesses the offerings by the sign of the cross frequently repeated: Jesus is nailed to the cross. The priest elevates the host: Jesus is lifted up on the cross. The priest elevates the chalice: the blood of Jesus flows from his wounds. The priest makes the *memento* of the dead: Jesus prays for all men, especially his executioners. The priest, striking his breast, prays for all sinners: Jesus converts the good thief.

Sentiments that ought to prevail in our hearts.—To excite within you a sentiment befitting this fourth part of the Mass, think that it is accomplished on Calvary. Bathed in the blood of your God, can it be possible that you will not feel an unutterable love? His blood flows: it flows by me, it flows on me, it flows for me. O blood! making atonement for my sins and for the sins of the whole world, wash and purify my soul and body. The utmost horror of every kind of sin, and an immense love for our sweet, holy victim: behold the twofold sentiment that should predominate in our hearts at the foot of the altar during the consecration, as it would have done at the foot of the cross during the crucifixion.

PRAYER

O my God! who art all love, I thank thee for having instituted the adorable sacrifice of our altars. Grant me the grace to assist at it as I should have done at that of Calvary.

I am resolved to love God above all things, and my neighbor as myself for the love of God; and, in testimony of this love, I will take care to be profoundly recollected during the time of consecration.

Lesson 22: Christianity Brought before the Senses (Continued)—Pater Noster through Communion

The priest, shut up in the sanctuary, has just, during the Canon, treated face-to-face with God regarding the interests of the people. At the conclusion of this series of prayers, he returns thanks through Jesus Christ, and raises his voice, saying: "Forever and ever." The people hasten to subscribe to all that the priest has just asked and done for them, and answer: "Amen." This word ends the Canon and the fourth part of the Mass.

Fifth part of the Mass.—The fifth part of the Mass is a preparation for Communion. Now, what are people who communicate? Have you ever been put this question? People who communicate are a large family that sit down to a table laid out on the confines of time and eternity, at which the inhabitants of the earth perform the most sublime, the most delightful, and the most social act possible to mere mortals, and at which they meet the noble inhabitants of the Jerusalem above: the very table of the common Father of angels and men, at which they may eat the bread and drink the wine that his tender solicitude has prepared for them. And O great God! what bread and wine are served up at this sacred banquet!

Pater Noster, with subsequent prayers and ceremonies. To recall this beautiful idea of a family sitting down at the same table, the Church wishes that her children should salute God with the sweet name of Father, and immediately she places on their lips the Lord's Prayer. But this prayer is so holy, and raises us to such a dignity, by letting us call God "our Father," that the Church considered it a duty to show in a short preface that it is only in obedience to the command of Jesus Christ himself that her children venture to say it.

While the priest pronounces it, let us take great care to excite in our souls a lively sentiment of humility and gratitude; for, "instructed by thy wholesome precepts and following thy divine directions, we presume to say: Our Father"—*Pater Noster,* etc. What a consolation to say the Lord's Prayer at a time when the Son of God, its author, is immolated on the altar in order to obtain for us from his Father all the petitions that it contains! The usage of reciting the *Pater* as a preparation for Communion is from all antiquity. May it come forth from our lips as it did from those of the man-God, the apostles, the martyrs, so many glorious saints during the last eighteen centuries!

In the Eastern Church, the *Pater* is said by all the people; and in the Latin Church, by the priest alone.[471] The Latin Church wishes that the priest alone should pronounce the Lord's Prayer, in a clear distinct voice, so that everyone may easily hear him. Yet, that the people may take some part in it, they are allowed to recite the last petition, which is to be regarded as a summary of all the others. Hence, in pronouncing the words, "Deliver us from evil," the faithful seem to say, "Deliver us from evil, that thou mayst always be glorified in us, that thou mayst alone reign in us, that we may do thy will, that we may obtain spiritual and temporal goods from thy bounty, that we may deserve the forgiveness of our sins by a sincere love of our brethren, and that our weakness may not be exposed to temptations." The priest answers: *Amen*—"So be it": may you be delivered from evil!

He explains this petition of the people by naming the evils from which we desire to be delivered, and the intercessors through whom we expect it—the blessed and glorious Mary, ever Virgin, Mother of God, the blessed apostles Peter, Paul, and Andrew, and all the saints.

Breaking of the host. Before this prayer and toward the end of the *Pater*, the deacon rubs the paten, that it may be in a more proper state. The priest takes it and holds it resting on the altar, so as to have it ready for making the sign of the cross. At the words, *Grant us peace*, he makes the sign of the cross on himself with the paten, and kisses it out of respect, as an instrument of peace, the ever-sacred vessel on which the adorable body of our Lord is soon to rest. He uses it at the same time to make the sign of the cross, because it was by the cross that the Savior destroyed everything opposed to our peace.[472] He puts the paten under the host, so as to be able to take up the host more easily. He then uncovers the chalice, genuflects in adoration, and, taking the host, breaks it into three parts over the precious blood, so that if any particles should become detached, they may fall into the chalice.

Why this breaking of the host? It is to set before us one of the most venerable memorials of religion. The Savior, when about to distribute to his apostles, took bread and broke it, saying: "Take ye and eat." It is therefore true that in the least of our ceremonies there is a treasure of pious reminiscences. This division of the host takes place in all the Churches of East and West.[473] One of the parts is put into the chalice. The second was formerly distributed to the people. The priest communicated with the third. In ancient times, the host consecrated by the priest was large and thick: it was possible to give a portion of it to the faithful. Nowadays, being smaller, the priest consumes it all. Little hosts serve for the Communion of the people.

The priest, taking between the thumb and forefinger of the right hand the part of the host that he is going to mix with the precious blood, makes the sign of the cross three times over the chalice from brim to brim, saying: "The peace of our Lord be always with you!" And the people answer: "And with your spirit!" The priest makes the sign of the cross over the Savior's blood; for it is by this divine blood that all things have been pacified.[474] He does so three times, in honor of the three Persons of the Blessed Trinity.

Kiss of peace. During the first six centuries, this wish of the priest, "the peace of the Lord be always with you!" was the signal for the *pax* which Christians used to give one another. You would then have seen all these children of the same family, called to the table of their common Father, the God of charity, tenderly embracing one another, in order to show that there was no bitterness, aversion, or coldness in their hearts, but the most sincere and lively charity. You would have heard the pagans exclaiming: "Behold how they love one another, and how they are ready to die for one another!" This infant society found in its charity the means of its victory over paganism; for union is strength. Men gave the holy kiss to men, women to women; and then all the family approached together to the table of the Lamb, at which, according to the holy doctors, the peaceful alone have a right to sit.[475]

If the Church, in her profound wisdom, has changed this affecting usage, she has retained some vestiges of it. At High Masses, we still see the deacon giving the subdeacon the peace which he has just received from the priest; for the priest, before giving the peace, kisses the altar, a figure of Jesus Christ, and formerly he used to kiss the holy host, in order to show that it was from the very heart of the Savior that he drew the peace. From the subdeacon this peace is next communicated to all the ecclesiastics present. Thus the spirit of the Church has not changed, and the faithful who attend Mass should at this moment ask the peace of God, and make an act of charity toward the neighbor, mindful of the words of their divine master: "If when you present your gift at the altar, you recollect that your brother has something against you, leave there your gift before the altar, and go and be reconciled with him; and then coming you shall offer your gift."[476]

But what is this peace, which the priest wishes the faithful, and which the faithful should ask? The peace of the Lord, *Pax Domini:* peace, the only temporal inheritance which the man-God bequeathed from the height of the cross to his children; peace of soul, which the world cannot give, because it is the fruit of a victory over our passions; peace with God and with our fellowmen; the peace of the world by submission to the gospel, and the peace of the Church by a cessation of persecution. The former is a disposition for Communion; the latter is its fruit. To present a lively image of this divine peace, the priest, while the people answer, "And with your spirit," drops into the chalice that portion of the host which he has been holding in his right hand.

Formerly alliances were sealed with the blood of victims, or with the blood of the contracting parties: each one took a little of the blood that had been mixed, and with it signed the agreement. And here it is in the divine blood, in the blood of the eternal covenant, that the priest seals the union, the peace of the faithful among themselves and with God. Thus, a perpetual and universal peace is what the Church asks by this prayer, as an effect of the august sacrifice offered by consecration and consummated by Communion.

The mixture made in the chalice of the species of bread and wine denotes: a) the union of God and man made in the incarnation, and called by St. Augustine the "mixture of God and man";[477] b) the mixture of God and man made by Communion on earth; and c) the mixture of God and man made by communion in heaven—a perfect, everlasting communion, through which, all veils having been removed, the saints will be confirmed in the peace and unity of God.

Agnus Dei. But how can we arrive at this desirable peace and divine unity if we have not a victim that will reconcile us with God by freeing us from the load of our sins? Alas! so long as the wall of division, raised by sin, stands, any union between God and man is impossible. The Church knows it. This is the reason why, addressing Jesus Christ, she invokes him as the Lamb, the victim of God. "Lamb of God," she says three times, "who takest away the sins of the world, have mercy on us, grant us peace!" She invokes him three times, to show by this earnest prayer and this mysterious number her infinite need of his clemency and grace in order to be reconciled with God in this world and perfectly united to him in the peace of heaven. When uttering these words, the priest strikes his breast, and the faithful ought to imitate him, in order to show that here, in our hearts, lies the only obstacle to peace, namely, sin, and to beseech the divine Lamb to come and take it away.

In Masses for the dead, the petition is changed: "Lamb of God, who takest away the sins of the world, grant them rest!" Wholly occupied with her departed children, the Church begs for them the only good worth seeking, the rest of heaven, and the priest does not strike his breast: since it is not for himself, but for his deceased brethren, that he asks peace.

Prayers before Communion. To become one body and one spirit with our Lord by Communion, it is necessary that among ourselves we should all have but one heart and one soul by charity. This important disposition the Church asks for us with new fervor. The priest, bowing, his hands joined on the altar, and his eyes modestly fixed on the God of peace who lies before him, makes a first prayer, which comes from the ninth or tenth century.[478]

This beautiful prayer is not said in Masses for the dead, because the peace that we ask for the Church militant does not befit the Church suffering. The priest, fearing lest his sins should be an obstacle thereto, asks it through the faith of the Church. Could anything be more just? It is faith that prays, and, the Church alone being the house of faith, the Church alone is the house of prayer. To the exclusion of all the sects, the Catholic Church alone has received the spirit of prayer. It is this chaste dove alone that moans, and its ineffable sighs are heard by the Lord, because they alone are formed by his Spirit.

In the early ages, the Church did not place any prayer here, because all the prayers that preceded Communion might be regarded as a sufficient preparation. But many holy priests, unable to consider the moment of the reception of the precious body of the Savior without a holy trembling, asked more earnestly the forgiveness of their sins and the grace to partake worthily of the Blessed Eucharist. This led to the introduction of several prayers, full of the most tender sentiments. The Church selected two of them, which, for six or seven hundred years, she has caused to be repeated daily.[479]

One reminds us that it is solely to the death of Jesus Christ that the world is indebted for its life. Now, we participate in the sacrifice of our Lord by Communion, as the Jews participated in the sacrifices of the law by eating the flesh of victims. The Eucharistic, that is to say, sensible Communion in the body of our Lord was instituted only as a means to communicate interiorly and invisibly in the grace and spirit of all the mysteries of the man-God.[480]

In the concluding prayer, the priest renews his sentiments of humility and compunction, and begs that the adorable body of our Lord may be to him a preservative against mortal sins, and a wholesome remedy for venial sins.

After these prayers, the priest, on the point of consummating the sacrifice, makes a genuflection in order to adore the immolated God. Having risen, he takes the holy host in his hands, and says, "I will take the bread of heaven, and call upon the name of the Lord." Where shall we find words more suitable to a soul full of love for the Savior and of desire to receive him? The priest wishes to be united to God. In his heart, there is the same sentiment that made Jesus say, when speaking of his passion: "With desire have I desired to eat this pasch with you."[481] But this sentiment of love is not all alone: it is accompanied by that of his own unworthiness.

What does the priest do? He annihilates himself, humbles himself before the thrice holy God; and, with the same confidence as the centurion whose words he borrows, he begs a miracle, which, cleansing him from his sins, may render him worthy of receiving his God. He strikes his breast, repeating three times: "Lord, I am not worthy that thou shouldst enter under my roof; say but the word, and my soul shall be healed." Yes, say but the word; and the messenger of thy omnipotent will, immediately setting out, will come and heal my wounds!

Communion of the priest. Meanwhile, in the depth of his humility, he remembers this command of the Savior: "Verily, verily, I say unto you, unless you eat the flesh of the Son of man and drink his blood, you shall not have life in you."[482] All is settled: confidence and love have won the victory, and the priest, making the sign of the cross with the holy host, takes the adorable body of the Savior.

This prayer lets us know that the body of the Word incarnate is given us as a pledge of the glory of heaven, as an earnest of a better life, as a viaticum to help us on toward our native land. The flesh and blood of the man-God become in our soul a kind of salt which preserves it from the corruption of sin, destroys in it everything earthly, makes it pleasing to God, and gives it a relish for heaven. Nourished with this food of immortality, the priest may view, without growing pale, the grave half open before him. He will go down into it without fear: the pledge of a future resurrection is deposited in his bosom.

After taking the holy host, the priest employs the moments which he requires for absorbing it in giving free course to his love and gratitude toward the Savior. As soon as he is in a way to speak, he returns thanks to the Lord. And what sentiment can be in a heart where Jesus dwells personally but a sentiment of gratitude and admiration? What words on the lips which he has just sanctified but a canticle of praise? The priest next uncovers the chalice, and genuflects in adoration. He then gathers up, to put them into the chalice, any particles of the holy host that may have remained on the corporal, and takes the consecrated cup.

Communion of the faithful. This is the time for the Communion of the faithful. We explained in the second part[483] of the catechism how the early Christians used to communicate.[484] It only remains for us to say a word on the ceremonies and prayers that nowadays accompany the Communion of the people.

By the mouth of the clerk or the deacon, the communicants make a general confession of their sins: *Confiteor*. This usage is more than five hundred years old. The priest turns toward them and asks pardon and eternal life for them. By the mouth of the minister, they all answer: "So be it"—*Amen!* The priest again asks the whiteness of innocence for the communicants. Their hearts answer: "May it be so"—*Amen!* Then, taking the sacred host, which he holds over the ciborium, the priest says, "Behold the Lamb of God, behold him who taketh away the sins of the world!" And he adds three times: "Lord, I am not worthy that thou shouldst enter under my roof; say but the word, and my soul shall be healed!" The priest approaches, and gives the Holy Communion, making the sign of the cross and saying: "May the body of our Lord Jesus Christ preserve thy soul to life everlasting!"

In many churches, the faithful answer: "So be it"—*Amen!* But if they do not say so everywhere with the mouth, they ought to say so from the depths of the heart. What more admirable or useful petition could they make? In Germany and some other parts of Christendom, the faithful who have just communicated are presented with wine and water to rinse the mouth. This very old custom is still observed at ordinations, and, in many places, on the day of a first general Communion.[485]

Out of respect for the Savior, the priest washes his mouth and fingers, so that they may retain none of the holy species: a venerable practice, which comes to us from the twelfth century. Previously, it was thought enough to wash the hands after Communion, and to throw the water into a *piscina*, a place consecrated for this purpose. Since then, the priest has made two ablutions, one with pure wine, and another with wine and water, which the clerk and the subdeacon pour on his fingers. But, while he is engaged with these external cares, his soul, united to God, maintains a holy converse with him. He asks: "What? Ah, what can or should a pilgrim soul, which is united to its God and Father, ask but that this union may last forever?" Such is the meaning of the two prayers that accompany the ablutions.

What more beautiful sentiments could the faithful who have had the happiness of communicating express in thanksgiving? But whether the assistants have communicated sacramentally or spiritually, they ought during these moments, so precious and so short, to keep company with their divine master, to adore him, to thank him, and to ask him confidently for whatever they need as regards soul or body. "The moments after Communion," says St. Teresa, "are the most precious in life."

Relations between the ceremonies of the fifth part of the Mass and the circumstances of the passion.—Here again, according to our custom, let us tell the relations which an ingenious and tender piety delights in finding between the ceremonies of the fifth part of the Sacrifice of the Altar and the circumstances of the sacrifice of the cross: let us not forget that our guide is always the amiable and holy bishop of Geneva. The priest says the *Pater*, consisting of seven petitions: Jesus, from the height of the cross, utters the seven memorable words that make up his last will. The priest divides the host: Jesus expires. The priest puts a part of the host into the chalice: the soul of Jesus descends into hell. The priest communicates: Jesus is buried.

Sentiments that ought to prevail in our hearts.—Let us now question our faith: it will inform us of the sentiment that should prevail in our souls during the fifth part of the Mass. Nothing more true than that here, on the altar, is the same Jesus who loved us so much as to give his blood for us, the same who said and who still says, "What will you that I should do unto you? My delights are to be with the children of men. Come to me all you that labor and are weary, and I will refresh you." Confidence—a boundless, childlike confidence: this is what ought to be in our hearts, and consequently on our lips. Let us ask for ourselves, for our relatives, for our friends, for all the world, without exception. What can he refuse us who gives us himself? O my God! how is it that we are not all most rich in spiritual goods, we to whom their source is daily opened with such amazing liberality? Ah, the fault is ours alone! But it is over: we shall henceforth have neither distrust nor tepidity with which to reproach ourselves.

PRAYER

O my God! who art all love, I thank thee for having permitted me to assist so often at thy adorable sacrifice. I ask pardon for all the irreverences of which I have been guilty.

I am resolved to love God above all things, and my neighbor as myself for the love of God; and, in testimony of this love, I will communicate either sacramentally or spiritually as often as I hear Mass.

Lesson 23: Christianity Brought before the Senses (Continued)—Communion through Last Gospel

Sixth part of the Mass.—The sixth and last part of Mass is the thanksgiving. Gratitude is a sacred duty among men: shame on him who would try to escape from it! He is branded as a monster. There is no more bitter insult than to say to one: "You are an ingrate!" Gratitude is also a duty commanded by religion. Did not our Lord loudly condemn those lepers who, after their cure, neglected to return and thank him? At Mass, he has vouchsafed to grant us the greatest of all graces. There was no fear that the Church, so tender a spouse, would fail to give him solemn thanks: she has done it in all ages. "After partaking of this great sacrament," says St. Augustine, "all concludes with thanksgiving."[486] What was practiced in his day is still practiced; and may our gratitude equal that of our ancestors!

The last part of Mass includes the antiphon of Communion, the prayer called the postcommunion, the *Ite Missa est*, the blessing, and the gospel *In principio* of St. John.

Communion of the faithful (continued) and the Communion antiphon.—In the beautiful days of the early Church, when all the people used to communicate, there were appropriate psalms sung during the distribution of the Eucharist. In the East, it was the canticle beginning thus: "As the hart panteth after the fountains of water, so doth my soul pant after thee, O God!"[487] In the West, it was Psalm 33: "I will bless the Lord at all times; his praise shall be ever in my mouth."[488]

We imitate this pious usage when, on our great solemnities, we sing psalms or canticles during Communion. What more beautiful? The banquets of the great ones of the earth are accompanied with music and song. Should not sweet melodies resound at the sacred banquet to which God himself, the host, the food, and the guest, invites his children? While the vaults of our temples ring with the canticles of our love, the angels, present at the divine banquet, relate in their manner the goodness of God and the happiness of man.

When the Communion was drawing to a close, the bishop made a sign to the leader of the choir, and the *Gloria Patri* was sung to conclude the festal hymn. The fervor of the faithful having unhappily diminished, the psalms were reduced to a verse, called an antiphon, because sung alternately by two choirs. Such is the prayer of the Mass that we call the communion.

The priest recites it at the epistle side; for, while he was covering the chalice again, the clerk removed the missal over here. This is the place best suited to the book, because it is on the side where the bishop and priest sit. The book would have been left here always if a mysterious reason had not determined that the gospel should be read on the north side, and if, from the time of the offertory, it had not been necessary to leave the side of the altar free on which the ablutions are made, cruets presented, chalice prepared, etc.; for the sacristy, from which everything required is brought, is generally on the same side.

Postcommunion prayer. The communion recited, the priest goes to the middle of the altar, and kisses it respectfully. Then, turning toward the people, he invites them to prayer and gratitude in these words: "The Lord be with you!" The people answer: "And with your spirit!" The priest returns to the missal, and, in the name of all, says, *Oremus*—"Let us pray." And he recites in a loud voice the postcommunion, which is a prayer of thanksgiving. Ah, if we knew the gift of God and the favor that he has just conferred on us, with what a deep feeling of love should we not say at the end of this prayer, *Amen*—"So be it"—eternal love, thanks, gratitude!

The number of postcommunions is the same as that of collects and secrets before the preface. In point of fact, it is right that we should return thanks as many times as we have made petitions. To postcommunions in Lent there is added a prayer, called a prayer for the people. It is preceded by an invitation given by the deacon: *Humiliate capita vestra Deo*—"Bow down your heads before God!" Whatever motive led to the institution of this prayer, whether it was said for the faithful who had not communicated or for sinners who were performing their penance, the assistants should, while it is being recited, humble their hearts and ask God to change and sanctify them.

After the postcommunion, the priest, having come back to the middle of the altar, which he kisses respectfully, turns toward the people and addresses his last good wishes to them: "The Lord be with you!" Oh, yes, may he be with you, pious Christians, who have come since break of day, like the faithful Israelites, to gather the manna fallen from heaven! Nourish yourselves with the sacred bread during the course of the day that now begins: pilgrims of eternity, you shall therein find strength to continue your journey to your fatherland! The Lord be with you to enlighten you, to guard you, to comfort you, to preserve for you the fruit of the sacrifice, and to remind you of what you have seen and done this morning! Penetrated with livelier gratitude than ever toward the priest who has been the minister of the great sacrifice, the people answer: "And with your spirit!" Such are the wishes that the pastor and the flock, the father and the children, give expression to at the moment of quitting each other. Do you know any better or more affecting?

Ite, Missa est. At length, the priest gives the signal for departure, saying: *Ite, Missa est.* The literal meaning of these words is: "Go, it is the dismissal," that is, "It is permitted you to leave, you may go." They have, as we already know, a higher meaning: "You may retire, the victim has been sent to heaven." At High Mass, it is the deacon that sings these words. He does so in the name of the priest or the bishop, whose principal minister he is. In the early ages, he warned the catechumens and sinners to leave the Church before the offering and the action of the sacrifice: it belongs to him therefore at the end of Mass to dismiss the faithful.

Formerly, *Ite, Missa est* was said when there was no other office after Mass: the people might then retire. But if there were any other prayers to be said or any ceremony to be performed, the priest or deacon, instead of *Ite, Missa est*, said, *Benedicamus Domino*—"Let us bless the Lord"; and in Masses for the dead, *Requiescant in pace*—"May they rest in peace!" Thus the faithful, instead of being warned that prayer was over, were engaged to remain in order to bless the Lord, or to entreat him to grant eternal rest and peace to the departed.

Nowadays, *Ite, Missa est* is said whenever the *Gloria in excelsis* is said at Mass. It is consequently regarded as a sign of joy and gladness. Such is doubtless the reason why it is suppressed on ferial days, and especially during Advent and Lent. On these occasions, *Benedicamus Domino* is said in order to invite the assistants to pray again, and to sanctify themselves by prayer, fasting, and penance. In Masses for the dead, *Requiescant in pace* is said, because the Church is wholly occupied with procuring for her deceased children the relief of which they stand in need.

The faithful, in reply to the *Ite, Missa est* or *Benedicamus Domino*, say: *Deo gratias*—"Thanks be to God!" Yes, they say, we retire with joy, and we bless, with hearts full of gratitude, the God who has laden us with benefits, by making us sharers in his holy mysteries! They imitate the apostles, who, having been blessed by their divine master, as he was ascending into heaven, returned full of joy, glorifying and thanking the Lord. After the *Requiescant in pace*, the people answer, "Amen," that is to say, "May it be as you desire, may the Lord hear your petitions, and give eternal peace to the souls suffering in purgatory."[489]

Mass is over. But it costs the priest something to quit the holy altar, and something to quit his faithful people. And the devotion of the priest and the people made two additions, which the Church subsequently authorized.[490]

The first is the following prayer, which the priest says for himself and for the people; he recites it in a low voice, with hands joined on the altar and eyes cast down: "May the homage of my total dependence be pleasing to thee, O Holy Trinity; and grant that the sacrifice which I, though unworthy, have offered in presence of Thy Divine Majesty, may be acceptable to thee, and, through thy mercy, may be a propitiation for me, and all those for whom I have offered it! Through Christ our Lord. Amen."

Blessing. This prayer being ended, the priest kisses the altar, raises his hands and eyes to heaven, and then, turning toward the people and extending his right hand, blesses them, by making the sign of the cross and saying: "May the Almighty God bless you: in the name of the Father, and of the Son, and of the Holy Ghost!" The people answer with their usual exclamation: "Amen!"—May God hear the petition that you have made for us! In Masses for the dead, the blessing is omitted: it cannot serve them since it is only for the assistants.

How beautiful are the ceremonies with which the priest accompanies this last blessing! He himself takes the blessing of Jesus Christ by kissing the altar, which represents him. He raises his eyes and hands to heaven, in order to show that it belongs to this eternal high priest, who sits at the right hand of the Most High, as the true Melchisedech, to bless the faithful people, the children of the true Abraham—to bless them for time and eternity, through the merits of his mysteries and his cross.

Gospel of St. John. The gospel of St. John is the second addition made to the Mass by the joint devotion of the priest and the faithful. From the beginning of the Church, Christians entertained the most profound veneration for the sublime words of the beloved disciple. St. Augustine did not disapprove of the custom, already established in his time, of laying this holy gospel on the heads of sick persons in order to cure them, and Pope Paul V commanded that, in visits to them, the gospel of St. John should be read, with imposition of hands. The pagans themselves, struck at the depth as well as the sublimity of the same gospel, used to say that it ought to be written in letters of gold in every place where men assembled, that it might be known to the whole world.

The faithful so earnestly desired that it should be read at the close of Mass that they expressly asked this in making foundations for churches.[491] The request soon became unnecessary. All priests recited the gospel before quitting the altar, and Pope St. Pius V made it a law to do so. It is recited every day, unless there is a double office on account of some festival. In this case, the gospel of the Mass that could not be said, is recited. For example, when the Assumption of the Blessed Virgin falls on a Sunday, the office of this solemn festival is celebrated; but the last gospel is that of the Sunday whose office is suppressed.

The recital of the gospel of St. John is accompanied with the same ceremonies as that of the ordinary gospel. At the beginning, the priest excites the attention of the faithful by saying to them: "The Lord be with you!" And the people answer: "And with your spirit!" The priest makes the sign of the cross with his thumb first on the chart containing the gospel, and then on his forehead, lips, and heart, in order to declare his love and his faith. He says at the same time: "Beginning of the gospel according to St. John!" The people answer: "Glory be to thee, O Lord!"

The priest resumes: "In the beginning was the Word, and the Word was with God, and the Word was God," etc.

When the priest says, "And the Word was made flesh," he makes a genuflection to honor the profound abasement of the divine Word, who, in order to redeem us, was pleased to humble himself so far as to take the form of a slave, that is to say, of man, the slave of the devil and of sin.

The idea of concluding the prayers of the holy sacrifice with the gospel of St. John is full of wisdom and piety. In point of fact, this gospel is a summary of all that the Word has done for us in eternity and in time. It shows him to us in the bosom of his Father, God of God, by whom all things were made, the life and the light of the world. It shows him come down on earth, the true sun of justice that shines on darkness and enlightens those who sit in the shadow of death. It reminds us that it is through him we are the children of God, for he was made flesh and dwelt amongst us that he might free us from the slavery of sin, and rescue us from eternal perdition. We have seen his glory in the crib, on Thabor, on Calvary, at the sepulchre; we see it daily in the Holy Eucharist: and we praise and bless him, because he is full of grace and truth.[492]

At the end of the gospel of St. John, all the people answer by the mouth of the clerk: *Deo gratias*—"We return thanks to God!" This short prayer is so holy, so perfect, and so worthy of God, that the celebration of the greatest of mysteries could not be closed with an expression more divine. "What can we think," asks St. Augustine, "what can we say, what can we write better than *Deo gratias*, 'thanks be to God'? No, we cannot say anything shorter, hear anything pleasanter, imagine anything nobler, do anything more useful or fruitful than what is expressed by the prayer, *Deo gratias,* 'thanks be to God!'"[493]

Oh, yes, thanks be to God, heaven is reconciled with earth! The august victim, expected during four thousand years, has just been immolated: God has received it by sacrifice; men, by Communion. Thanks be to the Father, who has given us his Son; thanks be to the Son, who has clothed himself with our nature; thanks be to the Holy Ghost, who has sanctified us in Jesus Christ! Thanks be to the three Persons of the adorable Trinity for all their gifts, for all their infinite mercies, of which the Catholic sacrifice is an abridgment!

Relations between the ceremonies of the sixth part of the Mass and the circumstances of the passion.—Let us terminate this last part of the Mass, like the preceding ones, with some pious comparisons between this part of the Sacrifice of the Altar and the circumstances of the sacrifice of the cross. The priest takes the ablutions: Jesus is embalmed. The priest, after the Communion, moves to the epistle side: Jesus rises again. The priest turns toward the faithful that he may say, *Dominus vobiscum*: Jesus appears to his disciples. The priest says the collect: Jesus converses several times with his disciples. The priest says the last *Dominus vobiscum*: Jesus bids farewell to his apostles and ascends into heaven. The priest blesses the people: Jesus sends down the Holy Ghost. The priest says the gospel of St. John: Jesus, crowned with glory, reigns triumphant in heaven and watches over his Church.[494]

Sentiments that ought to prevail in our hearts.—It is needless to say that gratitude is the sentiment that ought to prevail in our hearts during the last part of Mass. Do we wish to make this sentiment livelier? Let us rouse our faith by the following questions: Who has just been immolated? For whom has he been immolated? Why has he been immolated? By being immolated, what has he given me?

Let us meditate on these things, and having done so, can we avoid saying with St. Paul: "If anyone love not our Savior Jesus, let him be anathema!"[495]

How we should go away from Mass.—And now, how ought we to go away from Mass? What degree of sanctity ought to reign in our thoughts, in our desires, in our words, in our looks, in all our relations with God and the neighbor? Let us not forget ourselves.

Heaven, earth, and hell have their eyes fixed on us: heaven, to rejoice in our happiness; earth, to be edified by our virtues; and hell, to rob us of the fruits of the sacrifice. How much vigilance should we display!

Let us beware of rejoicing hell, grieving heaven, and causing the Christian name to be blasphemed among men. Let us live as we should have lived on the day of the crucifixion of the man-God, if we had been present at his immolation on Calvary. When leaving the church, we descend the same mountain, we have assisted at the same sacrifice. Shall we be like the Jews, who departed from Calvary blinder and more hardened; or like the centurion, who proclaimed aloud the glory of the Son of God; or like Mary and John, whose love for the Savior increased with the sorrows of which they were witnesses? Let us take our choice.

PRAYER

O my God! who art all love, I thank thee for letting thyself be immolated for me on Calvary, and for daily renewing thy sacrifice on our altars. I beseech thee to infuse into my heart the dispositions of thine own, when thou wast dying on the cross.

I am resolved to love God above all things, and my neighbor as myself for the love of God; and, in testimony of this love, I will depart from Mass profoundly recollected.

Lesson 24: Christianity Brought before the Senses (Continued)—Our Daily Festival

The days of the week considered from the standpoint of faith: They are festivals.—Sunday is the leading festival of Christianity. We have just explained in detail the divine office and the august sacrifice by which the Church wishes that it should be sanctified. In a certain sense, the other days of the week are also festivals. The universe is a temple, and man a priest, whose life ought to be one long festival: such is the idea of the fathers of the Church.

"Tell me," said Origen to the Christians of his time, "you who go to Church only on solemn days, are not the other days also festivals? Are they not also Lord's days, 'Sundays'? It is the affair of the Jews to distinguish days. Hence, the Lord declared to them that he held their calends and their days of rest in abhorrence. Christians, on the contrary, consider all days as Lord's days, and even as Easter days, because the heavenly Lamb is immolated for them daily, and they eat him daily. And if the sacrifice is made about sunset, according to the law of Moses, it is because the present life is like a day on its decline, a night that is to be followed by the day of the sun of justice, at whose rising we shall enter an ocean of joy, we shall begin an eternal festival."[496]

Two things follow from these beautiful words: a) that religion, completed by our Lord, has developed all the old law, so that, if the Jews had certain festivals, they were only a shadow of what should occur under the gospel, when every day would be a festival, on which men should abstain from offending God; and b) that festivals and life itself are only an apprenticeship for the joys of heaven—that time is the vigil of eternity, since it is only with a view to eternity that life is given to man or time to the human race—that we can always nourish ourselves here with the incarnate Word, as is done in heaven.

Keeping to the idea that life is only one long festival, on which we should be as pious and holy as may be expected on particular solemnities, Origen continues thus: "The Christian who understands his religion is convinced that every day is a Sunday for him, since he thereon gives his mind and heart wholly to the Lord; that every day is a Friday for him, and even a Good Friday, since he thereon subdues his passions and receives in his body the marks of the cross of Jesus Christ; that every day is an Easter Sunday for him, since he continually strives, by nourishing himself with the doctrine and the flesh of the incarnate Word, to separate himself from this world of corruption, and to pass into an invisible and incorruptible world; and, lastly, that every day is a Pentecost for him, since, risen in spirit with Jesus Christ, he has been carried with him to heaven, even to the throne of the Father, where he sits with Jesus Christ, and in Jesus Christ, by whom he receives the plenitude of the Holy Ghost."[497]

All the days of the year are therefore holy days, festival days. "But," adds the same Father, "as a great many Christians would not or could not resolve on spending their whole life as a single festival, it was necessary, in order to make allowances for weakness, to fix on some particular festivals. The Church, in her maternal solicitude, appointed them, so that the most distracted and lukewarm might thereon acquire new vigor, by disengaging themselves, at least for a little while, from the affairs of this world. Yet these days, according to the expression of St. Paul, are only parts of one day, parts of that continual festival which the just celebrate all their life and the blessed celebrate in eternity."[498]

Life is the vigil of eternity.—Such is the sublime idea that Christianity gives us of the world and of time. The world is a temple, and life is a festival, but a festival during which fallen man should strive to recover himself. To characterize the life of a Christian under the gospel, the doctors of the Church add:

"It is a truth equally important and indisputable that the religious worship of the deity had greater scope and liberty, and was less hampered by particular times, years, weeks, days, places, temples, and altars, in the first ages of the world than at any later period. We know with how many prescriptions it was straitened under the Mosaic law. The Church observes a mean between the synagogue and heaven or the state of innocence.

"Under the gospel therefore we are in a kind of intermediate state, which lets us regain some of our original innocence, but not all. What is more, we expect in the future life a liberty quite different from that of our first state, because God alone will there be our temple and we shall be his temple. We shall enter into his joy and into his rest, of which all the festivals of the state of innocence, the synagogue, and the Church herself, will only have been shadows. On festivals here below, God traces again in us by justification an image of our early purity as well as the liberty and happiness in which he created man. We thus acquire some traits of that perfect sanctity and liberty which he has prepared for us in heaven. The just therefore aspire now both to the first and the last state of the holy liberty of the children of God."[499]

How we are to celebrate it.—But how are we to make our life on earth a continual festival? how celebrate it worthily? We must, according to the idea of the fathers, bear in mind that the whole course of ages is only one great festival, all whose moments are consecrated to God; that, everything having come from God, everything belongs to him and should return to him; that, wherever we are, we are in the temple of God, we walk in his presence, we live in him and by him; that whether we eat or drink, or whatsoever else we do, we should refer all to God, we should give him the homage of all; that the love of truth and justice, which is the love of God himself, should fill our souls in joy as well as in sorrow, in prosperity as well as in adversity; that a divine flame should continually burn in our hearts as on an altar purer and richer than the holiest and grandest altar of earth.

The celebration of this perpetual festival, which makes up the life of the just and should make up the life of all mankind, finds no obstacle in manual labor, humble employment, servile work. For the just man, animated with charity, is free—free with the freedom of the children of God: no work of his is servile. Whether he prunes his vine, or tills his field, or sails over the sea, he does not cease to celebrate the continual festival of the just, since he does not cease in the midst of his occupations to love and praise his heavenly Father. If various works are forbidden on particular festivals, it is that temporal cares may not interfere with meditation and prayer.

The life of man here below is therefore a festival, but a festival that he ought to celebrate as a brave warrior, ever winning new victories; as a poor exile, ever journeying on toward his native land; as a fallen king, ever striving to reascend his throne. For the Christian, that is to say, for the man who understands his destiny, the festival of life is therefore, if we may so speak, a painful festival. But cheer up, O man! cheer up, O warrior, exile, king! in good time thou shalt bear thy palm, thou shalt see thy home, thou shalt wear thy crown!

Pagan names for the days of the week.—What deep philosophy in this idea that religion gives us of our temporal existence! How much it elevates our thoughts and affections! How much it ennobles us, and encourages us to virtue! Now, this splendid idea man had unfortunately lost. He had made his life a festival of devils, and his temporary existence was only an introduction to the horrible festival of hell. In his blindness, he had distinguished each day of the week by the name of some infamous creature or deity, to whose worship he consecrated it. The first of these days he dedicated to the sun; the second to the moon; the third to Mars; the fourth to Mercury; the fifth to Jupiter; the sixth to Venus; the seventh to Saturn. All these names, laden with shameful memories and defiled by horrible sacrifices, gave rise to crime after crime, and led guilty man farther and farther away from his Creator.

Christian names for the days of the week; profound wisdom of the Church.—The Catholic Church, the universal benefactress, hastened to destroy the gods and to banish their names from human speech. She designated each day of the week by a single word, *feria*, a word full of deep meaning, for it is the same as "festival" or "rest": festival, we know why; rest, because every day of life ought to be a cessation from the labor of sin, from the labor of ruin and disorder to which the human race rushed like a maniac after falling under the power of the devil. In the language of the Church, the first day of the week was called "the Lord's day," or "the first feria"; Monday, "the second feria"; Tuesday, "the third feria"; Wednesday, "the fourth feria"; Thursday, "the fifth feria"; Friday, "the sixth feria." The seventh day retained the name of "the sabbath," which means "rest," and which recalled the Jewish traditions and the Lord's rest after the creation.[500]

Thenceforth, life and the days marking it out told man by their new names the object of time, and the employments in which it should be spent. The Church left no stone unturned to banish from civil language the profane names given to the days, so well did she understand the effect of words, and so much had she at heart the rehabilitation of society. She wished to deprive paganism even of its last means of exercising its pernicious influence.

The quick genius of St. Augustine soon seized the idea of the Catholic Church. "Would to God!" he cried out, "that Christians were Christians in their language, and that we should never more hear the days of the week called by pagan names. Let us speak the language that is our own; let us not profane our lips with names that savor of idolatry. Let all our days warn us by their names that they are days of rest, festivals, and that our whole life is a festival consecrated to the God of all sanctity."[501]

Happy for Europe if she had followed in this matter, as well as in that of pagan studies, the advice of the great doctor! She would not have become pagan; and we should not be on the verge of frightful catastrophes, the well-deserved punishments of the apostasy of nations.[502]

Devotions connected with each day of the week: Sunday.—It was not enough for the Church to have banished the language of idolatry. A tender-hearted and intelligent mother, she knew well the weakness of her children. To keep their fervor continually exercised by new motives, a special devotion was attached to each feria by pious and ancient traditions. Sunday or the first feria was, of all times, particularly consecrated to the Lord.

Monday. In the beginning of the Middle Ages, Monday or the second feria was consecrated to the special worship of the Son of God, the eternal Wisdom. Later on, it was dedicated to the Holy Ghost, in order to implore his help at the beginning of the labors of the week. Lastly, it is now consecrated to the relief of the faithful departed; but this is a free and voluntary devotion, of which the Church approves, without prescribing it.

Tuesday. Tuesday or the third feria is generally consecrated to the worship of the holy angels, especially the guardian angels. Do you see how ingeniously piety strives to fill man with touching recollections, with noble ideas of himself, with deep sentiments of gratitude? Now, believe me, the man who is made grateful is made good.[503]

Wednesday. Wednesday or the fourth feria is the day chosen by piety to honor St. Joseph and to beg the grace of a happy death. Since the apostolic times, Wednesday has been an object of particular devotion both in the Eastern and the Western Church.[504] It used to be a station day, that is to say, a day of fasting and of assembly in places of prayer or at the tombs of martyrs. People went there very early in the morning and did not leave till after the hour of none, when the office and little fast of the day ended. This fast was called a "little fast," because it was three hours shorter than the fast of Lent, Quarter Tense, and the eves of great festivals, and it was not of such strict obligation, at least in the West.[505]

History of fasting and abstinence on Wednesdays and Fridays. The same exercises of piety and penance were observed on Friday, the sixth feria. Would you like to know why the Church consecrated these two days to revive the piety of her children by fasting and prayer? It was in memory of what had occurred to our Lord on the day before the eve and on the day itself of his passion. On Wednesday, she reminded her children of the council of the Jews in which it was resolved to put Jesus to death; on Friday, she showed them the execution of their murderous design. The Church therefore thought—and who can blame her?—that the crimes of men, the true cause of the death of the Son of God, would be a subject of grief and penance to her children on these days of the week, as his resurrection was a subject of consolation and joy for them on Sunday.[506]

The Greek Church, in spite of all the tribulations and revolutions from which she has suffered, has maintained to the present time the custom of fasting on every Wednesday and Friday of the year, with hardly an exception. In the Latin Church, the fast of these two days, having remained free till the ninth century, was then changed into a simple abstinence. That of Friday was soon afterward regarded as obligatory, and passed into a law. The abstinence of Wednesday and Saturday remained free till the fourteenth century. But the abstinence of Wednesday having been gradually done away with, that of Saturday grew so general that it became in many countries as settled as that of Friday.[507]

Thursday. To Thursday or the fifth feria there clings, as you are aware, a memory so consoling that the faithful have honored this day with special fervor. It was on Thursday that the Son of God instituted the Sacrament of the Blessed Eucharist, in which he bequeathed forever to the human race his flesh to eat and his blood to drink: an august sacrament, which made the Savior, triumphing in heaven, the companion of our pilgrimage and the prisoner of his love in our tabernacles. Since the institution of Corpus Christi, the Thursdays of the year seem to have been destined to renew this festival, as well by public offices as by private devotions. Nearly all the other Thursdays of the year have become in regard to Corpus Christi what all other Sundays are in regard to Easter; that is to say, the former are like a continual octave of the mystery of the Eucharist, as the latter are of the resurrection.

Friday. Friday or the sixth feria is consecrated to the passion. In part of Christendom, law courts were closed on this day;[508] for the fast thereon was observed as well in the East as in the West till the ninth century. At this period, it was changed into a simple abstinence. But the Church made so strict a law regarding this abstinence that she dispenses from it only when Christmas falls on a Friday.

With the abstinence, the faithful were accustomed to join on this day, about three o'clock in the afternoon, the recital of five *Paters* and *Aves*, in honor of the five wounds of our Lord.

Saturday. Saturday was, during many ages, kept like Sunday, and this for several reasons. First, to honor the Lord's rest after the creation, and to remind man that he too, an image of God, created in a manner during this life, will one day enter the sabbath or eternal rest figured by the seventh day. Next, it called to mind that the Savior had often chosen the sabbath to work cures, and to preach in synagogues. It was this last consideration that determined the emperor Constantine on making his law to have special honor paid to Saturday.[509]

History of fasting and abstinence on Saturdays. In the Church of Rome, this day was consecrated to fasting. The same was the case at Alexandria in Egypt. These two Churches, one founded by St. Peter, and the other by his disciple St. Mark, having the same practice, are a new proof of the fact to which their origin is traced. The ancient Romans said that St. Peter—it was during his first visit to Rome, whither St. Mark had accompanied him—before contending with Simon the Magician on a Sunday, fasted the previous Saturday, and ordered all the faithful to imitate him. In memory of the triumph won by the holy apostle over the champion of the devil, the usage of fasting on Saturday was retained:[510] it has been preserved during many centuries.

But if the fast was peculiar to the Church of Rome, it was not so with the abstinence. From the eleventh century—in a council at Rome in 1078—Pope St. Gregory VIII made it a law for the whole Church.[511] Yet this law was not observed everywhere. Several provinces of Christendom were permitted to continue the habit of eating meat on Saturday. In the fifteenth century, St. Antoninus, archbishop of Florence, examining the obligation of abstinence on Saturday, made this answer: "It is a sin to eat meat on this day in countries where the custom of not eating it is generally established; but a person living in a country where the contrary custom exists, as in Catalonia and many other places, need have no scruple about eating it there."[512]

In France, the law of abstinence on Saturday became general. There was no exception, save in some dioceses for the Saturdays between Christmas and the Purification. Hitherto, Spain has introduced no modifications as regards the liberty of eating meat on Saturday beyond this, that the intestines and extremities of animals may be used.[513] The abstinence of Saturday, though less general than that of Friday, should not be less religiously observed. The authority that prescribed both is the same: the authority of our holy mother the Church, of whom the Savior himself said: "If any one will not obey the Church, let him be to you as the heathen and the publican."[514]

As you see, Saturday has been held in great veneration among the faithful since the beginning of the Church.[515] Toward the close of the eleventh century—in 1095—Pope Urban II, wishing to draw down, through the intercession of Mary, the blessings of heaven on the Crusades, dedicated Saturday to her, and commanded that the office of the Blessed Virgin should be celebrated on this day.[516] Since his time, the faithful have made it a duty to consecrate Saturday in honor of Mary, so as to testify their affection and gratitude toward this divine Mother by fasting, assisting at the Holy Sacrifice of the Mass, or some other exercise of piety: nothing more tender or useful.[517]

Thus, every day of the week brings the Christian a new motive of fervor and sanctity. Do you not think that this way of distinguishing days is as moral as that of worldly people, who distinguish theirs only by the variety of their business or of their pleasures?

The Catholic calendar: Its beauty and utility.—What the Church did for every day of the week, she also did for the months and years. Set out from the principle that weak and inconstant man has continual need of new motives to excite him to virtue; that all states having their peculiar trials and duties, men of all states must have models of sanctity; that the life of man is an endless alternation of adversity and prosperity, in which there are few joys and many sorrows: and you cannot help admiring the Catholic calendar. What a high teaching of virtue, what an inexhaustible source of consolation, what a variety of motives and models, it presents to men of all times and conditions!

The heathenish impiety of the last century was well aware of the influence that it sought to destroy, when, in its blind hatred of Christianity,[518] it proscribed the calendar, and tried to replace our Christian festivals by festivals such as those of the Goddess of Reason; our Catholic models, by plants, agricultural implements, inanimate creatures; the names of our saints, by names such as that of Marat.[519] Time, and a very short time, did justice to this base project. Ah! if you love man—if you understand man, his destiny, his weakness, his struggles, his pains—let him look for examples, let him look for encouragement and consolation, where he can find them; and acknowledge that, after the worship of God, that of the saints is one of the most admirable institutions for which public morals are indebted to Catholicity.

Where can you find a richer or more varied succession of virtues than in the *Lives of the Saints*? They are simple virtues, within the reach of all, having as their object the happiness of all, suitable in every age and condition, offering to rich and poor, the fortunate and the unfortunate, works to imitate and the same reward to expect, and withal so divinely attractive as to move the soul to follow them, and to labor for the attainment of an end at once most social and most Christian.

Thanks to the Catholic calendar, there is no day of the year when the pilgrim of eternity, the exile of heaven, the combatant of evil, is abandoned to himself! There is no day when he does not receive in some manner a visit from a just man, who offers him all his good deeds as a tribute of respect. Thus, the religious year cannot pass without all the virtues of which man is capable being set before him, and the most perfect code of morals in every relation of life taught to him.

Christian parents! ah, you have perhaps too often forgotten the immense fruit that you might reap from such a worship for the happiness of your children. What an excellent lesson on equality, sobriety, obedience, charity, and modesty, would the daily reading of the *Lives of the Saints* be for them! How much more useful would their example be to them than that of the heroes of novels, or even that of the leading characters of profane history, so often disfigured by the imperfection of their works! How powerfully they would be urged on to do the good that they saw practiced before their eyes; for there is a strange secret grace, a kind of voice from heaven, accompanying the simple record of the works of the just!

It is impossible, especially at an early age, not to yield to the wish of being like them. How can we doubt that this wish, tended by a mother's care, will prove in children a germ of the purest virtue, and for parents a source of the most abundant consolations? Need we mention the names of St. Augustine, St. Ignatius, St. Teresa, and so many others who, on reading the *Lives of the Saints*, could no longer delay their return to religion? Need we recall those miracles of sanctity which will be the admiration of all time?

And then, again, see what a grand lesson on equity there is in the *Lives of the Saints*! The Catholic calendar is like a revelation of the judgment of God: all virtues are honored therein. Among our saints, you see not only hermits, pontiffs, and martyrs, but masters and servants, rich and poor, men of retirement and men of the world, magistrates and warriors, virgins and wives, learned and ignorant, Greeks and barbarians. Every condition, every clime, every century is represented. Every virtue, whether it comes from the East or the West, the hut or the palace, the past or the present, alike finds its place.

Has the favor of the lower or the higher order ever had influence here? Has wealth ever given a more distinguished rank or the sword of a despot ever written a name here? Is not the shepherdess of Nanterre, the humble Genevieve, here seated above the race of our queens? And if St. Louis is honored on our altars, was it his royalty that set him there? He was the support of the weak and the defense of the oppressed; he carried the poor in his heart; he loved God and men; he was just: behold why religion crowned him a second time! Thus, the hero vanishes before the Christian, and none of his virtues survive him but those which deserve to survive him, and to be set up as a pattern for all mankind.[520]

The Catholic calendar is therefore a school of all virtues, a guidebook from earth to heaven, a cicerone on the road of life, saying to man at every hour and in every tone of voice: "See the footprints that the saints left for you when they were journeying home. Follow them. On the right hand and the left are precipices."[521]

PRAYER

O my God! who art all love, I thank thee for having given me in the *Lives of the Saints* and day after day all the year round some new examples and new motives to sanctify me. Grant me the grace to profit of them for thy glory and the welfare of my brethren.

I am resolved to love God above all things, and my neighbor as myself for the love of God; and, in testimony of this love, I will daily read something from the *Lives of the Saints*.

Lesson 25: Christianity Brought before the Senses (Continued)—Advent Customs

The life of man ought to be a continual festival. Every day and every hour that goes to make it up ought to be sanctified, so that every moment of our existence may be a hymn to the glory of him who created us. But such is our weakness, such the multitude of our occupations, such the violence of our passions, that the Church, in her anxiety, fixed on some particular days and seasons when we should take more than ordinary care to purify our souls by prayer, fasting, and meditation on eternal truths. This is what we have seen in the foregoing lessons.

Advent.—In the first rank of these salutary periods, we must place the time of Advent. It is a time of prayer and penance, which the Church appointed to prepare her children for the birth of the Savior. What vigils are to ordinary festivals, what Lent is to Easter, what the four thousand years of the ancient world were to the coming of the Messias, that Advent is to Christmas. Four weeks of preparation will not seem too long to you, if you consider the excellence of the mystery that follows them. If the people of Israel should prepare so carefully to receive the law promulgated on Sinai, to cross the Jordan on their way to the promised land, to partake of weak victims, or to celebrate their figurative festivals, how do you think ought Christians to prepare to receive the God of heaven, the eternal Word, the supreme legislator, the spotless victim, the everlasting type of all festivals and sacrifices?

Antiquity of Advent; practices of devotion and penance. Full of these great ideas, the Church instituted Advent to smooth the way for the Messias into our hearts. The institution of Advent would seem as old as that of the festival of Christmas, though the discipline of the Church on this point has not been always the same. For several centuries, Advent consisted of forty days, like Lent: it began on St. Martin's day. Faithful to old customs, the Church of Milan kept up the six weeks of the primitive Advent, which had been adopted by the Church of Spain. At an early period, the Church of Rome reduced the time to four weeks, that is, to four Sundays, with the part of the week remaining before Christmas. All the West followed this example.

Formerly, a fast was observed throughout Advent. In some countries, this fast was of precept for everyone; in others, of simple devotion. The obligation of fasting is attributed to St. Gregory the Great, who had not, however, the intention of making it a general law. In the middle of the fifth century—462—St. Perpetuus, bishop of Tours, commanded that there should be three fast days weekly in his diocese from the festival of St. Martin to Christmas. This rule became general in the Church of France till the seventh century, after the holding of the Council of Mâcon in 581. The holy assembly prescribed that a fast should be observed on the Monday, Wednesday, and Friday of each week, from the feria or festival of St. Martin[522] to the Nativity of Our Lord; and that the offices, especially the Sacrifice of the Mass, should then be celebrated as in Lent. The use of flesh meat was forbidden every day during Advent.

The same abstinence was observed in other Catholic regions: as a pious donation proves for us. In 753, Astolphus, king of the Lombards, having granted the waters of Nonantula to an abbey of the same name, reserved forty pike to furnish his own table during St. Martin's Lent. We may hence infer that, in the eighth century, the Lombards observed the fast during the forty days before Christmas, or at least abstained from flesh meat.

Prayer and other practices of penance were joined to fasting. "Among us," says an ancient writer, "from the festival of St. Martin to that of Christmas, there is an abstinence from flesh meat commanded to all the children of the Church, as an indispensable condition for approaching the sacraments on the day of our Lord's birth."[523] Pope Boniface VIII, in the bull of the canonization of St. Louis, declared that this worthy successor of Charlemagne spent the days of Advent in fasting and prayer. Such was the conduct of the simple faithful.

As for religious, they fasted as in Lent: many of them continue the pious usage to this day. We shall add that it has always been so. It is they, whose days are all a preparation for eternal things, that adhere to the strict observances of preparation; it is they that, no longer engaged in the conflict, take care of their armor. And they whose life is a distraction, a series of pleasures and dangers, lay down their arms, and stand no longer on their guard against the enemy![524]

The Church neglects no means of reviving in her children the fervor of their ancestors. Is it not just? Is the little babe whom we expect less beautiful, less holy, less worthy of our love now than formerly? Has he ceased to be the friend of pure hearts? Is his coming into our souls less needed? Alas! perhaps we have raised there all the idols that, eighteen centuries ago, he came to overturn. Let us therefore be more wise. Let us enter into the views of the Church: let us consider how this tender mother redoubles her solicitude to form in us those dispositions of penance and charity which are necessary for a proper reception of the babe of Bethlehem.

Liturgy of Advent.—In the offices of this season, she lays aside her ornaments of joy and takes purple as a sign of compunction. The *Gloria in excelsis* is omitted at Mass; but her sadness is sweetened with hope. This is the reason why at Mass on Sunday she repeats the *Alleluia*. She dispenses with it on ferias, so as to remind us of penance—so as to say daily to Christians: "As all the days of Advent were days of fasting and abstinence with your ancestors, let them at least be days of repentance and prayer with you."

First Sunday of Advent. With a view to excite in our souls this twofold sentiment of hope and compunction, lo! one after another, the voice of Paul, the voice of Isaias, the voice of John on the banks of the Jordan, and the voice of the Messias himself, blend with the exhortations of preachers and the hymns of the Church. "It is time to rouse ourselves, the hour of our redemption is at hand, the night is past, the day begins to dawn. Let us make haste therefore to lay aside the works of darkness and to put on the armor of light. Let us walk honestly and decently, as befits the day. Yield not to vice, but clothe yourselves with our Lord Jesus Christ."[525] Such are the warnings given us by the apostle St. Paul in the epistle of the First Sunday of Advent.

To make this lesson more impressive, the Church reminds us, in the gospel, of the last judgment and the second coming of the Son of God. She seems to say to us: "If you wish to behold without fear the arrival of that God whom I announce to you, when he shall come as the supreme judge of the living and the dead, prepare to receive him now that he comes as a Savior. Happy shall you be if you take my advice; for see what dreadful things are to happen at his second coming! There shall be signs in the sun, in the moon, and in the stars. The nations of the earth shall be terrified. Men shall wither away in expectation of what is going to befall them. The pillars of heaven shall be shaken. Then shall the Son of Man be seen coming on a cloud with great power and majesty. As for you, when you witness these things, lift up your heads, for your redemption is at hand. Judge of this by a comparison of the fig tree and other trees. When you see them budding, you say that summer is near. In like manner, when you see what I announce to you, know that the kingdom of God is near. Verily, I say to you, this generation shall not pass away till these things are accomplished, heaven and earth shall pass away, but my words shall never pass away."

Could the Church find a truth more capable of striking souls with dread and obliging Christians to enter into themselves? But she wishes that with the tears of repentance and the fears of judgment there should be mingled the sighs and the consolations of hope. And hence, at the evening office, she lets them appear in the hymn, *Creator alme siderum*, whose notes and words express a deep but sweet melancholy:

> O mighty Creator of the stars, O eternal light of believers, O Jesus, the Redeemer of all, hear the petitions of thy servants!
>
> Thou who, impelled by thy love to keep the world from being lost through the malice of Satan, didst prepare a remedy for the afflicted human race!
>
> To expiate the crime common to the whole human race, thou didst come forth, a spotless victim, from the sanctuary of a Virgin, and go to the cross!
>
> At thy name—a name of power and glory—heaven and earth, trembling, bend the knee!
>
> O sovereign judge, secure us, we beseech thee, on the last day, under the armor of grace from on high, against the arrows of our enemies!
>
> Glory, honor, and praise be to God the Father, with the Son and the Comforter, forever and ever!

All the people, who in the morning trembled at the thought of the Valley of Josaphat, feel an exquisite thrill of hope in the evening on having a glimpse of the crib of Bethlehem; and a thousand innocent songs express their sentiments. Witness the popular canticle that young and old are so delighted to repeat in the evening at the fireside:

> Come, O divine Messias! and change our hapless days;
> Come, O source of life! come, come, come, etc.

Second Sunday of Advent. On the Second Sunday of Advent, the Church continues her instructions. They become more and more precise as the great event draws nigh: it is the gleams of light becoming clearer before the full break of day. In the epistle, the voice of the great apostle is again heard. He announces that the Messias is sent to fulfill all figures and to unite Jews and Gentiles in one fold.

The gospel sets before us the precursor pointing out, in the Person of Jesus Christ, the Redeemer expected during four thousand years. He knows the Lamb of God; but his disciples do not know him. Anxious for their instruction, he sent two of them to Jesus, with orders to ask this question and await an answer: "Art thou he that is to come, or are we to look for another?" Jesus, having wrought in their presence many miracles, by which, according to Isaias, the Messias should be recognized, answered them: "Go and tell John what you have seen. The blind see, the lame walk, the lepers are cleansed, the deaf hear, the dead rise again; to the poor the gospel is preached: and blessed is he that shall not be scandalized in me!"

Third Sunday of Advent. The nearer we come to the solemn moment when the Messias shall make his entry into the world, the more the Church multiplies her exhortations. On the Third Sunday, St. Paul again speaks to us in the epistle, and invites us to joy: the dawn of our deliverance shines bright above the horizon. He wishes that with joy we should unite prayer—in other words, that ardent desire which draws God to us and will open the door of our hearts to the Messias. In the gospel, St. John the Baptist, more than a prophet, no longer foretells the Messias, but says that he is already in the world. In point of fact, he was already among the Jews; and we adore him in his Mother's womb when we hear this gospel. The precursor adds a remark that is, alas! verified even to this day: "He is in the midst of you and you know him not."

Then, borrowing the voice of Isaias, he makes the vaults of our temples resound, as formerly he awoke the echoes of the Jordan, with these words: "The voice of one crying in the desert: Make straight the ways of the Lord, bring low the hills and fill up the valleys, that is to say, prepare your minds, your hearts, and your senses, for the reception of the liberator. Behold he cometh, and I am not worthy to loose the latchet of his shoe." And yet he who uses this language is the greatest among the children of men! Oh, how holy is our Lord, and how careful should we be in preparing ourselves to receive him!

Fourth Sunday of Advent. At length, on the Fourth Sunday, when the divine child is just about to enter the world, when this amiable spouse is already knocking at the door of our hearts, the Church concludes her instructions by saying: "All flesh shall see the Savior sent of God." These entrancing words mean: "Be ready, the times are accomplished, the sun of justice and truth is about to shine above the horizon; his light will burst over all men, without distinction of rich or poor, learned or ignorant; yet a moment, be ready." Hence, let us not content ourselves with admiring the wisdom with which the Church graduates her instructions during Advent: let us enter into her spirit, let us increase in fervor and recollection as we draw nearer to the birth of the Desired of Nations, who should also be the desired of our souls.

Festival of the Expectation. To make our sighs ardent, like those of the patriarchs, and to fix our thoughts on the wonderful event that is going to occur, the Church tells us to sing the great or O antiphons and to celebrate the festival of the Expectation. This twofold celebration begins on the 17th of December and continues until Christmas Eve. Before and after the *Magnificat* at vespers, we sing these solemn antiphons, commonly called the "O antiphons," because they begin with the exclamation "O." The day following that on which the first is sung, namely, the 18th of December, is the festival of the Expectation. Everything most glorious and at the same time most beautiful that the writers of the old and the new testament say of the Blessed Virgin, everything most proper to inspire us with filial confidence and affection toward the sweet Mother of the Desired of Nations, is found in the admirable office of this festival.

The O antiphons. The great antiphons, on their part, lead our thoughts and sighs to the divine child whom the Virgin of Juda is to give to the world. By their variety, they express the various characteristics of the Messias and the various wants of the human race.

Man, since his fall, has been a fool, with hardly any knowledge and with very little relish for true goods. His conduct excites alarm and pity: he has need of wisdom. The Church asks wisdom for him by the first antiphon: *O Sapientia*—"O Wisdom that camest forth from the mouth of the Most High, that attainest thy end mightily and disposest all things sweetly! come and teach us the way of prudence."

Man, since his fall, has been a slave of the devil: he has need of a liberator. The Church asks a liberator for him by the second antiphon: *O Adonai*—"O powerful God,

Leader of the House of Israel! who didst appear in the burning bush to Moses and give thy law on Sinai, come and redeem us by the strength of thine arm!"

Man, since his fall, has been sold to iniquity: he has need of a Redeemer. The Church asks a Redeemer for him by the third antiphon: O *Radix Jesse*—"O Root of Jesse! set up as a standard before the nations, in whose presence kings are silent, to whom the Gentiles will offer their prayers, come and redeem us, do not delay!"

Man, since his fall, has been a prisoner, locked down in the gloomy dungeon of error and death: he has need of a key to open the door. The Church asks a key for him by the fourth antiphon: O *Clavis David*—"O Key of David and Scepter of the House of Israel! who openest and none can shut, who shuttest and none can open, come and release the prisoner, the wretch that sitteth in darkness and the shadow of death!"

Man, since his fall, has been blind: he has need of sight. The Church asks sight for him by the fifth antiphon: O *Oriens*—"O Orient, Splendor of Eternal Light and Sun of Justice! come and enlighten those who sit in darkness and the shadow of death!"

Man, since his fall, has been a great ruin: he has need of a restorer. The Church asks a restorer for him by the seventh antiphon: O *Rex gentium*—"O King of Nations, God and Savior of Israel, Cornerstone uniting Jews and Gentiles in one building! come and save man, whom thou didst form from the slime of the earth!"

Man, since his fall, has bowed his head under the yoke of all kinds of tyrants: he has need of a just legislator. The Church asks a just legislator for him by the eighth antiphon: O *Emmanuel*—"O Emmanuel, our King and our Legislator, the Expected of Nations, the Object of all our desires! come and save us, O Lord our God!"[526]

Do you know anything more tender, or more replete with meaning, than these magnificent invocations? It seems to us, at all events, that one of the best preparations for the festival of Christmas is often to repeat these beautiful antiphons, and to let our souls be penetrated with the sentiments which they express. Oh, yes! if we wish to spend the time of Advent in a holy manner, let us unite our sighs with those of the Church, the patriarchs, the prophets, and the just of the old law. Let us adopt some of their burning words. Let us make them our aspirations every day, and, if possible, every hour of the day, so that God may be able to say of each of us, "Behold a man of desires," and he will hear us. If we prefer to do so, let us choose one of the following aspirations. They are equally proper to form in us those dispositions which the Church expects: "I beseech thee, O Lord, send him whom thou art to send!" "Come, Lord Jesus, and do not delay!" "O ye heavens, open, and let fall the dew!" "O divine infant Jesus, come and be born in my heart, to drive out sin and to place thy virtues there!"

To prayer, let us add greater recollection, a more constant vigilance. Let us enter our heart more frequently, to purify and adorn it, thinking that it is to become the cradle of the divine babe. But the great preparation is the renunciation of sin, especially mortal sin. What can there be in common between the Son of Mary and a heart defiled with iniquity?

Let us hear St. Charles exhorting his people to sanctify Advent, and apply to ourselves the words of this great archbishop:

"During Advent, we ought to prepare ourselves to receive the Son of God quitting the bosom of his Father, in order to become man and to converse with us. We ought daily to steal a little time from our affairs, that we may meditate on the following questions: Who comes? Whence does he come? How does he come? Why does he come? What should be the fruit of his coming? Let all our desires call on him with the just and the prophets of the old testament, who longed for him so much; and, to open a way for him into our hearts, let us purify ourselves by confession, fasting, and Communion.

"Let us not forget that formerly people fasted the whole Advent, regarding it as one Christmas Eve. They were right: the greatness and sanctity of this festival were well worthy of such a long vigil and so careful a preparation. We should all fast at least one or two days a week still out of devotion. We must pour more abundant alms into the hands of the poor at this season, when the eternal Father gives us his own Son as a great alms, a treasure of grace and mercy. We must also apply ourselves more earnestly to the performance of good works and the reading of pious books. Lastly, we must so dispose ourselves for this first coming of the Son of God that we may expect his second coming, not only without fear, but with that joyous confidence which always accompanies a good conscience."[527]

Several urgent motives induce us to follow the advice of this great apostle of modern times, and to sanctify Advent:

1. *Obedience to the Church.* "I am the voice of one crying in the wilderness: Prepare ye the way of the Lord, make straight his paths; the axe is laid at the root of the tree." This invitation, which the holy precursor addressed to the Jews, equally concerns men of all periods. Jesus Christ comes into the world for all men: it is therefore an indispensable duty of all men to receive him. Lest we should neglect a point so essential, the Church, ever occupied with the spiritual welfare of her children, and faithfully interpreting the divine oracles committed to her care, proclaims in the most pressing and solemn manner the invitation of the holy precursor during the whole of Advent. Judea is moved at the accents of the prophetic voice which resounds on the banks of the Jordan: priests, Levites, soldiers, publicans, sinners of every rank and condition, hasten in crowds to ask the baptism of penance. The same voice resounds in our temples. Have we less need of conversion? Have we less reason to fear the great God who now comes as a Savior, and who will one day come as a judge? Shall we let the Church weary herself in vain, telling us to prepare our hearts, "for all flesh shall soon see the Savior sent of God"?

2. *Gratitude to our Savior.* What was man before the incarnation of the Savior? What are we without him? Poor blind slaves—victims of the world, sin, and hell! And to enlighten us, to deliver us, to ransom us, to restore our lost rights to us, what did it not cost the Son of God? A God takes on himself the form of a slave, and undergoes all the miseries of our wretched humanity; a poor God, an infant God: Does this prodigy touch no chord in our hearts? Shall we who show gratitude to men for the least favors have none for a God who gives himself to us?

3. *Our own spiritual interest.* The fountain of graces never dries up; but great festivals are days when these graces are poured out more abundantly. The whole Church, animated with one spirit, then offers a more solemn homage to God, addresses him in more fervent prayer, and moves him by more sincere tears. Jesus Christ is born for our salvation; but he gives his graces only to those who come to him with a heart prepared to receive them. The dispositions that he finds in us are the measure of his benefits. Have we little or nothing to ask of him? Ah! let us enter into ourselves; let us question our past life, our present state, our purposes for the future: the abysses of our misery will make answer.[528]

PRAYER

O my God! who art all love, I thank thee for having established the holy time of Advent to prepare me for the festival of Christmas. Grant me the grace to spend it well.

I am resolved to love God above all things, and my neighbor as myself for the love of God; and, in testimony of this love, I will daily say during Advent: "O divine infant Jesus, come and be born in my heart!"

Lesson 26: Christianity Brought before the Senses (Continued)—Immaculate Conception

Immaculate conception of the Blessed Virgin: A dogma of faith.—On the 8th of December, the Catholic Church celebrates the festival of the Immaculate Conception of the Blessed Virgin. By "the immaculate conception of the Blessed Virgin," we understand that the Blessed Virgin, from the first moment when her soul was united to her body, was preserved from original sin and exempted from every stain.[529] A divine anathema, the just punishment of a great crime, has weighed for six thousand years on the whole human race, and the stain of sin accompanies the conception and birth of all children of the first of the guilty. Original sin is a sad inheritance, which is transmitted from generation to generation, and which will be so transmitted so long as there is one drop of the blood of Adam in the veins of the human race.

This dreadful and universal law, which condemns us to be born children of wrath, was once suspended, and it was in favor of Mary. Never, from the first moment of her existence, was the Virgin of Juda, the future Mother of the man-God, sullied with the least stain. Such is the miracle of which the Church celebrates the memory, such the benefit for which she thanks God, on the festival of the Immaculate Conception.

Mary was conceived without sin: this truth, before being a dogma of faith, was certain. The Church does not make new dogmas. What she believes today, she believed yesterday, she believed always. Only, she renders her belief more explicit and obligatory, by settling it in a solemn definition, according to the wants of various times.

With regard to the definition of the immaculate conception, the bishops of all parts of the world were consulted. They bore testimony to the belief of their people. The sovereign pontiff heard this testimony, and proved its universality; and, by his supreme authority, he defined that the immaculate conception of the Blessed Virgin is a dogma of the Catholic faith, which no one can ever more call in question, without falling into heresy.[530]

The infallible definition of the vicar of Jesus Christ does not rest only on the universality of testimonies, but also on their antiquity. In all ages, we find the belief, more or less explicit, of the immaculate conception. It must have been in very general existence and good credit among Christians, when Mahometans themselves should have consecrated the memory of it. Who would ever imagine such a thing as that the Alcoran[531] should be one of the first works in which it is recorded.[532] Yet such is the case. In the second century, Origen hints at it; and in the fourth, the brightest light of the Church, St. Augustine, never fails to except Mary when he speaks of original sin. "It is," he says, "out of respect toward Mary, and on account of the honor due to her Son, that we do not speak of her whenever there is question of sin."[533]

The Council of Trent, summing up the traditions of all Christian ages, thus expresses itself in its celebrated decree regarding original sin: "The Council declares that it does not intend, when there is question of original sin, to include in the decree the Blessed and immaculate Virgin Mary, Mother of God; but commands that, on this point, the constitutions of Pope Sixtus IV should be followed under the penalties therein attached."[534]

Now, in 1479, Sixtus IV had granted indulgences to those who should assist at the office and Mass of the festival of the Conception. Four years later on, he issued a constitution in which he forbade anyone to censure this festival, or to condemn the opinion of those who believed the immaculate conception. In 1622, the Holy See, by the mouth of Pope Gregory XV, forbade anyone to maintain, even in private disputations, that Mary was not conceived without sin.

Reason joins with tradition and authority. Why, I ask, would not God perform this miracle in favor of his Mother? "He could do it; it was becoming that he should do it;

therefore he did it."[535] This was the argument of a celebrated theologian of the Middle Ages, and all the children of Mary since his time have applauded its soundness.

1. *It became the Father*. Destined to be the Mother of Jesus, Mary was always, in virtue of the divine adoption, considered by the Father as his beloved daughter. It was therefore becoming that, for the honor of the Son, the Father should preserve Mary from all stain. The Father, too, had chosen this most dear daughter to crush the head of the infernal serpent: How then could he let Mary be first his slave? Lastly, Mary was destined to be the advocate of sinners: it was therefore proper that she should be free from all sin, so as always to appear spotless before God. "To appease a judge," says St. Augustine, "we do not send a person that is or has been his enemy: such a messenger would only increase his anger."

2. *It became the Son*. How can we suppose that the Son of God, sanctity itself, having it in his power to choose an immaculate Mother, always the friend of God, would wish to be born of one defiled by sin, for a time the enemy of God? "Moreover," says St. Augustine, "the flesh of Jesus Christ is the flesh of Mary." The Son of God would have been horrified to take a body in the womb of St. Agnes, or St. Gertrude, or St. Teresa, because these virgins, pure as they were, came into this world with the stain of sin. If the same had been the case with Mary, would not the devil have been able to reproach our Lord with the fact that the flesh with which he was clothed had been infected by his venom, that the Mother in whom he gloried had first been his slave? The Mother of God the slave of the devil!—oh, there is something so shocking in this, so offensive to pious ears, that it is impossible to listen to it. Lastly, St. Thomas says that Mary was preserved from all actual sin, even venial sin, because she would not otherwise have been worthy of God. But how much less worthy would she have been if she had been defiled with original sin, which makes us children of wrath in the eyes of God!

3. *It became the Holy Ghost*. Mary is the spouse of the Holy Ghost. If a skillful painter were allowed to choose a beautiful or an ugly spouse, according to the picture that he would himself make of her, what care would he not take to present a work of surpassing excellence, a work abounding in charms? Who will dare to say that the Holy Ghost would act otherwise with Mary, and that, having absolute power to make his spouse to his liking, he did not adorn her with all the beauty that he could give her and that became her? No, no, the Lord would not fail in such a way: witness the names that he gives her. After forming this masterpiece of his grace, he contemplates her with infinite delight, and says, "Thou art all beautiful, O my beloved! and there is no spot in thee; there are young maidens without number, but my dove alone is beautiful, alone is pure, alone is perfect among the daughters of her mother."[536] This means that all just souls are daughters of divine grace; but one among them deserves the name of dove, because she is spotless, and only one, because she alone was conceived in grace.[537]

Such are some of the authorities and congruities that, before the solemn definition of the Church, made the Catholic world admit the belief of Mary's immaculate conception. We see therefore that all those fathers of the Church and all those great theologians—the ornament of their age and the admiration of posterity—who so sincerely believed and so earnestly maintained this august prerogative of Mary, were not weak-minded men. Nor were all those doctors of the universities of France, England, Spain, and Italy, and all those knights of the military orders, who made profession of believing the immaculate conception of the Mother of God, and bound themselves by an oath to defend this belief, weak-minded men. Lastly, the bishop of Meaux was no weak-minded man when he said:

"The belief of the immaculate conception carries with it a secret influence that convinces pious souls. After the articles of faith, I know nothing more settled. Wherefore I am not surprised that the Paris school of theologians should oblige all its children to defend this doctrine…As for me, I am delighted to correspond this day with its views.

Having been nourished with its milk, I willingly submit to its ordinances, the more so as this is also what seems to me to be the will of the Church.

"She has a very honorable idea of the conception of Mary: she does not oblige us to believe it immaculate, but she gives us to understand that this belief is pleasing to her. There are some things that she commands, in which we make known our obedience; there are others that she recommends, in which we may show our affection. If we are true children of the Church, our piety will lead us not only to obey her direct commands, but even to yield at the least sign of such a good and tender mother's wishes."[538]

Those are truly weak-minded men who, running here and there, blame and reject what they do not understand, only because it does not suit their shallowness or their wickedness, or because the Catholic Church admits it.

History of the festival; wisdom of the Church. The festival of the Immaculate Conception justifies the words of Bossuet, and clearly shows the feeling of the Church on this point. In the East, the festival of Mary Immaculate was already old in the seventh century.[539] In the West, it reaches back beyond the twelfth. Celebrated at first by individual churches, it was earnestly supported and propagated by St. Anselm, archbishop of Canterbury, who died in 1109. Two hundred years later on, a council in London rendered it obligatory.[540] From Great Britain this festival passed over to the Continent, and spread rapidly in France, Spain, Italy, and other parts of Christendom. At length, in the fifteenth century, the Council of Bale, and, above all, Pope Sixtus IV, gave it more encouragement by the indulgences that were attached to it.[541]

The institution, apparently so slow, of a festival on which the most glorious of Mary's privileges is honored, gives rise to a reflection that applies equally to other festivals. As the Church did not of a sudden, or at her origin, decide all questions in regard to faith and morals, so she did not at once establish the various practices of her worship. She followed times, and adapted herself to the wants of the faithful. This is a new proof of her profound wisdom.

When the Church now defines truths of faith that are attacked, and in other days were not attacked, she is not, for all that, to be thought growing wiser. She does what former councils would have done, if they had been placed in the same circumstances. So with regard to festivals, confraternities, devotions, pious practices: they do not come from a silly and groundless presumption, as if we pretended to be wiser than our elders. Different times have different customs and wants. The Church knows them all, and takes care to satisfy them: no one knows better than a mother what suits her children.

In point of fact, we must judge of the Church, "the permanent incarnation of Jesus Christ,"[542] as of Jesus Christ himself. "As Jesus advanced in age," the scripture tells us, "he also advanced in wisdom and grace before God and men."[543] Not that the eternal Wisdom, though clad in our flesh, could make progress in knowledge or sanctity; but the Son of God, adapting himself to the laws of our nature, displayed more wisdom and sanctity from day to day, as he advanced in age, though from the first moment of his conception he was consummate wisdom and sanctity.

"We may say," adds the celebrated Thomassin, "that it is the same with the Church. This divine spouse, occasionally opening the treasures of tradition, brings to light some points of doctrine and practices of devotion that had not previously appeared, the time for their doing so not having come. The plenitude of the Holy Ghost dwells, and has dwelt since the beginning, in the heart of the Church. The eternal Wisdom[544] has always been, is now, and shall always be in and with the Church; but the Church does not display it outwardly save according to the counsels of divine providence. This loving providence infallibly attains its end, while disposing of all the means thereto sweetly.

It leads the human race as one man, and each man as the whole race, by the steps of different ages, and the speed suited to those different ages."[545]

Definition of the dogma of the immaculate conception: Appropriateness of this definition. For a long time, the Catholic world desired to see the belief of the immaculate conception, so dear to its heart and so honorable to its mother, placed among the dogmas of the faith. The Church knew the wishes of her children. But the Holy Ghost, who guides her, made her defer their accomplishment till the day marked out in the eternal decrees.

This ever-blessed day arrived. On the 8th of December, 1854, the sovereign pontiff Pius IX, in presence of two hundred bishops, assembled from all parts of the world, solemnly proclaimed in the Basilica of St. Peter the dogma of the immaculate conception of Mary. The Catholic world thrilled with extraordinary gladness and the Satanic world trembled with unexampled rage. Why so much joy on one side and so much fury on the other? Why should this dogma, which puts the finishing stroke to the glory of the ever Blessed Virgin, be defined in our age and not in some past or future one? What relation is there between this providential event and the necessities of our time?

God never makes guesses; and there is no effect without a cause. Now, a frightful cancer is at present eating away the world: it is Satanism or paganism. The two great symptoms of this evil are pride and pleasure, or rationalism and sensualism, but rationalism and sensualism such as the world has not seen since the establishment of Christianity. To say all in one word, the evil visible to everybody, the evil characteristic of our era, is the adoration of reason and the flesh, to an extent previously unknown.

What, in this crisis, is the providential object of proclaiming the dogma of the immaculate conception? With one blow this dogma strikes down rationalism and sensualism. Since the Renaissance, rationalism has attacked all the truths of faith, one after another: from negation to negation, it has come to deny everything, even the existence of God himself.

What does the dogma of the immaculate conception do?

To radical negation it opposes radical affirmation. The existence of God, the fall of man, the transmission of original sin, the necessity of a Redeemer, and the divinity of this Redeemer—the Son of Mary: all these articles of faith, and those which are derived from them, that is to say, Catholicity in its magnificent entirety, is affirmed by the single dogma of the immaculate conception of the Blessed Virgin.

If rationalism now brings back to the world the war cry of ancient paganism, "Believe nothing that Christianity teaches you," the dogma of the immaculate conception answers with the victorious cry of the martyrs, "Believe all that Christianity teaches you." Thus, Mary immaculate crushes the first of the infernal serpent's heads.

The second, sensualism, remains. "Adore your flesh: gratify all its concupiscences. Reject as an evil, abhor as a degrading stupidity, all kinds of mortification and penance, all the practices and precepts of the Church, which are intended to bring your senses into subjection, to reduce your body to servitude. Deny nothing to your inclinations: let this be your only law, your only religion, your only happiness." Behold what the pagan sensualism of our period preaches as it never preached before!

The dogma of the immaculate conception is diametrically opposed to this beastly doctrine. Pointing to the most exalted, the most splendid type of sanctity in a creature, our sister and our Mother, it cries out to man: "Behold your model. Be perfect as Mary is perfect, holy as she is holy, without spot or stain, without the shadow of spot or stain. Though you may not attain to a perfect resemblance with her, it is your duty to aspire to it; let this be the law of your existence, your religion, your happiness."

As we see, to the two negations of Satan returning triumphant to the world, the dogma of the immaculate conception opposes two precise, absolute, solemn affirmations. Wonderful power of this dogma! Henceforth it will be enough for a little Catholic child to say, "I believe that Mary was conceived without sin," in order to overturn with a breath all the scaffoldings of lies and deceits raised at so much cost during four centuries by Satan and his accomplices. Was there ever a remedy better suited to an evil, or more properly applied?

Influence of the festival. The day that calls to mind the dogma of the immaculate conception has necessarily a great influence on morals. Every year it brings before the whole world that truth whose importance we have just shown. Not to enter into other details, the thought that Mary is a rose which never faded, a mirror which the least breath never tarnished, sanctifies the imagination, by presenting to it the purest, sweetest, noblest ideas. Has it not then tended to the perfection of humanity to substitute so pure a type of woman for the infamous type presented by paganism? Mary and Venus: the distance between these two models is simply infinite!

On the day of the Conception of the Blessed Virgin, does not reason say to itself: "Why this astounding miracle in favor of Mary, which suspends the law condemning all the sons and daughters of Adam to be born in iniquity?—Why such perfect sanctity?" And reason here discovers, by the light of history, one of the deep counsels of providence for the restoration of the human race. "Today," it answers, "we begin the history of the Virgin of Juda, the Mother of the Emmanuel, the new Eve, the creature apart, in a word, Mary, the sublime type of woman in the Christianized world."

"Mary shall be the daughter of Adam, but she shall not be like us. We are defiled from the first moment of our existence. Mary shall be pure and spotless in her conception.

"She shall be born into this world of darkness and misery, but she shall not be born like us. We are born children of wrath. Mary shall be born a child of benediction, an object of ineffable love to the adorable Trinity.

"She shall live in this region of iniquity, but she shall not live like us, who are one moment the slaves of passion and the next the sport of gross illusions. Mary shall lead a life more angelic than that of the purest seraph.

"Mary shall die, but she shall not die like us. We undergo death in pain and anguish. Mary shall meet it as the weary meet rest, as the blind meet light, as prisoners meet liberty.

"Mary shall die not only in the love of God—this death is the portion of true Christians; not only for the love of God—this death is the portion of martyrs; but by an effort of the love of God—this death is the exclusive portion of the Mother of God.

"Mary shall be glorified in heaven, but not like us. We shall participate in the happiness of God himself according to our merits; but Mary shall be inundated with it, filled with it, as she was full of grace. Her throne shall be beside that of her Son. At her feet she shall see all that is not God."

Behold the divine type that religion today sets before us! It required nothing less than such a perfect model to render woman worthy of respect in her own eyes and in the eyes of man, so much was she degraded in the ancient world, and so much is she still degraded wherever the new Eve is not known. On the ever-blessed day of Mary's immaculate conception, a voice is heard saying to woman: "Look at the model set before you, be sure to imitate it!" And numberless graces are given to the young virgin, to the wife, to the mother, to woman in every station of life, that she may come nearer and nearer to this sublime model; and a thousand virtues bloom under Mary's smile! When woman has been rehabilitated, she rehabilitates the child, the family, man himself, to a great extent. She has found means to cross the immense space that separated ancient paganism from Christianity, and that still separates idolatrous from Christian nations.

Such is the salutary influence that reason discovers in the mystery of Mary conceived without sin. This is not all. Faith, coming to the help of reason, its child and pupil, acquaints it with another advantage of this mystery. It was necessary, says faith, that Mary should be free from stain, because she was one day to become the Mother of

God: her chaste womb was to become the tabernacle of the eternal Word. If the ark of the covenant was holy and covered inside and outside with the purest gold, because it was to contain the tables of the law, how much holier and purer should Mary be to carry within her the giver of the law?

After this lesson from faith, man exclaims, I understand it; Mary should be without stain. But what! is not the honor of receiving my God in person within me reserved also for me? In Communion, am I not associated in some manner to the divine maternity? And this Communion am I not obliged, under pain of death, to make? Is it not written that "unless you eat the flesh of the Son of Man and drink his blood, you shall not have life in you"?[546] Yes, it is necessary that I should communicate. But what is my sanctity, compared with that of Mary.

At this thought, profound sentiments of humility, a salutary remorse, generous resolutions are formed in the soul. Conduct is changed; and watchfulness, and gentleness, and tender piety, and obedience—what do I say?—all the virtues that make up the charm of life, the happiness of families, and the strength of society, burst out, as if by enchantment, at the remembrance of Mary conceived without sin, of Mary ever pure and spotless, because she was to receive her God. The senses, the mind, and the heart are regenerated, and man takes one step more toward the end for which he was made. Behold a new guarantee for the peace and welfare of the family and of society!

To render as great as possible the salutary influence of the divine model which this festival presents to us, the Church wishes that we should consider it from every point of view. She surrounds it with the most beautiful ornaments; she sets it, if we may so speak, in the most graceful positions, that each of us may study it at leisure and copy it exactly.

Liturgy of the Immaculate Conception. Thus, the Mass of the Conception shows us Mary uniting in herself all that is most splendid and noble. In the introit, the august daughter of the kings of Juda sings the glory with which the Lord has surrounded her: a glory which, surpassing all others, makes Mary the Creator's masterpiece. The epistle shows us the Almighty occupied with Mary from all eternity, and Mary telling, in language inimitably poetic, what the eternal Father has done for his daughter. The gospel crowns the favors of the Most High and the glory of Mary: it relates the mystery of the annunciation.

What transports of love, gratitude, and joy should be excited in the souls of the sons, and more especially of the daughters of Eve at the thought that all these treasures of grace are not only for Mary, but for us! Mary, the object of all the thoughts and delights of God from eternity; Mary, the liberatrix of the human race; Mary, beheld, desired, hailed from afar by the prophets; Mary, shining with a perfect sanctity amid the contaminated descendants of the first Adam, like a spotless lily amid thorns; Mary, the noble offspring of a long line of illustrious ancestors: such are the different lights in which the Church presents to us the child that is this day conceived. Do you know any means of exciting more respect, confidence, and love in our hearts; any means of sanctifying our imagination with purer or nobler ideas?

Manner of celebrating this festival. We now easily understand what we ought to do, in order to celebrate worthily the festival of the Immaculate Conception: a) thank God for having preserved Mary from the stain of original sin; b) congratulate her on this glorious privilege; and c) excite ourselves to a great confidence in her. Sanctity is the measure of the power that the saints have with God. What, then, is the power of this most Blessed Virgin, the holiest of creatures? What is her goodness toward us? She is our sister; she is our Mother; she is our advocate. These prerogatives were given her for the benefit of mankind: she has to make use of them for the glory of her Son, and the glory of her Son is the salvation of the human race.

We ought also d) to make up our minds to imitate the sanctity of Mary as much as possible, since, on the one hand, it is a means of pleasing her, and, on the other, we are called to receive into our hearts the God on whose account she was so sanctified; and e) to praise Mary, by daily laying on her altar a tribute of our filial tenderness. We may do so either by some little mortifications or by a few short but fervent prayers. Here is one, to which there is a hundred days' indulgence attached as often as it is piously said: "Blessed be the holy and immaculate conception of Blessed Mary the Virgin!"[547]

PRAYER

O my God! who art all love, I thank thee for having preserved our Blessed Lady from the stain of original sin. Grant me the grace to preserve my baptismal innocence all the days of my life or to recover it speedily.

I am resolved to love God above all things, and my neighbor as myself for the love of God; and, in testimony of this love, I will every day say three Hail Marys in honor of the immaculate conception.

Lesson 27: Christianity Brought before the Senses (Continued)—Ember Days, Vigils

Quarter Tense of Advent; antiquity of Quarter Tense or Ember days.—The third week of Advent brings the autumnal Quarter Tense. By *Quarter Tense* we understand three fast days that are observed at the close of each season: they are also called Ember days. If the antiquity of a practice, otherwise salutary, is calculated to render it venerable, I leave you to imagine what respect we should have for these days consecrated to penance, and with what religious care we should observe them. The institution of Quarter Tense dates from the early ages of the Church.[548] The synagogue itself offers us traces of it. The fasts of the seasons of summer, autumn, and winter are clearly pointed out by the prophet Zacharias.[549] Heiress to all the holy practices, as well as all the truths of ancient times, the spouse of Jesus Christ preserved, sanctified, and perfected the usage of fasting in each of the four seasons.

If we take a little trouble to study her conduct, we shall find that it bears the impress of supernatural wisdom; in other words, we shall see that she has a profound knowledge of man's condition here below, and is most anxious for his welfare.

In point of fact, what is man? He is a dethroned king, a degraded creature. So we are told by that strange mixture of greatness and baseness which we perceive in ourselves. There are two men within us always at war—opposed in thoughts, sentiments, and desires: the one good, aspiring to all that is noble and virtuous; the other bad, furiously inclined to all that is vile and criminal. Who shall win the victory? It is for us to decide. If we wish the good man to prevail over the bad, the spirit to triumph over the flesh, we must weaken the flesh, we must strengthen the soul: so reason tells us. Glory, freedom, and happiness are the reward of the victory of the spirit over the flesh. Remorse, shame, slavery, and woe in time and eternity are the inevitable consequences of the dominion of the senses over the spirit.

Again, what is man? He is a culprit. So we are told by all ages and all nations. So we are told by all the expiatory sacrifices that we meet wherever we turn, as well as by the innumerable miseries that overwhelm us. The work of a good God, man is miserable only because he is degraded, and he is degraded only because he is guilty.

Since we are guilty, we are bound to do penance. Yes, this is the declaration of reason as well as of faith. Every page of the old testament recalls the necessity of penance. The gospel confirms this unchangeable law. How often did the Savior of the world say that penance is an indispensable condition for salvation! Was it not from his lips that fell the words: "Unless you do penance, you shall all perish"?[550] Does not the Church, the infallible representative of the man-God, add that the life of a Christian ought to be a continual penance?[551]

Again, what is man? He is a being called to imitate a divine being, whose life, from the crib to the cross, was only one long penance. Thus, as men, as sinners, and as Christians, we are bound to do penance. Our obligation comes both from the natural and the divine law. We have no other means of reascending the throne from which we fell; of returning to the order from which we departed; of imitating the august model which, under pain of death, we must resemble.

But how is this penance to be done? And when? If you leave to every individual the care of solving these questions, you will soon witness a strange confusion of ideas, and then absurd, ridiculous, perhaps monstrous, practices. Ask history: in paganism, human sacrifices; in the beginning of the Church, the excesses of the Donatists and Gnostics; in the Middle Ages and since the so-called Reformation, the incredible follies of the Flagellants, Frérots, Anabaptists, Bearded Mummies, etc. Are they not all so many proofs of this sad truth?

In the course of time, you see the very precept itself of penance going to wreck. Such is man. His levity, his self-love, his concern about temporal things, his hunger after pleasure, his horror of whatever might be a check to his inclinations—what do I say?—all these things together will make an immense number forget the precept of penance. Though none may dispute its truth, yet they will find a thousand means of eluding it; it will be as if it were not.

He who created man knew his character too well not to provide for these inconveniences. Hence the Savior charged his Church to determine all the particulars regarding the precept of penance; to say to man with an infallible authority: "The divine precept of penance obliges on such an occasion, and, to comply with it, you must do so and so." Precious words! since they rouse negligent and calm timid souls, by acquainting them exactly with what God requires of them. How often do they keep man from the frightful misfortune of falling into the hands of his judge without having done the least thing to atone for a long life of uselessness, perhaps of wickedness!

Wisdom and goodness of the Church: Satisfactory works opposed to the three great concupiscences.—See next with what wisdom the spouse of Jesus Christ treats the disease of the sick man, whose cure is entrusted to her. This wisdom will be more evident if you reflect on the nature of the satisfactory works that the Church prescribes to us. Like the traveler left half dead on the road to Jericho, man received three great wounds: an inordinate love of riches, an inordinate love of honors, and an inordinate love of pleasures. These are his wounds, fearful wounds, mortifying wounds, which the apostle St. John, in language profoundly philosophical, calls the three great concupiscences.

What remedy is there for these evils, the fatal cause of all man's tears—and how many he sheds!—the source of all the crimes that disturb the world, and his crimes are such that they sometimes make one ashamed to bear the name of man? Search, and search again. In the meantime, we Catholics shall tell you. The remedy for covetousness is detachment; for pride, humility; and for voluptuousness, mortification.

Light-minded men, who smile contemptuously at the precepts of the Church, come, let us see: speak out! Can you tell us any other remedy? Man is sick: you know it, you say it, you pity him. Since you flatter yourselves with being wiser than Christianity, come, to business: cure him. I see you coming with a mouthful of pompous maxims to deafen him, and a handful of laws to throw at his head like a net for catching prey. Behind you I see ever so many police, chains, dungeons, and executioners. Ah! we know what all these remedies can do: they irritate and exasperate the sick man, and render his cure a thousand times more difficult!

Much more enlightened is the Catholic Church. With the sweet voice of a mother, she says to man:

"My son, since your father's fall, there have been two men in you. One, dragging you with all his strength toward gross enjoyments, strives to reduce you to the level of the brute; the other, continually withdrawing you from the dominion of the senses, strives to raise you toward God, and to make you aspire to what is most great, most noble, most worthy of you, namely, an inheritance of immortal glory and infinite happiness. With opposite intentions, sentiments, and desires, these two men, as you know, wage an unceasing war against each other: a war whose first scene was your cradle, and whose last will be your deathbed. This is the reason why the Holy Spirit calls you a soldier and your life a warfare.[552]

"You know, my son, that the good man in you should be always on his guard, and should labor with all his might to baffle the designs, and to break or blunt the murderous weapons of his adversary. There is no other way to win the victory, to secure happiness in this world and the next.

"Now, your enemy seeks to overcome you by raising in your heart a love of sensual pleasures. You shall therefore mortify your senses: you shall answer him by fasting. He endeavors to dazzle your eyes with the deceitful splendor of earthly goods. He says, 'Blessed are they that have these things.' You shall turn aside your head not to behold vanity. You shall answer him, 'Blessed is he whose wealth is the Lord'; and you shall give alms. Lastly, with increased cunning, he strives to awake in you that dreadful pride which, in the twinkling of an eye, changed beautiful angels into horrible devils. You shall cast yourself at the feet of your God. You shall acknowledge your nothingness and your dependence. You shall pray.

"Fasting, almsdeeds, and prayer: these, my son, are the weapons of which you must avail yourself. These are the remedies prescribed for you by the heavenly physician.[553] And I—I will tell you the time and the manner of using them."

And now, if there is anyone in the world not a son of Adam, not an heir to his corruption, let him at once dispense himself from these wholesome prescriptions. He has another nature than ours: the laws of humanity are not for him. But if all, without exception, find in themselves that law of the members which clashes with the law of the mind; if we all experience more or less in ourselves that sting of the flesh from which Paul himself, though rapt to the third heaven, was not exempt, how can we despise the sacred weapons with which all the saints conquered, and spurn the remedies which alone can effect our cure?

Such, therefore, is the wisdom of the Church in the remedies which she prescribes to us. Attacking our three great passions together, she never separates the three works opposed to them: fasting, almsdeeds, and prayer. The advantages of all this are not confined to ourselves: they extend to our neighbor. In the intentions of our tender mother, one of the objects of fasting is to deprive us of a portion of our food, so that we may relieve the poor.

Thus, in Christianity practiced according to the spirit of the gospel, every fast day is a day of dedication for the rich and of help for the needy. And thus, Catholicity is, by excellence, the religion of humanity and a law of love. And thus, the religion of Jesus Christ not only leads man to give what he possesses in superabundance to him who is in want, but it wishes a more perfect sacrifice, a kind of immolation of oneself for the miserable, by requiring of its disciples that, on every fast day, they should take something from their ordinary support to feed those who are hungry.

Many times a year it calls for a repetition of this voluntary sacrifice, sanctified by the precept of divine love, without which every virtue is imperfect and every motive selfish. We hereby see the true spirit of fasting, in the views of the Church. To fast otherwise, that is to say, to fast in the morning so as to make a more sumptuous repast in the middle of the day, or to fast by abstaining from flesh meat so as to partake with the same luxury of fish, is to fast after the manner of an epicure. To fast and not to join alms with fasting is, in a certain sense, to rob the poor of the savings of a repast: it is to corrupt the precept in its most sublime meaning, and to set an occasion of scandal, unfortunately too real, for the jests of the wicked.[554]

Crime of heretics and infidels.—But the heretics of the sixteenth century and the philosophers of the eighteenth are no less guilty for having accused Catholicity of those abuses which it condemns. What have they done by stirring up their disciples against the precept of fasting and abstaining? They have taken from sinners one of the most salutary means of repenting; from virtue, one of its strongest pillars; from social benevolence, one of its most ordinary practices. They have set man in opposition to the moral instincts of the world; for all peoples, without a single exception, have fasted, because they thought man responsible for his works to God, and obliged to satisfy for his offenses.[555]

Why Quarter Tense and vigils were established.—Very wise, then, is the Catholic Church in the general obligation that she lays on us to fast. She is no less so in fixing a fulfillment of this obligation at the close of each of the four seasons of the year. In effect, Quarter Tense was established: a) to ask pardon of God for the faults committed during the season that has just gone by; b) to thank God for the favors that he has granted us; c) to draw down on ordinations the graces of the Holy Ghost; and d) to help us to spend in a more Christian manner the following season.

1. Quarter Tense was established to ask pardon of God for the faults committed during the season that has just gone by. Alas! every season, while varying our enjoyments, only too often makes us vary our sins. Spring, which we ought to regard as a time of resurrection to grace, piety, and fervor, distracts our minds; absorbs our thoughts, by the care of temporal undertakings; and removes us from our last end, instead of bringing us nearer thereto. Perhaps it passes without our once uniting our heart and voice with those of all nature, in order to thank God, who, by a renovation of all things, provides for our subsistence, and offers us an image of the future resurrection. Summer raises the heat of the passions. The rich man gives himself on those beautiful days to tours of pleasure, and often to criminal enjoyments. The countryman violates by labor the days consecrated to the Lord. The heart of each is insensible to the varied presents that the Creator sends us. In autumn, the covetous man fills his barns with the goods of the Father of the family. There is no blessing on his lips for the God who has made the fields and meadows fertile. Winter sees costly parties, balls, and theatres. It also sees the tears of the poor, who are hungry and cold. Hard, pitiless selfishness reigns triumphant; and if, at this season, God is sometimes offended by the murmurs of the poor, he is much more so by the heartlessness of the rich.

Who among us, going down into the depths of his conscience, will not feel some touches of remorse? What season have we spent as Christians? Ah! I speak amiss: In what season have we not abused the benefits of God? Have we done penance? We have never thought of it. The Church, therefore, was wise in reminding us of its obligation, in prescribing its works, and in fixing its days. Without her, we should let our debts accumulate, and we should reach the gates of eternity as miserable bankrupts, carrying no other introduction to the supreme judge than a life of iniquity.

2. To thank God for the favors that he has granted us. Many are the benefits that our heavenly Father bestows upon us during the different seasons: each of them brings us his particular tribute of regard, and their succession places all nature at our service. Well, now, will you say that, for three months of unceasing liberality, three days of prayer and good works are too much? The heart that finds the burden of gratitude heavy is greatly to be pitied. Besides, our thanks are even for our own advantage. Ingratitude is like a scorching wind that dries up the source of grace, while gratitude opens our benefactor's hand.

3. To draw down on ordinations the graces of the Holy Ghost. No society without religion, and no religion without priests; but no priests useful to religion or to society without the virtues of their holy state. Though the Church had only this one reason to call her children to prayer, fasting, and almsdeeds during Quarter Tense, do you think that her command would not have been well founded? Are we not all concerned in having good priests? Is it not on their example and on their instructions that our virtue, the peace of families, and the happiness of the world, in a great measure, depend? Are they not appointed by the Lord himself for the salvation and the destruction of many in Israel?

On Saturday of Quarter Tense, the Church multiplies her prayers: there were formerly twelve lessons read at Mass, but the number has been reduced to five. The Church wishes to engage her children in useful meditations on the benefits of God, and to move them by the words of the prophet to ask the blessings of heaven more earnestly for those who are about to receive holy orders.[556]

4. To help us to spend in a more Christian manner the following season. It is not only useful but necessary for the traveler who makes a long journey to rest from time to time. It is not only useful but necessary for the soldier in the field to have some days of truce, when he may dress his wounds and repair his arms. By the same titles, it is not only useful but necessary for the Christian to have Quarter Tense.

Is he not both a traveler and a soldier? A traveler, the road of life, as we know full well, is not without fatigues and dangers for him. His soul must take breath. It does so by drawing near to God, and it draws near to God by prayer and the mortification of the flesh. A soldier, man unfortunately receives more than one wound in the conflict that he must maintain from the cradle to the grave. He needs remedies, and he finds them in prayer and fasting. Restored to health by these salutary observances, man may resume his journey and return to the combat with greater confidence. His thoughts raised above the earth, his affections purified and ennobled, labor becomes more meritorious for him and life sweeter. Hereby the family and society, besides being edified by good example, gain rest and happiness.

It was also to make us better and happier that the Church established the vigils or watches of great festivals. Formerly, the night preceding our solemnities was spent in the church: hence the name *watch*. We now term *vigil* the whole day preceding a solemnity, and on which fast and abstinence are observed. There are six vigils: those of Christmas, Easter, Pentecost, Sts. Peter and Paul, the Assumption, and All Saints.

How can we fail to admire the solicitude with which the Church prepares her children for the great festivals of religion? Prayer, fasting, works of charity: these are the means which she employs to weaken in us the life of the senses, and to give our souls the vigor, the purity, and the holy desires necessary for the more abundant effusion of grace that takes place on our solemnities. The word *vigil* is a whole instruction in itself: time is the vigil of eternity. Our life is a day of fasting, prayer, and labor. Eternity is the solemnity to which we look forward. If our age obliges us to fast, let us do so faithfully. If we are dispensed from the law, let us at least, on the eves of great festivals, offer some fervent prayers to God, make some serious reflections on ourselves, and frame some good resolutions.[557]

PRAYER

O my God! who art all love, I thank thee for having established Quarter Tense. Grant me the grace to enter fully into the spirit of this salutary institution.

I am resolved to love God above all things, and my neighbor as myself for the love of God; and, in testimony of this love, I will join alms with fasting and prayer.

Lesson 28: Christianity Brought before the Senses (Continued)—Christmas

Christmas: Its object.—The object of the festival of Christmas is the temporal birth of the Son of God. The eternal Word, equal in all things to the Father and to the Holy Ghost, he by whom all things were made, having become incarnate in the womb of the Virgin Mary, was born in a poor stable at Bethlehem, to save us: such is the touching mystery that the Church sets before us on this solemnity. To make us imitate a poor, humble, suffering God, here is what she says to us:

Four thousand years before, guilty and degraded man heard from the mouth of an offended God, who drove him out of the terrestrial paradise, these words addressed to the wicked serpent: "I will put enmity between thee and the woman, between thy race and hers, and she shall crush thy head."[558] These precious words were for many ages the only consolation of the descendants of Adam under their numberless sorrows. The Son of the woman by excellence, the conqueror of the devil, the repairer of the fall, the restorer of the human race, was the object of all their desires and sighs. Never was he more ardently or more generally desired than during the reign of Augustus; never was the city of Satan more powerful; never were the evils of the world greater. Thus, the time marked out for his coming had arrived. But it was necessary that his birth should take place with all the circumstances foretold by the prophets: among others, the Messias should be born at Bethlehem, so as to make it clear that he was of the royal race of David.

General enrollment. And lo! the emperor Augustus, wishing to know how many millions of men bowed beneath his scepter, commanded a general enrollment of his subjects. To preside over the difficult work of taking the census, he appointed twenty-four commissioners, whom he sent to all quarters of the world. Publius Sulpicius Quirinus, or, according to the Greeks, Cyrinus, was charged with the returns of Syria, on which Judea depended. The edict of this general enrollment commanded every one, the richest as well as the poorest, the strongest as well as the weakest, to go to the city in which he had been born, or to which his family belonged, there to be duly registered in Roman form.[559]

Fulfillment of prophecies. Now, Joseph and Mary, who were both of the royal family of David, went to the city of David, which was called Bethlehem. Their names were there inscribed; and the registers of the Roman Empire bear witness that Jesus, the Son of Mary, was a descendant of David, and thus the prophecies that had announced his coming were authentically verified.

Meanwhile, Joseph and Mary, having reached the city of their ancestors, looked about in vain for a lodging. Whether their poor appearance promised little reward, or that the public inn—*diversorium*—was already crowded with people, they were obliged to leave the city and seek a shelter in the country. They found it in a grotto or cave that served as a stable: here Mary brought forth the Redeemer of the world.[560] The circumstances of this divine birth having been related in the second part[561] of the catechism, we shall here content ourselves with describing the ever-venerable place where the great mystery was accomplished.

Description of the grotto of Bethlehem. "Before entering," says a modern traveler, "the superior of the convent put a wax candle into my hand and made me a short exhortation. This holy grotto is irregular, for it occupies the irregular position of the stable and manger. It is thirty-seven and a half feet long, eleven feet, three inches wide, and nine feet high. It is cut out of the rock. The sides of the rock are covered with marble, and the pavement of the grotto is likewise of precious marble. These decorations are attributed to St. Helen. The church receives no light from the outside: it is lighted by thirty-two lamps, sent by various Christian princes. At the farthest part of the grotto, on the eastern side, is the place where the Virgin gave birth to the Redeemer of mankind. This place is marked by a white marble slab, studded with jasper, and surrounded by a circle of silver, radiated like sunlight. We read these words going round:

Hic de Virgine Maria
Jesus Christus Natus Est.

"Here Jesus Christ was born of the Virgin Mary." A marble table, which serves as an altar, leans against the side of the rock, and rises over the spot where the Messias came into the world. This altar is lighted by three lamps, the most beautiful of which was given by Louis XIII.

"Seven paces southward from this point, you find the manger. You go down to it by two steps, for it is not on a level with the rest of the grotto. It is a low vault, sunk in the rock. A block of white marble, raised a foot above the ground, and hollowed like a cradle, tells us the very spot where the sovereign of heaven was laid on straw.[562]

"Two paces from this, opposite the manger, an altar occupies the place where Mary was seated when she presented the child of sorrows to the adoration of the Magi.

"Nothing can be more pleasing or devotional than this subterranean church. I heard an organ there, very well touched, play at Mass the sweetest and tenderest airs of Italy's best composers. These concerts entrance the Christian Arab, who, leaving his camels to graze, goes, like the ancient shepherds of Bethlehem, to adore the King of kings in a crib. I saw the inhabitant of the desert communicate at the altar of the Magi with a fervor, a piety, a religiousness unknown among Western Christians. No other place in the world can inspire more devotion. The continual arrival of caravans from all Christian nations, the public prayers, the prostrations, the richness of the presents sent by Christian princes, all excite feelings in your soul that are far, far better felt than expressed."[563]

When Joseph and Mary entered the grotto, they found there an ox and an ass, whose breath served to warm the infant. The scripture does not indeed mention this circumstance, but it rests on a common tradition, and is given down as certain by fathers of the Church most likely to be well informed regarding it. Such are St. Epiphanius, St. Jerome, St. Gregory Nazianzen, St. Gregory of Nyssa, and Prudentius. Baronius triumphantly defends this affecting tradition.[564]

Birth of the divine infant. It was in this cavern that Mary brought her divine Son into the world, without experiencing any of those pains which other mothers experience: she continued a Virgin before and after her delivery. Who can imagine the joy and respect with which she beheld and adored the Creator of the universe, become man for love of us? What a happiness for her when, contemplating him whom the angels adore, she pronounced for the first time those words which had never before been uttered by anyone but the eternal Father, "My Son!" With what reverence did she not touch him whom she knew to be her Lord! Who can describe the emotion of her virginal and maternal heart when she wrapped him in poor swaddling clothes and laid him on straw in the manger? With what ineffable kisses did she not overwhelm him! With what a holy awe did she not consider his face and his hands! With what sweet gravity did she not cover his little limbs![565]

St. Joseph, certain of the mystery, shared as far as lay in his power the sentiments of Mary. "He took the infant in his arms," says St. Bernard, "and lavished on him all the caresses that a heart inflamed with love could suggest."

At the moment when the prodigy was wrought, God wished that men and angels, earth and heaven, should come and render homage to their common Redeemer. But what happy mortals shall God first choose for such an honor? Augustus, who dost frame laws for the whole world; Herod, who dost rule in Judea; ye rich, who dwell in

Jerusalem and Bethlehem; ye emperors, kings, and princes of the earth: sleep on in your magnificent palaces! It is not you that the angels will awake with an invitation to the manger: you are not worthy of it. The new King must have courtiers that will know him, and you would not know him. He must have persons that will love the poverty of his birth, and you would not love it.

Adoration of the shepherds. Now, there were, in the neighborhood of the grotto, some shepherds[566] keeping the night watches over their flocks. Suddenly they saw an extraordinary brightness shining above them, and, in the midst of this glory, an angel, who said to them: "Fear not; for I bring you tidings that shall give great joy to all the people. This day, in the city of David, there is born to you a Savior, who is Christ the Lord. Behold the sign by which you shall know him: you shall find the infant wrapped in swaddling clothes and laid in a manger." At the same moment, the angel was joined by a multitude of the heavenly army, praising God, and saying: "Glory be to God on high, and peace on earth to men of good will."[567]

When the angels disappeared, the shepherds, struck with astonishment, said to one another: "Let us go over to Bethlehem, and see what is come to pass, as the Lord has made known to us." Without the least delay, they hastened toward the stable. Here they found the newborn babe, wrapped in swaddling clothes and laid in the manger. Mary and Joseph were near it. The shepherds, seeing all the angel had said accomplished, returned, praising and glorifying God.[568]

Thus, poor, simple, obscure men were the first to be made aware of the birth of the Messias, the first to whom God the Father granted the signal honor of laying their homage at the feet of his Son. This single fact contains a moral revolution. It is the beginning of that new order of ideas which is to change the face of the world. Wealth, despotism, and pride! your reign is at an end; that of detachment, charity, and humility begins!

The words of the angel to the shepherds, "Fear not, a Savior is born to you," the Catholic Church addresses annually to all her children, to you as well as to me. During Advent, she borrowed the voices of Isaias and John the Baptist to say to us: "Prepare ye the ways of the Lord; the moment draws near when all flesh shall see the Savior sent by God." Then, when the four mysterious weeks draw to a close, she appoints a last day of fast and preparation. "Sanctify yourselves," she says, "for tomorrow the Lord will do wonderful things among you."

Office of Christmas. That we may have a share in the happiness of the angels, she wishes us to spend the night in prayer. During those beautiful matins, she chants the promises made of old to the patriarchs and the prophets. She recounts both the misery of the human race, and the goodness of the Redeemer so often foretold. Suddenly a deacon comes down from the sanctuary, preceded by lights, and bearing the book that contains the fulfillment of all the promises, figures, and prophecies. Arrived at the jubé, he chants the genealogy of the Redeemer, the Son of God and the Son of Man.[569] To this sublime record of divine abasements, all voices make answer in the hymn of gratitude and love, *Te Deum!*

The priest ascends the altar, and ere long the babe of Bethlehem, again incarnate in the hands of his minister, will be present for the adoration and love of the faithful. The Communion draws near: it is a moment of ineffable delights. Then are joyous carols heard—precious remains of the lively faith and innocent piety of our ancestors. Happy with a happiness that is known only on this day, the new shepherds retire to their homes, praising and blessing God. Here a joyous, because an innocent, repast is prepared for them: the "Christmas treat" assembles friends and neighbors at the same table. And how could such people fail to love one another when they had just adored their common Savior, and partaken of the good things on his sacred table? How could they fail to rejoice when such great favors had been bestowed on them?

At break of day, the bell is again heard. For the second time the priest ascends the altar, and those who have kept watch during the night fill the church and render their homage to the divine infant. High Mass comes at length, after a few hours, to assemble all the faithful, and evening will find them again before the altar of the newborn God: always with new canticles and new emotions. How could it be otherwise? Is there any day more beautiful than Christmas day? Did ever any day bring to men what Christmas night brought to them under its shadows? On this night, a brother came to the miserable, a liberator to slaves, a friend to orphans, a master to teachers, a model to kings, a conqueror to death. Let men therefore rejoice in the Lord, as the earth rejoices every morning when the sun rises to set it free from darkness. Christmas is the bright aurora of our deliverance: Jesus Christ, in his birth, is the sun of justice rising on the world to scatter all the shadows of death.

See also what enthusiasm, what a holy delirium, appears in the office rang by our priests! Listen to them:

"O hill of Sion! leap for joy…Ye daughters of Jerusalem! put on your festive robes, and sing, sing new canticles.

"O Jerusalem! arise, shake off the dust from thy hair, break the chain from thy neck; arise, thy Savior is come.

"Thou wast sold, and lo! the Lord hath redeemed thee: sing, O Jerusalem! sing.

"The Lord said, Assur oppressed my people. Injustice and cruelty weighed them down. I must go and deliver them. Formerly I spoke, but now here I am.

"Plenty and peace come with the day of the Lord.

"Truth hath risen from the earth, and justice hath looked on us from the heights of heaven.

"Let us sing, therefore, let us sing new hymns to the Lord; let all the earth sing with us.

"Let us sing to the Lord and bless his name.

"Let us tell the whole world of the day of his salvation.

"Let the nations recount the wonders that he hath wrought, and let all people be joyful.

"Truly, our God is great: his name is worthy of praise, and his power is over all things that exist.

"What are the gods of strange nations in comparison with our God? Devils from the lowest depths. But our God, our God is he who made heaven and earth, the firmament with its stars and the sea with its waves.

"Let heaven therefore rejoice and let the earth be filled with joy, let the sea roll and heave as a sign of gladness, and let the fields and all the plants that grow therein thrill with delight; for the day of the Lord is come."[570]

Thus does the beautiful day of Christmas pass with Christians. If there is any punishment for the indifferent and the impious, it is to feel none of the joys of this solemnity, it is to see nothing more in this day than in any other day.

How to sanctify Christmas: Lessons of the crib. To avoid so great a misfortune, let us go to Bethlehem, and there, on our knees before the manger, ask ourselves: "What does this infant wish to do to me?" And those little limbs, and that wailing, and that straw, and those poor swaddling clothes will answer us: "He wishes to cure thee."

Am I, then, sick? Yes. My first father, on the day of his rebellion, received three dreadful wounds from the devil. The effects of these three wounds he transmitted to us: an inordinate love of riches, an inordinate love of honors, and an inordinate love of pleasures. This triple love is like a burning fever. For four thousand years the human race was continually raving: day after day it tossed about in fury on its bed of anguish. Seizing on all creatures one after another to appease the thirst that devoured it, it tormented them in a thousand ways, in order to make them give it a little relief. Then, falling at their feet, it besought them in suppliant tones to grant it the alms of happiness. Foolish prayers, useless efforts! And, in its despair, it cursed all creatures, it cursed life, it cursed itself, it cried out by the mouth of the "happiest" of mortals: "Vanity, lying, affliction, there is nothing but deception."[571] "The day of death is better than the day of birth."[572]

And, during all that time, man forgot God, forgot his end, forgot his nature. Created in honor and glory, he reduced himself to the level of the beasts. Like a fierce mountain torrent, fed from three sources, iniquity spread over the whole earth. There were rivers of blood and rivers of tears. Slavery reigned everywhere, and the devil had a long enjoyment of his insolent triumph.

And I have inherited the three diseases of my ancestors, and these diseases continually tend to break out worse in me. But lo! the divine infant is come to cure me. To the inordinate love of riches, honors, and pleasures, he opposes poverty, humiliation, and suffering. He says to me, "My son, detach thy heart from all these things: I am come down from heaven to instruct thee. The world, I know, preaches a doctrine contrary to mine. Well, of two things one: either I am deceived, or the world is deceiving thee.[573] But I am the eternal Wisdom; I cannot lead thee nor be myself led into error. Thy own reason, thy own experience, the experience of others, all will unite with my teaching to tell thee that riches, honors, and pleasures cannot make thee happy; they are fleeting, and thou art immortal; they are finite goods, and the desires of thy heart are infinite. And what would it cost me to tell thee to love riches, honors, and pleasures, so that thou mightest give thyself to them as much as thou didst wish? But this doctrine and this conduct would be thy ruin. I much prefer to disabuse thee. Be instructed therefore at my crib."

Oh, yes, let us listen with respect to the lessons of the crib. Let us love and practice them: this is the price of our happiness. Alas! it was on account of not knowing them that the ancient world was unhappy. It was on account of practicing them that men afterward enjoyed all the bliss and glory consistent with their state here below. It is on account of forgetting them that modern society has again become like a bloody arena, where armed combatants tear one another to pieces like wild furies. And all for what? For the sake of a little bit of metal called gold, or a little cloud of smoke called honor.

The Son of God comes therefore to remove from the heart of man the constant objects of his affections since the fall, namely: creatures. But, O my God! thou dost afflict me: I am made to love, I cannot live without loving. In saying thou shalt not love, thou givest me my death blow. Yes; but, O goodness! O wisdom! which I can never love or admire enough, to this command there is joined another: thou shalt love with all thy heart, with all thy strength, and with all thy soul—what?—not the finite, not deceit, not a vain shadow, but the infinite, the reality itself, God instead of creatures.

And behold how, to make this new object of love relished, to reassure man, who, since the anathema of the terrestrial paradise, used to tremble, run away, and hide himself at the very name of God, as much afraid to see him as to die, behold how this great God becomes a little babe, and presents himself to us under the most amiable form that can be imagined! O men! understand the lessons of Bethlehem, and you shall soon be restored to health. On the one hand, undeceive your heart, detach it from creatures; on the other, place your affections on the object that is presented to you—a God, your beginning and your end, your friend, your brother, bone of your bone and flesh of your flesh. What is needed for all this? A good will! The conditions of your God are not, you see, hard; for who has not or cannot have a good will? No learning, no nobility is required.

To cure me is therefore what this babe wishes. My heart, dost thou understand?

Allegory. Let us therefore love the babe of Bethlehem,[574] whose love ought so much the more to excite ours as it is absolutely gratuitous and transcends all imagination!

Listen, my soul: I will tell thee a story. A traveler, going along his way, trod on a little worm and crushed it. As he was regretting the poor thing's death, a stranger came up to him and said: "If you wish to restore this little worm's life, I will show you how to do it. You must consent to become a worm of the earth yourself, and to let four of your veins be opened. Out of your blood there will be a bath made, in which this worm will recover its life." "Do you take me for a fool?" answered the traveler. "What matter is it whether this worm is restored to life or not? I am not so simple as to give my life for such a purpose." This answer had so much the better grounds as the traveler was the son of a king, and the worm was not exactly a harmless little creature, but an ungrateful kind of asp, which, having been previously warmed in the illustrious young man's breast, had attempted to take away his life.

Nevertheless, the prince, moved with an infinite pity, consented to become a worm of the earth, and to lay down his life for the recovery of the reptile. And everyone hearing of this occurrence, said: "The prince was a fool of love!" What should have been the gratitude of the worm if it had been capable of reason!

Well, my soul! this is what the Son of God did for thee. Who art thou?—what is man but a worm of the earth, and a perfidious ungrateful worm? Thou art less before God than a worm before man. What did it matter to God if this rebellious nonentity remained in its sin, and was buried in hell, as it deserved? And yet this great God had so much love for thee that, in order to deliver thee from eternal death, he first became a worm of the earth, and then, in order to restore thee to life, he let himself be put to death, and made thee a bath of his adorable blood!

Yes, it is so, it is all of faith. Listen: "And the Word was made flesh, and he washed us in his blood, and he raised us up to life again."[575] And, after all this, my soul, thou canst forget him! Thou wilt have enough love for the animals that serve and amuse thee, and thou wilt have none for thy liberator! Oh, no, let it not be so; but let us say with a great heart: "If any man love not the babe of Bethlehem, let him be anathema!"[576]

Thus, an understanding of the mystery, gratitude, and good will are the dispositions for the festival of Christmas. Let us resolve to become "saviors": this is their end.

Establishment of the festival. We have now told in simple terms what the Son of God did for the human race. In memory of this miracle of love, the Church established the festival of the 25th of December; for it was at midnight on this very day, in the year of the world 4004, that the great event took place. St. Chrysostom proves with much force that the Church of Rome could know precisely the day of our Lord's birth, and acquaint the other Churches with it, because this birth occurred in the beginning of the general enrollment commanded by Augustus and made by Quirinus in Judea. Now, documents relating to acts of this kind were carefully preserved at Rome, in the imperial archives.[577] For the rest, we must go back to the early ages in order to find the origin of the festival of Christmas.[578]

One of the most celebrated of the year, it enjoys great privileges: the first, to suspend the law of abstinence, so that flesh meat may be used on Christmas day, even when it falls on a Friday or a Saturday;[579] and the second, to give priests the faculty of saying three Masses. The first Mass is said to celebrate the eternal birth of the Son of God in the bosom of his Father; the second, his birth of the Blessed Virgin Mary; and the third, his spiritual birth in our souls by faith and charity.

In former times, priests used to say several Masses every day: they had full liberty to do so, according to the impulse of their devotion. It was the Council of Salgunstadt, near Mayence, in 1002, that limited the number to three for each day and for each priest. But Pope Alexander II, who died in 1073, changed this usage, and gave no one liberty anymore to say three Masses except on Christmas day. The faithful cannot do better than assist at the three, but the Church does not lay this on them as an obligation: a single Mass suffices for the fulfillment of the precept.

PRAYER

O my God! who art all love, I thank thee for having sent thy divine Son to redeem us. Grant that we may understand, appreciate, and practice the lessons which he gives us at the crib.

I am resolved to love God above all things, and my neighbor as myself for the love of God; and, in testimony of this love, I will often say: "O divine infant Jesus! make my heart like thine."

Lesson 29: Christianity Brought before the Senses (Continued)—Christmastide

Christmas time.—The frosty season continues. Snow covers the fields. Most of the fine houses in the country have been deserted by their owners. The cottage door is seldomer opened. The laborer, surrounded by his family, sits near the fire. The rich are assembled in cities, where balls, plays, and banquets are multiplied for them. While the world leads its noisy crowds of worshippers from pleasure to pleasure, the Church, like a tender mother, gathers her children around her, and teaches them to imitate the God of Bethlehem. The affecting mysteries of his holy infancy are one after another presented to their adoration, and the rich find therein a lesson of charity and the poor a model of resignation. The hearts of the rich are touched, for it is in the name of the little infant Jesus that an alms is asked of them; and abundant relief comes to the needy, who tremble with cold or perish with hunger in their obscure retreats.

During the severity of winter, the charity of Christianity, as you see, fights against the selfishness of the world: at this season, our Christian festivals are multiplied. It follows hence that religion found means to have a greater number of holy works practiced, and to give millions of afflicted people a few moments of happiness. These festivals are so much the more charming, as they have existed from all antiquity; and the poor find special pleasure in thinking, as they look back on the past, that their ancestors rejoiced at the same period as themselves.

On the night of the birth of the Messias, the troops of children that used to adore at the manger, the churches lighted up and decked with flowers, the people that flocked round the cradle of their God, the Christians that made their peace with heaven in some quiet chapel, the joyous alleluias, the simple carols, the pealing of the organ and the bells, all offered us a pomp full of innocent charms. In Christian homes, Bethlehem, the grotto, the manger, the divine infant, and the shepherds afforded matter of story for many days to the white-haired grandfather, and led to pious reading every evening in presence of the whole family, seated round the blazing hearth.

Solicitude of the Church: Festivals of St. Stephen, St. John, and the Holy Innocents. But here come other festivals. On the day after Christmas, the Church celebrates the triumph of the first of her martyrs; on the next day, the festival of the apostle St. John, the beloved disciple; and then, the festival of the Holy Innocents: you know these thousands of young victims under two years of age, whom Herod's jealousy swept out of life, but who now, glorified in heaven, crowned with lilies and roses, play before the altar of the Lamb. The Church delights in setting all these miraculous triumphs before our eyes, to let us see the omnipotent virtue of the divine infant; for it was he that gave Stephen courage, kindled the flame of Christian love in the heart of John, and crowned the innocent victims of Bethlehem. While revealing to us the spirit of Christianity, all these glorious memories confirm our belief in the divinity of the Son of Mary.

Herein, the Church follows step-by-step the conduct of the eternal Father. To every humiliation of the Son, there corresponds a manifestation of his glory. Man never appears alone in Jesus Christ: God always appears at his side. He annihilates himself in the manger, but the hosts of heaven proclaim in song his birth. It will be the same throughout the whole course of his career: an astounding revelation of his divinity will accompany each of his abasements. Eight days after the festival of Christmas, the Church again assembles her children at the crib: a moving spectacle awaits us. The infant Jesus, the world's victim, hastens to offer to his Father the first drops of his atoning blood, which he is one day to shed entirely on Calvary: he is going to submit to the painful law of circumcision. Such is the memorable circumstance in the Savior's life that the Church honors on the octave day of his birth.

The object of our faith on this festival is the babe of Bethlehem receiving the mark of circumcision and the name of Jesus. Let us state the reasons for the ceremony of circumcision, to which the incarnate Word vouchsafes on this day to submit.

Circumcision: Reasons for the ceremony.—All the sons of Abraham should bear in their flesh the mark of the covenant that the Lord had made with this father of believers. The precept of circumcision rested on three principal reasons. It should be: a) the seal of the covenant into which the Lord had entered with Abraham; b) a distinguishing sign between the descendants of the holy patriarch and the other peoples of the earth; and c) a pledge of the blessings promised in the person of Abraham to all those who would faithfully observe the ordinances of the Lord. One of these blessings, and unquestionably the most precious, was the remission of original sin. Circumcision did not produce this effect by its own virtue, but by virtue of faith in the passion of our Lord, of which it was a figure: a salutary faith, which, by receiving circumcision, the adult professed for himself, and parents for their children. However, the circumcised child that happened to die did not go at once to heaven: it had to await the ascension of our Lord.[580]

Circumcision took place eight days after the birth of the child. It was the custom to comply with this duty, not in the Temple, but in private houses. There was no need of having priests or Levites for the ceremony: the father was generally its minister, sometimes the mother.[581] St. Epiphanius, born in Palestine, and better acquainted than anyone else with the sacred traditions of his country, says expressly that the Savior was circumcised in the stable of Bethlehem,[582] and probably by the hand of the Blessed Virgin or St. Joseph. Jesus, being God, could have dispensed himself from this painful ceremony of the Mosaic law; but he chose to submit to it for several reasons equally worthy of his wisdom and his love.

1. By subjecting his sacred Person thereto, he did away in an honorable manner with a rite that God had established only for a time.

2. He proved thereby that he had a truly human body, and confounded beforehand the sophisms of heresy, which, in spite of the evident proofs drawn from the actions and sufferings of his mortal life, would one day deny their reality.

3. By showing that he was a son of Abraham, from whom the Messias should come, he prevented any objections that the Jews might raise for the purpose of disputing with him the divine characteristics of the Messias under the pretense that he was a stranger, and he acquired the right of conversing among them for the salvation of their souls.

4. He became our model, taught us obedience to the laws of God, inspired us with a horror of sin, and made himself our victim.

Our duty on the festival of the Circumcision is to enter into the sentiments of the Savior, and to profit by the lessons that he gives us. For this purpose, let us strive to have a lively horror of sin, which subjects this tender infant to such a painful ceremony; let us sincerely detach ourselves from created things, keeping a strict watch over our senses, in order to preserve them from the seduction of external objects; and let us unite our heart with that of Mary. Who can tell what this tender Mother felt when she saw the first drops of her Son's blood? Let us, like Jesus and Mary, offer ourselves in sacrifice to the Lord. Let us faithfully and respectfully comply with all the holy practices that his law requires of us, and let us submit without a murmur to all the trials that his providence may send us. Thus shall we celebrate worthily so instructive and affecting a festival.

Name of Jesus: Its excellence and meaning.—It was usual among the Jews to give the child a name on the day of its circumcision. Was it not indeed just that at the moment when the Son of Man was enrolled among the children of God, honored with his friendship, laden with his gifts, and made the heir of his promises, he should take a name that would recall this glorious adoption and the sublime character corresponding to it? Our Lord was also pleased to take an august name when he was circumcised, in order to submit in all things not only to the law, but even to the pious customs of the people of God, and hereby to show us with what fidelity we should observe the practices and rites of holy Church.

But what name will he take? Who has a right to impose one on him? To fathers we must yield the right of naming their children: and the most suitable names are always those which best describe the essential qualities of the objects to which they are applied. It follows hence that no creature in heaven or on earth, not even Joseph or Mary, could worthily name the Son of God; for there was no one capable of understanding the excellence of his nature and the dignity of his functions. God the Father could alone give his Son a name that would be perfectly appropriate to him.

And behold! the eternal Father charges a prince of his court to convey from heaven to earth the name of his Son. The archangel Gabriel, honored with this august commission, comes and announces to Mary both her divine maternity and the name that she is to give the Son who shall be born of her.[583] This adorable name was also communicated by an angel to St. Joseph on another occasion.[584] Hitherto, it was known only to the eternal Father, angels, Mary, and Joseph: the moment for revealing it to the world has arrived.

Looking down from the summit of heaven on his beloved Son, who submits to the humiliating and painful ceremony of circumcision, God the Father suddenly breaks the silence, and gives him a name by which he declares him exempt from sin—declares him innocence itself, sanctity itself, the source of salvation for all mankind. Do you wish to know it? Bow your forehead in the dust; for at this name every knee must bend in heaven, on earth, and in hell.[585] *Jesus*, that is to say, "Savior": such is the name of the Son of God—a name of power, love, and victory![586]

A *name of power*. It reminds us of him by whom all things were made; the Word of God, who holds the world in the hollow of his hand; the King of kings and the Lord of lords, whose spiritual kingdom is of all times and all climes; the Lamb, for whom the centuries succeed one another, for whom kings and peoples, whether willingly or unwillingly, are like a staff in the hand of a traveler, or like servants under the authority of a master, servants whom he exalts and glorifies if they are faithful, and whom he destroys as a vessel of clay if they dare to rebel against him.

A *name of love*. The sweet sounds of the two syllables that make up the name of Jesus rouse our attention, and awaken our gratitude toward the author of our salvation, who became man to bring us near him; who was born in a stable; who wept; who was persecuted, calumniated, laden with reproaches, mocked, and crucified for us; who, to reconcile us with his Father, rose from the dead; who ascended into heaven, where he is our advocate and mediator; who, in fine, to console and strengthen us, made himself the companion of our pilgrimage, by remaining day and night on our altars.

A *name of victory*. *Jesus* means "Savior," "Conqueror," "Triumpher." Man and the world had fallen into the power of the devil, who, strong and well-armed, held his prey in chains for four thousand years. And God knows the use that he made of this power! The Son of God came down from heaven to drive out the usurper, to break the tyrant's scepter, to set free the enslaved universe: and his name reminds us of his victory. Jesus is our Savior in the fullest sense of the word.

A Savior of man in every respect. He saves our mind from the galling yoke of cruel, infamous, humiliating errors and superstitions; he saves our heart from the thralldom of its passions; he saves our body from the evils that oppressed it under paganism, and communicates to it the germ of a glorious immortality. He saves the child, the wife, the father, society: he saves all. Yet a little while after the Savior's arrival in the world, and it is transformed into nations. Nowadays, he prevents us from falling back into the abyss from which he drew us forth.

Jesus is always our Savior, and the Savior of the whole world. Without Jesus, the physical world would immediately return to chaos, outraged by our crimes;[587] without Jesus, the intellectual world would immediately shroud itself in the darkness of error, a darkness drearier than the gloom of midnight; without Jesus, the moral world would immediately plunge into a sea of vice and corruption, as a body hastens to dissolution when quitted by the soul, or as meat hastens to rottenness when left without salt. The histories of peoples, during the last eighteen centuries, are at hand to give testimony on these truths.

Sentiments that the name of Jesus ought to inspire. And now, is it hard to understand that the most perfect confidence, the most tender love, the most lively joy, and the most profound respect ought to be the sentiments of our heart when we pronounce the adorable name of Jesus? Let it be our first word on awaking, and our last when going to rest: let it lie all the night long as a seal on our lips. In our temptations, dangers, and afflictions, let us invoke the name of Jesus: it is all-powerful to gladden the soul and to put the devil to flight. Tertullian permits pagans to spill the blood of the Christian who, invoking the name of Jesus, would fail to drive out the devil from the body of a possessed person brought to him.[588]

Let us acquire the blessed habit of often using this holy name during life: we shall then feel no ordinary confidence in pronouncing it for the last time at the moment of death. Let us enter into the sentiments of a pious servant of God who used to exclaim: "O divine Jesus! to thee I commit my happiness, my life, and my death. Whatever I do will be done under thy protection and in thy name. If I wake, Jesus will be before my eyes; if I sleep, I shall breathe his holy love; if I walk, it will be in the sweet company of Jesus; if I sit, Jesus will be at my side; if I study, Jesus will be my master; if I write, Jesus will guide my pen, and my greatest pleasure will be to trace his adorable name; if I pray, Jesus will suggest my words and will mark my accents; if I be tired, Jesus will be my rest; if I be sick, Jesus will be my doctor and my comforter; if I die, it will be on the bosom of Jesus: Jesus will be my happiness, and his name will be my epitaph." We are bound to render homage to the name of Jesus, not only out of gratitude, but also in order to obey the eternal Father, who commanded that at this name every knee should bend in heaven, on earth, and in hell.[589] From this divine command is derived the most ancient custom that all the faithful show their veneration for the holy name of Jesus by bowing their heads as often as they pronounce it or hear it pronounced. In 1274, the Second General Council of Lyons confirmed this pious practice.

Later on, Sixtus V granted an indulgence of twenty days to those who, with sentiments of sincere contrition, bowed their head when pronouncing the holy name of Jesus. In 1587, the same pontiff granted to all Christians an indulgence of fifty days as often as in saluting one another they used the following formula, either in the Latin or in the vulgar tongue: *Laudetur Jesus Christus!*—"May Jesus Christ be praised!" or that they answered: "Amen," or *In saecula saeculorum*—"Forever!" A plenary indulgence was also granted at the point of death to those who, having been accustomed to invoke the names of Jesus and Mary, repeated these names in their heart, if no longer able to do so with their mouth. These indulgences were confirmed, in 1728, by Benedict XIII.[590]

Antiquity of the festival of the Circumcision.—The profound respect which the Church has always entertained for the Savior and his admirable name is a proof of the antiquity of the festivals established in their honor. Though mention of the solemnity of the Circumcision is found for the first time only in the Second Council of Tours, held in 567, yet we cannot doubt that it is more ancient, and reaches back at least to the fourth century.[591] As a matter of fact, this council says expressly that it only renews the statute of the ancient fathers. It made the festival more celebrated: longer prayers were commanded, and a fast prescribed, but only a half fast, whose observance was easily compatible with the solemnity. Formerly, it was usual to celebrate two Masses on this day: one in honor of the circumcision of our Lord, and the other in honor of the Blessed Virgin, so that the divine Mother might have a share in the festivals established after Christmas for the glory of her Son. Hence it is that we still find in the office and Mass many things relating to the Blessed Virgin.[592]

Acknowledge here the wise solicitude of the Church. The day of the Circumcision, which falls on the first day of the New Year, was a day of disorder among pagans. The Church opposed thereto the worship of Jesus suffering and that of Mary his Mother, the Mother of virgins; also, fasting and holy prayers.[593] The pagans honored on this day their goddess Strena or Strenua by an exchange of presents: of which custom we have still some remains in our Christmas boxes and New Year's gifts. These rejoicings, accompanied with a thousand excesses, began among the Romans on the 17th of December. During eight days, they celebrated the Saturnalia or festivals of Saturn. Slaves used then to eat with their masters: they had also leave to say whatever they pleased. The object of this superstitious custom was to perpetuate the memory of a supposed golden age, when there were no distinctions among men.

New Year's gifts and wishes.—The same people also celebrated the Calends or beginning of January in honor of their god Janus by spectacles no less extravagant than licentious. This god had imposed his name on the month of January. Such is the origin of these profane rejoicings on New Year's day and Twelfth day, and during the Carnival, to which so many Christians are not ashamed to abandon themselves: many councils have condemned them. We learn from St. Isidore of Seville and Alcuin that some churches commanded a fast for the 1st of January, so as to put a more effectual stop to these abuses.[594]

We have only a slight trace of the ancient custom on New Year's day left. Notwithstanding the pagan origin of present-making at this season, there is nothing in it nowadays contrary to Christianity. It may even become the happy occasion of a reconciliation between members of the same family, for it is calculated to draw closer the bonds of mutual charity. Let our care be to sanctify it by the purity of our intentions.

The same is to be said of good wishes for the new year. With many people, they are empty compliments. Why should we not make them holy? Why should we not turn them into a prayer? Why should we not sincerely wish one another a really happy new year—a good year in the sight of God—a year rich for heaven, sanctified by the love of God and our neighbor? Simple souls do so: Why should not we?

Our ancestors, more enlightened because more Christian than their children, used expressions much more perfect than ours. They would say to one another in their artless charity: "I wish you many happy new years and paradise at the end of your days." Perhaps you ridicule this formula! Well, tell us if you know another more worthy of a man or a Christian. Your contempt excites fear and pity: keep it to yourselves. Reserve your sarcasms for some false assurances or hollow conventionalities—the vain ceremonial of worldly people at the beginning of the new year. Let the formula of our ancestors be therefore on our lips and in our heart. Every other is imperfect or deceptive.

It is therefore laudable to wish a happy new year to all persons who are dear to us, or to whom we owe a special regard; but let us not forget him to whom our first addresses ought to be made. Yes, let us wish our heavenly Father a happy new year. Let us say to him with childlike simplicity: "My God! I wish thee a very happy new year, a year in which thou mayst be known, loved, and glorified by the whole world." Let us offer him our new year's gifts: our heart, a holy resolution for the year. Let us ask him for his gifts: he has stores of them. And let us leave the choice to himself: his hand, guided by his tender heart, will give us what he knows to be best for us.

Useful practice. Let us, above all, be faithful to the affecting custom established in a "Catechism of Perseverance" not unknown to you. You are aware that, on the first day of the year, the lady president herself makes a collection for the little infant Jesus. Money, oranges, sweets, etc., are received and offered as new year's gifts to the infant Jesus in the person of a poor little child chosen beforehand. There is no silliness in all this. Revive your faith. In the gospel, our Lord does not say, "The poor were hungry, the poor were thirsty," but he says, "I, yes I, your God, I was hungry, I was thirsty." It is therefore to the infant Jesus, identified with the poor, that your offerings are made. Adopt this kind practice, I pray you. It is well calculated to draw down the blessings of heaven during the year that is just beginning. And then it is so delightful to make happy a poor child that but for you would have to look, shivering with cold and perishing with want, at others of its own age enjoying themselves to their hearts' content amid the festivities of this long-expected season!

Lastly, the first day of the new year should inspire us with serious thoughts. Does the year now closing, now falling as a drop of water into the ocean of eternity, leave us pure from sin? What have I done for God and my soul? Am I better at the end of this year than I was at its beginning? Of what fault have I corrected myself? What virtue have I acquired? If I had now to give an account of the past, what merits should I have to present? And yet how many graces I have received!

A useful exercise for New Year's eve and New Year's day is to confess and communicate as if the moment of our viaticum had arrived. For this purpose, persons take a quarter of an hour to examine their conscience; they recite the prayers for the agonizing; they prepare for death—in a word, they endeavor to regulate the affairs of their conscience as merchants settle their accounts at this period and balance their books. How long, O my God! will the children of the world be more prudent than the children of light?

PRAYER

O my God, who art all love! I thank thee for having shed the first drops of thy blood for me on the day of the Circumcision. Grant me a great respect for thy holy name and a great confidence in it.

I am resolved to love God above all things, and my neighbor as myself for the love of God; and, in testimony of this love, I will every morning, on awaking, invoke the names of Jesus and Mary.

Lesson 30: Christianity Brought before the Senses (Continued)—Epiphany

Epiphany: Wisdom and utility of the worship of the infant Jesus.—Five days after the festival of the Circumcision, the heavy bells of our old cathedrals and the light ones of our hamlets are again set in motion. The inhabitants of town and country put on their best attire. The streets and roads leading to the church are thronged. Our altars display an extraordinary splendor. A new festival is come! For the third time within a fortnight, the Church summons her children to the cradle of Bethlehem. Ah! it is because mysteries of love succeed one another rapidly in this retreat of the newborn God.

"But why," asks the ignorant and reckless man of the world, "why bring continually before our eyes the sad sight of this manger, this stable, this infant weeping and moaning? Catholic worship is a worship that inspires only gloomy and sulky thoughts. It continually feeds the imagination of its disciples with the poor life of Jesus. It is a tiresome and sickening worship, far inferior to superstitious idolatry, which offered the pagans at least the smiling images of pleasure."

So much for accusations. Now for replies.

True, Catholicity continually reminds us of the poor life of Jesus; but what is there, O worldly sage! in such morality to scandalize you? Ask experience, cast a look on society, and tell me if this morality does not lead man better than your lessons to a contempt of wealth and pomp, and a respect for poverty. Is not your favorite dream equality among the members of the great human family? Well, tell me again if this morality is not an exhortation stronger than all your arguments, and more effectual in restoring the primitive equality of the children of Adam than all your charters and constitutions. Does it not give man better than your books a just idea of the true goods that he should desire and the true evils that he should fear? Is it not for the rich and great the most powerful of all motives to bring them near the poor man, to make them regard him as a mediator in the order of religion, and to put them on their guard against glorying in things which the Son of God and the justest of mortals have despised?

And as for the poor and oppressed, those who suffer and lament, those who, being cast off by the world, have God alone to witness their sorrows—and you know their number is great—well, is there for all these unfortunates anything more consoling than the stable of the infant God, his poor swaddling clothes, and the bareness of his manger? By wishing to deprive the miserable of this worship; by wishing to rob them of this divine cradle, these precious swaddling clothes, this poor manger—do you thus, O philosopher! show yourself a benefactor of humanity, or rather its most cruel enemy? While it is in the midst of your splendid rooms, your enchanting sights, and your grand banquets that you brave the severities of winter, oh! let religion console the poor man in want of food and fire, by showing him an infant—his model and his God—shivering and crying!

You also say that pagan worship was superior to ours, for it offered only the smiling images of pleasure. I admit that the worship of an abominable Jupiter or a shameless Venus would be more pleasing to the voluptuous; the worship of Juno more pleasing to the revengeful; the worship of Bacchus, more pleasing to drunkards; the worship of Plutus, more pleasing to misers; and that thus every passion, every vice would be delighted to see itself deified in the object of its desires. But, tell me, is this the way to make man better, consequently happier? Is this the way to make society more moral, consequently more tranquil and united? Has not man a strong enough inclination to evil already, without exciting him to it by the example of his gods?

Paganism, you say, was more smiling. But was it then to amuse and to distract us, or to glorify God and to make us better, that religion was established? Paganism was more joyous outwardly; but did it make man happier inwardly? Will you confound the riotous pleasures of the world with the calm pleasures of the mind and the heart? Paganism certainly satiated itself with the former, but it ignored the latter. Christianity does the contrary. It leads man to happiness by a surer way—that of privations. It does not make him go out of himself in order to attain a feeling of happiness: this feeling is within us, not without us. It is within man that true religion should place his sweetest enjoyments, and let him find the purest delights of virtue, contentment with himself, a profound peace, the repose of a good conscience, for which nothing else can supply, and which has never been known by the adorers of false gods or the panegyrists of deceit.[595]

Let the impious rave on. As for us, let us follow the Church to Bethlehem. Today is the festival of the Kings, or the Epiphany, that is to say, the Manifestation of the Infant Jesus.

Object of the festival of the Epiphany: Three manifestations of the Savior. On this great day, the Church celebrates three manifestations of the Son of God. The first is that which took place at his baptism, when the Holy Ghost descended visibly on him under the form of a dove, and a voice was heard saying: "This is my beloved Son, in whom I am well pleased."[596] The second is that which took place at the marriage feast of Cana, when the Savior wrought his first miracle by changing water into wine, a miracle by which he showed forth his glory, and in consequence of which his disciples believed in him. The third and most celebrated is that by which he revealed himself to the Gentiles and received the adoration of the Magi.

The union of these three commemorations on one day is of very ancient origin. It would seem that the Church, in the establishment of this triple festival of the Epiphany, or Manifestation of the Savior, had regard to the opinion of some holy fathers who thought that the three mysteries might have occurred on one day.[597]

The Magi. However, the thought of the Savior adored in the manger by the kings or Magi so prevailed that it gave its name to the festival, and appears almost exclusively in the office and hymns of the solemnity of the 6th of January. In effect, the manifestation of Jesus to the Gentiles was an extraordinary event, one that changed the face of the earth. Since the times near the deluge, the nations, having erred from the right way and bowed their heads to idols, were seated in the shadow of death. History tells of their abjection and their sufferings.

One people alone, entrusted with the true religion, had all the conditions necessary to live happy under the rule of God himself. Yet mercy pleaded in heaven the cause of the nations. It succeeded, and the infant God was born at Bethlehem. By calling strangers to his cradle, God wished to show that all mankind were destined to know, love, and serve him.

From the day on which the Eastern Magi came to adore the Son of Mary, there was no longer any privilege among the nations, no longer any special people of God. All peoples were the people of Jesus Christ; all nations were the chosen nation. Hence, the festival of the Adoration of the Magi is our festival; for we are the descendants of those who came from afar to adore the universal Redeemer. Our fathers were not the owners of the Land of Chanaan. To lead them into it, a star rose in the sky and went before them, as the pillar of fire went in other days before the soldiers of Moses.

The miraculous star. We ought to be very grateful to God for this prodigy. Without the star that shone before their eyes, we should have remained in the darkness and shadow of death. We ought therefore every year, on the return of the day of the Kings, to go to the foot of those altars which represent the manger of Bethlehem, and adore him who was born for the salvation of all; and, if we have no myrrh, or frankincense, or gold to offer him, let us not be disheartened, but call to mind that the shepherds adored the Son of Mary before the kings. And what had they to offer him but the homage of their purity and their faith?[598]

In the second part[599] of the catechism, we described the journey of the Magi.[600] It remains for us to give a few details regarding them and the star that guided them: everything on such subjects is interesting. Tradition informs us that, after their return into their own country, they took care to make a good use of the graces which they had received, and that they attained the glory of heaven, having preached Jesus Christ on earth by word and example.[601]

It also informs us that they were three in number, that they were kings,[602] and that they were named Melchior, Gaspar, and Balthazar. Melchior, the first of the Magi, was a bald old man, as tradition tells, with a large beard and some long white hair. He wore, when prostrating before the infant announced by the star, a robe of hyacinth or azure, a yellow or orange cloak, shoes of blue and white, and a royal mantle of various colors. He offered gold to the King Jesus. The second was Gaspar. He was young, beardless, and ruddy, and wore an orange robe and a red mantle. His shoes were of a hyacinth color. He offered frankincense to acknowledge the divinity of Mary's Son. The third was Balthazar. He was brown, had a large beard, and wore a red robe and a speckled mantle. His shoes were yellow. He offered myrrh to denote the Savior's mortality.[603] This tradition, regarding the appearance and costume of the Magi, may be piously believed, but we are not bound to believe it as of faith.

The prophecy of Balaam. As for the occupation of the Magi, we have said that they were kings, and they made astronomy their particular study.[604] Versed in old traditions, they recognized in the miraculous star the one that had been announced fifteen centuries before by Balaam. We know that the Israelites, on their entrance into the promised land, under the leadership of Josue, were everywhere triumphant. The fame of their victories, and yet more of the miracles that God wrought for them in the desert, spread alarm and anxiety among the people of Chanaan. The Moabites, above all, were struck with terror. Balac, their king, resolved on opposing this terrible nation with something else than useless weapons.

He accordingly sent deputies to Balaam, the son of Beor, who dwelt at Pethor, on the Euphrates, in Mesopotamia, and who passed for a diviner and enchanter. The chief of the messengers said to him in the name of the king his master: "Behold! people are come out of Egypt, who cover all the land and are encamped near me. Do you come therefore and curse these people, because they are stronger than I, so that I may see if I can by any means beat them and drive them out of my territory; for I know that those whom you bless shall be blessed and those whom you curse shall be cursed."

Balaam went. The day after his arrival, Balac led him to a high mountain, from which he could view the army of Israel. At this sight, Balaam, seized by the Spirit of the Lord, began to bless the people whom he had come to curse. Going on to prophesy, he said: "Behold what Balaam, the son of Beor, says; behold what a man whose eye is steady says; behold what he who hears the words of God, who knows the counsels of the Most High, who witnesses the visions of the Almighty, says! I shall see him, but not now; I shall gaze on him, but not near. A star shall rise out of Jacob. A scepter shall spring up from Israel, and it shall strike the chief of Moab. A ruler shall come forth from Jacob, and he shall destroy the remains of the city."

An unvarying tradition, common both to Jews and Christians, and dating from 3,500 years ago, has always admitted that Balaam pointed out the Messias in the words: "A star shall rise out of Jacob; a scepter shall spring up from Israel." The words of the prophet had resounded throughout the whole East. The remembrance of them was perpetuated from age to age, and, when the star appeared, the Magi, enlightened both by tradition and grace, set out on their journey to adore the glorious scion of Israel,[605] whom they found at Bethlehem with his divine Mother, and to whom they offered their gifts of gold, frankincense, and myrrh.

Faithful to the custom of Orientals, who used never to appear and even yet never appear before kings without offering them some gifts, the Magi laid deeply mysterious gifts at the feet of the infant Jesus. By gold, they acknowledged his royalty, his absolute dominion over the whole world, and his right to the tributes of all nations. By frankincense, they acknowledged his divinity; for incense is an emblem of adoration, of sacrifice, of the creature's annihilation before God. By myrrh, employed in embalming, they acknowledged his sacred humanity.[606] In these gifts, what a lesson for us! Let us carry to the divine infant the gold of charity and obedience, the frankincense of prayer and faith, and the myrrh of mortification and self-denial. These are the presents which he asks of us, and without which we cannot please him.

The Magi were the firstfruits of the Gentiles. It is from their arrival at Bethlehem that we date the new epoch of grace and benediction, when the sun of truth and justice rose on the whole world: a glorious epoch, of which the Church consecrated the memory by the solemnity of the Epiphany.

Antiquity of the festival of the Epiphany: Obligation and manner of celebrating it.—This festival is traced to the early ages. About the middle of the fourth century, it was already so solemn a one that, according to Ammianus Marcellinus, the emperor Julian durst not dispense himself from appearing thereon. This prince, being at Vienne on the Epiphany, thought himself bound to assist at the office of the day, lest he should betray his design of renouncing the Christian religion: this was in the beginning of the year 361.[607]

It was the same, a few years later on, with the emperor Valens. Though infected with Arianism, he thought that he should cease to be regarded as a Christian prince if he did not assist at divine service on the Epiphany. The immense concourse of people, the profound piety of the whole assembly, the magnificence of the ceremonies, the majesty of St. Basil, who celebrated the august sacrifice, all struck the heretical prince with such amazement and fear, especially when he saw himself excluded from the oblation, that he would have fallen in a faint if he had not been held up by one of the ministers of the altar.[608]

The festival of the Epiphany, though a most solemn one, is not preceded by any fast, because it is like a continuation of the festival of Christmas, and the Vigil of Christmas is in a manner the Vigil of the Epiphany. On this day, the Church sets before our eyes the grandeur of her decorations and the treasures of her poetry. The prophecies, the hymns, the evening psalms, all unite to sing with extraordinary enthusiasm the praises of the sun of justice rising on the nations, so long seated in the shadow of death. Ah! if we knew the gift of God, if we reflected on the state in which our fathers were and in which we ourselves should still be without the gospel, with what sentiments of gratitude should we unite our voices with the voice of the Church, our hearts with her heart, our prayers with her prayer, to thank him who vouchsafed to place our cradle in the midst of Christianity!

If these considerations affect us little, let us turn our eyes toward the many unfortunate nations, enslaved, degraded, bowed down to the hour that now is under the yoke of idolatry. Behold, they say to us, behold our abjection, our endless misery, our barbarism, our inhuman sacrifices: what we are, you once were, and you would still be without Christianity. Take care of what you have: the religion that brought you forth from barbarism can alone prevent you from relapsing into it.

Let us also question the nations that have lost the faith. What does the northern coast of Africa, formerly so flourishing, the land of Augustines, Cyprians, and Tertullians, say to us? What do Asia and Greece, watered by the sweat of holy apostles, say to us? Here were the fervent Churches of Antioch, Ephesus, Corinth, and Thessalonica; here dwelt an enlightened people, happy and free. What do you see instead of them? Ruins upon ruins. The crescent has taken the place of the cross; barbarism, that of knowledge; and slavery, that of freedom. Joy has been followed by sorrow, and prosperity by wretchedness.

From amid the remains of their ancient glory, these nations and cities cry out to us: "Ye peoples of Europe! we were your seniors in civilization. We first enjoyed the blessings of the faith. We were what you are, enlightened, happy, and free. Hold fast what you have: the religion that brought you forth from barbarism can alone preserve you from relapsing into it." Oh, no, my God! it is not without reason that thou dost encircle Christian nations with so many legions of idolaters and barbarians: thou wishest by this sight, at once so sad and so terrible, to instruct us and to make us grateful and faithful.

May these solemn lessons sink deep into our minds, and these dreadful miseries touch our hearts! But let us not confine ourselves to an idle pity: let us fly to the relief of these benighted people. Let a slight alms, seconding the heroic zeal of our missionaries, procure for these poor creatures, ransomed like ourselves by a divine blood, that happiness which we enjoy with perhaps too little gratitude. Who knows?—perhaps this is the cost at which we are to preserve the faith among us. To procure the light of the gospel for those who are buried in the darkness of error is, you may be quite sure, the true way of entering into the spirit of the festival of the Epiphany and celebrating it worthily.

The Magi also give us an example that we ought to imitate. Is it not time for us to show the same fidelity to grace? As often as God speaks to us, whether by his ministers, or by inspirations, or by revolutions, or by pestilences, or by benefits, it is a star that shines on our path, it is a voice that calls us to virtue. Let us follow it like the Magi, readily, generously, sincerely, and faithfully, and like them we shall find Jesus Christ. Having found him and laid at his feet the homage of our heart, let us return by another road: let us, the possessors of God himself and his grace, keep far from the Herods that would wish to put the child to death. These Herods, as everyone knows, are bad Christians, whose impious language and perverse example tend to rob us of our innocence.

Gratitude for our vocation to the faith; zeal for the propagation of the gospel;[609] a real desire to correspond with grace, so as to regulate our manners in all things according to our belief: these are the general dispositions with which we should enter on the worthy celebration of the festival of the Epiphany.

Office of Epiphany and the announcement of Easter. The office of this great day offers some particulars worthy of remark. Formerly at Mass, the priest or deacon, after singing the gospel, turned toward the people, and announced the day of Easter in these terms: "Let your charity know, my dearest brethren, that through the mercy of God and Jesus Christ, we shall celebrate the Pasch of the Lord on the ___ of the month of ___."

Here is the origin of this very old custom. In the second century, the day of Easter was appointed for all the Churches of the East and West; but there was no calendar yet. As the most able astronomers dwelt at Alexandria in Egypt, then a learned city, it was according to the astronomical tables sent every year by the patriarch of this city that the sovereign pontiff informed the metropolitans of the West regarding the day of Easter. In the council or synod that was held every year, each metropolitan pointed out the day of Easter for the coming year. The other bishops and priests present took a note of the date in their pocketbooks, and, before the close of the festivals of Christmas time, announced it to their flocks. They selected for this purpose the day of the Epiphany, the last of the solemnities of Christmas time, and the last great festival before Easter, so that the people assembled thereon in greater numbers might have a better knowledge of the august occasion.

At matins of the Epiphany, there was no invitatory, because on great festivals the people were called to the night office by the singing of the invitatory. When the watches of the faithful were done away with, and that of the Epiphany was one of the first to share this fate, on account of abuses that had crept in, the bishop and his clergy continued to say the office, but the invitatory, which would have no object, was dropped. It was allowed to remain on other festivals, because the people were still called to the night office. At length, when the night office was totally abolished, the invitatory was retained as a vestige of an ancient custom.[610] Thus, the suppression of the invitatory at the office of the Epiphany and its preservation on other festivals are monuments that recall all the discipline of the Church in the celebration of her holy watches.

The King's Cake. Lastly, on the day of the Epiphany there is something that may give us an opportunity of practicing the great virtue of Christianity—charity. The "Kings'

Cake," which assembles friends and neighbors around the same table, becomes for them an occasion of concord and peace, and of mercy toward the poor.

Oh how affecting is the custom, still kept up in good old families, of taking "God's part," that is to say, the part for the poor, before all others out of this royal cake! An immense cake is borne to the parish priest, who, on this day, joins in the festivities. He is requested to mark off the part for the poor and urged to make it very large. This part is set aside, and if by chance the bean is not found in the other portions given to the guests, then, to have the right of searching for it in the part for the poor, an alms must be given to the priest for the relief of the sick and distressed in the parish.

Blessed art thou, O holy religion! O loving mother! who dost allow thy children an innocent gaiety, but dost wish that all the members of thy large family should have a share in it.

PRAYER

O my God! who art all love, I thank thee for having called the Gentiles to the faith. Shed thy light on infidels, who know thee not, and on heretics who know thee amiss. Grant that, obedient to the voice of grace, we may never have the misfortune to lose the faith.

I am resolved to love God above all things, and my neighbor as myself for the love of God; and, in testimony of this love, I will help in the work of the Propagation of the Faith.

Lesson 31: Christianity Brought before the Senses (Continued)—Candlemas

From Christmas till the Purification, the Church keeps us in adoration before the babe of Bethlehem. She wishes that we should be deeply penetrated with its lessons; for the crib is a pulpit from which it eloquently instructs us. Forty days after the Savior's birth, she solemnly summons us together. But it is no longer in a stable that she offers the infant-God to our adoration. The Temple of Jerusalem is about to receive, for the first time, a victim worthy of the God therein adored. Let us set out for the holy city! Mary will lead the way, carrying her Son in her arms. The old man that steps along in the dust near her is St. Joseph, a virtuous descendant of the royal line of David.

Three mysteries.—On the 2nd of February, three mysteries are presented to our consideration: the Purification of the Blessed Virgin, the Presentation of Jesus in the Temple, and the Meeting with Anna and Simeon.

I. *The Purification.*—The son of a guilty father, man is defiled from the first moment of his conception: the giving birth to a defiled being causes the mother to contract a kind of defilement. A profound and terrible dogma: the source of humility, purity, and holy fear for parents; and the remembrance of which God wishes to be perpetuated from generation to generation. And behold this thrice holy God, dictating his laws to Moses, says: "Speak to the children of Israel, and say to them, 'If a woman bring a son into the world, she shall be unclean for forty days. She shall touch no holy thing, neither shall she enter into the holy place, till the days of her purification are over. If she bring forth a daughter, she shall be unclean for eighty days. When the days of her purification are over for a boy or a girl, she shall bring to the door of the tabernacle a lamb of a year old and a young pigeon or a turtle.'"[611]

The priest offered the lamb as a holocaust, to acknowledge the sovereign dominion of God and to thank him for the mother's happy deliverance. The pigeon or turtle was offered for sin. After this twofold sacrifice, the woman was freed from her legal uncleanness and reestablished in her former rights. The Lord, continuing to speak to Moses, added: "If the woman be not able to buy a lamb, she shall offer two turtles or two young pigeons, one for a holocaust and the other for sin, and the priest shall pray for her, and so she shall be cleansed."[612]

Humility and obedience of Mary. Mary, whose divine childbearing had only made her purer and more virginal, was certainly exempt from the precept relative to the ceremony of purification. Nevertheless, she subjected herself to it, and, keeping to the letter of the law, appeared at the Temple forty days after the Savior's birth. The imitator of her Son, who hid his divinity under the weakness of infancy, Mary wished to hide her august dignity of Mother of God, by comporting herself outwardly like ordinary women. Does the spirit of Jesus and Mary dwell in us?[613] The proud are eager to publish their superiority: How is it with us? The humble, content with the eyes of God, delight in obscurity: How is it with us?

Mary, being poor and the Mother of a child that, according to the prophecies, was to be born poor and to live poor, presented herself at the Temple with two turtles, as the law required. The daughter of David, the Mother of the Messias, can only make the offering of the poor! Oh, when I see poverty despised, I am indignant. There is often so much nobility in misery! Who can assure you that, under that ragged coat, there is not the son of a king, or, under that faded veil, the daughter of a queen? Perhaps some proud rich man of Jerusalem would have looked disdainfully on the couple that brought nothing to the Temple but the two little doves of the poor! Perhaps, in the front court, near the altar of sacrifices, the man with purple mantle and golden sandals would have disputed the ground with Joseph and Mary! And yet, thou stupid favorite of blind fortune! this man who carries the two birds is a descendant of thine own ancient kings; this woman, so timid, so beautiful, and so humble, is a daughter of David; this child—is the master of the universe! If he liked, he could with his little hand pull down the pillars of thy palaces, break the cedars of thy hills, and sweep away the riches of thy fields.[614] This offering, trivial as it seems to thee, is a thousand times more agreeable than thine! The heart that comes forward with it is a most perfect heart, and it is to the heart that God looks as the soul of sacrifice. Let us not forget this truth, and let an earnest, sincere charity give value to our least actions.

The Purification of Mary is therefore the first mystery that the festival of the 2nd of February presents to our consideration.

Custom of churching. Though Jewish rites have been abrogated since the promulgation of the gospel, the custom has prevailed among Christian mothers of imitating, on their first coming out after confinement, the example of the Blessed Virgin, who freely submitted to a law that did not concern her. They go to the church, in order to receive the blessing of the priest and to testify their gratitude to God. But Christian mothers do not go to the church with the intention that took the Jewish ones to the Temple: they go there in order to offer to the Lord a just tribute of praise and thanksgiving. Behold how Pope Innocent III expresses himself on this matter: "If women desire to enter the church immediately after their confinement, they do not sin by entering it, and they ought not to be prevented; but if, out of respect, they prefer to remain away for some little time, we do not think that their devotion ought to be blamed."[615] So far from blaming their devotion, the Church encourages it. Certain dioceses have a fixed number of days, after which the churching is to take place: people there should conform to the established rule. In districts where no settled custom or statute exists on this point, the Christian mother should fulfill this duty as soon as she can leave her house without endangering her health.

It is very proper indeed that her first visit should be to the church. Has she not to thank the Lord for her happy deliverance, and to beg his blessing as well on herself as on her child? Must she not ask the help of which she has need to rear up in virtue the child that she has brought into the world, and take a firm resolution to preserve its soul from sin? What would it avail her to be a mother if the fruit of her womb should fall into the power of the devil and perish forever? Let her therefore consecrate her child to the Lord.

The sacrifice that she makes will not fail to be accepted, if she enters into the dispositions that animated the Blessed Virgin on the day of her purification.

Ceremony of the churching of mothers. Nothing more proper to inspire them than the prayers used in the ceremony of churching. The Christian mother who comes to receive a blessing after her confinement stops at the door of the temple. Here she kneels, holding a lighted taper in her hand, in order to acknowledge her unworthiness to appear before God, and to show her ardent desire to share in his mercies. The priest, wearing a surplice and a white stole, comes to her, and, after invoking the name of the Lord, recites the twenty-third psalm: "The earth is the Lord's," etc. This beautiful canticle is admirably suited to the occasion. It recounts for the Christian mother the virtues that will procure for herself and her child the happiness of dwelling on the holy mountain of Sion. It reminds her of the absolute dominion of the Lord over all things in existence; consequently, of the boundless gratitude and perfect submission that are due to him. After giving the woman all these great lessons, the priest presents the end of his stole to her, and says, "Enter the temple of God, and adore the Son of the Blessed Virgin Mary, who gave you fruitfulness."

The priest presents the end of his stole to the woman: What is the meaning of this ceremony? The stole is an emblem of sacerdotal power. The priest, in presenting it to the woman, seems to say to her: "In the name of God, whose place I hold, be purified from any stains that you may have contracted. The Lord permits you to enter his temple. He accepts the homage of gratitude that you have come to render him."

The Christian mother, having arrived at the foot of the altar, goes on her knees, and thanks God for his benefits. Then the priest, reciting the *Pater*, calls down on the head of this new Eve all kinds of blessings from on high. Do you know any occasion when woman has more need of them? Is she not—frail creature!—appointed to train up a good citizen for society, a child for the Church, a brother for Jesus Christ, a saint for heaven? Is it not often on a mother's knees that the future of a man, the peace of families, and the happiness of the world are decided?

Full of these grave thoughts, the priest and the Christian mother begin, at the foot of the altar, in the presence of the God of angels, one of those dialogues which are to be found nowhere but in Catholic worship.

The priest says to the woman: "Do not lose courage; our help is in the name of the Lord."

By the mouth of the clerk, the mother answers: "Who made heaven and earth."

The priest: "O Lord! save thy handmaid."

The mother: "Thou knowest, O Lord! that she hopeth in thee."

The priest: "Send her thy help from thy holy place."

The mother: "From the summit of holy Sion protect her."

The priest: "Let the enemy have no power against her."

The mother: "And let not the son of iniquity come near to injure her."

The priest: "O Lord! hear my prayer."

The mother: "And let my cry ascend to thee."

The priest: "Let us pray. O Almighty and eternal God! who, by the happy delivery of the Virgin Mary, didst change the bitter pains of mothers into joy, graciously look upon thy servant, and grant, through the intercession of the august Queen of heaven, that she who this day comes into thy temple in order to return thee solemn thanks may arrive safe with her child at eternal beatitude. Through Jesus Christ our Lord," etc.

The mother: "Amen."

The priest then addresses some words of edification to her, in order to confirm the sentiments of gratitude and piety that have brought her to the foot of the altar, and to engage her to consecrate both her own life and the life of her child to the Lord; or some words of consolation, if, like Rachel, she weeps for her child already cut down by the scythe of death: he cheers her drooping spirits by reminding her of her happiness in being the mother of an angel.

Is there a Christian mother, one that understands her dignity and her duty, who can dispense herself from this beautiful ceremony? Let those dispense themselves from it who have no thanks to return to the Lord for the preservation of their days and those of their child, who are in no want of advice or consolation, who have no light, help, or blessing to ask from on high for the education of the immortal being that heaven has entrusted to them!

The priest concludes by sprinkling holy water on her, so as to render her purer, more faithful to her duty, and more worthy of the benefits of the Lord.

II. *The Presentation.*—The second mystery that the Church honors on the 2nd of February is the Presentation of the Infant Jesus in the Temple. You remember that the exterminating angel, who put to death all the firstborn of the Egyptians, spared those of the Hebrews. In memory of this event, and in order to show his supreme dominion over all creatures, God dictated the following law to Moses: "You shall consecrate to me all the firstborn of men and animals; for they belong to me. When your son shall one day ask you, saying, 'What is the meaning of this?' you shall answer him, 'The Lord brought us out of Egypt, out of the house of bondage, by the strength of his arm; for, Pharao being hardened and unwilling to let us go, the Lord slew all the firstborn in Egypt, from the firstborn of men to the firstborn of beasts. This is the reason why I sacrifice to the Lord all the firstborn of the male sex among beasts, and redeem all the firstborn of my sons.'"[616]

Firstborn sons were redeemed by means of a small sum of money, namely, five sides of silver. Mary therefore carried her Son to the Temple, to offer him to the Lord by the hand of the priest. She then gave the five sides to redeem him, and received him back into her arms as a deposit confided to her care until the moment when the eternal Father should again ask for him, to accomplish the work of the redemption of the human race.

Humility and devotedness of the infant Jesus. It is beyond doubt that the infant Jesus was not included under the law; "for if," says St. Hilary, "the son of a king and the heir of his crown is exempt from slavery, with how much greater reason was Jesus Christ, the Redeemer of our bodies and souls, free from the obligation of redeeming himself?"[617] But this divine Savior would give us an example of humility, obedience, and piety. He would publicly renew in the Temple the oblation that he had already made to his Father at the moment of the incarnation. On this day, Jesus Christ solemnly accepted tortures, the cross, the crown of thorns, the reed of ignominy, the robe of mockery, gall, vinegar, and death. The eternal Father, on his side, received a sacrifice capable of disarming his wrath, provoked by our crimes, and of rescuing our souls from the devouring fire that shall never be extinguished.[618]

Do you wish to enter into the spirit of this mystery, and how can anyone fail to wish it? From the foot of the altar, as from the depth of his cradle and the height of his cross, the Savior says to us, "I have given you an example, that you may do as I have done."[619] Let us therefore offer ourselves to God on this day with the great victim of the world: let us offer our two mites, our body and our soul. Poor as our sacrifice is, it will not, when united to that of the divine mediator, be rejected. Only let us beware of being guilty of rapine in the holocaust, that is to say, of reserving some of our affections for sin and creatures.

Let us now be candid: Have we ever offered ourselves to God without reserve? My heart! whose art thou at this hour, at the moment I consider these lines? Poor heart! thou hast perhaps been the victim of all kinds of strange gods one after another. For thee perhaps all things have hitherto been God, save God himself. It is over: thou shalt be God's alone henceforth and for—ever, is it not? Fear not, thou shalt be well received: thy God does not look at what thou hast been, but at what thou art and what thou wishest to be.

Sacrifice of Mary. The divine infant, our model in all things, would be presented in the Temple by the hands of his holy Mother. Let us also beg of Mary to take on herself the care of presenting us to God. She is the channel of grace. What thought more proper to give us the fullest confidence in her powerful mediation? And, I ask you, what can God refuse to Mary on this day, when she makes him the most heroic sacrifice that can possibly be imagined?

Let anyone say to a mother: "Here is a city that is going to be destroyed. A victim is needed to save it. Your dear son, the only object of your tenderness, is asked. He will be insulted, beaten, bruised, condemned, crucified. Do you agree?" I call all mothers to witness. There is not one but would rather die herself instead of her child, not one but would reject such a proposal with all the energy of her affections. And yet Mary, the sweet Mary, the most loving Mother of the most amiable Son, agrees to the request of the eternal Father: she consents. Behold the sacrifice that she makes on this day! And can you suppose that the just and good God, who so highly rewarded the figurative sacrifice of Abraham, would be ungenerous toward Mary, would close his eyes and his ears against her when she presents herself to ask him for something for us! Impiety, to think it; blasphemy, to say it!

III. *The Meeting with Anna and Simeon.*—The third mystery of which the 2nd of February recalls the memory is the meeting that took place in the Temple, of the holy old man Simeon and the prophetess Anna with Jesus and his parents. Mary had made her sacrifice. She had said to God: "I offer thee thy Son, who is also mine." She was going to descend the steps of the Temple and to take the road to Nazareth, when an old man met her. Simeon the just, who was earnestly longing for the Redeemer of Israel—Simeon, who had received a promise from God not to be taken out of the world before he had seen the Desired of Nations, took the divine infant into his arms, blessed it, and, returning it to its Mother, intoned this beautiful canticle: "Now, O Lord! thou hast only to let thy servant depart in peace, according to thy word; for mine eyes have seen thy Savior—that Savior whom thou hast prepared before the face of all people to be the light of the nations and the glory of Israel!"[620]

Tell us, Mary! what were the feelings of your maternal heart on hearing the blessings and the magnificent prophecies of the holy old man? O tender Mother! your joys will be of short duration. Listen again, Simeon has not ended: "This child has come to be the salvation and the ruin of many in Israel, to be a sign for contradictions; and thine own soul, O Mary! shall be transfixed with a sword of sorrow, that the thoughts shut up in the hearts of many may be revealed!"[621] And what are those thoughts? You shall one day know in the Garden of Olives, at Jerusalem, on the sorrowful way, at Calvary.

Mary, full of resignation, received her divine Son back into her arms. She was going to leave, when lo! a holy woman comes to proclaim in her turn the greatness of Jesus. In those days, there was at Jerusalem a prophetess named Anna, the daughter of Phanuel. She was far advanced in age and had been a long time a widow, having lived only seven years with her husband. This true Israelite spent her life in the Temple, praying and fasting, and performing good works: the Spirit of God was with her. When she had heard the canticle of Simeon, she also began to praise God, and to speak of the Savior to all that were expecting the salvation and redemption of Israel.

Happy old pair! We envy your lot: you found the Savior of the world; you saw him, you proclaimed his praises. Do we wish to have the same happiness? Let us go to the Temple, guided by the Spirit of God: we shall there find Jesus and Mary. It will be given us to enjoy their company and their conversation, and we shall then speak of them to all those faithful souls that expect in tears the salvation of Israel and the triumph of religion.

Origin of the festival of the Purification, or Candlemas.—The festival of the Purification is commonly called Candlemas, from the wax candles, *candelae*, that are lighted on it. The establishment of this festival, with its ceremony of lighted candles, is a new proof of the wisdom of the Church. In the month of February, pagan Rome used to celebrate the festival called Lupercalia, in honor of Pan, the god of shepherds, whose worship had been brought into Italy by Evander. This prince had consecrated to it the celebrated cave called Lupercal, at the foot of the Palatine Hill, in which, according to classic fable, Remus and Romulus were suckled by a wolf, and where the Church of Holy Mary of Deliverance now stands.

Early in the morning, the priests of Pan, called Luperci, went to the temple of their god, where they sacrificed a dog and some white she-goats. Then stripping themselves of their garments, and arming themselves with thongs of goatskin, they began to run through the city like madmen, and to strike all the people that they met on the way, especially women, who eagerly sought for this happiness. The object of this ceremony, they said, was the purification of the city. Hence came the name of the month, *Februarius*; for, among the Romans, *februa* meant "sacrifices of purification." Such were the festivals of that Rome which was so proud of its civilization.

There were still some remarkable vestiges of them in existence at the close of the fifth century. It was only in the beginning of the next century—512—that the infamous priesthood of the god Pan was totally abolished by the emperor Anastasius. Already in 496, Pope St. Gelasius had done what he could to destroy the too guilty ceremonies of the Lupercalia.[622] With this view, he established the festival of the Purification of the Blessed Virgin, thus opposing truly holy expiations to the unclean expiations of the pagans.[623] From Rome it passed over in a few years to Constantinople, where it was celebrated with extraordinary pomp and fervor, in order to obtain the cessation of a fearful plague that was carrying off five thousand persons in the city every day.[624] Nevertheless, several proofs go to show that the festival of the Purification was already known in a number of individual Churches. So that we may safely say its original institution is lost in the night of time.[625]

As for the procession of this day, which takes place with lighted candles, we must date its introduction beyond the sixth century. It was established in order to have a useful and edifying ceremony opposed to a pagan ceremony, full of superstitions and disorders: I refer to the doings on what the Romans designated the "amburbal festivals."[626] These ridiculous festivals, which recurred every five years, consisted in running through the streets and squares of Rome with lighted torches. The Romans, having subjected all the nations of the earth to their sway, had imposed a tribute on them which was paid every five years, after the quinquennial census. Having laid the money by in the treasury of the republic, they consecrated the month of February to running through the whole city with torches in honor of the infernal gods, to whom they thought themselves indebted for their conquest of the world.

Wisdom of the Church. The sovereign pontiffs destroyed this festival by another festival. On the 2nd of February, the people and clergy formed a grand procession, which shone with thousands of tapers, while the sweetest voices celebrated through the streets of the Eternal City the praises of the true conqueror of the world and his august Mother—the praises of the God of Calvary, who had given to Rome, instead of an empire of brute force, the more glorious, extensive, and powerful empire of faith. Setting out from the Church of St. Adrian, the whole population wended their way to St. Mary Major's, where they rendered homage for so many victories to Mary and Jesus her Son.[627]

All those lights which appear in processions, at Mass, and at evening devotions also remind us of the words in the canticle of Simeon: "This child shall be the light of Israel." Then each of the faithful, holding his lighted candle, recalls the dispositions of lively faith and ardent charity with which we should go to meet the divine Lamb, an affecting symbol, which may furnish all with an admirable subject of meditation. Have we ever seriously thought on this? If we had now to answer, should we not be obliged to say, "No!" But tomorrow, shall we not be able to say, "Yes!"

Dispositions for this festival. If we wish to celebrate the festival of this day well, let us deeply consider the three mysteries that it sets before us. Let us admire, and above all let us, imploring help, endeavor to imitate the profound humility of the Blessed Virgin. This virtue, the foundation, the guardian of all others, should be the constant object of our meditations and prayers, especially at the present day, when the world is perishing through pride and a spirit of independence. Let us contemplate the earnest and generous zeal of the infant Jesus. Let us beg of him to kindle some of its flames in our hearts. Let us lament that we have so little of it, especially in these evil times when there are so many occasions and motives for exercising it. Finally, let us join in the happy transports of Anna and Simeon. Let us learn from their example to prefer God and his grace to all that the world can offer us. And let us beg of God to give us a disrelish for everything that does not lead to him.

PRAYER

O my God! who art all love, I thank thee for having inspired thy Church to establish the festival of the Purification. Grant us the grace to imitate the admirable examples of humility and obedience given us by Jesus and Mary.

I am resolved to love God above all things, and my neighbor as myself for the love of God; and, in testimony for this love, I will carefully purify my intentions when going to church.

Lesson 32: Christianity Brought before the Senses (Continued)—Penance

Mysteries of the holy childhood: Wisdom of the Church.—As springtime strews the earth with flowers, so the Church scatters holy festivals, which are flowers in the life of Christian people, over the cold and dreary season of winter. See what a succession of joyful days: Christmas, the Holy Innocents, the New Year, the Kings![628] The world has also its festivals during this bitter season: suppers, dances, plays, all kinds of pleasures! Sources of dissipation and too often of immorality, the festivals of the world are select: the poor have no part in them. It is quite otherwise with Christian festivals: all the children of the great family are invited to them. The happiness of each one present is regulated, not according to his learning, dignity, or wealth, but according to the purity of his heart. From this point of view, also, there is nothing more social. And they are social because intended to make man happier, by making him better: not a virtue but they preach, not an honorable sentiment but they excite, not a useful lesson but they give!

Thus, during Advent, the Church took the voice of Isaias and the voice of John the Baptist, one after the other, to awake in the heart of man the sentiment of hope. "O fallen and exiled king!" she said to the human race, "one only good is left thee: it is hope. Hope, therefore; sigh, sigh on: behold, thy liberator cometh!" And this fall, and this redemption, and the characteristics of the Redeemer, and the means of profiting of the redemption, are they not the whole history of humanity? Do you know any higher lesson in possession of philosophy, or any better means of throwing light on the dark road of this life?

On Christmas day, the Church says to us by her thousand bells, her joyous hymns, and her splendid ceremonies: "After a long delay, the Messias is come: a little child is born to us; a Son is given to us!" And hearts are gladdened. And tenderness, and pious sympathy, and sweet tears, and a holy confidence, and all the sentiments that can be experienced toward an infant born for love of us, amid the gloom of a winter's night, in a damp cave, open to the piercing blasts of the north wind, affect the rich, console the poor, draw closer the ties of friendship among mankind, and lead to the practice of innumerable virtues!

But the Church does not forget the words of the divine master, saying: "Verily, verily, unless you become as little children, you shall not enter into the kingdom of heaven."[629] That she may form in Christians the character, the sentiments, and the virtues of a divine childhood, she presents to their meditation, for forty days, the Son of God in the swathing bands of his cradle. Hereby, the Church shows herself a most enlightened friend to society.

Whence arise, I ask, the frauds, the subterfuges, the hypocrisy, the selfishness, the spirit of unbelief and insubordination, all those hideous vices which poison the existence of so many persons, and which drag the world to the brink of ruin, if not because the admirable character of an evangelic childhood has almost entirely disappeared? Honor and gratitude to religion, which endeavors, by setting before us the model of an infant God, to remind us of those virtues which would quickly secure the happiness of individuals, families, and peoples!

Mysteries of our Lord's public life; obligation to imitate Jesus doing penance.—After teaching us to meditate on the first page of the life of Jesus, the Church passes on to the second. The Savior has advanced in age and wisdom before God and man: it is thus that we should also advance. Let us consider how we are to follow our leader in his new career. Here, we behold before us the history of the God-man's sorrows.

An expiator of our crimes, he would be seen humbling himself on the banks of the Jordan and receiving from John the Baptist the baptism of penance, fasting in the desert, exposed to the wicked attacks of the tempter, and, lastly, coming forth from his retreat in order to scatter around him the benefits of his example, his doctrine, and his miracles, amid the poor of Galilee, Samaria, and Judea. We, being guilty, should, like him, be expiators; that is to say, we should humble ourselves, fast, weep, and pray. And the Church wishes, in her maternal tenderness, that each of us should copy this second page of our divine master's life. Our salvation, nay, even our temporal happiness, cannot be had at any other price. She now publishes, therefore, the return of the solemn fast. Lent is going to begin. A creature, man owes homage to his Creator; a guilty creature, he owes expiation.

Answer to the objections of the world. The world, which understands nothing by the light of man's true condition here below, exclaims: "Your worship, a worship of abstinence and privation, will only aggravate the evils of our nature and accustom men to slavery!"

Catholicity is a worship of abstinence and privation. Yes, without a doubt, because it is a continual exercise of virtue, and virtue is not acquired without some difficulty or struggle. Open the records of history: run through the lives of all the great men that flourished in past ages, and see if a single one deserving of the name purchased a little renown in any other way than by great sacrifices. See what gave rise to so much manly courage: Was it not austerity of life, abstinence, privation, the spirit of sacrifice carried to heroism? All these things, therefore, have nothing in them but what is most natural to a well-ordered mind.

But how much does religion elevate the practice of them! Far from its being so painful a duty as you imagine for the Christian to multiply his sacrifices, that he may practice his faith, the cheering thought of obeying his heavenly Father, whose tender looks are fixed on him, and of vanquishing himself in the divine presence, makes the precept of abstinence sweet and easy. Henceforth, he desires nothing but an opportunity of proving to God his filial love and fear. This delicate sentiment, unknown to the children of the world, tells us to give joyfully to the author of nature a part of the gifts that we daily receive from his supreme bounty. Every heart with generous instincts understands how delightful is such an obedience.

The world says again: "Perhaps God does not command these privations, and, if he gives us good things, it is that we may use them in moderation all the days of our lives."

And why, I ask you, would God think this evidence of devotedness strange? If he gives us good things, is it that we may use them like beasts, without gratitude or love? But weak and finite beings as we are, how can we acquit ourselves of our obligations, if not by continual homage with the good things for which we are indebted to his liberality? All the peoples of the earth have anticipated us with this daily avowal of their submission and dependence. Heirs, though faithless, of primitive tradition, they preserved this part of their public worship even amid the darkness of paganism. And as there is no people without religion, so there is no religion without the worship of abstinence. Such is the unanimous testimony of the human race in favor of this part of our rites, which, though not rendering its observance more holy, nevertheless confirms its practice, as essential to public worship and dictated by the same spirit to all consciences. How false, then, is that worldly wisdom which would deprive religion of such a testimony, and lead men to enjoy all good things as if no God existed in the universe!

These good things, you say, were given us that we might use them in moderation all the days of our lives.

But to use them thus, do you think a wish enough? Frugality and temperance suppose a continual exercise of privation. Whosoever cannot sometimes abstain from the most lawful pleasures will not be able to stop when guilty pleasures begin. Virtue is nourished by sacrifices. Every abstinence, every privation that it imposes is a new pledge that it requires of our love and fidelity—a new cord by which it seeks to bind us to its holy laws. For such is the nature of the human heart that a first sacrifice disposes us to make a second, and at length nothing costs us any trouble, when we have to preserve, together with the pleasing remembrance of tried virtue, the esteem of ourselves and the fruit of long constancy. Thus, the laborer ends by having a passion for the field that he waters with his sweat; and the soldier for the war in which he sheds his blood. O men! whosoever you are, you will not be worthy of virtue unless you have a passionate love for it: and love does not pause to calculate.

General necessity of the law of abstinence. Privation and abstinence are therefore indispensable conditions for virtue. But man is so little disposed to check his inclinations that he lets himself go with his desires, like a dismasted vessel hurried along toward the rocks. The Church, which knows well what we are and loves us as a mother loves her children, provided for the levity of our minds. She raised a sacred barrier against our being carried away. Her laws on fasting and abstinence are the safeguard of the virtue of man and the happiness of society.

But this is not the only point of view from which we are to look at them. The Church, with eyes enlightened by faith, considered the depths of human nature. Man is guilty. Hence, the necessity on us all, kings or subjects, rich or poor, to satisfy for our offenses. It belongs only to sophists to address their disciples as impeccable, and to exclude from their code of morals whatever relates to man sinful and penitent.

The true religion should establish the everlasting rule of morals on other principles. Every fault requires a penalty, every crime a punishment, or we must banish from the human mind all ideas of justice. Now the Catholic who acknowledges himself guilty—and what man on earth can pretend to be innocent?—punishes himself for his offenses by a subtraction of those good things which he has abused. It seems just and reasonable to him that he should thus repair his excesses by austerities, and regain a control over his passions by training himself in habits contrary to those which have proved his ruin.

Tell me, after all this, if you see anything in Christian penance, in the Catholic Lent thus explained, that reason, when most enlightened, will not recommend to the man resolved to break with vice. There is not a philosopher but would be obliged to give the same advice to such of his disciples as wished to return from the errors of their ways. It would be easy to show that the moral code of Epicurus went as far: by privation it brought back the voluptuous to pleasure.[630] Hence, the general ends of fasting and self-denial are to render due homage to God, to give the soul a command over the senses, to strengthen virtuous habits, to atone for sin, and to turn away the scourges of the divine justice.

Preparations for Lent: Septuagesima, Sexagesima, Quinquagesima.—In order to prepare us for a solemn observance of the great law of penance, the Church invites us to meditation three weeks before the beginning of Lent. The three Sundays preceding it are respectively called Septuagesima, Sexagesima, and Quinquagesima. They bear these names because the first is the seventh Sunday before Passion Sunday, and the other two the sixth and fifth: as the first Sunday of Lent bears the name of Quadragesima because it is the fourth before Passion Sunday.[631] These Sundays and the days following them are a preparation for Lent. The Church wishes to make us anticipate, by her offices and by compunction of heart, the practices of corporal penance, and to make us enter into those sentiments which should accompany the fast of the holy quarantine.

During this time, the august spouse of the man-God reveals the magnificent characteristic of her Catholicity. "All times are mine," she tells us in her offices, "all the just are my children." And the three weeks preceding Lent are consecrated to honor the elect of ancient times: Adam and the other just before the deluge; Abraham and the patriarchs to Moses; lastly, the prophets under the old covenant. Among them she finds the great motive, the fundamental reason for the penance that is about to follow.

Hence, in the night office she traces for us the history of man's misery, caused by the sin of our first parents. At Mass, she wishes that we should regard ourselves as victims sentenced to death, that we should call to mind our many sins, so that, being convinced of the necessity of penance, we may find ourselves ready to embrace it at the prescribed moment. It is for the same end that she suppresses till Easter all joyful canticles, the *Alleluia*, the *Te Deum*, the *Gloria in excelsis*, and substitutes mournful chants and prayers in keeping with a time of affliction.

Prayers of the Quarant' Ore or Forty Hours. But while the Church is disposing us for the holy sadness of penance, the world accomplishes the terrible prophecy of the Savior. "The world shall rejoice," he said to his disciples, "and you shall lament."[632] "But woe to you that laugh,"[633] and abandon yourselves to guilty pleasures! To counterbalance the numerous crimes that are now committed, we have the solemn prayers of the Quarant' Ore. They occupy three days: Quinguagesima Sunday and the following Monday and Tuesday. Their institution dates from the sixteenth century. We are indebted for it to Father Joseph, a Capuchin, who began it at Milan about the year 1534—the very time when protestantism was committing such cruel outrages against our Lord in the sacrament of his love!

The eagerness of the Milanese for this affecting devotion was wonderful. If some regulations had not been made, the city would every year have been completely exhausted of wax, oil, and precious cloths for the ornamentation of churches. From Milan, the pious practice passed on to Rome, where it was welcomed with the same fervor by the people, and enriched with indulgences by the sovereign pontiffs Pius IV, Clement VIII, and Paul VI, which had the effect of spreading it thoughout the whole Church.[634]

The prayers of the Quarant' Ore or Forty Hours, accompanied with sermons, exposition of the Blessed Sacrament, and other pious exercises, serve: a) to appease the anger of God, provoked by the disorders of these evil days; b) to turn aside from follies, profanities, and debaucheries those who might be dragged away by the torrent of example and custom; c) to excite compassion among the faithful for our Lord, by encouraging them to meditate on the forty hours that elapsed between his condemnation and his resurrection; and d) to prepare us for the penance of Lent.[635]

The establishment of the Quarant' Ore only recalled the pious usages of antiquity. In effect, from the fifth century, the Church had established a Mass, with solemn litanies and fasts, in opposition to the abominable excesses of the Calends of January, and other days of pagan riot between the Epiphany and Lent, remains of which still exist among us. Later on, the three days before Ash Wednesday were called "Shrovetide," because, being connected with the application of public penance, people went to confession or were shrived as a preparation for a work so holy. When, by a cooling of ancient fervor, these days received the name of the "Carnival," the Church established the forty hours' adoration in order to atone for the crimes committed during them.

Ash Wednesday and public penance.—When, therefore, all the arrangements for the great fast are completed, the Church opens the holy quarantine with imposing ceremonies. On Ash Wednesday, the sacred minister appears in the holy place, wearing a dark cope. The members of the choir kneel down, and all together recite the seven psalms, so appropriately termed penitential. We shall here explain the origin and meaning of the ceremonies of this memorable day.

Every sin must be punished in this world or in the next: in this world by penitent man; or in the next by an avenging God. Convinced of the truth that the less we spare ourselves the more God will spare us, the early Christians and the holy penitents of all succeeding ages generously laid severe expiations on themselves. The Church entered into their views. The first day of Lent was chosen to put to public penance those who should be reconciled, that is to say, restored to the communion of the faithful at Easter.

The penitents began with confession. They then presented themselves at the church barefooted and in garments of mourning. Arrived before the bishop, with bowed head and tearful eyes, in a word, with every outward sign of sincere repentance, they humbly asked to be admitted to penance and absolution. The bishop, moved by their prayers and tears, clothed them with haircloth or sackcloth, put ashes on their heads, sprinkled them with holy water, and recited aloud over them the seven penitential psalms, all the clergy being prostrate on the ground.

The prayers ended, the bishops and priests rose and imposed hands on the penitents, in order to ratify their consecration to penance. The pontiff then addressed a pathetic exhortation to them, which he concluded by saying that, as God drove Adam out of paradise on account of his sin, so he was about to drive them out of the church for some time, while he urged them to have courage and to hope in the divine mercy. The procession began. The penitents marched along barefooted and in their sorrowful garb. Arrived at the door of the church, the bishop turned them out with the staff of the cross. They could not enter again till Holy Thursday, the day of their absolution. During this ceremony, so proper to excite tears, the clergy chanted the words that God addressed to man, when driving him out of the terrestrial paradise: "Thou shalt eat thy bread in the sweat of thy brow; remember that thou art dust and into dust thou shalt return."[636]

Originally, these dread formalities were only for great sinners, whose faults had given scandal; but, in the course of time, such among the faithful as were remarkably pious wished to take part in the public humiliations, so as to maintain their own penitential spirit. Some became general—chiefly that of putting ashes on the head. This is not, as we see, a superstitious custom, but a pious ceremony, practiced by the Church since the early ages of Christianity, and authorized by the example and recommended by the words of the patriarchs and prophets.[637]

Better still, there is no more striking emblem of the degradation and misery of man, and the consecration of our souls to exercises of penance. With what humility, compunction, and awe should we approach the sacred minister, who, on the part of God, is about to lay on our brow, youthful perhaps, the seal of death, and to write there in ashes the irrevocable sentence of our condemnation! You clever reasoners of all classes! find, if you can, a ceremony more proper to make man enter into himself—to make him return from that life of dissipation, wickedness, ambition, and selfishness of which you are in turn the witnesses and the victims. Instead of looking on our holy practices with a sacrilegious sneer, the most sacred of your duties, both as Christians and citizens, would be to authorize them by your respect and your example.

As for us, the docile children of the Catholic Church, let us enter deeply into the spirit of the ceremony of putting on ashes; let us permit our souls to be filled with the sentiments that it ought to inspire. What does it say to us? O fallen king! strive to understand the enormity of sin. Think on death. Do not spare thyself in the practice of mortification. Open thy heart to the liveliest compunction. Consecrate to tears and prayers the time that providence is pleased to grant thee, in order that thou mayest reconcile thyself with heaven and recover thy throne. "Remember, man, that thou art dust, and into dust thou shalt return!"

It is on the forehead that the sign of the cross is made with the ashes: this teaches us not to be ashamed of doing penance publicly, for love of our Lord, the truly just man, the great penitent of the world. Priests receive the ashes on the upper part of the head, lest, if they were put on the forehead, they should fall during Mass on the corporal or the altar. Priests also learn hereby that, though superior to others by the dignity of their office, yet they are like them by the frailty of their nature, for which death has no respect.

To these serious lessons the Church joins her maternal entreaties. "My children!" she says to us, "behold the day of salvation, behold the favorable time. Enter fervently on the holy career of penance. For many, this will be the last time. If you love your souls, make haste to unite your sufferings, your prayers, your fasts, with those of your divine Redeemer. Die to the old man, that you may be transformed into the new. Take my advice: labor to destroy within you the empire of the senses and of sin; labor to regain the empire of your souls, by regulating your wills according to the true spirit of our divine master—by practicing all those virtues of which he is a perfect model, especially humility, meekness, charity, mercy, and the spirit of prayer."

And then, our own debts are not the only ones that make penance a pressing duty on us. The sins of our brethren according to grace, and perhaps according to nature, and the punishments with which they are threatened, add to our personal obligations. Should not each of us be full of pity on beholding the disorders of the world? Should not each of us sigh, weep, and humble himself, on considering the prevarications of the body of which he is a member, and which has Jesus Christ for its head? This mourning is a duty inseparable from Lent, and finds place in the prayers and offices of the Church during this holy time.

How many sinners have been withdrawn from the way of perdition, how many calamities have been averted from society, by the prayers and fasts of the Church! The frightful spread of impiety and irreligion, the forgetfulness of the maxims of the gospel, the progress of vice, the triumph of worldliness: what subjects of sorrow and penance for a Christian soul! But, alas, such is the weakness of our faith that we have only a vague notion of the power of tears and prayers on the heart of God, and of the rigorous satisfaction that we owe to him for our sins. Do we wish to correct our judgment? Let us meditate on the example of the Ninivites. Let us above all meditate on the conduct of the Church in the imposition of public penance. The saints invite us to do so. It is time to read again a history more eloquent than any discourse.

Four orders of penitents. When public penance was in use, and it was so for nearly a thousand years, behold the spectacle presented by the Catholic Church![638] Around the holy place and in private houses, there were to be seen a multitude of Christians of both sexes—less guilty perhaps than we—clad in poor garments, their eyes full of tears, fasting, praying, and almost breaking the hearts of their brethren by sad evidences of the most bitter compunction. The penitents were divided into four classes: the weepers, the hearers, the prostrators, and the standers.[639]

The weepers stayed outside at the door of the church, and besought the faithful, when entering, to pray for them. They came to their place at the hours of offices, covered with sackcloth, and having their hair disheveled and ashes on their heads, so as to disarm by their humiliation the anger of God and to obtain the intercession of their brethren. Hence the Church, in all her Lenten offices, used to pray for the penitents: this affecting custom still exists. To add to their mortification, penitents of the first class often remained in the open air, but they were allowed to take shelter in the portico.

The hearers made up the second class of penitents. They were so named because, having fervently passed through the time prescribed for the first degree of penance, they might enter the church and listen to the instructions; but, like the catechumens, they were obliged to leave before the offertory.

The prostrators, or third class of penitents, had permission to remain in the church while some prayers were being said for them; but they were obliged to remain kneeling or prostrate: hence their name. Bishops and priests imposed hands on them, while saying prayers for them; and at the moment of the offertory the deacon ordered them to retire.

The standers were the fourth class of penitents. It was permitted them to remain standing and to join in the prayers of the faithful; but they could not make the usual offerings nor communicate in presence of the people.

No rank, however exalted, dispensed any person from the severity of the discipline. The example of the emperor Theodosius is a proof on this point. Fabiola, one of the most distinguished ladies of Rome, supplies us with another. Having been separated from her husband, she married a second time, as was permitted by the laws of the Empire; but no sooner did she learn that her conduct was contrary to the gospel than she renounced her second marriage. To atone for her fault, she submitted to the utmost rigors of canonical penance, in the sight of all Rome, before the gate of the Latin basilica, and went through her sufferings with a fervor and a compunction that still bring tears to our eyes.[640]

Besides the painful practices of which we have just spoken, to fast every day or very often on bread and water, to pray a long time prostrate with the face on the ground, to distribute a great deal of alms, and to abstain not only from all amusement but from all idle conversation were the chief exercises of public penance. How long did these severe trials last? Two years for theft, seven years for fornication, eleven years for perjury, fifteen years for adultery, twenty years for murder, one's whole life for apostasy.

And who then imposed such expiations on those early Christians, most of whom, born in paganism and living after their conversion among pagans, found themselves so much exposed to danger that, in our eyes, their falls would seem to call for indulgence rather than severity? Who treated them in so rough a manner? Their tender mother the Church, the spouse of the Holy Ghost: she who, guided by his counsel and filled with his love, shows herself in all things so kind and compassionate! And yet these Christians had no other God to serve, no other heaven to gain, no other hell to fear, than we! O enormity of sin! O sanctity of Christianity! O necessity of penance!

Thus, the recital of the penitential psalms and the procession that begins the office of Ash Wednesday remind us of the ceremony with which public penance used to be imposed. We now easily see the sentiments with which we should assist at them.

PRAYER

O my God! who art all love, I thank thee for having established the fast of Lent to purify my conscience, to strengthen my virtue, and to make me worthy of approaching thy holy table. Grant me the grace to keep the fast as a Christian.

I am resolved to love God above all things, and my neighbor as myself for the love of God; and, in testimony of this love, I will join fasting with prayer and alms.

Lesson 33: Christianity Brought before the Senses (Continued)—Lent

Social advantages of Lent.—To expiate sin, and consequently to destroy, as far as concerns each one of us, those heaps of iniquity which by day and night call down upon us the anger of God, are the great objects of fasting and penance. In the absence of any other consideration, this one alone makes a Catholic Lent a social necessity, more urgent in our sad days than ever before. Look around you! See how God, the Father of mankind, the Father of society, has become as great a stranger in the midst of his own children as the unknown God whom Athens adored in the midst of pagans—not only rejected by his own as formerly at Bethlehem, but betrayed as in the Garden of Olives, abused and mocked as at Jerusalem, and crucified again daily as on Mount Calvary; the Church, his spouse and our mother, the mother of modern peoples, in tears and mourning; society hideous with crimes and scandals—suicide, immorality, skepticism in every class, division in families, contempt of conjugal sanctity, hatred among brethren, want of faith; in short, the world, eaten to its very vitals by a monstrous indifference, which defies the most apostolic zeal, and would destroy hope, if hope were not immortal.

This is what we are come to. How, I ask you, are we to dispel the storms that so many crimes have raised around us? Worldly wisdom, always presumptuous, because always false, daily proposes some new means. It recommends society to the experience of diplomatists, to the bravery of soldiers, to stratagems, to physical force, to industry. Useless efforts! For it is written that all men in whom there is not the knowledge of God[641] are vain, blind, and powerless. The only means to save us, peoples and individuals, is to make our peace with heaven—to bring back God into society, into the family, into the heart of man. Now, the first step for this purpose—remember it well—is penance: "Be converted to me, and you shall be saved."[642] Penance, we repeat, is the great necessity of our period. Lent, intended to lead us to it, is therefore eminently social.

Special advantages of Lent for body and soul.—As the soul influences the body, so Lent, by curing the moral man, must necessarily promote the welfare of the physical man. The Church herself sings, in her offices, this new advantage of fasting;[643] and eminent physicians have proved the salutary effects of Lent on the health. It was not beneath the dignity of the Catholic Church, nor foreign to that spirit of charity which has always guided her, to have regard to bodily health when instituting Lent; for, as temperance and sobriety are the best supports of health, so fasting and abstinence are often the surest means to reestablish it. This remark is confirmed by experience. It was by continual fasts that so many of the ancient fathers of the desert preserved a vigorous and uniform health beyond the ordinary term of existence, living more than a hundred years in warm countries, where life is generally shorter than in temperate ones.

St. Paul, the first hermit, lived 113 years; St. Antony, 105; St. Arsenius, 120; St. John the Silent, 104; St. Theodosius the Abbot, 105; the two St. Macariuses, St. Paphnutius, St. Sabas, and St. John of Egypt, nearly 100. Medical science explains these astonishing facts. It declares that temperance is the mother of health, prevents all those diseases which are the result of weak digestion, renders external injuries less dangerous, soothes incurable evils, calms the passions, preserves the senses in their integrity, maintains the strength of the mind and the clearness of the memory, and lastly, as Cassian observes, is the foundation of virtue. All the saints who rose to the heights of evangelical perfection began with it.

Its practice is at first painful, because the resistance of the contrary habit must be overcome; but, when this is once done, it becomes a source of the purest pleasure, independently of the numberless advantages that attend it. In company with it, one need seldom send for the doctor. It keeps away all the diseases that arise from satiety. It supplies the simplest and surest means of restoring nature to freedom and activity. Generally speaking, an abstinence of two or three days produces the effect of a purgative with much less inconvenience and uncertainty.

A great many religious, leading a sober and regular life in their monasteries, have attained to extreme old age without the prescriptions of physicians or the drugs of apothecaries. Their principle was: when they felt themselves unwell, to abstain for two or three days—this usually sufficed to restore order. Hence, science in its most advanced state and the experience of all ages bear witness that fasting is the best remedy for most diseases, the surest safeguard of health, and the simplest and easiest means to prolong life.[644]

Harmony between Lent and springtime.—There would be no difficulty in seeing that our Catholic Lent should produce the most salutary effects, if one considered the time at which it is placed, namely, spring. Now, spring is the most favorable season to repair the disorders of health, occasioned either by the heats of summer or the intemperances of winter. The humors are then in motion. Everything that vegetates undergoes a kind of fermentation. Fresh herbs supply more wholesome juices than at any other season; and the best remedy for, or chief preservative against, most diseases is undoubtedly abstinence and a selection of vegetable food.[645]

Whoever has meditated on the profound wisdom and the maternal solicitude of the Catholic Church will easily admit that the care of our corporal health influenced her, as a secondary motive, in the institution of Lent. Always wise and good, the spouse of the man-God has sweetened her prescriptions on this point of discipline according to age and climate. Now that constitutions seem debilitated, she shows herself full of indulgence, and grants to our weakness many alleviations, of which it is proper to make account by being grateful for her kindness and faithful to the slight privations that she still imposes on us.

What more shall I say? The institution of Lent in spring offers us one of the most beautiful harmonies of the creation. While everything in nature moves, and the work of vegetation and renovation goes on in every part of the physical world, so as to bring about with the month of May the resurrection of all creatures, benumbed during the winter, the Church wishes that a similar work should take place in the spiritual world. The holy quarantine is a time when she plunges all her children into the sacred bath of penance, that they may there find either the life of grace or new vigor. In the distance she shows them a splendid table, to which all are invited. Here, served by the hands of angels, are the bread of immortality and the wine that refreshes, that purifies the blood of man, and produces virginity. And the great family leave the divine banquet renovated, strong in virtue, beaming with the smile of youth, ready to follow with a light step their divine guide on the way to heaven.

Tell me now, ye men accustomed to reflect! does not Lent, with its confession and Communion, solve in the best possible manner the great problem that at present torments the world, namely, what is the best means to make peoples moral, detached, and submissive, and kings just, righteous, and devoted? Would not a nation, coming forth in its entirety from a well-spent Catholic Lent, be fit for all virtues—like a royal eagle, which arrayed in new plumage, is not afraid of soaring to the greatest heights?[646] After all this, if there yet remains room for a sentiment in our heart, let it be occupied by the truest pity for men who do not understand, who censure, or who despise a Catholic Lent.

Protestants, more reasonable than our infidels, cannot help rendering homage to it.

"I remarked," says one of them, speaking of Italy, "that, notwithstanding the progress of vice, people of all classes restrained themselves very much during Lent. There was no longer any blasphemy or free speech to be heard as previously. Display, fashion, sumptuous repasts, had given place to modesty, austerity, a penitential exterior, edifying sermons every evening, numerous collections for the poor, a general appearance of compunction and amendment.

"I acknowledge that it was in Italy I best learned to appreciate the usefulness of Lent and to do justice to the motives of its institution. I cannot share the opinion of those who think that, men having at all times to lead a life conformable to the principles of faith, it is superstition to set aside a portion of the year for more than ordinary devotion. When we reflect on the difficulty of keeping men constantly within the bounds of duty, we are not slow to see how important it is to settle on some period of reasonable length during the year, in order to oblige them to enter into themselves and make serious reflections on their conduct, lest sin should cast its roots too deep and the habit of vice become too difficult to cure."[647]

Institution of Lent and the manner of sanctifying it.—From these general considerations, let us pass on to the institution of Lent and the manner of sanctifying it. Lent, or a fast of forty days immediately before the festival of Easter, is in many respects what is most holy among Christians, as well as most venerable on account of its ancient origin, its universality, and the numerous spiritual advantages that result from it. Our French word *Carême (Lent)*, formerly *quaresme* or *quarèsime*, is evidently a contraction of the Latin word *quadragesima,* by which the liturgy designates the holy quarantine.

This fast of forty days is an imitation of that of our Lord, though it is not observed at the period when the gospel places his. Our Lord began his fast immediately after his baptism, and the latter event occurred in the early days of January. But the Church wished to have this fast of forty days just before the festival of Easter, so as to prepare us, by a course of mortification, to celebrate worthily the glorious anniversary of the resurrection of Jesus Christ.[648]

Lent is an apostolic institution. Hence, the faithful of all ages have looked on its observance as a most sacred duty.[649] "There is no continent," says St. Basil, "no island, no nation, no city, no corner of the earth, however remote, where the Quadragesimal fast is not proclaimed. Whole armies, travelers, sailors, merchants, far from their own country, have heard it promulgated, and have congratulated themselves thereon. Let no persons therefore think themselves exempt from fasting. The angels take note of those who observe the law. Strive that your angel may write your name on his tablet, and do not desert the standard of religion…It is now that our Lord meets the devil in a general engagement, with all the forces of his army, formed of the inhabitants of the whole world. Happy are they who, by their courage, show themselves worthy of such a leader!…Kings and princes, clergy and lay people, nobles and plebeians, rich and poor, are now but one, when there is question of fasting. Would it not be a shame to consider as too heavy a burden that the whole Church takes up with joy?"[650]

Submission of our ancestors to the great law of Lent.—The Christians of the early ages hardly ate anything on fast days but herbs, roots, and legumes, or some fruit with bread and water. Some added a little uncooked fish. Whatever they took was of so common and cheap a kind that the expenses of the table were greatly lessened, and savings made in this way were, according to the advice of the fathers, changed into alms. They ate only once a day, toward evening. St. Fructuosus, bishop of Tarragon, going to martyrdom, refused a glass of wine and water that was offered him to increase his strength, saying that it was not yet the hour to break the fast: this was on a Friday, at ten o'clock in the morning.[651]

In the sixth century, the law of abstinence underwent some modification. A little wine was permitted to those who had a weak stomach.[652] From the seventh century, milk food was permitted in northern countries, where the season is not advanced enough to supply the necessary vegetables. Later on, the Church, always acting like a kind mother, sweetened her discipline yet more. In England and France, the use of butter for want of oil was tolerated. Nevertheless, many pious persons did not care to take advantage of this indulgence. The permission was granted only on condition of substituting alms or other good works.

That we may excite ourselves to fidelity in observing Lent, it will be well to recall some facts that prove the religious submission with which our ancestors observed the prescriptions of the Church. In the year 546, the supplies of wheat, wine, and oil failed at Constantinople, and the people were reduced to a state of much distress. The emperor Justinian, though a most religious observer of the fast, knowing the spirit of the Church, felt no difficulty in causing the shambles to be opened from the first week of Lent, and meat to be exposed for sale in every market. But the people preferred to endure all the pains of hunger rather than avail themselves of this indulgence. No one would buy any meat; no one would eat it.[653]

This religious submission continued from age to age. One of the towers of the Cathedral of Rheims has retained to this day the name of the Butter Tower, because it was built by the pious offerings of the inhabitants in return for permission to use butter during Lent, a permission which the archbishop had obtained from Pope Innocent VIII, in 1489, for his diocese.[654] Bourges and some other cities have also magnificent towers of the same origin. Let us acknowledge that the Church did not make a very ill use of the money obtained by dispensations on a few points of her discipline.

For the honor of the Diocese of Nevers, it is proper to mention the following fact. In the last century, the scarcity of legumes induced Monsignor Tinseau, bishop of Nevers, to permit the use of flesh meat during Lent. No person would take advantage of the permission: there were even respectful complaints about it. The people suffered on. To remove all their scruples, the Nevernese Francis de Sales gave at his house a great dinner, served up with dishes of meat. The example of the holy bishop could alone reassure consciences, and determine our pious ancestors on availing themselves of the permission. How changed are the times!

Wisdom of the Church in her regulations for Lent.—It is well to remark the profound wisdom of the Church in the modifications that she has made, according to climates and ages, on her discipline during Lent. Her chief intention was to retrench whatever bespoke too much luxury and delicacy in food, and to accommodate herself to the degree of fervor shown by her children. Hence, up to the fifth century, she forbade wine. The barbarians had torn up nearly every vine tree. Wine, being rare and costly, might be considered an article of luxury. The Church forbade its use during Lent. But vines were planted again, and wine became the drink of the mechanic as well as the merchant. The Church began by tolerating and ended by permitting it. Besides, the degree of goodwill apparent in her children demanded this condescension.

You afterward see her forbidding in some countries what she authorizes in others. Oil and certain fruits are permitted in warm countries where they are abundant, and milk food is forbidden; the contrary is the case in northern countries. Similarly, in dioceses near the sea, fish is permitted. Elsewhere it is forbidden, because it is scarce and may be regarded as too choice. Such are the data by which we must judge of the conduct of the Church. The variety at present to be found in *Regulations for Lent*, far from seeming whimsical to the enlightened man, is therefore a proof of solicitude, and of a profound knowledge of the human heart.

That which never varies is the obligation of doing penance during Lent. To maintain this obligation, the Church requires, if not the rigorous abstinence of other days, at least alms and prayers. Here again we have matter of praise and not of blame. As for the spirit of fasting, neither has it changed. By the mouth of St. Jerome, religion still blames those who, on a fast day, cover their tables with fine dishes. "What advantage," says this father, "do you derive from abstinence, if, at the same time, you choose the rarest and most delicate fruits? You make the richest conservatories send a supply to your sensuality: Is this the way to mortify yourselves? Common food is good enough for those who fast."[655]

Origin of the collation.—The spirit of religion and the discipline of each Church are the rules that ought to be followed in the practice of fasting. Nowadays, there is a slight collation permitted,[656] of which the origin was this: in 817, the Benedictines, assembled in general chapter at Aix-la-Chapelle, made a decree for their order: "If necessity require it, after hard labor, and on the day when the office of the dead is celebrated, the religious may drink, even in Lent, between meals and compline."[657]

When they assembled before the hour of compline, there was some pious reading or exhortation, called among themselves a "conference," in Latin *collatio*. Wine and water, blessed by the superior, were distributed in cups to all present after the reading, and sometimes during the reading. Hence the name *collation*, literally a conference, given to this slight refection.[658] This practice, having been adopted by lay people and tolerated by ecclesiastical superiors, became a little alleviation to the precept.

Age and circumstances that dispense from fasting.—As for the obligation of fasting, it extends to all the faithful who have reached the age of twenty-one years, unless grave reasons dispense them from it. Here again we must admire the wise solicitude of the Church. In the ages of fervor, the whole world fasted, even children; but the practice of the law varied according to age and constitution. In St. Thomas's time, the question was agitated at what precise period fasting could be conveniently reconciled with growth and constitution. After a mature examination, the Angelic Doctor fixed the age of fasting at the expiration of twenty-one years, that is to say, after the third septenary. His opinion, founded on a deep study of medicine, prevailed. Usage took the force of law, and nowadays serves as a rule in the Church.[659]

Among the grave reasons regarded as sufficient to dispense from fasting are the following: physical inability, such as that of the sick; exhaustion caused by great labor; the consideration of a greater good, as to attend the sick, to preach, etc. To secure the conscience, one should have recourse to the pastors of the Church: it is sometimes good to add thereto the advice of a pious and enlightened physician. A little derangement, a slight cold, a passing indisposition is not enough to dispense from fasting; on the contrary, poor diet is often the best remedy in such a case.

Under the title of fatiguing labors, likely to exhaust strength, we must not include those of barbers, tailors, jewelers, writers, compositors, etc. The regimen of poor laborers is, as Collet remarks, a perpetual fast. The same must be said of all those whose poverty prevents them from making daily what may be called a meal. Those who cannot fast ought to make up for not doing so by works of penance, more plentiful alms, longer prayers, and greater resignation under their sufferings.

Fasting, to be really useful, must be accompanied with alms, prayer, and a renunciation of sin and its occasions. We must therefore be earnest in attending to exercises of piety and to instructions; in preparing, by serious reflection on our lives, for a good confession; and, lastly, in making all our senses, which have been so many instruments of sin, fast. Here again we have a new occasion for admiring the wisdom of the Church.

She knew very well that fasting was not enough to make man enter into himself, and accomplish the work of his internal renovation. Hence, she took care to forbid during the holy quarantine whatever might lead him to dissipation. Shows of every kind were strictly forbidden during Lent by the fathers, by councils,[660] and even by emperors, who extended the prohibition to Sundays and holidays during the rest of the year.[661] Hunting and lawsuits were likewise forbidden. The suspension of hostilities also found place in the obligations of the time of penance.

Thus, our ancestors took Lent very seriously indeed. A great silence then came upon the world. Nothing more was to be heard but the great voice of the Church, calling her children to penance or imploring the divine mercy for them. Society, from the king on his throne to the least of his subjects, assumed the appearance of a penitent Ninive. Need we be surprised that Lent should have produced a complete renovation?

Effects of fasting.—O my God, my God! when shall we again behold the beautiful sight that society formerly presented, namely, town and country Christianized during the holy quarantine? "As a field," says St. Chrysostom, speaking in the large city of Antioch, "as a field cleared of weeds is better able to yield the crops expected from it, so the austerities of Lent, giving tranquility to the soul, dispose it for the practice of all virtues. No noise, no disorder during this holy time. We see no display of meats or eagerness of cooks to excite intemperance. The city looks like a chaste matron, the sober and dignified mother of a family. When I reflect on the change that has taken place everywhere in a few hours, I cannot help admiring the power of fasting. It purifies the heart and renovates the mind both of the magistrate and the private individual, the rich and the poor, the Greek and the barbarian, him who wears the diadem and the slave who obeys. I no longer perceive any difference between the table of the wealthy man and that of him who is reduced to the utmost misery. Everywhere simple fare, without luxury, without ostentation, and, what is most surprising, people go to a table thus served with more pleasure than formerly to that which was laden with the most tempting dishes and the most exquisite wines."[662]

If the holy quarantine no longer produces these salutary effects, we are not to attribute the blame to the Church. Her commands are no less formal, her exhortations no less pressing, her liturgy no less instructive. Wrapped in mourning garments from Ash Wednesday, she buries herself in the spirit of penance. Farewell to songs of joy, to ornaments of bright and smiling hue! The eyes and ears are struck only by sad images and plaintive sounds. The words of the prophets, who, from the depth of their solitude or the midst of Jerusalem, call Israel to penance, are heard on all sides. But behold another model, a more illustrious penitent, on whom the divine mother fixes the gaze of her children! This penitent is the Son of God.

Liturgy of Lent: First Sunday.—The gospel of the First Sunday of Lent shows him to us entering the desert, condemning himself to a fast of forty days, encountering the devil, and crying out to us: "I have given you an example, that you may do as I have done."[663] Retire into solitude; withdraw from the vain distractions of the world; fast; take up arms against the triple concupiscence—the love of pleasures, the love of riches, and the love of honors: it is by faith that you shall be conquerors. Oh, how well the Church knows us, when, as a proper beginning of Lent, she calls us to solitude!

As a matter of fact, amid the noise, the excitement, the whirl of society, there is little time for grave and serious thought: the inspirations that entrance the soul do not come in the public square. The Savior is to be found in the desert. Was it possible to choose a gospel better adapted to circumstances? In the evening, at vespers, the beautiful hymn of St. Gregory, *Audi benigne Creator*, is sung in sad and plaintive tones:

"Hear, O merciful Creator! the prayers accompanied with tears which we pour out during this sacred fast of forty days.

"Unerring searcher of hearts! thou knowest our weakness: grant the grace of pardon to those who return to thee.

"We have sinned much; but spare those who acknowledge their faults to thee: for the glory of thy name, cure those who are sick.

"Grant that we may so weaken the flesh by fasting that the spirit, having become sober, may abstain from all sin.

"Grant, O Blessed Trinity! O divine Unity! that the fasts which we consecrate to thee may be useful to thy servants. Amen."

It is, at the latest, on the First Sunday of Lent that the dispensations, authorized by the bishop, should be asked, if persons judge that they cannot observe the law in all its fullness. By the side of the rigors of penance, religion, ever kind and gentle as a mother, has established dispensations. When she commands, we must obey: this submission is what pleases God most. To ask not to fast or not to abstain during the whole Lent is an act of obedience. It is already to sever oneself from the pleasure of doing one's own will. It is to acknowledge the authority of the Church, to admit oneself her vassal. When, in minds and hearts, there is a strong inclination to independence and liberty, we must know how to make account of the least act of submission. In a fertile country, we pass by the richest meadows without pausing a moment to look at them. Whereas, in the desert we go into ecstasies over a tuft of grass; for it says, "There is still a little freshness here, all is not dead."[664] The ministers of a good God, priests never refuse dispensations to those who require and ask them.

Since the tenth century, the First Sunday of Lent has been called Brand Sunday. Whence came this singular name? *Brand* means "torch." Now, on the First Sunday of Lent, young people, chiefly those who had been a little too much diverted during the Carnival, presented themselves at the church with a brand or torch in their hand, as if to make public satisfaction, and to ask to be purified by receiving the penance that would be imposed on them by the pastors for the whole Lent until Maundy Thursday.[665] Ages of faith, happy ages! If our ancestors committed faults, they at least knew how to make reparation for them!

The thought of the last judgment, the power of prayer in the example of the Chanaanite woman, and the efficacy of penance in the parable of the paralytic are one after another presented to the meditation of the faithful in the gospels of the first week. See with what inimitable skill the Church graduates her instructions, and leads our hearts to sincere repentance!

Second Sunday of Lent. On the Second Sunday of Lent, the transfiguration of our Lord on Thabor is read at Mass. Like a mother who, to excite her little child to make a difficult step, holds out a reward before it, the Church, to encourage us in the practice of penance, hastens to show us the glory that will be its fruit. "If you suffer with Jesus Christ, you shall be crowned with him": behold what she says to us, as we enter on the course of mortification! How well this loving mother understands the feelings of her children!

After laying down the two great motives for all our actions, fear and hope, the last judgment and heaven, the Church has a good right to let her severe threats be heard by those who continue obstinate in their impenitence. She utters them in the gospel of the Monday of the second week of Lent. On the following days she warns us against the example of those perverse Christians who refuse to be converted during this holy time. She then recalls to our minds, in the parable of Lazarus and the rich man, the obligation of giving alms; then, the misfortune of those who reject Jesus Christ; then, in the divine parable of the prodigal son, the infinite goodness of God toward sinners. There is not a chord of our heart that she does not touch.

Third Sunday of Lent. On the Third Sunday of Lent, the Church gives us an instruction no less important, by reminding us that the essential act of penance is a good confession. The gospel of the Third Sunday is intended to make us avoid the danger, unfortunately too common, of failing in sincerity in the avowal of our faults. It represents to us, under the figure of a possessed deaf-mute, the sad condition of a sinner whose mouth is no longer open to prayer or to confession, nor his ears to the truth.

The perfect cleanness which our soul acquires in the salutary bath, figured by the cure of Naaman; the power of priests to bind and to unbind consciences; the infinite goodness of the Savior toward the most abandoned souls, as shown in the examples of the Samaritan woman and the adulteress: behold the subjects of the gospels of the third week! Do you know anything more proper to bring into a guilty heart that confidence which is so necessary for man, terrified at the thought of his judge, and overwhelmed with shame at the sight of his iniquities?

Fourth Sunday of Lent, or Laetare Sunday. The Fourth Sunday of Lent takes us another step toward the term whither the Church wishes to lead us. And what is that term? The nuptials of the Lamb. Our tender mother wishes to assemble all her children round the table of the Father of the family. Nothing has been omitted to provide them with the wedding garment. Today she sets before their eyes the festive hall, together with the angelic bread and the virginal wine that await them. The gospel of the Fourth Sunday recalls Communion, in the history of the multiplication of the loaves. "Faithful people!" says the Church, "you who follow the Savior in solitude and recollection, who forget all the affairs of life in order to hear his divine words, do not fear, he will take care of you: he will not let you faint on the way. Behold, to supply us with food, he is going to multiply the bread that gives immortality, the bread that comes down from heaven!"

Every week is marked by a recital of the most splendid and evident miracles of the Son of God. The sellers driven out of the Temple; the fury of the synagogue suspended at the pleasure of the God-man; the cure of the man born blind; Lazarus and the son of the widow of Naim raised to life: behold the miracles by which the Church takes care to confirm the greatest miracle of all, that of the Eucharist. We are all to participate therein, we must rouse our faith: Could she adopt a better means to succeed in preparing us for this great act? Let us follow step-by-step a mother so enlightened, let us meditate attentively on this course of instructions so well arranged, and our hearts will be filled with the dispositions necessary to profit of Lent and of the paschal Communion.

The Fourth Sunday of Lent is commonly called *Laetare* or "Rejoice" Sunday, from the first word of the introit of the Mass. It seems as if the Church, in the rest of the office, wished to choose those passages of scripture most proper to excite spiritual joy in her children, and to console them amid the evils of this life. A good mother, she blends joy with sorrow, and presents some solace to those who have courageously passed the middle of their holy and painful career.

In happier ages, she even permitted some outward rejoicings, worthy in all respects of Christian sanctity. But the world took possession of those innocent joys, which had never been intended for it; and, defiling whatever it touched, retained nothing of the festival of Mid-Lent but what would flatter the senses. He who did not fast had the effrontery to select those days of rest after the labor of fasting for giving guilty, or at least very unbecoming, parties and banquets!

PRAYER

O my God! who art all love, I thank thee for having multiplied the means of making me enter into myself during the holy time of Lent. Grant me the grace to profit by them.

I am resolved to love God above all things, and my neighbor as myself for the love of God; and, in testimony of this love, I will assist piously at the Lenten instructions.

Lesson 34: Christianity Brought before the Senses (Continued)—Passion Week, Holy Week

Passion Sunday and Passion Week.—The Church, after leading us into the desert with the Son of God, calls us on Passion Sunday to the sorrowful way which this divine Savior is about to tread from the Garden of Olives to Mount Calvary. The time for preparation for the funeral of the God-man is come. The Church is in tears: all things announce public mourning. She removes the canticle *Judica* from the Mass, as she does in Masses for the dead. No more any *Gloria Patri* in the responses, or in the invitatory of the office, or in the Mass. Purple crape covers the cross, the statues, and the pictures. The sacred ministers wear only sad ornaments—images of sorrow, preachers of penance.

In the Mass of Passion Sunday, the holy spouse of the man-God ascends with her weeping family to the summit of Calvary. Here, in the epistle, St. Paul describes for us the death of the great victim of the human race, and tells us that his sacrifice alone was capable of expiating sin; for the ancient sacrifices were only a figure of that of the cross. In the gospel, we are reminded both of the innocence and the divinity of the victim, and also of the crime of the hard-hearted Jews, who, notwithstanding the certainty of the Savior's miracles and the holiness of his doctrine, conceived the wicked design of putting him to death.

By showing his divinity in all its splendor to the plotting Jews, Jesus gives them a striking proof of his love; for he sets before them the most powerful motive not to lay sacrilegious hands upon him. He says to them what the prophet Jeremias said to their fathers: "Behold, I am going to be in your hands! Do with me what you wish. However, know that, if you kill me, you shall shed innocent blood against your own selves, against Jerusalem and its inhabitants; for I am truly sent of God."[666]

These serious words, which the Savior spoke to the Jews eighteen hundred years ago, he still addresses every year at the beginning of paschal time to all those who are willing to hear them. "Behold, I am going to be at your disposal. When I am in your heart, you will do with me what you wish. However, know that, if you crucify me again, you shall shed innocent blood against yourself; for I am truly the Son of God." Oh, how proper is this warning to make us enter into ourselves, so that we may carefully prove ourselves, as the apostle St. Paul desires, lest we should go to the holy table only to eat and drink our condemnation!

The gospel of the Mass tells us very plainly that the passion, Calvary, and the cross are about to become the absorbing thoughts of the Church. Hence, when all things in the holy temple bespeak mourning, the priests sing at vespers, to a slow and solemn air, the hymn of St. Fulgentius: *Vexilla Regis prodeunt.*

> Behold the standard of the great King,
> Behold the mystery of the radiant cross,
> Behold the mystery that shows us a God nailed to a cross,
> A God fastened for our sakes on an infamous gibbet!
> See the blood flowing from the Savior's side:
> It flows, mingled with water, to wash away our crimes.
> Now are fulfilled the words of David:
> A prophet, he said to the nations,
> It is by the wood that God shall reign.

O tree, which the King of kings bedewed with his blood;
O tree! shining and beautiful;
O privileged tree! thou wert chosen out of all,
And thou didst touch the sacred limbs of the saint of saints.
Oh, how blessed are thy branches—
They bore the ransom of the world!
It was on thy branches, as on a balance, that the divine body was weighed, and that it carried off the prey of hell.
Hail, O cross, our only hope!
O cross! in these days of the passion,
Grant an increase of piety to the just,
And obtain pardon for the guilty.

These last words are often repeated during the holy days that follow, and it will be the same with all others that can give rise to true compunction in the hearts of Christians. Let us yield to the suggestions of faith, and mingle at least our tears with the blood of our father, immolating himself for us.

From Monday, the gospel shows us the Savior occupied much less with the tortures that are being prepared for him than with the salvation of his enemies—calling them, entreating them to be converted in these pressing words: "If any one thirst, let him come to me. Yet a little while I am with you: I shall soon go to him who sent me. You shall then seek me and shall not find me."[667]

On Tuesday and Wednesday, we see in the gospel, on the one hand, the evil designs of the Jews appearing more and more, and, on the other, the man-God, always calm, suspending at his pleasure the fury of his enemies, and continuing his tender exhortations till the moment marked out for the powers of darkness.

The gospel of Thursday unveils all the loving mercy of the Savior's heart. It is the history of the penitent woman, who, having washed the Redeemer's feet with her tears, deserved to hear from him these consoling words: "Many sins are forgiven her, because she hath loved much."[668] O Jerusalem! if thou wert willing to shed them, a few tears would suffice to obtain thy pardon: behold what the Savior said to the Jews by this miracle of mercy! So true it is that our God is slow to punish, that he punishes only with regret and after having tried every means imaginable to bring back hardened sinners to their duty! And he is the Savior so good, whom the Jews wish to put to death as a wretched criminal!

Yes, such is the case; and the gospel of tomorrow will relate for us the plans, the debates, and the votes of that horrible council which decided on the death of the God-man.

Festival of the Compassion. If the heart of Jesus suffered from so much perversity, there was another heart that also felt the most bitter pain: it was Mary's. And the more surely and more deeply to move her children, the Church makes us honor on Friday the passion of the sweet Virgin. Yes, she wishes that we should take pity on this afflicted Mother, afflicted for our sake. She wishes that we should bring her the only consolation that she can or will receive—a sincere sorrow for our sins, a sorrow like that which a well-bred child feels on seeing its mother weep.

The festival of Compassion, intended to honor the dolors of Mary, whom the Church calls the Queen of martyrs, was prescribed in 1413, at the Council of Cologne, to make reparation for the blasphemies and outrages of the Hussites against the Blessed Mother of God. But the origin of this festival seems to ascend much higher. An ancient tradition, spread throughout the East, tells us that on the day of the passion, when the whole city of Jerusalem was in a tumult, the Blessed Virgin, separated for a while from her divine Son, met him again as he was ascending the hill of Calvary. The sight of this beloved Son, covered with wounds and blood, crowned with thorns, and carrying the instrument of his execution, made such an impression on Mary that she fainted away.

When we think on the tenderness of the best of mothers for the best of sons; when, above all, we think that the Savior, God as he was, fell into such an agony in the Garden of Olives that an angel should come to his relief: when, I say, we think on all this, we can easily understand Mary's faint, which is nowise inconsistent with her heroic courage.[669] However, this occurrence does not authorize painters to represent the Blessed Virgin fainting at the foot of the cross. No, the Mother of Jesus, who had said, "Let us go forward, behold him who is about to betray me," stood on Calvary.

But it is permitted to represent her, having her heart pierced with seven swords, symbolic of the seven great sorrows that she experienced during her life. These sorrows were the prophecy of Simeon, the massacre of the Innocents, the loss of the Child Jesus in the Temple, the carrying of the cross, the crucifixion, the taking down from the cross, and the burial. The seven founders of the Order of the Servants of Mary divided meditation among them on the dolors of Mary, and gave rise to this devotion and the pictures that express it.

In memory of the Blessed Virgin's pangs, there used to be a festival celebrated in France called the festival of the Swoon. It was most solemnly and widely observed in the fifteenth century. At Jerusalem, on the very spot where the accident occurred, there was a church built, of which only the ruins were to be seen in the sixteenth century. This proves the antiquity of the tradition which we have just mentioned. Children of the great Catholic family, behold therefore our father and mother, Jesus and Mary, plunged in a sea of sorrows! Will this sad sight say nothing to our hearts? It is for us, it is for our sake, that they suffer these unutterable pains. Tell me: Could the Church remind us, during Lent, of anything better calculated to detach our hearts from sin?[670]

On Saturday, the day after the Compassion, the gospel sets before us the Savior taking supper at the house of Lazarus, whom he had lately raised to life; Mary, the sister of Lazarus, pouring a perfume of great value on the God-man's feet; and the tender words with which the divine master prepared his disciples for the most cruel of all separations.

Speaking of Mary's act, our Lord said that it would be known and celebrated throughout the whole world. The prophecy has been fulfilled, and will be fulfilled to the end of ages. At Rome, an affecting custom perpetuated its memory for a long time. On the Saturday before Palm Sunday, the sovereign pontiff went to St. Peter's. Here he distributed alms of every kind to poor people and strangers, who were present in great numbers. The vicar of Jesus Christ then sent similar favors to the needy and sick in different quarters of the city, who could not come, or who durst not appear out.

Near the place appointed for these distributions, there was a small aqueduct, called the Sabbatine Form, in which the sovereign pontiff washed the feet of the poor to whom he gave alms. This was, as we have said, in memory of the act performed by Mary, the sister of Lazarus. It was also to shorten the ceremonies of Holy Thursday, among which the washing of feet held an important place.[671]

We have now arrived at the beginning of the great week. How much the Church has done to lead us by serious instructions and noble examples, the silence of recollection and the austerity of penance, to the sacred hill of Calvary! Without the penance of Lent, without the tears that we have shed, without the privations that we have undergone, without the white robe of innocence that repentance has given us, how should we dare ascend Golgotha in order to witness the death of a God? But if we have wept from the depth of our souls, if we have plunged ourselves in the bath of atoning blood, we are as pure as angels, and, like them, we may surround the cross.[672]

Holy Week: Its various names; piety of our ancestors.—The week beginning on Palm Sunday and ending on Holy Saturday bears various names. It is first called the "Great Week." There are two "great weeks" in the history of the world: one, when God created the universe, and each day was marked by some miracle of power; the other, when God repaired his work, created it in a manner again, purified it, brought it back to its early sanctity, by the blood and death of his Son. This second week, each day of which was distinguished by some miracle of love, is incomparably greater than the first.

"We call it 'great,'" says St. Chrysostom, "not because it has more days than other weeks, or because the days have more hours, but because of the number and the greatness of the mysteries celebrated during it; for it was on these days that the tyranny of the devil was destroyed, that death was disarmed, that sin and the curse were blotted out, that heaven was opened to man, who thereby became equal to the angels. Hence, the fasts and watches are longer, and the offices are more numerous."[673]

It is also called "Painful Week," because of the sufferings of our Savior; "Indulgence Week," because penitents were then admitted to absolution and to the communion of the faithful; "Xerophagy Week," because, during the six days of this week, only dry food was used, without any seasoning; lastly, "Holy Week," because of the holiness of the things then accomplished, and of the dispositions with which we should assist at them. And this last name, which is a volume in itself, generally prevailed. Let us show by our works that we fully understand its meaning, and, for this purpose, let us often call to mind the examples of our ancestors.

Formerly, all the days of this great week and the week following were so many festivals. Manual labor, business, and lawsuits were forbidden. The Roman emperors confirmed by decrees this admirable regulation of the Church.[674] St. Chrysostom had these imperial ordinances in view when he said to the people of Antioch: "It is not alone the pastors and preachers of the Church that recommend the faithful to honor and sanctify this week, but the emperors also command it throughout the whole earth, suspending all record and criminal trials, and bringing all civil and secular affairs to a standstill, so that these holy days may be free from all troubles, quarrels, embarrassments, and other distractions capable of preventing people from giving themselves leisurely and quietly to the pious exercises of religion and the spiritual welfare of their souls."[675]

Holy Week was also a time of indulgence and reprieve: Christian princes, either out of gratitude for the graces which God grants to mankind through the merits of our Lord's death or out of a desire of imitating in some manner his goodness, conformed their policy to that of the Church, which now reconciled public penitents. They opened prisons; they paid the debts of debtors, and set them free. "The emperor Theodosius," says St. Chrysostom again, "used to send letters of pardon to cities, setting prisoners free, and granting life to criminals on the days before the great festivals of Easter."[676]

The clemency of the emperors was regulated by prudence. No prisoners were allowed to be at large but such as would not prove dangerous to individuals or to society. The successors of the great prince whom we have named acted in like manner. Not content with writing to their officers, they made laws for the renewal of these favors every year. But we must hear the great St. Leo on this point.

"The Roman emperors," he says, "as a result of their piety and from an old custom, abase their majesty and suspend their power in honor of the passion and resurrection of Jesus Christ. They sweeten the severity of their laws and release persons guilty of various crimes, so that, on these days, when the world is saved by the mercy of God, they may represent to us his infinite goodness and imitate it in some manner by their clemency."[677]

And the holy pope, drawing religious consequences from this admirable conduct, immediately adds: "It is very just that Christian people should also imitate their princes, and that these great examples should move them to be indulgent among themselves during this holy time; for domestic laws ought not to be less humane than public laws. We must therefore forgive one another, overlook offenses and debts, put away all resentment, and be reconciled, if we wish to have a share in the graces which Jesus Christ merited for us by his passion and to celebrate worthily the festival of Easter."[678]

St. Augustine teaches us that this affecting custom was established in his time in Africa. In a sermon that he preached on Low Sunday, he exhorted the faithful to continue during the rest of the year a cessation from lawsuits, disputes, and enmities, and to preserve the spirit of peace and repose that had been prescribed them during the leisure days of Holy Week and Easter Week.[679]

France, formerly so pious, had adopted and religiously maintained the touching custom of letting prisoners free. In the last century, it still existed. On Tuesday of Passion Week, the last day of sitting, the parliament of Paris went to the prisons. The prisoners were questioned, and a great many of those whose cases were favorable, or who were not criminals of the worst class, were set at liberty. The same thing occurred on the days before the eves of Christmas and Pentecost.[680]

What do you think of this? Should not Holy Week, thus celebrated, have a great influence on public morals? Is it not true that religion, which seems to have no other end than the happiness of the next life, is marvelously well calculated to procure the happiness of the present life? Why should it be so little known and so little loved? Are not the evils of which we are the victims enough to open our eyes? Shall the voice of experience be forever despised?

As for us, the solemnity that the Church displays in the last week of Lent reminds us of our obligation to redouble our fervor. Whoever is so careless as to fail in this matter is unworthy of the name of Christian. To close the holy time of Lent as we should is the true means of gathering the abundant fruits of that penance which has been prescribed us, and of the sacred mysteries whose memory the Church celebrates.

PRAYER

O my God! who art all love, I thank thee for all the means of salvation that thou dost give us during Holy Week. Grant us the grace to enter fully into the spirit of the Church, so that this week may be truly a holy one for us.

I am resolved to love God above all things, and my neighbor as myself for the love of God; and, in testimony of this love, I will practice some particular mortification each day in Holy Week.

Lesson 35: Christianity Brought before the Senses (Continued)—Palm Sunday, Holy Thursday

Palm Sunday: Its various names.—Hitherto we have followed the man-God on his way gradually to Jerusalem, where he should soon shed his blood for the salvation of the world. Six days before his death he arrived in the town of Bethania, a short distance from the capital. Lazarus and his sisters had the happiness of giving him hospitality. Next morning, he set out for Jerusalem, mounted on a young ass, followed by its mother.[681] This circumstance, apparently so trivial, had not escaped the piercing glance of the prophets. Entering the city thus like one of the ancient judges or leaders of Israel, the Savior showed that he was truly the Prince of Peace, the Son of David, the envoy of God, announced by the oracles. The people were not mistaken.

As soon as his movements were known, a countless multitude gathered out to meet him, bearing palm branches in their hands, and filling the air with their acclamations:

"Hosanna to the Son of David! Blessed is he that cometh in the name of the Lord!" These words, as well as the branches strewed along the Savior's way, were a proof that the Jews regarded him as the Messias.[682] All the people accompanied Jesus to the Temple, where he delivered an admirable discourse to them, during which a voice was heard from heaven. This voice, as if of thunder, bore splendid testimony to his divinity. It was like God's last warning to the Jews, in order to keep them from imbruing their hands in the blood of the just one, and falling into the frightful abyss toward which the synagogue urged them.

During his triumph, the Savior, who knew the hard-heartedness of ungrateful Jerusalem, was touched with pity. On seeing the city, the gospel tells us, he wept over it. "If at least on this day," he said with a sigh, "thou knewest how to profit of my visit, if thou wouldst make thy peace with heaven—but no! all these things are hidden from thine eyes." And scalding tears rolled down the God-man's cheeks![683] A tender father, he weeps because he will be obliged to punish.

Procession. On Palm Sunday, the Church honors this triumphant entry of the Savior into Jerusalem. Before Mass, the palms are blessed and the procession begins. The branches borne are twigs of palm, olive, willow, box, and other trees most esteemed in the country where they are found. Some add flowers, according as the season furnishes them. Hence the various names of "Branch Sunday," "Palm Sunday," and the "Flowery Pasch."[684] The procession made before Mass is of the highest antiquity in the East. The general belief is that it took its rise in Palestine, from which it soon spread to other countries. In those remote days, it was called the "Palm Procession." About the sixth or seventh century, it passed over to the Latin Church. However, it was made before this period in the Church of Rome: it extended thence to the other churches.[685]

This procession is a commemorative figure of our Lord's triumphant entry into the city of Jerusalem. The passage in St. Matthew referring to this glorious entry is sung. After singing the responses and antiphons most appropriate for the occasion, a pause is made at the door of the church, which is found to be shut: this is not without a mystery. The Church rising suddenly to higher thoughts wished to represent to us, in the expressive language of her ceremonies, the state of the human race before the entry of Jesus Christ into the heavenly Jerusalem. Its gates were closed against men; but the angels dwelt within.

And behold, the children of the choir, the angels of the earth, have made their way into the church, and sing with their pure voices the eternal canticle: *Gloria, laus, et honor*—"Glory, honor, and praise be to thee, O Christ, our King, our Redeemer!" The faithful, who are outside, representing men banished from heaven, repeat the canticle of the angels: "Praise, honor, and glory," etc. Then the celebrant, an image of Jesus Christ, knocks at the door with the foot of the cross; for the cross was the key that opened heaven. Immediately the door opens amid the singing of a triumphant response: "When our Lord entered the holy city, the children of the Hebrews, prophets of the resurrection to life, sang, with palm branches in their hands, 'Hosanna in the highest!'"

In France, before our revolutionary troubles, the procession wended its way out of walled cities, and it was at a closed gate of the city that the ceremony now observed at the entrance of the church took place. This representation was much more natural, and agreed far better with the words used by the celebrant: *Attollite portas*—"Open your gates, ye princes; be ye lifted up, ye gates!"[686] These words refer to the removal of the holy ark from the house of Obededom to Sion. To understand their literal meaning, we must call to mind that the gates of Jerusalem, like those of other strong cities, were made like a harrow that rose and fell perpendicularly.[687]

With the priest, that is to say, with the Savior, the people who accompany him and whom he has gathered together on the way of life make their entry into the church.

Formerly, when the priest had crossed the sacred threshold, the children of the choir and such others as were within the church kissed their branches, in order to do homage to the glorious conqueror of death and of the devil. Nowadays, there is still an antiphon sung, which recalls the triumphant entry that the elect will make into heaven after the last judgment.

To bring this mystery more clearly before the senses, some churches used to have a magnificent ceremony. Before the procession, a richly adorned credence-table was prepared in the middle of the sanctuary, and the book of the gospels was laid on it, as if to represent our Lord. All the clergy assembled around it, in order to assist at his triumph. The branches distributed and the procession ready to set out, two deacons took the book of the gospels, laid it on a superb cushion, and bore it on their shoulders, as is done with shrines of holy relics. Preceded by the clergy, they advanced amid a multitude of tapers and the smoke of incense, and followed by all the people with branches in their hands. Hereto were added the crosses and banners of confraternities, and whatever else could give splendor to this representation of the triumphal entry of the Son of God. The procession ended in the same manner as it does at present.[688]

Origin of the chant, "Gloria, laus, et honor," etc. It is when the procession stops at the door of the Church that the *Gloria, laus*, etc. is sung. The origin of this canticle has something so interesting in it that it will be well for us to make it known. Theodulphus, bishop of Orleans, a pontiff illustrious by his virtues and talents, having been accused of conspiracy, Louis le Debonnaire ordered him to be arrested, and thrown into prison at Angers. During his captivity, he composed the celebrated hymn *Gloria, laus*, which contains seventy-eight verses. On Palm Sunday, Louis le Debonnaire, being at Angers, passed before the bishop's cell. The bishop was at the window, singing through the bars his joyous canticle. The emperor was so delighted with it, that he restored its author to liberty, and reestablished him in his see.[689]

Such, in a few words, are the special ceremonies of Palm Sunday. Now, you sublime geniuses! who find fault with the holy usages of the Catholic Church, do you know anything more proper to recall the ever-memorable event of Jesus Christ's triumphant entry into Jerusalem? Set to work: let us see what you can do. Find a better means of speaking to the senses, the imagination, the mind of a people; of captivating them; of awakening sentiments of faith and piety in their souls. And when I say *the people*, I mean all mankind, not excepting yourselves, you great philosophers! For, like all others, you have senses, and, to reach your hearts without fail, it is your senses that must be addressed. You are not angels: your conduct proves it. The wonderful influence, the fascination I should rather say, exercised on you by sensible things—gold, purple, rich furniture, embroidered garments, and sometimes creatures the most vile—is a clear sign that you are the people as much as your neighbors, and often much more.

As for us Christians, two sentiments should predominate in our souls during the procession of Palm Sunday: joy, on beholding the Savior's triumph and considering our own future reward, when we shall enter into the heavenly Jerusalem with him; and sorrow, on thinking that the same Jews, whose welcomes are so loud, will five days later on make the streets of Jerusalem resound with death-cries, and wake the echoes of Calvary with their blasphemous insults against him whom they today receive as the Son of David. Alas, how many Jews are there among Christians! Let us not be among the number. We should also carry the blessed branches to our houses, keep them there with great respect, use them for sprinkling holy water on our beds before going to rest, and regard them, according to the instructions of the Church, as preservatives against spiritual and corporal evils.

History of the passion read at Mass. The whole office of Palm Sunday is consecrated to honor the Savior. It is for this reason that the passion is sung at Mass. To bring this dreadful event home to us, the Church lets us hear three voices: the voice of the historian, who relates the facts, is that of the deacon; the voice of the Jew or the sinner, who accuses his God, and demands sentence of death against him, is that of the subdeacon; and the voice of the august victim, who maintains a calmness full of dignity, all the gentleness of a Lamb in the midst of his executioners, is that of the priest. We imagine ourselves present at the sad drama: and I know not how many sentiments of awe, indignation, piety, and admiration pass through our souls. We then feel something that we in vain look for in a mere perusal of the passion. O Catholic Church, how well thou understandest the nature of man![690]

Spy Wednesday; office of Tenebrae.—On Holy Monday, Tuesday, and Wednesday, the Church continues to remind us of various events that went before the Savior's passion. At length, on Wednesday evening the office of Tenebrae begins. It consists of matins and lauds for the next day, sung on the eve by anticipation. The name *Tenebrae* is given to this part of the office because, toward its close, all the lights are extinguished, as well to express the profound mourning of the Church as to represent the darkness with which the whole face of the earth was covered at our Lord's death. The extinguishing of the lights also recalls a historical fact of our beautiful Christian antiquity. The office that we say in the evening used to be said during the night, and lasted till morning. As day approached, the lights no longer needed were gradually extinguished.

These lights were and still are wax candles, placed on a triangular candlestick, at the left side of the altar. They are usually fifteen in number: seven on each side, and one on the top. Those on the sides are put out successively, one at the end of each psalm, beginning with the lowest on the gospel side, then the lowest on the other side, and so on alternately till none remain but the one on the top, which is left burning. They are of yellow wax, as prescribed by an ancient Roman Ordo, because the Church employs no others at funerals, or in great mourning.

But the one placed on the top of the triangular candlestick is usually of white wax, because it represents Jesus Christ. At the last verse of the *Benedictus*, it is taken down, and hidden behind the altar while the psalm *Miserere* and a prayer are being said. It is then brought forth again. This ceremony is a figure of the Savior's death and resurrection. The fourteen other candles represent the eleven apostles and the three Marys. Their extinction reminds us of the flight of the former and the silence of the latter during the passion.[691]

The number of candles, as well as the manner of arranging and extinguishing them, reaches back beyond the seventh century.[692] How great should be our veneration for a ceremony that so many pious eyes have contemplated! Would that it excited in us the same sentiments as in our ancestors! Let us remark, by the way, that the ordinary rites of the Church, especially on great festivals, are all of high antiquity.

The whole office of Tenebrae is shaded with the deepest grief. Invitatory, hymns, the *Gloria Patri*, blessings, all are set aside. Only four voices are to be heard: that of David, who bewails on his harp the outrages committed against his Lord and his Son; that of Jeremias, who, in lamentations equal to his sorrows, relates the destruction of Jerusalem and the torments of the august victim; that of the Church, whose tender words call her children to repentance—"Jerusalem, Jerusalem! be converted to the Lord thy God"; and, lastly, that of the holy women, who followed Jesus from Galilee, and who wept so bitterly as he ascended the hill of Calvary. Their tears, their cries, and their sad journey are represented to us by the two clerks who, on bended knees, and moving forward, sing, *Kyrie eleison*, interrupted with responses and sighs.

There is no leader to preside at the office of these three days; for it is written: "I will strike the shepherd, and the sheep of the flock shall be dispersed."[693] On all sides, sadness and sorrow. The bells are no longer heard, because the apostles, whom they figure, were silent during the passion. The office is followed by a confused noise—a doleful representation of the tumultuous advance and overthrow of the cohort that, armed with clubs and led by Judas, came during the night to lay hands on our divine Savior in the Garden of Olives.[694] The rattle that is used in monasteries, and in some churches, to call the faithful to the office during the last days of Holy Week, takes us back to ancient times, when boards were employed to announce pious assemblies.

Hereby the Church seems to say to us: "If my fidelity is such in retaining usages apparently so unimportant, what do you think is my care in preserving the deposit of holy truths entrusted to me? You may well rely on my solicitude. Do not be afraid, my children: I will not waste your patrimony." Such is the office of Wednesday.

Holy Thursday: Spirit and division of the office.—Holy Thursday is consecrated to honoring the institution of the august Eucharist. The Church shows us, on the one hand, the Son of God seeking amid the treasures of his love a new, incomparable, everlasting pledge of his tenderness for men; and, on the other, men occupied with thoughts of a cruel, outrageous death against this amiable Savior. On this day, it would be desirable to have many hearts. One is not enough for the opposite sentiments that are inspired by the contrast of which we speak; and this contrast the Church endeavors to make more striking. The morning office inspires joy and gladness; the evening office, the deepest sorrow. The former is divided into four parts: the absolution of penitents, the Mass with the blessing of holy oils, the stripping of the altars, and the *mandatum* or washing of feet.

The bishop, having arrived at the church, puts on his ornaments, takes his place in the middle of the choir, and here, accompanied by two priests, recites on his knees the seven penitential psalms. Then follow the prayers and verses in which the remission of the offenses of the penitents is asked. The bishop concludes with a touching prayer, in which he beseeches the Lord to open again the gates of the fold to the penitent sheep, so that the Savior may not lose the fruits of his blood, and that souls, redeemed at so dear a price, may not become the eternal victims of the devil. Then, turning toward the lower end of the church, formerly the place of penitents, the pontiff absolves them in the name of Jesus Christ, who died on the cross in order to deliver them from the chains of sin. This beautiful and holy ceremony is one of the remains of our venerable antiquity.

Absolution of penitents. During the days of public penance, penitents were, as we have seen, driven out of the church on Ash Wednesday. On the morning of Holy Thursday, these prodigal children were to be found at the door of the temple, covered with haircloth, and with ashes on their heads. They were led into the church with ceremonies, and presented to the sacred ministers. All fell prostrate, and the bishop made a short prayer over them. Then the deacon, speaking for the penitents—who, continuing prostrate, explained themselves only by sighs, tears, and groans—represented to the bishop that the time for mercy had come. He alluded to the mysteries of these holy days, in order to call to mind that God does not wish the death of the sinner sincerely converted, and that there was question of delivering from the dead those on whom Jesus Christ had vouchsafed to bestow life. The bishop, satisfied with the dispositions of the penitents, made them a short homily, and pronounced over them the formula of absolution. This ceremony ended, the newly reconciled took their places among the faithful, heard Mass, and participated with the rest in the holy mysteries. For it was the custom, and this custom lasted many ages, that all the faithful should communicate on Holy Thursday. Honor to those who still observe it![695]

The absolution given, the Mass begins. In the epistle, St. Paul reminds us of the dispositions necessary for receiving the Eucharist; and in the gospel, St. John traces for us the amazing humility and immense love of the Son of God: he shows him to us on his knees before his apostles, washing their feet. Humility and charity: such are the two great lessons that he gives us, and the essential dispositions for Communion. During the Mass, as has been the custom since the seventh century, the magnificent ceremony of the blessing of the oils takes place, which, in the main, comes from the apostolic times.[696] In vain shall we look elsewhere for anything more solemn or instructive.[697]

Blessing of the holy oils. The officiating bishop comes and sits down before a table prepared near the middle of the sanctuary. Deacons and subdeacons bring large urns, which they place in front of the pontiff. These urns are filled with the oils that are about to be sanctified and blessed: holy oils intended for young people who have just been born and sick people who are dying, for priests who are to be dedicated to God and kings who are to be consecrated and crowned; holy oils which flow upon us at our entrance into and our departure from this world—holy chrism at baptism and confirmation, and the last anointing at death.

As often as I have been present at the blessing of the holy oils, I have had very serious thoughts on seeing the bishop pray that the Spirit of God might descend upon them. I have said to myself: "Which of us shall be first anointed with this oil—a friend, a brother, or myself?" Oh, when such thoughts as these rush upon our minds, the ceremonies of the Church seem doubly holy! Serious thoughts are sisters to salutary thoughts.[698]

In blessing the holy chrism, the bishop must be assisted by twelve priests—all pastors, as far as possible—seven deacons, and seven subdeacons, so as to recall the time when the college of sacred ministers consisted of twelve priests, seven deacons, and seven minors, for the administration of the diocese and the service of bishop and people.

The pontiff and priests salute the holy chrism and holy oils separately, after their consecration, saying: "Hail, holy chrism," etc. That the salutation is either addressed to the Holy Ghost, the Sanctifier of all creatures, or that it ought not to be regarded as anything more than a mark of respect for things sanctified, is quite clear. It is figurative language, which paints the sentiment much better than ordinary language. Venerable in itself, this ceremony is still more so by its high antiquity. It is already mentioned in the sacramentary of St. Gregory the Great.

The tomb. When all the prayers have been said over the holy oils, the bishop ascends the altar again, and the host which he has consecrated for the next day is borne under a canopy and with great pomp to the chapel of the tomb. This tomb, adorned with all the care possible, is like the sepulchre in which our divine Redeemer rests. The faithful visit it to honor the Son of God, who suffered death to redeem us.

The visiting of "tombs" ought not to resemble a promenade. It ought to be grave and quiet. Piety and an indescribably religious melancholy ought to appear in our whole demeanor. When we arrive at the foot of a tomb, we should pour out our heart before the Savior. This is a good opportunity to say to him: "My God! I thank thee for having instituted the Blessed Eucharist for me, and admitted me to it so many times. I also thank thee for all the favors that thou hast granted in this church to me and to all others who have come here to pray since it was built. I ask pardon for the ingratitude with which thou hast been treated in thy adorable sacrament, as well as for the irreverences of which I and others have been guilty in this sanctuary."

We have said that, among the consecrated hosts, there is one held in reserve for the priest's Communion next day; for on Good Friday there is—properly speaking—no Mass said. The priest is content to recite the last part of the prayers, without the consecration. This is called the Mass of the Presanctified, that is to say, a Mass in which the host consecrated the previous day is consumed. This usage comes from the first ages of Christianity. By abstaining from the celebration of the Sacrifice of the Mass, the Church wished to testify her grief, and to fix all the attention of her children on the sacrifice of Calvary.

Stripping of altars. After Mass, the altars are stripped of their ornaments: they remain in this state till toward evening on Holy Saturday. Consider in all these sad ceremonies the profound affliction of the Church; also the nakedness and abjection of the Son of

God on the cross—for the altar has always been a figure of our Lord—and the rending of the veil of the Temple. Yield to the spirit of faith, and this ceremony will say more to you than any book.

The altars are also washed with wine and water. The first object of this is cleanliness. In the next place it represents that the body of Jesus Christ, the true altar of the world, streamed on the cross with blood and water. The better to indicate this mystery, the washing is accompanied with the recital of a penitential psalm, or a prayer in keeping with the passion.[699]

Washing of feet. The magnificent office of Holy Thursday concludes with the washing of feet. It is written that, when about to institute the Blessed Eucharist, the Savior humbled himself so much as to wash the feet of his disciples, and then said to them: "You call me Lord and master, and you speak well, for so I am. If then I, being your Lord and master, have washed your feet, you ought also to wash one another's feet. For I have given you an example, that you may do as I have done."[700]

Following the guidance of the divine master, the Church took this command of practicing humility in the lowest services as a lesson that should be observed to the letter. The early Christians practiced it, not only to renew the memory of what the Savior had done, but also to perform an act of charity. Hence, among them, the universal and sacred custom of washing the feet of guests.

In the course of time, when people of the world had ceased to wash the feet of their guests, the Church, not wishing to part with a custom so pious and instructive, made it a regular practice, intended to perpetuate the memory of our Lords's act from generation to generation. She wished that her principal ministers should wash the feet of the clergy, representing the apostles, or of the poor, as subjects toward whom it was proper to exercise that humility which the Savior so much recommended by his abasement.

And behold! for so many ages the world, on Holy Thursday every year, sees the greatest and most august—popes, bishops, emperors, kings, and queens—humbly prostrate before some poor people, washing their feet and kissing them respectfully, and considering themselves highly honored in being allowed to walk thus in the footsteps of the man-God. If some old Roman were to return to the earth and witness this spectacle, what would be his amazement! Where would he be who regarded the poor as most contemptible creatures, if he saw monarchs at their feet? This simple ceremony shows us that between us and pagans, between our ideas and theirs, Christianity has placed an infinite distance.

The ceremony of washing the feet is commonly called the "Mandy," or *Mandatum*. This name comes either from the command that the Savior gave his disciples to do among themselves what he had done to them, or from the antiphon: *Mandatum novum do vobis*—"A new commandment I give unto you," which is repeated between the verses of the psalm that is sung during the ceremony. In this antiphon there is another command much more important than the washing of feet—that which the Savior gave his disciples to love one another as he had loved them: a distinguishing precept of the Christian religion, and one which regards us all.

We must, therefore, especially on Holy Thursday, with all the good faith of people who do not want to deceive themselves, ask ourselves whether we love our brethren as Jesus Christ loved us. If our heart hesitates to answer—what do I say?—if it bears witness to some willful hatred or antipathy, how shall we dare to approach him who said: "If, when you come to offer your gift at the altar, you remember that your brother has anything against you, leave your gift there before the altar, and go first and be reconciled with your brother; then coming, offer me your gift."[701]

Such is the morning office of the Great Thursday: everything in it breathes love and joy. The evening office, called Tenebrae, like that of the previous evening, consists of the same parts, and plunges us again into sorrow.

PRAYER

O my God! who art all love, I thank thee for having instituted the Blessed Eucharist. I ask pardon for my little care in preparing to receive it.

I am resolved to love God above all things, and my neighbor as myself for the love of God; and, in testimony of this love, I will every month make some honorable amends to our Lord in the Blessed Sacrament.

Lesson 36: Christianity Brought before the Senses (Continued)—Good Friday

Good Friday: Object of this day's office.—Good Friday! At this name the Christian heart stands still: a shudder passes over you, and your imagination takes flight in spite of you to the summit of Calvary. Here comes the mob—I speak amiss, the people, for there are magistrates, priests, and old grey-headed men here, as well as children, women, and the poor. The noisy crowd wends its way up the hill, crushing and jostling to get near the scaffold, and enjoy more fully the victim's anguish. Lo! here is the victim himself, advancing with slow steps, for he is exhausted from loss of blood and weakened by tortures. Two criminals walk beside him, carrying on their shoulders the instruments of their execution. They are guilty; but you recognize the just one by the special severity displayed toward him. His head is crowned with thorns. His face is covered with blood and vile spittle. He is the object of the taunts of the multitude.

And yet this is Jesus, who went about doing good! Among the eager spectators are many who have had experience of his goodness: this one's father, mother, or sister, perhaps, has been raised to life; that one's servant or friend has been healed; on all, the treasures of the divine wisdom have been lavished. This is Jesus, who entered Jerusalem in triumph five days ago. On before him moved the same crowd, waking the echoes of Mount Olivet with their acclamations: "Glory to the Son of David! Blessed is he that cometh in the name of the Lord!" And today they shout and yell, and cry for his blood and his death!

What has happened? Has Jesus ceased to be what he was five days ago? No, but the hour marked out for the unchaining of the powers of darkness has come. The gloom of night has fallen on minds. The great murderer, the personal enemy of the incarnate Word, Satan has breathed his hatred into the souls of the people, and the people have bent like a reed before the wind. Meanwhile, the victim reaches the place of execution. Behold, he is stretched on the cross, nailed to it, raised up on it! The people laugh, the scribe shrugs his shoulders, the soldiers begin their game. Mary, for the Mother of Jesus is here, weeps, plunged in a sea of sorrows.

This is what passed eighteen centuries ago, on a hill near Jerusalem. The object of so many outrages, the victim of so many cruelties, was the eternal Word, the Creator of the universe, the only Son of God! And they crucified him!!! And you think that the Catholic Church has not done well in perpetuating, by a day of solemn mourning, the memory of the greatest of crimes! How can you be so deceived? It is not by forgetting crimes that one atones for them. And then, have we not to prevent them? What better means of inspiring a horror of them than a great expiation, perpetuated from age to age? Hereby, you may be sure, there is an immense service rendered to society.

Hence, since the consummation of the atrocity of Calvary, the Church has every year celebrated Good Friday in tears at all points of the Catholic world. She has been particularly desirous to celebrate it at the very spot where the fearful deed was done. In all ages she has wished that Christian tears should moisten on this day the ground that drank the Savior's blood. Listen to what still occurs at Golgotha on Good Friday; and in the history of the present, read the history of the past.

Good Friday at Jerusalem. "It was in 1832. The morning office was gone through with the most affecting ceremonies by the reverend Franciscan fathers, and I was present at it. At dinner, the whole community, with the Father Guardian at their head, ate on their knees: there was nothing served to them but some bread and water, and a few leaves of salad.

"At half past three, the fathers went to the office of *Tenebrae* as on the two previous evenings. It was the last time that I should hear at Jerusalem the voice of the prophet of Anatoth, and this idea made me still more alive to the earnestness and the tenderness of his complaints. You may sometimes have remarked how much more lively is the impression made by the words and wishes of those whom we love, when a moment of parting is come, especially if a deep conviction tells us that we shall never meet again. Then more than ever is the heart ready to burst, then are sighs heard, then are eyes bedewed with tears. It is a kind of suffering little different from that which snaps the chord of life. Such, and even more painful, was my anguish when Jeremias let me hear those words so perfectly in keeping with the sorrowful mystery of Good Friday, and with the thoughts that were passing through my mind:

"'The joy of our heart is at an end! our sweet concerts are changed into mournful sighs.

"'The crown is fallen from our head; woe to us because we have sinned!

"'This is why our heart has grown so sad; our eyes are troubled.

"'Because of the desolation of Mount Sion, the foxes wander about there today!

"'O Lord! thou remainest for ever; thy throne is from generation to generation.

"'Wilt thou always forget us; wilt thou keep away from us all our days?

"'Convert us to thee, O Lord! and we shall be converted; renew our days as in the beginning,' etc.

"To impress more deeply on minds the memory of the Savior's passion and death, and to excite more perfectly in hearts those feelings of compunction, gratitude, and love which they ought to awaken, the fathers have every Good Friday a ceremony quite in keeping with the genius of Orientals, and of which we find examples only in other missions of Asia, which have probably borrowed it from Palestine.

"By means of a large life-size figure, with movable head and limbs, ready to take any position desired, they represent the crucifixion and burial of Jesus Christ in such a manner as to make all their leading circumstances apparent. This ceremony, so touching and at the same time so dreadful, takes place toward the close of the day, in presence of an immense multitude of men, women, and children, drawn to it many by sincere piety and others by profane curiosity.

"The Fathers of the Holy Land, having assembled in the Blessed Virgin's chapel, left it about six o'clock, with one at their head who, attended by the young Arabs of the monastery, carried a large crucifix. The religious and the faithful, walking slowly in two rows, with taper in hand, recited in sad and plaintive tones the *Miserere* or the *Stabat Mater*.

"The procession stopped first at the altar of the Division of the Garments, and then at that of the Reproaches, to hear a few words, simple but full of unction, which a Spanish father delivered on the sorrowful scenes of the passion recalled by these two places. It afterward continued its course without interruption toward the summit of Golgotha. Here, the religious who carried the crucifix laid it aside respectfully at the foot of an altar, and the Spanish father, resuming his discourse, related for the weeping multitude the sad history of the sufferings and ignominies of the Savior until the moment when he was laid on the cross.

"At this moment, he ceased to speak, and, the image of Jesus having been fastened with nails to the wood, the cross was raised and fixed in the very place where once stood the true cross, on which the salvation of the human race was effected. Then the good father, his voice broken and almost stifled with sobs, described the last words and the last moments of the august victim, immolated on this spot to atone for our sins and to reconcile us with his Father. But it became more and more difficult to hear him. The crowd, already much excited by what had gone before, paid no further attention to anything but what it saw, and words hardly reached it amid the wailing and moaning, the cries and sighs.

"After a quarter of an hour given to sorrow, that it might have time to relieve itself, one of the fathers, provided with pincers and hammer, mounted to the top of the cross, lifted off the crown of thorns, and, while the brothers were holding up the body by means of white scarves passed under the arms, took out the nails from the hands and feet. The effigy was soon lowered, almost in the same manner as Christ himself had been lowered from the cross. The celebrant and the religious then came forward quietly in succession, fell prostrate, and kissed respectfully the crown and nails, which were immediately afterward presented to the veneration of the multitude.

"The procession soon set out again in the same order that it had ascended Calvary. The crown and nails were carried on a silver dish by a religious, and the effigy was carried by four others in the same manner as a corpse is carried to the grave. A pause was made at the Stone of Embalming, to imitate here the pious action of Joseph of Arimathea, Nicodemus, and the holy women. All needful preparations had been made: the stone was covered with a very fine white linen cloth, at the corners of which were vases of perfumes. The body, wrapped in a shroud, was laid here, the head resting on a pillow. The celebrant sprinkled some essence over it, burned some aromatics, and, after praying silently for a few moments, explained in a short exhortation the meaning of this station. Hence the road was taken to the church. The sacred effigy was laid on the marble of the Holy Sepulchre, and another discourse brought the ceremony to a close."[702]

In all other parts of the Christian world, Good Friday is no less religiously honored. For many ages it was kept without servile work like Sunday. The watches, mortifications, pious reading, and prayers of other days of the year were then greatly increased. The whole night was spent mourning in the assembly of the faithful, according to a custom handed down from the apostles or their early disciples.[703] No persons were exempted from the extraordinary watch and fast, save children under seven years. Even at the present day, notwithstanding the decline of faith, there is not a Christian family in which the children do not think it a pleasure and a duty to fast on Good Friday.

Division of the office.—The office of this day is of the highest antiquity.[704] To understand it well and to follow it with profit, we must know that it is divided into three parts:

1. *Lesson, tract, and the passion.* The first part consists of a lesson from the scripture, followed by a tract interspersed with verses in keeping with the occasion, and the passion. The Church has taken care to preserve in the office of this day all our beautiful antiquity: it breathes in every word and ceremony. Thus, the office begins with a lesson, because all Masses formerly began with lessons or readings from the sacred books. The lesson of Good Friday has no title, because Jesus Christ, who is our head, or our light, as the title throws light on the book and the lesson, is removed from us.[705]

Moses describes the ceremony of the paschal lamb, sacrificed and eaten with unleavened bread and wild lettuce by the people of God when about to quit Egypt, their garments tucked up, shoes on their feet, staves in their hands, and with all haste, because it was to be the Pasch, that is, the passage of the Lord. The paschal lamb was a figure of the Messias, and this lesson, which takes us back 3,500 years, reminds us that Christ was then what he is today, the faith and hope of the human race, and that the Catholic Church embraces all times.[706]

It was not without reason that the Church chose this lesson from Moses. She wished to show us that the law bore testimony to her divine spouse, and that he is really the object of the oracles and sighs of the ancient world.[707]

After the prophecy, the passion of our Lord according to St. John is sung. This singing is of high antiquity. We have already referred to the interlocutions that take place during it: the Jews, Pilate, Herod, the apostles, and Jesus himself, speak and answer in turn. At the words, "Bowing his head, he gave up the ghost," the singing ceases, a great silence falls on the church, and the faithful kiss the ground, which the Savior moistened with his blood.

2. *Solemn or sacerdotal prayers.* The second part of the office consists of solemn or sacerdotal prayers, which are not recited publicly on any day but Good Friday: they are very ancient; St. Leo tells that in his time they were recited wherever the Christian law had penetrated:[708] he believed them to be of apostolic institution. These prayers are ten in number. The priest at the altar, bending his knee and stretching out his hands, prays: a) for the whole earth and for holy Church; b) for our holy father the pope; c) for the bishop of the diocese; d) for all the sacred ministers and for all the faithful; e) for the king; f) for catechumens; g) for a remedy to all spiritual and temporal evils; h) for heretics and schismatics; i) for the Jews; j) for pagans and idolaters.

To mark her horror of willful apostates, and to distinguish them from the children that live within her pale and enjoy the advantages of her communion, the Church forbids her ministers to mention this sort of people in public prayers; but she makes an exception to her rule in the office of Good Friday, because on this day the Redeemer died for all mankind. Oh, yes, Good Friday is the great day of pardon! To set us an example of it, the Church, our mother, suspends her wise and holy prescriptions, and Jesus, our father, invites us from the summit of the cross to repeat along with him, for those who have done us evil, the words: "Father! forgive them, for they know not what they do."[709]

Between the prayers, one after another, the officiant says, *Flectamus genua*—"Let us bend our knees"; the deacon answers, *Levate*—"Rise up." But at the prayer for the Jews, who killed our Lord, the priest does not bend his knee. Hereby he shows a great horror for the deicide people.

3. *Adoration of the cross.* The third part of the office of Good Friday is the adoration of the cross.[710] When the sacerdotal prayers are ended, the celebrant lays aside his chasuble, moves to the epistle side, and receives the cross, covered with a veil, from the hand of the deacon. He now uncovers the cross a little, and sings the antiphon: *Ecce lignum crucis*—"Behold the wood of the cross!" The choir answers: *Venite, adoremus*—"Come, let us adore!" All the assistants fall prostrate. After two other like elevations, the cross is carried to a place before the altar, and the priest, barefooted, adores and kisses it. All the people imitate him. During this adoration, two chanters in the middle of the choir sing the words that express the ineffable love with which Jesus went forward to his execution. These words are called the *Improperia*, which here means, "Tender Reproaches," addressed by the heart of Jesus to the Jews when they were leading him to death.

Listen to them:

"O my people! what have I done to thee? or in what have I grieved thee? O my people! answer me!

"Because I brought thee out of the land of Egypt, thou hast prepared a cross for thy Savior."

Confounded at so much malice on the one side and so much goodness on the other, the Church, greatly affected, makes an act of adoration and love, like the heaving of a deep sigh: "O holy God! O holy and strong God! O holy and immortal God! have mercy on us."

These words are sung both in Greek and Latin: the Church shows us her catholicity. She wishes that all peoples, all tribes and tongues, should adore and love with her: it seems as if she cannot find any language sufficient to express her grief and to cry to God.[711]

The chanters continue: "Because I led thee forty years through the desert, and fed thee with manna, and brought thee into an excellent land, thou hast prepared a cross for thy Savior!"

The choir: "O holy God! O holy and strong God! O holy and immortal God! have mercy on us."

The chanters: "What more could I do for thee than I have done? Art thou not the vine that I planted and tended with so much care? Yet thou hast yielded me exceeding bitter fruits; for in my thirst thou hast given me vinegar to drink, and with a spear thou hast pierced thy Savior's side!"

The choir: "O holy God! O holy and strong God! O holy and immortal God! have mercy on us."

In this part of the office all is imagery, everything speaks to the senses. The simple words, "My people! what have I done to thee?" returning so often and so mournfully would touch hearts of stone.

It is in the midst of this anguish that kings, pontiffs, cardinals, archbishops, bishops, the old men of the sanctuary, the children of the choir, the rich, the poor, the faithful in general, come to adore the saving wood. We seem to behold weeping children let into the room where their deceased father has just been laid out, that they may kiss with respectful grief his venerable remains. Near the crucifix there is a copper plate, on which all place their alms; for it is not in a mourning journey that the poor can be forgotten.[712]

When going to adore the cross, how can we forbid ourselves the thought that we are traveling the sad road sprinkled with the Savior's blood? Let us open the ears of our souls to those tender reproaches which are addressed to Christians much more than to Jews, and which each of us should apply to himself. "My people! what have I done to thee, or in what have I grieved thee? Answer me." Christian soul, my child, my beloved! I delivered thee from captivity and fed thee with manna, and thou hast prepared a cross for thy Savior! I kept thee as the apple of mine eye—what more could I do for thee?—and thou hast prepared a cross for thy Savior!

We shall then have sorrow and love in our hearts, and tears in our eyes, and, if we can speak, tender words on our lips: and we shall return from Calvary like the centurion, striking our breasts, detesting our ingratitude, and resolving to die rather than ever again sadden a father so good!

The adoration ended, the Holy Sacrament is brought back in mournful silence. The priest communicates, vespers are sung in a grave tone, and the morning office concludes.

Useful exercise for the afternoon: The seven words.—At three o'clock in the afternoon, we must not fail to adore Jesus dying. In some countries, the people go in crowds to the church a little before this solemn hour. Everyone prays, everyone asks pardon for himself and for his brethren; and, when the clock strikes three, you see the whole multitude, in deep silence and emotion, falling prostrate and kissing the pavement of the temple. Now especially is it useful to meditate on the seven words which Jesus uttered from the summit of the cross. We are about to explain them briefly, and to show that these seven words are the Savior's last will, and a summary of religion; consequently, the basis of all our duties, and the pledge of our happiness in time and eternity.

1. *Father, forgive them, for they know not what they do.* Jesus is on the cross, and the crime of the Jews is evident. Nevertheless, he prays for them all without exception. He excuses them on the ground of their ignorance: they do not know the extent of the atrocity of which they are guilty. Thus, he does what he prescribed to us in the gospel: "Pray for

them who persecute you, love your enemies." The forgiveness of injuries or the love of enemies is the basis of public and private law. Such is the first article of our father's will.

2. *This day shalt thou be with me in paradise.* While people are mocking, denying, and forsaking Jesus, he hears one of the thieves making a petition to him with faith and confidence. It is enough. Jesus grants him pardon for a whole life of iniquity, and promises him that this very day he shall be with himself in the abode of blessed souls. All that has heretofore been said of the goodness of God grows pale before this promise. The infinite mercy of God toward the penitent sinner and the full confidence of the penitent sinner in the mercy of God are the basis of the moral order. Such is the second article of our father's will.

3. *Behold thy son; behold thy mother.* Jesus is about to die; but his holy Mother still engages his thoughts. He comforts her by telling her that she shall have another son instead of the one whom she is about to lose; and, to make St. John take great care of Mary, he tells him that she shall love him as a mother. The constant tenderness of children for their parents and the no less constant tenderness of parents for their children are the basis of the family. Such is the third article of our father's will.

4. *My God, my God, why hast thou forsaken me?* In the Garden of Olives, the Savior abandoned himself wholly to the will of his Father: he accepted all kinds of sufferings with the meekness of a lamb. He does not now belie himself. He only shows the extent of his sorrows, that we may not doubt he suffered, that we may understand how much he loved us, and that we may know to whom we should have recourse in our trials. Thus, Christian resignation in the midst of trials is the basis of public and private peace, the basis of every real virtue; consequently, the basis of all true merit for each one of us. Such is the fourth article of our father's will.

5. *I thirst.* At the moment of dying for the salvation of mankind, our Lord casts a divine glance into the future. He sees a countless multitude of souls that will make no account of his sufferings or his love, and this heartrending sight causes him to cry out: "I thirst." "I thirst for outrages, I thirst for sufferings; the cross, if needs be, to the end of the world, that I may save a few souls more!"[713] Thus, zeal for souls is the basis of all social relations. Such is the fifth article of our father's will.

6. *It is consummated.* "My Father is glorified; the reign of the devil is at an end; man, if he wishes it, is saved." Thus, the continual care to do the will of God in all things, according to one's state, is the basis of individual perfection. Such is the sixth article of our father's will.

7. *Father, into thy hands I commend my spirit.* "I have lived for my Father and I die for him: this is the secret of my coming into the world and of my departure out of it." Thus, the salvation of one's soul is the basis of all that is important in life. Such is the seventh and last article of our father's will.

What rich subjects of meditation are these seven words![714]

At the evening office, called *Tenebrae*, the mourning continues. The lamentations of Jeremias and the cries of the holy women resound through the temple. The Church is now like a widow weeping at the grave of her departed spouse.

PRAYER

O my God! who art all love, I thank thee for having delivered thine only Son to death in order to redeem me. Do not permit me to render the fruits of his passion useless to me.

I am resolved to love God above all things, and my neighbor as myself for the love of God; and, in testimony of this love, I will every Friday, about three o'clock in the evening, say five Our Fathers and five Hail Marys in honor of the five wounds of our Lord Jesus Christ.

Lesson 37: Christianity Brought before the Senses (Continued)—Holy Saturday

Holy Saturday.—Holy Saturday is consecrated to honor the Savior's burial. Up to Sunday morning, the time of the resurrection, the Church continues the weeping widow by the grave. Her offices are longer, but in the midst of her grief there are gleams of joy. We feel that she has faith in the consoling mystery soon to follow.

In the early ages, many churches made Holy Saturday a festival of precept. It was afterward reduced to the rank of a half-festival.[715] It is now nearly everywhere left to the devotion of the faithful. Notwithstanding these changes, the Vigil of Easter has always been the first of all vigils in dignity, as it is the first in antiquity. As a matter of fact, it is the longest of all and has the richest ceremonies. Formerly, the office of this vigil was joined immediately to that of the festival of Easter; for it was begun after the hour of none or about sunset, and continued till break of day on Easter Sunday, by the faithful of every state, most of them fasting since Friday and some since Thursday.

Even in places where the ceremonies were shorter or there were fewer catechumens to baptize, it was much recommended not to end the offices before cockcrow, which was the hour for offering the sacrifice, communicating, and breaking the fast of Lent. In this case, whatever time remained between the various blessings and Mass was employed in reading the lessons of the law, the prophets, or the Psalms, or in giving some instructions to the people. This usage, which ceased in the Latin Church only when the offices of the vigil began at the hour of terce, still exists among the Greeks. To this day they spend the whole night in the church, reading scripture, or singing, until the hour of the office of Easter, which they begin immediately after sunrise, without leaving the church.[716]

Object, excellence, and division of the office.—The office of Holy Saturday consists of six principal parts or ceremonies: a) the blessing of the new fire; b) the blessing of the paschal candle; c) the lessons; d) the blessing of the font; e) the Mass; and f) vespers. The most venerable antiquity breathes in every one of these beautiful ceremonies. The most touching records of the catacombs, of Constantinople, of Nice, of Jerusalem, of all the great Churches, are brought before our eyes. May the salutary impressions that they are well calculated to make sink deep into our souls!

1. *The blessing of the new fire.* It was an old custom, established in most churches from the fourth century, to daily bless, toward evening, the fire with which to light the lamps for the office of vespers.[717] The fire was taken from flint, rather than from the hearth of any house, in order to be blessed. This usage corresponds with the great idea of the Church, that all creatures having been vitiated, it is not fit to use them unblessed in the ceremonies of the divine worship. Hence, from the early ages, she did not use any profane or common fire in those public sacrifices or prayers which required lights. Is not this first ceremony of Holy Saturday very instructive? It cannot be explained without relating the whole history of the world, lost and saved.

The custom of blessing the new fire every evening was interrupted during the last three days of Holy Week, on account of the disarrangement in the order of the offices. It was decided therefore to hold over the fire of the evening till next day, by keeping the last of the candles lit. This usage, common at first to the three days, was later on confined to Holy Saturday, in such a manner that the blessing of the new fire became a ceremony proper to this day.[718]

It begins the office, and is performed with great solemnity of prayers; for this new fire is to the Christian an image of the new law, the law of grace and love that is about to spring from the tomb of Christ, as the old fire is an image of the old law, quenched in the blood of the Savior. When therefore the clergy reach the choir, the Litany of the Saints is intoned. The Church wishes that her children, already crowned in heaven, should take part in the joy with which the appearance of the new law fills the earth, and that by praying for their brethren here below, they would obtain for them the grace to observe, as they did, the commands of this immaculate law, and thus arrive at the same happiness.[719] During the chanting of the Litany, the priest blesses the new fire. Such is the first part of the office of Holy Saturday.

2. *The blessing of the paschal candle.* The paschal candle was originally a pillar on which the patriarch of Alexandria wrote out the date of Easter, and the dates of the movable festivals depending on this great solemnity. Alexandria being the city possessed of the best astronomers, the bishop used to consult them every year, and, according to their decision, acquaint the pope, and through him the whole Church, with the first Sunday after the fourteenth day of the moon of March. In those times, people wrote on wax, and it was on a kind of pillar of this material that the patriarch of Alexandria drew up a list of the principal festivals of the year. The pope received this canon[720] respectfully, blessed it, and sent similar ones to the other churches, which received them with the same honors.

This waxen staff was soon changed into a torch, which helped to give light on Easter night, and it was at the same time regarded as an emblem of Jesus risen. Pope Zozimus approved of this usage, and led to its general establishment by ordering all parish churches to bless a candle on Holy Saturday.[721]

The paschal candle is lighted with the sacred fire. It must not be lighted otherwise, any more than the candles for the offices and Mass of Easter Eve. Every other fire is declared strange and profane, like that which provoked the Lord against Nadab and Abiu, and which caused their ruin. The blessing of the paschal candle dates from the highest antiquity. It is already to be found in the works of St. Ennodius, bishop of Pavia, who lived in the beginning of the sixth century.[722]

This very high candle is placed on a candlestick in the middle of the sanctuary, before the altar. It is lighted at the office of Holy Saturday, at Mass, and at vespers; during the whole of Easter Week; and at Mass and vespers on Sundays and festivals till the Ascension. On this day, it disappears immediately after the gospel at High Mass: the Savior, rising from the earth, now returns to heaven.

All these details show sufficiently the mysterious meaning of the paschal candle. It is the first symbol of the resurrection of our Lord that the Church proposes to the faithful on Holy Saturday. It reminds them at the same time that their divine Redeemer is the light of the world. Hence, nothing more magnificent or celebrated in the liturgy than the formula employed to bless it. The opening words are: *Exultet jam angelica turba*, etc.

"Let the angels of heaven, let the hosts above exult and thrill with gladness, and let the sound of trumpets proclaim our joyous sacrifice!

"Let the earth be filled with bliss, and let it revel in the glorious light that has burst upon it!

"And do thou, our mother, holy Church, rejoice too: thou art all radiant with the divine light that shines upon the world!

"Let the holy place resound with the joyful transports of the people, and let the acclamations of earth ascend to heaven!"

The rest breathes the same enthusiasm. This blessing is worthy of the genius of St. Augustine, to whom it is attributed.[723] In vain shall we look elsewhere for more graceful or poetic images, nobler language, or a more beautiful chant. It is in this inimitable blessing that we find those amazing words: "O truly necessary sin of Adam, since Christ has blotted it out by his death! O happy fault, which merited for us so great a Redeemer!" It is the deacon that sings this beautiful announcement of the festival of Easter; for the blessing of the paschal candle has always been part of the ministry of deacons, even in presence of the officiating priest or bishop. The deacon is now the herald of heaven, as it were, coming to announce to the Church the glorious resurrection of her spouse and the splendid proofs of his mercy, as well as the happiness of man, reconciled to God by the accomplishment of the great work of the redemption.

The five grains of incense that he fixes in the candle, in the form of a cross, are an emblem of the five wounds of our Lord, and of the spices with which he was embalmed.[724] The prayer that the Church uses in blessing them leaves no doubt on this matter. It also shows us the efficacy of the blessed candle, as of all other sanctified things, to banish the devil, scourges, and diseases. This is the reason why little pieces of wax used to be taken from the paschal candle and distributed to the faithful after Mass on Low Sunday. They burned them in their houses, fields, and gardens, as preservatives against lightning, winds, hail, wild beasts, and the craft of the devil. Instead of these pieces of wax, Rome blesses, on the morning of Holy Saturday, little waxen lambs, which she distributes at the Mass of Low Sunday, with the same intentions.[725]

Before taxing the faith of our ancestors with simplicity, it should be proved that the Church is not infallible—or that we have nothing to fear, especially at the present day, from the snares of the devil—or that God is not the master of nature, and cannot attach his favors to whatever conditions he pleases. As for us, let us admire the infinite goodness of our heavenly Father, who vouchsafed by these weak means to supply his children with arms against their enemies, and thus made our preservation and that of whatever is dear to us depend on our confidence in him. Henceforth, when we see the paschal candle lighted, let us think seriously on rising again to life with our Lord; and when, from Easter to the Ascension, we see it shining before our eyes, like the bright pillar that led Israel toward the promised land, let us ask ourselves whether we walk faithfully in the footsteps of the risen Savior toward the true promised land.

3. *The lessons.* We have seen that anciently the office of Easter did not end sooner than cockcrowing, that is to say, after midnight of Easter day. In churches where there were few catechumens to baptize, the time remaining from the blessing of the new fire and the paschal candle till Mass was employed in chanting lessons from scripture. They were so many instructions for the faithful. That all might take an interest in them, they were sung in two languages, then quite common, Greek and Latin. To prevent monotony, and to speak in turn to the minds and hearts of her children, the Church had appointed that these lessons should be interspersed with canticles or responses, and also with collects proper to excite piety. The same thing is still observed at the present day. All these lessons, twelve in number, relate to baptism, whose great festival is Holy Saturday.

Could the Church find a better time than that between the death and the resurrection of the Savior to celebrate the baptism of the faithful and the resurrection of the children of God? Is there not question of representing the passage that is made from the death of the old man or sin, buried in the Savior's tomb, to the new life that the new Adam procures for us by the grace of baptism? When therefore the deacon has ended the blessing of the paschal candle, he lays aside his dalmatic, and, clad in his alb and stole, ascends the jubé and sings the first lesson. The others are sung by clerics of an inferior order. It is, as we have said, to the great mystery of our regeneration that the Church wishes to apply the meaning of these twelve lessons, which are called prophecies. As a sign of mourning, they have no titles.

The first is taken from Genesis, and describes the creation of the world, and chiefly that of man, made to the image of God. This image, blotted out by sin, is restored by the baptism of Jesus Christ, through the merits of his passion and resurrection.

The second is the history of the deluge, by which all those who were not in the ark, a figure of the Church, perished.

The third is the history of the sacrifice of Abraham, wherein we see the submission of Isaac, who, being under the power of his father, whose arm was guided by the Lord, represented a neophyte submissive to the minister who, with imposition of hands and holy unction, makes him renounce his first life in the waters of baptism.

The fourth is the history of the miraculous passage of the Israelites through the Red Sea, which was a way of life and salvation to them, as baptism is to catechumens.

The fifth is taken from Isaias. By the mouth of the sublime prophet, the Lord, after showing the nature of the inheritance that he promises to his adopted children, invites all the world to embrace religion, whose door is baptism.

The sixth is a prophecy from Baruch. The prophet tells the children of Israel that they have been led away captive only for having abandoned the Lord. He then shows them the way to return to life and liberty. This represents the human family become slaves by original sin, and set free by baptism.

The seventh is taken from that part of Ezechiel where he treats of the general resurrection of mankind, a resurrection mysteriously effected by baptism.

The eighth is that passage of Isaias where he says that seven women will take hold of one man, asking only that they may have the honor of bearing his name, in order to be delivered from reproach. Do you see all nations running to baptism, and taking the name of Christian, in order to be delivered from the shame and the horrors of paganism?

The ninth, taken from Exodus, recalls the visit of the destroying angel, who spared the houses marked with the blood of the lamb. Happy the catechumens over whom, after baptism, the devil will no longer have any sway!

The tenth is the history of the prophet Jonas, who, thrown to the waves and swallowed by a sea monster, came forth full of life after three days. Truly this is man, devoured as it were by the infernal serpent, and rescued by baptism!

The eleventh is taken from that part of Deuteronomy where it is said that Moses wrote his second canticle and taught it to the children of Israel a short time before his death. A warning to those who are about to be baptized not to be unmindful of their engagements!

The twelfth is the history of the three young Hebrews cast into a burning furnace for refusing to adore the statue of the king of Babylon. The protection of God over the baptized, who have become his children!

4. *The blessing of the font.* This means the blessing of the water to be used for baptizing catechumens. The usage of blessing the water for baptism comes from the origin of the Church. We have a proof of this in the writings of the fathers of the fourth and even of the third century.[726] When the catechumens had passed their last examination, made their triple renunciation, and received the bishop's unction, they were taken to the font in order to be blessed.

The whole assembly of the faithful, carrying lighted tapers, walked in procession to the singing of the litanies, which were repeated three times by five or seven choirs when the assistants were numerous,[727] or three, five, or seven times by two choirs. Hence came the names *ternary*, *quinary*, and *septenary*, given to these litanies. Returning from the font, the ternary litany was sung: it is still said at the present day.

When therefore the prophecies are ended, all the clergy set out in procession toward the font, singing the litany. Arrived at the baptistery, the priest blesses the water. Nothing more venerable, instructive, or efficacious than the holy prayers that he employs! He begins by calling to mind, in a magnificent preface, the wonders that God has wrought by water. Then plunging his hand into the basin of the font, he divides the water in the form of a cross, and asks God to fill it with the virtue of the Holy Ghost and to make it fruitful by grace. He afterward pours out some of it toward the four quarters of the world, to show that the whole world should be bedewed with it; that is to say, that all peoples should, according to the divine promise, be called to baptism. He breathes three times on the water, imploring our Lord to bless it with his own mouth, and to withdraw it from the power of the devil.

He sinks the paschal candle into it three times, in order to show that it is by the merits of the Savior, dead and risen again, of whom the candle is a figure, that it will have virtue to preserve our bodies and souls from the snares of the enemy, and to remit venial sins, by exciting sentiments of contrition and the love of God in hearts. He lets fall some drops of this wax into the water that has just been blessed, in order to show that the virtue of Jesus Christ remains with it. He then separates the water that is to be reserved for baptism. When it is in the font, he mixes some holy chrism with it, and reminds us of the grace that baptism will produce in those who receive it. "May this water," he says, "by this mixture be sanctified, made fruitful, and obtain the virtue of remitting sins and regenerating souls for life eternal, in the name of the Father," etc.[728]

Formerly, after the blessing, the priest would go and sprinkle some of the blessed water on the assistants: the same is still done at the present day. All the faithful then had, and they still have, leave to take some of this water and carry it to their houses. It is used as a safeguard against spiritual and corporal dangers. What a shame not to have some of this holy water in houses, not to know where to find it, when there is question of administering the sacraments to the sick! The blessing ended, all take their way back to the choir, singing the litany. It was now, in the early Church, that the newly-baptized were led in procession to the altar, clad in their white garments, holding lighted candles in their hands, and accompanied by their godfathers and godmothers. At the altar, they received the Blessed Eucharist and partook of the milk and honey of innocence.

5. *The Mass*. The Mass begins immediately after the return to the choir. It has no introit, because all the people have entered. In the early ages, they used to be at the church from the day before. The Mass is very short, on account of the length of the preceding offices. The *Alleluia*, suppressed since the beginning of Lent, reappears as a sign of joy; but it is followed by a tract, a song of sadness, because the great mystery of the resurrection is not yet accomplished.

6. *Vespers*. It is the same with vespers. A single psalm of two verses suffices for them; but how well chosen is this psalm! "Let all the nations of the earth," cries out the Church, "praise the Lord! Praise him all ye peoples! because his mercy is manifested to us, and the truth of his promises remaineth forever."[729]

By *the nations*, the prophet means "the Gentiles," and by *the peoples*, "the children of Israel," previously separated, but united on this great day in Jesus Christ, to make only one family henceforward. This is the reason why the prophet, seeing in the future the great mystery of unity—baptism—by which Jews and Gentiles, receiving the same Spirit, shall become the children of God, cries out in a holy transport: "His mercy is manifested to us!" Yes, to us all, to you and to us! How touching is the word *us!* May it inflame our hearts with that truly Catholic charity of which it is the expression!

On Holy Saturday, let us bury ourselves in the tomb with our Lord: let us leave the old man there. Let us go back to the solemn nights of the early Church when baptism was conferred. Let us renew our promises. Let us wash our baptismal robe in the tears of sincere repentance, that we may be able, on Easter day, to go to the nuptial feast of the Lamb.

PRAYER

O my God! who art all love, I thank thee for having vouchsafed to die and to be laid in a tomb for me. Grant me the grace to divest myself of the old man during Lent, that I may rise again to the life of grace on Easter Sunday.

I am resolved to love God above all things, and my neighbor as myself for the love of God; and, in testimony of this love, I will ask myself on Holy Saturday whether I am dead or not to the old man.

Lesson 38: Christianity Brought before the Senses (Continued)—Easter Day

Festival of Easter, or the Pasch: Its object and its excellence.—Pasch![730] This is a word that has come down to us through more than thirty centuries; a word that has been heard amid the deserts of Egypt, by the slopes of Sinai, on the banks of the Jordan, in the Temple of Jerusalem, in the catacombs of Rome, in the basilicas of Constantinople and Nice, in the cabins of the savages of America, in the huts of the negroes of Central Africa, on the burning plains of China, on the snowcapped mountains of Tartary: an immortal word, like the event that it expresses!

Pasch! This is a solemnity that, for thousands of years, has filled East and West with joy. It is the festival of the whole world; it is the festival of the human family. How comes it to pass that it makes so many millions of hearts beat in unison? Because it commemorates an event of general and mighty interest.

Would you wish to know the origin of this truly Catholic solemnity? The people of God were groaning under the tyranny of Pharao. But at length, the hour of their deliverance struck. The angel of the Lord passed over the land during the night, and slew the firstborn of every house on which he did not see the blood of a lamb. All this was figurative. The lamb was Christ; Pharao, the old serpent, the tyrant of the human race since the fall; and the Hebrew people, all mankind. Behold the reason why the Jews celebrated by a perpetual festival the memory of this passage of the angel, and of the sacrifice of the lamb that saved them from the sword! Behold the reason why, the figure having given place to the reality, the Church now celebrates by a perpetual festival the sacrifice of the true Lamb and his passage from death to life, the defeat of the devil, and the deliverance of the human race!

Shall we not in vain look through the annals of peoples for an event so worthy of being remembered, and so capable of filling with gratitude, enthusiasm, and love anyone that carries in his head an idea of faith, or in his breast the heart of a man?

Pasch means "passage": you know the reason. The man-God had scarcely returned to his Father when the apostles hastened to establish a solemn festival to commemorate his pasch, that is to say, his glorious passage from death to life. We see them arranging their journeys, shortening or lengthening their evangelical visits, so as to celebrate at Jerusalem, the very place of the event, this solemnity of solemnities. It was similarly celebrated in all countries converted to Christianity. Our festival of Easter is therefore of apostolic institution: a point on which no one has ever raised any doubt. Such an origin ought to be a new title to our veneration.

Unanimous on the celebration of the solemnity, the primitive churches did not agree on the exact day to be chosen for it. From the middle of the second century, this affair gave rise to great controversies. The Christians of the West would hold the festival only on the Sunday after the fourteenth day of the moon that follows the spring equinox, so as not to keep with the Jews in the celebration of this solemnity. The Christians of the East, on the other hand, asserted that it was necessary to celebrate Easter on the fourteenth day of the moon after the equinox. In reading the history of the contests that took place on this point, shallow-minded men are inclined to regard them as silly. Let them have patience to hear us for a moment, and they will see that the Catholic Church is not moved without grave reasons.

There are some points of secondary importance in discipline, wherein variety may and even ought to be admitted, according to ages and countries. This variety shows out the beauty of the Church and the unity of the faith. There are also some essential points in discipline which ought to remain unchanged. Now, the time of Easter is one of those important points on which unity is necessary.

In effect, there is not question here only of one day, but of all the other great days that depend on it, comprising a good part of the Christian year. The fast of Lent, for example, and the festival of Pentecost depend absolutely on the day of Easter. Was it not proper that the Church, spread over all the world, should weep at the same time and rejoice at the same time? Is there not more strength in this general agreement of all the members of the great Catholic family than in isolated efforts?

While some would be honoring with their tears and penances the passion of the Son of God, others would be celebrating his resurrection with all the signs of gladness and joy! How, I ask, could such a spectacle be endured? And then, if the Church is one, if she ought to love unity—the noble seal of her heavenly origin—in all things, ought she not to love it and to seek it much more earnestly in the celebration of that mystery which, having united all mankind to God, made us all but one body in Jesus Christ?[731]

I can understand, you say, that all the churches of the East should agree in the celebration of Easter; but what need is there that East and West should agree? You seem to think, I answer, that there is an immense distance between East and West, and that this distance makes up for all inconveniences; but surely you forget that East and West are only one body in religion, one and the same Church! You forget that there are always a great many Westerns in the East, and a great many Easterns in the West! You forget that in the border countries of East and West this distance no longer exists!

Imagine what an embarrassment, what confusion, what a strange medley there would be if in one province or city some bewailed the death of the Savior and others were rejoicing at the same time, some fasted and others forbade fasting, some were covered with sackcloth or haircloth and others appeared in festive dress! How many dangers might you expect to result to the public peace! It would be necessary to keep in concord not only intelligent and virtuous people, with sense and charity enough to be satisfied or at least to bear their differences patiently, but also ignorant and carnal people, easily scandalized and provoked by one another.

For all these reasons, which certainly cannot appear light to any but the unreflecting, nearly all the churches yielded to the sentiment of Pope Victor, until such times as the First Council of Nice fixed, by an irrevocable decree, the oneness of Easter day throughout the whole world. We have enlarged on this point of our history purposely, so as to show, once for all, the profound wisdom of the Church, and the gravity of the motives that induce her to act, to resist, to approve, and to decide on all occasions.[732]

"The festival of Easter," says St. Gregory, "is the solemnity of solemnities, because it raises us from the earth into eternity, which it enables us to enjoy beforehand by faith, hope, and charity."[733] This day inspires an unspeakable joy, not known on other days. Man loves life passionately: he feels that he was created immortal. Whatever strengthens his belief in immortality, whatever restores him his right to life, whatever breaks the arrow of death, makes a deep impression on him. The festival of Easter, which is the triumph of life over death, which shows us man resuscitated, Jesus Christ destroying for himself and for us the empire of death, always excites the liveliest joy and produces the sweetest contentment.

Its harmony with the season. Add that on this festival the Christian receives by Communion a sensible pledge of his glorious immortality. Add also that all nature harmonizes with religion in repeating this consoling dogma to him. It is in spring, that is to say, at the very time when everything in the material world is born again, that we celebrate the mystery of our resurrection to grace first, and then to glory. In the absence of a book, all creatures may instruct us. Not a blade of grass but says to us: "You shall rise again!"

"You shall rise again!" This is also what the Church says to us by the eloquent voice of her ceremonies. Let us enter the holy temple. All the signs of mourning have disappeared. The altars are decked out with extraordinary magnificence. Ornaments of gay colors and rich embroidery reappear with the sacred ministry. Every face is bright. The bells are all in motion. The inhabitants of the city arrive in crowds at the portico of the old cathedral, as those of the country throng to the door of the simple village church. The song of joy—the *Alleluia*—that word of the language of heaven, fallen on earth for our festive days, resounds on all sides, is repeated every moment, is varied again and again, is modulated into every key; and when hereto are added the rays of a beautiful sun, avoid, if you can, those feelings of hope and delight which it is the mission of this great day to inspire!

Division of the office.—The office of Easter is divided into four parts: the morning procession; Mass; vespers; and the evening procession.

Formerly, when the great day began to dawn, all the faithful, men and women, young and old, rich and poor, hastened to the church. The priest intoned the canticle of the resurrection, and kissed an image of Jesus Christ risen. He then gave the "kiss of love" to the most important man of the assembly, who communicated it to the next, and so on till it reached the most remote from the sanctuary. The women did in like manner among themselves. The person who gave the kiss, said: "Christ is risen"; and the person who received it answered: "He is truly risen!" From the church, the embraces passed out to the streets, the fields, the houses: wherever people met, they gave the "kiss of love," without any other distinction than that of sex.

This was kept up for three days in the same manner and with the same words. Beware of looking on it all as a vain ceremony: our ancestors took religion very seriously indeed. For the most part, they chose this occasion to be publicly reconciled, and to begin again that life of peace and charity which should distinguish the children of him who said: "By this shall all men know that you are my disciples, if you love one another."[734] This affecting custom still exists in Poland. During the festivals of Easter, a Pole who meets another says to him: "Jesus Christ is risen!" The other answers: "Yes, Jesus Christ is truly risen!" And they embrace on the street or the road. Among us, it is nowadays reduced to the kiss of peace that the ministers of the altar give one another before Communion.

1. *The morning procession.* To perpetuate the memory of the resurrection of the Savior and the baptism of the catechumens, we have also, as the ancient liturgists say, a procession before Mass and a sprinkling of holy water. This twofold ceremony is renewed every Sunday, because all the other Sundays of the year are a continuation of the festival of Easter.[735]

In former days, the Easter procession was made with all the pomp and circumstance calculated to recall the Church's intention in establishing it. She wished to represent the apostles and disciples going from Jerusalem to Galilee, whither Jesus had told the holy women that he would precede them. And behold the pastors, at the head of the flock, set out for the station, that is to say, the point where the procession should come to a stand, and then return to the church!

In the simple language of our ancestors, this station was called "Galilee." It was a place richly adorned, like the repositories on the festival of Corpus Christi. Here, the choir, surrounded by all the people, endeavored to surpass themselves in songs of gladness. The whole assembly answered with an enthusiasm that often evoked tears of joy. Scripture antiphons were succeeded by canticles, of which the principal was: *Salve, festa dies*—"Hail, festive day!" Intoxicated with a holy joy, all the faithful returned in admirable order to the church, to assist at the adorable sacrifice.

2. *Mass.* From beginning to end, the Mass of Easter Sunday breathes gladness. During it is sung that ancient hymn which, though simple in words, is so full of poetry, and so much in keeping with everything else inspired by Christianity: *Victimae paschali laudes*, etc.

"O people! fall prostrate, adore the paschal victim, adore the Lamb that saves the sheep!

"Adore the Christ, adore him who reconciles earth with heaven!

"Oh, what a wonderful due between life and death!

"The master of life dies. But death shall be conquered, and the crucified shall take up life again, as a garment that belongs to him, and that he has only laid aside!

"What didst thou see, Mary? Tell us; what didst thou see on the way?

"I saw the sepulchre of the living Christ. I saw the glory of the risen Christ. I saw angels, heavenly witnesses, with white shining robes; they showed me the empty tomb, and I heard them saying to me: 'He is not here.'

"Christ, my hope, is risen: he goes before you into Galilee.

"We know it: Christ is truly risen. O victorious King! have mercy on us."

The gospel of the Mass contains in a few words the history of the resurrection, and of the apparition of angels to the holy women: two facts which have been fully related in the second part[736] of the Catechism.

Though the office of Easter Sunday is wholly consecrated to the festival of the resurrection, yet there used to be a kind of suspension in it for that of the baptized, whose festival, beginning on Holy Saturday, ended only after the Saturday following. Now, the office of the baptized began with a litany, whose first words were: *Kyrie, eleison.* Such is the reason why the vespers of Easter day used to begin with *Kyrie*, and not with *Deus in adjutorium*. This ancient usage is preserved in the Diocese of Besançon.[737]

3. *Vespers.* The two psalms at vespers, *Laudate pueri* and *In exitu*, likewise refer to the office of the baptized, so that on Easter day the Church, divided as it were between joy at the resurrection of her divine spouse and joy at the increase in the number of her children by baptism, seems not to know which to think of. A spouse and a mother, she passes from the empty tomb of her beloved to the cradle of her newborn babe. She sings, she praises, she thanks. She reminds the baptized of the inestimable favor which they have received, and tells them of the joy with which her heart overflows. Formerly, during Easter Week, the neophytes, clad in their white garments, used to be daily led to the sacred font.

4. *Evening procession.* At the procession, two psalms were sung. The one going to the font was *Laudate, pueri*—"Children, praise the Lord!" Praise him when you visit the place where he gave you birth! The other, coming from the font, was: *In exitu Israel*—"When Israel was leaving Egypt." This is the hymn of the great deliverance, of which that of the Israelites was only a figure. What think you? Do not all these lately baptized, returning from the sacred waves which gave them life and destroyed the power of Satan, seem to you like the children of Israel, after the passage of the Red Sea, coming up from the brink of the deep, and, at the remembrance of their miraculous escape and the overthrow of Pharao, intoning with a transport of delight the beautiful canticle of Moses? "Let us sing to the Lord, for he hath made a glorious display of his power. The horse and the rider he hath thrown into the sea: the waves swallowed them up."[738]

To celebrate the festivities of Easter worthily, we must enter into the spirit of the Church and of her holy ceremonies. A lively faith in the great mystery of the resurrection; a boundless love for the Savior, who was pleased to be born, to live in this wretched world, to die, and to rise again for us; a great desire of one day rising glorious with him; lastly, a sincere and constant will of keeping ourselves in the state of grace, which we have entered by the paschal Communion, so that one may be able to say to those who seek us among the wicked or the tepid what the angels said to the holy women, when speaking of our Lord, "He is risen, he is not here";[739] such are the dispositions that we ought to bring to the celebration of this great day. Woe to us if we do not treat all this seriously!

Easter Week.—Formerly, Easter Week was one continual festival: it was particularly on account of the neophytes that these seven days were so observed. The Church wished to give her new children a solemn welcome. She also wished to strengthen them by heavenly succor against the attacks that they should have to endure after baptism. "Our Lord," says St. Chrysostom, "was tempted after his baptism. New believers need not expect better treatment from the sworn enemy of holiness and justice. We therefore strengthen them for seven days."[740]

To the end of the week, they wore their white garments; they put them by only on Low Sunday, called for this reason, *In albis depositis*—"the Sunday when white is laid aside." During this whole week, as well as during paschal time and on all the Sundays of the year, people prayed standing in memory of the Savior's resurrection.

On Easter Sunday, there are only three psalms and three lessons said at matins, on account of the length of the other offices, not a moment of which the early Christians could bear to lose. It is the same during the octave of the festival; for it was customary to do every day of the week what had been done on the festival itself.[741] By these three psalms, the Church wishes to remind neophytes that in baptism they have received faith, hope, and charity, and also to make them return thanks to the three adorable Persons of the Blessed Trinity for having granted them these virtues, the exclusive portion of adopted children, the precious germs of glory and immortality.[742]

PRAYER

O my God! who art all love, I thank thee for having given me in the glorious resurrection of thy Son a pledge of my glorious resurrection on the day of judgment. Grant that we may now rise to the life of grace, so as hereafter to rise to that of glory.

I am resolved to love God above all things, and my neighbor as myself for the love of God; and, in testimony of this love, I will prepare with the greatest care for my Easter Communion.

Lesson 39: Christianity Brought before the Senses (Continued)—Marian Devotion (1)

Annunciation of the Blessed Virgin: Its excellence, its object, and its influence.—The Annunciation of the Blessed Virgin is the festival that the Catholic Church celebrates on the 25th of March. Among the great events of which religion consecrates the memory, this undoubtedly stands in the foremost place. It is like the first link in that long chain of wonders which go to make up the work of human redemption. Pentecost, the Ascension, Easter, Christmas, all suppose the Incarnation of the Word, and the Incarnation of the Word supposes the Annunciation of Mary. This festival is therefore referred chiefly to the Blessed Virgin.[743] Recollect your thoughts, and see how far behind this solemnity are all the festivals of the nations! Above all, see how powerful is religion to raise up the thoughts of man: it carries them away to infinity!

God, as an omnipotent being, can act independently of his creatures; but, to give man, even fallen man, a high idea of the dignity of human nature, God usually takes him as a companion in the works that he performs outwardly. He associates Moses to his omnipotence in order to deliver the Hebrews from the slavery of Egypt: he charges him to publish his law, and appoints him mediator of the covenant that he makes with his people. He associates the prophets to the lights of his infinite intelligence in order to reveal to the world the secrets of the future and his supreme will. Later on, he associates twelve poor fishermen to the mission of his divine Son, namely, the conversion of the world. Today he is going to associate a humble virgin to the accomplishment of the most amazing of prodigies. His Son, the eternal Word, has resolved to clothe himself with our nature. This divine Son, he who made all things, can dispense with the aid of any creature; but no, he wishes to take a body formed of the substance of a woman.

Now, there is question of announcing to this privileged woman the choice that God has made of her to be his Mother. The archangel Gabriel is sent as an ambassador to Mary, in order to ask her consent. See how respectfully God treats us! The festival of the Annunciation is intended to celebrate the memory of this embassage, the most important and instructive ever known. For who sends the ambassador? The King of kings. Who is the ambassador? A prince of the heavenly court. Whither is he sent? To a little city of Galilee, called Nazareth. To whom is he sent? To her who is the greatest, the most august creature that earth has ever seen or ever shall see. Who is she—a queen, the mistress of the world? No, a virgin of a royal race, but poor and unknown, who derives from her inviolable purity of soul and body and her perfect devotedness to God a lustre that the most glorious scepter could never give.

O human reason, shattered reason! learn a lesson. The choice of a poor virgin for the accomplishment of the most ineffable of mysteries is a clear proof that in the eyes of God the honors and riches of the earth are nothing, and that there is no true greatness but what proceeds from sanctity. Do you understand this?[744]

Let us now place ourselves in the company of the heavenly ambassador, and see how he delivers his message. Arrived in the presence of Mary, he says, "Hail, full of grace!" It was not the first time that angels had appeared to women. Sara and Agar had been honored with visits from them; but nowhere do we see such marks of respect as the angel Gabriel gives to Mary. "Hail, full of grace"—as if he should say: "Hail, thou who art the most pleasing of all to the Most High! Abraham, Isaac, Jacob, the patriarchs, the prophets, the Baptist, the greatest of the children of men, had grace, but in measure; as for thee, Mary, thou hast it in all its fullness!"

The ambassador adds: "The Lord is with thee." But what art thou saying, O holy archangel? Was not the Lord with Moses by his power, with the prophets by his wisdom, with David by his goodness; and is he not with all creatures by his immensity? Do not thy latter words weaken thy former ones? Not at all. The Lord is with Mary, not only as with creatures, as with David, as with the prophets, as with Abraham—not only as with all the just, by that sanctifying grace which makes them children, or with the elect, by that special protection which leads them to the term of their happiness; but he is with Mary in the reality of the adorable Person of the Word, who is about to make for himself a body of the substance of this Virgin, in whose womb, as in a new ark of the covenant, he is to rest for nine months with his divinity and humanity. It is thus that the Lord is with Mary. I now understand how the latter eulogy agrees with the former.

Gabriel continues: "Blessed art thou among women!" What! Adam, Noe, Abraham, Moses, David, the prophets—were not they blessed? Sara, Rebecca, Rachel, Debbora, Anna the mother of Samuel—were not they blessed? Yes, but not like Mary. Their blessing was limited: it was common to many; it was intended for a particular purpose.

But the blessing of Mary is the blessing of blessings, the fullness of all others, an exceptional and incommunicable blessing. She is blessed among women, because she is a mother and a virgin at the same time, and because God makes use of her in preference to all other persons of her sex to remove the curse incurred by the human race. Hence all nations will forever call her "blessed."

What impression did these words, the most flattering that ever fell on woman's ear, make on Mary? Mary was troubled. Yes, the Virgin of Juda is troubled, because she knows that praise is an ordinary artifice of those who lead others astray. The new Eve is troubled, because she remembers that the first Eve was ruined by flattery. Behold, therefore, how she observes a modest silence, and thinks with herself what this salutation may mean!

How many innocent souls have been ruined through not imitating the precautions of Mary! Henceforth, Christian maidens! learn to distrust praise, and to turn a deaf ear to the enchanting voice of the flatterer. Mary is troubled, not only because she is pure, but also because she is humble. Humble souls cannot endure praise. They know themselves; they despise themselves. They refer to God whatever is estimable in them. Such a one was Mary! And we—are we troubled when we hear ourselves praised?

The angel, perceiving the uneasiness of the humble and chaste Virgin, hastens to calm it. "Fear not, Mary!" he says to her. "The power of the Almighty shall overshadow thee: thou shalt conceive and bring forth a Son, whom thou shalt name Jesus. He shall be great; he shall be called the Son of the Most High; he shall have the throne of David, his father; he shall reign forever in the house of Jacob."[745]

Thus Mary, without ceasing to be a Virgin, is to become the Mother of God: here is the mystery. Will she consent to it? "Ah," cries out St. Augustine, "consent, O holy Virgin! consent; do not delay the salvation of the world."[746] Think that we shall have a Savior when thou givest thy consent! The sweet and humble Mary bows to the will of God, and, in accepting the title of Mother of God, also accepts that of Queen of martyrs. "Behold," she says, "the handmaid of the Lord; be it done unto me according to thy word!"[747]

This moment the mystery of love, promised to the earth four thousand years before, is accomplished. The Word of God becomes incarnate, that is to say, takes a human body, formed of Mary's purest blood, and a human soul, which is no sooner united to him than it enjoys the most august privileges, knowing past, present, and future. God has a worthy adorer, and the world an all-powerful mediator. Is not this an event that well deserves to be called to mind by a solemn festival from generation to generation?

Virgins and wives, maidens and mothers, women whosoever you are! it is you especially that ought to celebrate this festival with a fervor and a gratitude quite enthusiastic. Mary's exaltation is your glory. Do you remember what you were under paganism? Degraded, branded slaves. Do you know what you still are wherever Christianity has not set you free? In India, victims to be burned; in Africa, beasts of burden to be worn out with toil; everywhere, the most contemptible of creatures. But, thanks to Christianity! when man saw that God honored woman, when he saw that in Mary God honored woman so much as to make her his own Mother and the Queen of angels, he also honored woman.

It is for woman, in her turn, to keep the place that Christianity has given her. The more she shows herself like Mary, the more shall she secure affection, respect, power, freedom, and happiness for herself. Hence, I can never tire of admiring that instinct which leads girls to be devout to Mary. I say *instinct*, because they do not all perhaps know how important for them is devotion to the Immaculate Virgin.

When I see them in their white dresses gathered round an altar of Mary, I am inclined to say to them: "If you knew the gift of God![748] If you knew how much you owe to Mary, oh, how much you would wish to be like her, and how quickly you would run in her footsteps to the imitation of her virtues! Do not forget that devotion to Mary is your safeguard: liberty, honor, regard, life, you owe all to it!"

Origin of this festival. We need not be surprised that, since the origin of Christianity, the worship of Mary has held so high a place in the piety of Christian men, and especially of Christian women. We see it everywhere associated to the worship of the Savior: Jesus has his temples, Mary has hers; Jesus has his servants, Mary has hers; Jesus has his festivals, Mary has hers. That of the Annunciation, celebrated at first in a few places, spread, from the apostolic times, wider and wider. It is already to be found in an ancient martyrology of the Western Church, attributed to St. Jerome.[749]

The approval of Church after Church made up at length a universal consent, and established a usage that was sanctioned by the Tenth Council of Toledo, held in 656. It calls the Annunciation the great festival of the Mother of God. In 692, the Council of Constantinople confirmed this festival for the East. It had already been established there, though it is impossible to say at what period. It fell on the 25th of March, nine months, to the very day, before the birth of the Savior; "for," says St. Augustine, "it is an old tradition, adopted by the Church, that the incarnation of the Word took place on the 25th of March."[750]

Sentiments that this festival ought to inspire. To celebrate this festival well, let us unite in congratulating Mary, not only in having been chosen to be the Mother of God, but also on having faithfully corresponded with her sublime vocation. Let us likewise resolve to correspond with ours. Let us beg of Mary to help us to know it; and, that we may hear the voice of God, let us imitate the recollection of this sacred Virgin: let us love her modesty and piety. Let us thank God for the graces of which the mystery of the annunciation and incarnation has been the source for the human race in general, and for ourselves in particular. But above all, when we think on Mary's most sublime prerogative, on the supreme rank to which God this day raises her, let us conceive a noble pride in having such a Mother, and let us permit our souls to expand with the most childlike confidence in her who has never been invoked in vain.

Let us, with a pious author, say to her:

"O great Princess! you have already given me much; but what you have given me is very little in comparison with what you can give me, and what I propose to obtain from you. All kinds of legislatures give children a right to the property of their mother: it is on this right that I take my stand. Let us look to our accounts, I pray you, and see which of us is indebted to the other.

"From the moment when you were raised to the incomparable dignity of Mother of God, you were put in possession of all the treasures of heaven, as their absolute mistress; and who can imagine how great, rich, and powerful you then became? But, if such is the case, you must agree with me that, whatever you give your children, there always remains with you much more to give; for your treasures are inexhaustible mines.

"Well, these treasures, permit me to tell you, are superfluous for you. Nay more, however liberal you may be in dispensing them to poor creatures like us, you are not the less rich. You must let me add something else: it is, that they were entrusted to you only on condition that you should share them with the miserable who would have recourse to you. And sure you know well that God never raised you so high unless to be the refuge of the wretched.

"Now, then, dear Mother! let me take an innocent liberty. It seems to me that I have put you in such a predicament that you cannot say, 'No.' Either you must welcome me tenderly—base, wicked, sacrilegious wretch as I am—or you must oppose the merciful designs of that God to whom you are under so many obligations, and prove a traitress in the employment confided to you. Have you anything to answer, or rather are there any better reasons to lay before you? I commit the case to you. Decide."[751]

Ave Maria. The words of the angel Gabriel that we have explained above, "Hail, full of grace, the Lord is with thee, blessed art thou among women," make up the first part of the *Ave Maria.* The following ones, pronounced by St. Elizabeth, when she received her cousin's visit, "And blessed is the fruit of thy womb," make up the second. The Church, another Mary, another spouse of the Holy Ghost, completed the Angelical Salutation many centuries ago by adding the well-known words: "Holy Mary, Mother of God," etc. The occasion of her doing so was this:

In 431, a general council had assembled at Ephesus to anathematize the heresy of Nestorius. The day on which the council was to pronounce on the divine maternity of Mary, the people, uneasy and excited, crowded the streets, and thronged round the magnificent temple that the piety of the dwellers by the sea had raised under the invocation of Mary. It was here that two hundred bishops were examining the propositions of Nestorius, who had not dared to come and defend them, so little did he rely on the justice of his cause or the soundness of his arguments. The multitude that waited in the portico of the temple and the adjoining streets observed a profound silence. Yet alarm was to be read on the expressive faces of those Greeks, whose looks reflect so well the feelings of their souls.

A bishop makes his appearance. He announces to the dumb and eager crowd that the anathema of the council has been hurled against the innovator, and that the most Blessed Virgin is gloriously defended in her august prerogative of Mother of God. Then transports of joy break out on all sides. The Ephesians, and the strangers gathered together from all the cities of Asia, surround the fathers of the council, kiss their hands, and burn the most exquisite perfumes in the streets through which they pass. The city is quickly illuminated. Never was joy more general or sincere.

It is believed that it was in this Council of Ephesus that St. Cyril, in concert with the holy assembly of fathers over whom he presided, reduced to its present form the last part of the Angelical Salutation: "Holy Mary, Mother of God," etc.[752]

Mary attaches particular value to the Angelical Salutation, because it reminds her of the joy she felt on learning from the angel Gabriel that she was to become the Mother of God. We should therefore address it often to her. Whoever salutes Mary will also be saluted by her, and Mary's salutation is always a sign of some favor. The Mother of God can refuse nothing to anyone that comes to her with the words of the *Ave Maria*.[753]

Devotion to Mary.—The devotion of the *Ave Maria* consists in the following practices:

1. Saying every day, at rising and going to rest, three *Aves*, with the face bowed to the ground, or at least on bended knees, adding to each *Ave* this short prayer: "O Mary, by thy pure and immaculate conception, purify my heart and my senses!" One then asks Mary's blessing, like that of a Mother, as St. Stanislaus Kostka used to do, placing himself in a special manner under her protection, that she might preserve him from all sin during the day or the night. For this purpose, it will be good to have an image of the Blessed Virgin near one's bed.

2. In saying the *Angelus* morning, noon, and evening. It was Pope Urban II that, in a council held at Clermont, in 1095, decided that every day the bell should be rung morning, noon, and evening, and the Angelical Salutation said each time. His chief aim was to gain Mary's protection for the Crusades. These holy wars are past and gone, but the life of the whole Church, the life of each Christian, is a crusade. The motives for repeating the *Angelus* are therefore unchangeable. Popes John XXII, Calixtus III, Paul III, Clement X, and Benedict XIII have strongly recommended this practice, and enriched it with indulgences.[754]

Formerly, at the first sound of the bell, all the faithful fell on their knees and recited the *Angelus*. Why should the weakening of faith be such today that most Christians are ashamed thus to salute their Mother? Honor at least to those who continue faithful to this pious practice! Yes, honor to them, for a son can never be dishonored by honoring his mother! Honor to St. Charles Borromeo, the restorer of the old usages of piety, who, though a prince of the world and a prince of the Church, was not ashamed to come down from his carriage or his horse, and acquit himself of this duty in the open street!

During paschal time, we recite, instead of the *Angelus*, the antiphon *Regina Caeli*, enriched with the same indulgences. It is said standing, in memory of our Lord's resurrection: the same is done with the *Angelus*, and for the same reason, from vespers on Saturday till Sunday evening.

A suttee at Benares.—We have remarked that Mary's exaltation is the glory and the safeguard of woman. To enable persons of her sex to understand what they would still be if God had not honored them in Mary, we are going to tell what they are wherever Christianity has not introduced the saving worship of the new Eve. A single example will suffice: that of a "suttee" at Benares.[755]

It appears from reports made in the English House of Commons that the horrible custom of burning Indian widows with their husbands still exists. During the years 1835, 1836, 1837, and 1838, there were counted no fewer than 2,610 women who perished victims of this monstrous superstition in the British Indies.

In presence of such facts, the question is asked how is it possible that, in a country more than a century under the rule of a civilized people, such abominable excesses can be tolerated. Yet the answer is easy. Powerful as the English have been to subject a population of a hundred million souls, they have not been so powerful as to overcome a religious prejudice. To succeed herein, the only arms are those of persuasion. But heresy cannot persuade. It has not received the words of life, the words that civilize nations. Not to it was said: "Go, teach all nations!" Hence, the end of the world will come before Anglican protestantism destroys the influence that Brahmins exercise over the credulous Indians.

"These druids of Hindostan," says Dr. Gilchrist, "hide under an exterior of meekness and humility the fury of a tiger." An account of a late sacrifice of this kind, made particularly interesting by the events that were its consequence, is given by Sir W. C. Mallet, the East India Company's representative at Poona.

We borrow from his report the following details, almost in his own words:

Young Poolesbay had married a distinguished man of Poona, who died after five years of marriage. As soon as his death was known, the widow, aged nineteen years, found herself surrounded by Brahmins, who urged her to conform to the established usage, threatening her, in case of refusal, with disgrace in this world and everlasting pains in the next.

It was in vain that her brother, who loved her tenderly, and who, in the society of Europeans, had imbibed more humane sentiments, tried to save her from such a dreadful fate. Wholly under the influence of the Brahmins, and carried away by superstitious fears, she agreed to give herself to the flames. "It is better," she said, "to burn for one hour than for all eternity."

The sacrifice was appointed to take place on the next day, at five o'clock in the evening. An immense multitude, consisting of Brahmins, the governor's guard, and the people, wended its way toward the house of the suttee. She came forth, accompanied by her relatives. She was of middle height, but of elegant appearance. Her noble and expressive features gave her an air of dignity, which the solemnity of the occasion rendered still more remarkable. Her flowing hair was adorned with flowers, and her eyes fixed on heaven seemed lost in the contemplation of eternity.

She walked through the town, scattering leaves of goolod and betel plentifully along the way. Arrived at the Mooth, a river that passes near the town, she made her last ablutions there, and sat down on the bank. A parasol, held over her head, protected her from the heat of the sun, while one of her companions fanned her, by shaking a silk handkerchief before her face. She was surrounded by her relatives, a few friends, and the principal Brahmins, to whom she distributed two thousand rupees, and the rich jewels with which she was adorned, reserving only common ornaments, that is to say, a ring through the nostrils and a gold bracelet on each wrist. This distribution over, she placed herself in an attitude of prayer and invocation, her hands joined and raised above her head, while, not far off, about a hundred yards, the pile was being prepared to burn her.

The funeral structure consisted of four posts, ten feet high, and fixed in the ground so as to form a right-angled space nine feet long by six broad. A platform of planks, laden with as many small logs as it could hold, was made fast by ropes to the upper ends of the posts. Above this, a heap of wood, covered with straw and the dry branches of an odoriferous shrub, rose to the height of four feet. Three sides of the top were blocked up with the same materials, but the fourth was left open in order to give entrance to the victim.

These preparations ended, Poolesbay went forward, followed by her friends. After some steps, she paused, renewed her acts of devotion, and drew to one side a little in order to make way for the corpse. This, carried from the banks of the river where it had been laid, was placed on the grate with a large quantity of sweets, dry confectionery, and a paper bag of sandalwood sawdust. The suttee then walked round the pile three times, and, placing herself on a square stone, which is always used on these occasions, and which has the shape of two feet roughly cut on it, received the last farewells of her friends.

With an affectionate look, she passed her right hand over the heads of those to whom she was attached. Then, stooping, she embraced them tenderly, and set out for the fatal pile...She paused a moment at its entrance. For that single moment, the love of life seemed to make her hesitate...But fanaticism triumphed. She ascended the steps with a steady foot, lay down beside the body of her husband, and was immediately hidden from the sight of the spectators by the straw that was used to close the entrance and that was set fire to.

After a few seconds, the unfortunate Poolesbay gave a dreadful cry. Touched by the flames, pain made that vain firmness vanish which had heretofore supported her. The sentiment of self-preservation returning with all its force, she threw herself against the weak barrier already more than half consumed, got out, and rushed to the side of the river, as to a place of refuge where she could not be reached by the terrible element that seemed to pursue her. But the poor creature was not to escape the fate that was in store for her, and that she had asked of her own will.

The priests ran off in pursuit of Poolesbay, and were not slow in overtaking her. Then a frightful struggle ensued. The Brahmins endeavored to drag her to the pile. She, aided by her brother, offered the greatest resistance to their efforts. She cried out in the most heartrending manner, and implored the help of the crowd, kept in awe by the governor's guard; but her voice was drowned by the sound of trumpets, which, at a given signal burst out all together.

Wearied by her efforts, she lost consciousness, and in this state was carried off to the pile. All the spectators of this tragic scene now united to hasten it to a close. Some cut away with a hatchet the ropes that held the platform; others brought armfuls of goolod and dry branches to feed the flame; and thousands of hands, provided with torches, set fire to the pile on all sides. During this time, the victim's brother had been dragged away, uttering, in his despair, threats of revenge against the murderers of his sister...

Some time after all this, the roar of cannon and the peal of trumpet announced to the inhabitants of Benares the approach of a great religious solemnity. The streets of the town were strewn with flowers, and eager crowds hurried to the temple of Brahma. The festival of the procession of Juggernaut had drawn to Benares, not only all the people of the surrounding districts, but also many fanatics, who, from the most remote parts of Hindostan, came to seek a holy and glorious death within sight of their idol.

At an appointed hour, the gates of the temple opened to let out the procession.

Amid the splendors of Eastern display, an enormous car, drawn by elephants and carrying a colossal bronze figure, covered with precious stones, moved forward, accompanied by Brahmins. A troop of young girls scattered flowers along its way, and the piercing notes of the trumpet, the lively and voluptuous dances of the company that preceded the car, the most precious perfumes burnt in honor of the deity and seeming almost to embalm the air, all excited the enthusiasm of the multitude to the highest and wildest degree. They raised frantic shouts, and loudly applauded the devotedness of the Fakirs. "Brahma! Brahma!" they cried out, and disputing with one another the glory of dying for their god, they cast themselves on the ground before the idol, which crushed them in its passage. Suddenly, a cry "Poolesbay! Poolesbay!" was heard from a young man, who, breaking forth from the crowd, rushed toward one of the Brahmins, the one that had presided at the sacrifice of his sister, caught him in his arms, and threw him under the blood-spattered wheels of the car.

The act was done so quickly, so unexpectedly, that it could not possibly have been prevented, and the criminal might easily have escaped, if he had wished to take advantage of the general stupor; but he had no idea save of fully gratifying his revenge. He stood his ground, contemplating with delight the mangled body of his victim. The people recovering from their first alarm, gathered round the young man. They were ready to tear him to pieces, in order to appease the wrath of their idol, when the Brahmins interposed between him and the populace. They brought forward some men of the governor's guard, and placed the prisoner in their hands. The procession immediately returned to the temple.

In snatching the brother of Poolesbay from the fury of the multitude, the Brahmins had not been moved by pity, nor by any feeling of justice: they wanted to reserve to themselves alone the punishment of the culprit. It was necessary that the severity of his sentence should be proportioned to the enormity of his crime, so as to strike the minds of the people, who, having been witnesses of an attack unknown in the annals of Hindostan, should tremble with fear on remembering the expiation of the sacrilege. The college of Brahmins having been assembled, a long discussion took place on the kind of punishment that should be inflicted on the suttee's brother. The most ancient documents were examined. Every memory was questioned. At length, the punishment of the wall was decided on.

The young man, his head having been shaved, was led out of the town to the middle of a vast plain. Here he was held erect, whilst a wall was built close round him, rising to the height of his neck, and thus exposing his bare head to the full rays of a scorching sun. In this state he was left a prey to the most frightful sufferings. After a few days the vultures of the mountains came and broke in with their bills the poor wretch's skull, plucked out his brain and eyes, and devoured all the flesh on his head. When the expiatory monument was visited, there was nothing any longer to be seen but some blood-stained remains.[756]

What a horrible chain of crimes and atrocities! What a frightful tyrant is the devil! How he treats man when his slave! O Christian religion, which hast destroyed his empire, be blessed forever, be forever blessed!

PRAYER

O my God, who art all love! I thank thee with my whole heart for having chosen the Blessed Virgin to be the Mother of thy Son. Grant me the grace to correspond with my vocation as the Blessed Virgin corresponded with hers.

I am resolved to love God above all things, and my neighbor as myself for the love of God; and, in testimony of this love, I will often bless the passing hour by saying a Hail Mary.

Lesson 40: Christianity Brought before the Senses (Continued)—Marian Devotion (2)

Practices of Devotion to Mary.—Life here below is a warfare. This is true of man, is true of society, and above all is true of the Church, which is a society of the first order. In this warfare, begun in the terrestrial paradise to end only on the threshold of the heavenly Jerusalem, God watches over the Church his spouse and man his beloved child. Providence takes care to proportion its aids to the violence of the attacks, so that victory always remains with religion, that is to say, with the truth, with virtue. We have seen it in every age opposing to heresy a defender of truth, to scandal a victim of atonement and a model of the virtues attacked, in short, bringing to every evil a suitable remedy. When ordinary means do not suffice, it steps in with a direct and sovereign action that secures new triumphs for the truth.

But above all other remedies, there is one applicable to all evil. Above all other defenders, there is one whose power and goodness are equal, and who, ever ready to do battle, infallibly gains the victory. This is Mary—Mary, who crushed the old serpent's head, and triumphs over all heresies and scandals. Hence, the Church varies to no end the means of invoking Mary and securing her help.

Wisdom of the Church. In her youthful days, she composed the Angelical Salutation. Later on, she instituted religious orders, appointed to implore by day and night the favor and protection of her who is never invoked in vain. Other ages saw spreading far and near the devotions of the rosary and the scapular.

We should never be done, if we tried to relate all the testimonies of the truth that the Church, in her afflictions and dangers, has always put her chief hope in Mary. Is it not because her wants are today more urgent and her risks greater that the Church, while preserving her ancient devotions, establishes and approves new means of drawing on her the gracious looks of the all-powerful Queen of heaven? When victory is closely disputed, a general calls up all his battalions, makes use of all his resources.

Month of Mary.—Among the practices reserved for these latter days, we must put the month of Mary in the first place. The devotion of the month of Mary took its rise in Italy toward the close of the last century. Some pious souls, grieved at the disorders that used to return more numerous and serious with the delightful season of spring, were inspired to obtain pardon for them and to stay their course. They raised their eyes to the Virgin of virgins. While the lovers of the world were retiring to their villas, surrounded with all the perfumes and flowers of the month of May, there to seek guilty pleasures, these chaste doves, these plaintive turtles were sighing out ineffable prayers before an altar of Mary. Here, we say it without fear, was one of the most touching contrasts of the religious world.

Oh, yes, very just and very happy was the thought of consecrating to the purest of virgins the month of May, the month of flowers, the most beautiful month of the year; consequently, the one that draws us most to the pleasures of the senses. Oh, yes, it was to oppose to a terrible evil, returning every year, an admirable remedy, also returning every year.

What do they know of the secrets of God who, with the levity of ignorance, despise or censure these salutary devotions? They do not know, then, that the existence of the moral world, as well as that of the physical, depends on an equilibrium of forces! They do not know, then, that it is expiation that places a counterpoise to crimes in the scales of the divine justice, and that the greater the crimes the more perfect should be the expiation!

As for us, to whom these laws are known, children of the Catholic Church, let us enter into the spirit of our mother, and, that the month of May may not be an ordinary month for us, let us verify in all its extent the meaning of the title *month of Mary*.

What then—you ask—is the meaning of the words, *month of Mary?* And I—I ask you what is the meaning of these words, *the Lord's day*, by which you refer to Sunday? You answer that *the Lord's day* means a day belonging to the Lord; a day which ought to be wholly consecrated to the worship of the Lord; a day on which temporal affairs ought to be forgotten, that one may think of the Creator, of the soul, of eternity; a day on which the Lord is particularly well pleased to hear our prayers; a day, in short, of great audiences and great favors.

In the same manner, the *month of Mary* means, according to the language of piety, a month belonging to Mary; a month of great audiences and great favors; a month whose every hour should be consecrated to the worship of this amiable Mother, to congratulate her on her happiness, to meditate on her power and goodness, to implore her protection, and to copy her virtues. We must, therefore, not to be guilty of theft against Mary, consecrate to her during this beautiful month all the emotions of our heart, all our thoughts, all our words, all our intentions, all our works. How can we consecrate all these things to her? By making her an offering of them, and by doing everything for her, by her, with her, like her.

Month of Mary! Ah, let us not belie this beautiful name! Let not the month of perfumes and flowers be a month of stains and dead works! Let it not be a month of vanity, dissipation, tepidity, sin, but truly the month of Mary: this name tells all. From the first day to the last, let us say to ourselves, "If Mary were in my place, how would she act?" What would be the modesty of her looks, the affability of her manners, the sweetness of her words, the promptitude of her obedience, the charity of her conversation, the recollection of her prayer, the purity of her intention, the sanctity of her behavior?

In these simple words, there is a hidden treasure of light and strength. The soul that knows how to profit of them will soon be completely transformed, almost without perceiving it.

The Church, anxious to encourage every wise practice of piety, hastened to enrich the devotion of the month of Mary with indulgences. By a rescript of the 21st of March, 1815, Pope Pius VII, of holy memory, granted to those who observe the month of Mary an indulgence of three hundred days for every day of the month, and a plenary indulgence for that day on which they communicate.[757]

Confraternity of the Scapular.—The month of Mary is only a particular form of that devotion which the Christians of all ages have professed for the sacred Mother of God. Before this new institution, many others existed in her honor. One of the most ancient, as well as celebrated, is the Confraternity of the Scapular. It was inspired and revealed by the holy Virgin herself to the blessed Simon Stock, sixth general of the Carmelite Order, about the beginning of the thirteenth century.

The blessed Simon, a descendant of the noble family of the Barons Stock in England, was born at Hestford, Kent, in 1164. Illustrious by his birth, Simon was not slow to become still more so by his piety. Scarcely had he attained the age of twelve years when he retired into an immense forest, where he had no other lodging than the hollow trunk of an old oak tree. Out of the little space at his command he made an oratory, furnished with a crucifix, an image of Mary, and a psalter. Here the holy youth renewed all the austerities of the ancient hermits. Water from a rock was his drink; herbs and roots, his food.

Simon had led the life of a recluse for twenty years, when two English nobles, returning from the Holy Land, brought with them out of Egypt some religious of the Order of Mount Carmel. Penetrated from his childhood with the most sincere devotion to the Blessed Virgin, Simon was very much affected at the piety shown by the new religious toward the august Queen of heaven, and he joined them before the close of the year 1212. Having made his profession in the Carmelite Order, he set out for the East and remained six years in Palestine. Returned to Europe, he was chosen general of his order, which, under his guidance, made rapid progress in the West. On invitations that he received to go over to France, he embarked for Bordeaux, where he died on the 16th of July, aged about sixty years. He was buried in the cathedral, and was soon afterward honored among the saints.

This venerable religious, who had entertained from his earliest years a truly filial confidence in Mary, was one day in prayer, when the Queen of heaven appeared to him, surrounded by a multitude of blessed spirits, and holding in her hand a scapular of the Order of Carmel. She gave it to him with these words: "Receive, my dear son, this scapular of thy order, as the distinctive sign of my confraternity, and the mark of the privilege that I have obtained for thee and the children of Carmel. Whosoever dies while piously wearing the scapular shall be preserved from eternal flames. It will be a sign of salvation, a safeguard in danger, and a special pledge of peace and protection till the end of time."[758]

Though magnificent, this first promise was only a part of what the blessed Simon had asked. To answer him fully, the holy Virgin made him a second promise in favor of Carmelite religious, and members of the Scapular Confraternity. To make the matter more sure, she appeared to Pope John XXII, and said to him according to the very tenor of the bull: "John, vicar of my Son! it is to my solicitations with my Son that you are indebted for the high dignity to which you have been raised. As I have withdrawn you from the ambushes of your enemies, I expect from you an ample and favorable confirmation of the holy Carmelite Order, which has always been singularly devoted to me...If, among the members of the Order or the Confraternity who quit this world, there be any whose sins deserve purgatory, I, as a tender Mother, will go down to them in purgatory on the Saturday after their death. I will deliver such as I find there, and will bring them to the holy mountain, the happy abode of eternal life."[759]

Here four questions present themselves: 1) Are apparitions possible? 2) What is the meaning of the Blessed Virgin's twofold promise? 3) Could the Blessed Virgin make this promise? 4) Did the Blessed Virgin make this promise?

1. *Are apparitions possible?* Not only for the Catholic, but also for the man of good sense, this question is more than fully solved. Take up the old and the new testament, and you will there find incontestable proofs that apparitions are possible. An angel appeared to Abraham in order to call him into the Land of Chanaan. The Lord himself appeared to him in order to announce to him the birth of a son and to reveal to him the destruction of five infamous cities. An angel appeared to Josue immediately before the taking of Jericho. Gedeon, Manue the father of Samson, Samuel, Tobias, Daniel, and Judas Machabeus received by heavenly messengers the commands of the Lord. In the new testament, the archangel Gabriel appeared to the Blessed Virgin in order to announce to her the mystery of the incarnation. An angel warned Joseph to go into Egypt. An angel appeared to St. Peter and delivered him out of prison. We should be a very long time indeed before coming to an end, if we wished to relate all the angelic apparitions of which there is mention in scripture. Now scripture, we must remember well, is the most certain book in existence: one whose authenticity rests on the testimony of two great bodies of people, mortal enemies to each other, Jews and Christians; also, on the testimony of many millions of martyrs.

And then, cannot God reveal himself to his creature? Can he not choose for this purpose such an interpreter as pleases him? What man has a right to tell God that he cannot do so? Is his power to be restrained by the narrow limits of our minds? Can he do nothing but what we understand? But if God could let angels appear to men, why, pray, could he not grant the same privilege to the Queen of angels? That Mary may appear to her children and communicate to them the wishes of heaven is a truth confirmed by faith and reason, which all men will admit, except those who have neither one nor other.

2. *What is the meaning of the Blessed Virgin's twofold promise?* Our divine Mother promises, in the first place, to save from the pains of hell those who die wearing piously the scapular.[760] Does this mean that in whatsoever state, even the state of mortal sin, a member of the Scapular Confraternity dies, he will not fail to be saved, provided only he dies wearing the scapular? Such an interpretation is revolting, shocking.

On the one hand, it is often the style of the scripture to attribute salvation to a thing that really leads thereto, but at the same time does not suffice if other things be omitted. Thus, the apostle St. Paul attributes salvation at one time to faith, and again to hope; and Tobias attributes it to alms.[761] On the other hand, the bull of John XXII, in which the promise is found, does not say that to escape hell it suffices to wear the holy scapular, without practicing any good works. It says quite the contrary.[762]

The meaning of this promise is therefore that the Blessed Virgin will obtain for her clients the grace not to be surprised by death in the state of mortal sin, though it should be necessary on many occasions to prevent by a miraculous interposition some dreadful accident in order to save them from death, or to prolong the life of the sick and bring about a favorable moment for their conversion and salvation. Behold the natural and only lawful meaning to put upon Mary's promise.

To obtain its fulfillment, we must join with the duties of the confraternity the still more essential duties of a Christian. We must avoid sin, and not expose ourselves to the danger of being overtaken by death in the enmity of God. It is by these marks that the true servant of Mary is known.

The Blessed Virgin promises, in the second place, that she will come and deliver out of purgatory the wearers of the scapular on the first Saturday after their death.[763] There is nothing repugnant in this. First, God can make the pains of purgatory more acute, and compensate for shorter duration by greater severity. Again, parents in their families and rulers in their states have certain days for granting their favors. The Church herself has many days appointed for granting a plenary indulgence, that is to say, the remission of the temporal penalties due to our sins. Why should not the Blessed Virgin do likewise?

3. *Could the Blessed Virgin make this promise?* Every Catholic answers: "To be sure she could! Mary is most powerful, and is all goodness."[764]

Whoever reflects on the rights of the best of mothers and the power that she ought to exercise over the best of sons, will answer again: "Yes, indeed, Mary could." "There is nothing wanting to her on this point," says St. Bernard, "neither the power nor the will. Besides, this promise, explained in its true sense, contains nothing but what is most orthodox. It honors Jesus Christ by showing us his affection for Mary. It honors Mary by showing us her charity for mankind."

4. *Did the Blessed Virgin make this promise?* Two voices answer: "Yes, Mary made this promise."

The first of these voices is that of the Church. What have not sovereign pontiffs done that no doubt should remain on minds regarding the truth of each part of this promise? Consulted on the first, which refers to the pains of hell, John XXII, in a bull issued expressly in 1316, declares that it has been examined with the weights of the sanctuary and found most true. As for the second, which refers to the pains in purgatory, he declares that, in an apparition, the Blessed Virgin has made the promise personally to himself. The better to establish these things, he publishes another bull in 1322, wherein he renews the previous one. Since the time of this pontiff, we count twenty-two popes, his successors, who have solemnly explained themselves in the same sense on the subject of the Confraternity of the Holy Scapular. Lastly, an annual festival is celebrated, in virtue of the decrees of sovereign pontiffs, throughout the whole extent of the Catholic Church, to perpetuate the memory of this glorious promise, and to glorify Our Lady of Mount Carmel or of the Holy Scapular.[765] Do you know, even humanly speaking, any authority more worthy of respect?

The second of these voices is that of God himself. God never authorizes error or deceit by miracles: it would be out of keeping with his sanctity to do so. Now, of all the practices of piety that have been inspired to honor Mary, none has been more visibly authorized by splendid miracles. It would take volumes to relate them all: we must be content with one.[766] Here is an authentic fact, which was juridically proved—proved so carefully that we think it a duty to quote from the original document drawn up regarding it:

"On the 19th of August, 1667, at the camp of Brugelette, after noon, in presence of M. Maximilian de Sausse, Count of Mastaing—the Reverend Father Joseph, prior of the Carmelites of Brugelette—Father Barnabas of St. Paul, sub-prior—Father René of St. Teresa—Father Thomas of St. Peter, etc., there appeared Vincent Matthieu, called in his nom-de-guerre *Maison-Dieu*, gendarme of my lord the Dauphin, and Nicolas Pierrot, called *La Plaine*, trumpeter of gendarmes, who deposed that, having had a quarrel, the said Vincent Matthieu fired a pistol at the said Nicolas Pierrot, distant ten feet or thereabouts; but happily, the ball having met his scapular, he received only a slight bruise, which was seen by the assistants and witnesses, though the said ball had pierced his coat and shirt, and was found a third flattened at the middle of the stomach and three good inches below the ribs.

"Louis Amelot, gendarme of the same company, a native of Auxerre, saw the shot fired. Jean Cadot, Lord of Orgeneuvilles, of the same company, was also a witness thereof, and saw the scapular stuck to the bruise. The surgeon found the ball inside the shirt. M. Brojart, quartermaster, and M. de Lestre, brigadier, were witnesses of this. M. Visancourt was also a witness of it, and saw the shot fired. The chaplains of the Count de Broglie and the Marquis de Fervaques saw the bruise, and the holes in the coat and shirt, made by the ball.

"Now, the said Vincent Matthieu and Nicolas Pierrot, after forgiving each other and embracing like true Christians, deposed to this occurrence on oath, as also all the bystanders, who saw the bruise, the flattened ball, and the holes in the coat and shirt, praising God and the good Virgin for having let appear so evident a miracle of her protection by means of her scapular.

"This 20th of August, 1675.

"Signed Mastaing, Count.

"Matthieu, called *Maison Dieu.*

"Nicolas Pierrot.

"Louis Amelot.

"J. Cadot, Lord of Orgeneuvilles.

"Brojart.

"De Lestre.

"J. De Visancourt.

"A. Héliaud, Chaplain.

"A. Viomart, Chaplain of the Queen's Light Cavalry.

"Father E. Antonie du Pain, Guardian of the Recollects of Château-Vilain, declares the above to be most true."

Then follow attestations signed by the officers of the regiment, including the colonel. Lastly, we have the attestation of the surgeon, which runs thus:

"I, the undersigned, surgeon-major of my lord the Dauphin's guard, having come to Nicolas Pierrot, trumpeter, in the belief that he must have been wounded, found the ball inside his shirt, it having pierced the coat and shirt of the said trumpeter, and I saw only a slight bruise: which cannot have happened without a miracle, seeing that it was right over the stomach.

"Signed Nuet."[767]

This fact, and a thousand others, prove that God has authorized by splendid miracles and apparitions both the promises of the Blessed Virgin and the devotion of the scapular.[768]

To obtain the first privilege of the holy scapular, that is to say, the grace of a happy death, and to share in the indulgences of the confraternity, the merits of the Carmelite Order, and the protection of the Blessed Virgin, it is necessary to be a member of the Confraternity of the Holy Scapular. For this purpose, two conditions must be fulfilled: a) to receive the blessed scapular from the hands of a priest who has the power of giving it; and b) to wear it round the neck day and night, in health and in sickness, in life and at death.[769]

These are the only obligations necessary and common to all the members. The Church imposes no extraordinary prayers, abstinences, or fasts on them. It is enough for them to be Christians, that is, to join to the title of servants of Mary the virtues that distinguish the servants of her Son.

To enjoy the second privilege, that is, to have a speedy release out of purgatory, it is also necessary for all the members to observe the chastity proper to their state: virginal chastity in the state of celibacy; conjugal fidelity in the state of marriage; and continence in the state of widowhood.

Moreover, for such as can read: to recite daily the canonical office of the Church, or the little office of the Blessed Virgin,[770] according to the Roman Breviary. In case of grave hindrance, one is not bound thereto; but it is proper to have recourse to one's confessor, so as to obtain a settled commutation. The confessor may, for example, make this commutation consist in the daily recital of the *Ave Maris Stella*, the *Magnificat*, or the *Salve Regina*, which are parts of the Carmelite office. For such as cannot read: to supply for the office by a) not failing in any of the fasts prescribed by the Church; and by b) abstaining from flesh meat on Wednesdays, in addition to Fridays and Saturdays, except on Christmas when it falls on any of these days. In case of grave hindrance, the abstinence does not bind; but here again one ought to obtain a commutation from the confessor, according to the wish of the Holy See.[771]

Such are the obligations of the Confraternity of the Scapular. If it is not the easiest devotion, there is none more honorable or more advantageous.

Compare it with all human associations, even those into which the proudest people are anxious to be admitted. All the orders of chivalry, however honorable they may be, set only a man before me as their founder, and only transitory goods as their advantages. It is otherwise with the august Confraternity of the Scapular: from whatever point of view I consider it, I find it most honorable and most advantageous.

Honorable by its origin. The most beautiful, amiable, and powerful Queen—Mary—was its foundress.

Honorable by its antiquity. It has existed for nearly seven hundred years, in spite of persecutions and revolutions.

Honorable by its members. It is by thousands that we must count the popes, cardinals, patriarchs, bishops, priests, emperors and empresses, kings and queens, noble knights, and illustrious scholars and saints that have made part of it, from St. Louis, who received the scapular at Mount Carmel, to Louis XIV, who did not seem very weak-minded, and who, before the most splendid court in Europe, and in the bloom of youth, received the badges of Mary's service. There is no Christian worthy of the name but would wish to share the same honor. This is the glorious senate that we join, when we take the holy livery of Carmel.

Honorable by the testimony that the two most important authorities in existence have rendered and continually render to it: the authority of God, speaking by miracles, and the authority of the Church, speaking by her pontiffs.

Advantageous by the twofold privilege of a good death and a speedy deliverance out of purgatory. O mortal men, creatures of a day! who hasten along the road to an awe-inspiring eternity, compare, compare the happiness of making this great journey safely with the advantages that are offered by human associations, and say on which side lies the superiority. Will you say that you do not believe? Truly, you are to be pitied! What reason have you not to believe? Do you mean to tell us that you are far more intellectual geniuses than all those crowds of great men whose names adorn the rolls of Carmel? You do not believe! And it is necessary that people should believe you, in preference to the two greatest authorities, God and the Church! Ah, begone from us with your pretended unbelief! It is a long time since we learned the certain marks of folly; and, if we had not learned them, you would teach them to us.

Advantageous by the innumerable indulgences with which it is enriched. People would consider advantageous that human association which should give its exiled members a right to return to their native land; its imprisoned members, a right to be set free; its insolvent members, the means to discharge their debts. Such, in a higher order, is the Confraternity of Carmel.

Advantageous by the share that it gives in the good works of one of the holiest orders in the Church and of all the members of the confraternity. Do you know the Carmelite Order, consisting of religious of both sexes, an order of sublime virtue, which has outlived so many centuries? Have you ever seen a cloister of Carmelite nuns, those angels of the earth whom the angels of heaven contemplate with delight, now recollected in the sanctuary and again engaged in manual labor, clad in coarse garments, and sleeping on beds that would make your delicacy shudder—those who are so holy, often the dearly-beloved children of wealthy houses, sometimes the daughters of kings? What treasures of grace do they lay up every day and every hour! Well, these treasures they are willing to share with you! Have you ever seen a Carmelite friar: here, a holy priest, bringing down on the altar the great victim, the source of every grace; there, a humble cenobite, prostrate in his cell, praying and mortifying himself for the world; elsewhere, a zealous missionary, carrying to the most distant regions the light of the gospel, and bedewing with his sweat and his blood the land that he has just conquered for Jesus Christ? Count, if you can, his merits, and those of thousands of his brethren during the course of seven hundred years. Well, you will have a share in these merits of every kind—martyrdoms, Masses, watches, fasts, tears, prayers, macerations, labors, sacrifices—if you are received into the Confraternity of the Scapular!

What more shall I say? Lift up your eyes to the bright host of Carmelite disciples: popes, bishops, pastors, friars, nuns, emperors, kings, princes, great and little, rich and poor, the elite of the Church during seven centuries. Calculate their good works, and, if you wear the emblems of Carmel, say: "I have a special share in all these goods!" Once more, do you know any association more honorable or more advantageous?

Ye men that seek the glory of wearing the decorations of kings, there is question here of wearing the insignia of the greatest and most amiable Princess in existence. And you pause! And you blush! Away, away, miserable souls, be yours the toys of human distinction! As for us Christians, with truly noble hearts and minds, be ours the most beautiful decorations, the most honorable uniform: children of Mary, be ours the uniform of our august Mother! May a virtue proved in battles for the faith make us worthy of the honor of wearing it!

As often as our scapular meets our view, let us say to ourselves: "Whose image is this?"—*Cujus est imago haec?* In memory of Mary, and after the example of the wise

Boleslas VI, king of Poland, let us entertain sentiments worthy of our Mother. This prince wore day and night round his neck a likeness of his father, as if it should be the witness and guide of his conduct. Had he to pronounce a sentence or to decide on some matter of importance, he would first gaze steadfastly on the little portrait of his father, and utter such admirable words as these: "Father, never let me prove false to your blood; never let my mouth pronounce a word or my hand perform a deed unworthy of your name, and of the high rank in which you have set me!" In the same manner, at the sight of your scapular and the image of Mary joined to it, exclaim: "O Mother, never let me do anything unworthy of your name, or that would dishonor the title of your adopted child!"[772]

The rosary.—It remains for us to speak of another devotion in honor of Mary, nearly as old as the last, and no less authorized, no less widely spread, no less useful: we allude to the holy rosary. In the beginning of the thirteenth century, St. Dominic preached against the Albigenses—dreadful heretics, who were laying waste the South of France. He endeavored to bring the stray sheep back to the truth, and to keep in the fold such as were on the point of quitting it. His success did not correspond to the ardor of his zeal. It was then that Mary, who triumphs over all heresies, appeared to him, and told him to establish the devotion of the holy rosary. On this condition, she promised him a plentiful harvest.[773]

The devotion of the rosary consists in reciting the Our Father 15 times and the Hail Mary 150 times—in all saying the five decades of the beads 3 times. It is intended to honor the fifteen principal mysteries of our Savior and his holy Mother. These fifteen mysteries are divided into three classes: the joyful, the sorrowful, and the glorious. When saying the beads the first time, we honor the five joyful mysteries, namely: the annunciation of the Blessed Virgin, the visitation, the Savior's birth, the presentation of Jesus in the Temple, and the finding of Jesus in the Temple. When saying the beads the second time, we honor the five sorrowful mysteries, namely: the Savior's agony in the garden, the scourging, the crowning with thorns, the carrying of the cross, and the crucifixion. When saying the beads the third time, we honor the five glorious mysteries, namely: the resurrection of our Lord, the ascension, the descent of the Holy Ghost, the assumption of the Blessed Virgin, and the coronation of the Blessed Virgin in heaven. We should meditate during each decade on the mystery attached thereto.

This was what St. Dominic did: he taught the people to meditate while praying. And was it not an admirable idea to join the two most beautiful prayers that human lips can utter with mysteries the most august and most proper to touch the heart? It was at Toulouse, in 1208, that he instituted the rosary, and began to preach it. The success of the preaching of the rosary was so rapid that it surpassed all hopes and astonished Rome itself. People ran in crowds to take part in the recital of the rosary. They pressed round the pulpit of truth to hear a development of the mysteries. They kissed the chaplet, watered it with their tears, and interrupted its recital with their sobs.

In a little while, the churches cannot hold the congregations. St. Dominic is obliged to go everywhere through town and country, and everywhere his inspired words work wonders. The eloquent panegyrist of Mary's rosary has soon changed hearts by a very simple formula of prayers; and all people celebrate with him the sanctity, glory, and power of the Mother of God. Like the scapular, the rosary, spreading quickly, counts ere long among its members popes, kings, illustrious captains, in a word, all the noblest representatives of Catholic genius and piety; and rich indulgences are attached to it.

As for the festival of the Holy Rosary, its origin was this: on the 7th of October, 1571, which was the first Sunday of the month, the Christians won a great victory over the Turks—that of Lepanto. It was a death blow to the Ottoman power. In memory of this event, which saved Europe, Pope St. Pius V wished that thanks should every year be returned to the Blessed Virgin,[774] under the title of Holy Mary of Victory.

Some years later on, Gregory XIII ordered that a solemn festival, under the name of that of the Holy Rosary, should every year be kept on the first Sunday of October, because the victory had been won on the first Sunday of this month, at a time when the faithful were reciting the rosary with singular fervor for the happy issue of the battle. Clement XI made the office of the rosary universal, so as to perpetuate the memory of our Blessed Lady's protection.[775]

Nowadays more than ever before, the state of the Church, of society, and of the family calls for Mary's help. It is time, it is more than time, to associate ourselves with all those who invoke her. Man, the family, society, can no longer go to God but by Mary; man, the family, society, devoted to Mary will no longer be lost. This is the declaration of bygone ages, the assurance of our own experience, the testimony of faith: What more do we need?[776]

PRAYER

O my God! who art all love, I thank thee for having given us so many practices of devotion toward the Blessed Virgin. They are a powerful means of salvation, of which I beg the grace to profit.

I am resolved to love God above all things, and my neighbor as myself for the love of God; and, in testimony of this love, I will join the Confraternities of the Scapular and the Rosary.

Lesson 41: Christianity Brought before the Senses (Continued)—Rogation Days

Rogation days: Procession.—"During the course of spring, the Church displays in our country districts a pomp whose innocent beauties harmonize well with village manners. Behold the Rogation days. On these days of prayer, the peasant sees with joy his heart opening under the influence of religion, and his fields under the showers of heaven. Happy he who will gather a rich harvest, and whose humble heart will bend under the weights of its virtues, like the stalk under its load of grain! The village bells are ringing: the people quit their work. The vinedresser comes down from the hill, the laborer hurries from the field, the woodcutter comes forth from the forest. Mothers, shutting the doors of their cottages, set out with their children. Little girls forget their spindles, their lambs, and their fountains, in order to join in the festival.

"People assemble in the parish cemetery on the green graves of their ancestors. The only clergyman to be present at the ceremony soon makes his appearance. He is an aged pastor, who is known only by the name of *Curé*, and this venerable name, in which his own has been lost, does not indicate the minister of the temple so much as the laborious father of the flock. He comes from his retreat, built near the abode of the dead, over whose ashes he keeps watch. He is stationed in his presbytery as a sentinel on the frontiers of life, to receive those who enter and those who leave this region of sorrows. A well, a few poplars, a vine twining round his window, and a few doves make up the inheritance of this king of sacrifices.

"Meanwhile, the apostle of the gospel, vested in a simple surplice, gathers together his lambs in front of the large door of the church. He delivers to them a discourse—doubtless very beautiful, if we may judge by the tears of those who listen to it. He often says, 'my children,' or 'my dear children': herein lies the secret of this village: Chrysostom's eloquence."[777]

After the exhortation, the antiphon, "Arise, O Lord, help us and deliver us," is intoned. All present kneel down, and the Litany of the Saints is begun. At the invocation, *Sancta Maria, ora pro nobis*, the procession moves off, continuing to sing the litany.

"The standard of the saints, the ancient banner of chivalrous times, opens the way for the flock that follows with its pastor in whatever order it finds convenient. On they go by shady roads, often much torn by the wheels of rustic cars and carts; on over barriers raised by fallen oaks; on past hawthorn hedges, where the bee buzzes or the bullfinch and the blackbird whistle. The trees are covered with blossoms, or with leaves in all the freshness of youth. The woods, the valleys, the rivers, and the rocks hear one after another the hymns of the children of toil. The denizens of the fields, amazed at these canticles, come away from the new wheat, and stand at a short distance to witness the passing of so much rural pomp."[778]

The procession generally makes two rests—at two crosses erected in the country. The time of delay is employed in invoking the saints, beseeching them to be our interpreters and intercessors with God. Hence, the Litany of the Saints is sung, and, if the route is long, some penitential psalms. Alas! we have often abused the gifts of God! The fruits and crops gathered last year, perhaps, afforded many persons the means of offending him who made them grow. How can we better obtain new ones than by a sincere repentance, and a loving confidence in the mercy of God?

All these sentiments the Church endeavors to excite in the hearts of the faithful, by placing on their lips the canticles of the penitent king. "Oh, you," she seems to say to them, "that bear the burden of the day and the heat, do you wish that your land may be made fruitful by your sweat? Water it first with the tears of repentance."

As for the Litany of the Saints, never could it be better introduced than on this occasion. From the height of their thrones, the happy citizens of the heavenly Jerusalem contemplate their brethren in the midst of toils and trials. They have not forgotten what they were themselves, travelers and laborers like us, and they are implored to obtain for the land that fertility which is necessary for our existence. Man here acknowledges his dependence. "I plant and water," he says, "but God alone can give the increase."[779] Accordingly, he raises his suppliant hands to the Lord, that, by the intercession of all the saints, especially the patrons of the parish, he may move him to pour down his blessings on the earth, to moderate the heat of the sun, to send rain and dew in their measure, to dispel clouds, and to keep away storms and hail.

The procession returns at length to the village. All the people throng into the rustic temple, where the old pastor celebrates Mass in order to fertilize by the blood of Jesus Christ and by prayer the fields, vineyards, and meadows. The sacrifice over, all return to their work: religion does not wish that the day on which we ask earthly goods of the Lord should be a day of idleness. With what hope does the farmer drive his plough along the furrows, after imploring the help of him who guides the sun on its course, and keeps in his treasury the soft breezes of the south and the warm gentle shower!

But one day of prayer is very little: it is perseverance that ensures success. Now, it is particularly between May and September that the crops are exposed to danger. Hence, the Church, attentive to the wants of her children, calls them daily to prayer during this long interval, as the true means of turning away the evils that threaten their hopes. From the Finding of the Holy Cross, the 3rd of May, till its Exaltation, the 14th of September, the priest recites every morning before Mass the passion of our Lord Jesus Christ.[780] What prayer could be more efficacious? It reminds God of the sufferings of his Son, and beseeches him in virtue thereof to open his hand and bless the earth.

Passion Sheaf. While this reading is going on, the bell is heard, and the laborer in the field and the vinedresser on the hill should unite with the priest in order to implore the Lord to yield to his entreaties and to bless their labors.[781] In gratitude for his prayers, the "Passion Sheaf" is offered to the priest: Was ever anything better deserved? Is it not right that man should share his crop with him whose prayers have kept it in existence or increased its abundance? For the rest, it is less to the priest than to God himself that this mark of gratitude is shown; and do we not know that gratitude for favors received is a sure title to receive new ones?[782]

Laws of nature under the influence of prayer.—When an infidel hears of prayers to keep away storms or hail, or to obtain rain or fine weather, he smiles contemptuously. "If you had studied like me the laws of nature," he seems to say to the Catholic Church, "you would know full well that they are unchangeable, and that the prayers of poor little creatures, such as men are, cannot have any influence on physical phenomena. Electricity, for example, is necessary to the world, as fire or light, and since the world cannot dispense with electricity, how can it dispense with lightning? In the same manner, you would know that physicists have found, by a series of close observations, that in any particular country there fall so many inches of rain every year. If you knew all this, how would you dare to insult science, and to make your Rogation prayers?"

Thank you, doctor, for the lesson on physics that you have just given us! The Catholic Church ought to be very grateful to you; for no one believes more firmly than she does in the influence of prayer on the phenomena of nature. Let us see, however, whether your knowledge is as certain as you suppose.

1. I have a very strong prejudice against you on one account; namely, that all people have prayed. Yes, always and everywhere I behold supplications, processions, and sacrifices, to turn away the scourges that threaten the world.[783] Among the Hebrews, prayer was made to turn away hail and storms from the harvest. Among the Romans and all other nations, civilized and barbarous, ancient and modern, prayer has been made for the same end. You cannot deny facts, doctor!

It is only a prejudice, do you say? If I am not mistaken, this means that you alone know more than all the rest of the world. But who are you, I ask, to say: "Poor human race! thou art only a fool!" And are not you yourself a part, though a very small part, of the human race? Is your knowledge any more in comparison to its knowledge than a sepulchral lamp to the sun? If you imagine the human race convicted of folly, who are you, I ask again, you, an imperceptible atom, to pretend to be alone right, and to lay down your assertions as axioms? Until you show me your letters of infallibility, I prefer to be mistaken with the human race, with the Catholic Church, than to be right with you; and do not be offended if I continue praying to God in order to be preserved or delivered from temporal evils.

2. You say that the world requires electricity, and hence the lightning flashes so many times a year; and that so many inches of rain must fall every year, because the earth requires it. This time I will not return you any thanks; for your fine system of unchangeable laws leads us straight to fatalism, and makes man a mere statue. You degrade me; and I will not recognize in any man or system the right to place me on a level with a machine.

The world is not a clock to me, and myself a part of its wheelwork. Above its laws, with all their pretended invariability, I behold a lawgiver. You will search a long time, I think, before you find laws without a lawgiver. Now, this lawgiver all people salute with the name of *Father*—a Father most good, most great, and most free—and I believe with all peoples that it is well to address God as we address a king or a father, and that prayer has the power to obtain graces and to prevent evils.

3. You tell us, doctor, of a certain number of storms with thunder and lightning, and a certain quantity of rain due in each country in the course of a year. I do not know how you manage your studies; but, to tell you the truth, an experimental knowledge on this matter seems to me impossible: at least, I cannot understand how you should attain to any degree of certainty, even approximative, regarding it. Be that as it may, there is question here only of an ordinary year. Well, where do you place the limits of your period of test? At a distance of ten years or a hundred years, as you like. But how, in good earnest,

can you conclude from what happens during so short a space of time that the same thing must happen invariably during all ages. A law, I say, is recognized by the permanence of its effects. Now, ten years or a hundred years are not, in comparison with thousands upon thousands of years, enough to establish a law.

But I want to give you fair play. I will admit then that, in each country, there must fall exactly the same quantity of water every year. This is to be an invariable law. The distribution of this water will, if you permit me so to speak, be the flexible part of the law. Now you see that, with all your invariable laws, we may very well have floods and droughts, general rains for the whole world, and exceptional rains for such persons as can ask them.[784] We pray, therefore, not that the olive may grow in Siberia, but that the olive may not perish in the fields of Provence. We pray, not that the quantity of water needed every year may be lessened, but that this water may fall at the proper times and places.

4. In my turn, if you will let me give you a lesson, or rather a friend's advice, I shall say to you: Take care, doctor. You are in bad company; and, believe me, it is not well to go with the mob. Now, every other examination aside, the morals of the men who support your system are an argument against its soundness, and above all against its goodness. Your masters are those very philosophers who strive to degrade the rest of mankind after having degraded themselves: the history of their lives and of their writings leaves no doubt on this matter. They speak only of invariable laws, I am aware; but their anxiety is to keep man from praying, and they adopt a very sure means of succeeding therein. Now to keep man from praying is to destroy the idea of a wise, powerful, free, and good God, who rules the world, and the idea of those relations which unite us with him as children with their father. It is to destroy the religious bond, which alone ennobles man; for there can be no religion without prayer. Hence comes, as we know, the anger of those unbelievers when moralists tell us that temporal scourges are divine punishments.[785] Yet moralists are right. Scourges are intended to beat us; and we are beaten because we deserve it. We can undoubtedly avoid deserving it, and, even when we have deserved it, we can obtain pardon. Ask your masters, doctor, whether they have anything more reasonable to say to us. While awaiting their reply, we shall hope that this is one of those pretty numerous cases in which philosophy, after long and tiresome wanderings, comes at length to find rest in full belief. For my part, I do not despair of seeing the philosophers and physicists of our day coming in a body to this happy end; and I sincerely trust, doctor, that you will be among the number.

As for us believers, who have the happiness of dwelling quietly within the pale of Catholic truth, it only remains for us to renew our faith in the influence of prayer on physical laws and phenomena. We are just going to do this, by studying the history of the Rogation days.

History of Rogation days.—The observance of the Rogation days owes its origin to a variety of calamities that befell the city of Vienne in Dauphiné. For more than half a century, not a year nor even a season passed without Dauphiné and Savoy being afflicted with some new evils. So many misfortunes, sometimes succeeding one another, sometimes coming together, had reduced these provinces to a state of extreme desolation. Earthquakes were almost of daily occurrence, and the strongest buildings could not resist such severe shocks. Never had fires been so numerous. Wild beasts came out of the woods in broad daylight and made their way into the streets and squares, as if to defy man and the elements.

The public alarm was continually increasing, when, on Easter night, in the year 469, while all the people were assembled in the great church with their bishop, St. Mamertus, for the celebration of the solemnities, the city hall, a magnificent building that stood on a hill, took fire. Everyone began to fear for his own house, when he saw how furiously the flames spread. All the faithful left the church to provide for their safety. The divine service was abandoned, and the holy bishop remained alone before the altar.

Happily, for the city of Vienne, St. Mamertus did not believe that the laws of nature are unchangeable. In the liveliness of his faith and charity, he offered up prayers and tears to appease the wrath of God: he besought him to put an end at last to so many evils, which hindered the people from serving him with due affection and fidelity. Day was scarcely beginning to dawn when the great conflagration suddenly ceased. The joy produced by this wonderful occurrence brought back all the people to the church, in order to continue the office. Having concluded the august mysteries and returned thanks to God for so evident a favor, the holy bishop told his flock that prayer and penance were the true remedies for the evils with which the city and province were afflicted, and that, during the general fright, he had vowed rogations for this purpose.

The rogations were litanies or supplications, which should consist in a solemn procession, accompanied with public fasts and prayers. Everyone applauded the pontiff's pious idea; and, with the general consent of clergy and people, the three days preceding Ascension Thursday were chosen for the fulfillment of the vow. The holy bishop appointed as the station or halting place of the first procession a church outside the city, but not very far. All the inhabitants went thither with great devotion in humble and penitent garb, mingling their tears and sighs with the singing of psalms. St. Mamertus, seeing the zeal of his people, appointed a more distant station for future processions.

This pious institution did wonderful good. With that spirit of earnestness which, in the ages of faith, never failed to characterize devotional exercises, it spread beyond the city and Diocese of Vienne.

The bishops of Gaul, considering the wisdom of this practice, thought that they could not do better than adopt it. St. Caesarius, bishop of Arles, who presided in the Council of Agde in the year 506, speaks of the Rogations of St. Mamertus in such a manner as to lead us to suppose that, in his time, they were established in the provinces subject to the Visigoths. From the beginning of the sixth century, they were received in the other parts of Gaul that made up the states of Clovis I, king of France. Since that time their observance has never been interrupted among us. It passed over to Spain in the seventh century; and to Rome at the close of the eighth, under Pope Leo III. In France, they used to be real pilgrimages, or very long processions. At first, there was no work done on the three Rogation days. Later on, the obligation was limited to assisting at the procession and Mass.

What must be done to sanctify them. The fast prescribed in former times is nowadays confined to abstinence.[786] To observe this abstinence is the first way to sanctify the Rogation days. To assist at the processions is the second. Established for the preservation of our temporal goods, the pious and edifying ceremonies of these days imperatively demand the presence of all, rich and poor. Would it not be melancholy to see only a few women and children following the pastor, while he is going to implore for all the people the blessings of heaven?

What! You selfish men, who go to your labors when the Church calls you to prayer, do you then forget that neither he who plants nor he who waters is anything, but he alone who gives the increase? Do you forget that it will avail you nothing to rise before the dawn, if the Lord build not the house? And you indifferent men, who, from the doors of your shops and stores, watch, with arms folded and perhaps an impious sneer, the passing of our processions, have you then nothing to fear or to seek? Do you command the winds, the floods, hailstorms, thunderbolts, and earthquakes? You imagine perhaps that God has no longer in his treasures anything with which to punish your daring contempt. O just heaven! to what blindness, even regarding our material interests, do not irreligion and indifference lead!

As for us Christians, who know the influence of prayer, let us consider it our duty to assist regularly and modestly, with sentiments of compunction and penance, at the processions of the Rogation days, begging of God that we may make a holy use of the good things which we ask of his liberality.

Procession of St. Mark's day.—The Church of Rome, which had received the Rogations from us, gave us in its turn the Great Litany, or St. Mark's Procession. In November, 589, the Tiber overflowed its banks with such fury that it threatened to destroy the city of Rome. When retiring, it left in the country an infection that ended in a violent plague. Pope Pelagius II was one of the first to fall a victim to it, and his death was followed by a general desolation. St. Gregory the Great, the successor of Pelagius, understood that it was necessary to appease the anger of God by extraordinary prayers, fasts, and penitential tears. He exhorted his people to second his efforts by a sincere change of life. The pious inhabitants of the Eternal City responded enthusiastically to the pontiff's appeal.

To have some order in the crowds of the faithful who should walk in procession with public prayers, Gregory divided the clergy, the religious, and the people into seven bodies. Hence the name of the Septiform Litany,[787] given to St. Mark's procession. The public prayers were continued for three days, and the processions were out on march from nine o'clock in the morning. All the streets and squares of the city resounded with *Kyrie, eleison*—"Lord, have mercy on us!" Though in less than an hour on the first day there were eighty persons, stricken by the plague, seen to fall down and die, yet so sad a spectacle could not dishearten St. Gregory. The holy pope's faith soon obtained its reward: at the end of three days of procession, the plague ceased.

It is now a long time since the three processions were reduced to one, fixed for the 25th of April, St. Mark's day. From the beginning of the ninth century, it was generally established among us.[788] In Rome and in some dioceses of France, the abstinence is still obligatory on this day. The Rogations, the Processions of St. Mark's day, all those public prayers, make us admire the maternal solicitude of the Church. Not only do the spiritual wants of her children touch this good mother's heart, but she takes a deep interest in their temporal wants, and neglects no means of relieving them. Like her divine spouse, she may say, in the fullest sense of the words, what no sect can ever say: "I went about doing good."[789]

PRAYER

O my God! who art all love, I thank thee for watching so carefully over our temporal concerns. Grant that we may obtain, by the fervor of our prayers, the good things needful for our life, and, above all, the grace to use them for thy glory.

I am resolved to love God above all things, and my neighbor as myself for the love of God; and, in testimony of this love, I will assist piously at the Rogation processions.

Lesson 42: Christianity Brought before the Senses (Continued)—Ascension Thursday

Ascension Thursday: Object of this festival.—We have seen the Son of God coming down from heaven, born, living, and dying, to redeem man, to repair his work so sadly injured by the first fall. It was forty days since the divine repairer had proved his resurrection to the most incredulous. To enjoy rest after the sufferings of his humanity, he should have remained a shorter time on earth. But no: his love for us kept him away from the angels. "He was like a royal exile, whose ban had been removed, but who did not wish to return immediately to his native land, because, during his banishment, he had cherished a tender love for the men among whom he suffered."[790]

If he leaves us today, it is all for love. The noble conqueror is going to take possession of the kingdom won by his blood, and to place humanity on a throne of immortal glory. Would you wish to be witnesses of the accomplishment of this mystery, which crowns the work of our redemption? Let us set out for Jerusalem.

Behold the Savior, surrounded by his disciples! He is near Bethania, a little town on the side of Mount Olivet, about fifteen furlongs from Jerusalem, whence the man-God had started on his triumphant entry into the deicide city. An old tradition tells us that he went to take leave of his dear friends, Lazarus, Martha, and Mary, who lived in Bethania.[791] With them, he climbs this mountain, lately the scene of his agony. We observe it on the road between Jerusalem and Jericho: it is the highest in the neighborhood of the city of David; its sides are covered with verdure; its summit is crowned with vines and olives.

Arrived at the summit, the Son of God stops, and says to his disciples, gathered in a circle round him, "All power is given to me in heaven and on earth. Go ye therefore in my name through the whole world, and preach the gospel to every creature. Teach all nations, baptizing them in the name of the Father, and of the Son, and of the Holy Ghost. Show them how to observe all things whatsoever I have commanded you. Behold I am with you all days even to the consummation of the world."[792]

At the same time, he opened their minds, that they might understand the scriptures, and see that everything foretold of Christ by the prophets had been accomplished in his Person. "Witnesses of all these things," he added, "you must not forget them. I will send down on you the gift of my Father that has been promised to you; but do you stay in the city until then—until you are endued with power from on high."[793] To console them for his departure and to show them that love guided all his steps, he had said to them previously: "It is advantageous for you that I go; if I go not, the Spirit will not come to you."[794] What! my Savior! is thy sensible presence therefore an obstacle to the communications of the Holy Ghost? Thy words seem to indicate it: What is their meaning?

Necessity of the Savior's Ascension: Its history. In the beginning, it was necessary to detach the apostles from the love of sensible things by the love of the sensible presence of the Son of God, clothed with our flesh. But the Savior wished to attach them only for a time to his sensible presence, in order to accustom them gradually to the love of justice, truth, charity, humility, and all other virtues, of which he gave them so many admirable lessons, and set them such a divine example. The sensible love of our Lord is useful, and even necessary to beginners. It would at length prove prejudicial to those who should pass from spiritual childhood to a more perfect age and state, wherein they should love Jesus Christ as God, as the eternal truth, as incorruptible justice and sanctity. This is the reason why the divine master ascended into heaven. Otherwise, the apostles would not have been able to love him with a purely spiritual love, and consequently would not have been able to receive the Holy Ghost.[795]

The supreme moment draws nigh. The great teacher of the human race is about to deprive the world of his visible presence; the divine mouth will soon be closed. It was a Thursday, about noon, the fortieth day after the resurrection.[796] The Savior, casting a last look on his holy Mother and his disciples, stretched out his hand and blessed them. Immediately, he began to rise from the ground. As, in his resurrection, he had come forth from the tomb by his own power, so, in his ascension, he rose without requiring a fiery chariot like Elias, or any other extraneous help whatsoever. A bright cloud, symbolic of his glory, received him, and, in a little while, this new triumphal chariot hid him from the view of his friends.

While they were still gazing after him, lo! two angels, like two handsome young men, appeared to them and said: "Ye men of Galilee, why stand ye here with eyes fixed on heaven? This same Jesus who hath just left you, will one day come again as you have seen him ascend."[797]

The disciples, having therefore adored him and kissed the traces of his feet, returned full of joy to Jerusalem, where they remained in company of the Blessed Virgin, awaiting the fulfillment of the promise that the Lord had made to them, and praising God daily in the Temple. Such was the departure of the Son of God from this earth, which his mighty hand had drawn from nothingness on the day of the creation, and which he had bedewed with his blood on the day of the redemption.

The Savior's footprints. It was from the highest point of Mount Olivet that the Savior ascended into heaven. He left there the prints of his divine feet: on the very spot where he touched the earth for the last time. Many centuries have looked at them there, kissed them respectfully, and bedewed them with tears of repentance and love. St. Jerome, Sulpicius Severus, St. Paulinus of Nola, and St. Optatus are unexceptionable witnesses to this miraculous fact.[798] To their authority is joined that of the great St. Augustine. "People go to Judea," says the illustrious bishop of Hippo, "in order to adore the footprints of Jesus Christ, which may be seen at the place from which he ascended into heaven."[799]

During the siege of Jerusalem under Titus, the Roman army was a long time encamped on Mount Olivet, without the movements of its soldiers and horses, which could not fail to tear up the ground, being able to efface these sacred footprints. They were to be seen so plainly in the time of the empress Helena, mother of Constantine the Great, that, when this pious princess built the magnificent Basilica of the Ascension on the very part of the mountain from which, as was known, our Lord had ascended into heaven, it was proposed to pave them over with marble, but there was no succeeding in the effort to do so. Everything put there was repelled by an invisible power, and at length the place had to be left uncovered, as it had been found. It was henceforth one of the greatest objects of devotion to Christians, who, from all the provinces of the Empire, and from foreign countries, went in crowds to visit the holy places.

St. Jerome relates another splendid miracle that occurred here. "When the workmen were trying to finish the roof of the Ascension Basilica," says the great doctor, "they found it impossible to complete the vault that rose directly over the place of the Savior's footprints. They had to leave open the space through which he had passed away from the earth and been received into the cloud. This let the faithful contemplate the way by which the Son of God had ascended into heaven."[800]

Matters were still in the same state about the close of the seventh century, when a French bishop, named Arculphus, visited the holy places.[801] In the Middle Ages, the building was destroyed during the wars with the Saracens. Last of all, the Rev. Father Geramb, in his *Journey to Palestine*, expresses himself thus: "At the top of Mount Olivet we find a mosque, on whose site there was formerly a magnificent church, built by St. Helena, at the place from which Jesus Christ had ascended into heaven after his resurrection. This mosque, which threatens to become a ruin, is surrounded by miserable houses, occupied by Turks. At the center, in a kind of chapel, there is to be seen the print made on the rock by the Savior's left foot, when he was quitting the earth to ascend into heaven. We are assured that the Turks took away the print of the right foot and buried it, in order to remove it afterward into the mosque of the temple. As for the print of the left foot, it exists in such a manner as to leave no doubt about it, though a little worn by the numberless kisses of pilgrims during so many ages, and perhaps by some pious thefts that a strict watch could not always prevent."

The Son of God, who has just laid the prints of his feet on the rock, as everlasting monuments of his stay on this earth, sanctified by his blood, advances rapidly toward the heavenly Jerusalem. But what invisible multitudes adorn his triumph! He is accompanied by the souls of the ancient patriarchs, the holy prophets, all the virtuous people against whom heaven has heretofore been shut: he raises them up with himself, leading captivity captive. All these captives, now delivered, follow their Redeemer in his triumph, singing his victory. Jesus, having snatched them out of the power of the devil, leads them with him to heaven as trophies of his victory, as rich spoils taken from the enemy, as the prize of his adorable blood, as the ornament and glory of his triumph. "How great, how splendid a procession, at which the apostles were not yet worthy to assist!" exclaims St. Bernard.[802]

Suddenly, the eternal gates open. Who can describe the amazement of the angels when they see human nature placed above them—at the right hand of God himself; when they see Jesus Christ, who, as man, has been ignominiously judged and put to death on earth, now acknowledged as the Lord of the whole universe and the supreme judge of mankind?

Subjects of joy on Ascension Thursday. On this day, the Church of earth, uniting with the Church of heaven, goes into transports in celebrating the triumphs of her spouse. The office of the Ascension breathes the liveliest joy. In some places, it is accompanied with a procession. This was established to represent the journey of the apostles from Jerusalem to Bethania and thence to the summit of Mount Olivet, in order to see our Lord ascend into heaven, as well as their return to Jerusalem, in order to prepare themselves for the descent of the Holy Ghost. For these reasons it is made only after terce, that is, about nine o'clock. In effect, it was at this time that the Savior, accompanied by his disciples, wended his way up the holy mountain.

On Ascension Thursday, let us call to mind all the circumstances of this journey. Let us imagine that we ourselves accompany the Savior, and let us yield to the emotions of a lively faith. Above all, let us not forget that eighteen centuries go before us in the celebration of this festival.[803] Let the example, the piety, the loving tears, and the holy desires of our ancestors rush in upon our memory, and, believe me, this procession will no longer prove useless to us.

Yet should not the mystery of the ascension, so proper to excite joy among the blessed spirits, be a subject of grief to us, poor orphans on earth? "What part have I in these solemnities?" cries out St. Bernard.[804] What! you forget, O great saint! that every step our Lord took was dictated by love. Here are some reasons why we should rejoice:

1. Jesus Christ ascends to heaven in order to take possession of his glory and to enjoy the fruits of his sufferings. For a highborn child, can there be any greater subject of joy than to see its father, victorious over his enemies, entering into possession of the repose and glory that he has merited by many fatigues and conflicts; to see him honored, exalted, blessed by the whole world?

2. Jesus Christ ascends to heaven in order to send the Comforter, that Spirit who should regenerate the world as he had made chaos fruitful on the day of creation. "If I go not," says the Savior, "the Paraclete will not come to you."[805] If our Father deprives us of his sensible presence, it is not to leave us orphans, but to fill our souls with the precious gifts of the Holy Ghost. Let us therefore pray and sigh, to the end that the divine Comforter may find us worthy of his inspirations. Let us ask of him to enlighten our understanding and to purify our will. The serpent belonging to Moses devoured all the serpents of the magicians: in the same manner, the divine Spirit should consume all our sensual appetites and inclinations. On this great day, let us say to the Lord for ourselves and for the whole world: "Send forth thy Spirit, and they shall be created; and thou shalt renew the face of the earth."[806] It has great need thereof!

3. Jesus Christ ascends to heaven in order to open its gates and to prepare places there for us. The second Adam, he opens heaven, shut against the human race by the fault of the first Adam. With what sweet hope ought not our hearts now to beat! I have a place in heaven! I, a poor creature, covered perhaps with rags; I, a beggar; I, a shepherd; I, a laborer; I, a child; I, an unknown wayfarer, despised perhaps by the world—I have a place in heaven!

O devil! jealous of the happiness of our first parents, how well thou hast been conquered! See: our nature was condemned to misery; suddenly it is exalted, the heavens are opened to it! We were unworthy of life, and we are called to immortality! In Jesus Christ, that human nature which thou didst degrade holds the highest place in heaven, and what was the object of thy sacrilegious jeers is adored by the angels. Look! that same human nature which thy rage pursued, whose ruin thou didst think complete, is now crowned in heaven: it occupies thy place and that of thy wicked angels; it is in heaven and thou art in hell! Congratulate thyself now on thy jealousy and thy lies.

Thus, in Jesus Christ, we are today the possessors of heaven; for he ascended there as our head, as our leader. Where the head is, there the members ought also to be. A leader supposes someone to follow; and this someone is you, is I myself, is the whole human race. Our Lord died for all mankind.

4. Jesus Christ ascended to heaven in order to guard our places there. Not content with having traced out for us the road to the heavenly Jerusalem, with having opened its gates, with having prepared places for us there, the Savior wished to secure the possession of those places for us. What is he doing in heaven? An advocate, he continually pleads our cause. "My little children," says the beloved disciple, "I write these things to you that you may not sin. But if any one sin, let him not lose heart. We have an advocate with the Father, Jesus Christ the just, who shed his blood, not only for our sins, but for those of the whole world."[807]

An eternal high priest, he reconciles us with his Father by presenting to him the wounds in his adorable hands and feet. Again, continuing on earth the sacrifice of his body and blood, he stands unceasingly as a lightning conductor against the thunderbolts of the divine vengeance. The firstborn among his brethren, and we are his brethren, he gives over to us his sacred titles to an eternal inheritance. God, he has a right thereto by his nature; man, he has a right thereto by his blood. Heaven is his conquest: and it was for us that he conquered it.

How to celebrate this festival: Its harmony with the season. Let us, therefore, follow the noble eagle that today soars heavenward: we are its little ones. It stretches out its wings, inviting us to go with it. "But remember," says St. Augustine, "that pride does not ascend to heaven with a God of humility, nor avarice with a poor God, nor luxury with a God of sorrows, nor impurity with the Son of a Virgin, nor vices with the Father of virtues." Let us lift up our hearts; let us break away from the affections that degrade us; let us mount higher and higher: *excelsior!* All nature encourages us; it, also, seems anxious to go to heaven. See at this season of the year all those myriads of young birds which, coming forth from their nests, try their first flight toward the sky; see the plants, which push their tender stalks upward; see the trees with arms outstretched to the clouds! *Sursum corda* is the cry of all creation!

St. Augustine remarks another harmony between this festival and the season in which it is celebrated. "God, the author of nature and grace," he says, "wished to make some relation between the mysteries of his Son and the seasons of the year. The Redeemer comes into the world when the days are shortest and will just begin to lengthen, in order to tell us that he finds the world in darkness and brings light to it. He dies and rises again at the time of the full moon. This planet, which, by its many changes, is a figure of perishable things, is then quite dark on the side turned toward heaven, and has light and beauty only for the side turned toward the earth. However, it begins again to hide its face from the earth and to turn toward the sun, that all its brightness may be for heaven. This spectacle is in perfect harmony with the death and resurrection of the Savior, by which we turn toward heaven, toward the sun of justice, all the inclinations that we have for the earth. The Son of God ascended into heaven and sent the divine fire of his Holy Spirit about the time when the sun is in its apogee, that is to say, when it is most elevated and also most distant from the earth: a new harmony, which reminds us that it was only after Jesus Christ had risen far from the earth that he spread over the world the brightest flames of his charity."[808]

These admirable relations, whose reality is well known by minds accustomed to reflect, are proved to every man by comparison with the divine laws. In effect, since the author of grace is also the author of nature, was it not becoming that he should place a harmony between these two great works, so that the changes occurring in nature and the very sight of the universe should, far from distracting us, lead our minds to thoughts of religion?

If there be added to this observation what we have said of the history of the human race, wherein God has also been pleased to write in large letters the truth of the Christian religion, it will be concluded that nature, the annals of the world, and the economy of the Church are three wonderful books, between which there exists a most admirable harmony: books which bear testimony to one another, and in which God has most clearly written all that is necessary to detach our thoughts and affections from this world, and to raise them to heaven with Jesus Christ.[809]

The festival of the Ascension dates from the times of the apostles; and the early ages of the Church saw the establishment of the procession that still takes place on this day in memory of our Lord's journey with his apostles to the summit of Mount Olivet, where, having blessed them, he quitted the earth in their presence.[810] This festival is the last of the solemnities relating to our Lord, and recalls the happy end of his pilgrimage on earth.[811] Thus it ought to be with each of us: children of God, we ought to return to God. Life can have no higher aim.

PRAYER

O my God! who art all love, I thank thee for having ascended into heaven in order to open it for me and to prepare a place there for me. Grant me the grace to succeed in being reunited to thee.

I am resolved to love God above all things, and my neighbor as myself for the love of God; and, in testimony of this love, I will often look up to heaven and say: "There is a place up there waiting for me."

Lesson 43: Christianity Brought before the Senses (Continued)—Pentecost

Pentecost: Greatness of this festival.—A skillful architect desires that people should approach a palace through long avenues, and a wise mother makes her child expect for a long time the reward that is to crown its young virtues. Thus does the Church wish that her great solemnities should be preceded by a long preparation. Herein we see a great knowledge of the human heart. Advent prepares us for Christmas; Lent for Easter; paschal time for Pentecost. "We prepare for the festival of Easter," says Eusebius, "by forty days of fasting, and we dispose ourselves for Pentecost by fifty days of a holy gladness."[812]

Why so much joy? The same historian tells us. "At Easter," he says, "baptism is received; at Pentecost, the Holy Ghost is received, and this is the perfection of baptism. The resurrection of Jesus Christ strengthened the apostles: it was Pentecost that perfected their charity, and made them invincible. On this day, the Holy Ghost was given to the Church with all the fullness needed to subjugate the whole world. Wherefore, I regard Pentecost as the greatest of festivals."[813] The ten days before it are consecrated by pious Christians to recollection and prayer. They shut themselves up in the upper chamber with the Blessed Virgin and the apostles, that they may prepare to receive the Holy Ghost with the abundance of his gifts.

However, these preparations do not seem enough to the Church, so great is her desire to make us worthy of the favors of her divine spouse. She appointed for Pentecost a most solemn vigil, whose office bears a close relation to that of Easter Eve. The reason is easily understood. It was on these two glorious and ever-memorable nights that the sacrament of regeneration used to be administered to catechumens. In the early ages, the office began with twelve lessons, which, like those of Holy Saturday, were intended to instruct catechumens. Nowadays, there are only six read. They also relate to baptism and the law of grace.

In the first, we are reminded of the promise which God made to Abraham, that he would reward his obedience and faith, and bless in his race all the nations of the earth. Now, it was on the day of Pentecost that this promise was fulfilled by the effusion of the Holy Ghost, whom our Lord, the Son of Abraham according to the flesh, sent down on the world.

The second recounts the miraculous passage of the Red Sea, a figure of the more miraculous passage by which the human race, regenerated in the waters of baptism, escapes from the power of the devil, and finds itself on the road to the true land of promise.

The third announces the entry of the Jews into this land, the object of all their desires, and relates the last advice of Moses to his people, if they wish to enjoy the prosperity promised by the Lord for their good behavior. The same advice is given on the part of the Church, the same assurances on the part of the Holy Ghost, to new Israelites standing on the borders of the eternal country.

The fourth speaks of the eagerness of the nations to enter into an alliance with the Jews, whose happiness they envy: a lively figure of the zeal with which pagans would run to baptism, and make that good and fruitful vine from which the Church begs of God to keep far away the thorns of sin.

The fifth shows the false greatness and prosperity of infidel nations. It exhorts the Jews to take the Lord and his law as their richest treasure. This is a lesson of the highest importance for Christians, especially the newly baptized.

The sixth describes the celebrated vision of Ezechiel. We behold an immense plain covered with human bones; these bones moving, uniting, and forming the bodies of men; and these men returning to life at the breathing of the spirit: a striking image of the human race at the appearance of the gospel, and of the new life communicated to it by the Holy Spirit.

Nothing more magnificent than these lessons; nothing grander than their instructions.[814] Next come the procession, the blessing of the sacred font, and the Mass without the introit, as on Holy Saturday. The eve of Pentecost is accompanied with a fast, which already existed in the eighth century.[815]

All these preparations for our Catholic Pentecost are not the least exaggerated, if we reflect on the excellence of this festival. And first, by the greatness of its object, it leaves all profane festivals far behind. Then it surpasses the Jewish Pentecost as much as the law of grace surpasses the law of fear, as much as the accomplishment of the mystery of our redemption surpasses the types and figures thereof.

The third Person of the adorable Trinity descending on the world to regenerate it, as at the creation he descended on chaos to make it fruitful; the divine Redeemer putting the finishing touch to the great work that was the object of all his mysteries; a new people destined to adore God in spirit and in truth, from the rising to the setting of the sun; the face of the earth renewed; Jewish figures replaced by the reality; paganism struck dead; the covenant of God with all mankind, promised during four thousand years, at length perfected: such are the wonders, such are the subjects of meditation and praise, to be found in the festival of Pentecost.

And you wish that the Catholic Church should not be all gladness in celebrating it! But one should be as dull as an indifferentist not to feel his heart beat with gratitude and joy on the return of this memorable day. What! is not the festival of Pentecost the festival of civilization? Christian nations! answer. From what period do those new ideas, lights, morals, and institutions date, which have changed the face of the earth, substituted the law of charity for the brutal right of might, and made you what you are? If, ungrateful, you pretend to forget it, the Catholic Church takes care to tell you again of it, as she has told of it to the generations that went before you, and as she will never cease to tell of it to the generations that will come after you. For the last eighteen centuries, she has celebrated the festival of Pentecost, and you, rich and poor, kings and peoples, should unite with her to do honor to this day, as you do honor to your birthdays. The upper chamber in Jerusalem was your cradle. Thence came that intellectual superiority, that sublime morality, of which you are so proud.

Let us now call to mind the circumstances amid which this mystery was accomplished. After the ascension of their divine master, the apostles returned to Jerusalem, where they awaited the fulfillment of his promise. They withdrew to a cenacle, that is, to an upper room, shut off from other rooms. In Palestine, the houses having a flat roof, the highest room was the largest as well as the most retired. It was here that the Jews had their private oratories.[816]

It is believed that the apostles assembled in the house of Mary the mother of John Mark, that fervent disciple of whom St. Luke speaks.[817] No matter what was the exact place of their assembly, they represented the Universal Church. They were in expectation of some favors from their divine master, when, on the tenth day after his ascension and the fiftieth after his resurrection, the Holy Ghost descended on them. It was a Sunday, the day after the Jewish Pentecost, to the end that the new law might be published at the very same time of the year that the old, which should make way for it, had been given on Mount Sinai.

But see what a difference!

Difference under the old law and the new law. The old law had been promulgated in the midst of thunder and lightning, and with the peal of trumpets. It threatened offenders with death. It was written on tables of stone. It tired, by the numerousness of the practices to which it subjected, a gross, ignorant people, who should be brought to obedience more by fear than by love.

The new law, on the contrary, is a law, not of terror, but of grace, destined to be written, not on stone, but on the human heart. The work of the Holy Ghost, who is the source of consolation, sweetness, and love, it could not be promulgated with that dreadful pomp which accompanied the promulgation of the Mosaic law. God had been long enough served by slaves: he wanted children.

Therefore, on Sunday, the day of Pentecost, about nine o'clock in the morning, as the disciples were all together, they suddenly heard a noise like that of a mighty wind coming from heaven. It filled the whole house.[818] This signal of the arrival of the Holy Ghost is intended to rouse their attention: it is full of mystery. The wind coming from on high, the harbinger of holy inspirations, is the breath of grace, which maintains our spiritual life, as the air maintains our physical life. Its impetuosity shows the power of grace in changing and vivifying hearts. If it fills the whole house, it is because the Holy Ghost offers his gifts to people of every country, and he transforms us into new beings, penetrating all our faculties.

This first prodigy is followed by another. There come down from heaven tongues of fire, which part and rest on the heads of all the members of the happy assembly. It is the Holy Ghost himself, who is pleased to take outward forms emblematic of the amazing effects that he produces inwardly in souls. I behold him, at the Savior's baptism, appearing under the form of a dove, in order to denote the innocence and zeal that are the fruits of the sacrament of regeneration. Today his presence is manifested under the form of tongues of fire, an eloquent figure of that unity of belief and love which is about to make of all mankind but one family.

Fire enlightens, tends upward, transforms into itself whatever it seizes: similar effects are produced by the Holy Ghost in our souls. This fire appears under the form of tongues rather than of hearts, to let us understand that the gifts of the Holy Ghost are poured out on the apostles, not only that they may love God, but also that they may make others love him, communicating to them by their words the fire of their charity. This form also announces the gift of languages, which will enable the apostles to communicate with the different nations, in order to preach the doctrine of their divine master[819] to them.

Here we behold the Savior repairing the last effects of sin. The descendants of Noe, having resolved on building the Tower of Babel, were scattered by means of a confusion in their language. The punishment of pride, this confusion in language brought about a confusion in ideas and a forgetfulness of holy traditions. It also led to hatreds and endless divisions among peoples. The gift of languages at the publication of the gospel is a happy presage of the speedy meeting of all nations in unity of belief and love, to make henceforward but one large family, declaring the glory of the Lord from the rising to the setting of the sun.[820]

Effects of the Holy Ghost on the apostles.—The descent of the Holy Ghost wrought a twofold miracle in the apostles: an internal miracle and an external miracle.

An internal miracle. All their faculties were enriched with the gifts of God. Enlightened by a divine light, their understanding penetrated without difficulty into the meaning of the ancient prophecies and the sacred books, as well as into the mysteries of faith and all other revealed truths. The magnificent system of Christianity, with its end and means; the astounding gentleness of their master, and his excessive love for mankind; the depth of the counsels of God, and his unlimited power in the various dispensations of his grace: all these abysses, previously unfathomable to the most perfect creatures, lost their darkness for the apostles. As for their hearts, divine love so penetrated them that it banished thence every trace of anything impure, and filled them with the choicest graces and the most sublime virtues. To say all in one word, the Holy Ghost changed them into new men.

An external miracle. The authentic proof of this internal change was the external miracle in their conduct. Do you now see these twelve Galileans, these uneducated fishermen, speaking and writing with an eloquence, a dignity, and a wisdom that throw genius into raptures; quoting with precision, as necessity requires it, and applying with the utmost justness, the most difficult passages of the holy books? All this showed clearly to the most incredulous that they did not speak of themselves. What it showed no less clearly was their courage and their zeal for the glory of God.[821]

A strange sight! Behold twelve fishermen, of whom, a few days ago, the boldest thrice denied his master at the voice of a maidservant; behold these men, I say, who face magistrates, kings, the whole world sworn against them! "See," says St. Chrysostom, "how intrepidly they behave! They triumph over every obstacle, as fire triumphs over straw. Whole cities rise up against them; nations make a league to destroy them; wars, wild beasts, the sword, and the stake threaten them. Vain efforts! They are moved by none of these dangers, which seem to them like idle dreams or harmless pictures. They are unarmed, and they crush armed legions. Illiterate men, they dare to discuss topics with a host of orators, philosophers, and sophists, and confound them. Paul alone lays low the pride of the Academy, the Lyceum, and the Portico: the disciples of Plato, Aristotle, and Zeno are struck dumb before him."[822]

And to render, before the eyes of all ages, an authentic testimony of this twofold miracle, wrought in the apostles, behold, Judaism and paganism fall to the ground, and Christianity rises on their ruins. We repeat, and be sure not to forget it, Pentecost is the date of that moral revolution the most amazing of which history preserves a record. This fact is always living, always speaking, consoling the faith of some, grieving the infidelity of others, preaching to all the love of a religion that has changed the face of the world.

Effects in us. These wonders, which the Holy Ghost wrought on the memorable day of his coming, he still works in well-disposed souls.[823] External gifts have never ceased in the Church: only they are less common, because they are no longer so much needed. But internal gifts, which are always needed, we can always obtain. The Church invites us to ask them, above all days on Pentecost. She is right: now more than ever before is the Holy Ghost indispensable to the world. Wherefore, in the office of this great day, the tender mother of Christians, the protectress of society, the Catholic Church places on the lips of her children and sings along with them the following prose, so proper to draw down the Holy Ghost into hearts:

Veni, Sancte Spiritus, et emitte coelitus lucis tuae radium.

Come, O Holy Ghost, enlighten us more and more; let the rays of thy heavenly light continually shine upon our eyes.

Veni, Pater pauperum; veni, dator munerum; veni, lumen cordium.

Come, thou Father of the poor. Alas! we are poor, especially in regard to the goods of the future life. By this title, we are doubly worthy of thy visit, and of the gifts of thy pity and thy bounty. Pour them out on us in abundance, O thou who art the light of hearts and the distributor of all gifts.

Consolator optime, dulcis hospes animae, dulce refrigerium.

We drag out a miserable life in toil and trouble. In vain do we look for consolation among men. We find only tormenting comforters, who make our ills worse, and leave us under our load of sorrow. O consoling Spirit, thou art the best of friends, the only one that offers a sweet retreat to the afflicted soul, the only one that obtains for it some pleasing refreshment.

In labore requies, in aestu temperies, in fletu solatium.

In thee we find rest after our labors, shelter from the heats of summer, strength against the violence of our passions. Thou wipest away our tears in this sad journey from time to eternity.

O lux beatissima! reple cordis intima tuorum fidelium.

O bright and joyous light! thou dost spread a sweet serenity over souls that are faithful to thee. Sometimes a sad gloom settles on them: fill them with that gladness which accompanies thee.

Sine tuo numine, nihil est in homine, nihil est innoxium.

Without thy divine help, we have nothing, we can do nothing, we are nothing: all that is in us is weakness and misery.

Lava quod est sordidum, riga quod est aridum, sana quod est saucium.

Purify in us whatever is defiled; water these dry and withered hearts; heal the wounds of our souls, by applying effectual remedies to them.

Flecte quod est rigidum, fove quod est frigidum, rege quod est devium.

Bend this rebellious and heedless heart; triumph over its resistance and obstinacy; make it pliable under thy gentle inspirations. Melt that ice which makes it so cold in regard to objects that ought to inflame it with love. Alas! it wanders in the ways of iniquity: bring it back into the paths of justice.

Da tuis fidelibus, in te confitentibus, sacrum septenarium.

We put all our trust in thee: Where else should we put it? Grant to thy servants the seven precious gifts that lead to heaven: Wisdom, understanding, counsel, fortitude, knowledge, piety, and the fear of the Lord—all the graces of which we have such urgent need.

Da virtutis meritum, da salutis exitum, da perenne gaudium.

Adorn our souls with solid Christian virtues, which alone are meritorious in thy sight. Lead us to the happy term of salvation: to that glory, to that joy, to those delights which will never end.

Amen. So be it.[824]

It is needless to say that the festival of Pentecost comes from the apostles, and that it has always been celebrated with the greatest pomp. Let us only add that in the Middle Ages, those ages of lively faith, which form so strange a contrast with our age of cold indifference, there was a usage for the day of Pentecost that made a kind of sacred drama. When the choir were intoning the admirable prose that we have just explained, a burst of trumpets resounded throughout the church, in imitation of the impetuous wind mentioned by St. Luke. At the same time, the roof of the temple let fall a great many sparks, together with all sorts of flowers, and especially leaves of red roses—emblems of joy and of the variety of languages spoken to the nations by the apostles. Lastly, doves let loose on purpose flew through the whole church—touching images of that Spirit who is all strength and mildness.

Let us imagine to ourselves therefore a numerous congregation of the faithful assembled in a spacious nave at the hour when, to the singing with one mind of this beautiful sequence, were joined the loud peal of trumpets, a shower of flowers, numberless fiery sparks expiring above their heads, and the noise of the flapping wings of the doves: we shall then understand how delightfully those souls of ardent faith identified themselves, by going back a few centuries, with the disciples, the apostles, the holy women, and Mary, the Mother of Jesus, in the upper chamber of Jerusalem. What miracles of devotions and sacrifice might not be expected from souls thus roused and vivified!

In those moments of holy enthusiasm, the Christian of the thirteenth century found nothing impossible to his love. Crusades, religious institutions, Gothic cathedrals, are eloquent witnesses to the strength and constancy of that divine love with which he was transported. Well may we exclaim with the pious Cardinal Bona: "Here is love seen… He who comes down from heaven in the fire natural to him shoots forth at the same time his flaming darts!"[825]

Dispositions for celebrating Pentecost. Let us conclude with a reflection useful in regulating our conduct. An ardent desire of receiving the Holy Ghost, and, what is still more important, a disengagement from all inordinate affection to creatures are the means essential to draw this divine Spirit into our souls. See how jealous he is! Assuredly, there could be no sensible attachment more holy or lawful than that of the disciples for their divine master. Yet this attachment should be in some degree banished from their souls before the Holy Ghost could take possession of them. "If I go not," said the Savior to them, "the Paraclete will not come to you."[826]

If then it is certain that the too great attachment of the apostles to the sensible presence of our Lord's humanity was an obstacle to the descent of the Holy Ghost on them, who will be so presumptuous as to flatter himself with the prospect of a visit from the divine Paraclete so long as he remains the slave of his body? To persuade oneself that heavenly sweetness can be combined with the pleasures of the senses, divine balm with poison, the light of the Holy Ghost with the darkness of the world, would be a strange error. What relation is there between truth and falsehood, between the fire of charity and the ice of worldly affection? No, no: the more a man becomes carnal, the farther the Spirit of God departs from him. This is the reason why Christianity is nowadays departing so far from many people. And they say, Christianity is worn out! Blind people, it is they themselves that are worn out!

PRAYER

O my God! who art all love, I thank thee for having sent the Holy Ghost on the apostles, and, by means of them, on the whole world. Never permit that I should contristate this divine Spirit within me.

I am resolved to love God above all things, and my neighbor as myself for the love of God; and, in testimony of this love, I will be much afraid of resisting the inspirations of grace.

Lesson 44: Christianity Brought before the Senses (Continued)—Trinity Sunday

General festival of the Blessed Trinity: Antiquity and universality of this festival.—The Blessed Trinity! Of all religious festivals, this is the oldest, though in one sense it is the newest. By creating the universe, God built himself a temple, and by forming time, he consecrated to himself a festival; "for the Lord made all things for himself."[827] The creature cannot but belong to its Creator and be consecrated to his glory. Now, it is one God in three Persons that is the Creator of every being and of all time. It is therefore true that no religion can, in the main, have any other object than the worship of the Creator of the universe, and consequently of one God in three Persons, who is this Creator. The consecration of the world and of time to the glory of the adorable Trinity had been violated and profaned by paganism. Our Lord, the great restorer, came on earth to repair the consequences of sin, and to bring all things back to their primitive institution. And behold, creatures and time were consecrated anew to the glory of the Blessed Trinity!

Restoration of all things in the name of the Blessed Trinity.—1. *Intelligent creatures.* The Word made flesh ordained that all nations should be regenerated in the name of the Trinity: "Go, teach all nations, baptizing them in the name of the Father, and of the Son, and of the Holy Ghost."[828] Since then the Catholic Church has never ceased to baptize in the name of the three august Persons. And how often, from our cradle to our grave, does she make over us the adorable sign of the Trinity! Are we strengthened by the grace of confirmation? It is in the name of the Holy Trinity. Are our sins forgiven in the sacrament of penance? It is also in the name of the adorable Trinity. Are the body and blood of the Savior presented to us as food? It is likewise with the sign of the most Holy Trinity.

Are the sick anointed with holy oil, are priests ordained, are people married? It is always in the name of the Blessed Trinity. If we receive the blessing of pastors or pontiffs, if we begin a holy office, if the Church addresses prayers to the Most High, it is always with an invocation of the three Persons of the adorable Trinity. Does she sing canticles of joy or hymns of sorrow? She always concludes them by rendering glory to the Father, the Son, and the Holy Ghost. So much for intelligent creatures.

2. *Inanimate creatures.* It is also in the name of the Trinity that all inanimate creatures are sanctified. From one end of the Catholic world to the other, you see the sign of the cross consecrating water, fire, air, earth, salt, wood, stone, iron, linen—in a word, whatever the Church wishes to purify and to withdraw from the common mass. It is the sign of the cross that recalls all these things to their primitive sanctity and disengages them from the evil influences of the devil, by imprinting on them anew the seal of their origin, the seal of the adorable Trinity. Ah, what deep mysteries there are in the sign of the cross, of which the Catholic Church alone has retained the frequent use! Here is

the whole history of the world, its creation in a state of sanctity, its profanation by sin, its restoration by our Lord—by the Blessed Trinity. So much for inanimate creatures.

3. *Time*. By baptism, men become children. Their body becomes a temple; their soul, a priest; their whole life, a festival in honor of the Blessed Trinity. Now, the succession of all individual lives, forming the life of the human race, makes up time. Therefore, by the baptism of man, time is in one sense already consecrated to the glory of the Blessed Trinity; for all our thoughts, words, and actions ought to be referred to the glory of the three divine Persons, and to make up, as it were, a continual hymn in their praise.

Final object of Catholic worship. It belongs in a still more direct sense to the same object, since it is to the Blessed Trinity that the Catholic Church consecrates every moment of her existence. There is not a day of the year nor an hour of the day but, by the lips of her ministers or her children, she is rendering homage to the Trinity. She has even prescribed a formula called the Doxology to honor at every turn the three adorable Persons—Father, Son, and Holy Ghost: a sacred formula, which concludes her psalms, responses, and hymns.

What shall we say of her festivals? See how splendidly our solemnities, which serve as landmarks for time, demonstrate this truth, that the Blessed Trinity is the end of all Catholic worship! What nobler end? Thus, the festivals of the saints and of the Queen of saints are referred to Jesus Christ, of whom all the blessed are members: it is in relation to Jesus Christ that we honor them. In the same manner, it is in relation to the adorable Trinity that we adore Jesus Christ himself, who is essentially united to, or rather is one substance with, the Father and the Holy Ghost. The divine Persons are inseparable, even in our devotions and our worship.[829]

To throw more light on this sublime doctrine. If we honor the Son of God becoming incarnate in the womb of Mary, we immediately see the Father and the Holy Ghost taking part in the accomplishment of this mystery. If we honor Jesus Christ suffering, we immediately see the Father, who delivers him to death, and the Holy Ghost, who, like a divine fire, consumes this innocent victim.[830] If we honor Jesus Christ rising from the dead, we see the Father, who raises him up, and the Holy Ghost, who leads him to a new life.[831] If we honor the Savior ascending into heaven, we see the Father in the glory that surrounds his rest, and the Holy Ghost, whom he sends. Lastly, if we honor our Lord hiding himself, and causing himself to be adored in the Eucharist, we see in him a victim that we cannot honor but by uniting ourselves therewith, and thus immolating ourselves to the Father, the Son, and the Holy Ghost.

Is anything else needed to make us understand that there is no festival in the Christian religion but is truly a festival of the Blessed Trinity, since all the others are only means to honor the Blessed Trinity, and steps to raise us to it as the true and only term of our worship?

Particular festival of the Blessed Trinity. Hence, when there was question of establishing a particular festival of the Blessed Trinity in order to satisfy the devotion of those who sought it, great doctors and great saints were heard to remonstrate. "All the festivals of the year," they said, "being only parts of the general and perpetual festival of the Trinity, is it not superfluous to institute a particular festival, subject to the annual revolution of the others? Is there not reason to fear that a particular festival will lead to forgetfulness of that general and perpetual festival which ought continually to occupy the minds and hearts of Christians? Does it not look like limiting what ought to have no limits, and reducing God himself to the condition of the saints, that is to say, of his own creatures, by establishing a special festival for him? Is it not to ignore the fact that there are no festivals, or temples, or altars, but belong solely to the Blessed Trinity?"

From all these motives, the Catholic Church, acting with that consummate prudence which distinguishes her, was a long time without admitting a particular festival of the Holy Trinity. Pope Alexander II, who ascended the papal chair in 1061, wrote thus: "The festival of the Trinity is differently observed by different Churches; but the Roman Church has no particular festival of the Trinity, because she honors it every day and every hour of the day, all her offices containing its praises and concluding with a tribute of glory to it."[832]

However, the Church of the Eternal City, the mother and mistress of all others, not censuring a particular festival of the Trinity, her daughters that had adopted it continued to celebrate it. According to general belief, it was established in the ninth century by a few bishops, who at first only proposed to supply new food for the piety of their flocks. It was with this view that Stephen, bishop of Liege, caused an office to be written for it about the year 920.

Some neighboring Churches received it, and the festival of the Blessed Trinity spread so much that the abbé Rupert, who lived in the beginning of the twelfth century, speaks of it as a festival adopted in his time, and takes up a whole book with an explanation of its mystery.[833] Its celebration, previously left to the devotion of particular Churches, was fixed for the octave of, or First Sunday after, Pentecost: the change was gradually accomplished in the thirteenth century.[834] This Sunday was chosen for two reasons. The first because it was vacant, that is, it had no office. In effect, the ordination that took place on the previous Saturday began only after the office of vespers and lasted far into the night, especially when the number of clerics to be ordained was large. Oftentimes the ordination was prolonged even to break of day, so as to seem made on Sunday, and that thus the Sunday might have a kind of office that would prevent it from remaining vacant.[835] But as pious persons asked a sacrifice for this day, the office and festival of the Blessed Trinity were placed on it. The second reason was to remind the faithful that the Trinity is the end and consummation of all festivals and mysteries, even those of our Lord.[836]

At length, the Roman Church, seeing that a particular festival of the Blessed Trinity did not interfere with the general and perpetual festival of the three adorable Persons, decided on adopting it herself; but this was only in the fourteenth century, under the pontificate of John XXII. This pope attached it irrevocably to the Sunday after Pentecost, and caused its office to be substituted for that of the octave, which was thenceforth concluded at none on the Saturday of Quarter Tense. The Church assigns to the particular festival of the Blessed Trinity only a secondary rank among the festivals of the year—doubtless not to injure the general festival, and in order to show our inability to celebrate this august mystery worthily. It is so much elevated above our thoughts that the general chapter of Citeaux, held in 1230, while ordering that the festival of the Trinity should be observed in all its houses, forbade any preaching thereon by reason of the difficulty of the matter.[837]

Dogma of the Blessed Trinity: Influence of this mystery.—However, incomprehensible as the mystery of the Blessed Trinity is, it certainly is not useless as a rule of morals. Like the sun, on which we cannot fix our eyes, but whose light dazzles us, and whose existence is evident, the dogma of the Blessed Trinity offers us on all sides the most convincing proofs of its truth. Without mentioning here the references so often made to it in scripture, or the numerous figures under which God gave a glimpse of it to the ancients,[838] we see around us and bear within us images of this mystery.

The sun, for example, offers you light and heat: the sun, the light, and the heat are distinct things, and yet they are all of the same substance and the same age. Created to the likeness of God, man also bears graven on himself the image of the Blessed Trinity. Our soul has three faculties: memory, understanding, and will. These three faculties belong nevertheless to the same substance, and began with it.

Model of our duties toward God. We have also said that the mystery of the Blessed Trinity is far from being useless in the regulation of our life. O men! understand how much this dogma ennobles you. Created to the image of the august Trinity,[839] you ought to take it as your model, and form yourselves thereby: this is a sacred duty for you. Now, you adore a Trinity whose essential characteristic is holiness, and there is no holiness so high but you may reach it by the grace of the sanctifying Spirit, the substantial love of the Father and the Son. To adore the Blessed Trinity worthily, you ought therefore, as far as human weakness permits, to be holy like it.

God is holy in himself, that is to say, there is no sin or shadow of sin in him. Be ye holy in yourselves. God is holy in his creatures, that is to say, he has laid the seal of his holiness on them, and he cannot endure evil or sin in them: he pursues it with unwearied zeal—now mild, now severe, always paternal. Be ye also holy in your works, and holy in your neighbors, either by taking care never to scandalize them or by trying to keep or to deliver them from sin. "Be ye holy," says the Lord to us, "for I am holy."[840] And again: "Be ye perfect as your heavenly Father is perfect; do good to all as he does it to all, making his sun to rise on the good and on the bad, and causing the rain to fall on the fields of the just as well as on those of the unjust."[841]

Model of our duties toward our neighbor. A model of holiness, consequently of our duties toward God, the Blessed Trinity is also the model of our charity, consequently of our duties toward our neighbor. We ought to love one another as the three divine Persons love one another. Such is the command of our Lord himself. This admirable union was the object of the last petitions that he addressed to his Father after the institution of the Blessed Eucharist. He asked that we might be one among ourselves as he is one with his Father. By this holy union, the fruit of grace, he wishes people to acknowledge that his Father sent him on earth, and to distinguish those who belong to him. "May they be one," he says, "that the world may know that thou hast sent me! By this shall all men know that you are my disciples, if you love one another."[842] "What dost thou ask of us, O divine master," exclaims St. Augustine, "but that we should be perfectly united in heart and will? Thou dost wish that, by grace and imitation, we should become what the three divine Persons are by the necessity of their being, and that, as all is common among them, so the charity of Christianity should divest us of all personal interests."

Who can tell the wondrous efficacy of the mystery of the Blessed Trinity? Thanks to it, we see, in the midst of pagan society, in the midst of a society of selfishness and hatred, the early Christians, those faithful disciples of the three august Persons, having but one heart and one soul; and we hear the astonished pagans crying out: "See how much these Christians love one another; see how they are ready to die for one another!" If there are yet a few drops of Christian blood in our veins, let us imitate our ancestors; let us be united by charity; let us have the same sentiments, as we have the same faith, the same baptism, the same Father.[843] Let our hearts and our goods be in common by charity. Thus shall that holy society which we have with God, and in God with our neighbor, be perfected on earth, until it is consummated in heaven.

Model of our duties toward ourselves. We also find in the Holy Trinity a model of our duties toward ourselves. The object of all these duties is to reestablish in us that order which was disturbed by sin, to place the flesh under the spirit and the spirit under God; in other words, to renew in us the harmony and sanctity that characterize the three august Persons. Each of us ought to say, "I am the image of a thrice holy God. How noble I am! What respect I ought to have for myself! what fear of degrading this sacred image in myself or in others! what eagerness to restore it, to perfect it more and more!" Yes, the few words, "I am the image of God," have inspired more virtuous deeds and prevented more wicked ones than all the fine maxims of philosophers!

Look at Francis Xavier. Nothing more celebrated than the expression that he used to be continually repeating: *O sanctissima Trinitas*—"O most Holy Trinity!" During more than ten years, the echoes of the East were awakened by this mysterious exclamation, which was the war cry of the St. Paul of modern times. To excite himself to the gigantic war that he had undertaken against Indian paganism, Francis Xavier considered the august image of the Holy Trinity disfigured in so many millions of men, and he cried out: *O sanctissima Trinitas!*

A divine fire then took possession of him, his breast heaved, and tears flowed from his eyes. With the quickness of lightning he traversed unknown regions, pulled down idols, and scattered miracles around him. And on thousands and thousands of brows he poured the regenerating stream and restored the disfigured image of the most Holy Trinity. Neither death nor hunger, nor thirst, nor the powers of men, nor the powers of hell could stay or cool his zeal in repairing the spoiled image of the three august Persons: *O sanctissima Trinitas!*

What shall we say of the sentiments of gratitude that the contemplation of this great mystery excites? The Father, who created us; the Son, who redeemed us; the Holy Ghost, who sanctified us: Do you know any subject more proper to elevate and purify our affections, or to give dignity to our conduct? Modern nations! it is to the mystery of the august Trinity that you are indebted for not being bowed down at the feet of idols. If you dare, say that you are indebted to it for nothing.

As for us Christians, let us honor the Blessed Trinity by all the homage in our power. Let us often say that beautiful prayer: "Glory be to the Father, and to the Son, and to the Holy Ghost, as it was in the beginning, is now, and ever shall be, world without end. Amen."[844] Three persons sometimes enter into a holy union, and agree to say together or separately every day—morning, noon, and evening—the *Gloria Patri* seven times, followed by an *Ave Maria* once, in honor of the Blessed Trinity. This is a devotion authorized by the Church and enriched with great indulgences: among others, a plenary indulgence on two Sundays each month.[845] It is a good means of repairing the blasphemies of the wicked.

Let us celebrate joyfully the particular festival that the Church has consecrated to the three adorable Persons; but let us remember that our whole life ought to be one continual festival in their honor. Let us adore this incomprehensible mystery in the silence of annihilation. Let us imitate the three divine Persons by our charity and sanctity, and let us be full of gratitude for the good things that we have received from them. Let us take care to renew our baptismal vows on this day, and to awake within us a lively zeal for our own perfection and for the sanctification of our neighbor. It is thus that we shall enter into the spirit of the Church, that we shall fulfill the duties of creatures toward the Creator, and that we shall perfect within us the august image of the Blessed Trinity.

PRAYER

O my God! who art all love, I thank thee for having revealed to us the mystery of the Blessed Trinity. Fill our souls with gratitude toward the Father, who created us; the Son, who redeemed us; and the Holy Ghost, who sanctified us.

I am resolved to love God above all things, and my neighbor as myself for the love of God; and, in testimony of this love, I will often ask myself whose image I am.

Lesson 45: Christianity Brought before the Senses (Continued)—Corpus Christi

Corpus Christi: Antiquity and universality of this festival.—We may say of the festival of the Blessed Sacrament that it dates from the origin of the world, like the festival of the Blessed Trinity. The patriarchs celebrated it by offering up sacrifices figurative of the great victim. All peoples also renewed the memory of it on their bloodstained altars; for it was from the primitively revealed idea of a spotless victim, capable of expiating crime, that the idea of sacrifice came to the human race. How, I ask you, could such a strange thought have entered the mind of man as that God would be appeased by the blood of a beast? Thus, all the ancient sacrifices were figurative of the great sacrifice of Calvary. It matters little that the knowledge of this profound mystery was altered by paganism: the fact is no less certain.[846]

But it is especially since the publication of the gospel that the festival of the Eucharist has become continual on the earth. The apostles, faithful to the command that their divine master had given them of renewing the mysterious sacrifice of the last supper and celebrating it in memory of him, made the festival of the Eucharist as old and as widespread as the Church. Setting out from this period, the divine blood has never ceased for a single moment to flow in all quarters of the world.

Its place in Catholic worship. See the admirable harmony that exists between the festivals of Pentecost, the Trinity, and the Eucharist! On the festival of Pentecost, the Church begins by celebrating her birth. Then comes the festival of the Blessed Trinity, whose daughter she is, and whose image she wishes to be: so she declares. Hence, on Trinity Sunday she earnestly implores the first of Christian virtues—charity—as the gospel of the day shows. Before her shines the festival of the Blessed Eucharist, which is her treasure and her life. But as it is not enough to be born, nor even to have a prospect of food, she reminds us, on the Sunday within the octave of Corpus Christi, of the obstacles and dispositions in regard to receiving the Holy Eucharist.

Thus, the adorable Trinity is the essential and primary object of all religion and of all festivals; and the august Eucharist is the perpetual sacrifice, and the holiest worship that we can render to the Trinity. In other words, every year is a festival of the Trinity, which we adore, and of the Eucharist, by which we adore it.

Need we after this be surprised that so much slowness was shown in appointing particular days for honoring these two great mysteries? If at length the Church did so, her intention was not to exclude the Trinity or the Eucharist from other festivals, or to oppose their perpetual festivals. So far from it, she wished to confirm these two fundamental truths in the minds of all people: a) that the three divine Persons are the only objects of our honor and adoration during the whole course of the year, everything else being honored only in regard to them; and b) that the most essential honor rendered to the Blessed Trinity on all festivals is the sacrifice of the body and blood of our Lord. Hence, God is the term of Catholic worship; and Jesus Christ is the mediator between God and man, the high priest of Catholic worship. This is the whole of the liturgy, the sum total of religion. What more sublime, and at the same time so simple? Where shall we find a richer source of noble thoughts, lofty sentiments, generous resolutions? O my God! how much are they to be pitied who know neither the beauties nor the riches of Christianity!

Institution of a particular festival in honor of the Blessed Sacrament.—Formerly, Holy Thursday was the festival of the Blessed Sacrament, and it is so still. This is the reason why our ancestors in the faith went to Communion every Holy Thursday; why the Mass of Holy Thursday is still accompanied with all the pomp and ceremony of a great festival, though the Church is then in grief and mourning; and, lastly, why there is only one Mass said on Holy Thursday, thus recalling the last supper more vividly. All the other priests wait to communicate from the hand of the celebrant, as the apostles communicated from the hand of our Lord.

The time came when Corpus Christi should be added to Holy Thursday, in order to honor the august sacrament of our altars. Here again behold how much in harmony with all the wants of religion and society are the institutions of the Church! It was the thirteenth century. Men would soon be met so bold as to attack the most amiable of our mysteries, that which is like the heart of Catholicity, and consequently the foundation stone of society. To the blasphemies and outrages of innovators, there should be opposed a splendid manifestation of faith in the real presence of our Lord among men; to their sacrilegious mockeries, an authentic testimony of respect and love; to their horrible profanations, a solemn expiation. Wickliffe, Zuinglius, Calvin! guilty foes of the mystery of love, it is against you and your unfortunate followers that the great festival of Corpus Christi shall be established!

God wills it. But to whom shall he make known his design? Here let us pause a moment to consider the application of the divine law formulated by the great apostle when he says, "God hath chosen the weak and foolish things of this world to work his wonders."[847] All glory belongs to God. He is jealous of it; he resigns it to no person: and this is the reason why he employs the commonest means for the attainment of the greatest ends. The weakness of the instrument proves the skill of him who uses it, and obliges man to cry out: "To God alone be all honor and glory!"[848] This law is fulfilled, not only in the order of religion, but in all others. As an occasion presents itself, it will not be amiss to prove by facts what we have just said.

Search the history of the world. A whole people groan under the slavery of Pharao: What instrument will God choose to deliver them? An obscure shepherd of Madian—Moses. A dreadful giant spreads consternation through the army of Israel: Who will strike him down? A young shepherd of Bethlehem—David. Holophernes and Aman threaten to exterminate the holy nation: Who will break the pride of these haughty men? Two humble women—Judith and Esther. There is question of making the pagan world fall on its knees before the cross: Who will accomplish this prodigy? Twelve poor fishermen. St. Gregory VII, St. Ignatius, St. Teresa, and St. Vincent de Paul come next, like so many monuments raised along the highroad of time, informing us that the divine law is ever in force: "God chooses the weak things of the world to work his wonders." So much for the religious order.

Now for the social order. There is question of uniting peoples separated by immense oceans, and of rendering voyages possible across a trackless and almost boundless expanse of water: What means will God employ to work this new prodigy? A little magnet and steel—the compass. It is necessary to discover a world lost in the midst of the ocean: Who is called to this glory? An obscure fisherman of Genoa—Christopher Columbus. In war, what does the God of hosts take to produce the most astounding effects? A little saltpeter—gunpowder. In commerce, if he wishes to enrich whole provinces and to afford a livelihood to millions of people, what will he consider enough? A silkworm. In the various arts and industries, what does he select to work incredible wonders? A little boiling water—steam. Man, the image of God, aspires to a kind of ubiquity; he wishes to be instantly present by his words at every point of the globe: What does God give him to satisfy his desire? A spark—electricity.

And are you surprised that he observes the same conduct in the supernatural order? Ah! it is here especially that he should hide the means, so as to let his almighty hand appear more plainly. To be brief, God is everything in the order of grace and in the order of nature, and he wishes this to be known. A lesson too often forgotten! which says to all, kings and subjects, rich and poor, learned and ignorant: "If you wish to be employed in anything great, be humble!"

The blessed Juliana. This law received a splendid illustration in the establishment of the festival of Corpus Christi. As we have said, it was in the thirteenth century. At this time, there lived in the shade of a lowly cloister a nun forgotten by the world and by herself. It was on her that the Almighty cast his eyes for the accomplishment of his magnificent design, as he had cast them on Mary for the accomplishment of the incarnation.

Near the village of Liege there was a convent of the Hospitallers of Mount Cornillon. Among the chaste doves that dwelt there was a young novice, sixteen years of age: a humble girl, born at the village of Retina, in 1193. Her name was Juliana. This earthly angel being one day in prayer, the spouse of pure souls, he who loves to communicate himself to humble hearts, made known to her that he wished a festival to be established in honor of the sacrament of his love. Whether through timidity or through fear of illusion, the pious child kept this revelation hidden deep in her heart for nearly twenty years. Only, she endeavored to supply for what the Church had not yet done, by redoubling her devotion toward Jesus in the Blessed Sacrament.

In 1230, having been elected prioress of the convent of Mount Cornillon, she felt herself more earnestly urged to lay open her mind. The first person to whom she spoke was a canon of St. Martin's, Liege, very highly esteemed by the people on account of the holiness of his life. She persuaded him to communicate the affair to theologians and pastors of the Church. The canon fulfilled his mission very zealously, and succeeded with most of those to whom he addressed himself.

He interested in this pious undertaking the bishop of Cambrai and the chancellor of the Church of Paris, but above all the provincial of the Dominicans of Liege, who afterward became cardinal and archdeacon of Liege, bishop of Verdun, patriarch of Jerusalem, and finally pope, under the name of Urban IV. The blessed Juliana, assured of the approbation of so many persons eminent for their learning and piety, caused an office of the Holy Sacrament to be composed, of which she herself gave the idea and plan, and had it approved of by the principal theologians of the country.

In 1246, the bishop of Liege declared in his synod the establishment of a special festival of the Blessed Sacrament, and ordered its public and solemn celebration throughout his whole diocese. A serious illness prevented him from putting the finishing stroke to this arrangement by a command that he was on the point of publishing. Nevertheless, he did not die without having the satisfaction of seeing the office of the new festival celebrated in his presence. The canons of St. Martin's were the first who solemnized it in the city of Liege—in 1247. But holy works must suffer contradiction. God permits it that the instruments he employs may attribute their success to him alone. This precious seal was not wanting to the work of the blessed Juliana. A persecution of which she was the object, joined with the death of the bishop of Liege, suspended the celebration of the new festival.

In the meantime, Juliana herself died, and it seemed as if her efforts were to die with her. This fate was inevitable if the movement had only been the work of man. But in 1258, two years after her death, a recluse of the city of Liege, who had been her intimate friend, earnestly pressed the new bishop to use his influence with the pope for the establishment throughout the whole Church of the festival of the Blessed Sacrament, such as it was observed in St. Martin's of Liege. The elevation of Urban IV to the pontificate was regarded as most opportune for this undertaking, the end and the means of which he had previously approved. However, according to the wise custom of the Roman Church, the vicar of Jesus Christ took time to examine an affair of so much importance. Delays followed delays, until at length a splendid miracle put an end to the holy father's hesitation, and hastened the settlement of the matter.

Miracle of Bolsena. Urban IV, accompanied by the Sacred College, was at Orvieto, a small town about sixty miles from Rome, and near Bolsena. In the last-mentioned place, a priest, while celebrating Mass in the Church of St. Catherine, which still exists, let some drops of the precious blood fall accidentally on the corporal. To remove the traces of this occurrence, he folds and folds the sacred linen in such a way as to absorb the adorable blood. The corporal is afterward opened; and it is found that the blood has penetrated all the folds and left everywhere a figure of the sacred host, perfectly drawn, in the color of blood. The rumor of what has happened arrives in a few hours at Orvieto. By the command of the sovereign pontiff, the miraculous linen is brought to this town. The miracle is proved, and the corporal, enclosed in a reliquary, one of the masterpieces of the Middle Ages, is kept to this day in the cathedral.

Meanwhile, the holy father, mindful of the entreaties made to him regarding the establishment of the festival of the Blessed Sacrament, institutes this solemnity, and commands it to be celebrated with all the pomp of festivals of the first class. He assigns it the Thursday after the octave of Pentecost, and this for two reasons: a) it is the first Thursday free from the offices of paschal time; and b) it is becoming to take the day of the week on which our Lord instituted the Eucharist. We are ignorant of the year and the place in which the bull of institution was given. We only know that the brief addressed by Urban IV to the blessed Eva, a recluse of St. Martin's, Liege, is dated 11th of August, 1264.[849]

Object and office of this festival. The chief motives of the institution of this festival were, as expressed in the bull, to confound the malice of heretics, to repair the outrages committed against our Savior, and to declare aloud the Catholic faith in the real presence. "Without doubt," adds the pope, "Holy Thursday is the true festival of the Holy Sacrament; but on this day the Church is so very much occupied in bewailing the death of her spouse, in reconciling penitents, and in consecrating the holy chrism, that it was good to take another day when she might manifest all her joy and supply for what she could not do on Holy Thursday. For the rest, all the solemnities of the year are the solemnity of the Eucharist; and this particular festival has been instituted only to make up for the faults of which we may have been guilty on the general festival."[850]

The festival of Corpus Christi once established, the only question was to find a poet worthy of the mystery of love. Providence had him ready. At this time, there shone one of the brightest geniuses that ever appeared in the world: he was called Thomas of Aquin. This great man, the glory of his age, surnamed the Angelic Doctor, on account of the purity of his life as well as the sublimity of his doctrine, being then at Orvieto, received an order from Urban IV to write an office for the Holy Sacrament.[851]

The saint set to work, and, yielding to the inspirations of his heart, composed the office that is sung even to this day: an imperishable masterpiece, wherein poetry, faith, and piety strive for the palm. Hence it is justly regarded as the most regular and admirable of all the offices of the Church, as well for the strength and the elegance of its expressions, which in turn convey sentiments of the most tender charity and the most precise doctrine regarding the Eucharistic mystery, as for the exact proportion of its parts and the closeness of its relations between the figures of the old testament and the realities of the new.

Like a grain of mustard seed, the work of the blessed Juliana of Mount Cornillon had gradually sprung up from the humble cell of a convent to the pontifical throne. It was to grow still more, but with time and amid storms.

Urban IV having died on the 2nd of October, 1264, God permitted that one of his immediate successors should not press the execution of his decree. For forty years there were few churches, besides that of Liege, in which the new festival was celebrated. It remained thus neglected till the time of the General Council of Vienne, assembled in 1311. It was herein that, to give the festival of Corpus Christi all the splendor and stability that it deserved, Pope Clement V confirmed the bull of institution issued by Urban IV. The august solemnity was eagerly accepted by all the fathers of the council, in presence of the kings of France, England, and Aragon. Such is the history of the festival of the Blessed Sacrament: a glorious triumph appointed in reparation for the outrages done to our Lord in the most august as well as the most amiable of all our mysteries.[852]

Procession: Dispositions for assisting at it. The most splendid part of the offices of Corpus Christi, that which most distinguishes this festival from all others, is the solemn procession. The Savior is herein borne along triumphantly with all the pomp and magnificence possible. This procession, established by Pope Urban IV, was earnestly recommended by the holy Council of Trent.[853] Everything helps to render it solemn: it seems as if all nature wished to take part in it. It is the time of beautiful days; it is the season of roses and lilies; it is the period when millions of little birds, still covered with the down of their youth, attempt their first flight and their first song. There is nothing more graceful than the procession of the Blessed Sacrament in villages, where the fields, the trees, and the meadows, in all the splendor of their attire, reflect their beauty on the rustic repository; nothing more imposing in inland towns, where the boom of cannon mingles with sacred hymns; nothing more solemn in maritime towns, where the wide ocean gives some idea of the infinite.

But what must I do to correspond with the wishes of that God who is borne in triumph? First, assist at the procession. Man always does himself honor by humbling himself before God. And then, ought not gratitude toward that God Savior who vouchsafes to travel through our streets and our squares, scattering benefits around him as of yore, draw me along in his footsteps, and chain me as it were to his chariot? Proud men! who scorn to walk in the train of the great King, who imagine yourselves degraded by taking part in our processions, you are not always so hard to please. Is it not you that we see, vile slaves, chained to the chariot of ambition or voluptuousness, and following through the mud the tortuous windings of its wheels?

I will therefore assist at the procession. The presence of my God tells me how respectfully and recollectedly I ought to do so. His goodness speaks to my heart and asks my gratitude. The flowers scattered along the way, the clouds of incense rising to the sky, and the holy canticles resounding through the air invite me to a return of love, to a spirit of sacrifice, to thanksgiving, to prayer. And these repositories that I meet from time to time, by making me admire the infinite condescension of the master of the universe, who is pleased to rest in them, will tell me that my heart ought also to be a repository from which the purest virtues should exhale their perfumes. I will therefore give free play to my faith: no more is needed.

The noisy heedless crowd, who sometimes almost block up the passage of the august cortege, will be a new motive of compunction and fervor to me. I will say, not like James and John, the sons of thunder: "Master, will you that we call down fire from heaven on their guilty heads?"[854] I will utter in sighs the tender words of the divine Lamb: "Father, forgive them for they know not what they do."[855]

Thus, a faithful child of the great Catholic family, I will not, like so many, be ashamed to honor and to follow my father. He will remember me when he comes as supreme judge of the living and the dead; and, if my heart hold fast to him, I shall take part in that solemn and last procession which will rise glorious toward heaven, under the leadership of Jesus triumphant, while the proud despisers of Jesus humbled will sink, overwhelmed with shame and confusion, into the fiery abyss. Gratitude, compunction, thanksgiving, and reparation will occupy my mind and heart during the procession, all the rest of the day, and till the end of the octave.

Miracle of Faverney. We cannot better conclude this lesson than by relating one of those numerous miracles by which our Lord has vouchsafed to strengthen the faith of his children in the reality of his presence in the august Sacrament of the Altar.

In the year 1608, that unfortunate time when the Church was still bewailing the sacrilegious attacks which the Calvinists, up in arms, had long made in France on the very Person of our Lord, whose real presence in the Holy Sacrament they refused to acknowledge, it pleased the divine goodness to make known, for the consolation of the faithful and the confusion of heretics, the truth of this august mystery by a most splendid miracle.

In consequence of certain indulgences granted by our holy father the pope, the Benedictine monks of Faverney, a small town in the Diocese of Besançon, were accustomed, on the eve of Pentecost, to adorn a chapel in their abbatial church. On the altar stood a tabernacle, which contained two consecrated hosts, enclosed in a silver monstrance. This year, on the 25th of May, the Blessed Sacrament had been exposed. Night having come and everyone having gone away, the doors of the church were closed. On the altar of the chapel were two lighted candles. The sparks that fell from them, as there was much reason to believe, set fire to the ornaments.

A thick smoke soon spread on all sides; nearly everything in the chapel was burnt—cloths, steps, tabernacles, etc.: little more was left than ashes and pieces of charred wood. But who can tell the sentiments of the religious when they entered the church the next day? Seized with fear, they lifted up their eyes, and, above the heap of hot cinders, beheld the monstrance miraculously suspended in the middle of the church.

The fame of the prodigy immediately spreads. A multitude of persons, belonging to Faverney and its neighborhood, rush to the scene. The crowd is immense. The monstrance, containing the two holy hosts, remains suspended in the air. On Tuesday, the third festival day of Whitsuntide, many priests came with their parishioners to celebrate Holy Mass in this church. One of them was saying it at the high altar. The august sacrifice was on the point of being accomplished when the candle burning before the Blessed Sacrament suddenly went out. It was relighted; it again went out. It was again relighted; it went out a third time. This occurrence led all present to fix their eyes on the monstrance, that they might see what was going to happen. After the first elevation, at the moment when the priest was laying the sacred host on the altar, the monstrance, which had remained suspended in the air for thirty-three hours, gradually descended, and settled on a corporal placed beside the chalice.

How admirable is thy providence, O my God! By this miracle, it was pleased to preserve our ancestors from the errors of the Calvinists. It was pleased to confirm them more and more in the Catholic religion, by making known to them in a most miraculous manner the truth of all that the Church teaches us regarding the Blessed Sacrament, Mass, and indulgences, so many articles of our faith that Calvinists reject.

In the juridical investigation that Monsignor De Rye, then archbishop of Besançon, caused to be made on this matter, he received the depositions and signatures of fifty persons among the most respectable of those who had witnessed the miraculous occurrence. Every year, the office of the 30th of October recalls it to the memory and the gratitude of the faithful in the Diocese of Besançon. As for us who write these lines, time shall never efface from our mind the solemn procession on the day after Pentecost by which the town of Faverney annually celebrates the memory of this miracle. In 1827, it was given us to bear in our hands the miraculous host, and to offer it to the adoration of an immense multitude of people.

PRAYER

O my God! who art all love, I thank thee for having instituted the festival of the Blessed Sacrament. Grant me the grace to celebrate it with all the piety necessary to indemnify thee for the outrages of which thou art the object in the adorable sacrament of thy altars.

I am resolved to love God above all things, and my neighbor as myself for the love of God; and, in testimony of this love, I will assist at benediction every day during the octave of Corpus Christi.

Lesson 46: Christianity Brought before the Senses (Continued)—Sacred Heart

Festival of the Sacred Heart: Object and motive.—Behold a new festival, still more touching if possible than that whose history we have just related. The festival of the Sacred Heart! At this name, all the tenderness of Christian souls is moved. What, then, is the festival of the Sacred Heart? What is its object? What is its motive?

1. *What is the festival of the Sacred Heart?* And I—I ask you, what are the festivals of the Nativity, the Resurrection, and the Ascension, but festivals of our Lord himself, to which these mysteries gave occasion, and on which we commemorate some great events in the Redeemer's life? What, too, is the festival of the Blessed Sacrament but one of the festivals of our Lord, the motive of which is the memory of the institution of the Eucharist? What, then, shall the festival of the Sacred Heart of Jesus be? Nothing but one of the festivals of our Lord, to which his immense charity for mankind gave occasion; and this charity is represented or symbolized by a heart of flesh. The answer to the first question also solves the second.

2. *What is the object of this festival?* We must know that all Catholic festivals have for their particular object and matter some intelligent persons, as the Blessed Trinity—Jesus Christ, God and man—or a saint. It is not a mystery, it is not the memory of a benefit, it is not the virtue of a saint that is the material object of any festival whatsoever: all these things are only occasions and motives thereof. Hence, the material object of the festival of the Sacred Heart is the same as on all other festivals of our Lord: that is to say, it is our Lord himself.

3. *What is the motive of this festival?* It is at once the immense charity of the Savior for mankind, and his Sacred Heart, which is the symbol and the victim thereof. Such was the end, such the intention of the Church in the institution of this solemnity. We see all this clearly in the double office that she gave it: one for the kingdom of Poland, and another for the kingdom of Portugal.

In the first, she expresses herself thus: "That the faithful might honor with more devotion and fervor the charity of Jesus Christ suffering, under the symbol of his Sacred Heart, and gather more abundant fruits therefrom, Clement XIII permitted certain churches, which had petitioned on the matter, to celebrate the festival of this most holy Heart."[856] The veneration of the charity of Jesus Christ, under the symbol of his Sacred Heart, was therefore one of the motives for the concession of this festival.

In the second, approved for the kingdom of Portugal, the Church proposes another motive. It is expressed in the invitatory: "Oh come, let us adore the Heart of Jesus, the victim of charity!"[857] The Heart of Jesus, the victim of charity, was therefore another motive for the concession of this festival, and we cannot doubt that the real heart of Jesus Christ is here referred to.

Let us therefore conclude by saying, the charity of the Savior for mankind, and his real physical heart, which was its victim and which represents it as a symbol, are the motives of this new festival of the man-God.

If we were asked why this festival is not called the festival of Jesus Christ, but the festival of his Sacred Heart, we should answer that, in order to distinguish them from one another, the names of the different festivals of our Lord are taken, not from their object, but from their motive. Thus we say the festivals of the Nativity, Epiphany, and Ascension, because their motives are the birth of the Savior, his adoration by the Magi, and his return to heaven, though our Lord is always their object.

If we were asked again why the charity of the Son of God toward mankind is honored under the symbol of his Heart, and not under any other symbol, we should give a very natural reason. Does not experience tell us that the heart is that portion of the human body which feels most the passions of the soul? This may arise from the fact that the heart is the great motive power of all our humors. It follows hence that motions ought to be more sensibly felt at the place where the material cause acts, at the source of vital motion. Be all this as it may, the sensations, the emotions, the beatings that the heart is subject to, in consequence of the love that dwells in the soul, are so many unimpeachable witnesses to a correspondence existing between the material heart and the spiritual soul.[858]

Hence, the universal custom among mankind of taking the heart for love. And this custom is founded on the holy scripture itself, where we see that the infinite love of God is sometimes expressed under the symbol of a human heart. God says to Heli: "I will raise me up a faithful priest, who shall do according to my heart";[859] whereby we see that the heart is put in the place and as a symbol of the will or the love of God. Other examples of this mode of speaking are not rare in holy writ.

Lastly, if we were asked what worship the Catholic Church renders to the material heart of Jesus Christ, we should answer that she renders a worship of *latria* or adoration to it. In effect, the heart of our Lord is adorable, as his sacred body is adorable, on account of its hypostatic union with the divinity. For it is evident that the worship of adoration rendered to the material heart of Jesus Christ is due to it precisely because it is the Heart of Jesus Christ, God and man, and because in this heart of flesh we honor our Lord altogether, without separation or division. "I believe," says Muzarelli, "that we can express the manner of this worship in a few words by saying that the material heart of Jesus Christ is adored with a worship of *latria* in Jesus Christ, with Jesus Christ, and because of the excellence of Jesus Christ"[860]

Difference between devotion to the Sacred Heart and devotion to the Blessed Sacrament. It is on the festival of which we speak that the adorable Heart of our Lord is specially honored, and this leads us to answer another question that may be addressed to us: What difference is there between devotion to the Sacred Heart of Jesus and devotion to the Blessed Sacrament? Well, in devotion to the most Holy Sacrament, the motive is to honor the sacred flesh of Jesus Christ united to the Word, and by this union made truly worthy of the adoration of angels and men. In devotion to the Sacred Heart, the essential motive is to honor the heart of Jesus united to the divinity; above all, to acknowledge that love with which he was consumed for mankind, and to make him reparation for what he has suffered and what he is still every day pleased to suffer from mankind in his sacrament of love, the most wonderful invention that ever issued from his divine Heart.[861]

History of the festival of the Sacred Heart: Its harmony with the wants of the Church and of society.—Let us now come to the origin of the festival of the Sacred Heart, and its harmony with the wants of the Church and of society. If Belgium had the glory of bestowing on the Catholic world the festival of the Blessed Sacrament, France was chosen to give it that of the Sacred Heart. In Belgium, I see a holy child to whom God vouchsafes to communicate his designs. In France, he chooses a humble virgin to make her the confidante of the secrets of his divine Heart. Thus, at a distance of four centuries, I still behold the accomplishment of the great law in virtue of which "God chooses the weak things of this world to work his wonders."[862]

In the seventeenth century, there lived in the Visitation Convent at Paray-le-Monial, Charolais, a holy nun, named Margaret Mary Alacoque. A model of wisdom, submission, and penance, this earthly angel was one day in adoration before the holy altar during the octave of Corpus Christi, when the God of pure souls appeared to her, and, showing her his adorable Heart, said: "Behold this Heart, which has loved men so much that it has spared nothing, but gone on even to the wasting and consuming of itself in order to let them see its love. In return, I receive nothing from most people but ingratitude, which appears in the contempt, the irreverences, the sacrileges, and the coldness that they have for me in this sacrament. But what is still more painful to me is that hearts consecrated to me treat me thus. Wherefore I ask thee that the first Friday after the octave of the Blessed Sacrament be consecrated as a special festival to honor my Heart, by making it a solemn reparation, and by communicating on this day with the intention of atoning for the unworthy treatment that it has received while it has been exposed on altars."[863]

At the same time, the Savior promised his humble handmaid that the most abundant treasures of grace would be given to those who should devote themselves to the worship of his Sacred Heart.[864]

The seal of the works of God, I mean contradiction, was soon laid on the new devotion. Scarcely had the venerable Margaret Mary spoken of her revelation when she was treated as a visionary. Contempt, mockery, penances, all kinds of annoyances were tried; but nothing could make her withdraw her words. Like the apostles, she might say: "We cannot but speak what we have seen and heard."[865]

Hitherto, all had taken place within the convent. The storm became far more violent when the revelation transpired outside. The Jansenists, above all, attacked the proposed devotion with the fiercest rage; and the pastors of the Church remained in suspense till the will of heaven should appear with new evidence. This moment was not far distant, but the humble servant of God did not live to see it. On the 17th of October, 1690, she sank into the tomb, bearing with her the crown of thorns that the Savior gives as a favor to his dearly beloved spouses. This crown was changed in heaven into a crown of glory, and soon the earth also changed its sentiments and its language regarding both the servant of God and the devotion to the Sacred Heart.

Heaven let its powerful voice be heard—the voice of a miracle. In 1720, Provence was ravaged by an unexampled plague. Marseilles was the first place attacked, and in a very short time this large city lost half its inhabitants. Monsignor de Belzunce de Castelmoron, bishop of Marseilles, seeing how inadequate were all human resources, resolved on having recourse to him who holds in his hands the keys of death and hell, and on opposing to the anger of God the merits of the Sacred Heart of his divine Son.

O hero of charity, you are right! Seek in the public worship of our Lord's Heart a remedy for an evil that has no remedy on earth, and you shall not be mistaken. The holy bishop exhorted all his clergy to enter into the spirit with which he was himself animated. He ordered that the festival of the Heart of Jesus should thenceforth be solemnized on the first Friday after the octave of Corpus Christi, and that it should be celebrated as one of the greatest festivals of the year. He went still further: he made a solemn and public consecration of his diocese and himself to the Sacred Heart of Jesus. His prayer was heard. From that day, the evil, previously so great, began to decline very much, and in a little while it disappeared altogether. These things the magistrates of the city acknowledged and attested in an authentic act. But God had in reserve a still more marked protection for the fervor of the pontiff and his people.

In May, 1722, the plague, which was supposed to have long departed, broke out anew in the city, and filled it with a strange consternation. Death, the king of terrors, erected his throne in the midst of this large city, yesterday so eager for business and pleasure. Abandoned by those who could flee, Marseilles soon presented the image of a battlefield, full of dead and dying. Then was to be seen again that sublime devotedness which always comes forward in public calamities, so long as Catholicity holds sway. Monsignor de Belzunce renewed all that St. Charles Borromeo had done in Milan. Here again a sublime conflict, worthy of the gaze of angels and men, between the fury of the disease and the zeal of charity! Here again dangers faced, the dying ministered to, the poor relieved! Here again priests dying by hundreds near the plague-stricken, and with their last breath exhorting others to die! Here again fearful sufferings and ineffable consolations! Here again a want of wood for coffins and of porters for cemeteries! But the priests nowhere failed to relieve and to console.

It was from Marseilles that Belzunce wrote thus:

"I am still, by the grace of God, left standing amid the dead and dying. All around me are fallen: of all the ministers of the Lord that accompanied me there remains only my chaplain. During eight days I have seen two hundred dead bodies putrifying under the windows of my house. I have been obliged to walk through the streets, all without exception, bordered on each side with corpses half putrified and torn by dogs, and the middle full of the chattels of the plague-stricken: the ground everywhere in such a filthy state that one would hardly know where to put his foot. A sponge—wet with vinegar—to my nose, and my soutane tucked up under my arms, I have been obliged to step over these infected corpses in order to keep clear of them, and to confess and comfort the dying thrown out of their houses.

"I am, as it were, without confessors. The priests have wrought prodigies of zeal and charity, and laid down their lives for their brethren. All the Jesuits but three or four are dead. Some of them came a long way to die here. Thirty-three Capuchins are dead. Father De la Fare, notwithstanding his great age, has escaped, so that at least one Father of the Holy Cross may survive the others. Twenty Recollects and as many Observantins have died in the service of the sick; many Discalced Carmelites and Minims; and some Great Carmelites. I will not speak of my own dear ecclesiastics that have sacrificed themselves. I look upon myself as a general that has lost the best part of his troops."

Two hundred and fifty priests of the Diocese of Marseilles and the neighboring dioceses had actually succumbed, and, after the malady, there daily arrived new ones, who envied the fate of the former.

When the contagion seemed on its decline, Mgr. De Belzunce caused an altar to be prepared in the middle of the Corso. It was All Saints' day. He came forth from his episcopal palace barefooted and with a rope round his neck, like St. Charles Borromeo, and, preceded by the priests and monks that were left, went and fell on his knees before that God who punishes and pardons. Here he sang: *Parce, Domine, parce populo tuo!* praying earnestly for his flock. Oh, who can tell the emotion both of pastor and people on such an occasion? The supplications continued, and on the 15th of November, Mgr. De Belzunce gave benediction to the whole city from the top of a steeple, amid the pealing of bells and the roar of cannon, which warned all the inhabitants to put themselves in prayer. This imposing spectacle spread a religious awe among the people.

Notwithstanding so much charity on the part of the pastors, and so many tears and prayers on the part of the faithful, heaven remained insensible, and the scourge continued its ravages: the glory of taking it away was reserved for the Heart of Jesus. In effect, this Sacred Heart became a second time the happy refuge of the holy prelate. At his solicitation, the magistrates in a body made a vow to go every year, in the name of the city, to the Church of the Visitation on the festival of the Sacred Heart, in order to honor there this worthy object of our love, to receive the Holy Communion, and to offer a white wax candle, four pounds weight, adorned with the arms of the city, and also to assist at a general procession that the prelate proposed to establish forever on the same day. This vow was pronounced publicly before the altar of the cathedral church by the chief man of the municipal magistrates, in the name of all, on the festival of Corpus Christi, before the procession of the Blessed Sacrament, which the bishop held in his hands, the magistrates being on their knees before him. All the people joined in a vow from which they expected with a lively faith the best results.

It was heard in a manner that filled the city with admiration as well as consolation. From this day, all the sick began to grow well, and no other person was attacked by the plague. Distrust, which, on these sad occasions, often does more mischief than the scourge itself, gave place to the utmost confidence, the inhabitants of Marseilles believing themselves safe under the protection of the merciful Heart of the Savior. The evil vanished to such an extent that, six weeks afterward, the virtuous pontiff said in a letter that he published to excite his diocesans to gratitude: "We at present enjoy such perfect health that—what is unexampled in a city so large and populous as this, and may be regarded as a prodigy—we have hardly had any deaths in Marseilles for some time past, or any kind of sickness whatsoever."

Full of gratitude for this second favor, which appeared still more sudden and miraculous than the first, Mgr. De Belzunce hastened to fulfill his promise, and established in perpetuity a general procession for the festival of the Sacred Heart of Jesus. All these facts are proved by the charges of this prelate, and by the resolutions of the municipal authorities of Marseilles.

To the voice of heaven, in favor of devotion to the Sacred Heart, was soon joined the voice of the Catholic Church, its infallible echo. After the usual informations, and we know how long and strict are the informations of the Court of Rome, Pope Clement XIII approved of the festival and office of the Sacred Heart for the kingdom of Poland. Some years later on, the kingdom of Portugal begged and obtained the same favor. Already the bishops of France, after a deliberation on the subject in an assembly of the clergy in the year 1765, had almost generally adopted the devotion of the Sacred Heart in their dioceses. From this period, it went on spreading till the pontificate of Pius VI.

This great pope, of holy and glorious memory, gave a new approbation to this salutary devotion, and condemned those who had the hardihood to oppose it.[866] The festival of the Sacred Heart was fixed, according to the revelation of the venerable Margaret Mary, for the first Friday after the octave of Corpus Christi. To give it more splendor, the churches of France make its solemnity on the second Sunday of July.

Let us now speak of the propagation of devotion to the Sacred Heart. This devotion extends to all parts of the world with amazing rapidity. Religious societies are formed with the special object of honoring the Sacred Heart of the Savior. Already one of these congregations evangelizes the vast archipelago of Oceania; and another, among women, sharing the zeal with which Jesus Christ inflamed his apostles, sends various colonies into the immense Diocese of Louisiana, in order to second, as far as becomes it, the labors of the missionaries who go to enlighten with the light of faith the savages of the Mississippi and the Missouri. Not far from the banks of the latter river, the young Indian is heard singing the praises of that divine Heart which is outraged on the banks of the Seine.

Why this speedy propagation, why the revelation of the devotion to the Sacred Heart in these latter times? Here we must admire the providence that guards the Church, and the harmony that God maintains between the wants of the world and the developments of religion. Attacked, denied, changed by numerous heresies which were the daughters of paganism, the dogmas of faith were about to become the objects of the sacrilegious sneers of the philosophy of the last century. God, the soul, heaven, virtue, religion, all these things should in future be regarded by most people as only matters of doubt or contempt—vain abstractions, without any influence on conduct; in a word, the monster of indifference should spring up from the midst of blood and ruins, and drag man to the foot of an idol, one single idol, gold! And the heart of man, made to love, should be given up to indescribable anguish, and society to endless convulsions!

It is at this supreme moment that our Lord shows his divine Heart to man and to society. Like a father who, after trying all the tender expressions that language can supply and all the other means that paternal love can suggest, in order to bring back a dear son from the edge of a precipice, calls suddenly to this ungrateful child, and opening his breast, says, "Look! Behold my heart! If you know any other heart that loves you with a more sincere love, go, give yours to it, and break your father's."

This is what the Savior, the father of men, does at the moment when they are about to plunge into the frightful gulf of indifference and impiety. "O men!" he seems to say, "forget all that I have done for you—my crib, my exile, my blood, my cross; but, since you are made to love, you need a heart. Behold mine! In return, I ask yours. It is impossible that your heart should keep all alone by itself, since it cannot live without loving, nor love without selling or bestowing itself. If your heart is to be sold, who can buy it better than he who is its beatitude, its end, its eternal reward? If it is to be bestowed, who deserves it better than he who made it? The world, impiety, heresy, indifference, and money ask your heart to change it into a hell; I ask your heart to change it into a heaven, even in this life. Take your choice."[867]

While the Son of God spoke thus, the devil stirred up the fanaticism of his agents, and societies were organized in secret to snatch the hearts of men from the man-God. The hour of darkness was come, and the spirit of frenzy, seizing on a great many guilty people, hurried them toward the abyss. But in this deadly conflict God will not be overcome. Lo! the Sacred Heart rallies round it all that is good and pure on earth, and prayers mount to heaven like clouds of sweet incense! The divine justice, it is true, will take its course in regard to the obstinate, but a counterpoise will be put in the scales, and faith will not perish.

Confraternity of the Sacred Heart. In effect, under the pontificate of Pius VII, there was established in Rome, the center of Catholicity, a strong and numerous association in honor of the Sacred Heart. Others were likewise formed in the various dioceses of Christendom; but that of Rome became the central point toward which all the others turned, if not in deed, at least in intention and desire. This admirable devotion, which spreads from Rome into all other places, even the most remote, and which is everywhere practiced with all the public exercises of a worship that does not dread the light, is opposed to the dark, hidden, secret machinations of anti-religious and anti-social societies.

The devotion of the Sacred Heart is in perfect harmony, not only with the present wants of religion and society, but also with the great laws of the moral world. All beings descended from God should ascend to him again through the medium of the heart of man, and the heart of man itself should ascend to him through the medium of the Sacred Heart of Jesus. Hence devotion to this Sacred Heart is the center of union, the place in which all other devotions meet, and lose themselves like rivers in the ocean. All holy institutes and religious orders, united among themselves by a pure affection in the Heart of Jesus, acknowledge that, under different names, they have issued from it, their common source, and that they should return to it, or rather that they should never leave it, as light never leaves the sun, which gives it birth and sends it forth.[868]

And now, since we must have a heart, who among us will refuse to choose—what do I say?—to accept that of Jesus? For he offers it to us. What does he ask in return? Only one thing—our heart. Is it too much? Heart for heart: On which side is the advantage? Let us hasten, therefore, to join the Association of the Sacred Heart of Jesus. Many graces and few obligations: such are the conditions proposed to us.

Thus, there is a) a plenary indulgence on the first Friday or the first Sunday of each month; b) a plenary indulgence on the festival of the Sacred Heart; c) an indulgence of seven years and seven quarantines on the four Sundays preceding this festival; d) an indulgence of sixty days for each good work performed during the day; and e) a plenary indulgence at the point of death, provided one invokes with his heart, if he cannot do so with his lips, the holy name of Jesus.[869] The associates, according to a rescript of Pius VII, dated 20th March, 1802, must every day recite devoutly one Our Father, one Hail Mary, one I believe, and the following aspiration or any other that has the same meaning:

Sweet Heart of Jesus, I implore
That I may daily love thee more!

We may also, with great advantage, keep the month of the Sacred Heart, as we keep the month of Mary: it is June that has been dedicated by Catholic piety to this beautiful and touching devotion.[870]

PRAYER

O my God! who art all love, I thank thee for having revealed to the world the devotion of the Sacred Heart of Jesus. Grant us the grace to make a due return for the burning love that this divine Heart bears us.

I am resolved to love God above all things, and my neighbor as myself for the love of God; and, in testimony of this love, I will become a member of the Association of the Sacred Heart.

Lesson 47: Christianity Brought before the Senses (Continued)—Visitation, Assumption

Wisdom of the Church in celebrating festivals of the Blessed Virgin.—Nations preserve by monuments the memory of great events in their history, and highborn children consecrate by joyous festivals the noble deeds of their parents or the remarkable circumstances of their own lives. Shall we be surprised that the members of the great Catholic family have perpetuated by monuments and festivals the memory of the chief events in the lives of their father and mother, Jesus and Mary? The only question that can be asked is why the festivals of the Blessed Virgin do not date from the early ages. Oh, beware of imagining that there was any forgetfulness on the part of the Church! The bright flame of the most tender and filial piety toward Mary burnt in her heart from the day of her birth, but the times would not let her manifest it. The delay with which, in spite of herself, she approached the public celebration of the festivals of the Queen of heaven is a new proof of the divine wisdom that characterizes her conduct.

The Church, born among the Jews, grew up among pagans. While her early disciples, gathered in small numbers round a single altar, were offering their hearts to the one only God, millions of people fell prostrate before thousands of altars, raised to a host of contemptible deities: with the pagans, everything was God save God himself. In those dismal ages, what was thenceforth the chief mission of the Church? It was to bring back men to the unity of God. Accordingly, she was very cautious in regard to honoring the Blessed Virgin, lest she should give occasion of rendering excessive honor to her, or of renewing under another form that idolatry which it was necessary to crush. The pagans had adored and were still adoring ever so many goddesses, the mothers of their false gods. Was there not reason to fear that they would easily pass on to the adoration of the Mother of the true God? Such was the danger that should be guarded against.

Herein, the Church complied with the wishes of Mary herself, who sought nothing more earnestly than that her Son alone should be adored in spirit and in truth throughout the whole earth. What do I say? God himself seemed to authorize this conduct. While he was crowning with glory the deaths and the tombs of martyrs, he left the death and the tomb of Mary, as well as the glorious circumstances of her divine life, in a kind of oblivion. Ever faithful to himself, and full of solicitude for the welfare of his children, he had acted in like manner toward Moses, whose death and burial he wished to be unwitnessed, lest the Israelites, ever prone to idolatry, should make him a God.[871]

Providence of God, who draws good out of evil. But the long-desired moment came when the Church could give free play to the transports of her love for Mary. Here again we ought to admire the wisdom of God, who draws good out of evil and the glory of religion from the attacks of his enemies. On the one hand, Nestorius had dared to dispute Mary's august title of Mother of God; on the other, the fear of idolatry had been removed by the establishment of Christianity. The wise reserve that had been practiced hitherto might become dangerous, and the Church hastened to publish the sublime prerogatives of Mary, in order to oppose the outrages that heretics committed against her. Temples were built under the invocation of her name, and festivals instituted in her honor. But here again the Church acted only by degrees, always having regard to the wants of times and places.

Origin of the festival of the Visitation.—It is thus that on great occasions, when there is question of reviving the piety of nations, of averting some calamity, of obtaining from heaven some signal favor, we see her introducing now a new festival and again a new devotion in honor of the all-good and all-powerful Mother of God. The festival of the Visitation, for example, had indeed been celebrated in the Order of St. Francis from the middle of the thirteenth century (1263), and in the East from a very remote period; nevertheless, it was only under the pontificate of Urban VI that it became universal. This pope, of glorious memory, ordered it to be solemnized with special fervor, and even to be prepared for by a fast, so as to obtain through Mary's intercession the extinction of the great schism of the West, which was then desolating the Church. Urban VI having died before publishing the letters of institution, it was his successor Boniface IX that published them in 1389, changing the obligation of fasting into a simple counsel. At length, the Council of Bale, in 1441, fixed its date for the 2nd of July.[872]

Lessons given us by the Blessed Virgin. The object of this festival is to honor Mary paying a visit to her cousin Elizabeth, and to set the Blessed Virgin before us as a model for our charity toward our neighbor. Could the sovereign pontiff that instituted it find an example more capable of inducing the two parties then formed in the Church to give each other the kiss of peace? Now, this festival has lost nothing of its efficacy or its appropriateness. On the one hand, it is always equally proper to inspire us with charity toward our neighbor, and to give us rules for the practice of this virtue; on the other, peace is perhaps more disturbed nowadays than ever before. Let us therefore take directions for our conduct from the account that the gospel gives us of the Blessed Virgin's visit to her cousin.

At the time of the mystery of the annunciation, the archangel Gabriel told Mary that her cousin Elizabeth had conceived miraculously, and that she was then in her sixth month. The Blessed Virgin concealed, out of humility, the amazing dignity to which the incarnation of the Word in her womb raised her; but, full of joy and gratitude, she wished to go and congratulate the mother of John the Baptist. It was the Holy Ghost who inspired her with this resolution, for the accomplishment of his designs in regard to the precursor of the Messias, who was not yet born. "Mary set out therefore, and went into the hill country, to a city of the tribe of Juda; and, having entered the house of Zachary, she saluted Elizabeth."[873]

The distance from Nazareth, where Mary lived, to Hebron, where Elizabeth lived, was some sixty or seventy miles.[874] Yet the holy Virgin did not hesitate a moment to undertake the journey; and, though weak and little accustomed to endure such fatigue, nothing could stay her. What urges her thus? It is a burning desire to be useful to a virtuous family, and to make them sharers in the grace that she carries with her.[875] Let us remark that the evangelist, when speaking of Mary's departure, says that she went "with haste,"[876] but as for her return, he points out no eagerness therein, and is content to say:

"Mary abode with her about three months, and returned to her own house."[877] Children of Mary, what an example of prompt and generous charity does our Mother here give us!

This desire to be useful to mankind did not leave the Blessed Virgin when she entered into heaven. Very far from it: it only grew stronger. For Mary now knows our wants better, and pities our miseries more. She wishes to help us even more than we ourselves wish to be helped. "So much so," says St. Bonaventure, "that she considers herself offended by those who neglect to have recourse to her; for all her desires are to give to mankind in general the same favors as she lavishes on her special servants."[878]

Enlightened by the Holy Spirit, Elizabeth understood the ineffable mystery of the incarnation that had been wrought in Mary, though the latter, out of humility, did not wish to discover it. Transported with joy, the mother of the precursor cried out: "Blessed art thou among women, and blessed is the fruit of thy womb!"[879] Then turning her thoughts on herself, she added: "And whence is this happiness to me that the mother of my Lord should come to see me?"[880] An example of the holy joy and gratitude that we should feel when we receive a visit from our brethren! Oh, how loudly does the behavior of Elizabeth condemn all disdain, all coldness, all refined insincerity! In condemning these things, is it not ourselves, perhaps, that it condemns?

Elizabeth tells the cause of her joy: "For behold, at the moment when thy salutation sounded in my ears, the infant in my womb leaped for joy. Oh, how happy thou art to have believed, because thou shalt see the accomplishment of all that was spoken to thee by the Lord!"[881] An example of what we should praise in our brethren: not temporal advantages, not bodily graces, not talents, but the gifts of God—virtue! John the Baptist was sanctified in his mother's womb. He had the use of reason, and knew by a supernatural light who had come to visit him. This knowledge filled him with such joy that he leaped in Elizabeth's womb. And who was the dispensatrix of this favor, and the instrument of this first miracle of Jesus in the supernatural order? Mary; yes, Mary, who later on obtained the first miracle of her Son in the natural order.

O Mary, how powerful thou art; but, above all, how good thou art! Since thou art the dispensatrix of all the favors of heaven in the order of nature and in the order of grace, thou art therefore the hope of all mankind, and mine in particular. Thanks be to God my Savior, who hath made thee known to me, and who hath been pleased at the same time to teach me the means of going to himself! Thou art this means, O august Mother of God; for I am well aware that it is to the merits of Jesus and thy powerful intercession that I owe my salvation!

O my Queen, who didst go so willingly to the habitation of St. Elizabeth, come also to the habitation of my poor soul! Make haste: thou knowest better than I how much it suffers, and how many dangers surround it. Thou knowest that it is a prey to a thousand inordinate desires and a thousand evil habits, and that the plague of sin has left in it some sad remains that may lead it to eternal death. Thou canst make it rich, O dispensatrix of the treasures of God! Thou canst heal it of all its infirmities! Come, therefore, often to me while I sojourn in this valley of tears, but especially at the hour of my death!

But if we wish to be favored with the blessed visits of the Queen of heaven, let us often pay her a visit ourselves, by addressing our prayers to her, either at the foot of her image or in a church dedicated to her. "Believe me," says St. Anselm, "we shall find grace sooner by addressing ourselves to Mary than by addressing ourselves to Jesus himself: not that Jesus is not the source of every grace, but, by having recourse to Mary, she will pray for us, and her prayers will have much greater influence with her Son than ours."[882]

Let us therefore not leave the feet of this divine treasurer, who has charge of so many graces, and let us always repeat to her with St. John Damascene: "O Mother of God! open to us the gate of mercy, by continually praying for us; for thy prayers are the salvation of men, and the only thing that we have to do, in turning to thee, is to beg thee to ask and obtain for us the graces that thou knowest us most to need."

This is what Brother Rainauld, of the Order of Dominicans did, as may be seen in their chronicles.[883] This pious servant of Mary was sick, and he implored her to cure him. The Queen of angels, accompanied by St. Cecilia and St. Catherine, appeared to him, and said with the greatest sweetness: "My son, what do you wish me to do for you?" Surprised at this question, the religious was a good deal embarrassed, and did not know what to answer. Then one of the saints accompanying the Blessed Virgin said to him: "Rainauld, you do not know how you ought to act. Ask nothing; only abandon yourself to Mary, and she will obtain for you a greater favor than you would have chosen." The sick man obeyed, and he was cured.

To the praises that the humble Mary receives from Elizabeth, what reply does she make? She refers all glory to him who has done great things to her. "My soul," she says to her cousin, "doth magnify the Lord,...for he hath vouchsafed to look down on the lowliness of his handmaid."[884] An example of the manner in which we should receive praise!

After three months spent with Elizabeth, Mary takes the road back to her humble city. The wants of her relatives have determined the length of her stay. An example that condemns idle conversations, and needlessly prolonged visits!

O Mary! I return thee thanks for the admirable example that thou dost set before me on this day. Thou dost teach me how to sanctify some of the most important things in life, namely, conversations and visits, which are the occasions of so many sins for a great many people. I wish to avoid, like thee, all vain, profane, and useless discourse. I will banish from my language all those silly puerilities which degrade the soul, dwarf the mind, and distract the heart.

The Assumption: Origin and tradition.—The festival of the Visitation is celebrated on the 2nd of July. Six weeks afterward, that is to say, on the 15th of August, comes the solemnity of the Assumption. Behold the glorious triumph of Mary! But, before describing it, let us tell the origin of this beautiful day. The gospel teaches us that the most Blessed Virgin was confided by our Lord to the beloved disciple, and tradition adds that she dwelt with him in the city of Ephesus, that she was the oracle and comfort of the apostles, that she lived (according to the best established opinion) to the age of seventy-two years, and that she died at Ephesus.[885]

The Church, instructed by the apostles, has always believed that the august Mother of God was taken up, body and soul, into heaven immediately after her death, and that she is there seated on a throne inferior only to that of God himself. Without being an article of faith, this belief, first expressed obscurely by the fathers of the early ages, went on developing itself like many other truths: so much so that it nowadays receives the homage both of East and West.[886]

The belief of the Church is founded not only on the testimonies that we have cited, and a thousand others that might be cited, but also on an old tradition, very widely spread through the East. Some days before calling his divine Mother to him, says this tradition,[887] the Lord sent her the archangel Gabriel. Then was heard in the place where she lay a sweet harmony, which was a sign to the holy apostles that Mary was about to leave them. At this supreme moment, breaking out into new tears and sighs, they lifted up their hands, and said to her with one voice: "O thou, who art our Mother! thou art leaving us to go to heaven; give us thy blessing, and do not abandon us, for we are weak and miserable!" Mary, turning her dying eyes on them, said, as if to bid them her last farewell: "Be blessed, my sons; I will never cease thinking of you!" And soon the apostles saw the Savior, accompanied by his angels, coming to receive the soul of his divine Mother.

Meanwhile, one of the apostles had been unable to be present at Mary's death, and to receive her last blessing. He only arrived three days after her happy departure. Full of sorrow and regret, he besought the sacred college to open Mary's tomb, that he might rest his eyes once more on her. It was opened accordingly. But, O prodigy! the sepulchre was empty, and some lilies, symbols of purity and virginity, had sprung up in the place where the chaste body had been laid: that immaculate body, which was too holy to remain in the grave, and which angels and archangels, seraphs and cherubs, bore away on their wings when the voice of God woke it from its short sleep.[888]

This beautiful tradition has inspired a multitude of Christian artists, and given occasion to some glorious masterpieces. Our large church pictures often show us heaven, thronged with the blessed, who carry crowns and palms to the daughter of David, about to be declared their Queen. The tombstone is thrown aside, and among the folds of the shroud may be seen the flowers that have sprung up miraculously.[889]

The happy death of Mary, followed by her elevation body and soul into heaven, was an event too important in itself and too glorious for our august Lady not to induce the Church to consecrate the memory of it by a solemn festival. In effect, if a want of documents does not let us show the celebration of this festival from the age of the apostles, we find it in the fourth century.[890] The Council of Ephesus, by securing to Mary her sublime title of Mother of God, gave much authority to the worship that the faithful already rendered to her, and consequently increased the solemnity of her Assumption. It was soon celebrated throughout the vast empire of Charlemagne, and thus became a Catholic festival.[891]

The Assumption is preceded by a fast and followed by an octave, which shows the greatness of this solemnity. It bears two names. Some fathers have called it the "Blessed Virgin's Sleep or Rest"; others, more commonly, the "Assumption of our Lady"; the Church has long adopted the latter denomination.[892] Now this word *assumption* points out very clearly the difference between the manner in which the Blessed Virgin ascended into heaven, and that in which our Lord himself ascended. Our Lord ascended by his own power; Mary, by the power of her Son.[893]

Triumph of Mary: Her goodness and power. What pen can describe Mary's triumphant entry into heaven? When the Savior had accomplished the work of redemption by his death, the angels sighed for his return to heaven, and continually repeated to him in their concerts these words of David: "Arise, O Lord; come to thy resting place, thou and the ark of thy sanctification."[894] The ark of thy sanctification! that is to say, thy divine Mother, whom thou didst sanctify by dwelling in her. The Lord was at length pleased to comply with the wishes of the inhabitants of the heavenly Jerusalem, by calling Mary to dwell among them.

But if he had judged it proper that the ark of the old covenant should be brought with so much pomp into the city of David, what pomp should he not display at the entry of his Mother into the city of God? It was not enough to have a group of angels as her escort. The King of angels would himself accompany her, with all the heavenly court. The Son of the Eternal, who is also the Son of Mary, descends from heaven, and, coming to his Mother, addresses her in these sweet words: "Arise, make haste, my beloved, my dove, my beautiful one; for the winter is now past, and all its severities are gone. Come from Libanus, my dearest Mother, come and take the crown prepared for thee."[895]

Mary quits the earth; but, thinking of the many dangers and miseries to which she leaves her children exposed, she turns toward them her looks of pity and love, in order to tell them that she will not forget them amid the splendors of her glory. Jesus stretches out his hand to her, and Mary, rising with him through the air, above the clouds, beyond the spheres, arrives at the abode of the blessed. The eternal gates open, and the maid of Juda enters heaven, of which she is to be Queen.

The saints and angels have no sooner contemplated her than, amazed at her beauty, they cry out with one voice: "Who is she that cometh up from the desert, radiant with so many graces and virtues, and advanceth, leaning on her beloved? Who is she that hath the Lord himself to wait on her?" And unanimous acclamations reply: "This is the Mother of our King; this is our Queen; this is the saint of saints, the beloved one of God, the spotless dove, the most beautiful of creatures!" And all the hierarchies of heaven, the angels, the archangels, the virtues, the powers, the principalities, the dominations, the thrones, the cherubim, and the seraphim, and all the orders of saints, the patriarchs, the prophets, the martyrs, the virgins, etc., proclaiming her praises, lay their immortal crowns at her feet.

But those who ran to her most eagerly were our first parents, Adam and Eve. "Beloved daughter," they said to her, "thou hast repaired the evil that our fault caused to the human race. Thou didst win back for the world the grace that it had lost. Thou didst crush the head of the serpent that had conquered us. It is by thee that we have been saved. Blessed art thou!" In what terms did the authors of her being, St. Anne and St. Joachim, salute her! And Joseph, her spouse—what human tongue can tell the joy with which he beheld her glorious entry into heaven?

Words also fail to tell with what love and graciousness the most Holy Trinity welcomed her: how the Father received her as his daughter, the Son as his Mother, and the Holy Ghost as his spouse. The Father calls her to share his power, the Son his wisdom, and the Holy Ghost his goodness. And the three divine Persons place on her brow a diadem of twelve stars, brighter than rubies or diamonds, and, leading her to her throne, at the right hand of Jesus, declare her Queen of heaven and earth, and command angels and all other creatures to recognize her as such, and to serve and obey her in everything.[896]

Saying of the blessed Berchmans. And what does Mary do on her lofty throne? The mediatrix of the human race with her Son, she intercedes for us; she pleads our cause; she fills her hands with heavenly favors, and distributes pardons, blessings, and graces far and near. Mary is a Queen, but a Queen of clemency and mercy: her goodness has no bounds, and her power is equal to her goodness.[897] In return for granting us her protection, what does she ask? Hear one of her greatest servants. The blessed Berchmans, laden during his whole life with the most signal favors of this august Queen, is at the point of death. The community assemble round his bed, and the superior orders him, in the name of obedience, to tell his brethren what he has done and what should be done to merit the astonishing graces with which Mary has favored him. "What Mary asks," replies the dying saint, "is very little indeed: 'The slightest homage, provided it is constant.'"[898]

Need more be said to excite in our hearts a childlike confidence in this good Mother? Let us therefore address ourselves to her in all our wants of body and soul. Let us, above all, implore her, through the merits of her blessed death, to obtain for us a good end, and to see that we shall quit this life either on a Saturday, a day that is consecrated to her, or within the octave of one of her festivals, a favor that she has obtained for many of her servants: among the number, especially St. Stanislaus Kostka, who died on the very day of the Assumption.

History of St. Stanislaus Kostka. This holy young man, who had always professed a filial attachment and sincere devotion to Mary, was present, about the beginning of August, at a sermon preached by Father Canisius to the novices of the Society of Jesus. He exhorted them always to live as if they had reached their last day, and were on the point of appearing before the divine tribunal. The sermon over, Stanislaus said to one of his brothers that he felt something like a warning from God, which told him that this should be the last month for him. Whether God had actually revealed it to him or that it was merely the effect of fancy, the event justified the prediction. Four days afterward, as he was going to St. Mary Major's, he said to a father of the Society, with whom he conversed of the approaching festival of the Assumption, that it seemed to him as if there must have been a new paradise seen in the celestial country on the day of this event, by reason of the glory of the Mother of God, crowned Queen of heaven and of angels. "And if it is true," he added, "as I firmly believe, that the same solemnity is renewed every year, I hope to be present at the next celebration of it."

Chance, or rather providence, had given Stanislaus, as his protector for the month, the martyr St. Laurence, and it was rumored that he had written a letter to Mary, his Mother, begging her to obtain for him the favor of being present at her festival in paradise. On St. Laurence's day, he communicated. He then besought the saint to present his petition to the Queen of angels and to obtain a happy reply to it. That very evening, he was taken ill with a fever. Though it was not at all violent, he was no less convinced that his prayer had been heard and that the hour of his death drew nigh. As he lay on his bed, he could be heard repeating, with evident satisfaction, these words: "I shall never rise again." Afterward, he turned to Father Aquaviva, who was close by, and said to him: "Father, I really believe that St. Laurence has obtained from the Blessed Virgin for me the favor of being in heaven on the festival of her Assumption." But the father paid no attention to him.

On the eve of the festival, though the illness still seemed far from serious, the saint said to one of the religious that the following night he should no longer be in this world. "Ah! Brother," replied this religious, "it would be a greater miracle to see you die here than to see you perfectly restored." But, about noon, the state of the patient changed very suddenly: he began to have cold sweats, and his strength forsook him altogether. The superior hastened to him. Stanislaus begged him to order that he should be laid on the bare ground, so as to die as a penitent.

To please him, he was wrapped in a blanket and laid on the ground. Here he confessed, and received the holy viaticum, amid the tears of all who surrounded him. On the arrival of the Blessed Sacrament, his face was seen to brighten up with a heavenly joy and to become like that of a seraph. He also received extreme unction, and, during all this time, he did nothing but pray, lift his eyes to heaven, and kiss or press to his heart an image of Mary.

A father having asked him what need he had of the beads that he held in his hand, since he could no longer say them, "They help to console me," he answered, "for they belong to my Mother." "You will soon be consoled," remarked the father, "by humbly kissing the hands of Mary herself in the abode of the blessed." At these words, the saint's face brightened up again, and he raised his hands on high as if to show his gladness at the thought of soon being with Mary. The divine Mother next appeared to him, as those present could perceive, and a few moments afterward, at daybreak, on the 15th of August, he passed away without pain to the peace of the blessed. He ceased to press the image of Mary to his heart, only to go and kiss in heaven the feet of his amiable patroness.

And we, too, let us on the day of the Assumption show our joy at having in heaven a Mother so powerful, so good, and so easily pleased. Let us prepare for her festival by a novena. Let us receive the Holy Communion, as if it were our viaticum, to obtain the grace of a happy death. To make thoroughly practical our sentiments of devotion and our exercises of piety toward Mary, let us ask ourselves seriously by what means she arrived at such a degree of honor and bliss. The dignity of Mother of God was doubtless something very great; yet it was not this that God crowned in Mary. Fidelity to grace; such was the measure of her glory, and such will be the measure of ours. Children of Mary, let us imitate our Mother, and take today as our motto: "To do little things well!"

PRAYER

O my God! who art all love, I thank thee for having given me in Mary a Mother so powerful and so good. Grant me the grace to deserve her tenderness by a constant fidelity in imitating her virtues, her humility, her purity, and her love for her divine Son.

I am resolved to love God above all things, and my neighbor as myself for the love of God; and, in testimony of this love, I will take the Blessed Virgin for my special friend.

Lesson 48: Christianity Brought before the Senses (Continued)—Marian Feasts

The Nativity of the Blessed Virgin: Origin of this festival.—If the Catholic Church celebrates the assumption of Mary with so much pomp and joy, why would she not also consecrate her blessed birth by a solemn festival? On the 8th of September, she summons all the faithful to the cradle of this divine child. According to the most exact calculations and the most venerable traditions, Mary was born in Nazareth, during the reign of Herod, at the time when this wicked prince was endeavoring to destroy the royal race of David, so as to render impossible the fulfillment of the prophecies, which announced that the Savior of the world should come of the family of Jesse. This occurred in the twenty-second year of the reign of Augustus; under the consulship of Marcus Drusus Livius and Quintus Calpurnius Piso; and consequently in the year of Rome, 738.

The birth of the Blessed Virgin took place on the 8th of September, as is established by the authorities that we have cited, and it was not without a mystery that this day was chosen to give the world a new Eve. A tradition, preserved among the Hebrews, tells that the first Eve was created on this day. A miracle of grace and beauty, the first Eve ravished Adam's heart and completed his happiness. On the same day, the new Eve, of whom the first was only a figure, appeared on the earth, and, if we may so speak, presented to the eyes of God, by her incomparable grace and beauty, the most ravishing spectacle that he had ever contemplated.[899]

However, for reasons set forth in the preceding lesson, and for others also drawn from the wisdom of the Church, which develops with the progress of time the means of rousing the piety of her children, the festival of the Nativity did not appear, at least with any splendor, from the origin of Christianity. The chief and most ancient monument that we have of it is the sacramentary of St. Leo the Great and some of his predecessors, in which we find, as well as in the sacramentary of St. Gregory, the festival of the Nativity of the Blessed Virgin, with Mass and prayers proper thereto.[900]

Before the seventh century, it was generally celebrated throughout the Church, and before the end of the ninth, it was one of the most solemn in France.[901] The town of Angers seems to have distinguished itself in this matter, by its piety toward Mary and by the pomp with which its inhabitants observed the Nativity. Hence it comes, according to very probable conjectures, that the neighboring provinces call this festival "Angevine," as taking its origin from *Anjou*.[902] The East soon rivaled the zeal of the West; and, from the middle of the twelfth century, we see the festival of the Nativity celebrated there with the same pomp as the greatest solemnities of the Church.[903]

The very name *Nativity* shows the object of our devotion. If highborn children look forward eagerly to the return of a loved mother's birthday and celebrate it with the greatest delight, rivaling one another in offering her bouquets and congratulations, I leave you to imagine with what sentiments the hearts of the children of Mary should thrill on the return of the day that gave them such a Mother. Parents also celebrate with rejoicing the birth of their children, and the anniversaries thereof. This custom, proper to keep alive the family spirit, is very affecting and laudable. Yet does it not seem more just to weep over children when they arrive in this valley of tears, considering that they are born, not only without reason or merit, but also children of wrath, defiled with sin, and condemned to sorrows and death?

Hence the Catholic Church, rising with all the pride of faith above the sentiments of nature, celebrates, not the birth, but the death of her children. See the profound wisdom of her language: she calls the death of her saints their nativity or birth! In effect, it is on the day of their decease that the elect quit this dying life in order to be born to a true life, an immortal and glorious life. To this great rule, our Catholic liturgy knows only two exceptions: St. John the Baptist and the Blessed Virgin. It celebrates the festival of the former on the day that he came into the world, because he came sanctified and confirmed in grace. With much greater reason should it celebrate the nativity of the latter, who appeared on the earth full of grace and enriched with all the gifts of God.[904]

Exempted from the law of original sin and predestined for the divine maternity, it is beyond a doubt that Mary was the most beautiful soul that ever came forth from the hands of the Creator, as, excepting the incarnation, she was the most perfect and most worthy work of the Almighty in this world. "For," says St. Thomas, "God proportions his graces to men according to the dignity he intends for them. Wherefore Mary, before being Mother of God, received from on high all the graces that should render her worthy of this eminent prerogative."[905] This is the reason why the archangel Gabriel saluted her with the words: "Thou art full of grace."

Let us also salute her "full of grace." Children of Mary, let us today gather round her cradle, and address our prayers and our homage to our amiable Mother. Young as she is, she both sees and hears us. What confidence we ought to have! Can a mother refuse anything to her children on her birthday? If we are guilty, she will ask pardon for us. If we are just, she will obtain perseverance for us. Do we want to win her heart? Let us imitate her virtues. Little children especially! come and see this holy child, your Mother and your model. She loves and desires above all things the lilies and roses of purity. O young people! who are so much indebted to Mary, she calls you to her cradle, and to the study of her early years.

Confidence inspired by Mary in the cradle: Words of St. Ambrose. "Come," says St. Ambrose, "and set before your eyes the virginal life of Mary: it will be like a mirror in which you shall see the model of chastity and every other virtue. The first motive of imitation is always the nobility of our instructor. Now, who is more noble than the Mother of God?...She was a virgin in body and soul, and of a purity incapable of guile. She was humble of heart, grave in her language, wise in her resolutions. She spoke seldom, and said only what was necessary. She read the books of the law assiduously, and put her trust, not in perishable riches, but in the prayers of the poor. Always fervent, she wished to have God alone as the witness of what passed in her heart. It was to him that she referred whatever she did and whatever she had.

"Far from causing the least trouble to anyone, all had experience of her kindness. She honored her superiors, and entertained no feeling of jealousy against her equals. She shunned vainglory, acted according to reason, loved virtue ardently. Her looks were all gentleness; her words all affability; her whole conduct bore the impress of modesty. There was nothing to be remarked in her behavior but what was becoming. Her gaiety had no levity. Her voice did not show the least sign of self-love.

"Her exterior was so well regulated that it was a picture of her soul, and a perfect model of all virtues. Her charity toward the neighbor knew no bounds. She practiced long fasts, and chose as her food not what might flatter sensuality, but what was needed to support nature. She consecrated to exercises of piety many moments that were intended for sleep. If she left her house, it was only to go to the Temple, and always in the company of her parents."[906]

And let all of us Christians, whatever our age or our condition, rejoice with the child Mary that she has been born so holy, so dear to God, so full of grace! Let us rejoice, not only on her account, but on our own; for the grace that she brings with her into the world is no less for us than for her. Let us beware of losing confidence in Mary or devotion to her; for she is the channel of all heavenly blessings.

When Holofernes wanted to get possession of Bethulia, he began by cutting off the aqueducts. When the devil wants to enter a soul, he first tries to deprive it of devotion to Mary, quite sure that, the channel of grace having been turned aside, it will soon lose the light and fear of God, and at length its eternal salvation. Hence, whatever the state of our soul may be, whatever the number or the enormity of our offenses, let us have recourse to Mary. The refuge of the most abandoned sinners, she will stretch out a helping hand to us, and will save us. From the depth of our miseries, let us send up to her a cry that her heart cannot resist: *Memorare, O piissima Virgo Maria*—"Remember, O most pious Virgin Mary," etc.

The Memorare. Need we relate that story which has become so celebrated, and which would alone suffice, though we had not the testimony of all ages, to make us rely on Mary in our greatest wants, as the ship trusts to its anchor amid the storms? Under Louis XIII, there lived in Paris a holy priest named Bernard, or the Poor Priest. His goods he had consecrated to the poor, and his life and the tenderness of his heart to wretches that human justice struck with its sword. Now it happened that a criminal, condemned to be broken alive upon the wheel, was unwilling to hear mention of confession. This news was brought to the Poor Priest, who immediately ran to the prison.

Led into the cell, he salutes the prisoner, embraces him, exhorts him, suggests sentiments of confidence to him, and threatens him with the anger of God; but nothing makes any impression. The criminal does not even deign to look at him, and seems deaf to all that is said. The confessor begs him at least to join in a very short prayer to the Blessed Virgin, which he declares he has never recited without obtaining what he sought.

The prisoner makes a gesture of contempt, and refuses to say it.

Father Bernard does not cease reciting it from end to end. But, seeing that the obstinate sinner has not so much as uttered a word, his charity urges him, his zeal inspires him, and, holding up to the hardened man's mouth a copy of this prayer, which he always carries about with him, he endeavors to put it in, saying: "Since you will not say it, you shall eat it!"

The criminal, encumbered by his chains and scarcely able to defend himself from this importunity, promises, at least for the sake of being let alone, to recite it. Bernard goes on his knees along with him, and again begins the *Memorare*. The prisoner has scarcely pronounced the first words when he feels himself completely changed. A flood of tears bursts from his eyes.

He begged the holy priest to give him time to prepare for confession; and, as he recalled the wanderings of his life in the bitterness of his soul, he was so touched both by the enormity of his crimes and the greatness of the divine mercy that in that same hour he died of grief.

This example, so often brought forward in the course of ages, shows how useful the protection of her whom the Church has named the Refuge of sinners may be to those who invoke it. Let us only remember that, as a general rule, it is respect, tenderness, a filial affection for our Mother, and above all an imitation of her virtues, that will make us worthy of her favors.

The festival of the Holy Name of Mary.—On the Sunday within the octave of the Nativity, the festival of the Holy Name of Mary is celebrated. Pope Innocent XI, by his decree of the year 1683, rendered this festival, previously confined to Spain, obligatory on the Universal Church. In this order, so sweet of itself to fulfill, we must also recognize a testimony of the Church's gratitude toward Mary. The Queen of virgins always showed herself the personal enemy of Mahometanism, a grossly sensual religion. In the sixteenth century, she had plunged it beneath the waves of Lepanto; but having partly escaped on this dreadful occasion, it was now again threatening Christendom.

In 1683, the grand vizier, at the head of a formidable army, lays siege to Vienna, one of the ramparts of the Church. John Sobieski, at the head of his Poles, rushes to the defense of the besieged city. On the morning of the battle, he puts himself, as well as his army, under the protection of the Blessed Virgin. All the troops kneel down, while Sobieski serves Mass in the convent of the Camaldolese, praying all the time with arms stretched out in the form of a cross. "It was here," says a Christian warrior with profound truth, "that the grand vizier was beaten." On coming out of the church, Sobieski gives orders to sound the charge. The Turks, terror-stricken, betake themselves to flight, and abandon everything, even the grand standard of Mahomet, which the conqueror sends to the sovereign pontiff as a mark of homage to Mary.

How can we tell the respect that the name of Mary, at once so powerful and so beautiful, is entitled to? Let the ages of faith instruct us! First, it is believed that God himself revealed it to the parents of the Blessed Virgin.[907] For many centuries it was forbidden to women, even of the royal blood, to bear the name of Mary. Alphonsus VI, king of Castile, being about to marry a young Moorish princess, who should receive a name at her baptism, forbade that of Mary to be given her, though she earnestly desired it.

In the marriage agreement between the Duchess Mary Louisa of Nevers and Ladislaus, king of Poland, it was stipulated that the princess should lay aside the name of Mary and retain only that of Louisa. Casimir I, another king of Poland, made the same terms when he married Mary, a daughter of the Duke of Russia. Hence came the custom, so long preserved in Poland, that no woman, of any condition whatsoever, should bear the name of Mary. These examples show us what veneration we ought to have for this august name, as the victory of Sobieski shows us with what confidence we ought to pronounce it. Let us say therefore: "O Mary, O name under which no one should ever despair!" *O Maria, O nomen sub quo nemini desperandum!*[908]

The Presentation of the Blessed Virgin: Object of this festival.—Children of Mary! let us now quit her cradle. Here she is again, still very young, hastening to the Temple of Jerusalem, whither the voice of God calls her. Let us run after her, and celebrate the festival of the Presentation.

The Presentation is a festival established by the Church to consecrate the memory of a solemn journey that Mary made while yet a child. A constant tradition, which dates from the early days of Christianity, teaches us that the Blessed Virgin, when about three years old, was presented in the Temple of Jerusalem, where she consecrated herself wholly to the Lord.[909] Favored with the plenitude of her faculties, she made to God a vow of virginity, and was the first to raise that sacred standard which has since rallied round it so many legions of virgins. It was a usage among the Jews to consecrate children to the service of the Temple, and to have little girls brought up under the tutelary shadow of the holy edifice. Mary, knowing that her father and mother, faithful to this sacred usage, had promised the Lord, when asking him for a child, to offer it to him, regarded herself as happy in anticipating their vow. She wished of herself to consecrate herself to the Lord, and was the first to ask them to go and fulfill their promise. "Anne did not hesitate to yield to her desire," says St. Gregory of Nyssa. "She led her to the Temple, and offered her to the God of Abraham."

But let us see in what manner Anne and Joachim made to God the sacrifice of what was most dear to them in this world. They set out from Nazareth for Jerusalem, carrying in turn in their arms their beloved daughter, still too young to endure the fatigue of a journey of ninety miles. With them walked a small number of relatives. But the angels, says St. Gregory of Nicomedia, served them as a suite, and accompanied in crowds the pure young Virgin who was going to offer herself at the altar of the Lord.

When the holy company arrived at the Temple, the sweet child turned toward her father and mother, kissed their hands, and asked their blessing. Then, without the least hesitation, she mounted the steps of the sanctuary, and ran to offer herself to the high priest. How beautiful, how solemn was that moment! God himself celebrated that memorable day, on which he saw his chaste spouse enter the Temple; for never had a creature so pure and holy been offered to him.[910] And when Mary had consecrated to her God both her soul and her body, without reserve and forever, with what love might she exclaim: "My beloved to me, and I to him!"[911]

Her appearance. Let us too enjoy this enchanting spectacle, contemplating the portrait that St. Epiphanius, born in Palestine, has preserved for us of this admirable child. "Mary," he says, "was on all occasions full of reserve and gravity. She spoke rarely, and listened courteously: she was most affable and respectful toward all around her. She was a little above the middle height. Her color was somewhat like that of gold or wheat; her hair flaxen; her eyes bright, with oval, olive pupils. Her eyebrows were arched, and of a most pleasing black; her nose long; her lips rosy, and her words ineffably sweet. Her face was neither round nor sharp, but a little long. Her hands and fingers were also somewhat longer than usual. Her garments were most simple, and of the natural color of the stuff from which they were made. Lastly, a divine grace breathed in all her movements."[912]

Her life in the Temple. Who will now describe Mary's angelic life in the Temple? "The holy child," says St. Jerome, "regulated her moments thus. From morning till the third hour of the day, she spent her time in prayer. From the third hour till the ninth, she worked. She then returned to prayer till the moment of taking her repast. She strove with all her might to be the first at the holy watches, the most exact in observing the law, and the most humble, the most perfect in virtue, among her companions. No one ever observed in her the least sign of anger, and all the words that fell from her lips were so full of sweetness that it was easy to recognize the Spirit of God in them."[913]

Origin of this festival. The act that Mary had performed of presenting herself in the Temple was too important and instructive for the Catholic Church to omit consecrating it by a solemn festival. The East was first to celebrate the Presentation. We already find it in the constitutions of the emperor Emmanuel Comnenus, in the middle of the twelfth century, 1143. Two centuries later on, in 1374, after the Crusades, this festival passed into the West, under the reign of Charles V, king of France.

See in what terms this religious monarch writes of it to the doctors and students of the Navarre College, Paris! "I have learned from the chancellor of Cyprus," he says, "that the Presentation of the Virgin in the Temple, when she was only three years of age, is very solemnly celebrated in the East on the 21st of November. This same chancellor, being ambassador of the king of Cyprus and Jerusalem at Avignon, told the pope how religiously this festival is observed by the Greeks, and presented its office to him. The pope examined the office himself, and also caused it to be examined by cardinals and theologians. He approved of it, and permitted the celebration of this festival, which he solemnized himself with an immense concourse of people. The same chancellor having come to France and presented the office to me, I had the festival celebrated in the holy chapel: many prelates and other lords were present, and the papal nuncio preached an eloquent sermon."[914]

Such was the way in which the festival of the Presentation passed from the East into the West, and especially into France, where it was observed by the command of the pious monarch whose words we have just heard. The successors of Gregory IX, to whom the office of the Presentation was presented by the ambassador of Cyprus, enriched with many indulgences this beautiful feast, which has taken rank among the solemnities of the Church.[915]

Mary as the type of Christian woman: First as a Virgin.—This is the place to make some reflections on the life of the new Eve, and the salutary influence of her example. On all her festivals, Mary appears as the model and type of Christian woman. A daughter, a wife, a mother, and a widow, Mary passes through all the states of woman, so as to be a universal model. But in Mary a sublime quality prevails over all others, and exists from her cradle to her grave; namely, virginity. In effect, it is to virginity, or at least to conjugal purity, that the honor, esteem, and rehabilitation of woman are attached. Let her never forget it! What alone entitles woman to respect, and makes her the object of a kind of worship and veneration, is modesty. Such, we repeat, is the first condition of woman's restoration and salvation.

Mary as a daughter. A daughter, Mary teaches woman the means of preserving her most beautiful ornament, the spotless lily of innocence; namely, to conceal herself under the shadow of the sanctuary. A tender piety, and flight of the world: such make up the second condition of woman's restoration and salvation.

Mary as a wife. A wife, Mary teaches woman the means of acquiring an extraordinary ascendancy over her husband, which, removing in her regard the anathema pronounced against Eve, enables her to exercise again all that sway which she ought to have for the happiness of the family, her own happiness, and the happiness of society.[916] The meek Mary obeys, prays, labors, and is silent. Joseph speaks, and Mary sets out for Bethlehem, Egypt, Nazareth, or Jerusalem. Meekness, obedience, prayer, labor, and silence: such make up the third condition of woman's restoration and salvation.

Mary as a mother. A mother, Mary appears for the first time in the world only to perform a work of charity. There is question of carrying a blessing to the family of her cousin: she flies, as it were, over the hills. Charity, good works, oh, yes! this is woman's department in Christianity. It is her vocation. God has given her in abundance all that she requires to fulfill it with success. Tenderness, gentleness, insinuating ways, activity, courage—nothing is wanting to her. Charity: such is therefore the fourth condition of woman's restoration and salvation.

A mother, Mary teaches woman the means of fulfilling the most sacred of her duties. From the crib to the cross, you see her inseparably attached to her Son. How can Christian mothers be told more eloquently that on their knees lies the future of the world, that in their hands the coming centuries are prepared? Let not your care, let not your eyes, any more than your heart, quit man for a moment: man, whose life is to make your happiness or your misery, and that of many others! Education, education that takes place at the knee and by the fireside: such is therefore the fifth condition of woman's restoration and salvation.[917]

A mother, Mary teaches woman to suffer. To flee into Egypt, trembling for her Son; to offer him, while yet young, to God; to consent beforehand to the tortures of Calvary; to stand at the foot of the cross: such is the life of Mary, the Mother of God. Suffering in every form, suffering from the birth of her child unto death: such is the life of a mother. To bear sufferings like Mary, meekly and silently, with courage and perseverance: such is the sixth condition of woman's restoration and salvation.

Mary as a widow. A widow, Mary teaches woman the great secret of the hidden life. Domestic virtues, wholesome advice, long prayers, and good works, so much the more meritorious before God as they are hidden from the eyes of men: such make up the seventh condition of woman's restoration and salvation.

A daughter, a wife, a mother, and a widow, and always a virgin: such does Mary appear to us in her relations with this lower world. These affecting relations, so perfectly realized by Mary, were only an expression of her more sublime relations with the upper world. She is the daughter of the Father, the Mother of the Son, and the spouse of the Holy Ghost, and all this in a manner ineffably wonderful. And woman also, to be what she ought to be in regard to man and society, ought to be like Mary in her intimate relations with the upper world. Like Mary, though in a different manner, she ought to be the daughter of the Father, the mother of the Son, and the spouse of the Holy Ghost.

On this condition, she will have that salutary sway in the lower world with which Mary was invested for the salvation of the human race.

In effect, if you read history, you will see many new "Marys" who, from age to age, exercise a most amazing influence on men and nations. Monica, Clotilda, Blanche, Adelaide, Matilda, Elizabeth, and many others, are authentic monuments of the truth to which we refer. The worship of Mary is therefore the salvation and glory of woman, and by woman of society.

Influence of the worship of the Blessed Virgin. This worship of the sweetest, the fairest, and the purest of virgins also spreads over Catholicity an indescribable charm, a nameless grace, that ravishes the heart and fills it with confidence. We delight to think that near God we have a mediatrix who is our sister, whose blood is the same as that which flows in our veins, whose purely human nature approaches so near to our weakness, and whose divine maternity gives her a kind of sway over the Almighty himself. In a word, we delight to see Mary pressing both God and man to her motherly heart, and saying to each, "My son!"

See how this consoling thought is reproduced in the Christian world. Man felt the need of not losing sight of it for a single moment, and he wished to meet it at every step and under every form. Without speaking of hymns, canticles, and litanies, in which he lavishes the sweetest titles on Mary, consider those thousands of masterpieces inspired by the worship of the Queen of angels, the Mother of God and men. Travel Europe: stand before the old monuments, question them, ask them who made them rise out of the earth with all their wonders. A voice will come forth from the stones, from traditions, and from annals, to tell you that it was the worship of Mary. Yes, it was this touching worship that adorned the Catholic world with so many magnificent churches, so many rich abbeys, so many noble hospitals, so many poetic memorials!

Without leaving our own France, formerly so Christian, see how many basilicas, how many chapels, how many hospices there are under the invocation of our Lady, and what sweet names are given to the divine Virgin! Here it is Our Lady of Good Succor; there, Our Lady of Mercy; further on, Our Lady of All Joys, or Our Lady of Gladness; yonder, Our Lady of All Help; at the hospital, Our Lady of the Seven Dolors; where the fallen lie, Our Lady of Victories; in the depths of the valley, Our Lady of Peace; on the mountaintop, Our Lady of Grace; near the surging waves, Our Lady of Good Harbor, or Our Lady of Guard; elsewhere, Our Lady of Deliverance, Our Lady of Snows, Our Lady of Rocks, Our Lady of the Hill, Our Lady of Lilies, Our Lady of the Angels, Our Lady of Comfort, Our Lady of Puy, our Lady of Fourvières, Our Lady of La Salette, Our Lady of Lourdes, etc.

Such are some of the beautiful titles of the patroness whom our ancestors chose. "The sons of the Franks and the Gauls, those men of action, of battles and conquests, our ancestors, who during so many ages went about through the world, setting kings on thrones, had put their fiery valor under the protection of a heavenly woman. All covered with the dust and the gore of combats, Old France fell on its knees before the statues of Mary, and often placed the image of the Virgin on its white flags... Verily, it was a noble spectacle, to see the strong and the brave thus honor a Mother and a child, and oppose what is sweetest in heaven to what is most terrible on earth!"[918]

And God himself took care to justify, to authorize, and to encourage the worship of Mary by splendid miracles. It would be too long to relate them all: we should have to write out the annals of every people, of every city, and even of every family. One will suffice.

The victory of Lepanto.—The day at Lepanto will always be a glorious proof of the protection of the Mother of God in favor of those who invoke it. For nearly a century, the Turks had been spreading terror through all Christendom by a succession of victories, which God permitted in order to punish the sins of Christians, and to revive their faith, half dead. Selim, the son and successor of Soliman, emperor of Constantinople, having made himself master of the island of Cyprus, came with a powerful army against the Venetians, and promised himself nothing less than the conquest of Europe. The holy pope Pius V, alarmed at the danger that threatened Christendom, joined with the Venetians, the Genoese, and the Spanish, to resist the common enemy. Though the league was not very strong, the Christians, relying on the protection of the Blessed Virgin, did not doubt of the success of their enterprise.

From the outset, the pope commanded public fasts and prayers in order to appease the divine justice. All Europe prayed: the faithful ran in crowds to the Church of Our Lady of Loretto, there to implore the assistance of heaven, through the intercession of the Mother of God. The holy pontiff, when sending his blessing to the general, Don Juan of Austria, assured him positively of victory. He ordered him at the same time to dismiss all such soldiers as seemed animated only by the prospect of plunder, as well as all persons whose morals were irregular, lest their crimes should draw down the divine vengeance on the army.

The pontiff's order is religiously executed. All the troops, without a single exception, approach the sacraments with a lively faith. A stop is put to cardplaying. Blasphemy is forbidden under pain of death. The papal nuncio blesses the fleet solemnly, and thousands of brave men, assured of the protection of heaven, set sail for the East. The sovereign pontiff, on his side, lifts up his hands to heaven like another Moses, and endeavors by fervent prayer to draw down the blessing of God on the Christian arms.

At length, on the 7th of October, 1571, the two fleets meet in the Gulf of Lepanto. The Turks charge the Christians furiously, and seem at first to gain some advantage. But he who holds victory in his hands does not delay to declare for the Christians. The infidels are completely beaten. They lose more than thirty thousand men and nearly all their war material. The Christians find immense booty, and set free some fifteen thousand captives, detained on board the ships of the Mahometans.

The holy father had a revelation of the victory at the very moment that it was won. He was then engaged in business with the cardinals. Suddenly he leaves them, and opens the window. After looking toward the sky for a few moments, he says to them: "There is no more time to speak of business; we should rather think of returning thanks to God for the victory that he has just granted the Christian army."[919] This fact, extraordinary as it is, was proved in the most authentic manner, and is related as indisputable in the process of the holy pope's canonization.

Pius V was so convinced that this victory was the effect of the Blessed Virgin's special protection that he instituted the festival of Our Lady of Victory, which was afterward transferred to the first Sunday of October by his successor, Gregory XIII, under the title of the festival of the Holy Rosary. It was also on this occasion that Pius V inserted in the Litany of the Blessed Virgin the words, *Auxilium Christianorum, ora pro nobis*—"Help of Christians, pray for us!"

PRAYER

O my God! who art all love, I thank thee for having given us in Mary a Mother so good and powerful. Grant us the grace to love and imitate her.

I am resolved to love God above all things, and my neighbor as myself for the love of God; and, in testimony of this love, I will invoke Mary in all my trials and temptations.

Lesson 49: Christianity Brought before the Senses (Continued)—Worship of the Cross

What a cross is.—What is a cross? A cross is a book that contains the whole history of God, man, and the world.

The history of God. The universe, with all its wonders, is a book that, no doubt, relates eloquently the omnipotence of him whose mere word drew all creatures forth from nothingness.

The order and harmony of so many worlds tell me the infinite wisdom of him who arranges, as if for play, all the wheels in the mighty machine of the universe.

Lucifer and his rebel legions cast in the twinkling of an eye from the splendors of heaven into the gloomy depths of the abyss; Adam and Eve, the rulers of the visible world, uncrowned, dethroned, banished, sentenced to pain and death with all their race; the earth covered with the waters of the deluge; Sodom burnt; nations dashed to pieces for their crimes: these things tell me the dreadful severity of God's justice.

The sun, rising every day for the wicked as well as for the just, tells me the inexhaustible goodness of God. But all these things are only the alphabet of the knowledge of God: the cross is its summary. A thousand times more eloquently than anything else, it tells me the power, the wisdom, the justice, and the goodness of God. The cross is therefore the most splendid manifestation of God and his adorable perfections.

The history of man. Wars, divisions, national and domestic hatreds, and the conflict that I continually feel within myself, tell me, no doubt, that man is degraded, and that he is degraded only because he is guilty. But what is the depth of my degradation? The cross alone teaches me this, since it alone tells me what atonement had to be made for me.

Divine revelations, the teachings of the prophets, and the numberless graces shed on the world tell me very well the value of a human soul in the eyes of God, but the cross does so infinitely better. Presenting to my sight a God dying on a gibbet, it says, "See, O human soul, how much thou art worth"—*Anima, tanti vales!* It is therefore true that the cross tells me more of my nature, my corruption, the means of my rehabilitation, and the value of my soul, than all revelations and books. The cross is therefore a summary of the knowledge of man.

The history of the world. Historians relate for me the lives of nations, the periods of their glory and decay, their influence for good or evil; but the general tendency of centuries, the providential end of all the peoples that succeed one another on the stage of this world, the cross alone tells me.

Alone, it shows me the history of the human race, like a magnificent epic poem. The cross rallies under its arms all the centuries. It embraces the old world and the new: it saved the one by hope, and it saves the other by faith. Standing on Golgotha, look out into the future: all the peoples are going to pass before you. One moment they will come, sword in hand, to oppose the triumph of the cross; the next you will see them resting under the shade of this beautiful tree, or buried, so as to be born again, in the waters of baptism. Are there any at the ends of the earth that do not think of coming to it? It flies to them, and its apostles write their names with their own blood on its immortal rolls.

Above all peoples and all histories, the cross shows us God holding in his hands the heart of the world, and moving states, the Church, and men, at his pleasure, in the sphere of their destiny. The cross—always the cross! Everything serves for its progress, everything leads to its victory, both in ancient and modern times. The cross is therefore a summary of the knowledge of the world and of man.

Again, what is a cross? A cross is all Christianity brought before the senses in its means of success and in its spirit. It is an imperishable monument to the divinity of our religion. Go back nineteen centuries; question the nations of former days; ask them what is a cross. Jews and pagans will answer you that it is an instrument of punishment for slaves; an object of malediction, shame, and horror.[920]

Question the nations of our own days; ask them what is a cross. They will answer you that it is an object of love and veneration. And if you lift up your eyes, you will see it on the ridges of houses, on the tops of mountains, along the highroads, in deserts and in public squares, in town and in country, on the necks of princesses for ornament and on those of simple villagers for consolation, over the brows of monarchs and over the graves of beggars, in the palace and in the cabin, in temples and in courts.

Whence came this strange revolution in sentiments and ideas? Why and when did honor begin to be given to the cross? What cross was the first honored? If you put all these questions to the simplest Christian child, he will tell you of the great cross that was raised, eighteen hundred years ago, on the summit of Calvary—the cross on which our Savior Jesus died. This was the first cross honored in the world, and the only one that deserves to be honored; for all others are honored only in regard to it, as it itself is honored only in regard to the God whose blood purpled its branches and its stem.

Ah! I am no longer surprised at the Christian's reverence for the cross. Every man, whosoever he is, ought to fall on his knees before it; for, remember what I am going to say, the cross is the first tree of liberty, the palladium of thrones, the standard of civilization, the book of great sorrows and great lessons—consequently of great lights and great consolations. It was the cross that vanquished cruel, despotic, infamous paganism. The cross alone dispelled and still dispels the darkness of ignorance. The countries where it shines are full of light, like those on which the sun sends down his glorious beams. The cross is devotedness, is the spirit of sacrifice, is all that secures the existence of families and of society. Shame on the men, woe to the men, that pass before the cross without thinking it worth their while to salute it! Shame on those, woe to those, who banish it from its place over the hearth at home! A son is not ashamed of a virtuous father, even when he has ceased to be virtuous himself.

The Catholic Church, the loving spouse of the God of Calvary, has always regarded the cross as her most precious and beautiful jewel; who will tell the honors with which she surrounds it? Not a ceremony of her worship wherein you do not find the memory of the cross! As if all this homage of every day and every moment was not enough, she established two particular festivals to honor the cross: that of the Finding and that of the Exaltation. Let us relate their history.

Festival of the Finding of the Cross: Its history.—Constantine the Great, who had triumphed over his enemies by the miraculous power of the cross, entertained feelings of the liveliest gratitude toward Jesus Christ. St. Helena, his mother, shared the pious sentiments of her son. Hence, their great veneration for the places that the Son of God had honored by his presence, his instructions, and his miracles. It was to satisfy her devotion that the pious empress, though nearly eighty years of age, visited Palestine in 326.

Having reached Jerusalem, her soul was filled with an earnest desire to find the cross on which the Son of God had suffered for our sins; but there was nothing to show where it lay. Tradition itself threw little light on the subject. The pagans, out of hatred to Christianity, had striven to destroy all knowledge of the place where the body of the Savior had been buried. Not content with having heaped up an immense quantity of stones and rubbish, they had also built a temple of Venus there, so as to make it appear that the faithful were honoring this infamous deity when they came to offer their adorations to Jesus Christ. They had also profaned the place where the mystery of the resurrection had been accomplished, by raising there a statue of Jupiter, which existed from the reign of Adrian to that of Constantine.

Helena, resolved on sparing no efforts to succeed in her pious design, consulted the inhabitants of Jerusalem, and all others from whom she might expect any information. She was told that if she could discover the Savior's sepulchre, she would not fail to find the instruments of his death. In point of fact, it was the custom among the Jews to dig a hole near the place where the bodies of persons condemned to death had been buried, and to throw in there whatever had been employed in their execution. Articles of this kind were held in horror, and people hastened to cast them forever out of their sight.[921]

The pious empress immediately ordered the temple to be pulled down, and the statue of Venus, as well as that of Jupiter, to be broken in pieces. The place was cleared out, and, after digging for some time, the holy sepulchre was found. At a short distance lay embedded three crosses, together with the nails that had pierced the Savior's body, and the title that had been fixed to the top of the cross. Evidently, one of the crosses was that sought, and the other two those of the malefactors between whom the Son of God had died. But how were they to be distinguished? The matter was so much the more difficult as the title was lying apart—not attached to any of the three.

In this embarrassment, it was considered a duty to have recourse to St. Macarius, bishop of Jerusalem. He directed the three crosses to be borne to the house of a lady of quality who had just died. This was done. Having addressed God in fervent prayer, he applied the three crosses singly to the deceased. At the touch of the first and the second, death refused to give up its prey. But the third put it to flight, and the lady awoke full of life.[922]

St. Helena showed the greatest joy at the miracle that had made known the true cross. She built a church on the very spot where this sacred treasure had been found, and deposited it there with great veneration, having provided an exceedingly rich case for it. However, she kept a portion of it for the emperor, her son, which he received at Constantinople with much respect. With another portion she enriched a church that she built in Rome, under the name of the Holy Cross of Jerusalem.

To the same church in Rome, she made a present of the title of the Savior's cross. It was laid on the top of an arch, where it was found in 1492, enclosed in a leaden box. The inscription which, as St. John says, was in Hebrew, Greek, and Latin, appears in red letters and on whitened wood. The colors have faded very much since the end of the fifteenth century. The last letters of the words *Rex* and *Judaeorum* are gone, together with the part of the board belonging to them. Such as it is, this board is nine inches long; but originally it was twelve.

The most considerable portion of the cross, left in Jerusalem under the care of the holy bishop Macarius, to be handed down to posterity, soon became an object of general veneration, as we learn from the lives of St. Cyril of Jerusalem, St. Porphyrius of Gaza, and others. Pieces were often cut from it for pious persons, yet the sacred wood suffered no diminution thereby: this fact is related by St. Paulinus in his letter to Severus. Twenty-five years after the discovery of the cross, St. Cyril of Jerusalem said that the wood thus cut in little pieces was spread over the whole earth, and he compared this prodigy to that which the Savior wrought when he miraculously fed five thousand men in the desert.

The church built by St. Helena was called the Basilica of the Holy Cross, on account of the precious treasure of which it was in possession. He who had care thereof was always a venerable priest. The Basilica of the Holy Cross was also called the Church of the Sepulchre, or the Church of the Resurrection, because there was a chapel there, built over the sepulchre or cave in which the body of the Savior had been buried, and which was in a garden near Mount Calvary. We may judge hereby of the size of the basilica. It covered the sepulchre, extended to Mount Calvary, and included, not only the rock of Golgotha, but the very spot where the cross of our Lord had been planted at his crucifixion. This edifice was enclosed within the boundaries of Jerusalem when the city was rebuilt.

We have spoken of the title that was placed on the cross of the Savior. It was customary among the Romans to have a notice carried before malefactors on their way to execution, telling the crime for which they had been condemned to death. Suetonius, speaking of a criminal, says, "Before him was carried a title, on which the public might read the cause of his punishment." Dio assures us of the same thing. See what Eusebius relates of Attalus, a martyr in Lyons: he was led round the amphitheatre, a tablet borne before him with the words: "Attalus a Christian," written on it.

Conformably to what was practiced among the Romans, Pilate ordered a title to be carried before the Savior to Mount Calvary, and fastened to his cross: it set forth the cause of his execution. He wished people to understand from this title that Jesus Christ was put to death only for having aspired to the sovereign power. But everything here was guided by providence. Our Lord was really the King of the Jews, the Greeks, and the Romans: it was written in the languages of these three peoples, that they might read it, and render their homage to him who alone had a most just claim to such a title.[923]

Origin of the festivals of the cross. Let us now speak of the origin of the festivals of the cross. In memory of the cross that appeared miraculously to Constantine, there was a festival established from the fourth century: it was celebrated on the 14th of September with great pomp by the Churches of East and West.[924] This festival acquired a new solemnity after the discovery of the true cross by St. Helena; for these two events were united on the same day in the devotion of Christians. In the seventh century, the recovery of the cross gave occasion to the establishment of a new festival, which the Latin Church celebrates on the 14th of September. Since that period, the festival of the Finding of the Cross, that is, its discovery by St. Helena, has been kept on the 3rd of May.

We shall relate in a few words how this precious treasure was got back from the Persians. In 614, Chosroes, king of Persia, took Jerusalem and carried off the true cross. By the ordinance of heaven, the case that contained it was not opened, and the bishop of Jerusalem's seal remained intact. Fourteen years afterward, the Persians having been conquered by the emperor Heraclius, the first condition imposed on them was to restore the cross. The condition was accepted, and the cross was restored.

The emperor brought back this precious relic to Constantinople, where he made his entry with the greatest magnificence. In the beginning of the next spring, 629, he embarked for Palestine to deposit this same relic in Jerusalem, and to return thanks there to God for his victories. A truly Christian prince, he wished to carry the true cross on his shoulders when entering the city, and to accompany this ceremony with all the pomp possible; but he suddenly felt himself stopped and quite unable to advance. The patriarch Zachary, who walked by his side, represented to him that so much splendor did not agree with the humiliations of the Son of God when he carried his cross through the streets of Jerusalem. "You wear," he said, "your imperial ornaments, and Jesus Christ was poorly clad; you have a rich diadem on your head, and he had a crown of thorns; you walk in shoes, and he walked barefooted." The emperor immediately laid aside his costly robes, his crown, and his shoes, and, following the procession with an exterior that bespoke poverty, he was easily able to carry the cross to the place where it had been before.

The seals having been again examined and found whole, the silver case was opened. The holy relic was then venerated, and shown to all the people. We learn from ancient writers that this portion of the true cross consisted of different pieces, and hence it is that they speak of it only in the plural number. The ceremony to which we refer was performed with the greatest piety, and was attended with several miraculous cures. The practice of exposing this sacred relic to the veneration of the faithful, long before its recovery out of the hands of the Persians, was observed with much devotion. The portion of the true cross kept at Constantinople was exposed in like manner.

Advantages of the worship of the cross.—Let us also, children of the Catholic Church, honor the cross, as highborn children honor the portrait of their father—what do I say?—as they honor the most affecting pledge of his love. Let worldlings have their way in accusing religion of saddening us by continually setting before our eyes a mournful object. They do not know that, with the faithful Christian, the cross is joy, is glory, is the wisdom of God.

It was from the summit of the cross that our Lord gave peace to all good people, and a peace that the whole world of the wicked cannot tear from their souls. It was from the summit of this cross that the Son of God, both priest and victim, drawing all the just to him, bringing close together the earth of heaven and the heaven of earth, taught us to suffer and to die. And this cross, by which the Redeemer of the world triumphed over death and hell—this cross, which gives value to virtue and secures for it an immortal crown—this cross, round which all those rally who are baptized in Jesus Christ, you would destroy the worship of throughout the world!

Ah! if you love the human race, or if you have the heart of a patriot, leave the cross on the pinnacle of the palace, to recall the rich and great to the paths of penance; leave it on the roof of the cottage, to instruct the poor in patience and resignation; leave it to all men, because all men have pride to crush, have passions to subdue, and because, to teach them to esteem what is of any worth and to trample under their feet all the vain prejudices of the world, there is no better master than Jesus Christ dying on the cross.

But if we wish that the cross should serve us, if we wish to press it lovingly and hopefully to our lips at death, if we wish it to keep guard over our grave and to be a pledge to us of a glorious resurrection,[925] let us often read this divine book, let us write its lessons deeply on our hearts. Let him who wishes to acquire the science of the saints draw near to the cross. There he will be able to drink in the most sublime and pathetic doctrines ever given to men. Jesus crucified is, beyond all else, the model of virtue and the book of life. St. Paul studied this model and this book continually, because he found in the cross alone all the truths that it was proper for him to know. All Christians worthy of their glorious name imitate the apostle, and confirm the same principle.

Where did St. Bernard find his ardent love of God and fervent piety? Was it not in the sufferings of his Redeemer on the cross? Where did St. Augustine obtain the knowledge that made him one of the lights of the Church, if not in the wounds of Jesus, as he himself tells us? It was the book of the cross that inspired St. Francis with a seraphic love. St. Thomas, who cast himself on every occasion at the foot of his crucifix, was indebted to it for his admirable wisdom.

"St. Bonaventure," says St. Francis de Sales, "seems, when writing, to have had no other paper than the cross, no other pen than the lance, and no other ink than the precious blood of Jesus Christ. With what an overflow of tenderness does he not exclaim: 'It is good for us to be with the cross! Let us make three tabernacles here in Jesus crucified: one in his feet; another in his hands; and the third in his sacred side. Here shall I dwell—here shall I watch, read, and meditate—having this divine book always before my eyes, to study the science of salvation during the whole day, and even during the night as often as I awake!'"

The prophet Jonas rested with delight under the shade of the ivy bush that the Lord had prepared for him. What then ought to be the delight of a Christian when he rests under the shade of the cross! Protected by this sacred wood, we may say: "Let Jonas rejoice under an ivy bush; let Abraham make ready a repast for angels under a tree in the vale of Mambre; let Ismael be heard under a tree in the desert; let Elias be fed under a juniper tree; as for us, our consolation and joy will be to remain under the branches of the cross!"

The foregoing remarks have acquainted us with the great advantage of the knowledge and love of the cross of our Lord and his sorrowful passion. An excellent means of securing this inestimable advantage for Christians was to speak to their senses, setting before their eyes and making them travel the sorrowful way that the Savior trod, laden with his cross, from the praetorium to Calvary. The Church did this by establishing the pious practice of the Way of the Cross.

The Way of the Cross.—The devotion of the Way of the Cross, that is, the devotion which leads the Christian, praying and weeping, to go over the ground walked by his

God, laden with the instrument of his execution, is as old as Christianity. From the time of the apostles, and after the example of the apostles and Mary, Christians visited this ever-celebrated place. When the gospel had passed beyond the boundaries of Judea, the devotion drew new pilgrims from all parts to Jerusalem. The wars of the Romans, the dissensions of the Jews, the destruction of Jerusalem, and the profanations of emperors could scarcely interrupt the visits and the adoration of the faithful.

Of a truth, they were often obliged to present from afar and in secret their homage to the sacred places; but they never forgot or abandoned them. Divine providence watched over those things the memory of which was faithfully preserved. The patriarchs of Jerusalem easily handed down traditions, and the most important memories of the Holy Land still existed when religion came, in 313, to adorn with its splendor the diadem of the Caesars.

In the footsteps of St. Helena, Christians thronged of Jerusalem from all the countries of the known world. The Holy Land was covered with them. Bethlehem, Nazareth, the Jordan, and Jerusalem were continually receiving the homage of their faith and love. They spent whole months and years near these monuments: some even fixed their abode here altogether. The traces that the foreheads and knees of pilgrims left here in the course of time bore witness to the true situation of the places consecrated by the events of our Savior's passion. Their pious thefts, though injurious to monuments that had been raised there, also served to show the right spots.

Kings and princes visited them in their turn.[926] At length, the holy places having fallen into the hands of the Saracens, Europe was seen arming to regain them. During the ninety years that Christians had been masters of them, they spared nothing to honor in a becoming manner these monuments so dear to their hearts. From the time that they lost them, providence always raised up some faithful guardians for them, guardians so much the more reliable as their creeds were different and their communions divided. Thus, from the origin of Christianity down to our own days, the chain of pilgrims to Jerusalem has never been wholly broken. People always wished to travel the way sprinkled with the blood of the man-God; and innumerable graces have, in all ages, rewarded this evidence of faith and gratitude.

The benefits related on returning from the holy journey set hearts on fire. Everyone wanted to go in his turn; but this was impossible. Hence the majority would have been deprived of the consolations, indulgences, and other favors attached to the pilgrimage to Jerusalem, to the real Way of the Cross, if the Church, at once a mother attentive to the wants and wishes of her children and the supreme dispensatrix of all the merits of the Redeemer, had not supplied for them by a pious practice, brought to the doors of all the faithful.

This practice, called the *Via Crucis* or Way of the Cross, is nothing else than a figurative journey of that which our Lord made, laden with his cross. To render this representation as striking as possible, there are pictures set up from distance to distance—showing us the most tender scenes in the passion, from the moment when our Lord leaves the praetorium of Pilate to go to Calvary. These stations, known from scripture and tradition, are twelve in number, to which the descent from the cross and the laying in the sepulchre have been added, thus raising the number to fourteen. Such is the origin of the devotion called the Way of the Cross, and such is the idea that we ought to have of it.

As for our motives to practice this excellent devotion, the principal are these:

1. *The authority of the Church.* Twenty-two sovereign pontiffs have approved and recommended the devotion of the Way of the Cross, and enriched it with numerous indulgences. Among all, one of the greatest popes that ever occupied the chair of St. Peter—namely, Benedict XIV—was distinguished for his zeal in extending this practice

throughout Christendom. He regarded it as a most proper means to reform morals and to maintain piety.[927]

2. *The desire of our Lord.* The old and the new testament are full of texts by which this divine Savior invites us often to call to mind his humiliations. The apostles seem unable to preach anything but Jesus, and him crucified. The saints of all ages have made the passion of our Lord the ordinary subject of their meditations. With what happiness will Mary herself see us think on the sufferings of her beloved Son! A mother, can she be indifferent to the tears that we shed over the sorrows of her child?

3. *Our own interest.* Pious meditation on the cross dispels the darkness of the understanding. What lights regarding God, his power, his justice, and his mercy, our greatness and our misery, and also the enormity of sin, beam from the cross! It touches the heart. The sight of a crucifix, or meditation on the passion, is more proper to convert souls and to make them love God than the most terrible truths.

And then, are not the extraordinary indulgences attached to the Way of the Cross a powerful motive to practice this devotion? According to a concession of Pope Innocent XI, the Way of the Cross is enriched with all the indulgences granted at various times by sovereign pontiffs to the visiting of all the holy places in Palestine.[928]

We need not speak of the manner of going round the Stations. It is sufficiently explained in little manuals on the subject. Let us, in conclusion, be content with admiring the wonderful solicitude of the Catholic Church in continually bringing her children to the bloodstained footprints of their father. How much wisdom and love there is in so doing! And you who read these lines! you will correspond with her pious care, will you not?

PRAYER

O my God! who art all love, I thank thee for having redeemed us by thy cross. Grant that, like the apostle St. Paul, we may know nothing but Jesus, and him crucified.

I am resolved to love God above all things, and my neighbor as myself for the love of God; and, in testimony of this love, I will often ask for the science of the cross.

Lesson 50: Christianity Brought before the Senses (Continued)—Worship of the Angels

Origin of the worship of angels.—The worship of angels is as ancient as the world. We see them invoked in the old testament.[929] The Catholic Church, the heiress of all true traditions, ennobled and consecrated from her origin the worship of the holy angels. The fathers of the East and West are unanimous on this point.[930] Nevertheless, heretics having risen up who rendered an idolatrous worship to the angels, the Eastern Church thought it a duty to be somewhat reserved in the honors that she offered to these blessed spirits, lest the sectaries should take occasion therefrom to become more attached to their errors. But the Western Church, having nothing of this kind to fear, explained herself more freely in regard to the invocation of angels.[931]

It is certain that they were invoked long before festivals and temples were dedicated to them. No particular day was set apart for them, because their worship was in a manner incorporated with all public prayers; consequently, with all the festivals of the Church. There is mention made of the angels in the preface and the Canon of the Mass. In the psalter, of which the canonical office consists, the memory of the angels is very often renewed. The Litany of the Saints, which comes from the highest antiquity, and which is, as it were, an abridgment of the general prayers of the Church, names the angels after Mary, their august Queen.

In the same manner therefore as the Blessed Trinity, the Holy Sacrament, and all the saints were honored by a general festival before the establishment of a particular solemnity, there was a general festival for all the angels, whose worship is connected with everything in the Catholic liturgy, before any particular solemnity or temple was dedicated to them.

Nevertheless, the Church, full of gratitude toward those ministering spirits who watch over her defense and labor for the salvation of her children, established three special festivals in order to pay them the tribute of her piety. The first and second are those of St. Michael, the prince of the heavenly host; the third is that of all the holy angels in general and the angel guardian in particular. Let us tell in a few words the origin of these solemnities.

Festivals of St. Michael.—During the time that the Creator had marked out to try the fidelity of the angels, a great many, filled with pride at the consideration of their own excellence, rose up against the author of so many sublime gifts, and, from a feeling of jealousy, protested against the dogma of the incarnation. The archangel St. Michael hurled the rebels into the abyss by the irresistible power of the name of God. This victory is expressed in the very name of the archangel: *Quis ut Deus?*—"Who is like God?" St. Michael has always been regarded as the defender of faithful nations. The ancient protector of France, he was chosen as patron of the military order established under his name, in 1469, by King Louis XI.

In 493, the glorious archangel appeared on Mount Gargano, in Italy.[932] Nothing could be more consoling or celebrated than this apparition. A solemn festival, observed on the 8th of May, perpetuates the memory of it.

From time immemorial, another festival has been celebrated in honor of the same archangel. On the 29th of September, the Church reminds her children of the power and the benefits of the prince of the heavenly host. This festival was formerly most solemn in many countries of the West.

Here is what we read in the ecclesiastical laws published in 1014 by Ethelred, King of England: "Let every Christian who is of age fast three days on bread and water and raw herbs before the feast of St. Michael, and let every man go to confession and to Church barefoot...Let every priest go three days barefoot in procession with his people; and let everyone's food for three days be prepared, without anything of flesh however, and let all this be distributed to the poor. Let every servant be dispensed from labor these three days, that he may celebrate the feast better, or let him only do what is necessary for himself. These three days are the Monday, Tuesday, and Wednesday next before the feast of St. Michael."[933]

Though St. Michael alone is named in the title of this festival, it would seem from the prayers of the Church that all the holy angels are the objects of it. Hence comes a truth very proper to draw closer the bonds of charity that unite us. The Church evidently desires that we should honor the angels and saints, and that we should celebrate their festival in a spirit of unity and universality, considering them all as one body, the body of Jesus Christ, or as one saint, the saint of saints.

It is difficult to honor one member without this honor being communicated to all the other members of the same body. The glory and the joy of each one are common to all, and whatever is common to all in general is proper to each one in particular. "If one member rejoices, all the others rejoice with it,"[934] says St. Paul. Thus, the festival of each saint is a festival of every other saint. It was for this reason that the festival of all the apostles was formerly kept on a single day, because we cannot celebrate the festival of one of them without all the others sharing therein.[935]

These reflections are still more necessary in regard to the angels, whom we honor all in general on St. Michael's day. The Church does not let us name more than three angels, whose names are given in scripture, and yet she wishes that we should honor many millions of them. It is not therefore by particular festivals that we are to fulfill our duty toward them, but by being firmly convinced that, when we mention or revere one of them, we include all the others, as all making up one holy city, of which each represents the majesty and preeminence.

Means of honoring the holy angels.—Let us say a word of the worship that we render to the angels, and the manner of celebrating their festival. Supreme worship, called *latria*, belongs to God alone, and we cannot give it to any creature without falling into idolatry, and being guilty of the crime of high treason against the Divine Majesty. An idolater is one who offers sacrifice to a being that is not God, or who transfers to that being, either directly or indirectly, any attribute of the deity. But there is an honor of an inferior order which is due to certain creatures on account of their superiority or their excellence.

Such is that honor which the law of God itself commands us to render to our parents, to kings, to rulers, to all persons constituted in dignity. Such is also that honor, blended with a deep sentiment of religion, which, according to the holy books and the law of nature, is due to priests or the ministers of the Most High, and which kings, even the most wicked, often rendered to the prophets, though the latter were obscure men, contemptible in the eyes of the world.

This honor, as we see, differs widely from that which belongs to God alone. It cannot be an injury to him; for it is referred to creatures only insofar as their perfections are the gifts of the divine bounty. When we show respect to an ambassador, we honor the master who has entrusted him with a part of his own authority, and it is this master who is the remote object of the sentiments that we manifest. The scripture comes to the support of the law of nature on this point: "Render to all men what is due to them:...honor to whom honor belongs."[936] "Give honor," says St. Bernard, "to everyone according to his dignity."

As for the manner of celebrating the festivals of the angels well, we ought, if we would enter into the spirit of religion, a) to thank God for the glory with which he loads these sublime creatures, and rejoice at the happiness which they enjoy; b) to show our gratitude to the Lord for that, of his mercy, he has entrusted the care of our salvation to these heavenly spirits, who let us continually feel the effects of their zeal and their tender solicitude; c) to join them in praising and adoring God, in asking him for grace to do his will on earth as they do it in heaven, and in laboring for our salvation, by an imitation of the purity of these blessed spirits, to whom we are so closely united; and d) not only to honor them fervently, but to implore the help of their intercession confidently.

Festival of the Guardian Angel.—It remains for us to speak of the guardian angel. And first, tell me, O men! whosoever you are, if you know anything more proper than the festival of the Guardian Angel to give a high idea of himself to the son of Adam, to this being who creeps in the dust, who bedews the road of life with his tears, and who, borne down by the weight of a corrupt nature, inclines to all that is vile and abject? Do you, I repeat, know anything better to ennoble him in his own eyes, and to make him sacred in the eyes of others?

"Remember, O son of dust!" says the Church to him on this day, "that thou art the son of the Eternal! The monarch of worlds hath deputed a prince of his court to attend on thee, and said to him: 'Go, take my son by the hand; watch over all his steps; let me know his wants and his wishes. By day, keep near him as he moves, and by night, stand at the pillow of his bed. Bear him up in thy arms, lest he dash his foot against a stone. He is entrusted to thy care: thou shalt lead him to the foot of my throne on the day that I have fixed for receiving him into my kingdom, his eternal inheritance." Behold a few of the many things that are said to us by the festival of the Angel Guardian!

How could the Catholic Church, repairing all things, forget to celebrate such a festival? Oh, no, she is not so unmindful! On the contrary, she has done everything to render sensible, and, as it were, always present the belief of the guardian angel. From our cradle to our grave, she speaks to us of the prince of the heavenly court who watches over the defense of our body and our soul, who sees all our actions, and who gives an account of them to God, the Father and judge of all mankind.

All this, however, was not enough for her solicitude. She appointed a special festival to honor the guardian angels of her children. It was Ferdinand of Austria, afterward emperor, who, in the beginning of the seventeenth century, obtained leave from Pope Paul V for the establishment of the office and festival of the Guardian Angel.[937] Soon spread throughout the whole Church, this touching solemnity has never since been interrupted.

In point of fact, are not the motives we have to celebrate it always the same, that is to say, always powerful, always numerous, always dear to generous hearts? It even seems that the farther we advance in life and the nearer the world draws to its end, the more imperative do the reasons become for honoring the good angels. In the last times, the devils will be unchained, and will make the most fierce and dangerous attacks on Christians. Who will take care of them but the good angels? Moreover, is not every day of our existence and the world's existence the witness of some new benefit bestowed by the guardian angels? Are not these new benefits so many titles to our gratitude and our respect?

Duties toward our guardian angel. "To fulfill the duties imposed on us toward our guardian angel, we must," says St. Bernard, "render him a triple homage: that of reverence, that of devotion, and that of confidence. We owe him reverence for his presence, devotion for his charity, and confidence for his vigilance. Penetrated with respect, walk always with circumspection, remembering that you are in the presence of angels, appointed to guide you in all your ways. Wherever you are, no matter how secret the place, always respect your angel guardian. Would you dare to do before him what you would not do before me?"[938]

We should not only respect our tutelar angel, but love him. He is a faithful guardian, a true friend, a powerful protector. Notwithstanding the excellence of his nature, his charity leads him to charge himself with our defense. He watches over the preservation of our body, which the devils have sometimes the power to injure; but what does he not do for our soul? He instructs us, he encourages us, he exhorts us interiorly; he warns us of our duties by secret reproaches. He fulfills toward us the duties of an office like that of the angel who led the Jews into the promised land; he does for us what the angel Raphael did for young Tobias; he serves us as a guide amid the dangers of this life. With what sentiments of gratitude, reverence, docility, and confidence should we not be penetrated for our guardian angel! Can we ever sufficiently thank the divine mercy for the benefits that it has bestowed on us?

Tobias, reflecting on the signal favors that he had received from the angel Raphael, said to his father: "What reward can we offer him that will bear any proportion to the good things with which he has laden us? He guided me away and brought me back safe; he himself obtained the money from Gabelus; he introduced me to the woman whom I have married, he banished the devil from her, he filled her father and mother with joy; he delivered me from the fish that was going to devour me; he let yourself see the light of heaven. It is by him that we have received ever so many favors. What then can we give him for all that he has done to us?"[939]

Tobias and his parents, touched with the liveliest gratitude, fell prostrate on the ground, and lay upon their face for three hours, praising God. Let us endeavor to enter into the same sentiments. "Let us," says St. Bernard, "love the angels tenderly in God—those blessed spirits who will one day be our companions and coheirs in glory, and who are now our tutors and guardians. Let us be devout and grateful, toward such protectors; let us honor them as much as we are able."

We should also have a loving trust in the protection of our guardian angel. "However weak we are," continues St. Bernard, "however miserable our condition, however great the dangers surrounding us, we need fear nothing under the protection of such guardians...As often as any affliction or temptation assails you, implore the help of him who guards you, who guides you, who assists you in all your trials."

But, to deserve his protection, we ought above all things to avoid sin: faults, even venial, grieve him. "As smoke," says St. Basil, "puts bees to flight, and a bad smell does the same with doves, so the infection of sin drives away the angel appointed to guard us."

Let us hear what the God of angels says, and let his words be the rule of our conduct and the support of our hope. "I will send my angel," says the Lord, "that he may walk before you, that he may keep you on your journey, and that he may bring you into the land that I have prepared for you. Respect him, listen to his voice, and take great care not to despise him, because he will not forgive you when you sin, and my name is in him. But if you listen to his voice and do whatever I shall tell you by his mouth, I will be an enemy to your enemies and will afflict those who afflict you. My angel will walk before you, and will lead you into the land that I have prepared for you."[940]

PRAYER

O my God! who art all love, I thank thee for having sent thy angels to guard me: grant me the grace to be myself an angel before thee by the purity of my heart and by my readiness to do thy holy will.

I am resolved to love God above all things, and my neighbor as myself for the love of God; and, in testimony of this love, I will every day say fervently the prayer to my guardian angel.

Lesson 51: Christianity Brought before the Senses (Continued)—All Saints

Festival of All Saints: Wisdom of the Church in the division of her year.—Our mother the Church had the skill to represent in the division of her year the whole history of the human race. The four weeks of Advent, which terminate at the birth of the Savior, remind us of the four thousand years during which this divine Messias was expected. The time between Christmas and Pentecost sets before us the hidden, public, and glorious life of the Redeemer: this part of the year concludes with the Ascension of Jesus Christ into heaven and the Descent of the Holy Ghost. The interval from Pentecost to All Saints tells us of the pilgrimage of the Church on earth: this new part of the year ends in the festival of heaven.

During the long space of time last mentioned, we see the heavenly traveler speeding her way toward the blessed land, gathering together the elect from the four winds, and, that she may console herself in her exile and encourage herself amid her conflicts, celebrating one after another the festivals of her martyrs, her confessors, her virgins, and the angels who keep watch over her. All the gospels of this period breathe the charity, the zeal, the virtues, the hopes of a mother all tenderness and solicitude. Thus does she reach the end of her annual course, sowing along her way the seeds of salutary lessons and a noble example.

When, therefore, autumn is come, and the vinedresser fills his cellars, the farmer lays up the heavy sheaves in his barns, men gather in joyfully their goods of every kind, fruits of their sweat and their toil, the Church cries out to all her children on earth: "Eyes and hearts above!" Then, opening a little the gates of the heavenly Jerusalem, and letting a few rays of that ineffable glory which God has in store for his saints shine down on them, she says with her sweet motherly voice to all, rich and poor, learned and ignorant: "These good things which you are putting by are hardly an image of the good things awaiting you beyond the grave. Labor is indeed a condition of your earthly existence, but, while laboring for time, labor for eternity, sow virtues and you shall reap merits. Take noble views: heaven with its palms and its crowns, heaven with its eternity of glory and its torrents of delights, heaven alone is worthy of your care!"

And see how, in her own eloquent language, she speaks of the joys of our dear fatherland! The epistle of All Saints' day encourages our weakness: it tells us that heaven is filled with persons of every tribe, and tongue, and nation; that the saints were all that we are—weak, tempted, sinners even, in a word, children of Adam, like us; and that it only remains for us to be one day what they are.

The gospel shows us the conditions on which heaven will be given to us. It consoles us by teaching us that the simplest virtues, from humility, which delights in lying hid, to patience, which calumny puts to the severest tests, are so many royal roads that lead to the city of happiness. Let us read again with new attention the words of the sacred text.

"At that time, Jesus, having gone up into a mountain, sat down amid his disciples, and taught them thus:

"Blessed are the poor in spirit (that is to say, those who are humble and detached), for theirs is the kingdom of heaven.

"Blessed are the meek, for they shall possess the land.

"Blessed are they that mourn, for they shall be comforted.

"Blessed are they that hunger and thirst after justice, for they shall be filled.

"Blessed are the merciful, for they shall find mercy.

"Blessed are the clean of heart, for they shall see God.

"Blessed are the peacemakers, for they shall be called the children of God.

"Blessed are they that suffer persecution for justice's sake, for theirs is the kingdom of heaven.

"Blessed are you when men revile and persecute you, and speak all kinds of calumnies against you for my sake."[941]

With a wisdom of language that we can never sufficiently admire, the Church calls the exercise of those virtues to which heaven is promised, of those virtues within the reach of all, the eight beatitudes. Yes, beatitudes of man even on earth, where they secure his heart against the storms of the three great passions that tyrannize over the human race, and throw society into convulsions: an inordinate love of riches, an inordinate love of honors, and an inordinate love of pleasures. Hence, to make man happy through all eternity, religion only asks him for leave to make him happy in time.[942]

Full of such thoughts as these, let us on the festival of All Saints transport ourselves to the holy Jerusalem. There we shall see a host of witnesses, who, from the bright thrones on which they sit, contemplate and encourage us. Poor banished children, we shall be reminded by the palm branches in their hands that life is for us, as it was for them, a warfare. We are the combatants; the saints are the spectators; heaven is the crown. But the saints are not idle spectators. Our brethren and our friends, they encourage us by looks and gestures, they help us by their powerful prayers, they lift us up when we fall, and they embrace us if we win the victory, and applaud the great King who sets on our head the conqueror's crown.

Thus, in the magnificent office of All Saints, all the prayers of the Church tend to encourage us, while the splendor of her ornaments and the majesty of her ceremonies give us a faint idea of the entrancing beauties of the eternal festival.

Office of All Saints. To awake in our hearts a lively feeling of hope and joy is the object of the Church in the morning offices. But the festivals of earth are imperfect; the joys of our exile are mixed with sorrows: and lo! to complete the impression, the evening office leads us to a deep melancholy. It is full of sighs. There are tears in the choir. There are solemn canticles. The psalms seem to take a particular meaning in harmony with the dispositions of exiled man, uncertain of his salvation. In the hymn, we address ourselves to our Lord, the King of saints; to Mary, their Queen; and to all the orders of the blessed. We implore them to remember us, to bring us to them, and, in the meantime, to spread through the Church militant that charity which forms the happiness of the Church triumphant.

The antiphon at the *Magnificat*, by which we salute heaven for the last time, is a burning sigh after the happy land above. All is over. The gates of the heavenly Jerusalem, half-opened for a moment, close on our tearful eyes, and the Church calls us to a spectacle quite different. Such is, in a few words, the spirit of the Catholic liturgy on the festival of All Saints. But it is time to relate the origin of this solemnity.

Origin of this festival: Sentiments that it ought to inspire. From the early ages, the Church annually celebrated the festival of each martyr. On this day, the faithful assembled at the place where the Christian hero had won his victory. They surrounded his tomb, the stone of which served as an altar; and the august sacrifice was offered there in thanksgiving.[943]

Soon, the number of martyrs increasing, it was no longer possible to assign a particular festival to each one. The difficulty became much greater when the Church had given to heaven a countless multitude of solitaries, virgins, and confessors, whose sanctity was proved from day to day by splendid miracles. These reasons led to the establishment of one festival, which was consecrated to honor, first, all the martyrs, and afterward, all the saints in general. Let us here enter into a few details.

Marcus Agrippa, son-in-law and favorite of Augustus, had built a magnificent temple and dedicated it to Jupiter the Avenger.[944] He wished hereby to pay court to the emperor, who had just won the famous victory of Actium over Antony and Cleopatra. This temple was called the Pantheon, either because all false deities were worshipped in it, or because its shape represented the heavens, called by the pagans, the "abode of all the gods." This masterpiece of pagan architecture is a kind of half globe; its height is nearly equal to its breadth; its diameter is 158 feet. It has no pillars or windows: the light descends by a large round opening in the top. Most of the pagan temples were destroyed; but the emperor Honorius wished that the Pantheon should be let stand, as a monument of the former magnificence of the Empire.

In 607, Pope Boniface IV had it opened and cleaned. He dedicated it under the invocation of the Blessed Virgin and all the martyrs, which obtained for it the name of *Sancta Maria ad Martyres*. It was called the *Rotunda*, on account of its shape. The day of the Christian dedication of this famous temple was one of the most solemn that Rome ever witnessed. The sovereign pontiff appeared in all the ornaments of his dignity, followed by a great many of the clergy and an immense crowd. On the previous day, a large quantity of bones and other relics of martyrs had been taken from the catacombs. They were borne to the basilica in twenty-eight magnificently adorned chariots. How much more admirable was this triumph of the heroes of the faith than that of pagan consuls and emperors![945]

About the year 731, Pope Gregory III consecrated a chapel in St. Peter's Church, in honor of all the saints. Since those days, the festival of all the blessed inhabitants of the heavenly Jerusalem has always been celebrated in Rome. It seemed to be only for Rome, on account of the Pantheon and of the surprising quantity of relics transferred thereto. But Pope Gregory IV, having come into France in 836, engaged Louis le Debonnaire to cause it to be celebrated in his states. The prince consented willingly, and soon the festival of All Saints was universally adopted. Sixtus IV gave it an octave in 1480.[946]

The solemnity of All Saints was established therefore: a) to honor all the saints, for each of whom it is impossible to have a particular festival, either because their names are written only in the book of life, or because their festival has no day fixed for the faithful; b) to thank God for the benefits with which he loads the elect; c) to excite us to imitate their example; d) to encourage our weakness and to confound our tepidity, by setting before our eyes a multitude of saints of both sexes, and of every age and condition, and making us contemplate the ineffable happiness which they enjoy and to which we are invited; e) to implore the goodness of our heavenly Father in favor of his children on earth through the merits of his children in heaven; and f) to give us an opportunity of repairing the faults that we may have committed in the celebration of each particular festival.

How to celebrate this festival worthily. To celebrate the solemnity of All Saints worthily, it suffices to think that it is a family festival, the festival of our relations and friends, and that it is one day to be our own festival. We are the children of saints! Behold the balm that the divine goodness pours on the wounds—so many, alas! and so deep—of poor humanity! Can it be that we shall not regard the earth with disgust when we reflect that, by the divine mercy, we are capable of attaining to an extraordinary happiness which will never end. How shall we not then renounce whatever might tend to deprive us of our felicity, and adopt every means calculated to secure its possession? How shall we not be inflamed with an ardent desire of seeing ourselves admitted into the company of God's friends and crowned with them in eternal glory?

A general, who had risen by his bravery and good conduct from the lowest to the highest ranks of the army, used to delight in conversing familiarly with the soldiers under his command. "I too," he would say to them, "carried the musket and kept sentry like you. I led exactly the same kind of life as you, and went through the same fatigues." He would tell them how in sieges he had dug trenches and carried fascines; how he had always been foremost to scale the wall or to attack a dangerous post. He would relate in detail the various means by which he had passed through the grades of sergeant, lieutenant, captain, and colonel, on to general.

It is not easy to conceive how much the soldiers were roused by such discourses, or what a deep impression was made on them by the example before their eyes. They could no longer complain of fatigues or dangers. They regarded such things as matters of joy or ambition, as means of advancing to a position like that of their general. Yet they knew well that nothing could be more uncertain than the object of their hopes, that the least promotion was to be purchased only by very great dangers, and that, when they had the most happy and glorious success on their side, reward and distinction were something so extraordinary, so dependent on a variety of circumstances, so subject to the caprices of fortune, that they could not reasonably expect them.

It is quite otherwise in the great affair of our salvation: success depends on our own hearts. Immense as is the glory to which we aspire, it is God himself who invites us to it, and who will gladly be our light and our strength on the way. We are sure, with the help of his grace, which will never fail us, except through our own fault, that we can reach this happiness, which will have no end, and which surpasses all that we can imagine. How many saints already possess it! They have marked out for us by their example the road that we are to follow. They were what we are, wayfarers on earth: they had the same nature. "Elias," says the apostle James, "was subject to the same infirmities as we are."[947] Yet they were all sanctified.

In vain shall we allege the obstacles that we have to surmount: the saints found themselves in the same circumstances, and perhaps in more delicate ones. How many had to struggle against the attractions of pleasure, the snares of greatness, the seductions of flattery, the injustice of enemies, the horrors of prisons, the rage of persecutors, the cruelty of executioners! Not only did they triumph over all these difficulties, but they made them means of salvation: they thence became more attentive in watching over themselves. Their very faults turned to their advantage, making them more fervent in prayer, more mortified, more penitent, more earnest in the practice of good works.[948]

Such are the footprints that the saints have left behind them on their way home;[949] we must walk therein to reach the same place. If we want motives to do so, let us often remember this truth: it costs more to be damned than to be saved.

On the great day of All Saints, we render to the blessed inhabitants of heaven that worship which all Christian nations have rendered to them, and which all future ages will render to them when we are no more. Founded on the word of God and general tradition, the worship of the saints is imperishable. This is not the place to develop its nature. We know that Catholics do not adore the saints: they honor them as the friends of God, as powerful and faithful protectors, whose prayers obtain more surely than ours the graces that we require.

History of the beatification and canonization of saints.—What is less generally known is the history of the canonization of saints, that is to say, the manner of proceeding in order to prove their sanctity. We shall be happy if what we are going to say thereon help to make us admire more and more the profound wisdom and consummate prudence of the Catholic Church. Interesting in themselves, the following remarks seem to us particularly useful in that they complete the history of All Saints.

Let us first explain some words that perhaps we have often heard without attaching any precise meaning to them: servant of God, venerable, blessed, saint, beatification, canonization.

Servant of God. In the language of the Catholic Church, the Christian who has died in the odor of sanctity is thus named.[950]

Venerable. This term is applied to one whose reputation for sanctity has been judicially confirmed,[951] or, strictly speaking, whose process of beatification has been begun.[952]

Blessed. This term is applied to one who has been beatified, that is, whose sanctity has been declared by a solemn judgment, and to whom the sovereign pontiff permits worship to be rendered in certain places or in certain religious orders, up to the time of solemn canonization.[953]

Saint. One who has been canonized, that is, the worship of whom is permitted throughout the whole Catholic world.[954]

Beatification. After what has been said, it is easy to see that beatification is an act by which the sovereign pontiff declares that a person is happy after death. In consequence of beatification, the pope grants to certain persons or countries the privilege of honoring with a definite worship someone who has been beatified, without incurring the penalties threatened against those who offer a superstitious worship. Saints who are beatified, or declared blessed, are honored with a worship less solemn than those who are canonized. They cannot be chosen as patrons. Their office has no octave. The day of their office cannot be a festival of obligation. We cannot show our regard for them, as for others, by a votive Mass.[955]

Beatification has been introduced since canonization came to be attained only after a long series of investigations. Up to the time of Pope Alexander VII, who occupied the Holy See in the middle of the seventeenth century, the solemnity of the beatification of saints was made in the church of their order, if they were religious, or in that of their nation, if they had one in Rome. It was the same pope who first ordered the beatification of saints to take place in the Basilica of St. Peter, and the first that did so take place was that of St. Francis de Sales, on the 8th of January, 1662.[956]

Canonization. According to the etymology of the word, *canonization* means "the act by which someone is placed in the canon or catalogue of the saints." As a matter of fact, the ceremonies of canonization in the early ages of the Church consisted in writing the saint's name on the sacred diptychs, that is, on tablets which were read at Mass, and which contained the names of the Blessed Virgin, the apostles, and other saints: blessed names, which we still recite every day during the august mysteries, in memory of this ancient usage. The name of a saint having been placed on the diptychs, churches or oratories were erected in his honor, and the holy sacrifice was offered up there to thank God for his triumph and to implore his intercession.

If we now wish to explain the word *canonization* according to its present acceptation, we shall say that canonization is a lawful, solemn, and definitive declaration by which the sovereign pontiff places in the canon or catalogue of the saints a person who has been beatified, and authorizes his or her worship in the Universal Church. The term *canonization* is not as old as the thing itself, since we do not find it before the twelfth century, and the first who uses it is Uldaric, bishop of Constance, in his letter to Pope Calixtus II for the canonization of Bishop Conrad.[957]

Canonization itself is as old as the Church. The right of canonizing belongs essentially to her. In effect, since God permits and desires us to honor the saints, he should give his Church the right and the means of proving their sanctity. Otherwise, the world would very soon relapse into superstition and idolatry, from which Christianity has drawn it forth. Hence, the cogent reasoning of Catholic theologians: it is heresy to deny the authority of the Church and the sovereign pontiff in reference to the canonization of saints; for it is heresy to deny that the saints ought to be invoked. Therefore, the Church has the right to canonize saints, that is, to distinguish those whose sanctity entitles them to the worship and the veneration of their brethren.[958] We see that she acted thus from her origin, in those beautiful ages when, as protestants themselves admit, the Roman Church was the only true and faithful spouse of Jesus Christ. The first saints canonized were martyrs.

Let us admire how maturely and prudently the Church tested their sanctity before authorizing their worship. When Christians found one of their brethren thrown into chains or dragged before some tribunal on account of the faith, they endeavored to obtain all the particulars of his examination. For this purpose, they employed one or other of two means. a) They mixed without being known among the pagans, attended the trial, and collected with religious care both the questions and answers, which they wrote down after returning to their homes. On the day of execution, they were present at the appointed place, and heard the last words and saw the last deeds of the martyr. They thus became fit witnesses as to his sacrifice. To cite only one example, it is to this first means that we are partly indebted for the history of the martyrdom of St. Tarachus and his companions. In the absence of such evidence, b) our ancestors had recourse to the clerks of courts, from whom they purchased leave, often at a very high price, to take a copy of the law proceedings. The first three parts of the Acts of St. Tarachus, whom we have just mentioned, cost two hundred denarii: this sum was paid to the clerk of the proconsular registers in Asia.

But, in whatever way the Acts of Martyrs were procured, an account thereof was first of all sent to the bishop of the diocese in which the saint had suffered death. After having examined it well, the bishop sent it to the metropolitan: to him was reserved the ecclesiastical judgment by which a public worship was decreed to the martyr. The ecclesiastical judgment was strictly necessary; and, according to Dusaussay, cited by Benedict XIV, the metropolitan did not give it until he had consulted his suffragan bishops.[959]

The same course and the same formalities were observed in the canonization of confessors, that is, of servants of God who had confessed the faith, not by their blood, but by the heroism of their virtues.[960] It was only after the ecclesiastical judgment, proving the sanctity of the servant of God, had been pronounced, that canonization was proceeded to. As we have already said, it consisted simply in setting his name on the diptychs of the saints, which were read at Mass.

Such was the manner of canonizing up to the twelfth century. But, from the time of Pope Alexander III, who occupied the Holy See in 1161, this discipline was changed for grave reasons, which it would take too long to explain here;[961] and the right of beatifying and canonizing was reserved exclusively to the sovereign pontiff.

Since that period, and according to present discipline, the manner of proceeding in the beatification and canonization of saints is as follows: when a person has died in the odor of sanctity, and it is rumored that he works miracles, the bishop of the place, authorized by the Holy See, draws up, on the evidence of trustworthy witnesses, a statement of facts proving the fame of sanctity and miracles.[962] This is sent to the Congregation of Rites, in Rome. Here it is examined with great care. If there seem to be grounds for further action, the sovereign pontiff is informed of it, and he appoints a cardinal of the Congregation of Rites to be "relator of the cause." It is the duty of this cardinal to procure all the documents necessary to throw light on the matter, and to acquaint the Congregation with them. Those who are deputed to seek the judgment of beatification or canonization are called "postulators of the cause."

The Congregation of Rites then forms a regular court. The following are the parties who appear in it:

1. A president. This is the cardinal who is the relator of the cause.

2. Two advocates for. These are the cardinals who are the postulators of the cause.

3. Two advocates against. These are called the "promoter" and the "sub-promoter of the faith." The office of the promoter of the faith consists in raising all the difficulties imaginable on facts and on laws, so that the truth may be discovered, and, if necessary, that the cause may be brought to nothing. The sub-promoter is the promoter's counselor. He takes an oath of secrecy, and it is with him that the promoter confers on all the objections that may be proposed against the cause in question. The sub-promoter assists at discussions, and examines all the documents, so that he may be able to judge of them by himself, and rake difficulties out of them.

4. Several notaries or clerks, who take an oath to transcribe the depositions and other documents with the most scrupulous fidelity.

5. An archivist, who keeps the documents of the process under lock and key. Several copies of these are made: one for the notary, one for the secretary, and one for the promoter of the faith.

6. An interpreter. It sometimes happens that documents are drawn up in a foreign language. To translate them, the cardinal relator of the cause chooses, with the consent of the promoter of the faith, an interpreter, who takes an oath to translate them faithfully. At the same time, a trustworthy person is secretly appointed and sworn to examine the translation carefully.

7. Able jurisconsults, so as to study all questions bearing on law, that may arise during the course of the arguments.

8. Physicians, surgeons, mathematicians, and natural philosophers, who are consulted when there is question of miracles, and who are obliged to give their answers in writing.

Such is the constitution of this court, which has to judge of the most solemn cases wherein man can appear.

Let us come to the manner of proceeding with the investigation. First, no one concerns himself about the beatification of a servant of God until fifty years after his death. This general rule permits of exception only in some very rare cases of a sanctity quite extraordinary. It was very glorious for St. Alphonsus Liguori to have been, in our times, the object of such an exception. The Sacred Congregation of Rites begins by examining the works of the servant of God, if he has written any. The least proposition contrary to the Catholic faith or to good morals suffices to put an end to his cause forever. The examination of the works over, the course of the procedure is suspended for ten years, so as to give opinion time to develop itself, and the Congregation time to discover works of the servant of God that might have escaped its knowledge.

At the end of ten years, the postulators of the cause beg remissorial letters. These are letters or bulls by which the holy father appoints commissioners to search, at the places where the servant of God lived, into the heroism of his virtues and the certainty of his miracles. These virtues are the three theological virtues—faith, hope, and charity; and the four cardinal virtues—prudence, justice, fortitude, and temperance.

The search over, the Sacred Congregation passes in review the reports of the commissioners, the depositions of witnesses, justificatory documents, etc. Scrupulously studied in the Congregation, the process, with all its documents, is next submitted to the examination of a Consistory, or general assembly of all the cardinals, archbishops, and bishops of the Court of Rome.[963] Meeting follows meeting. The sovereign pontiff presides at several of them; asks the opinion of all the cardinals and other consultors, without giving his own; recommends himself to their prayers, and commands public ones; in a word, omits no means of gaining light. If, after all these precautions, the vicar of Jesus Christ is convinced, he publishes a bull that gives authority to proceed to the ceremony of beatification.

We now ask if there can be found on earth a tribunal that acts with more wisdom and prudence. Either the truth regarding facts, and the plainest facts, cannot possibly be proved, or we must admit that, with so many precautions and untiring searches, it will necessarily come to light. Hence, there is no honest man who doubts of the validity of Catholic canonizations, even independently of the assistance of the Holy Ghost.

Speaking of this matter we shall relate a well-known anecdote, which dates from the last century. One of the greatest men of that period, Pope Benedict XIV, being as yet only Cardinal Lambertini, was appointed relator in a cause of beatification. As he was one day busy in his cabinet with an enormous bundle of papers, two English protestants called to pay him a visit. The conversation had scarcely begun when a messenger from the holy father brought the cardinal an order to come immediately to His Holiness. The cardinal begged his noble visitors to excuse him, and, engaging them to wait, said to them: "If you like to examine this bundle, you will not find the time so long." The proposal was accepted. Procedures, depositions of witnesses, accounts of miracles, all sorts of documents were ransacked, scrutinized, and pondered during the absence of the cardinal, who was delayed much longer than he had expected.

"Well," said he on his return, "what do you think of our procedures?"

"If the person referred to in the documents that we have examined," answered the two Englishmen, "be not canonized, you will never canonize anybody."

"Do the proofs then seem sufficient to you?"

"And more than sufficient!"

"We are harder to please than you. If we do not receive other evidence, the case will come to nothing."

And the two Englishmen, to whom the cardinal had given an idea of the precautions taken by the Congregation of Rites in affairs of beatification, went away with one prejudice less, saying aloud that the saints of the Roman Church had no alloy in them, and that they themselves, honest people as they thought themselves to be, should not like to have their probity put to such a test.

Ceremonies of beatification and canonization. It remains for us to speak of the solemn ceremonies of beatification and canonization. That is truly a glorious day when, convinced by the evidence of heaven and earth—in other words, by miracles and a long series of juridical proofs—of the sanctity and eternal happiness of one of her children, the Church places him on her altars, and presents him to the veneration of the world. The sovereign pontiff, from the height of his throne, as lasting as the truth on which it rests, publishes a bull to announce this great day. The Eternal City is stirred. A thrill of delight passes through the Catholic world, and numerous pilgrims set out from distant lands to be present on so joyous an occasion. A plenary indulgence is granted to all the faithful who, having received the sacraments of penance and the Holy Eucharist, assist at the Solemn Mass to be celebrated for the beatification, in the Vatican Basilica, that is, in St. Peter's Church.

This august temple is adorned with a taste and magnificence unexampled, even in Rome itself, save on such a day. On its front you behold, at a great height, in the midst of the brightest lights, an image of the saint, who rises to heaven, borne up by angels. Underneath shine, framed in gold, the arms of the reigning pontiff; also, those of the king in whose state the blessed one was born, and those of his native city. If he was a religious, the emblems of his order are added.

Should you cross the sacred threshold, you imagine yourself in heaven. Your feet rest on rich carpets. The pillars all round the immense temple are hung with large festoons of crimson velvet. Pictures in gilt frames, devices wherein gold and silk blend their brightest hues, and sentences in letters of gold, placed to the right and left, remind you of the sublime virtues of the saint. At the farther end of the temple, high above the altar or confession of St. Peter, is hung a picture of the saint, ascending to heaven, his head surrounded with an *aureola*; but this picture is still veiled. It will soon be uncovered.

On each side of the altar are thrones ranged in a curve—bright with gold and purple, and intended for the cardinals, the prelates of the Roman Court, and the consultors of the Sacred Congregation. Near the Sacred College appear galleries richly adorned, where kings and queens, princes and princesses, strangers of distinction, whom the august ceremony draws from various parts of the Catholic world, will be placed. To throw light on this magnificent spectacle, there shine, in all parts of the temple, candelabra, lustres, and chandeliers—a perfect blaze. With so much to dazzle the eyes are blended soft clouds of incense, an emblem of prayer. At regular distances appear superb vases of flowers, which yield the sweetest perfumes, and on the altars are gold and silver pans, which burn the most exquisite aromatics.

If, on this unique festival, the senses are gratified, the imagination, mind, and heart are flooded with the purest joys. To give more life to the solemnity, several choirs of musicians, placed in different parts of the vast basilica, accompany with their instruments the melodious accents of the most beautiful voices that can be brought together.

When the hour of the ceremony draws near, the pontifical guard arranges itself round the sanctuary, so as to add to the pomp of the occasion, and to maintain the utmost order. Meanwhile all the cardinals, all the prelates of the various Congregations, and all the generals of orders take their places. In the reserved galleries appear the privileged personages who should occupy them, and more than one king perhaps thinks himself happy in assisting at the triumph of one of the humblest of subjects. At length, the large doors of the immense basilica turn on their hinges, and a countless throng of people rush in, like a mighty wave, to overspread its floor. All these anxious spectators, whether foreigners or natives, Catholics or dissenters, await the proceedings of the day in religious silence.

Suddenly, the cardinal grand master of ceremonies appears, wearing a rich cope and a miter. He advances, accompanied by two canons of St. Peter's; ascends with them to a high platform; and reads in a loud voice the brief of the holy father for the beatification of the servant of God. The reading over, the cardinal celebrant comes to the foot of the altar, accompanied by the deacons and subdeacons of the Roman Church, and intones the hymn of triumph—the *Te Deum*. The last note is still on his lips when an invisible hand draws aside the veil that covers the blessed one's picture, suspended above the altar.

At this sublime moment, cardinals, pontiffs, kings, princes, magistrates, all the immense crowd of people, fall on their knees and bow down their heads to the ground in veneration of the holy image. And a thousand musical instruments, breaking forth at once, make the vaults of the temple ring with harmonious sounds; all the artillery of the Castle of St. Angelo joins its deep base with the sharp staccato bursts of the musketry, and with the joyous peals of all the bells of the Eternal City. O solemn moment, happy are they who have once in their life experienced the indescribable feelings that thou dost inspire! O august triumph, how far dost thou leave behind thee all the triumphs of ancient Rome, with its elephants, and its ivory chariots, and its hosts of chained slaves! Here, at least, there are no tears, or, if there are any, they are tears of gladness.

The prostration ended, the choirs continue and complete the *Te Deum*. The first deacon now sings the verse: "Pray for us, blessed N." And the choirs answer: "That we may be made worthy of the promises of Jesus Christ." The cardinal celebrant adds a prayer composed in honor of the blessed one, whose image he incenses. Then, having put on the pontifical robes, he offers the holy mysteries in honor of the newly beatified inhabitant of heaven. The Mass over, the procurator of the cause distributes to each of the assistants an image of the blessed one, painted or stamped, framed or gilt, more or less richly according to circumstances.[964] Such are, in a brief form, the ceremonies of beatification.

As we have said, they date from the period when the Church judged it proper to proceed to canonization only by a long series of investigations. Beatification is, in point of fact, canonization begun. To pass from one to the other, it is necessary that, since his beatification, the blessed one should have wrought miracles.[965] When they are known, the Congregation of Rites begins again, in regard to these new miracles, the informations, the searches, the procedures, that had taken place for beatification. It is only after they have been proved that canonization is decided on.

The ceremonies of canonization differ little from those of beatification.[966] On the day appointed for it, Rome shows the same enthusiasm, and St. Peter's is adorned with the same splendor. In the morning there is a magnificent procession, which bears along in triumph the image of the blessed one who is about to receive the last honors that the Church of earth can render to her children. On the return of the procession, at which the sovereign pontiff assists in person, he ascends his throne, prepared in the Basilica of St. Peter. The consistorial advocate, in the name of the cardinal procurator of the cause, advances and beseeches His Holiness to admit into the number of the saints the blessed one on whose process judgment has been given. To this petition the prelate secretary of briefs for princes answers in the name of the pontiff: "We should pray earnestly in this great affair, that the Lord may grant us his light."

The multitude go on their knees, and invoke all the saints of heaven by singing their litany. The consistorial advocate advances again, and begs canonization. To this second petition the prelate secretary answers: "We should redouble our entreaties and prayers." And the Spirit of light is addressed, that Spirit who guides the Church, and who shall be with her all days even to the consummation of the world: the *Veni Creator* is sung. The advocate presents himself a third time before the pontifical throne, and solicits canonization. Then the sovereign pontiff pronounces the solemn sentence by which he declares and defines that such a blessed one is to be placed in the rank of the saints. This decree is succeeded by the singing of the *Te Deum*. Then follows a Mass in honor of the new saint, celebrated by the vicar of Jesus Christ.

In the evening, after vespers, the sovereign pontiff goes again to St. Peter's, accompanied by all the Sacred College. There, in the midst of an immense congregation, he adores the Blessed Sacrament. Moving then to the altar where the relics of the saint lie, he addresses fervent prayers to him, and takes up his image, kisses it respectfully, and presents it to the homage of the eager crowd.[967] And sweet tears flow with prayers; and looks of love and sentiments of confidence, and transports of joy, ascending toward the saint, begin for him on earth that glorious triumph which will henceforth last to the end of ages. At length, when night, descending on the seven hills, spreads its dark veil over the Eternal City, a new spectacle begins. Bonfires and magnificent illuminations crown the joy of a people intended for the greatest of spectacles, and make Rome more beautiful and a thousand times happier than in the days of the triumphs of its Caesars.

But the happiness of the Romans extends beyond the limits of their city. The canonization of a saint is an extraordinary event, whose echoes are heard to the ends of the Catholic world. Millions of hearts dilate at this happy news. Rich and poor rejoice equally. It says to both: "The gate of heaven is still open; its tabernacles are free to all!" And every one delights to hear that voice which comes from his conscience, and says to him: "I too may be a saint!" Who can tell how much fallen courage this consoling voice has raised, how many heroic deeds it has inspired?

Oh, yes! let us say it, the solemn ceremony of beatification or canonization is very, very moral. There is then on earth a tribunal at which virtue, persecuted, downtrodden, slandered, at length finds justice. Here, no exception of persons: whether you are rich or poor, learned or ignorant, a master or a servant—whether you have been born amid the snows of the North or amid the burning heats of the South, in Europe or in Asia, in the hut of the African negro or in the wigwam of the American Indian, in the fair city of Rome or in the islands away beyond Japan, it matters not.

Have you practiced in a heroic degree all the virtues that are the basis of society and religion—in other words, have you been a heroically docile child of your heavenly Father and a benefactor of your brethren? It is enough. This is all that is asked about, all that is examined into, to place you on the altars of the Catholic world, to make your name immortal, and from generation to generation, to obtain for you, a poor shepherd or a humble laborer, honors that many monarchs, with all their power, shall never obtain.

PRAYER

O my God! who art all love, I thank thee for having destined us for the bliss of heaven. Grant us the grace to deserve it.

I am resolved to love God above all things, and my neighbor as myself for the love of God; and, in testimony of this love, I will often say to myself, I shall try to be a great saint.[968]

Lesson 52: Christianity Brought before the Senses (Continued)—All Souls, Funerals

All Souls' day: Its harmonies.—On the day of All Saints, the Church undertakes to move all the fibers of our heart. We see that she wants to strike a great blow—to inspire a disgust for the earth, a desire of heaven, and a tender compassion, a universal charity among all her children. If, on the morning of this memorable day, the pomp of her ceremonies and the gaiety of her hymns are an expression of unmixed joy, in the evening her canticles are blended with deep sighs. In a little while, the spectacle already modified changes altogether. Joyous chants are followed by sorrowful ones; ornaments of mourning take the place of copes strewn with golden flowers; and lo! we soon see nought in the temple but a funeral monument, covered with tears and bones.

What is all this? A new festival, the festival of the faithful departed! The Church, a tenderhearted mother, wishes that this day should be a family festival. She appears to us in three different states: triumphant in heaven, exiled on earth, and groaning in the midst of expiatory flames. And the canticles of heaven, and the sighs of earth, and the cries of purgatory, which on this day succeed and answer one another, make us remember that mysterious bonds unite all the children of Jesus Christ in one body; that the three Churches, like three sisters, help, encourage, and comfort one another, until the day when, meeting in heaven, they shall thenceforth form but one Church, eternally triumphant. What a magnificent harmony!

There is another that it is impossible not to remark. How well chosen is the day for celebrating the memory of the dead! Those birds which migrate, those days which shorten, those leaves which fall and are swept along the roads by the cold north wind, that sky which lowers, those gray clouds which tell of the coming frost, are not all those signs of decay and death marvelously well calculated to fill our soul with the serious thoughts that the Church wishes to inspire?

This is not all yet. Like the others, and perhaps more than the others, the festival of All Souls draws closer the ties of the family. One might have seen formerly, and in the country one may still see, brothers and sisters, friends and neighbors, meeting on this day in the cemetery to pray, to weep, and to give alms, in order to obtain peace for their dear deceased. We cannot doubt but if, in the course of the year, there rise some clouds of division among these people, they disappear on this day. For we are never more ready to love one another than when we pray and weep together.

Not long ago, in certain cities,[969] a watchman, traveling the streets all the night, used to stop at every twenty steps, ring his bell, and cry out: "Awake ye that sleep: pray for the departed!" Why is it that such touching usages should have disappeared? Since we began to forget our dead, we have become cold toward the living. Selfishness has withered hearts—selfishness, which degrades man, disturbs the family, and destroys society.

Its origin, foundations in tradition, and its establishment. But it is time to speak of the establishment of the festival of All Souls. From the beginning, the Church prayed for all her children on the day of their decease. Her prayers were supplications for those who needed them, and thanksgivings for the martyrs. Sacrifices and supplications were renewed on the anniversary of their death. Tertullian expressly says so: "We celebrate the anniversary of the nativity of the martyrs."[970] And further on: "According to the traditions of our ancestors, we offer the sacrifice for the departed on the anniversary of their death."[971] Other fathers give us the same testimony.[972]

Yet more, the Church, which has always shown herself so kind and considerate toward her children, had, from the beginning, two ways of praying and offering the sacrifice for the dead: one, for each individual or for a few individuals in particular;[973] the other, for all the dead in general, so that her charity might embrace those who had no kindred or friends to acquit themselves of this pious duty on their behalf.[974] She acted thus before the time of St. Augustine. "It is a very old and generally received custom in the Church," says this father, "to pray for all those who have died in the communion of the body and blood of Jesus Christ."[975]

However, we do not see that there was a special festival to recommend all the dead to God. But we see the foundations on which it could be established. For if the Church, from her birth, prayed and sacrificed for some of the dead in particular and for all in general; if, in all liturgies and in all the Masses of the year, there was prayer for the dead: is it not evident that on these foundations a special festival could be established in order to fulfill this duty toward the departed with more care and attention?[976]

The thing really took place, and the everlasting glory of Franche-Comté, then known under the name of Burgundy, will be to have set on foot this pious institution.[977] Descended from one of the noblest families of Burgundy, the Blessed Berno, pastor of Baumeles-Messieurs, near Lons-le-Saulnier, had founded the Abbey of Cluny. This illustrious daughter, inheriting a great deal of her mother's pity for the dead, hastened to adopt the general commemoration for the departed. It made a perpetual decree on the matter in the year 998.

The Chapter of Cluny speaks thus: "It was commanded by our venerable father Odilo, with the consent and at the request of all the brethren of Cluny, that as, throughout the whole Church, the festival of All Saints is celebrated on the 1st of November, so in all our monasteries a commemoration of all the faithful departed should be made on the next day. After the chapter on All Saints' day, the dean and cellarers shall give an alms of bread and wine to all those who present themselves. After vespers, all the bells shall be rung, and the vespers for the dead shall be chanted. The Mass shall be solemn, the brethren shall chant the tract, all shall offer individually, and twelve poor persons shall be fed. We wish this decree to be observed forever, as well in this place as in all others that depend on it; and whosoever will observe this institution like us, shall share in our good intentions."[978]

The pious practice soon spread to other Churches. That of Besançon was the first to adopt it. Her patrimony seemed returning to her, consecrated by the suffrages of the servants of God. Ere long the general Commemoration of the Dead on the day after All Saints was adopted by sovereign pontiffs, and became common to the Universal Church.

Let us conclude what we have to say on the origin of this festival by a remark very proper to show the immense charity of the Church our mother. The general Commemoration of the Departed is only a supplement to all the other festivals, offices, and sacrifices of the year. It has this character in common, not only with the festival of All Saints, but also with those of the Blessed Trinity and Corpus Christi. As a matter of fact, on all festivals, in all the offices and sacrifices of the year, we render supreme honor to the Trinity by the adorable Sacrifice of the Eucharist, in which our Lord is immolated with all his saints, who are named therein, at least in general. Hence, particular festivals of the Trinity, the Eucharist, and all the saints were established only as a supplement to the general festival, in order to renew the attention and fervor with which we ought to celebrate it during the whole year. It is the same with the general Commemoration of the Dead. The Church instituted it to supply for the prayers and sacrifices which are daily offered for them, and to warn us that we ought continually to acquit ourselves of our duties toward them with new attention and piety.

We need not here go over again our explanation of the motives that we have to pray for the dead.[979] We shall content ourselves with offering one thought to the reflections of Christians.

Petitions of the departed. The glory of God, charity, justice, and our own interest are the powerful motives that urge us to pray for the departed. May we accomplish this duty, which both nature and religion lay upon us, in such a manner as to hush that plaintive voice, that accusing voice, which is ever rising from purgatory and striking on the ear of the attentive Christian: *Hominem non habeo, hominem non habeo*—"I have no man, I have no man."[980]

The first to utter these painful words was the paralytic mentioned in the gospel. Powerless in all his limbs, this poor wretch had for eight-and-thirty years been chained to the banks of the Probatica Pond. Continually before the eyes of the crowd, whom curiosity or a desire to be healed brought to this celebrated place, his misery was known to all Judea. And in this crowd there were no doubt relations, acquaintances, friends of his, if the unfortunate have any friends. What did he ask in order to be delivered? Only a little help from a kind hand, which would put him into the pond when the angel of the Lord stirred its salutary waters. Yet he had to wait long for this slight service: he implored it in vain for eight-and-thirty years.

Tell us: Is not this a lively image of the souls in purgatory? Held down by the divine justice in cruel sufferings, they anxiously expect and loudly implore the help of some kind hand that will break their chains, and enable them to enter the city where sorrows are unknown. These poor sufferers are our brethren. Everything around us recalls their memory: the places that we visit, and the houses that we live in, and the property that we enjoy, and the very name that we bear, and the mournful ceremonies that we assist at, and the graves that we may see every day! Yet these dear departed souls are not relieved!

Ask them why they are suffering, some twenty, others perhaps thirty or forty years. Their answer will be that of the paralytic: "Alas! I have no one to help me—*Hominem non habeo!* I did indeed leave relations on earth, but I see that I did not leave friends. I did indeed leave a wife on earth, but I see that she quickly dried her tears: my name is no longer on her lips, my memory no longer lives in her heart—*Hominem non habeo!* I did indeed leave children on earth, children whom I overwhelmed with the most tender caresses, whom I brought up at the cost of many a toilsome hour and bitter sweat, but I see that they no longer care to think of their father—*Hominem non habeo!* Yet what I ask is very little: some prayers, some alms. This is all, and I ask it in vain. Slaves to pleasures and employments, all have forgotten their dead, their dearest ones! *Hominem non habeo*—I have no one to help me!" Oh, may this accusing voice, this heartrending complaint, touch our souls, and lead us to procure glory for God, peace for the dead, and for ourselves the reward of mercy: "Blessed are the merciful, for they shall find mercy!"

Christian funerals.—This is the place to say a word on Christian funerals. The Church, which consecrates our cradle, and which surrounds with so august a protection the little stranger that arrives in this valley of tears, neglects no means of procuring respect for man when, having reached his journey's end, he sinks into the grave, there to undergo that sentence which condemns him to return into dust.

I am very much struck by our funeral ceremonies. On one side, I see parents, or children, or friends in tears; I hear the solemn knell; I find nought in the holy temple but signs of mourning. On the other, behold! the Church sings, always sings. What a contrast! Can a mother sing at the death of her child, and is not the Church the most tender of mothers? Ah, there is not a doubt but the Church loves us with a love so much the greater as she is more enlightened! Let us endeavor to understand her heart.

The guardian of the promises of immortality, she proclaims them loudly in presence of death. If there is some sadness in her voice, there is also joy. She weeps, but happier than Rachel, she is comforted, and she comforts us too, because she knows that her children will be restored to her. Hence, in the tears of friends I behold nature, and in the chants of the Church I behold faith. The former cries out sadly, "I must die"; the latter comforts it, saying, "Thou shalt rise again!"

When therefore the Christian soul has quitted the body, the bell warns the faithful to pray for their brother. To excite their fervor, the tolls are repeated at intervals up to the moment when that which belongs to the earth is returned to the earth. Before removing the body, the priest, sprinkling holy water on the coffin, says, *Requiem aeternam*, etc.—"Give him, O Lord, eternal rest, and let thy light never fade from his eyes!" The *De profundis* is then recited in two choirs. In effect, there are two voices in this mournful canticle: the voice of the uneasy soul, afraid of the judgments of God, and the voice of the soul that feels new hope springing up at the sight of the redemption of the Lord, which effaces all the iniquities of Israel.

The removal of the body takes place in processional form. The cross, which is the pledge of our hope and the sign of our resurrection, is borne in front. At length, the corpse reaches the church, the church where the Christian career begins and ends. What a resemblance between the cradle and the grave, between baptism and burial! In the midst of the mournful scene, we perceive candles burning. These are a sign of the faith and charity of the deceased; an emblem of his future return to a better life; a pledge that the sadness of the Christian shall be changed into joy. Thus, the present life and the future life, time and eternity, meet at the coffin: one with its tears and its deceitful hopes; the other with its consolations and its glorious promises.

The Mass begins, and in a little while the grave voices of the chanters make the sacred vaults resound with the prose, *Dies Irae*. Nothing more proper to freeze one with awe than this poem on death and the last judgment! It is as much for the instruction of the living as for the relief of the departed that the Church causes it to be sung. Death, with its graves and its cold clay, and the judgment, with its dreadful signs and its severity, come forward in turns. Then, to cheer somewhat the alarmed soul, a last word, a word of hope breaks on the ear and sinks into the heart as the sentiment that ought to prevail. "To redeem me, thou didst suffer on the cross. Ah, let not such great agony be fruitless! O just judge, the avenger of crime, forgive me before thou dost summon me to thy court! I groan as a wretched culprit. I am ashamed of all my offenses. O God, spare a guilty suppliant! Merciful Jesus, grant rest to the departed!"

The author of this masterpiece was, as is generally believed, Cardinal Malabranca, of the family of the Ursins, who lived in the thirteenth century.

After Mass, the clergy range themselves for the absolution round the coffin, and the response, *Libera me*—"Deliver me, O Lord," etc., is sung. In this mournful and touching prayer, it is the dead man that speaks. We imagine that we hear Jonas crying out to God from the depths of the sea, from the bowels of the monster that has swallowed him up alive: "Deliver me, O Lord, from eternal death on that dreadful day when thou shalt come to judge the world by fire!"

Moved by his cries, the Church, his mother, answers him by the mouth of the celebrant: "Lord, have mercy on us!"

The choir: "Christ, have mercy on us!"

The priest: "Lord, have mercy on us!" He then intones the *Pater*, which is said in a low voice. He now walks round the coffin, and sprinkles it with holy water: this is the last purification for the departed soul. He next incenses it, and this reminds us both of the prayer of the Church for her deceased son, and of the good odor of the virtues which this Christian practiced and which rose to heaven like the smoke of perfumes. Will it be thus with you who read these lines? What answer does your life make?

The moment of departure for the cemetery is come. Farewell, holy church, in which I received baptism; farewell, sacred pulpit, from which the words of salvation fell on me like a precious dew; farewell, tribunal of mercy, at which I so often received, together with pardon for my faults, a fatherly advice and an ineffable consolation; farewell, blessed table, at which my God fed me with his immortal flesh; farewell, my relations, my friends, my children, farewell till the great day of the general resurrection! Behold what is said by this last departure from the church for the cemetery!

Hence, the tears and even the cries of kindred are redoubled at this solemn moment. What does religion do now? With a sweet, and we were going to say a joyful, voice, she gives the signal to start, singing these beautiful words: *Deducant te angeli*—"May the angels lead thee into paradise; may the martyrs meet thee, and introduce thee into the holy Jerusalem; may the choirs of angels receive thee, and make thee a sharer with Lazarus, formerly poor, in eternal rest and bliss!"[981]

Thus, while weeping nature regards a cemetery as merely the end of a journey—a cemetery with its sad mysteries of decomposition and putrefaction—religion, radiant with immortality, shows us paradise with its boundless joys and endless glories, and a new word of consolation will be spoken over the grave. The priest, throwing a little clay on the coffin, says: "Let dust return into the clay from which it was taken, and let the spirit return to God who gave it! May he rest in peace! Amen!"

After a last sprinkling of holy water, the grave is closed, and the cross which surmounts it tells the passerby that here lies the body of a Christian who lived full of hope, and who awaits with confidence the day of the general resurrection.[982] Consoling thoughts! A blessing be upon thee, O holy religion! In this grave, surmounted by a cross, the Christian resembles a weary traveler, who rests himself sweetly under a shady tree till the hour comes when he shall rise again.

PRAYER

O my God! who art all love, I thank thee for the tenderness with which thou hast inspired thy Church for the departed. Grant us the grace to do for them all that we would wish to be one day done for ourselves.

I am resolved to love God above all things, and my neighbor as myself for the love of God; and, in testimony of this love, I will consecrate every Monday to prayer for the dead.

Lesson 53: Christianity Brought before the Senses (Continued)—Dedication of Churches

Festival of dedication.—If, as we have proved, religion has reason to bless the least things used in its worship, it could not fail to consecrate places intended for the offering of its sacrifice and the accomplishment of its august mysteries. Hence, we see that the consecration of temples was practiced under the old law. We know with what pomp and circumstance the royal Solomon made the dedication of the first Temple raised in the world to the glory of the Most High. And this Temple contained nothing but vain shadows: the tables of the law, some of the manna of the desert, and Aaron's miraculous rod! Within its cedar walls only a carnal people should kneel; on its brazen altars, only the blood of animals should flow; and through its golden vaults, only the voice of prophets should resound.

In a Catholic temple dwells the God who dictated the law. A people of adorers in spirit and in truth fills its sacred precincts; its altar is wet with the blood of the Redeemer of the world; its vaults reecho with the voice of the master of the prophets. Would the Catholic Church not consecrate her temples by ceremonies whose holiness should correspond to the holiness of the edifice itself? She could not fail to do so.

And behold! this divine spouse of the man-God no sooner comes forth from the catacombs, where during three centuries she has hidden her august mysteries, than she hastens to build and to consecrate temples to God, the conqueror of the Caesars. "The persecutions of preceding emperors," says Eusebius, "had destroyed all our churches; but under Constantine we repaired this loss with advantage. It was delightful, it was the fullness of joy, for the Church to see a countless number of temples being built and rebuilt on all sides. All the power and wealth of the new emperor were displayed on this occasion. Hardly anything was thought of in all the cities of the Empire but the superb temples that were rising, and that bishops were dedicating to the glory of Jesus Christ."[983]

But whence do you think the joy came that the solemnity of dedications caused to the Church? Was it from the material temples that were offered to her divine spouse? No: what enraptured her soul was the concord, respect, and charity that, uniting all men, as they then united our ancestors in the faith, made them a living and eternal temple within those material and perishable temples. "Visible temples," says the spouse of Jesus to us, "are only an image; the real temple is the union of emperors, bishops, peoples, provinces, and kingdoms, all Christians among themselves, offering themselves together to the Lord with the divine and immortal victim, who is my divine spouse. It is with a view to render this truth plain that many bishops assemble for the dedication of material temples. A figure of my spiritual temple, a building is consecrated by them, in which the saints of the earth, imitating the saints of heaven, shall meet to sing psalms, to praise God, to hear the divine word, to sacrifice, and to admire what is most august in my ceremonies."

Let us follow in detail these august ceremonies, and we shall see whether the Church of earth could better represent the temple of heaven, that true temple in which angels and men are the living stones, and whether she could better teach her children that they ought to make in Jesus Christ but one body, one soul, one heart, one temple, one altar, one living and undying host, by charity. As there is no virtue more social or indispensable than charity, with its great spirit of sacrifice, we must admit that our ceremonies, which levity ridicules, are admirably proper to preach it to the world.

Ceremonies before and after the opening of a church.—How magnificent is the language that the Church addresses to us in the dedication of her temples! "The eternal Word," she says, "uniting himself hypostatically with a human body, which is a portion of the earth, engaged himself, as it were, to consecrate all the rest of the earth, and to make it one immense temple. The Word alone could attempt such a masterpiece, and he did so only by becoming man, building up for himself a temple on earth, and changing all the earth into this same temple. It is on this account that I employ so many ceremonies and so much magnificence in the dedication of my temples, which are only an image of this divine and miraculous temple."[984]

Docile children of the Church, let us study in a spirit of faith and piety the consecration of our sanctuaries. This ceremony, one of the most imposing in Catholic worship, may be divided into two parts: the first what precedes, and the second what follows, the opening of a church. The first tells us that we are exiles on earth, and that we ought to make every effort to reach our heavenly country. The second gives us a figure and a foretaste of the joys of the glorious Jerusalem. Thus, the whole ceremony is like a beautiful epic poem that describes for faith and the senses the whole life of the human race in time and eternity.

First part: From the beginning of the ceremony to the opening of the church. Let us say at the outset that the power of consecrating churches belongs exclusively to the bishop. He prepares for its exercise by fasting. The reason is because he represents the eternal pontiff, who opened heaven for us by fasting and sufferings. The relics of the saints that are to be placed in the principal altar of the new temple are enclosed in a vase, which is sealed with the greatest care, and laid between candles on an elegantly adorned table, but outside the church. Behold man exiled from heaven!

The bishop, wearing a white cope and accompanied by his clergy, approaches the relics, to implore near them the mercy of God. For this purpose, he recites the seven penitential psalms, the true sighs of repentance and hope. When they are ended, the procession moves to the large door of the church. The door is shut: there is no person inside but the deacon, wearing an amice, girdle, and white stole. He is a figure of the apostle St. Peter, to whom the keys of heaven were delivered.

The bishop, struck at the greatness of the undertaking, cries out: "O Almighty God, Father, Son, and Holy Ghost, be in the midst of us!" Pontiff, clergy, and faithful immediately fall on their knees to implore the assistance of their brethren in heaven. These powerful advocates are invoked by their names, one after another, in the Litany of the Saints. Trusting in their help, the consecrator proceeds to the opening of this figurative heaven. He blesses salt and water with the usual prayers, exorcisms, and signs of the cross. We have elsewhere explained both the meaning and the efficacy of holy water, salt, and exorcisms. The powers of darkness, which have profaned the world and shut heaven, are about to be dispossessed.

With the water that he has just blessed, the bishop makes an aspersion on himself, the clergy, and the people. To purify himself, so as to be more worthy of consecrating the house of God, and to purify the clergy and the people, so that their prayers may be more fervent and acceptable: such is evidently the object of this first ceremony. He now sets out, preceded by two acolytes, and moves round the church, sprinkling the walls on the outside with holy water, and continually repeating these words: "In the name of the Father, and of the Son, and of the Holy Ghost." During this time, the choir sings the antiphon: "The house of the Lord is built on the top of the mountain, and is raised above all the hills. All nations shall come to it, and say, 'Glory be to thee, O Lord!' They shall come with joy, bearing sheaves in their hands, and saying, 'Glory be to thee, O Lord!'"

The bishop, having returned to the front of the church, recites a prayer in which he beseeches the Lord to take this temple under his protection, and to make it a house of holiness and prayer. Then, with his pastoral staff, he strikes the door once, saying: "O princes, open your gates! Be ye lifted up, O eternal gates, and the King of glory shall enter in!" The deacon, who is inside the church, asks: "Who is this King of glory?" The bishop answers: "He is the strong and mighty God; he is the God of hosts."

The deacon does not open the door. Then the bishop sprinkles the walls of the church a second time, while the choir sings the antiphon: "O Lord, bless this temple which thou hast raised to the glory of thy name! From the height of thy throne, hear the prayers of those who come to adore thee here! O Lord, if thy people be converted, do penance, and pray to thee in this place, hear their desires from the height of thy throne!"

After making the circuit of the church a second time, the bishop recites a prayer to beg of God that all those who assemble in this church may taste the sweetness of peace and concord. He strikes the door a second time with his crosier, saying: "O princes, open your gates! Be ye lifted up, O eternal gates, and the King of glory shall enter in!" The deacon asks again: "Who is this King of glory?" The bishop answers: "He is the strong and mighty God; he is the God of hosts."

The door of the church is not opened yet, in order to remind us that it was not without resistance our Lord Jesus Christ vanquished the devil, and put an end to the sway that he had so long exercised on earth.

The bishop goes round the church a third time, sprinkling holy water on the walls "in the name of the Father, and of the Son, and of the Holy Ghost." Then the choir sings this new antiphon: "O master of the universe, O thou who hast all things in abundance, but didst wish that thy temple should be raised in the midst of us, O Lord, preserve thy house forever from all defilement! Thou hast chosen it, O my God, that thy name may be invoked in it, and that it may become a place of supplications and prayers. Keep it always undefiled."

The bishop, on returning to the front, asks God to bless and sanctify what he is going to bless and sanctify; and that the devils may quit this temple, and the angels of peace enter it, never more to leave it.

He then strikes the door of the church a third time, saying the same words: "O princes, open your gates," etc. The deacon, after his answer, opens the door. In this triple journey, you will find a memorial of the Blessed Trinity; of the triple hierarchy of the elect—virginity, continence, and marriage; and, in the three strikings of the door, of the triple power of Jesus Christ over the physical and moral world—by creation, redemption, and glorification. How many bitter pains and labors did the acquirement of his inheritance and ours cost him!

Before entering the church, the bishop makes the sign of the cross with his crosier on the threshold, in order to show that it was by the death of Jesus Christ that hell was closed and heaven opened. In performing this ceremony, he says, "Behold the sign of the cross! Let all vain phantoms be gone!"

The clergy follow the bishop into the church; the faithful remain outside. If the people were to enter in a crowd, there would be an end to the decorous progress of the ceremony. Such is, doubtless, one reason why the assistants are not introduced. There is another, full of mystery. The church represents heaven. When, after his resurrection, Jesus Christ entered it, he was followed only by the just whom he had delivered from limbo; but when, at the end of time, he completes the dedication of the eternal Jerusalem, he shall enter it at the head of all the elect.

"Peace to this house," says the bishop as he sets foot in the church; and the clergy sings an antiphon, imploring this peace so necessary for the happiness and salvation of man. The antiphon ended, all kneel down in the middle of the church, and the bishop intones the hymn, *Veni Creator*, to ask the light and help of the Holy Spirit.

The saints are again invoked by reciting their litany. This is followed by the *Benedictus*. During this canticle, the bishop traces with his crosier, on two lines of ashes, which run in the form of a St. Andrew's cross[985] from one end of church to the other, the letters of the Greek and Latin alphabets.[986] On one line are the Greek letters, and on the other the Latin. They are so placed that the four first and last letters, of the two alphabets, correspond with the four corners of the church.

The union of Greek and barbarian, that is to say, of all mankind, in the Church, the power of the cross, and the victory of the apostles are brought to our minds by this expressive ceremony. It is followed by another no less solemn or instructive. The pontiff is going to bless the altars, and the walls of the church on the inside. He will not use the water that he has employed to sanctify the outside of the temple. He blesses new water, in which he mixes salt, ashes, and wine. As it is Jesus Christ who opens heaven for us, and gives holiness to our churches, in which he vouchsafes to dwell, the water and salt, ashes and wine, symbols of his humanity and divinity, his ignominy and glory, his death and resurrection, recall this twofold truth.[987]

After a magnificent prayer, in which the bishop enumerates all the qualities of the water that he has just blessed, and the wonderful effects that he expects from it, he approaches the altar, if he is to consecrate it, and, while the psalm, *Judica me*—"Judge me," etc., is being sung, takes some of the water and with it makes five crosses on the table of the altar, one in the middle, and one at each of the four corners, saying: "Let this altar be sanctified in honor of Almighty God, the glorious Virgin Mary, and all the blessed, under the name and in memory of St. N., in the name of the Father, and of the Son, and of the Holy Ghost."

He then goes round the altar seven times, and sprinkles it with the holy water, reciting the psalm, *Miserere mei, Deus*—"Have mercy on me, O God," etc. Here all is mysterious. The bishop conjures the Almighty to hear him, by pouring down his blessings on the stone whereon the adorable victim is to be offered. But he must persevere in prayer, since it was only when Jericho had been gone round seven times that the Lord heard the petitions of Israel, and overturned the walls of this city.

In the mind of the Church, the altar also represents our Lord himself. All the ceremonies and prayers of consecration tend to identify, as far as possible, the material with the spiritual altar. These seven turns tell us both of the seven great virtues of our Lord and the seven journeys of the divine shepherd in search of his sheep, as the five crosses made on the altar, with three unctions of oil, represent to us his five wounds, so many sources of grace, and the three fundamental virtues of Christianity—faith, hope, and charity. The incense that accompanies these things is an emblem of prayer.

The bishop sprinkles the walls of the church inside with the same holy water three times, first the lower part, then the middle part, and lastly the upper part, beginning on the eastern side; and, while he is returning to the altar, he blesses the floor. This ceremony tells us that to outward purification must be added purity of soul; that there is nothing defiled in heaven; and lastly that our Lord, setting out from the east, sanctified the whole world. The clergy, during this time, sing several psalms, which recall the heavenly Jerusalem, and the blessings that the Lord has in store for his elect.

After this ceremony, the bishop recites several touching prayers, but above all a preface, to which a translation would do but feeble justice, and in which he sets forth all the favors, all the graces, all the benefits that he implores the Lord to pour down on those who come to adore in this temple. So much being ended, he makes with the last-mentioned water and some lime and sand a cement, which he blesses, and which he will soon employ in sealing up the relics of the saints in the altar.

Second part: from the opening of the church to the end of the ceremony. The moment is come to introduce these precious relics into the church. A procession is formed to bring them, with the singing of psalms and antiphons in their honor. Priests carry them on their shoulders. They and the bishop walk round the church on the outside, and, during this triumphal march, the faithful cry out in a transport of enthusiasm: *Kyrie eleison*—"Lord have mercy!"

Then the bishop addresses a pious exhortation to the faithful on the dedication or consecration of churches, and causes a decree of the Council of Trent, having reference thereto, to be read by the archdeacon. He next beseeches the Lord to take possession of his temple, whose door he marks with a triple sign of the cross, made in holy chrism. Meanwhile, the procession enters the church. The faithful follow the clergy, and all together move in the traces of the relics that are about to be deposited in the tomb of the altar.

No one can witness this spectacle without being deeply moved by it. It bears you away to the last great day, when the supreme judgment having been pronounced, the company of the elect shall rise toward heaven in the footsteps of their divine leader. The emotion is so much the more profound as antiphons and psalms are sung that breathe gladness and recall the endless happiness of the blessed. The bishop recites a prayer, after which he consecrates the tomb with holy chrism, and immediately lays the holy relics in it, together with three grains of incense.

This ceremony reminds us that in the early Church the august sacrifice was offered on the martyr's tomb—a precious usage, the memory of which is preserved by placing relics in the altar, and which was doubtless established in accordance with the vision of the apostle St. John in the Apocalypse. "I saw under the altar," he says, "the souls of those who had been put to death for the word of God, and for the testimony that they had rendered, and they cried out with a loud voice, saying, 'O Lord, who art holy and true, how long wilt thou delay to do us justice?'"[988] The three grains of incense show our respect for the holy relics, and our wish to surround them always with the perfume of our prayers.

The bishop now consecrates the stone that is to close the tomb of the holy relics. He fixes it on the sepulchre with the cement that he has made and blessed. Then, anointing it again with holy chrism, he says, "Let this altar be sealed and sanctified in the name of the Father and of the Son and of the Holy Ghost; and let peace always surround it." Immediately afterward, he incenses the altar on every side in the form of a cross, and recites this beautiful prayer: "We beseech thee, O Lord, that our prayer may ascend to thee as an incense of sweet odor, and thy faithful people shall be laden with blessings. Let all those who, at the foot of this altar, offer up their prayers or participate in the sacrifice, obtain help in the present life, forgiveness of their sins, and the grace of eternal salvation."

There is a cross engraved on the stone that contains the relics, and, as you look at it, you call to mind the great words of the Savior: "Thou art Peter, and upon this rock I will build my Church," etc.

A priest, who has received the thurible from the hand of the bishop, never ceases, till the end of the consecration of the altar, to shake out its perfumes around the altar. The Church instituted this ceremony in order to teach us that we ought never during our whole life to grow weary of praying, and of edifying our brethren by our virtues. The choir intones some psalms, and, while they are doing so, the bishop consecrates with the oil of catechumens the table of the altar. Anointings, signs of the cross, incensings, and various prayers unite in this eloquent ceremony. At length, pouring out holy chrism and oil of catechumens on the altar, he rubs it with his right hand, and invites the people to ask the Lord that, from his lofty dwelling place in heaven, he may vouchsafe to consecrate and to bless this altar on which the holy oil has just been shed, and to receive graciously the petitions and oblations that the faithful shall here present to him.

Meanwhile, twelve crosses have been impressed on twelve pillars of the church. This number recalls that of the apostles, appointed by our Lord to be the pillars or foundations of the truth. From the beginning of the ceremony, lighted candles burn before these crosses, to remind us that the Savior is the light of the world. The pillars have been blessed, but they are not yet consecrated. The bishop draws near, and, making with holy chrism an unction on each of the crosses, says, "Let this temple be sanctified + and consecrated + in the name of the Father and of the Son and of the Holy Ghost, in honor of God, the glorious Virgin Mary, and all the blessed, under the name and in memory of St. N." He gives three shakes of the thurible at each cross, and goes to the foot of the altar, there to address a fervent prayer to God, accompanied with a blessing.

When a warrior takes possession of a fortified city, he sets up his banner there, and, as it floats above the ramparts, it declares the victory of the conqueror. Do you now understand the meaning of these crosses, engraved on the walls of the temple? But the mystery of the holy unction that accompanies them perhaps you do not understand. This unction reminds you of the inward grace that sweetens the cross of the Christian, and that will one day change it into a crown of pearls and diamonds.

The consecrator having returned to the foot of the altar, there are twenty-five grains of incense presented to him to bless. With these grains, he makes five crosses: one in the middle of the altar, and the others at the four corners. He places on them little tapers, one on each, shaped also like a cross, and intended to burn by the four ends. These grains of incense and these tapers are symbols of the virtues that ought to adorn and to consume the hearts of Christians. Such is the first offering that the bishop makes to the Lord on the altar that he has just consecrated. If ever you be witnesses of this mysterious ceremony, you will enter into the spirit of the Church, saying to God: "Yes, I offer thee my heart. Grant that faith, hope, and charity may consume it, as fire consumes wax, and that the good odor of my virtues may edify the earth and rise toward heaven!"

While the candles and the incense are burning on the altar, the bishop and the clergy, prostrate, sing the following antiphon, which perfectly expresses the spirit of this ceremony: "God be praised! Come, O Holy Ghost, replenish the hearts of the faithful, and enkindle in them the fire of thy love!"

Meanwhile, one of the assisting priests gathers up respectfully the ashes of the incense and candles, to throw them into the piscina, and the bishop recites a prayer and a preface asking God to confirm in heaven what he has just wrought on earth, and to grant that the sacrifice offered in this temple and on this altar may always be pleasing to him. At length, to complete this solemn consecration, the bishop traces with holy chrism a cross in the middle of the front part of the altar, and others at the joints of the four angles that support its table. This unction is accompanied by two prayers that seem a summary of all the other prayers employed during the august ceremony.

Immediately, the altar is furnished with its ornaments: the bishop blesses them, if they have not been already blessed. A number of candles are lighted, which give a new charm to the scene. Hitherto, there were none lighted but those suspended before the crosses of the pillars and those of the acolytes. This house is no longer a house of darkness, but of light: these flames teach those who come here to pray that they are not children of darkness and the night, but of light and the day, and consequently that they must not sleep like others, but be sober and watch.[989]

The august ceremony concludes with the Holy Sacrifice of the Mass. It is on the new altar that the bishop pronounces the all-powerful words of consecration: words which open heaven and bring down into this temple that God whose abode it shall henceforth be.

If the faithful wish to assist with fruit at the consecration of a church, they must understand it. This is the way to enter into the spirit of those beautiful prayers and mysterious actions so much in keeping with their condition and their wants. As we have shown, the first part of the ceremony, which is performed in the church, out of their presence, tells them that they are exiles on this earth, and that they should constantly endeavor to reach their heavenly country, while the second part, which takes place before their eyes in the temple, is a figure and a foretaste of the joys that they shall find in the blessed city of heaven.[990] Thus, every act of the consecrating pontiff is a lesson on holiness to them.

"In effect," says St. Bernard, "churches are consecrated only on account of our bodies, our bodies on account of our souls, and our souls on account of God." Our bodies are therefore living temples, which ought to be much holier than material ones. They have been purified by the waters of baptism; marked with the seal of God, who writes his law in our hearts; touched by the unction of the Holy Ghost in the sacraments; enlightened by the lights of the gospel, that we may never engage in any work of darkness; and, lastly, blessed, since the Lord has freed them from the shameful yoke of the passions, and promised them a glorious immortality. Hence it is that he shows himself so jealous of the holiness of these living temples. "If any man violate my temple," he says, "I will destroy him; and you are my temple."

The dedication of our churches reminds us that we are not only the temple of God, but its architects and its guardians. By these titles, we should do for our living temple whatever is done for a material temple. We ought to build it up by faith, hope, and charity; to adorn it by the practice of good works; to place an altar in it, whereon we may daily offer sacrifice; to open and to close it at proper hours; to repair it; and to keep it always in a state worthy of the majesty of the God who dwells in it. Do we act thus? Shame, shame! How many people are there who take more care of their stables or their cowhouses, the abodes of beasts, than of the temple of their soul!

Reasons that urge us often to visit the church. O men, whosoever you are, living temples of a thrice holy God, if you want to preserve undefiled or to purify speedily this august sanctuary, come often into the holy temple! I pity you, if you think little of it. The son that forsakes the paternal roof is not a good son; nor will he ever make a good brother, a good husband, a good father, or a good citizen.

Ye just, you have no surer or more sacred refuge than the temple of the Most High! If you keep far from this holy place, if you turn your eyes from heavenly objects to rest them on the vanities of the world, your soul will soon be swept away by the torrent of evil customs. Weak stalks, you shall soon be broken. Pillars detached from the sanctuary, you cannot stand alone: you shall fall to the ground and thereby be shattered to pieces. The purest water soon loses its clearness; the motion of an insect disturbs it; a breath of wind ruffles it: your heart is an image of this water.

If the temple of the Lord is a place of prayer and consolation for the just man, it is a place of light and peace for the penitent sinner. Here he was born again; here he was made a child of God, a brother of Jesus Christ, and an heir of heaven; here he renounced the world and its pomps: he cannot hide from himself that he is continually violating his engagements, and that the Holy Ghost no longer dwells in him. Here he beholds those sacred tribunals at which, moved by the words of a zealous confessor, he a hundred times promised God to change his life and to put a check on his passions. There his eyes rest on the altar at which he so often nourished his soul with the adorable body and blood of Jesus Christ, who died on the cross to deliver him from the slavery of sin and the tyranny of the rebellious angel. Yonder is the pulpit from which the bread of evangelical truth was so often broken and distributed to faithful souls, and in which his pastors, explainers of the law of God and the science of salvation, contended with the disorders of his life and showed him the dreadful consequences of it.

What more shall I say? On the holy flagstones there lies prostrate a pious soul, a virtuous man, a true Christian, whose piety condemns him, whose example confounds him. As he walks over the ashes of his ancestors, he himself feels that he dishonors them by the foulness of his life. From the depths of their graves, which seem to open up before him, his fathers reproach him with his wickedness and his stubbornness. Lastly, it is death itself that bursts out with a great noise from the bowels of the earth, dragging after it coffins, bones, and shreds of winding-sheets, smeared with blood and mud: it presents itself to his eyes as a frightful specter, digging the grave that is soon to receive him. The whole temple, in short, accuses him, and speaks to him of his ingratitude and of the benefits of God. After a little while, a fear of everlasting pains, joined with a sorrow for having offended God and having been so long his enemy, produces in the soul of the sinner a beginning of love, which, continually increasing, appeases remorse, restores peace, and becomes the principle of justification.

Let sinners therefore go into temples, and ask pardon at the feet of him who is the resurrection and the life. The evil is great, habits are deep-rooted; but Jesus Christ will remedy all, and justice shall reign where iniquity abounded.[991]

Every church is dedicated under the invocation of a saint. Our good mother gives him to the inhabitants of a parish as a protector and a model. He is one link more between the Church of earth and the Church of heaven. It is needless to say that the faithful ought to celebrate the festival of their patron with a holy joy, and with a sincere desire to walk in his footsteps. In every saint's life, no matter what may be our condition, there are some virtues for us to imitate.

PRAYER

O my God! who art all love, I thank thee for having chosen thyself an abode among us. I beg pardon for the neglect and the irreverence with which thou art treated in our churches.

I am resolved to love God above all things, and my neighbor as myself for the love of God; and, in testimony of this love, I will endeavor to be as respectful as the angels in our churches.

Lesson 54: General Summary—Religion in Time and Eternity

We are coming to the end of our task. We have followed religion from its origin down to our own days, and everything tells us that it is preeminently the work of God. The need of a restorer after the fall of Adam is incontestable. The fact of the promise of a Redeemer has been demonstrated, and from the time of this promise belief in the Redeemer was necessary. During four thousand years, the Messias, to be sent by God for the salvation of men, was continually brought before their minds by promises, figures, prophecies, and preparations. At length, the Desired of Nations arrives: the eternal Word becomes man for love of us. In him and by him are fulfilled all the promises, are realized all the figures, and are verified all the prophecies of the old testament.

The new Adam, he is really the Savior of the world. He is the only center round which all ages, past and future, assemble. His life and his works have been presented to our admiration and our imitation. The law of grace is his work: henceforth we must attach ourselves to him by faith, hope, and charity. After showing the conditions and the object of our union with the new Adam, we explained in detail what would destroy and what would perpetuate it.

Here appeared the Church of Jesus Christ; and we have seen Christianity established, preserved, propagated, and brought before the senses during all the centuries of the Christian era. Therefore it—the Roman Catholic Church—is the only depositary of the only good and true religion.

Hence flow three propositions, a magnificent summary of this work, and of all demonstrations on religion. a) There is one true religion, or for the last six thousand years the human race has lost the use of reason. b) The true religion is to be found in Christianity, or nowhere. c) Christianity is to be found in the Catholic Church, or nowhere.

Thus, after passing down the sixty centuries that separate us from the birth of man, and crossing in imagination all the centuries that remain, we arrive at the threshold of eternity. Here time ceases; here ends all that belongs to time. Will the case be the same with religion? No: religion will last when the centuries will be no more; for the relations of which it is the expression are as unchangeable as the natures of God and man on which they rest.

What, in effect, is religion but the bond that unites man with God? Now, between a father and a son, between a mother and a daughter, there exists a sacred, indispensable, and unchangeable bond. Who will dare to deny it? Therefore, between God, a Creator and Father, and man, a creature and child, there exists a bond, and this bond, sacred and unchangeable, will exist as long as it will be true that God is the Creator and Father of man, and man the creature and child of God. Now, this will be true for all eternity. Therefore, religion will exist forever and ever: *in aeternum et ultra.*

Before saying, or rather that we may say, what religion will be in eternity, we must call to mind what it was and what it is in time. Let us recollect ourselves: the history that we are going to enter on is less its than our own.

Religion, the only source of happiness in time.—In the beginning, God created the world and man: the world for man, and man for God. God, essentially good, made a good work: he could not do otherwise. Hence, the book of books tells us that, casting a look over his works in their magnificent entirety, "God saw that all the things he had made were very good."[992] Man especially, the masterpiece of his hands, was very good. Intelligence, love, innocence, immortality, and happiness were his portion.

Happiness in his mind. He knew clearly all that he ought to know: God, himself, and creatures, from the fiery globe that hung above his head to the lowly hyssop that crept beneath his feet. He knew all the beings and all the riches of his vast dominions, and over all he exercised a sway that was absolute, and was as gentle as it was great. And this teaching which religion gives us regarding our first state is so true that we find it at the head of the genesis of every people.

Happiness in his heart. He loved with a deep, pure, calm love all that he ought to love: God, himself, and creatures. And his heart was the sublime medium by which the whole world, submissive to his laws, returned to God.

Happiness in his senses. Around him nature full of vigor, of life, of gigantic productions in harmony with his powers; above him, a cloudless sky; before him, a thornless land, flowers whose perfume and beauty were unmixed with defect, and fruits whose delicious juices would keep him in everlasting youth. No sickness then, no weakness, no fears, no sighs, nothing that could afflict the mind, disturb the heart, or impair the senses.

So much happiness man owed to religion—to the sacred bond that united him, a creature and child, with God the Creator and Father, truth, goodness, life, immortality, perfect happiness. Meanwhile, the hour of crime arrived. Sin entered the world, and happiness fled from it. A thick mist overspread the mind of man. Concupiscence, like a fierce fever, worked into the marrow of his bones; the bright looks of his face grew dim; the strength of his senses was undermined; and death appeared before him, waiting for its prey. Farewell, clear light of the mind; farewell, pure love of an innocent heart; farewell, beauty of body; farewell, calm empire of the world; farewell, strength of organs; farewell, immortality; farewell, happiness!

As Lucifer, that great dragon, when driven out of heaven, drew with him into the abyss a multitude of bright seraphs, so man in his fall drew with him the whole creation, which had been subject to him. All beings were weakened; animals saw their most gigantic species disappear; plants lost their virtues, and flowers their perfumes; thorns grew up instead of roses, and man and the world were no longer anything but a great wreck.

Religion, which had constituted all the happiness of innocent man, came forward to repair the misfortunes of guilty man. A tender mother, she sets out with him from the garden of delights, accompanies him in his exile, wipes away the tears that flow from his eyes, speaks to him of hope in the midst of his punishments, and, seated by his deathbed, soothes the last pangs of his agony. O men! whosoever you are, who believe yourselves endowed with the faculty of thought, we beg of you to say, with your hand upon your heart, to whom is fallen man indebted for whatever knowledge, virtue, nobility, hope, or happiness he has retained or has recovered.

Take the human race at every period of its existence; follow it into every place; question it in every region that it has occupied or that it still occupies: What answer? Facts, but facts as plain as the sun at midday, will speak to your eyes.

Again, who preserved among men, buried as they were in idolatry, some remains of justice, equity, morality, and subordination? Do I hear you say it was philosophy?

Ah! do not oblige us anymore to draw aside the veil of its misery and shame. What were the lights that the ancient world owed to philosophy? What did it teach that religious tradition had not first taught? But why do I speak thus? What ideas were there, even slightly just, regarding God, the soul, the creation of matter, the sovereign felicity, or the end of man—ideas kept among idolatrous peoples by religion, like a small inheritance kept by a father for a prodigal and rebellious son—that philosophy did not alter, condemn, or discredit, by mixing up with them ever so many sophisms and absurdities?

Come with me to the schools of the philosophers—the preservers, according to you, of truth in the ancient world. Question them on a truth that interests both you and me in the highest degree. Here we are in the school of Democritus; ask him: "What is the soul?" The great laugher will answer you: "It is a fire." The Stoics will say that it is an airy substance; others, an intelligence. Heraclitus, the great weeper, will tell you that it is a motion. With Thales, it is a breath, an emanation from the stars; with Pythagoras, a motive number, a monad; with Dinarchus, a harmony. These call it blood; those, a spirit; twenty others, as many other different things. Hence, for every answer to the question, "What is the soul?" only endless contradictions and silly reveries from the philosophers!

But let it pass that they do not understand the nature of the soul. Do they agree better about the rest, for example about its properties? "It is immortal," says one. "No," says another, "it is sentenced to death." According to this man, it will exist for some time. According to that one, it will pass into the body of a beast. "Yes," says someone else, "but not to remain there: it must undergo three transmigrations altogether, and one transmigration may settle its state of existence for a thousand years." What good people, who cannot prolong their own existence beyond a hundred years, and yet promise thousands of years to others!

How shall we speak of these opinions? Shall we say that they are chimerical, foolish, absurd, monstrous? If what these people declare to us is true, why, let all of them use the same language; let one confirm what another asserts: I shall then be glad to listen to them. But when we see them divided on the nature of the soul, are we to tear it into pieces that we may continue such a shocking dispute?

How then shall I address these teachers? This one makes me immortal: what a happiness! That one makes me mortal: what an affliction! Another resolves me into the most minute atoms: behold me water, behold me air, behold me fire! After a little, I am no longer water, nor air, nor fire; I become a deer or a dolphin, I sport amid the woods or the waves. When I begin to examine myself, I grow afraid: I cannot tell what is my name—whether I am a man, or a dog, or a wolf, or a bull, or a bird, or a serpent, or a dragon, or a chimera, so numerous are the metamorphoses to which it has pleased philosophical gentlemen to subject me. Transformed into all the beasts of the earth, wild and tame—into all the animals of the land, the sea, and the air, of so many different shapes, quiet and noisy, sagacious and stupid—I roam, I swim, I fly, I creep, I rest; and now here comes Empedocles, who is going to turn me into a plant![993]

Question all these famous masters on other truths, the bases of moral order and of society: they understand them no better. And the only words that rise to your lips on quitting their tiresome schools are those of a man who knew them well. "There is no absurdity, however shocking," says Cicero, "that is not brought forward by some philosopher!"[994]

And now do you really believe that these philosophers, who bear so close a resemblance to mountebanks that argue in the public squares,[995] preserved in the ancient world those principles of justice and equity which maintained a little harmony among men, broke occasionally the chains of some slaves, and dried up a few tears? Was it of philosophy that Job, the patriarch of sorrow, born and living in the midst of heathenism, asked consolation? Where is the poor man, oppressed with misery, or the slave, torn with stripes, that ever said: "O holy philosophy, comfortress of the afflicted, come to my aid!"?

If the philosopher whom they call their master, Socrates, wants at the moment of drinking hemlock to sweeten the bitterness of his fate, is it philosophy that he invokes? No; it is religion—religion which preserved and which brings to him the consoling dogma of the immortality of the soul. Conclude therefore with us that whatever truths and principles, and, consequently, whatever virtues and consolations there were in the ancient world, they came from religion, and not from philosophy.

But lo! the day dawns when this truth, that man owes everything to religion, is about to appear with the greatest clearness. Do you remember what the world was eighteen centuries ago? Was the night of error dark enough? Was slavery hard and cruel enough? Was man corrupt and wretched enough? Was woman, was the child, was the slave, was the prisoner, were the poor, degraded and downtrodden enough?

Well now, tell us whether it was from schools of philosophy or rather from the upper chamber that the light issued which dispelled the darkness of error, and drove far away, as birds of evil omen, those numberless devils at whose feet the ancient world lay trembling, and whose altars it bathed with human blood. Who again acquainted man with the origin of things? Who taught him the unity of God? Who told him with certainty that he has a soul; that it is immortal, spiritual, and free; that it came from God, and must return to God? Who proclaimed the sacred duties on which society was founded? Who substituted for the brutal right of might the sweet law of charity?

Who told kings that they were made for the people, and not the people for them; that their power is a charge; that their devotedness should reach even to self-sacrifice? Who, showing them a cross, reminded them that the King of kings died thereon for his people? Who told the peoples of the world that they ought to respect their kings, as the ministers of God for good; that if they resisted them, they should be resisting God himself; that they ought willingly and obediently to shed their blood, if necessary, on the field of battle? Who, showing them a cross, reminded them that the first of subjects, or rather the Son of the eternal Father, died thereon out of obedience?

This is not all. Who burst asunder the chains of slavery from one end of the earth to the other? Who did away with the combats of gladiators? Who taught man to respect his fellow man? Who saved children from the murder, exposure, and sale authorized by ancient laws? Who raised woman from her deep abjection, and of a poor degraded wretch made her the noble companion of man?

Who changed the law of nations and made war, savage as it was, as humane as it could be? Who substituted the maxim, "Mercy to captives," for the bloody motto of the ancient world, *Vae victis*—"Woe to the conquered"? Yes, woe: for their inevitable portion was slavery, or death on their conqueror's tomb, or slaughter in the arena of the amphitheatre.

What more shall I say? Who ennobled the poor to such a degree as to make them sacred? Who provided palaces for their misery and their old age? Who brought down to the bedside of the sick, so disgusting and despised, young princes and princesses, born on the steps of the throne, and made them proud to bear the name of the servants of the poor?

Among all these works, which, O philosophers, do you claim for yourselves? Which did you inspire? Tell us whose is the glory. Ah! it is time for you to renounce your indefensible and deplorable errors. Prostrate yourselves before the amiable daughter of heaven, who made the world what it is, less the blotches with which you have covered it; who watched over your cradle as she watched over mine; who enlightened your mind as she enlightened mine; who ennobled your heart as she ennobled mine; and who, if you wish it, will again come to console you when all others flee far from you.

It is time to cease pursuing her with your blasphemies and your hatred. Tell us: What evil has she ever done you? What evil has she ever done the world? If, then, wicked passions come again to tempt your heart, and to call you out under the banners of the enemies of religion, answer them, and you have every reason to do so, that which the human race itself has answered for six thousand years: "She has guided me during the last six thousand years, and she has never done me any harm. How could I think of offending my mother and my queen, to whom I am indebted for everything—knowledge, virtue, freedom, and life?"

This homage of filial piety, let us hope, is in your heart, and it will soon—will it not?—be on your lips; but to whom will you address it? I hear you sometimes speak of different religions: one would say that you did not know on what altar to offer incense. It is true that many societies dispute the honor of being the depositaries of that religion to which the world is indebted for everything. Would you wish to settle all your doubts? Follow us: the work will neither be long nor difficult. See which of these societies has scattered on the human race the benefits that I have hastily sketched for you.

Conclude without a moment's hesitation that the one from which the world has received them is the true society, the only depositary of good doctrine. In effect, a doctrine which civilizes men, which alone makes them better, that is to say, pious in regard to God, just and kind in regard to their brethren, and chaste and humble in regard to themselves, is a good and the only good doctrine. But it is good only because it is true; it is true only because it is divine: and you have found the true society or the true Church.

Which is the religion that makes man happy?—What now are those societies which, during the last eighteen hundred years, have presented themselves to the world as the true depositaries of the word of life? I see the Roman Church; then I see Arianism, followed by Mahometanism and protestantism, and, last of all, I see pagan philosophy returning to the world.

With your hand upon your breast, answer us! Was it Arians, Mahometans, protestants, or philosophers that went down into the amphitheatres of ancient Rome, to cement with their blood the foundations of modern society, and to create that civilization which is the glory and the happiness of the world? No: it was the children of the Roman Catholic Church.

Was it Arians, Mahometans, protestants, or philosophers that peopled the vast solitudes of Thebaid, to give the world so many wonderful examples of virtue, and to teach it to apply to society, to the family, and in all the details of private conduct, the great lessons of Christianity? No: it was the children of the Roman Catholic Church.

Was it Arians, Mahometans, protestants, or philosophers that, at the cost of innumerable fatigues and privations, in contempt of tortures and death, set out to plant among the nations of former times the standard of civilization and religion—the cross? No: it was the children of the Roman Catholic Church.

Arians, Mahometans, protestants, and philosophers! how could any of you have wrought these wonders? You were not yet born. All was done before you came. The world was already resting peacefully under the shade of the Christian tree: many generations had already been nourished, during their stay on earth, with its wholesome fruit.

What of Arianism? When at length you came, what did you do? What truth did Arianism preserve? What social principle did it proclaim when it denied Jesus Christ, the principle of every truth and every duty, and consequently of all society? What people did it draw forth from barbarism? What part of the world did it make more moral, more happy, more prosperous? What is the sum total of its benefits? Nought. What is the extent of the evils that it caused? I see divisions, quarrels, and outrages in every part of the world where it appears. Behold the works of Arianism!

Its doctrine therefore is not good. It is not good because it is not true, and it is not true because it is not divine. Arianism therefore is not the true society, the society that preserves the good religion.

What of Mahometanism? And Mahometanism—what are its works? The son of an Arab, a brigand and a libertine, it advances with a sword in one hand and a cup of pleasure in the other, saying: "Believe or die!" And I see towns on fire from the end of Asia to the center of Africa. I see man transformed into a machine under the iron hand of a blind fatality; the slavery of conquered peoples; the degradation of woman; the contempt of art and science; all the darkness of barbarism. I see the tribes that are subjected to the Mussulman doctrine suddenly arrested in their onward march, and becoming a living petrifaction, as it were, of humanity. Behold the works of Mahometanism!

Its doctrine therefore is not good. It is not good because it is not true, and it is not true because it is not divine. Mahometanism therefore is not the true society, the society that preserves the good religion.

What of protestantism? Pretended reformers of the sixteenth century! it is now your turn. Let us see what are your titles to the confidence and the gratitude of the world. Luther, Zuinglius, Calvin, Henry VIII! do not be afraid; I will not speak of your private lives: every modest soul knows why. There is question here only of your religious work.

You set yourselves up to reform the Roman Church, which had itself reformed and civilized the world, and which had preserved the intellectual and moral superiority thereof for fifteen centuries. Well, tell us: What abuses did you correct? What new virtues did you bestow on the earth?

What consolations did you bring to human misery? Where are the Sisters of Charity that you sent to the pillow of the dying, to the cradle of the abandoned child, to the poor man laid on straw? What new dogmas did you teach? What principles calculated to guard society and religion did you proclaim? What sacred sanction did you give to faith—to faith, the basis of religious, political, civil, and domestic order? What am I saying? A sanction to faith! You destroyed it, by deifying human pride and proclaiming individual infallibility.

And, in consequence of your principles, whole peoples were to be seen marching, with a sword in one hand and a torch in the other, to kill, to burn, and to pillage. Europe was shaken to its foundations. Germany, England, Switzerland, and France were drenched for more than half a century with the blood of their citizens. Scandals of every kind multiplied: adulteries, robberies, daring violations of every law that gave protection to man's character, property, and life.

While the torrent was still raging, you sank into the grave, and your disciples, divided into a thousand opposing sects, anathematized and slaughtered one another. They scattered around them professions of faith as numerous as the leaves of trees, and filled the human mind with a restless activity that urged it on to the wildest dreams and the most guilty theories: so much so that, thanks to them, a broad denial has been given to Jesus Christ, the source of all truth, of all morality, and consequently of all civilization. Hence, complete chaos, realizing on earth an image of the abyss below, where no order, but everlasting horror, dwell.

Again, what people have you civilized? What savages have you drawn forth from their forests? For a century, there have been a hundred million Indians bowed down under the yoke of English protestantism. Go and see if they have made one step, one single step, toward civilization. Tell us, ye zealous Anglicans and Methodists: Do not all the superstitions that you found in India still reign there? Ah! to civilize peoples, it is not enough to have factories for gathering up the produce of their sweat and stores of bibles for distributing to them. Some other things are needed, which alone can civilize them: namely, on the lips truth, and in the veins blood to shed. And the blood of martyrdom is what you never had!

Hence, in regard to civilized peoples, disunion, skepticism, murder, pillage, revolution; in regard to savage and barbarous peoples, utter helplessness; no good, and much evil: behold the effects of protestant doctrine! This doctrine therefore is not good. It is not good because it is not true, and it is not true because it is not divine. Protestantism therefore is not the true society, the society that preserves the good religion.

What of philosophy? Shall we now speak of philosophy? We might dispense ourselves from doing so. What we have said of ancient philosophy applies in every particular to modern philosophy. The same confusions, the same variations, the same contradictions, the same absurdities; and, as a consequence, the same moral disorders, the same political convulsions, the same contempt of all the truths and maxims that have civilized the world. For the rest, modern philosophers are condemned out of their own mouth. "Truth," they say, "is never hurtful." "This," answers one of themselves, "is the best proof that what you say is not the truth."[996]

Struck with barrenness in regard to every kind of good, what has philosophy done? Where are the hospitals that it founded, where are the really useful establishments that it created? Where is the people that it drew forth from barbarism? Where is the civilized nation that it rendered more moral, more tranquil, and consequently more happy? Where is the young man whose morals it purified, whose disorders it corrected? Where is the father that it made more vigilant, the wife more faithful, the citizen more loyal, the magistrate more upright, the trader more honest? What do I say—where is the virtue, however small, however lowly, that it taught, that it sanctioned, or that it practiced?

But if philosophy was powerless for good, it was all-powerful for evil. "It was it," yes, truly it, say its adepts, "that did all that we see."[997] And what do we see? The world shaken to its foundations; all the bonds of society, civil and domestic, torn asunder in scorn; torrents of blood; mountains of ruins; crimes, the very thought of which makes one shudder; man become flesh, become a brute with a human face, and with no other life than that of animal sensations. Behold the works of philosophy; for a philosopher is a man who holds that he has a right to believe nothing and to do whatever he pleases!

This doctrine, fruitful in errors, crimes, and revolutions—this doctrine, which gives up society as a prey to ambition, power, and cunning, is therefore not good. It is not good because it is not true, and it is not true because it is not divine. Philosophy, therefore, is not the true society that preserves the good religion.

And what of Roman Catholicism? It is therefore true that the Roman Catholic Church alone had civilized the world before the birth of Arianism, Mahometanism, protestantism, and philosophy. The Roman Catholic Church, therefore, was before their birth the only true society, the only depositary of sound doctrine, and consequently of the good religion.

Since the days of these new arrivals on the earth, has her beneficent mission ceased? Bulgarians, Russians, Prussians, Tartars, Hungarians, Normans, all ye formidable peoples of the North! so long the scourge of Europe, tell us who it was that first met you and sweetened your ferocity. Who took you by the hand and showed you how to become intelligent? Who made you human beings first and then Christians?

And later on, ye Iroquois and Illinois! ye savages of North and South America! who planted the civilizing standard in the midst of your forests? Who taught you to put an end to your feasting on human flesh, and to your bloody sacrifices? Who brought you into the company of the nations, and made you sit down at the banquet of civilization? In our days, who still civilizes the unheeded tribes of Oceania, and the remains of the American Indians, bowed down under the yoke of horrible superstitions? Who sends her children to bedew with their blood those distant lands, and to prepare a rich harvest for an approaching future? Is it any of you—Arians, Mahometans, protestants, philosophers?

Without leaving our own Europe, who covers our kingdoms from end to end with all those institutions in which we do not know whether to admire more the immense good that they effect in regard to persons of both sexes and of all ages and conditions, or the heroic devotedness and heavenly cheerfulness of those visible angels who, day and night, watch over a mass of human wretchedness with a solicitude more tender than that of a young mother over the cradle of her firstborn? And then in the epidemics that lately decimated the Old and the New World, who flew to the bedside of the sick? Who held an ear close to their infected mouth in order to receive their last sigh? Was it you—Arians, Mahometans, protestants, philosophers?

It is therefore true that since the appearance of these other societies—the pretended guardians of the true religion—the Roman Church alone has magnificently continued her civilizing mission, which she had begun before their birth. Her doctrine therefore has not ceased to be good, and exclusively good. But it is good only because it is true, and it is true only because it is divine. The Catholic Church therefore has not ceased to be the only society established to preserve Christianity.

Do you now know the society that has charge of the true religion? Yet, to enable you to distinguish it from all false sects, we have brought forward only one proof—a most plain proof, it is true, and consequently most suitable for the people, namely, that "the tree is known by its fruits." What would it be if we wished to fall back upon all our resources, and to develop for you the intrinsic marks of truth, which all agree with the Roman Church, and not one of which agrees with Arianism, or Mahometanism, or protestantism, or philosophy?

These marks, to tell them to you in a few words, are unity, sanctity, apostolicity, and catholicity. The inalienable seal of the truth is to be one, holy, of all times, and of all places. Now try, I pray you, if you can find a shadow of unity, sanctity, or universality in Arianism, Mahometanism, protestantism, or philosophy!

O holy Roman Church! the only guardian of truth, virtue, and civilization among mankind, who will now refuse to join his voice with that of St. Augustine, saying to you?—"O Catholic Church! O true mother of Christians! it is you who not only teach men to adore one God, and thus banish idolatry from the face of the earth, but also show them how to practice charity toward one another in such a perfect manner that all human miseries, however various they may be, find therein an efficacious remedy.

"It is you who, in turn, simple with the child, firm with the young man, calm with the old man, declare the truth, and train to virtue, according to the strength of the body and capacity of the mind.

"It is you who subject woman to man by a chaste and faithful soul, not in order to gratify beastly passions, but to preserve the human race, society, and the family.

"It is you who give man a superiority over woman, not that he may despise her, but that he may be her support, and may direct her according to the laws of the most cordial love.

"It is you who subject children to parents by a willing service, and who give parents a holy sway over their children.

"It is you who unite children to one another by the bond of religion, stronger and more sacred than that of blood.

"It is you who, while respecting the laws of nature and the inclinations of the heart, draw closer by a mutual charity the ties of marriage and of friendship.

"It is you who teach servants to obey their masters, less from fear than from love.

"It is you who make masters kind and compassionate toward their servants, by the thought of a supreme God, the master of all.

"It is you who unite, not only by the ties of society, but by those of fraternity, citizen to citizen, nation to nation, all men, wheresoever they may be, to one another, by the memory of their common cradle.

"It is you who teach kings to be devoted to the welfare of their peoples, and peoples to be submissive to the authority of their kings.

"It is you who tell with the utmost precision to whom honor is due, to whom affection, to whom respect, to whom fear, to whom consolation, to whom warning, to whom exhortation, to whom reprimand, to whom correction, to whom punishment, showing that all these things are not due to all, but that charity is due to all and wrong to no one."[998]

And what does religion, what does the Roman Church, wish in molding us to virtue, and in providing for all our wants? She wishes to repair gradually, in regard to all the generations that appear on the earth, the sad consequences of original sin and of all other sins. She wishes to restore to our mind some of the knowledge that it enjoyed in the state of innocence; to our heart, purity and a control over the senses; and to our senses themselves, some of their first power and integrity. Since quitting the terrestrial paradise, religion has led man from light to light, as a mother leads her child from the bewildering darkness of its early years to the full and clear development of its reason.

Religion, the only source of happiness in eternity.—But the work of rehabilitation, which has been so well continued, and a picture of which we have drawn in all the preceding portions of this catechism, is only begun on earth. Its perfection is reserved for eternity, and thither religion leads us. It is there that all things will be perfect. It is there that we shall see something far better than that golden age of which a faint remembrance is preserved even among pagans: we shall see heaven. It is time to tell what heaven is. The picture which we are going to draw of it will, though very imperfect, suffice we think, to excite our desires, to support our courage, and to make us say with the apostle: "No, all the pains of time, all the sacrifices that religion imposes on us, are not worthy to be compared with the glory and the happiness that await us in heaven."[999]

What is heaven? What light is to the blind man, who has once seen it, and who longs to see it again; what health is to the sick man, who is tormented with cruel pains; what peace is to the miserable, who spend their days and nights in grief; what the recovery of his throne is to a fallen king; what a clear, fresh stream is to a thirsty and weary traveler; what a return to his native land and to the bosom of a dearly beloved family is to an exile; lastly, what a deliverance from all evils, the full and perfect enjoyment of all goods, the sweet rest of never-ending bliss and glory, are to man gnawed by insatiable desires, to man overwhelmed with sorrows and labors, to man condemned to tears, sickness, and death: that, and much more, is heaven to the human race!

Heaven is the accomplishment of all the desires of God, creatures, and man; it is the restoration of all things in a state of absolute perfection; it is the eternal repose and quiet of order.

1. *In regard to God.* Heaven is the accomplishment of this desire expressed by the Son of the Eternal, instructing the human race: "Father, thy kingdom come, thy will be done on earth as it in in heaven."[1000] Heaven is for God the full enjoyment of his works; the perfect manifestation of his glory, power, goodness, wisdom, and other ineffable perfections. It is the intercourse of a fond Father with affectionate children: it is the immense, eternal overflowing of his love for them, and the immense, eternal overflowing of their love for him. It is the union of man with God, and of God with man: a union without confusion of natures, so that God and man, united without being confounded, shall forever enjoy, in an ocean of unspeakable delights, the plenitude of their being. In a word, heaven is the place where God "shall be all in all."[1001]

2. *In regard to creatures.* Heaven is the accomplishment of this desire expressed in their name by the great apostle: "All creatures groan, and travail in pain, expecting their deliverance from corruption, and a share in the glory of the elect, to whom alone they shall thenceforth be subject, and who shall no more make them, in spite of themselves, subservient to iniquity."[1002] Creatures therefore, as Catholic doctors conclude, sigh after their liberation and renovation, not their destruction or annihilation. As for their substance, they shall therefore not be destroyed, but merely purified by the fire of the last day: like gold, which is not destroyed by being passed through the crucible, but purified and made brighter and more durable.[1003]

Who will describe the beauty and perfection of the new earth and the new heavens? The eagle of the schools, whose angelic purity obtained for him a glimpse at things hidden from the profane, St. Thomas, speaking of the elements after the general resurrection, tells us that water shall be like crystal, the air as pure as the clearest sky, fire as bright as the sun and stars, and the surface of the earth as transparent as glass.[1004] Always equally enlightened, the earth will enjoy a sweet unchanging temperature. The stars and the elements, always the same in themselves and in regard to us, will have none of the imperfections that we perceive in them at present.[1005]

The earth, it is true, will be deprived of some mixed bodies, inseparable from its present condition, but it will not be less perfect. It will have all that can contribute to its perfection in the state of stability and incorruption wherein it shall then be, though deprived of some beauties that became it in its former state of imperfection. The ornaments that become the house of a private individual no longer become it when it is made the palace of a great prince.[1006]

3. *In regard to man.* Heaven, as we have said, is the accomplishments of all his lawful desires. It is the accomplishment of the desire expressed by the royal prophet in the name of the whole human race: "I shall be satisfied when thy glory shall appear."[1007] To prove this, we only need two principles. First: heaven is a perfect deliverance from evil, and a perfect enjoyment of happiness without mixture and without end. Second: man will in heaven be true man, that is to say, body and soul. Heaven will therefore be complete happiness for body and soul. Such is the definition that an instinct, as general as it is strong, gives to the human race.

A thing too little remarked, though very remarkable, this is the reason why man desires heaven with all his twofold might, spiritual and corporal. Created for happiness, he is always and irresistibly gravitating toward it, as the magnet toward the pole, and all nature toward its center. From the cradle to the grave, this wretched, degraded being seeks his rehabilitation, his deliverance from evil; this dethroned king seeks his crown; this fallen god remembers the heavens, and seeks them everywhere. Urged on by an irresistible force, he goes about everywhere, asking heaven, that is to say, happiness, from whatever he meets.

Ask him what is the object of his toils, his sighs, his troubles, his sacrifices, his virtues, and even his crimes. Always and everywhere he will tell you that it is happiness, that is to say, heaven. During the six thousand years that he has spent on the globe, nothing has been able to check the impetuous force that drives him on toward happiness, that is to say, heaven. On the contrary, the older he grows, the more eager he becomes; for the farther he wanders away by corruption from the true heaven, the more strenuous are his endeavors to find that imaginary heaven of which his passions rave to him.

Why those heaps of ruins with which the earth has been strewn during so many centuries? Why those frightful convulsions, those frequent revolutions, which end only in bitter disappointment, without ever satisfying man's obstinate desire of happiness? What is the last cry after all these things? Happiness, heaven, which man implores of whatsoever he supposes able to give it to him.

Lawful desires, but vain efforts! If he seeks heaven, he seeks it amiss, or rather he places it where it is not; and this is one of the sad consequences of his degradation. What would you think of a man who, standing on the bank of a smooth lake, and suddenly noticing therein the image of the moon, should jump into the water to lay hold on it? Would you not call him a big child? The more he grasps and struggles, the less are his hopes of success. And the end of all his efforts is fatigue, despair, death. O big child! lift up thy head, and do not seek at thy feet what is above thee: what thou pursuest is only an image of happiness! Nothing is more true than that the happiness which man finds in creatures is only a shadow, or, if you choose, a faint image of the happiness of heaven.

In effect, what are the pleasures that man desires for his body and soul?

Fulfillment of the body: A beautiful dwelling.—First, man desires for his sojourn an exquisite site, a place surrounded with all the beauties of nature: fertile land; a clear, calm, cloudless sky; no extremes of heat or cold. See how little account the rich make of journeys and expenses occasioned by the search for such a situation! When they find it, they seem to have reached their hearts' content. They congratulate themselves on their good fortune, and write thereof to their friends and relations, whom they wish to rejoice with them.

Well, what is heaven? It is the full, eternal satisfaction of this desire. For, when time is over, there will be new heavens and a new earth. Purified by fire, they shall have all the qualities corresponding to the nature of our bodies, become impassible and immortal. Oh, how ravishing shall their beauty be! And then, under those new heavens and on that new earth, there shall be none of the things that disturb the quiet of your dwelling place now, however happy it may appear to you: no robbers to threaten your property or your life, no famines, no floods, no fires, no plagues, no evils whatsoever.

A *spacious dwelling*. What else does man ask for his body? A spacious habitation; gorgeous rooms; rich furniture. See the wonderful activity that he causes in order to procure them! Can you tell how many arts and trades are employed for this purpose? Masons, stonecutters, carpenters, joiners, gilders, cabinetmakers, artisans of every class unite to adorn his residence. Nearly all the metals are called in: iron, silver, copper, lead. What choice slate and marble! What elegant curtains and carpets! And when he comes to occupy this sumptuous abode, he thinks himself happy!

Now, heaven is the full, eternal satisfaction of this desire. Listen to the description given you of the abode of the elect by the beloved disciple, whose eye had the happiness of contemplating it. "And the angel took me up in spirit to a high mountain; and he showed me the city, the holy Jerusalem, coming down from God. It was lighted by the brightness of God himself; and its light was like to a jasper stone, even as crystal. It had a great and high wall, in which there were twelve gates, and at each gate there was an angel. The wall was built of jasper stone, and the city was of pure gold, like to clear glass, and the foundations of the city were of precious stones. The twelve gates were twelve pearls: each gate was made of one of these pearls. And the street of the city was of pure gold, as it were transparent glass."[1008]

Splendid garments. Man, what else do you desire for your body? Splendid garments. We know, alas! how much value you attach to them, and how much pride—I was going to say vanity—they inspire you with. In heaven these ignoble spoils of animals, which you carry about with you to hide your shame and to defend your weakness, all these liveries of primitive degradation will be no more. Your body, shining with all the graces of a never-ending youth, will be its own garment.

What are the other goods that you desire for your body? Health, beauty, agility, life.

Health. How great are the efforts of man to preserve the first of these goods, or to recover it when lost! Expenses, journeys, privations of every kind seem nothing to him; and if, at the cost of so many sacrifices, he obtains once more that health which will soon fail again, he imagines himself, even though a poor outcast of society, happier than the greatest monarch in the world. Now, in heaven man shall enjoy perfect health. All his organs, at present so corruptible, shall be so perfect that nothing shall ever change them, and they shall serve the soul in all its operations with marvelous ease.

Beauty. For his body, man desires beauty: natural deformity is sometimes as hard to bear as death. He envies those who have beauty. He delights to think that he has some share of it. And if this frail, imperfect beauty is often threatened, oh, what care does he take to repair it, what precautions to stay the ravages of time! Now, in heaven, man, delivered from evil and all the consequences of evil, will reappear with a beauty of which we can form no idea. "In the grave," says St. Augustine, "all the bodies of the saints shall lose their defects. Man shall arise in the vigor of age. His beauty shall then shine with all its brightness, and he shall enjoy an everlasting youth."

Agility. For his body there is another good that man desires, especially in our days, with the utmost ardor: it is agility. He wishes to be no longer troubled with distance. The weight of matter annoys him: at any cost, he must be rid of it. His genius is taxed, and wonders crown his efforts. Steam lends him its extraordinary power, and electricity its amazing speed. The mountains fall down before him. With a swiftness far greater than that of a bird, he flies over immense distances. He aspires to make the circuit of the globe with the quickness of thought, and the success which he has attained and that of which he still dreams cause him indescribable joy. Well, heaven is the accomplishment of this desire of agility which torments us. Our bodies having become spiritual, they will no longer be an obstacle to the activity of the soul, which will transport them whithersoever it wishes with the quickness of thought.

Life. For his body, man also desires life. Oh, were he to set his hopes on immortality, which is endless life, what would he not do to procure it? Judge thereof by the eagerness that he shows to lengthen his days, and by the excessive fear that he has of dying. See how he fights against sickness, how he struggles with death! The measure of his efforts to escape is the measure of his love for life. Well, heaven is the accomplishment of this desire, the strongest and most imperious of the human heart. There, immortal life, a life accompanied by all joys without any mixture of sorrow: behold what is promised to us!

Beauty, health, agility, life: such are the great goods that man desires for his body, that he seeks, that he pursues, that he buys at any cost. Religion leads him to the possession of them. She gives them to him in heaven.

For each of his senses, man also experiences desires that nothing here below can satisfy, and that become a torment to him. The eye desires to see all that is beautiful, the ear to hear all that is harmonious, and so on with taste, smell, and touch. We should write the history of the human race from its first to its last page, if we wished to relate all that man has done to gratify his senses. What lives wasted, what rivers of bloodshed, what mountains of gold and silver squandered, to procure pleasure for the senses! Heaven gives all this, or rather heaven is all this in perfection, without any mixture of imperfection or shadow of vicissitude.[1009]

First, the pleasure of seeing. The saint shall see the new heavens and the new earth, incomparably more beautiful than the former ones. They shall see that holy city which Tobias and, after him the apostle St. John, having no terms to express its magnificence, picture to us as a city built of gold, and adorned with all kinds of precious stones. They shall see one another, and as, according to St. Paul, their bodies shall be reformed on the model of that of Jesus Christ,[1010] they shall be so bright and beautiful that they shall not yield to the sun in brightness and beauty.

This is no exaggeration. The Savior's body, to which all others shall be made like, was one day seen by St. Paul brighter than the sun at noon. Does not the Savior himself say, that "the just shall shine as the sun in the kingdom of their Father"?[1011] What contentment, therefore, shall they have when they see their hands, their feet, all the members of their body so resplendent that, wherever they may be, they shall have no need of a lamp or a star to give them light!

But they shall not only have the satisfaction of seeing their body thus radiant with glory: they shall also see with the greatest pleasure the bodies of the other saints, and especially those of our Lord and his Blessed Mother. If the sun, as it rises, rejoices all nature, what joy will it be to each one of the blessed to see all those living suns, I mean all those bodies which will attract and charm the eyes, as well by the admirable disposal and exact proportion of their members as by their extraordinary brightness! For the rest, one will not then have to turn away the eyes in order to defend them from too great a light; for they shall be impassible, and he who so strengthens the eyes of the soul that they can look fixedly on the deity will also strengthen those of the body in such a manner that millions of suns will not be able to dazzle them.

We may add for the pleasure of sight what St. Augustine says, that the holy martyrs shall have some glorious mark on that part of their body which suffered most. Thus, on St. Stephen's head shall be seen a crown made up of as many diamonds as there were stones thrown at him. St. John the Baptist, St. James, and St. Paul, who were beheaded, shall have a collar of wonderful beauty and inestimable value. St. Bartholomew, flayed alive, shall be arrayed in purple far more splendid than that of kings. Lastly, to omit mention of the others, we shall see the glorious wounds of St. Peter and St. Andrew, who were crucified: they shall be as bright as the stars. But he who shall surpass all the other martyrs in brightness, without eclipsing them however, shall be the King of martyrs, who shall shine among them as the sun among the stars.

Secondly, the pleasure of hearing. It is certain that those luminous bodies of the saints in heaven shall have the organs needed to hear and to speak; for all the apostles, with a great many disciples and women, saw the Savior after his resurrection, and spoke to him, and he answered their questions. We learn also from the book of Tobias and the Apocalypse of St. John that there shall be canticles sung in heaven to the praise of the Lord. These canticles, so sweet and ever new, shall wondrously rejoice the saints, and shall please them so much the more as their voices shall be more beautiful, as he whose praises they sing shall be more worthy thereof, as the place shall be better suited for such concerts, and lastly, as the audience shall have more delicate ears and be assembled in greater numbers.

Who then can conceive the excess of their happiness when, rejoicing in an unchangeable peace and burning with the love of God, the supreme benefactor, they shall excite one another to praise him forever? St. Francis, as we learn from St. Bonaventure, having heard for some little time the sweet sounds of a lute touched by an angel, was so ravished therewith that he imagined himself in another world. What pleasure then shall it be to hear millions of voices, accompanied by as many instruments, which, divided into two choirs and continually answering one another, shall sing forever and ever the praises of God!

Thirdly, the pleasure of smell. Heaven shall be a city filled with the most exquisite perfumes. We know for certain that the bodies of many saints have yielded such a pleasing odor after their death that no person had ever felt the like. This, according to St. Jerome, is what occurred with St. Hilarion. For, ten months after he had been buried, his body was found as entire as if he were alive, and from it there issued a miraculous fragrance, which made some people suppose that he had been embalmed. The same thing is related of St. Servulus, that poor paralytic of whom St. Gregory makes such a great eulogy. When dying, he spread around him a heavenly perfume, which amazed all those who were present. There are innumerable other examples of this wonder. Hence we may conclude that if bodies whose souls enjoy glory exhale a divine odor even in the grave, the case will be very different in heaven when they shall be living and glorified.

Add what the same St. Gregory writes of his aunt St. Tharsilla, that at the very moment of her death the room in which she lay was filled with such a sweet perfume that it seemed as if the author of all sweetness was there present. Let those therefore who have a liking for sweet scents begin to feel from afar off the pleasure that they shall experience in paradise, amid the flowers of that delightful garden.

Fourthly and fifthly, the pleasure of taste and the pleasure of touch. It is true that in heaven there will be no material, corruptible food. Nevertheless, the sense of taste, elevated and purified like the other senses of man, will have its action and its pleasures, conformable to the place and the condition of the blessed.[1012] Heaven is described to us as a wedding feast, or as a city flowing with torrents of delights. What enjoyment for the sense of touch, especially when we consider the good health of the bodies of the risen just!

Let us judge by a comparison. When here the body is covered with ulcers or oppressed by some other disease, the sense that suffers most, or the only one that suffers, is the touch. In the same manner, when the body is sound and strong, it is also the touch that derives most pleasure therefrom. The touch shall therefore have its beatitude, and shall have it forever, when, after the resurrection, the saints, having become immortal and impassible, shall enjoy the most perfect health. What would not the great ones of the world give to be always free from gout, calculus, lumbago, headache, and dyspepsia? What ought they not to give, what ought they not to do, in order to gain heaven, from which every kind of disease and pain will be banished forever?

Still more: though the risen bodies shall consist of flesh and bone, yet they shall be spiritual, that is to say, they shall be so submissive to the soul that they shall move about at its wish; they shall ascend, descend, go everywhere with amazing speed; they shall pass through the thickest walls as easily as if they were spirits and not bodies. As therefore this sense is the only one that suffers when heavy terrestrial bodies are obliged to descend from a height, to climb a hill, or to run a race, so it alone shall enjoy the pleasure that the facility of going everywhere without ever being tired can cause to a glorified body.

Behold in what manner the blessed shall be delivered from the slavery of this corruptible flesh! To travel more quickly or securely, never shall they have need of horses, or coaches, or firearms, or any other things whatsoever, because they shall go, as it were, in the twinkling of an eye from pole to pole, and whithersoever they fly they shall have nothing to fear. Would to God that even those persons who are not yet capable of relishing spiritual sweetness would at least think of these sensible goods, and, by dint of thinking of them, come to esteem and to seek them! They might at length rise higher, and thus make with the divine help a step toward eternal bliss.

Fulfillment of the soul.—If from the pleasures of the senses, which, such as we have described them, would surely satisfy the desires of the most ambitious man, we pass on to spiritual pleasures, infinitely purer and nobler, we may well cry out with the apostle: "No, no, the eye of man has never seen, his ear has never heard, his heart—large as it is—has never desired anything like what God has prepared for the elect."[1013] Let us try to form an imperfect idea of it.

For his memory. For his memory, man desires clear and delightful recollections. One of our greatest miseries and most bitter regrets is to forget either wholly or in part what we have seen, heard, or learned. Well, in heaven what satisfaction shall it be for the saints when their memory, become full and perfect, recalls to them, on the one side, the infinite blessings that God bestowed upon them for body and soul, for time and eternity, and, on the other, the almost continual dangers from which he delivered them at every period and in every occupation of their life! Can they think on his goodness in preserving them from mortal sin and the pains of hell on so many occasions when they were nearly falling into them without returning him a thousand thanks?

But will they think on this goodness forever, and make it a subject of boundless and endless gratitude? Ah! if they were capable of forgetting it, would the prophet exclaim: "The mercies of the Lord I will sing forever"?[1014] And would St. Augustine say that in the city of God there will be nothing more charming than this canticle, nothing which will show out more admirably the grace of Jesus Christ our Redeemer?

What shall we say of the vicissitudes of times that they shall have always present to their imagination? Will it not be a very pleasing thing, when they see God, to see in God all that has previously occurred in the world—so many various events that providence caused or permitted, and infallibly guided to its own wise ends? Will not this be that impetuous river of which David speaks, that river which is always flowing and "rejoices the city of God"?[1015] Could the rolling centuries be in any way better represented than by this river, which is most rapid in its course, and which will never stop until it is lost in the great ocean of eternity?[1016]

For his mind. For his mind, man desires knowledge. And you see him undertaking long journeys, crossing seas, climbing mountains, going down into the depths of the earth, wasting himself with study! Why? To know one truth more. And when he has had a glimpse through a thick veil at one of the beauties of the spiritual world, he considers himself happy!

Yet what is this truth or this beauty? What are all the truths that we can discover here below, or all the beauties that seem to bewitch us in creatures? "Footprints of the Creator," says St. Thomas—*Vestigia Creatoris!* If a lady of surpassing beauty, walking by the seaside, should lay on the sand such beautiful footprints that the kings of the earth would raise armies and wage war to gain possession for them; that the most avaricious would give all their treasures in exchange of them; and, lastly, that all men would quit their occupations in order to gratify the single passion of looking at them, placing therein their supreme felicity, what judgment would you form of the beauty of this lady, seeing that the very prints of her feet could have so many charms as to throw the world into confusion? Would you not say that she should be a most amazing miracle of beauty, far beyond anything that the human imagination can conceive?

O God of love! what then are we to think of thy ineffable beauty, since all men toil unceasingly and even fight to death with one another, enchanted as they are by thy footprints? Why do kings and emperors make war, if not for the possession of human greatness and glory? And what is greatness or glory, what are kingdoms and riches, but thy footprints on the sands of this earth—*vestigia Creatoris?*

Why do so many people run over land and sea in search of gold and diamonds, if not because they are passionately fond of these things? And what are these things but thy footprints on corruptible matter—*vestigia Creatoris?*

Why have the greatest philosophers and the noblest geniuses of the world at all times found so much pleasure in studying the secrets of nature, if not because they met with ravishing beauties in them? And what are all these beauties but a few of thy footprints on creatures—*vestigia Creatoris?*

If then the mere marks of thy feet, laid as it were upon the sands of time, have a beauty that rouses the courage of all, a splendor that excites the passions of all, a charm that wins the minds and hearts of all and sets the whole world in commotion, who can imagine what it is to see thy face, O my God! the inexhaustible source of all beauty?[1017]

Well, heaven is the full, complete, eternal satisfaction of this insatiable desire to see what is beautiful. There we shall see that beauty which is the source of all other beauties. We shall see it not as in a mirror, but face-to-face and without a veil. We shall see it in itself, and in it the secrets of all events. We shall know why God created the universe. We shall understand the mystery of all those revolutions of our globe which astonish and defy science. We shall see why the Lord permitted the fall of the first angel, as well as that of the first man, and why he gave a Savior to the latter, and not to the former.

We shall know why, among so many nations, he chose for his beloved people the descendants of Abraham, though he foresaw that they would be most intractable, and would persecute his Son and even put him to death like a criminal on a cross: thus accomplishing, in spite of themselves, the design that he had formed to save all the nations of the earth.

Lastly, we shall know in particular why, at all times, he permitted an innumerable multitude of the good to suffer persecution in this world, and it will be seen that his whole object was to let them merit by patience the glory that he was preparing for them. And all together we shall bless him forever, when we see our crosses changed into crowns; and we shall say with the prophet: "As much pain and distress as we suffered, O Lord, with so much consolation and joy hast thou filled our souls."[1018] What think you, men of science? Shall the delights of heaven become tedious? And if you tire yourselves out for less, how does it come to pass that you will do nothing at all for more?

For his heart: To love and to be loved. What is it that man desires for his heart? To love and to be loved. And who will tell what he does to satisfy this imperious want of his being? Sacrifices, labors, dangers, privations cost him nothing: everything, even death itself, seems sweet to him, provided he be loved. He offers his heart to whatever comes in his way, to gold and silver, to honors, to his kind, to the very animals. He is happy when it is accepted and he finds a return of love. Well, heaven is the full, complete, eternal satisfaction of this desire. There we shall see beauty itself, an ocean of beauty, the infinite good, the eternal source of every other good, and in it all created beauties and goods.

And then, what makes the special charm of friendship is that secret sympathy, that tender regard, that wonderful fondness which produces between some souls an attraction so strong that they seem struggling to break all their other bonds and to go to be knit to one another. But what is this in comparison with the sympathy that attaches God to the soul and the soul to God? It is so great on God's side that it drew him down from heaven to earth. It is so strong in the soul that the soul cannot possibly be happy without being united to God.

In heaven this sympathy will be such that, if we may so speak, it will endeavor to transform us into God; so that, according to the expression of the apostle St. John, we shall "be made perfect" in him, made "like to him."[1019] Made perfect in God, made like to God: Can you imagine such happiness? What think you, men that burn with love? Shall the delights of heaven become tedious? And if you tire yourselves out for less, how does it come to pass that you will do nothing at all for more?

Examine again what are the other desires of man. Glory and power. Yes, glory and power!

Glory. To arrive at glory, every way, no matter how difficult, is good to him. Ask the scholar, who wastes himself in painful studies, the soldier, who is going to shed his blood on the battlefield, and the ambitious man, who watches night and day for a fortunate moment, what are they seeking? All will answer you: "Glory! glory! without it life is nothing to us!" Well, what glory there is in heaven! To be known, esteemed, and loved by God himself, as well as by the angels and saints![1020] On the brows of virgins, doctors, and martyrs, I behold a bright, unfading *aureola*, varied according to distinction of virtues and degrees of merit:[1021] a crown which shall give rise to no feeling of jealousy; a crown which, justly deserved, shall be the joy of those who wear it!

And power. We have not words to tell with what ardor, especially in this world, man desires it. Ask the heaps of ruins, the rivers of blood, the dreadful convulsions, of which we are the victims. A voice will come forth from them, saying to you: "See what man does to arrive at power!" And, in fact, of all the passions the strongest is unquestionably that of ruling. Royalty passes for a good that contains all the other goods most eagerly sought after by men: influence, honor, wealth, independence. Hence it is that kings, when they wish to show an exceeding affection and liberality, think that they can offer nothing more than the half of their kingdom. Thus, Assuerus said to Esther: "What wilt thou? What is thy request? Though thou shouldst ask the half of my kingdom, I will give it to thee."[1022] Herod, in the same sentiments, said to the daughter of Herodias: "Ask of me whatsoever thou pleasest, and I will give it to thee, though it should be the half of my kingdom."[1023] Hence also it is that both ancient and modern history are full of examples that show the extremes and excesses to which the passion for sway leads. We know that Julius Caesar had often on his lips this saying from Euripides: "If ever any one can break an oath, it must be for the purpose of reigning; in all things else behave as an honest man." Agrippina, the mother of Nero, having consulted astrologers as to the destiny of her son, received this answer: "Your son shall be emperor, but he shall put his mother to death." "No matter," she exclaimed in a transport of delight. "Let me die, provided he shall reign."

From these instances and thousands of others, we see that among all the goods of this world there is none so much esteemed or desired as sovereignty. Yet reason and faith teach us that the kings of the earth cannot reign for a long time, that the throne is often a Calvary, that kingdoms here below soon come to an end, and that the kingdom of heaven alone shall last forever.[1024]

Heaven is therefore the complete, eternal satisfaction of this desire to reign, which torments the heart of man. Associated with the King of ages and of worlds, the saints shall be kings in the fullest extent of the word. What the Almighty can do by himself, they shall be able to do by him. They shall reign, over their totally vanquished enemies, the devil and his angels, the wicked and their passions; and also over all nature. Domination and independence, honors, riches, and pleasures, crowns and scepters, all the belongings of royalty shall be theirs, and this without strife or fear.

For the rest, let no one imagine that the glory of paradise shall be lessened in any manner because so many millions of the blessed shall share it. This kingdom does not resemble those of the earth, which are lessened in proportion as they are divided, and in each of which only one person rules. The kingdom of heaven has this advantage, that it is all for the just who possess it, and all for each one of them without any division: like the sunlight, which shines on the eyes of all, and which enlightens each man in particular as much as all men in general.

In heaven, all the desires of man shall therefore be satisfied, but in a manner far surpassing anything that we can imagine.[1025] O men, my brethren, beings of a day and candidates for eternity! be therefore more ambitious. Lift up your eyes toward heaven, and, when you think on the earth, and its honors, and its riches, and its pleasures, say: "I am greater than all these things, I am born for greater goods"—*Major his sum et ad majora natus!* Be steadfast in this noble ambition, and heaven is yours.

Blind, deaf, senseless are we, if, for vile and abject goods, and which are to last only a little while, we quit others of infinite value, and which are to last through all eternity; if for the shadow we sacrifice the reality, wasting ourselves in seeking heaven where it is not, and refusing to seek it where it is! O my God, I beseech thee in thy mercy to cure our blindness! Open the eyes of our minds; grant us understanding, and correct our errors! What will the light of reason, which distinguishes us from beasts, avail us, and what profit shall we draw from the light of thy countenance, which shines upon us, if we still continue as blind as ever in the most important of all affairs?

It is therefore true, as we have endeavored to show throughout the whole course of this work, that religion, which procures for man all the happiness that is to be found on earth, also leads him to infinite happiness, without mixture and without end.

It is therefore true that, in order to render man happy through all eternity, religion only asks permission to render him happy on earth.

It is therefore true that God is a Father, who created man the king and the high priest of the universe; who loaded him with glory and joy; and who, after having been grossly insulted by this favored creature, has never ceased for a single moment, in spite of so much ingratitude, to do him good. Since the beginning of the world, he has been continually laboring to repair the evil that his guilty child did himself in withdrawing from his Father; continually consoling and encouraging him; continually moving heaven and earth to supply him with the means of recovering his lost happiness. And this happiness, but increased far more than a hundredfold, made perfect to overflowing, he will one day restore to him forever. May we all come to enjoy it!

The author's declaration.—Now that our task is ended, there remains for us one very pleasing duty to fulfill—the duty of a respectful son toward the best of mothers. We regard it as our glory here to follow holy examples.

It was the 7th of March, 1274. In a little cell at Fossa Nuova, a celebrated abbey of the Cistercians, in the Diocese of Terracina, there lay dying, on a poor bed, a traveler who had arrived a few weeks previously. This traveler was the light of his age, the prince of scholars, the Angel of the Schools: he was called Thomas of Aquin. At the mournful toll of the bell, all the inhabitants of the monastery had hastened to the church: the last sacraments were about to be administered to the Angelic Doctor.

When he saw the holy host in the priest's hands, the dying saint raised his failing voice, and before receiving the God of truth, declared his inviolable attachment, his filial obedience to the Catholic Church, the pillar and the ground of truth on earth. "I firmly believe," he said, "that Jesus Christ, true God and true man, is present in this august sacrament. I adore you, O my God and my Savior! I receive you, O you who are the price of my redemption and the viaticum of my pilgrimage; you, for whose love I have studied, labored, preached, taught! I hope that I have never advanced anything contrary to your divine word; but if this has happened to me through ignorance, I now publicly retract it, and submit all my writings to the judgment of the holy Roman Church."

To us also it is pleasant, it is glorious to imitate this great man in his filial submission to the Church. The duty that he fulfilled, how much more readily ought we to fulfill—we, to whom a consciousness of our own weakness suggests so many reasons for fearing that there may have escaped from our pen some of those involuntary errors which are the sad heritage of humanity! It is therefore with our whole heart that we submit this catechism, and our other works,[1026] to the judgment of the holy Roman Church. A child and a minister of the infallible spouse of the man-God, we regard it as our happiness and our glory to say: "Her faith shall always be ours; we believe with her, we hope with her, and we love with her; we condemn whatever she condemns, and we approve whatever she approves." Such are our dispositions, and, with the help of God, such shall be our dispositions till our last breath, convinced as we are that "no one can have God for his Father if he has not the Church for his mother."[1027]

ENDNOTES

1 Vatican I, Dogmatic Constitution *Dei Filius de fide catholica*, Ch. 4

2 Pope Benedict XIV, Apostolic Constitution *Etsi minime*, n. 13

3 Cf. Pope St. Pius X, Encyclical *Acerbo nimis*, n. 27

4 Cf. Ex 23:21

5 Cf. 4 Kgs 4:9-37

6 Cf. Ps 98:5, 9

7 Lk 10:16; Mt 10:40. See Bergier, *Dictionnaire de théologie*, art. *Culte*; and Jauffret, *du Culte public*.

8 It is derived from *car*, *ker*, *cor*, "the heart," and *moneo*, "to warn," "to manifest," "to make known." See Bergier, *Dictionnaire de théologie*, art. *Cérém*.

9 It would not be easy to frame an idea of the monstrosities that have sprung and that still spring up from the ignorance and fanaticism of heretical sects. Let us take one example out of a thousand.

In 1827, in the government of Saratof, district of Atkarsk, village of Koneny, thirty-six persons, of various ages and both sexes, belonging to the Sect of the Savior, deliberately put themselves to death in order to secure their salvation.

A peasant, named Ignatius Nikitin, put to death the women Anastasia Wasilief, Eudoxia Iliine, and Matrona Federof. He was then put to death himself by Alexander Petrof, who had already slaughtered the wife and children of this Ignatius Nikitin, the peasant Moses Ivanof with his children, and the peasant James Ivanof.

After this carnage, Alexander Petrof went off to find his mother-in-law in order to persuade her to let herself be put to death. She would not consent, and, having learned that her children were among the victims, went to see them. In the meanwhile, Petrof went to the house of Van Youchkof, who urged him to let himself be sacrificed. Petrof consented, and, kneeling down beside a block, placed thereon his head, which Youchkof cut off with a hatchet.

Among the victims, there were old men of seventy and children of two years. This sect has many adherents in the government of Nijni and still more in that of Kostroma; but its center is the district of Danilof, in the government of Yaroslaf.

A peasant, named Michael Kourtin, of the village of Slobodistch, district of Viaznekof, government of Vladimir, aged sixty-seven years, put to death, in 1855, his son Gregory, aged seven years, believing that he should thereby perform an act pleasing to our Savior.

He gave himself up freely into the hands of the officers of justice, and related for them all that he had done. Here is a summary of his disclosures.

"I belong," he said, "to the Sect of the Savior; so did my father and mother, and also my grandfather. I have never confessed nor communicated in any church. I have induced my wife to join my sect, and never permitted her to receive the sacraments of the Church. On the 27th of November, 1853, a feast of the Blessed Virgin, I prayed a long time with tears, thinking that there was no salvation for men on earth and that they should all be lost.

"During the night, my grief became so intense that I never closed an eye and had to rise many times. I lighted tapers before images, and prayed on my knees, with tears, in order to obtain my salvation and that of my family. It came into my mind to save my son Gregory from everlasting perdition.

"As this child, seven years old, was very bright and cheerful, and more intelligent than is usual for his age, I was afraid lest, after my death, he should renounce the faith and be lost in the eternal gehenna, and I decided on putting him to death in order to convey him safely to the kingdom of heaven.

"At daybreak, I got up and began to pray toward the East, asking the Savior for a sign. I said to myself that if, after praying, this thought should return to me once more from the right side, I would then offer my son in sacrifice to God; but, if it came to me from the left side, I would then do nothing. For we believe that thoughts which come to us from the right side are from the good angel, and those which come to us from the left are from the devil. After praying for a long time, this thought came to me from the right side, and I returned to my cabin with joy in my soul."

At this time, the child and the mother, who loved her son very tenderly, were in a deep sleep.

Michael awoke his wife, and, in order to have her out of the way, sent her on a message to a village about a mile off.

Then, left alone with his son, he awoke him.

"Rise, my little Gregory, and put on a white shirt, that I may look at you."

"Papa," answered the child, "I have no white shirt; mamma has not made me one yet."

"Well, put on mine; it will do as well."

According to the belief of the sect, it is a sin to die in a colored shirt.

"All right," answered the child, and he put on his father's shirt.

"That will do," said Michael. "Now lie down on the bench till I look at you."

The child lay down, and the father put a rolled-up cloak under his head for a pillow. Then this father, suddenly lifting the shirt, gave the child several stabs in the stomach with a table knife that he had hidden in his sleeve.

The child began to struggle. To shorten the sufferings of his son, the father ripped his bowels open with one great cut. The child was no longer able to offer any resistance, but he did not die immediately. At this moment, the first beams of the rising sun fell suddenly on the poor victim's face. At this sight, the father stood confounded; his hands trembled, and the knife fell from his grasp. He cast himself on his knees before the images, and began to beg of God to accept graciously this victim.

Then returning to his son, he said to him, "My dear little Gregory, in the name of Christ, forgive me the evil that I have done you."

The child, who was dying, but was still conscious, replied, "Goodbye, papa."

The father then ordered him to repeat these words: "Father, God will forgive you." The child said, "Father, God will forgive you."

Then the murderer lighted candles and recited the prayers for the recommendation of the soul. He told his son to repeat after him the Hail Mary. The child kept doing so till the third time with a weak voice; he could not finish it the third time, and was silent.

The peasant was on his knees before the images and his son lay bathed in blood, when the unfortunate mother returned. Learning from one word what had just occurred, seized with terror, and overwhelmed with grief, she fell on the ground before the corpse of her son.

The murderer, who was still on his knees, then rose and said to his wife, "Go to the starosta (the mayor) and tell him all. I have made a feast for the saints."

When the neighbors, informed by the wife, entered, they found Michael Kourtin on his knees before the images and in prayer. At the sight of the neighbors, he said to them, "I have finished my business. Go to the court, and the justice of the peace, and say that I have slain my son. I have made a feast for all the saints."

Michael Kourtin was arrested, and, while preparations were being made for his trial, he starved himself in prison.

We have taken this account from the *Moscow Gazette* (a journal of our own times, 1868, n. 25), which borrowed it from the *New Times*.

You see what need these people have to be instructed and evangelized. The Russian clergy are dumb, and the Catholic clergy are forbidden to speak. Hapless people, so circumstanced!

—J. Gargarin, S. J.,

A Russian by birth, and one who knows his country well.

10 A pagan author, Festus, calls "rituals" those books which taught the ceremonies for the consecration of cities, temples, and altars, and we call at present "ritual" the book which prescribes the mode of administering the sacraments.

The rite followed by the Churches of Spain from the beginning of the eighth till about the end of the eleventh century is called the Mozarabic Rite. The Arabs having possessed themselves of Spain in 712, the Spaniards who lived under their rule were called "Mozarabs," that is to say, "Outer Arabs," in order to distinguish them from Arabs by descent. According to Cardinal Bona, the word *Mozarab* means "mixed with the Arabs": *cum Arabibus mixti*. This rite is also called the Gothic Rite, because it was followed by the Goths, become Christians and masters of Spain in the time of the Moors.

Sacramentary. We call a "sacramentary" the book which contains the prayers and words that bishops and priests recite, when celebrating Mass and administering the sacraments.

Missal. Everyone knows that this is the book which contains what is said at Mass during the course of the year. We speak of the Roman, the Milanese, the Gothic or Mozarabic Missal, to denote the Missal used in different places.

Antiphonary or *Antiphonal*. We call thus the book which contains what is to be sung by the choir during Mass, because the introits have as their title *Antiphona ad introitum*.

Roman Ordo. This is the book which shows the manner of celebrating the Mass and the offices of the principal days of the year, especially the last four days of Holy Week and the octave of Easter.

Ordinary of the Mass. This is the name given to what is said at every Mass, in order to distinguish it from what is peculiar to festivals and other days of the year.

Hours. These are books which contain prayers of various kinds, in addition to the offices of the principal festivals and the ordinary of the Mass. We call them "hours" because the ecclesiastical office is divided into different hours: matins, lauds, prime, terce, sext, none, vespers, and compline.

11 See Bergier, *Dictionnaire de théologie*, art. *Liturgie*, and Père Le Brun, *Cérémonies de la Messe*, p. 1.

12 Cf. Rom 1:20

13 Council of Trent, Session 22, "Doctrine on the Sacrifice of the Mass," Ch. 5

14 Cf. *Encyclopédie*, art. *Religion*

15 Cf. Ez 20:5ff; Jer 7:22ff

16 Cf. Bergier, *Dictionnaire de théologie*, art. *Cérémonies*

17 See *Perpétuité de la Foi*, Arnaud, Renaudot, Le Brun.

18 In France, how many towns and villages still bear the name of *Moutier* or *Moustier*, which comes from *monusterium*, "a monastery"!

19 *Génie du Christianisme*, Pt. 4, Ch. 1

20 See Bergier, *Dictionnaire de théologie*, art. *Cérémonies.*

21 What we say of ceremonies must also be said of discipline. The discipline of the Church is an outer network in regard to government. It is founded on the decisions and canons of councils, on the decrees of popes, on ecclesiastical laws. Whence it follows that the regulations wise and necessary at one time may not be useful at another. Certain abuses or circumstances, unforeseen cases, etc., have often required the making of new laws and sometimes the abrogation of old ones. All this has necessarily introduced changes in the discipline of the Church (Cf. Bergier, *Dictionnaire de théologie*, art. *Discipline*).

22 Ps 44:14

23 Cf. Ps 44:15

24 Augustine, *Epistle 36*

25 Cf. Augustine, *Contra Faustum*, Bk. 20, Ch. 4, n. 21

26 Cf. Council of Trent, Session 22, "Doctrine on the Sacrifice of the Mass," Ch. 8

27 Cf. Nm 22:41; *Mém. de l'Acad.*, p. 63

28 Cf. Bergier, *Dictionnaire de théologie*, art. *Eglise*

29 Cf. Bergier, *Dictionnaire de théologie*, art. *Culte*

30 Someone has said that whoever does not dress well on Sunday is an infidel.

31 Cf. Gn 35:2

32 Cf. Ex 19:10

33 Cf. Bergier, *Dictionnaire de théologie*, art. *Culte*

34 Cf. Ps 121:1

35 Cf. Clement of Rome, *First Epistle*, Ch. 41; Ignatius of Antioch, *Epistle to the Magnesians*, Ch. 7; Clement of Alexandria, *The Stromata*, Bk. 7, etc.

36 "It is certain," says the celebrated antiquary Bottari, "that the little chapels of the catacombs were the rude types of the churches and basilicas that were built afterward": *E certo che queste cappelletti...furono un rozzissimo abozzo delle chiese e delle basiliche edificate dipoi* (t. 3, p. 75). See our *Histoire des Catacombes*, in which we have given a detailed description of subterranean churches, and shown that they, not pagan basilicas, were the patterns of our churches.

37 We take as our guides the antiquaries of Rome. They are more to be relied on than any others: the reason is easily understood. See Mamachi, t. 1.

38 This vestibule was called *nartex*, that is to say, "rod" or "baton," because of its long shape.

39 Claustrum.

40 Atrium.

41 Cf. Gn 35

42 Cf. Ibid.

43 Cf. *Summa Theologiae*, III, q. 65, a. 1, rep. 8. See our *Traité de l'eau bénite.*

44 Nartex interior.

45 Navis.

46 The Church of Saint-Etienne du Mont, Paris, still possesses a most remarkable ambo.

47 If, in the celebration of marriage, this order is reversed, it is that the husband may be at the right of the wife, whose head he is.

48 It is still general in Italy.

49 Chorus.

50 Translator's note: Sometimes called a "screen," "grate," or "lattice."

51 Bema vel sanctuarium.

52 From the Greek *απσις*.

53 Chrysostom, *Homily 3 on Ephesians*

54 "Never did the Church," says the abbé Pascal (letter to M. Didron), "prescribe with severity that temples should be turned toward the East...St. Paulinus, who lived in the fourth century, admits that the most general custom is to turn churches toward the East; but he is so far from discovering in this custom a liturgical rule that he causes at the same time to be built in Tyre a Christian temple which he turns exactly in an opposite direction—toward the West. Hence, therefore, an ordinary custom as much as one pleases; but an invariable rule, never. I am now going to state a fact of very great importance. The most august church in the Catholic world, the cathedral of cathedrals, St. John Lateran's, the type of all the temples of Christianity—toward which of the cardinal points is it turned? Toward the West. The magnificent Basilica of St. Peter, the first collegiate church in the world, stretches out its vast naves and its long apse toward the West. The ancient church of St. Clement directs its three apses toward the same point. It would therefore be quite contrary to the spirit of the Church to regard as a constant and absolute rule what was never anything but a matter of pure convenience and option." This is true; but the celebrant who says Mass at the papal altar turns toward the East.

55 *Cripta*, "a cave," "a vault," "a grave."

56 Monumentum arcuatum.

57 In Italy, the end of it has been that altars bear exclusively the name of *confessions*. Thus we say "the confession of St. Peter," to designate the altar or tomb of the prince of the apostles. Sometimes the altar, that is to say, the tomb, is wholly detached, and is placed in the center of the grotto. Hence have come "Roman altars," that is to say, altars moved forward into the sanctuary, and around which one can walk.

58 See the description of this church in the *Trois Rome*, t. 2.

59 Cf. M. Raoul Rochette, *Tableau des Catacombes*

60 St. Jerome bears witness to this custom: *Cum alii cereos lampadesque, alii choros psallentium ducerent* (*Epistle 108 to Eustochium*, n. 29). See Bottari, t. 3, p. 67-68.

61 On the lamps, paintings, etc., see our *Histoire des Catacombes*.

62 *Microlog.*, Ch. 11

63 Loculi.

64 The necessity of perpetuating the memory of the catacombs has been such that architects, rather than sacrifice it, have preferred to derogate from the rules of their art in the construction of our churches. "An inconvenience to architecture," says M. Raoul Rochette, "is the multiplication of little side chapels around Christian churches, as private confessions or memorials of martyrs, whose worship is associated with that of the principal saint or patron. This usage, born with the Church herself in the depths of the catacombs, had a more decided influence on the general arrangement of Christian basilicas than any circumstance taken from the genius of worship. For so many memorials of martyrs, whose number gradually increased beyond all measure, beyond all proportion, in the same temple, it was necessary to open private chapels in the side naves. These private chapels became so many independent monuments in the midst of the principal monument, and, if we may so speak, basilicas within basilicas. The consequence was, in plans as well as in elevations, frequent interruption of those straight lines which are not only the chief merit of works of architecture, but also the chief element of the impressions of grandeur that they produce" (*Tableau des Catacombes*, p. 91).

65 Cf. M. Raoul Rochette, *Tableau des Catacombes*, p. 185

66 Cf. Gregory of Nyssa, *Oration, De Laudib. Theodor.*; Paulinus of Nola, *Natal*, i, *de Ornat cl.*; Gregory the Great, *Register of Epistles*, Bk. 9, Epistle 9; Gregory Nazianzen, *Epistle 49*

67 Cf. Polydore Vergil, *De Inventoribus Rerum*; Onuphrius, *Epist. summ. Pontif.*

68 *Cloche*, "a bell," comes from the German *clocke* or *glocke*. This word seems to express the sound of the instrument. The *sonnettes* were not used to call people to prayer. Apropos of this, the grave cardinal Bona relates an amusing story from Strabo:

A lute player arrived in one of the islands of Greece, to give proof there of his musical ability. All the people gather round the performer, and wait to hear him; but, scarcely has he taken a few notes from his instrument, when the sound of a little bell is heard, and the multitude rush off as fast as their legs can carry them. The poor musician's audience is reduced to one, who is somewhat hard of hearing. "I congratulate and thank you," says the lute player to him, "for alone remaining to hear me; but why do the people in your country run away when they hear the sound of a bell?" "And did the bell ring?" asked the deaf man. "Yes." "Good day!" and he began to run with all his might, shouting back to the disappointed musician, "It is the fish market!"* (Durantus, *De Ritibus Ecclesiae Catholicae*, Bk. 1, Ch. 21).

* Cardinal Bona, *Rerum liturgicarum*, Bk. 1, Ch. 22, p. 192.

69 Cf. Cardinal Bona, *Rerum liturgicarum*, Bk. 1, Ch. 22
Instantis quod signa canens, det Gallus Eoi,
Et revocat famulas, ad nova pensa manus.
—Alciatus, *in Emblemate*

70 Cf. Council of Cologne, Can. 14

71 Cf. Cardinal Bona, *Rerum liturgicarum*, Bk. 1, Ch. 22

72 *Roman Pontifical*

73 Cf. Modern science has annihilated the pretensions of the "philosophical" science of the last century. It has proved clearly that the bell does not attract the thunderbolt, which falls at least as often on plains as on heights. See *l'Histoire de la Foudre*, by Dr. Boudin.

74 Nm 10:9; Cf. Durandus, *Rationale divinorum officiorum*, Bk. 1, Ch. 22, n. 4

75 See *Génie du Christianisme*, Pt. 4.

76 Cf. Rom 8:22

77 Cf. Jn 12:31; 1:29

78 1 Cor 15:28

79 Gn 1:31

80 Cf. Rom 8

81 1 Tm 4:5

82 Cf. Ex 15

83 4 Kgs 2:21

84 Cf. Tb 8

85 Cf. Leviticus, passim

86 Cf. Mt 14

87 1 Tm 4:4-5

88 Cf. Bergier, *Dictionnaire de théologie*, art. *Bénédiction*

89 See our *Traité de l'eau bénite.*

90 Cum igitur hodie Dominus ad mortuos descenderit, ea de causa hic colligimur, ob id ipse etiam locus coemeterium (*κοιμητηριον*) nominatus est: ut discas, mortuos, et eos qui hic siti, non mortuos, sed somno consopitos esse et dormire. Nam ante Christi adventum mors nomen mortis habebat…"Mors vivo requies" (Cf. Jb 3:13). At postquam Christus venit, et pro mundi vita mortem subiit, mors non amplius vocatur mors, sed somnus et dormition…qua de causa et locus coemeterii, quasi dicas *dormitorii*, nomen invenit. Utile enim hoc nomen est et philosophiae plenum. Quando igitur huc mortuum ducis, ne ipse te concidas; non enim ipsum ad mortem sed ad somnum ducis; sufficit tibi nomen hoc ad calamitatis solatium et levamen (Chrysostom, *Homily, De Coemeter. Appellat.*, n. 1, p. 469ff, op. t. 2, P. Prior, edit. Gaume).

91 Gn 3:19

92 Until the time of the French occupation, all persons were buried there; since then, only a part of the population.

93 Cf. Bergier, *Dictionnaire de théologie*, art. *Cimetière*

94 Jb 19:21

95 Jn 11:25

96 *Tibia* is the name given, in anatomy, to the principal bone of the leg.

97 These various ceremonies take place when the bishop himself blesses the cemetery.

98 All these ceremonies are accompanied with magnificent prayers and poetic prefaces, as may be seen in the Pontifical.

99 J. B. Rousseau

100 Mt 25:41

101 Visum est autem sanctae synodo, praecedenti doctrinae de poenitentia adjungere ea quae sequuntur de sacramento extremae unctionis: quod non modo poenitentiae, sed et totius Christianae vitae quae perpetua poenitentia esse debet, consummativum existimatum est a patribus (Council of Trent, Session 14, "On the Sacrament of Extreme Unction," Introduction).

102 *Festus, festivus.* See Du Cange.

103 Cf. Gn 35

104 To give justice to this observation, it is not necessary that the same harmony should reign in all climes: the shape of the earth and the course of the sun render it impossible. Some people have summer while we have winter. It is enough that this harmony should be perfect at the center of Catholicity. Here we meet with the perfection of relations.

105 Homo cum in honore esset, non intellexit: comparatus est jumentis insipientibus et similis factus est illis (Ps 48:13).

106 On the matters treated of in this fourth part of the catechism, see the following authorities, consulted by us: Justin Martyr, *First Apology*; *Second Apology*; Tertullian, *Apology*; *Prescription against Heretics*; *De Corona Militis*; Clement of Alexandria, *The Stromata*; *The Paedagogus*; Augustine, *City of God*; *Genesis according to the Letter*; *Contra Faustum*; Innocent I, *Letter to Decentius*; *Apostolic Constitutions*; Isidore of Seville, *De Ecclesiasticis Officiis*; Durandus, bishop of Mende, *Rationale divinorum officiorum*—of which it is said, *Caeteri libri utiles, iste necessarius*; Duranti, first president of the Parliament of Toulouse, his excellent treatise *De Ritibus Ecclesiae Catholicae*; Cardinal Bona, *Rerum liturgicarum libri duo*; Boldetti, Canon of St. Mary's in Transtevere, *Osservasioni sopra i cimiteri de' santi martiri ed antichi Christiani di Roma*, fol.; P. Mamachi, a Dominican, *De' Costumi de' primitivi Christiani*; *Antiquitates Christianae*; Le Brun, *Cérémonies de la Messe, Liturgies de toutes les Eglises*; Thomassin, *Traité des Fêtes*; Baillet, *Fêtes mobiles*; Bergier, *Dictionnaire de théologie*; Jauffret, *du Culte public*; M. Raoul Rochette, *Tableau des Catacombes*; M. Thirat, *Esprit des Cérémonies de l'Eglise, Rituel romain*, etc.

107 Cf. Ex 20:8-11; Dt 5:12-15

108 From that incessant application to labor which has no regard for the holiday, and which is the daughter of luxury and industrialism, that is to say, of selfishness carried to excess, the following consequences have resulted: it is the chief magistrate of a large manufacturing town who points them out in an official report on the causes of pauperism: a) endless competition; b) cheats in production; c) bad faith; d) the ruin of artisans; e) the monopoly of monster establishments; f) an increase in the number of failures; g) beastliness among workpeople; h) destruction of family life; i) the absence of any moral bond between master and servant.—See our work: *La profanation du Dimanche, considérée au point de vue de la Religion, du bien-être, de la santé,* etc.

109 *Génie du Christianisme*, Pt. 4

110 See, in the second part of this work, what we say on Sunday, Lesson 49 [i.e., Volume XI of the Tradivox series, p. 381-392].

111 We read in the Catholic epistle of St. Barnabas: "We spend the Sunday in joy, the day on which Jesus rose from the dead"; *Diem Dominicam laetitia agimus, in quo Jesus resurrexit a mortuis* (Ch. 15). Tertullian says, "We do not allow any fasting on Sunday"; *Die Dominico jejunium nefas ducimus* (*De Corona Militis*, Ch. 3; *Apology*, Ch. 16).

112 The early Christians prayed standing on Sunday, in memory of the resurrection and as a sign thereof. They prayed kneeling on other days in memory of the fall of Adam and their own falls. *Christiani orant genuflexi omnibus feriis et diebus, idque ad memoriam lapsus Adae et omnium posterorum ejus, exceptis dominicis et tempore paschali, quando stantes orant in honorem et representationem resurrectionis Christi, ut docet sanctus Justinus*, q. 115. *Unde, inquit, talis in Ecclesia consuetudo? quia utriusque nos oportuit jugem obtinere memoriam, et ipsius per peccatum lapsus nostri, et gratiae Christi nostri, per quam a lapsu resurreximus: quapropter genuum per sex dies inclinatio, symbolum et nota est lapsus per peccata nostra. Quod vero die dominico genua non flectimus, signum est et designatio resurrectionis per quam gratia Christi a peccatis et a morte, quae ab illo interfecta est, liberati sumus.*

113 Eighty years after St. Justin, Tertullian wrote thus: "Commendable old men preside. Each of us brings monthly his little tribute, when he pleases and as he pleases, according to his means; for no person is forced. All is voluntary. We have thus a kind of pious fund, which is not wasted in repasts or useless dissipations: it is spent in the support of the needy and on the decent accompaniments of their burial; it maintains poor orphans, servants worn out by age, the shipwrecked. And when Christians are

condemned to the mines, banished far from their country, or kept in prison solely for the cause of God, it brings them relief in many ways" (*Apology*, Ch. 39).

114 Justin Martyr, *First Apology*, Ch. 65-67. See Mamachi, *De' Costumi de' primitivi Christiani*.

115 Cf. Le Vicomte Walsh, *Tableau poétique des fêtes Chrétiennes*

116 Mt 18:20

117 Precationes fiant mane, tertia hora, sexta, nona, et vespere, atque ad galli cantum (*Apostolic Constitutions*, Bk. 8, Ch. 34; Cf. Durandus, *Rationale divinorum officiorum*, Bk. 3, Ch. 11, p. 733).

118 Jerome, *Epistle 107 to Laeta*, n. 9

119 Cf. Jerome, *Epistles to Marcella*

120 Augustine, *Sermon 1, Feriae quartae; 56, de Tempore.*—See also Basil, *Homily, In Martyr. Julittam*; Augustine, *Epistle 109*, etc.

121 Ps 118:164

122 Isidore, *De Ecclesiasticis Officiis*, Bk. 1; Rabanus Maurus, *De Institutione Clericorum*, Bk. 2; Basil, *De Instit. Monach.*, Bk. 1; Jerome, *On Psalm 118*; John Cassian, *Conferences of the Desert Fathers*, Bk. 3, Ch. 4. It is a pleasure to us to quote the following lines, which give the reasons for the different hours by showing the mystery that is honored in each of them:

Matutina ligat Christum qui crimina solvit;
Prima replet sputis; causam dat tertia mortis;
Sexta cruci nectit; latus ejus nona bipertit;
Vespera deponit; tumulo completa reponit.

123 Jerome, *On Job*, Ch. 43

124 See also, on the other harmonies of the number *seven*, Varro, *Eorum qui inscribuntur hebdomades*, Bk. 1, and our *Traité du Saint-Esprit*, t. 2; Basil, *Homily 2, in Hexaem.*; Gregory Nazianzen, *Oration 94, in Sanct. Pentecost.*; Augustine, *City of God*, Bk. 2, Ch. 37; *De Genesi ad Litteram*; *De Genesi contra Manichaeos*, Bk. 1.

125 This is the reason why it is called the "breviary."

126 Apoc 4:8

127 Sunday excepted, when the first nocturn consists of thrice four psalms, to recall a sacred number, which it would take too long to explain here.

128 Cf. Vegetius, *De re militari*, Ch. 8

129 Cf. Hilar., *On Psalm 118*; Ambrose, *On Luke*, Bk. 7

130 Praeponatur ei probae fidei, et morum ac pudicitiae virgo veterana, quae illam doceat et assuescat exemplo ad orationes et psalmos nocte consurgere (Jerome, *Epistle 107 to Laeta*, n. 9).

131 Durandus, *Rationale divinorum officiorum*, Bk. 5

132 Adhuc te loquente ecce adsum (Cf. Is 58:9).

133 Some authors give a more ancient origin to the *Gloria*: they attribute it to the Council of Nice.

134 Ps 99:2

135 Cf. Augustine, *On Psalm 63*; Gregory Nazianzen, *Poem 20*

136 Cf. Col 3:16; Eph 5:19; Eusebius, *Ecclesiastical History*, Bk. 2

137 Cf. Socrates, *Historia Ecclesiastica*, Bk. 6

138 Cf. Jn 4:23

139 Cf. Durandus, *Rationale divinorum officiorum*, Bk. 5

140 Cf. Ps 32:2

141 Cf. Gal 6:2

142 Cf. Is 6:2-5

143 The word *Domne* is a contraction of *Domine*: we trace it back to the ninth or tenth century. *Dicat diaconus, 'Jube, Domne,' non 'Domine,' nam hoc Dei est, illud homini praeclaro* (Gavanti, *Thesaur. Sacr. Rit.*, Pt. 2, t. 6, p. 94, in-4: Venitiis, 1685; see also St. Peter Damian).

144 Durandus, *Rationale divinorum officiorum*, Bk. 5

145 The three psalms that follow the canticle make but one.

146 In some churches, the lauds of Sunday had eight psalms. It would take too long to explain the reason for this difference. See Durandus, *Rationale divinorum officiorum*, Bk. 5, Ch. 4.

147 Cf. Durandus, *Rationale divinorum officiorum*, Bk. 2, Ch. 7

148 Cf. Durandus, *Rationale divinorum officiorum*, Bk. 5, Ch. 5

149 Amalarius Fortunatus, *De Ecclesiasticis Officiis*, Bk. 4, Ch. 2

150 Editor's note: The Symbol of St. Athanasius, *Quicumque Vult*, is included in full in Volume VI of the Tradivox series.

151 Cf. Ignatius of Antioch, *Epistle to the Trallians*

152 Cf. *Apostolic Constitutions*, Bk. 8, Ch. 34

153 *Quo tempore eversio fuit, eodem rursus facta reparatio* (Cyril of Jerusalem, *Catechetical Lecture 14*; Cf. Theophylactus, *On Matthew, ad ca verba: A sexta autem hora, etc.*) Here are some other harmonies: *Propter protoplastum Adam...(Christus) sexta hora in crucem ascendit, sexto die saeculi, in sexta hora ejusdem millenarii, et sexta hebdomadis et sexta hora sexti diei, etc.* (Anastasius Sinaita, *Commentary on the Hexameron*, Bk. 7). See our *Histoire du bon Larron*.

154 Cf. Basil, *The Longer Rules*, q. 37

155 Cf. Durandus, *Rationale divinorum officiorum*, Bk. 5, Ch. 5

156 Cf. *Apostolic Constitutions*, Bk. 8, Ch. 34

157 Cf. Jn 19:28

158 See the explanation of matins in the last lesson.

159 *Compline* means "complement," because this hour completes the office.

160 Le Vicomte Walsh, *Tableau poétique des fêtes Chrétiennes*, p. 33

161 Cf. Basil, *The Longer Rules*, q. 37; Clement of Alexandria, *The Paedagogus*, Bk. 2, Ch. 4; Isidore, *De Ecclesiasticis Officiis*, Bk. 1, Ch. 21

162 Christianus alter Christus.

163 Cf. Bergier, *Dictionnaire de théologie*, art. *Langue*

164 Cf. Council of Trent, Session 22, "Doctrine on the Sacrifice of the Mass," Ch. 8

165 Except the Canon or ordinary of the Mass, the translation of which is contrary to the intentions of the Church.

166 See Cardinal Bona, *Rerum liturgicarum*, Bk. 1, Ch. 5, p. 33.

167 Cf. Durandus, *Rationale divinorum officiorum*, Bk. 5, Ch. 11

168 Cf. *Annal. de Phil. Chrét.*, Anno 1830

169 Cf. Augustine, *Confessions*, Bk. 6

170 Cf. Basil, *On Psalm 1*; Lactantius, *The Divine Institutes*, Bk. 6, Ch. 21; Chrysostom, *On Psalm 41*

171 Cf. Ruff., *Hist.*, Bk. 10, Ch. 35, 42; Theodoret, *Ecclesiastical History*, Bk. 3, Ch. 1

172 Cf. 4 Kgs 2; 1 Kgs 16; Dn 3

173 Mt 21:9

174 Cf. Eph 5:19

175 Cf. *Epistle* 97. See also the Council of Laodicea, Can. 15; Fourth Council of Carthage, Can. 10; Council of Agde, Can. 21; Council of Aix, Can. 132, 133, etc.

176 Cf. Lebeuf, *Traité hist. du chant*, Ch. 3

177 Cf. *Génie du Christianisme*, t. 2, Ch. 40

178 Augustine, *Confessions*, Bk. 9, Ch. 6

179 *Etudes de la Nature*, t. 3, p. 506

180 Oblatio rei sensibilis a legitimo ministro facta Deo, per realem immutationom, ad agnoscendum supremum ejus dominium nostramque subjectionem. Communia sacrificia proprie dicuntur, quando circa res Deo oblatas aliquid fit, sicut quod animalia occidebantur et comburebantur, quod panis frangitur, et comeditur et benedicitur. Et hoc ipsum nomen sonat: nam sacrificium dicitur ex hoc quod homo facit aliquid sacrum (*Summa Theologiae*, II-II, q. 85, a. 3, rep. 3).

181 See on all these matters the excellent work of Père De Condren, *l'Idée du Sacerdoce et du Sacrifice de Jésus-Christ*, p. 48; and *Summa Theologiae*, I, q. 45, a. 5.

182 Cf. Ps 50:7

183 Cf. M. de Maistre, *Eclaircissements sur les sacrifices*, p. 396

184 Cf. Macrobius, *Saturnalia*, Bk. 1, Ch. 7

185 Cf. M. de Maistre, *Eclaircissements sur les sacrifices*, p. 413

186 Mal 1:10-11

187 Sacerdos Patris Catholicus (Tertullian, *Against Marcion*, Bk. 4, Ch. 9).

188 Cf. Heb 10:5ff

189 Origen, *Homily 1 on Leviticus*, n. 3

190 Cf. Col 1:19-20; Eph 1:10; Heb 9:23

191 Pelisson, *Traité de l'Euchar.*, p. 182, Paris, 1694.—Hence it was that the early Christians preferred to die rather than eat flesh offered to idols: this would have been to sit down at the table of the devil and join him in his repast.

192 Cf. Council of Trent, Session 22, "Doctrine on the Sacrifice of the Mass," Ch. 2-3

193 Jn 6:54

194 Adhaereat visceribus meis…ut in me non remaneat scelerum macula (Liturgy of the Mass).

195 Cf. M. de Maistre, *Eclaircissements sur les sacrifices*

196 Una enim eademque est hostia, idem nunc offerens sacerdotis ministerio qui se ipeum tunc in cruce obtulit, sola offerendi ratione diversa (Council of Trent, Session 22, "Doctrine on the Sacrifice of the Mass," Ch. 2).

197 Cf. Jn 10:17-18

198 Augustine, *City of God*, Bk. 8, Ch. 27

199 Cf. Council of Trent, Session 22, "Doctrine on the Sacrifice of the Mass"

200 Cf. Ibid.

201 Coenam suam dedit, passionem suam dedit (Augustine, *On Psalm 21*).

202 Cf. 1 Cor 11:26

203 Passio est enim Domini sacrificium quod offerimus (Cyprian, *Epistle 63, ad Caecilium*).

204 Ps 110:4-5

205 Cf. Augustine, *Confessions*, Bk. 9, Ch. 12-13

206 Significans passionem Domini Jesu, cujus quotidie vescimur sacramento (Ambrose, *On Psalm 43*).

207 Cf. Alphonsus Liguori, *Selva*, t. 2, p. 197

208 Cf. Council of Trent, Session 22

209 In hoc mysterio salus mundi tota consistit (Odo, *Opusc. 2*, Ch. 28).

210 Per quam terrarum orbis consistit (Timothy of Jerusalem, *Orat. de Proph.*).

211 Non minus videtur facere Deus in hoc, quod quotidie dignatur descendere super altare, quam cum naturam humani generis assumpsit (Bonaventure, *De Instit.*, Pt. 1, Ch. 11).

212 In qualibet Missa invenitur omnis fructus quem Christus operatus est in cruce. Quidquid est effectus dominicae passionis, est effectus hujus sacrificii (Aquinas, *Commentary on Isaiah*, Ch. 6).

213 Tantum valet celebratio Missae, quantum valet mors Christi in cruce (Chrysostom, *Apud Discipul., Sermon 48*).

214 Lk 10:13

215 See what we have said on the manner of hearing Mass in the second part of the catechism, Lesson 49 [i.e., Volume XI of the Tradivox series, p. 389-392].

216 Cf. Eusebius, *Ecclesiastical History*, Bk. 8, Ch. 8

217 Pope Stephen, *Epistle, ad Hilar*. See also Tertullian, *On Monogamy*, Ch. 12; Origen, *Homily 11 on Leviticus*, Ch. 20; Jerome, *Commentary on Ezekiel*, Bk. 13, Ch. 46; Cardinal Bona, *Rerum liturgicarum*, Bk. 1, Ch. 24. See particularly on this subject *Summa Theologiae*, III-Sup., q. 40, a. 7.

218 Agg 2:9

219 Cf. Jerome, *Epistle 60 to Heliodorus*

220 Amictus.

221 Amicire.

222 Cf. Durandus, *Rationale divinorum officiorum*, Ch. 2; Durantus, *De Ritibus Ecclesiae Catholicae*, Bk. 2, Ch. 9

223 Mt 26:68

224 Alba.

225 See Apulaeus in his *Apology*. The same, *Milesian Fables*, Bk. 2. Ovid, when speaking of the priests of Isis says:

Nec tu linigeram fieri quid possit ad Isim
Quaesieris.

And elsewhere:

Nunc dea linigera colitur celeberrima turba. Scheffer says the same thing of the Pythagoreans (*De Italica Philosophia*, Ch. 14).

226 Apollonius, being questioned on this custom, answered: *Vestem quam e morticinis plerique ferunt non puram esse ratus Pythagoras, linea veste usus est* (*Apud Philos.*, Bk. 8).

227 Alba, lineum vestimentum, longissime distat a tunicis pelliceis, quae de mortuis animalibus fiunt, quibus Adam vestitus est post peccatum, et novitatem vitae significat, quam Christus et habuit et docuit et tribuit, de qua dicit apostolus: 'Exuite veterem hominem' (Rupert, *De Div. Offic.*, Bk. 1, Ch. 20; Innocent III, *De Myst. Missae*, Bk. 1, 36).

228 Durantus, *De Ritibus Ecclesiae Catholicae*, Bk. 2, Ch. 9

229 Cingulum.

230 Cf. Rabanus Maurus, *De Institutione Clericorum*, Ch. 13; Bernard, *Sentent.*; Bede, *Collectanea*; Cardinal Bona, *Rerum liturgicarum*, Bk. 1, Ch. 27

231 Manipulum.

232 Cardinal Bona, *Rerum liturgicarum*, Bk. 1, Ch. 27

233 Ibid.

234 Stola.

235 Council of Laodicea, Can. 28. The use of the stole in the sense that we have just mentioned was already known to the Romans. Our ancestors did not invent a new fashion. The stole had been an ornament of the Roman ladies. Its length distinguished them from women of low condition or character. To win the favor of the people, Aurelian was the first that gave them the *orarium*, so that, when the emperor passed along, the people might wave it in the air and thus show their joy (Vopisc., *in Aurelian*).

236 *Casula* or *planeta*. *Casa* means "a house," and *casula*, "a small house." The chasuble was formerly round, and of such goodly size that it wrapped up the whole body. It was like a small house, in which a man might dwell; hence, its name (Isidore, *Etymologiae*, Bk. 19, Ch. 24). *Planeta*: the chasuble, which had only one opening for the head to pass through, and had nothing to keep it steady, might easily turn round the neck. It was therefore a circulating garment, and it thence came, naturally enough, to be called "a planet" (Honorius of Autun, *Gemma animae*, Bk. 1, Ch. 207).

237 Dalmatica.

238 Colobia.

239 Cf. Isidore, *Etymologiae*, Bk. 19, Ch. 22; Cardinal Bona, *Rerum liturgicarum*, Bk. 1, Ch. 24

240 Tunica.

241 Cf. Honorius of Autun, *Gemma animae*, Bk. 1, Ch. 229

242 Superpelliceum.

243 Cf. Cardinal Bona, *Rerum liturgicarum*, Bk. 1, Ch. 24

244 Pluviale.

245 Cf. Roman Ordo

246 Cf. Durandus, *Rationale divinorum officiorum*, Bk. 3, Ch. 1

247 Quas aures habeat, aut quid in hoc homini simile sit, nescio (Cicero, quoted by Gellius, *Noctes Atticae*, Bk. 13, Ch. 21).

248 Cf. M. Thirat, *Esprit des Cérémonies de l'Eglise*, p. 272

249 Caligae, sandalia.

250 Compagia. See Trebellius Pollio, Julius Capitolinus, and *Hist. de l'Acad. des inscript.*, t. 11.

251 Omnis presbyter missam celebret ordine romano cum sandaliis (*Capitul. Carol. Magn.*, Bk. 5, Ch. 219).

252 Tunicella, dalmatica.

253 Chirothecae.

254 Cf. Roman Ordo

255 Annulus.

256 Cf. Jer 22; Trebellius Pollio, *in* M. *Septim.*; Duranti, *De Ritibus Ecclesiae Catholicae*, Bk. 2, Ch. 9, n. 27ff

257 Roman Ordo

258 Mitra, cidaris.

259 Cf. Honorius of Autun, *Gemma animae*, Bk. 1, Ch. 214

260 Cf. Eusebius, *Ecclesiastical History*, Bk. 5, Ch. 24

261 Cf. Innocent III, *De Myst. Missae*, Ch. 60; Antoninus, *Summa Theologica Moralis*, III, t. 20, Ch. 2; Steph. Eduens. episc., *De Sacram. Altar.*, Ch. 11

262 Pedum, seu baculus pastoralis.

263 Cf. Roman Ordo

264 Cf. Glos., *in Can. disciplinae*, dist. 45. On the various significations of the crosier, we feel pleasure in quoting the following lines:

In baculi forma, praesul, datur haec tibi norma,
Attrahe per primum, medio rege, punge per imum;
Attrahe peccantes, rege justos, punge vagantes;
Attrahe, sustenta, stimula, vaga, morbida, lenta.
—Glos., *de Sacr. Unct. D. Unic.*

265 Pallium.

266 Cf. Cardinal Bona, *Rerum liturgicarum*, Bk. 1, Ch. 24. See the account of the blessing of the pallium in *Trois Rome*, t. 2, January 21.

267 Cf. Isidore of Pelusium, *Epistle 136*

268 Cf. Gregory the Great, *Register of Epistles*, Bk. 2, Epistle 54

269 Auctor vetus, *Rit. eccl.*, *S. R. E.*, Bk. 1, t. 10, Ch. 5

270 Gremiale.

271 Cf. *Cerem. episc.*, Bk. 1, Ch. 11

272 Cf. Durandus, *Rationale divinorum officiorum*, Bk. 3, Ch. 18, n. 5

273 We know the old saying: "The king is dead—long live the king!"

274 Cf. Ex 19:6; 1 Pt 2:9

275 Cf. Augustine, *City of God*, Bk. 10, Ch. 8

276 Cf. Jerome, *Epistle 52 to Nepotian*; Gregory of Tours, *Glory of the Confessors*, Ch. 1; Paulinus of Nola, *Nat. 3, S. Felicis*

277 Cf. Hincmarus Remens., *in Capitul.*; Bede, *Ecclesiastical History of the English Church*, Bk. 5, Ch. 11; Athanasius, *Apologia ad Constantium*; Eusebius, *Life of Constantine*, Bk. 5

278 Cf. Tertullian, *Against the Valentinians*, Ch. 3

279 Editor's note: See Volume XI of the Tradivox series, p. 271.

280 See Burchard, *Decret.*, Bk. 5, Ch. 9.

281 Durantus, *De Ritibus Ecclesiae Catholicae*, Bk. 1, Ch. 7. This date is most useful in determining the age of glass cups for the Eucharist, found in the catacombs. See our *Histoire des Catacombes*.

282 Translator's note: That is, if not of gold.

283 Cf. Roman Ordo

284 These chalices were called "ministerial chalices."

285 *Amulae* or *hamae*.

286 Some authors assert that the vessels sold by holy bishops were neither ciboriums nor chalices, but other vessels belonging to the Church. I do not know on what grounds such an opinion rests.

287 Cf. Thiers, *Exposit. du Saint-Sacrement*, Bk. 2, Ch. 1, sub fine; *Histoire des Sacrements*, t. 11, p. 296; M. Thirat, *Esprit des Cérémonies de l'Eglise*, p. 244

288 At least in many churches.

289 Cf. Basil, *De Spiritu Sancto*, Ch. 27

290 *Omnis creatura...sanctificatur per verbum Dei et orationem* (1 Tm 4:4-5). See our *Traité de l'eau benite.*

291 Cyprian, *Epistle 70*

292 Cf. *Microlog.*, Ch. 41

293 See their grave testimony in Duranti, *De Ritibus Ecclesiae Catholicae*, Bk. 1, Ch. 12.

294 The spirit-rapping, etc., that are now going the round of the world, become pagan again, are a splendid justification of the Church in her antidemoniacal proscriptions.

295 Cf. Gelasian Sacramentary, 238

296 The Sunday procession is of the highest antiquity. It is said to have been introduced by Pope St. Agapetus in the sixth century; but would seem to have been of earlier origin, since St. Jerome makes mention of it. *Die tantum Dominico ad ecclesiam procedebant, ex cujus habitabant latere, et unumquodque agmen matrem propriam sequebatur, atque inde pariter revertentes* (*Epistle 108*, "Epitaph for Paula," Ch. 19. See Duranti, *De Ritibus Ecclesiae Catholicae*, Bk. 2, Ch. 10, p. 352; Rupert, *De Div. Offic.*, Bk. 7, Ch. 20; *Meunier, Traité des processions; Eveillon, de Proces. Ecclesiae.*).

297 Cf. 2 Kgs 6

298 Cf. 3 Kgs 8

299 Cf. Mt 21. See also Ex 15; Jdt 15-16; Est 4; Jl 2.

300 Cf. *Hist. univ. de l'Eglise*, t. 5, p. 250

301 Habet et pax martyres suos.

302 Debitricem martyrii fidem (Tertullian, *Scorpiace*, Ch. 8).

303 Cf. Tertullian, *On Baptism*, Ch. 5; *De Corona Militis*, Ch. 7, 15

304 On the procession of the pagans, see Brisson, *de Formulis* and the *Trois Rome*, t. 3, *description du grand cirque.*

305 Cf. Boldetti, *Osservasioni sopra i cimiteri de' santi martiri ed antichi Christiani di Roma*, Bk. 11, Ch. 16, p. 529

306 Mt 18:20

307 Cf. Nm 10:9-10

308 Cf. Tertullian, *Ad Uxorem*, Bk. 2, Ch. 4; Jerome, *Epistle 8*; *Epistle 29*; *Epistle 13*; Basil, *Epistle 34*; Nicephorus, *Church History*, Bk. 10, Ch. 35; Bk. 12, Ch. 45; Bk. 14, Ch. 47; Bk. 4, Ch. 3; Baronius, Anno 398, Anno 1065; Gregory of Tours, *History of the Franks*, Bk. 4, Ch. 5; Augustine, *City of God*, Bk. 22; Ambrose, *Sermon 20*; *Sermon 21*, etc.

309 The use of lamps and other lights in churches, in religious ceremonies, and in processions, comes from the most remote antiquity (Cf. Ex 25; 3 Kgs 7; Gregory the Great, *Dialogues*, Ch. 30; Gregory of Tours, *Glory of Martyrs*, Ch. 20, 79).—Torches are placed at sepulchres to indicate that the deceased Christians won a victory over their enemies (Cf. Gregory Nazianzen, *Oration 2, in Julian.*; *Oration 7, in mort. fratris*; Chrysostom, *Homily 70, to the People of Antioch*, etc.).

310 On all this matter, see the interesting details given by Durandus, *Rationale divinorum officiorum*, Bk. 4, Ch. 6.

311 Mk 16:7

312 Mt 28:10

313 We speak of the old custom.

314 Cf. Le Brun, *Cérémonies de la Messe*; Pére de Condren, *Idée du Sacerdoce*, etc.

315 As the Sacrifice of the Altar, like that of Calvary, is offered for four ends—to expiate, to adore, to impetrate, and to thank—we may also divide the Mass into four parts: the first, to expiate, from the beginning to the offertory; the second, to adore, from the offertory to the consecration; the third, to impetrate, from the consecration to the communion; and the fourth, to thank, from the communion to the end.

316 Ite, Missa est.

317 Cf. Cardinal Bona, *Rerum liturgicarum*, Bk. 1, Ch. 1

318 *Summa Theologiae*, III, q. 83, a. 4, rep. 9

319 Soror nostra Euprepia, sicut bene recordaris, titulum domus suae pauperibus assignavit, ubi nunc commorantes missas agimus (Baronius, Anno 166).

320 Cardinal Bona, *Rerum liturgicarum*, Ch. 3, p. 13

321 Cf. Innocent III, *De Myst. Missae*, Bk. 11, Ch. 13

322 Cf. Le Brun, *Cérémonies de la Messe*, p. 112

323 See Duranti, *De Ritibus Ecclesiae Catholicae*, Bk. 2, Ch. 15, p. 375.

324 Cf. Durandus, *Rationale divinorum officiorum*, Bk. 4, Ch. 8

325 Cf. t. 14, *Opusc.*, p. 267

326 The same comparisions, with a few variations, are also found in Bellarmine, *Dottrina Cristiana*; *Summa Theologiae*, III, q. 75, a. 6; Turlot, *Catéch.*, Pt. 4, Lesson 18, p. 639.

327 Cf. Apoc 6:9

328 Cf. Cardinal Bona, *Rerum liturgicarum*, Bk. 2, Ch. 22

329 Cf. Ex 30:34ff

330 Cf. Tertullian, *Apology*, Ch. 30; Arnobius, Bk. 2

331 Cf. Lk 7:46

332 Cf. Jn 12:3

333 Cf. *Apostolic Canons*, Can. 4; Liturgy of St. James, etc.

334 Cf. Pontifical. Damas. et Metaph., *in Vita S. Nicolai.*

335 *Euch. Graec.*, p. 2

336 Cf. Dionysius, *Ecclesiastical Hierarchy*, Ch. 3-4: Symeon of Thessalonica, *De Templo*; *Summa Theologiae*, III, q. 83, a. 5, rep. 2

337 Augustine, *Homily 6 on Apocalypse*, Ch. 10, n. 3

338 See Père Menard, *Catechis.*, p. 271.

339 Liturgy of John Chrysostom, Euch., p. 52

340 Cf. Evagrius, *Ecclesiastical History*, Bk. 4, Ch. 7

341 Apoc 5:8

342 Cf. Cant 1:11

343 Cf. Gn 27:27

344 Cf. 3 Kgs 10:2

345 Cf. Cochin, *Cérémonies de la Messe*, p. 222

346 Cf. Le Brun, *Cérémonies de la Messe*, p. 157

347 Cf. Rhenan, *ad Tertull. de Coron.*

348 Cf. Amalarius Fortunatus, *De Ecclesiasticis Officiis*, Bk. 3, Ch. 5; *Lib. Pontif.*, Ch. 10

349 Cf. Mt 13:17; Lk 10:24

350 Maximus, *Exposit. liturg.*

351 Cf. *Rit. Laud.*, p. 98; Roman Ordo

352 Council of Vaison, under Leo I, Can. 5

353 The *Apostolic Constitutions* add: "Let the people, at each of the things which the deacon proposes, say, *Kyrie, eleison*, and especially the children" (Bk. 8, Ch. 6).

354 Cf. Augustine, *Append.*, p. 44

355 Cf. Athanasius, *De Virginitate, vers fin.*; *Apostolic Constitutions*, Bk. 7, Ch. 47

356 Cf. Gregorian Sacramentary

357 Lk 2:14

358 Cf. Durandus, *Rationale divinorum officiorum*, Bk. 5, n. 15. See our *Traité du Signe de la Croix.*

359 Cf. Remigius of Auxerre, *Exposit. Missae*

360 Cf. Ps 27:2

361 Cf. Tertullian, *Apology*; *On Prayer*, Ch. 16

362 Formerly, when there were processions on fast days, the people went to a church, where they awaited the bishop, who began with the prayer called *Ad collectam*, that is to say, "At the assembly," or, "On the assembly"; and then they went to another church, where Mass began. The celebrant said, *Oremus*—"Let us pray." The deacon said, *Flectamus genua*, so that the assistants might go on their knees for a little while, during which everyone prayed in silence. The deacon then said, *Levate*. On rising, the celebrant said the prayer, in which he set forth the petitions of the assembly (Cf. Gregorian Sacramentary, Ch. *Jejun.*, p. 34; Cardinal Bona, *Rerum liturgicarum*, Bk. 2, Ch. 5).

363 Cf. Cardinal Bona, *Rerum liturgicarum*

364 Cf. Justin Martyr, *Second Apology*

365 Hence the names *lectricium*, *lectorium*, *legeolum*, given to the desk from which it was read.

366 Cf. Acts 13, 15

367 Tertullian, *Apology*, Ch. 39

368 Justin Martyr, *First Apology*, Ch. 67

369 Cf. Eusebius, *Ecclesiastical History*, Bk. 5, Ch. 1

370 Cf. Cardinal Bona, *Rerum liturgicarum*, Bk. 5, Ch. 7

371 Cf. Durantus, *De Ritibus Ecclesiae Catholicae*, Bk. 2, Ch. 18. St. Jerome's book is entitled *Comes*, or *Lectionarius*; Pamel., t. 2, *Liturgicor.*—*Seriem vero et ordinem lectionum, atque epistolarum et evangeliorum quae singulis diebus per annum in missae sacrificio legi debent, communis eruditorum sententia est, paucis licet negantibus, S. Hieronymum disposuisse in libro, quem Comitem inscripsit* (Cardinal Bona, *Rerum liturgicarum*, Bk. 2, Ch. 6, n. 2, p. 23).

372 Heb 1:1-2

373 Cf. Durantus, *De Ritibus Ecclesiae Catholicae*, Bk. 2, Ch. 18; Alcuin, *De Celeb. Missae*

374 Cf. Rabanus Maurus, *De Institutione Clericorum*, Bk. 1, Ch. 33

375 It was St. Jerome that, as we said above, arranged, at the request of Pope Damasus, the psalms, gospels, and epistles in their present order. Popes St. Gregory and St. Gelasius added prayers, responses, and verses. St. Ambrose added graduals, tracts, and the Alleluia. He did so to nourish the piety of the Catholics of Milan, who had to keep watch in their churches lest the Arians should gain an entrance.

376 Cf. Hugh of St. Victor, *Specul. eccl.*, Ch. 7; Alcuin, *De divin. Offic.*, Ch. *De Septuagesima*

377 Cardinal Bona, *Rerum liturgicarum*, Bk. 2, Ch. 6, p. 368

378 Augustine, *On Psalm 148*; *On Psalm 118*

379 Durantus, *De Ritibus Ecclesiae Catholicae*, Bk. 2, Ch. 20

380 Bonaventure, *De Exposit. Missae*, Ch. 2

381 Non habebat ultra spiritum (3 Kgs 10:5).

382 Cf. Radulf. Tungrensis, *prop.* 23, Cornel. Schultingus, *Biblioth. eccl.*, t. 1, Bk. 2, Ch. 6-7

383 Cf. Cardinal Bona, *Rerum liturgicarum*, Bk. 2, Ch. 7

384 Cf. Augustine, *On Psalm 113*

385 Cf. Roman Ordo

386 Cf. Amalarius Fortunatus, *De Ecclesiasticis Officiis*, Bk. 3, Ch. 5

387 Cf. Cardinal Bona, *Rerum liturgicarum*, Bk. 2, Ch. 7

388 Cf. Sozomen, *Church History*, Bk. 7

389 Cf. *Append. Ad Sacr., S.*, p. 358

390 This is what has always been recommended since any kind of support came to be used in the church. The length of the office not permitting everyone to stand, the custom of using a staff was introduced about the year 800. It continued to be used in the ninth, tenth, eleventh, and twelfth centuries. It then took the shape of a crutch. The crutches were called *reclinatoria*, as being more easy to lean upon. At a later period, forms and stalls were made, and the slight support called a *misericorde*, on which one might rest without appearing to sit. But at the gospel, all laid aside their staffs or crutches, and stood up as servants before their master (Amalarius Fortunatus, *De Ecclesiasticis Officiis*, Bk. 3, Ch. 18). The Eastern Christians still use crutch-like staffs, which they lay aside at the gospel. (See Le Brun, *Cérémonies de la Messe*, p. 225.)

391 Remigius of Auxerre, *Exposit. Missae*

392 Cf. Is 14:13

393 Cf. Cardinal Bona, *Rerum liturgicarum*, Bk. 2, Ch. 7

394 Cf. 2 Cor 2:14

395 Cf. Justin Martyr, *Second Apology*

396 Praeconium

397 See Jauffret, *du Culte public*, p. 244.

398 According to an old tradition, each of the apostles would seem to have composed one article of the Symbol:
Peter: "I believe in God, the Father Almighty."
John: "Creator of heaven and earth."
James: "I also believe in Jesus Christ, his only Son, our Lord."
Andrew: "Who was conceived by the Holy Ghost; born of the Virgin Mary."
Philip: "Suffered under Pontius Pilate; was crucified, dead, and buried."
Thomas: "He descended into hell; the third day he arose again from the dead."
Bartholomew: "He ascended into heaven, and sitteth at the right hand of God, the Father Almighty."
Matthew: "From thence he will come to judge the living and the dead."
James, the son of Alpheus: "I also believe in the Holy Ghost; the holy Catholic Church."
Simon: "The communion of saints; the forgiveness of sins."
Jude: "The resurrection of the body."
Matthias, concluding: "And life everlasting."

399 Cf. Theodorus Lector, *Collectaneorum*

400 Cf. Third Council of Toledo, Can. 2

401 Berno Augiens, *de Rebus ad Mis. per.*, 1.

402 Cardinal Bona, *Rerum liturgicarum*, Bk. 2, Ch. 8

403 Augustine, *On Psalm 31*, n. 18, etc.

404 Cf. Cardinal Bona, *Rerum liturgicarum*, Bk. 2, Ch. 8

405 Amulas.

406 Oblata.

407 Fontem.

408 Cf. Roman Ordo

409 All the faithful offered bread, wine, oil, and whatever else was necessary for the celebration of the holy mysteries and Communion. When that which was required for this purpose was taken away, the ministers of the altar lived on the remainder, together with other alms given to the Church. The variety in the bread and wine offered for consecration was not without its inconveniences. The Church approved of the idea that only one person should offer the bread, wine, and lights necessary for the sacrifice, and that the rest of the faithful should offer in money whatever their devotion urged them to give for the support of ecclesiastics. Hence our "offerings" at High Mass on Sundays. We have still a vestige of the custom here mentioned in Solemn Mass for the dead, when bread, wine, corn, candles, and money are offered. This act is not one of mere liberality, but one that corresponds to what has always been practiced in every sacrifice, for which the offerer should provide the host, and to a custom most religiously observed by the ancient faithful.

410 Fleury, t. 4, p. 244

411 Cf. Augustine, *Retractions*, Bk. 2, Ch. 11

412 Cf. *Apostolic Constitutions*, Bk. 8, Ch. 12

413 Cf. Gregory of Tours, *History of the Franks*, Ch. 23; Cardinal Bona, *Rerum liturgicarum*, Bk. 7, Ch. 12

414 Pallium. Cardinal Bona, *Rerum liturgicarum*, Bk. 4, Ch. 27. In Italy there is no card, which goes to show more clearly the origin of the pall.

415 Cf. Durandus, *Rationale divinorum officiorum*, Bk. 4, Ch. 30, n. 15

416 See the Liturgies of St. James, St. Basil, and St. Chrysostom; Justin Martyr, *Second Apology*; Cyprian, Bk. 2, Epistle 3, etc.; Cardinal Bona, *Rerum liturgicarum*, Bk. 2, Ch. 9.

417 Cf. Apoc 17:15

418 Cf. Cyril, *Epistle 63*

419 Mixtura Dei et hominis (Augustine).

420 Council of Tribur, Can. 19, held about 895.

421 Prv 23:1-2; Cf. Ecclus 31:12. See hereupon the magnificent commentaries of the fathers in Cornelius a Lapide, on Prv 13:1-2 and Ecclus 31:12.

422 Augustine, *Sermon 31*

423 Cf. 1 Jn 3:16

424 Tertullian, *Against Marcion*, Bk. 4, Ch. 9

425 1 Jn 2:2

426 Jn 13:35

427 Cf. Acts 4:32

428 Cf. Paulinus of Nola, *Epistle 41 to Augustine*

429 Cf. Ibid.; Eusebius, *Ecclesiastical History*, Bk. 5, Ch. 24

430 Cf. 1 Cor 10:17

431 In the Diocese of Besançon, there is no blessed bread distributed on Easter Sunday, because, every one being supposed to partake of the reality on this day, the figure becomes useless.

432 Chrysostom, *Sermon 22*

433 Tertullian, *Apology*, Ch. 39

434 Si nos natalitia celebramus, etc., quanto magis nobis dies iste observandus, quem si quis natalitium totius naturae humanae appellet, non errabit! (Chrysostom, *Sermon 22*).

435 Cf. 1 Cor 16:2

436 Chrysostom, *Sermon 25*

437 Cyril of Jerusalem, *Catechetical Lecture 23*

438 Dionysius, *Ecclesiastical Hierarchy*, Ch. 53

439 Cf. Liturgy of St. Chrysostom, *Euchol. Graec.*, p. 60

440 Cf. Cardinal Bona, *Rerum liturgicarum*, Bk. 2, Ch. 9

441 Cf. Père de Condren, *Idée du Sacerdoce*, etc.

442 Cf. Steph. Eduens., episc., *de Sacr. altar.*, Ch. 12

443 Cf. Miss. Illyric.

444 *Ordin. Catrtusian.*, Ch. 26, n. 21

445 Undo estis omnes fratres? De uno patre, Christo; do una matre, Ecclesia (Arnobius, *On Psalm 133*).

446 Cf. Augustine, *Epistle 54 to Januarius*

447 Cyprian, *On the Lord's Prayer*, n. 31

448 Some particular churches have added others of less ancient date, but which should be authorized by the Holy See.

449 Cf. Liturgies of Sts. James, Basil, and Chrysostom

450 Cf. Concilior. t. 4

451 Cf. Is 6:3

452 Cf. Apoc 4:8

453 Cf. Liturgy of St. James; Cyril of Jerusalem, *Catechetical Lecture 23*

454 Cf. Gregory of Nyssa, *Orat de non diff. Bapt.*, p. 302

455 Cf. Pope Vigilius, *Epistle, ad Praefect. Bracar.*; Cyprian, *On the Lord's Prayer*; Innocent I, *Epistle, ad Decentium*

456 Council of Trent, Session 22, "Doctrine on the Sacrifice of the Mass," Ch. 4; Cf. Can. 6; Can. 9

457 Cf. Strabo., *de Reb. eccl.*, Ch. 22

458 See M. Thirat, *Esprit des Cérémonies de l'Eglise*, p. 333; Le Brun, *Cérémonies de la Messe*, p. 410.

459 Cf. Le Brun, *Cérémonies de la Messe*, p. 441

460 Cf. Le Brun, *Cérémonies de la Messe*; Condren, *Idée du sacrifice*

461 Chrysostom, *Homily 3 on Ephesians*

462 Chrysostom, *Homily 61, to the People of Antioch*. The elevation took place then only before Communion.

463 "A mystery of faith": words of the Savior, preserved by tradition. Oh, yes, the sacrifice of the man-God is indeed a great mystery of faith: a mystery of faith for all ancient times preceding the Messias, which expected it; a mystery of faith for all succeeding times, which believe it, though human reason cannot fathom it!

464 Cf. Lk 22:19; 1 Cor 11:24-25

465 Cf. Le Brun, *Cérémonies de la Messe*, p. 471

466 Cf. Lk 22:19; 1 Cor 11:24-25

467 Cf. Le Brun, *Cérémonies de la Messe*, p. 488; Cardinal Bona, *Rerum liturgicarum*, Bk. 2, Ch. 13

468 Cf. *Apostolic Constitutions*, Bk. 8, Ch. 12

469 Here are some decisions, useful to priests who celebrate Mass for the departed, as well as to the faithful who desire to gain indulgences.

The Roman Congregation of Rites gave its decision lately on various cases of indulgences. The text of the questions and answers runs thus:

Quaeritur 1: Utrùm sacerdos satisfaciat obligationem celebrandi Missam pro defuncto, servando ritum feriae vel cujuscumque sancti etiamsi non sit semiduplex vel duplex?

Quaeritur 2: Utrùm qui privilegium habet personale pro quatuor Missis in hebdomadis singulis, debeat cum paramentis nigro colore celebrare, diebus non impeditis, ut possit indulgentiam plenariam pro animabus defunctorum lucrari?

Quaeritur 3: Utrùm qui celebrat in altari privilegiato pro singulis diebus, debeat semper uti paramentis nigris, diebus non impeditis, ut indulgentiam privilegii consequatur?

Quaeritur 4: Utrùm ad lucrandam indulgentiam plenariam, Orationi: "O bone et dulcissime Jesu...concessam, necesse sit aliam orationem addere pro intentione summi Pontificis?

Quaeritur 5: Utrùm ad indulgentias applicandas crucibus, rosariis, etc., alius ritus sit necessarius praeterquam signum crucis a sacerdote qui hanc facultatem accepit factum?

Quaeritur 6: Utrùm indulgentia concessa cadat solum in Christo ex aere, ligno vel alia quaque materia facto, ita ut possit ex una cruce in alia transferri absque periculo amittendi indulgentiam ipsi collatam?

Sacra congregatio indulgentiis sacrisque reliquiis praeposita ad superiora dubia, sic respondendum esse censuit.

Ad primum.—Affirmative.

Ad secundum.—Negative.

Ad tertium.—Ut in secundo.

*Ad quartam.—Affirmative.**

Ad quintam.—Negative.

Ad sextum.—Affirmative.

In quorum fidem, etc. Datum Romae ex secretariâ ejusdem sacrae congregationis indulgentiarum die 11 Aprilis, 1840.

Loco + sigilli.

—C. Card. Castracane, praefectus.

Hanibal Ginnasi, secret.

* In accordance with a decision of Pius IX.

Here are some new solutions:

Dubium I. Per Decretum S. Congregationis indulgentiarum datum die 12 junii 1822 conceditur confessionem sacramentalem peractam infra hebdomadam ante festivitatem suffragari posse ad indulgentiam lucrandam.

Quaeritur 1: An verba infra hebdomadam—significent octo dies tantum, quae festivitatem immediate praecedunt; an vero hebdomadam illam totam et integram, quae ante festum decurrit, ita ut ex. gr. confessio facta die Dominica suffragetur ad lucrandam indulgentiam die sabbati hebdomadae sequentis, in quam diem festum incideret, tametsi tunc 13 dies inter confessionem et festivitatem intercessissent.

Quaeritur 2: An confessio octavo die ante festivitatem peracta vi hujus indulti suffragetur tantum ad unam indulgentiam lucrandam, an vero per hanc confessionem aliae etiam lucrifieri possint indulgentiae quae infra praedictum tempus occurrent, et ad quas lucrandas sacramentalis confessio caeteroquin requireretur.

Dubium II. Quaeritur an, cum in Bulla vel Brevi quo conceditur indulgentia, confessio tanquam conditio sine qua non praescribitur, necesse sit ut sacramentalis absolutio poenitentibus detur ad indulgentiam lucrandam.

Sacra congregatio indulgentiis sacrisque reliquiis praeposita respondendum esse censuit

Ad dubium primum:

Ad primum.—Affirmative quoad primam partem; negative quoad secundam.

Ad secundum.—Negative quoad primam; affirmative quoad secundam.

Ad dubium secundum:

Respondetur: Negative.

In quorum fidem, etc. Datum Romae ex Secret. ejusdem sacrae Congregationis Indulgentiarum die 15 decembris 1841.

—*C. Card. Castracane, praef.*

470 This prayer is found in the most ancient liturgies. Cardinal Bona, *Rerum liturgicarum*, Bk. 2, Ch. 14; Durandus, *Rationale divinorum officiorum*, Bk. 2, Ch. 43.

471 Cf. Gregory the Great, *Sermon 58 on Matthew*, Ch. 6; *De Orat. Dom.*, Ch. 10

472 Hence it comes that in many churches, one gives the paten to be kissed at offerings saying: *Pax vobis*—"Peace be to you!"

473 Cf. *Euchol. Graec.*, p. 81; Amalarius Fortunatus, *De Ecclesiasticis Officiis*, Bk. 3, p. 635; Cardinal Bona, *Rerum liturgicarum*, Bk. 2, Ch. 15

474 Cf. Col 1:20

475 Cf. Jerome, *in Epist. ad haec verba: Salutate invicem in osculo sancto.*

476 Mt 5:23-24

477 Mixtura Dei et hominis.

478 Cf. Roman Ordo, *Microlog.*, *Illyrian Mass*, etc.

479 Cf. Le Brun, *Cérémonies de la Messe*, p. 597

480 "This is the ordinary course," continues Père De Condren, whose words we have just cited. "Though grace is often received before and without Communion, but not without regard to Communion, the very reception of grace is an interior Communion in the merits, spirit, and grace of Jesus Christ. Wherefore, St. Augustine thought this Communion necessary even for children in order to be saved: not that he thought that baptized children who died without receiving the body of Jesus Christ by the mouth under the appearance of bread would fail to attain salvation, but because there is so close a bond and so strict a dependence between baptism and the Eucharist that the necessity of the former includes the necessity of the latter—the request, so to speak, the right, the desire, and the necessity of the Eucharist being contained in baptism as the necessity of food is inseparable from the life of a child that has just been born, that cannot preserve its life without food, and that makes known its wants and wishes by every means in its power. This is the reason why, in former times, the three sacraments, baptism, confirmation, and the Eucharist, were seldom separated" (*L'idée du sacerdoce de Jésus-Christ*, p. 386).

481 Lk 22:15

482 Jn 6:54

483 Editor's note: See Volume XI of the Tradivox series.

484 See also on this subject, the interesting details given by Duranti, *De Ritibus Ecclesiae Catholicae*, Bk. 2, Ch. 55.

485 Cf. Le Brun, *Cérémonies de la Messe*, p. 636

486 Augustine, *Epistle 149*

487 Ps 41

488 Cf. Cardinal Bona, *Rerum liturgicarum*, Bk. 2, Ch. 17

489 Cf. Le Brun, *Cérémonies de la Messe*, p. 642 et suiv.; Durandus, *Rationale divinorum officiorum*, Bk. 6, Ch. 55, 57; Durantus, *De Ritibus Ecclesiae Catholicae*, Bk. 2, Ch. 56; Cardinal Bona, *Rerum liturgicarum*, Bk. 2, Ch. 20; M. Thirat, *Esprit des Cérémonies de l'Eglise*, p. 377

490 Cf. *Microlog.*, Ch. 22

491 Cf. Le Brun, *Cérémonies de la Messe*, p. 673

492 Cf. M. Thirat, *Esprit des Cérémonies de l'Eglise*, p. 384; Le Brun, *Cérémonies de la Messe*, p. 676; le P. de Condren, p. 410

493 Augustine, *Epistle 72*

494 Translator's note: For many other interesting particulars regarding the ceremonies of the holy sacrifice, see *A History of the Mass and its Ceremonies in the Eastern and Western Church*, by Rev. John O'Brien, A. M.

495 1 Cor 16:22

496 Origen, *Homily 10 on Genesis*

497 Origen, *Contra Celsum*, Bk. 8

498 Ibid.; Cf. Jerome, *On Galatians*, Ch. 4

499 Clement of Alexandria, *The Stromata*, Bk. 7, n. 512

500 From the beginning, she manifested her wish, which, by the instrumentality of Pope St. Sylvester, became a formal law. *Sabbati et dominici diei nomine retento, reliquos hebdomadae dies feriarum nomine distinctos, ut jam in Ecclesia vocari coeperant, appelari voluit* (*Roman Breviary*, 31st Dec.).

501 Una sabbati, dies dominicus est; secunda sabbati, secunda feria, quem saeculares diem Lunae vocant; tertia sabbati, tertia feria, quem diem illi Martis vocant. Quarta ergo sabbatorum, quarta feria, qui Mercurii dies dicitur a paganis, et a multis Christianis: sed nollemus; atque utinam corrigant et non dicant sic. Habent enim linguam suam qua utantur. Non enim et in omnibus gentibus ista dicuntur: multae gentes aliter vocant: melius ergo de ore Christiano ritus loquendi ecclesiasticus procedit (Augustine, *On Psalm 93*, n. 3, opp., t. 4, pars alter, p. 1428, édit. Gaume).

502 On the causes, propagation, and effects of modern paganism, see our work *La Révolution*, 12 vol. in octav.

503 Cf. Amalarius Fortunatus, *Divin. Offic.*, Bk. 4, Ch. 13

504 Cf. Epiphanius, *Adversus Haeresus*, Bk. 3, n. 22

505 Cf. Albaspin., *Obser.*, Bk. 1, Ch. 16; Tertullian, *On Prayer.*—*Jejunia sane legitima, id est quarta et sexta feria, non sunt solvenda, nisi grandis necessitas fuerit, quia quarta feria Judas de traditione Domini cogitavit, et sexta feria crucifixus est Salvator* (Jus Can., *de Consecr.*; dist. iii, c. 16).

506 Cf. Augustine, *Epistle 36 to Casulanus*, n. 30; Baronius, Anno 34, n. 168

507 Cf. Thomassin, *Des jeûnes*, Pt. 2, Ch. 15, n. 3-5

508 Cf. Sozomen, *Church History*, Bk. 1, Ch. 8

509 Cf. Eusebius, *Life of Constantine*, Bk. 4, Ch. 18

510 Cf. Cassian, *Institutes of the Coenobia*, Bk. 3, Ch. 9-10

511 Cf. Grat., *Decr. de consecr.*, Bk. 5, c. 31; Lup., tit. 5, Comm., p. 167-168

512 In Italia in sabbato abstinetur ab esu carnium, et qui tali die sine causa rationabili, puta infirmitatis, comederet carnes, peccaret mortaliter, quia faceret contra consuetudinem talis patriae. Extra Italiam in multis partibus, ut in Catalonia, non est talis consuetudo abstinendi in illa die a carnibus, unde comedentes ibi carnes non peccant (Antoninus, *Summa Theologiae*, Pt. I, tit. 17, Ch. *unic.*, § 4, edit Venit., 1582).

513 Cf. Marian., *Hist. Hisp.*, Bk. 5, Ch. 6; Bk. 11, Ch. 24.—We must add that in Spain there is a pontifical concession, called the *cruzada* or "crusade," in virtue of which one may, by the help of a small sum of money, be dispensed from the law of using only "meager fare" on Saturday. The very great heat of the climate rendered this grant in some measure necessary.

514 Cf. Mt 18:17

515 Cf. Amalarius Fortunatus, *Divin. Offic.*, Bk. 4, Ch. 17

516 Cf. Moreri, art. *Office*

517 To enter deeper into the intention of the Church and to second the very providential work of the Propagation of the Faith, we can now add to these pious intentions by consecrating Sunday to prayer for the conversion of Europe in general; Monday, Oceania; Tuesday, Africa; Wednesday, Asia; Thursday, England and Russia; Friday, America; and Saturday, France.

518 The evident proof that hatred of religion caused the Republican to be substituted for the Catholic calendar is set forth in the two fragments following:

A resolution of the 13th Germinal, year VI (3rd April, 1798), says expressly that "the observance of the French calendar is one of the means best calculated to efface the memory of sacerdotal rule."

A message of the 18th Germinal, year VII (8th April, 1799), adds that "the calendar is intended to root superstition out of the hearts of the people, by making decadal festivals general in all the communes."

See our work on the *Revolution*, in which we give all the details relative to the publication of the Republican calendar.

519 We here present the calendar of the "one and indivisible" Republic, whose year began on the 22nd of September. It is a document already very rare, and a more than ordinary proof of the Satanic wickedness of the pretended reformers. Here then are the models, the subjects of meditation, that they set before French citizens! I am not imposing on you. Read:

VENDEMIAIRE. First or Vintage Month.		BRUMAIRE. Second or Foggy Month.		FRIMAIRE. Third or Frosty Month.	
1	Grape.	1	Apple.	1	Rampion.
2	Saffron.	2	Celery.	2	Field-turnip.

Vendemiaire. First or Vintage Month.		Brumaire. Second or Foggy Month.		Frimaire. Third or Frosty Month.	
3	Chestnut.	3	Pear.	3	Chicory.
4	Colchicum.	4	Beet.	4	Medlar.
5	Horse.	5	Goose.	5	Pig.
6	Balsam.	6	Heliotrope.	6	Lamb's lettuce.
7	Carrot	7	Fig.	7	Cauliflower.
8	Amaranth.	8	Scorzonera.	8	Honey.
9	Parsnip.	9	Beam-tree.	9	Juniper.
10	Tub.	10	Plough.	10	Pickaxe.
11	Potato.	11	Salsify.	11	Wax.
12	Immortelle.	12	Caltrop.	12	Horseradish.
13	Pumpkin.	13	Jerusalem artichoke.	13	Cedar.
14	Mignonette.	14	Endive.	14	Fir.
15	Ass.	15	Turkey.	15	Rokbuck.
16	Jalap.	16	Skirret.	16	Whin.
17	Pumpion.	17	Cress.	17	Cypress.
18	Buckwheat.	18	Leadwort.	18	Ivy.
19	Sunflower.	19	Pomegranate.	19	Savin.
20	Winepress.	20	Harrow.	20	Mattock.
21	Hemp.	21	Bacchante.	21	Sugar-maple.
22	Peach.	22	Azarole.	22	Heather.
23	Turnip.	23	Madder.	23	Reed.
24	Amaryllis.	24	Orange.	24	Sorrel.
25	Ox.	25	Pheasant.	25	Cricket.
26	Aubergine.	26	Pistachio.	26	Pine-Apple kernel.
27	Allspice.	27	Macjone.	27	Cork.
28	Tomato.	28	Quince.	28	Truffle.
29	Barley.	29	Sorb.	29	Olive.
30	Cask.	30	Roller.	30	Shovel.

Nivose. Fourth or Snowy Month.		Pluviose. Fifth or Rainy Month.		Ventose. Sixth or Windy Month.	
1	Turf.	1	Spurge-laurel.	1	Colt's-foot.
2	Coal.	2	Moss.	2	Cornel.
3	Bitumen.	3	Butcher's-broom.	3	Wall-flower.
4	Sulphur.	4	Snowdrop.	4	Privet.
5	Dog.	5	Bull.	5	He-goat.
6	Lava.	6	Laurestine.	6	Wild-spikenard.
7	Vegetable ground.	7	Touchwood.	7	Alatern.
8	Manure.	8	Mezereon.	8	Violet.
9	Saltpetre.	9	Poplar.	9	Marceau.
10	Flail.	10	Hatchet.	10	Spade.
11	Granite.	11	Hellebore.	11	Narcissus.
12	Clay.	12	Broccoli.	12	Elm.
13	Slate.	13	Laurel.	13	Fumiter.
14	Sandstone.	14	Filbert-tree.	14	Hedge-mustard.
15	Rabbit.	15	Cow.	15	She-goat.
16	Silex.	16	Box.	16	Spinach.

Nivose. Fourth or Snowy Month.		Pluviose. Fifth or Rainy Month.		Ventose. Sixth or Windy Month.	
17	Marl.	17	Lichen.	17	Leopard's-bane.
18	Limestone.	18	Yew.	18	Chickweed.
19	Marble.	19	Lungwort.	19	Chervil.
20	Fan.	20	Pruning-knife.	20	Cord.
21	Plasterstone.	21	Treacle-mustard.	21	Mandrake.
22	Salt.	22	Bay-plant.	22	Parsley.
23	Iron.	23	Dog-grass.	23	Cochlearia.
24	Copper.	24	Knot-grass.	24	Easter-daisy.
25	Cat.	25	Hare.	25	Tunny.
26	Pewter.	26	Woad.	26	Dandelion.
27	Lead.	27	Hazel.	27	Sylvia.
28	Zinc.	28	Cyclamen.	28	Maiden-hair.
29	Mercury.	29	Celandine.	29	Ash.
30	Riddle.	30	Sledge.	30	Dibble.

Germinal. Seventh or Budding Month.		Floreal. Eighth or Flowery Month.		Prairial. Ninth or Grassy Month.	
1	Primrose.	1	Rose.	1	Lucerne.
2	Plane-tree.	2	Oak.	2	Asphodel.
3	Asparagus.	3	Fern.	3	Clover.
4	Tulip.	4	Hawthorn.	4	Angelica.
5	Hen.	5	Nightingale.	5	Duck.
6	Blite.	6	Columbine.	6	Balm-mint.
7	Birch.	7	Lily of the Valley.	7	Rye-grass.
8	Jonquil.	8	Mushroom.	8	Turk's-cap.
9	Alder.	9	Hyacinth.	9	Wild-thyme.
10	Cover.	10	Rake.	10	Scythe.
11	Periwinkle.	11	Rhubarb.	11	Strawberry.
12	Hornbeam.	12	Sainfoin.	12	Betony.
13	Morel.	13	Golden staff.	13	Pea.
14	Beech.	14	Dwarf cherry-tree.	14	Acacia.
15	Bee.	15	Silkworm.	15	Quail.
16	Lettuce.	16	Comfrey.	16	Carnation.
17	Larch.	17	Pimpernel.	17	Elder.
18	Hemlock.	18	Yellow-basket.	18	Poppy.
19	Radish.	19	Orach.	19	Linden.
20	Hive.	20	Hoe.	20	Fork.
21	Judas-tree.	21	Thrift.	21	Bluebottle.
22	Cos-lettuce.	22	Crown-imperial.	22	Camomile.
23	Large chestnut-tree.	23	Borage.	23	Woodbine.
24	Rocket.	24	Valerian.	24	Cheese-rennet.
25	Pigeon.	25	Carp.	25	Tench.
26	Lilac.	26	Spindle-tree.	26	Jasmine.
27	Anemone.	27	Chive.	27	Vervain.
28	Pansy.	28	Bugloss.	28	Thyme.
29	Bilberry-bush.	29	Charlock.	29	Peony.
30	Grafting-knife.	30	Crook.	30	Cart.

Messidor. Tenth or Harvest Month.		Thermidor. Eleventh or Hot Month.			Fructidor. Twelfth or Fruit Month.
1	Rye.	1	Spelt.	1	Plum.
2	Oats.	2	Mullein.	2	Millet.
3	Onion.	3	Melon.	3	Puff-ball.
4	Veronica.	4	Darnel.	4	Winter-barley.
5	Mule.	5	Ram.	5	Salmon.
6	Rosemary.	6	Shave-grass.	6	Tuberose.
7	Cucumber.	7	Artemisia.	7	Sugar-melon.
8	Shallot.	8	Carthamus.	8	Dog's-bane.
9	Wormwood.	9	Mulberry.	9	Liquorice.
10	Reaping-hook.	10	Watering-pot.	10	Ladder.
11	Coriander.	11	Panic-grass.	11	Watermelon.
12	Artichoke.	12	Saltwort.	12	Fennel.
13	Gillyflower.	13	Apricot.	13	Berberry.
14	Lavender.	14	Basil.	14	Walnut.
15	Chamois.	15	Sheep.	15	Trout.
16	Tobacco.	16	Marshmallow.	16	Citron.
17	Currant.	17	Flax.	17	Teasel.
18	Chick-pea.	18	Almond.	18	Blackthorn.
19	Cherry.	19	Gentian.	19	Tagette.
20	Park.	20	Sluice.	20	Creel.
21	Mint.	21	Carline-thistle.	21	Sweet-briar.
22	Cumin.	22	Caper-bush.	22	Nut.
23	Haricots.	23	Lentil.	23	Hop.
24	Alkanet.	24	Elecampane.	24	Sorgo.
25	Guinea-fowl.	25	Otter.	25	Crawfish.
26	Sage.	26	Myrtle.	26	Seville orange.
27	Garlic.	27	Colza.	27	Golden rod.
28	Vetch.	28	Lupin.	28	Maize.
29	Wheat.	29	Cotton.	29	Large chestnut.
30	Pipe.	30	Mill.	30	Basket.

SANS – CULOTTIDES				
Festivals.				
I. Virtue.	II. Genius.	III. Labor.	IV. Opinion.	V. Rewards.

520 See Godescard, *Préface de la Vie des Saints*, le *Spectaeteur français au dix-neuvièms siècle*, and Jauffret, *du Culte public*.

521 Haec sunt vestigia quae Sancti quique revertentes in patriam nobis reliquerunt (Bede, *Sermon 18, de Sanct.*).

522 Cf. Martène, *de Antiq. Eccl. discipl.*, Ch. 10, n. 5

523 Rainald, Anno 1287, n. 64. Insuper de consensu uxoris suae reginae per totum Adventum, per totam Quadragesimam, ab usu matrimonii mutuo absti nebant; insuper in solemnitatibus quibus communicare debent (Duchesne, t. 5, p. 448).

524 Cf. *Fêtes Chrét.*, p. 46

525 Cf. Rom 13:11-14

526 See Durandus, *Rationale divinorum officiorum*, Bk. 6, Ch. 11.

527 Charles Borromeo, *Acts of the Church of Milan*, p. 1012

528 See Thomassin, *Célébration des Fêtes*; Godescard, *Avent.*

529 Per conceptionem hic intelligitur; ipsa animae infusio et unio cum corpore debite organizato...quae scilicet fit illo ipso instanti, quo rationalis anima corpori omnibus membris ac suis organis constanti unitur (Benedict XIV, *De Festis*, p. 536).—Beata virgo in eo puncto, quo anima corpori unita est, ab originali peccato munda fuit et immunis (Ibid.).

530 The words of the bull *Ineffabilis* run thus:

"For the honor of the holy and indivisible Trinity, for the glory of the Virgin Mother of God, and for the exaltation of the Catholic faith and the spread of the Christian religion, We, by the authority of our Lord Jesus Christ, that of the blessed apostles Peter and Paul, and Our own, declare, pronounce, and define that the doctrine according to which the Blessed Virgin Mary was, from the first moment of her conception, and by a special grace and privilege of Almighty God, granted in consideration of the merits of Jesus Christ, the Savior of the human race, preserved and exempted from every stain of original sin, has been revealed by God, and is, as a consequence, to be firmly and constantly believed by all the faithful.

"If, therefore, any persons, which God forbid, should have the presumption to think otherwise in their hearts than has been defined by Us, let them learn and know that they have made shipwreck of the faith and quit the unity of the Church; and moreover that if, by writing or in any other outward manner they should dare to express those sentiments of their hearts, they incur, *ipso facto*, the penalties rightfully imposed."

531 Editor's note: The Quran.

532 Cf. Bergier, *Dictionnaire de théologie*, art. *Mahomet*

533 Augustine, *On Nature and Grace*, Ch. 36, n. 42

534 Council of Trent, Session 5, "Decree concerning Original Sin," Can. 5

535 *Potuit, decuit, ergo fecit* (Scotus, who died in 1308).

536 Cf. Cant 6-7

537 See the *Glories of Mary*, by St. Liguori. It contains a great many passages from the fathers of the Church on the immaculate conception, t. 2, p. 1. See also the numerous works published since the proclamation of the dogma and setting forth the evidence of tradition.

538 Bossuet, first sermon on the conception.

539 Cf. Benedict XIV, *De Festis*, p. 547, n. 17

540 Venerabilis Anselmi praedecessoris nostri, qui post alia quaedam ipsius antiquiora solemnia, Conceptionis solemne superaddere dignum duxit, vestigiis inhaerentes statuimus, et firmiter praecipiendo mandamus, quatenus festum Conceptionis praedictae in cunctis ecclesiis nostrae Cantuariensis provinciae festive et solemniter de caetero celebretur (Council of London, Anno 1328).

541 Cf. *Extravag. comm.*, Bk. 3, tit. 12, Ch. 1

542 An expression of the celebrated theologian Moehler, in his "Symbolic," Vol. 2.

543 Lk 2:52

544 Cf. Mt 28:20

545 Thomassin, *Des Fêtes*, p. 217

546 Jn 6:54

547 Rescript of our holy father Pope Pius VI, 21st November, 1793.

548 Cf. Baronius, Anno 57, n. 126-127; Isidore, *De Ecclesiasticis Officiis*, Ch. 37-38; Rabanus Maurus, *De Institutione Clericorum*, Bk. 2, Ch. 19, etc.

549 Cf. Zac 8:19

550 Lk 13:3

551 Cf. Council of Trent, Session 14, "On the Sacrament of Extreme Unction," Introduction

552 Cf. Jb 7:1

553 Haec tria remediorum genera spiritualiter commendavit nobis coelestis medicus, eleemosynam scilicet et jejunium et orationem, quibus tanquam medicinalibus antidotis possemus inveterata mala curare, praesentanea pellere, et servando salutem, futura cavere (Augustine, *Sermon, in Vigil. Pentec.*).

554 This is no arbitrary interpretation of the precept of fasting: it agrees exactly with the intention of the Church. On fast days, say the holy canons, alms are to be given. Everyone should give to the poor the food and drink which he would have used himself if he had not fasted. Fasting, without watches, alms,

and prayer, is hardly of any value. *Diebus jejunii eleemosyna facienda est, vel cibum et potum quo quisque uti deberet, si non jejunaret, pauperibus eroget. Pene non valet jejunium quod orationes, vigiliae et eleemosynae non commendant* (Ex Capitular. Theodulph. Aurelan., episc., ap. 797, Can. 34, 38).

Let us hear St. Leo: "What is there more effectual than fasting to disarm the enemy of salvation, to subdue the passions, to resist the seductions of vice? Fasting is the food of virtue. It inspires good thoughts and holy desires. It silences the carnal appetite and renovates the spiritual man. But as the vigor of the soul is not maintained by fasting alone, we must, in order to please God, accompany it with works of charity. All that we retrench from sensuality must be given to virtue. Thus shall our abstinence become the support of the poor" (*On the Fast of the Tenth Month*, Sermon 11).

555 See Jauffret, *du Culte public*, p. 205.

556 Cf. Rabanus Maurus, *De Institutione Clericorum*, Bk. 2, Ch. 24

557 See Thomassin, *Treatise on Fasting*, Pt. 1, Ch. 18; Pt. 2, Ch. 14.

558 Cf. Gn 3:15

559 *De ea descriptione sub Caesare Augusto nihil reperias apud profanos rerum scriptores; neque id mirum. Unam enim tantummodo ejus imperatoris historiam habemus accurate scriptam, cujus pars decem admodum annos complectens, in qua descriptio ipsa contineri debuerat interiit, ut bene advertum Casaub., Tillemont., Calmet.*, etc. (Benedict XIV, p. 392, n. 2). This is what the learned pontiff said, and, taking his words literally, he was right. But the famous marbles of Ancyra give us a palpable proof of the enrollment of the Empire made by Augustus. These valuable monuments show even three successive enrollments made by orders of the same emperor, as may be seen in Père Magnan's work, *Problema de anno nativitatis Christi*, which records the ancient inscription, p. 261.

The difficulty is to reconcile a) the words of St. Luke, who says that this first enrollment was made by Cyrinus or Quirinus, president of Syria: *Haec descriptio prima facta est a praeside Syriae Cyrino* (Lk 2:2); b) the words of Tertullian, who says that the enrollment was made in Judea by Sentius Saturninus: *Sed et census constat actos sub Augusto tunc in Judaea per Sentium Saturninum* (*Against Marcion*, Bk. 4, Ch. 19); and c) the words of the historian Josephus, who places the departure of Saturninus from Judea in the last year of the reign of Herod, and mentions Quintilius Varus as his immediate successor, and Publius Sulpicius Quirinus or Cyrinus as the immediate successor to Quintilius Varus. This statement of Josephus would make the enrollment in question occur about ten years after the birth of our Lord; for it cannot be doubted that our Lord came into the world either in the very year of Herod's death or the year before. *Anno ipso, quo natus est Jesus, vel proximo, certe obiisse Herodem, optimorum chronologorum sententia est* (Huet., Domonst., Evangel., Prop. 9, Ch. 10, n. 9).

The first part of this difficulty is removed by saying that Publius Quirinus made the enrollment of Judea twice: the first time as extraordinary commissioner or procurator of Syria, on which Judea depended, and this in the name of the emperor and under the government of Caius Sentius Saturninus, governor of Syria. This answer reconciles the texts of St. Luke and Tertullian perfectly. *Si enim Cyrinus vir consularis cum potestate extraordinaria missus est ab Augusto ut censeret Judaeam, Saturnino ejus provinciae praeside, ecce tibi jam Cyrinus Judaeam descripsit, ut scribit Lucas, eaque descriptio vere dici potest facta sub Sentio Saturnino, quod testatur Tertullianus* (Benedict XIV, p. 394). The Greek terms that St. Luke uses are most favorable to this explanation (Magnan, p. 303).

The second part of the difficulty is removed by saying that Publius Quirinus made the enrollment of Judea a second time, as governor of Syria, of which Judea was a part. We have perfectly good grounds for saying, in accordance with the marbles of Ancyra and the testimony of Suetonius, that Augustus *censum populi ter egit* (In Aug., Ch. 27), and, in accordance with the testimony of Tertullian, cited above, that there were several enrollments ordered by Augustus. We have equally good grounds for saying that Quirinus made the enrollment of Judaea, as governor of Syria. In point of fact, here, according to the medals and historians of the time, is the list of the governors of Syria about the period of our Lord's birth: Titius, till the eleventh year before the vulgar era; Quintilius Varus, till the first year before the vulgar era; Volusius Saturninus, till the sixth year after the vulgar era; and Publius Quirinus, till the twelfth year after the vulgar era.

As we see, Publius Quirinus figures much among the governors of Judea. He appears only in the sixth year after the vulgar era, and this is one of the reasons why the learned Père Magnan, in his work *Problema de anno nativitatis Christi*, asserts that our Lord was born eight years before the vulgar era. The second enrollment made by Quirinus took place ten years after the birth of our Lord, on an occasion of which we are now going to speak. Archelaus, the son and successor of Herod, having displeased the Romans, the emperor dethroned him, sent him an exile to Vienne, and directed Quirinus, the governor Syria, to confiscate his property and to draw up a census of Judea. *Decimo autem principatus Archelai anno...Caesar... misit eum Viennam in exilium, quae est urbs Galliae, muletatum prius omni pecunia...caeterum ditione Archelai contributa Syriae, missus est illò a Caeare vir consularis Quirinus, qui censum ageret per Syriam, et ipsius Archelai domum venderet...Quirinus in Judaeam venit jam attributam provinciae Syriae, ut percenseret facultates civium, et Archelai pecunias in potestatem suam redigeret...Quirinus autem, venditis et confiscatis Archelai facultatibus, peractoque censu, qui incidit in annum trigesimum septimum post victum a Caesare in actiaca pugna Antonium*, etc. (Josephus, Bk. 17, Ch. 15). The word *prima* (*descriptio prima*) is employed by St. Luke, because, according to St. Justin, Quirinus was the first commissioner of Judea: *Quae sub Quirino primo vestro in Judaea procuratore* (*First Apology*, Ch. 34); and also to distinguish the first enrollment from the second, which was made by the same Quirinus, and of which we have just spoken.

According to commentators, the word *prima* is moreover employed by St. Luke to designate the most celebrated or the first general enrollment, made by Augustus alone, and not with colleagues, like the other two. This construction agrees exactly with the statement in the gospel: *Exiit edictum a Caesare Augusto* (Lk 2:1). Now the enrollment, made by Augustus alone, is the second commanded by the emperor: which puts the gospel into perfect harmony with the marbles of Ancyra. In effect, it is there said:

1. That Augustus made the first enrollment of the Empire with his colleagues, under the consulship of Marius Agrippa, twenty-eight years before the vulgar era.

In consvlatu. Sexto. censvm popvli. collega M.
Agrippa egi.

2. That he made the third with his colleague Tiberius, under the consulship of Sextus Pompeius and Sextus Appuleius, fourteen years after Jesus Christ.

...Consvlari. cvm. Imperio. Lvstrvm.
...Collega. Tib. Ca...Sex Pompeio. et. Sex.
Appvleio. cos.

3. That the second he made alone, under the consulship of Caius Marius Censorinus and Caius Asinius Gallus.

Imperio. Lvstrvm. solvs. feci. Censor...
...sinio...
Cos...

See Cornelius a Lapide, *On Luke*, Ch. 11, v. 2. Let us sum up in a few words what has been said. To reconcile all existing monuments with the gospel text, here is the way in which we must read the history of the general enrollment of the Empire, during which the birth of our Lord occurred. Eight years before the vulgar era, under the consulship of Caius Marcius Censorinus and Caius Asinius Gallus, the emperor Augustus, having no colleague in the government, and wishing to ascertain the population of the Empire, commanded a general census of the Roman world. He published the decree regarding it in the beginning of April, and sent commissioners into the provinces with authority to make it. He himself made it at Rome, as the Ancyra marbles inform us. About two or three months afterward, Sentius Saturninus received in Syria the order to proceed to the enumeration. He published it himself at Antioch, and sent commissioners into the various parts under his government to execute it. Publius Quirinus went into Judea, and there made the enrollment about the close of the year, according to the universal tradition of the Church since the time of the event (P. Magnan, p. 278).

560 Quoniam Joseph non habebat in vico illo Bethleem, quo diverteret, in specum quemdam prope vicum divertit, et cum illi essent ibi, peperit Maria Christum (Justin Martyr, *Dialogue with Trypho*).

561 Editor's note: See Volume XI of the Tradivox series, Lesson 2.

562 The manger itself in which the Savior was laid is of wood, and is preserved at Rome in the Church of St. Mary Major. It was brought thither in the seventh century, with some stones cut from the rock in the cave of Bethlehem, as has been shown by Benedict XIV, *De Canonis*, Bk. 4, Pt. 2. See the description of the manger, as it exists at present in the *Trois Rome*, t. 1, Dec. 25.

563 Chateaubriand, *Itinéraire dc Paris à Jérusalem*, t. 2, p. 157

564 Cf. Baronius, Annal., Anno 1, n. 3. We found it at Ancona, engraven on a tomb of the fourth century. See the *Trois Rome*, t. 3.

565 Cf. Bonaventure, *Life of Christ*, Ch. 10

566 Tradition tells us that they were three in number. See *Trois Rome*, t. 1; the *Pifferari*; and Sandini, *Hist. famil. sacr.*

567 Lk 2:14

568 Cf. Lk 2:20

569 Mt 1:16. In examining the genealogies of our Lord given by St. Matthew and St. Luke, we see that two branches of the family of David, by Solomon and his brother Nathan, are united. This takes place a) in Salathiel and his grandson Zorobabel; and b) in the Person of Jesus, the Son of Mary. Hence, Jesus sprang from the root of Jessé. He was consequently the Son of David and Solomon, and the heir of the promises made to both.

But as the evangelists teach us that Jesus is not the Son of Joseph, but of Mary, there are several difficulties raised here.

1. Why does St. Matthew give the genealogy of Joseph and not of Mary? It is answered that among the Hebrews it was not usual to draw up the genealogies of women. This fact is known by the constant practice of scripture, and by the testimony of fathers and rabbis, who say formally: "The mother's family is no family." (See their texts in the Bible de Vence, t. 19, p. 168, édit. in-octav., Paris, 1829.)

2. How is anyone to conclude that Jesus is a descendant of David and Solomon, because Joseph is a Son of David? It is answered that, Jesus being the son of Joseph, either by adoption, or simply as the Son of Mary, his spouse, Joseph having received him and brought him up as his Son, Jesus hereby entered into all the rights of the family of Joseph. The usage of adoption was known among the Hebrews from the time of Abraham (Cf. Gn 16:2; 48:5; Ex 2:10; Est 2:7-15). Although Jesus, therefore, were to be regarded only as the adopted Son of Joseph, this would suffice to give him a right to the character of the Son of David, and to act as heir of the promises made to this family. But there is a still stronger reason: namely, that Mary was of the same family and house as Joseph; for the law directed that daughters should marry in their own tribe, and, as far as possible, in their own family. It obliged them to do so even when a daughter was the only heiress of her family. Now, it is a most ancient tradition of the Church that Mary was an only daughter (Hilar., *On Matthew*, Ch. 1; Eusebius, *Ecclesiastical History*, Bk. 1, Ch. 7; etc.).

3. How could Joseph have two men as his father—Jacob, of the race of Solomon, and Heli, of the race of Nathan? It is answered that Jacob was Joseph's father according to nature, and Heli his father according to the law, that is to say, by adoption. In effect, St. Matthew says that Jacob begot Joseph, while St. Luke says merely that Joseph was of Heli, as he says at the head of the genealogy that Adam was of God (or belonged to God), though Adam was not the son of God. This opinion, founded on the authority of nearly all the fathers, is also related by Julius Africanus, who lived in Palestine in the beginning of the third century, and he assures us that he held it from some relatives of the Savior according to the flesh. Here is the way in which they explain this pedigree. Nathan, a descendant of David by Solomon, and Melchi, a descendant of the same David by Nathan, married, one after the other, a woman named Escha. Nathan had Jacob by her, and Melchi had Heli by her. Heli married, and dying childless, Jacob took to wife his widow, in virtue of the law of Moses (Cf. Dt 25:5-6). From this last marriage came Joseph, who was thus the son of Jacob according to nature, and the son of Heli according to the law.

4. How can it be proved that Jesus is a descendant of David and Solomon, admitting even that St. Luke gives the genealogy of the Blessed Virgin, since, on this supposition, Mary descends from Nathan and not from Solomon? It is answered, first, that the scripture does not formally say God promised that the Messias should be born of the race of Solomon according to the flesh, but only of the race of David. It is answered, next, that the two branches of Nathan and Solomon being united in Salathiel and Zorobabel, the blood of David meets in these two persons, so that the branches which spring from them are equally of each stock. The Heli of St. Luke and the Jacob of St. Matthew are both sons of David, Solomon, and Nathan. Hence, no matter how we consider our Lord, we always see that he comes from David, and that he unites in his Person all the rights of this noble family, as well by Joseph's side as by his mother Mary's. (See the Bible de Vence, *Dissert, sur la généalogie de Jesus-Christ*, t. 19, p. 170 et suiv.)

570 Le Vicomte Walsh, *Tableau poétique des fêtes Chrétiennes*, p. 64

571 Cf. Eccles 1:2; Jer 16:19

572 Cf. Eccles 7:2

573 Christus elegit quod salubrius judicat, vos eligitis quod reprobat, quis prudentior e duobus?...Aut iste fallitur, aut mundus errat (Bernard, *Sermon 3, in Nativ. Dom.*).

574 *Amemus puerum de Bethleem; amemus puerum de Bethleem!* "Let us love the babe of Bethlehem; let us love the babe of Bethlehem!" This was the motto, and, as it were, the war cry of the seraphic St. Francis.

See Alphonsus Liguori, *Bethléem ou l'Ecole de l'enfant Jésus*, in-18. We shall in vain look for anything more instructive or affecting.

575 Cf. Jn 1:14; Apoc 22:14; Eph 2:6

576 Here comes the great chronological question. Everyone knows that there are two principal chronologies founded on the Bible: the chronology of the Septuagint and the chronology of the Hebrews. The first is met in the Greek translation of the holy books made by the seventy-two Jewish doctors sent for this purpose into Egypt, under Ptolemy Philadelphus, about 250 years before Jesus Christ. In following this chronology, we must place the birth of the Savior about the year of the world 5504; or, according to the old compiler of the Roman martyrology, in the year of the world 5199: *Anno a creatione mundi, quando in principio creavit Deus coelum et terrain, quinquies millesimo centesimo nonagesimo nono.* The second rests on the Hebrew text of the holy books. It places the birth of our Lord in the year 4004 or thereabouts. Between the two chronologies, there is a difference therefore of about 1,500 years. This difference arises from the

fact that the Septuagint gives to the partriarchs of the first and second ages of the world several hundred years more than the Hebrew text allows them.

"To know," says Benedict XIV, "in what year of the world our Lord was born, we must therefore examine whether we should follow the Hebrew text with which the Vulgate agrees, or rather the Septuagint version. We answer that it is far better to follow the Hebrew text. First, the Roman Church follows the translation called the Vulgate, edited by St. Jerome more than 1,300 years ago, and approved by the holy Council of Trent. Now, the Vulgate agrees, as We have said, with the Hebrew text of the scripture. Next, the Septuagint version is evidently faulty; for, in the fourth chapter of Genesis, it places the death of Mathusala 14 years after the deluge. In point of fact, according to the Septuagint writers, Mathusala begot Lamech in the 269th year of his age, and Lamech begot Noe at the age of 88 years. Hence, at the birth of Noe, Mathusala would be 355 years old. Now, as the deluge began in the 600th year of Noe's age, it is clear that Mathusala was then 955 years old; and as Mathusala lived 969 years altogether, it follows that he lived 14 years after the deluge, which is quite false. In effect, St. Peter says formally that only eight persons survived the deluge: Noe, his wife, his three sons and their three wives: *Quando expectabant Dei patientiam in diebus Noe, cum fabricaretur arca, in qua pauci, id est octo animae, salvae factae sunt per aquam* (1 Pt 3:20). This error, and others besides, being fully proved, We say that, among the great variety of opinions which have been given on the year of our Lord's birth, and which amount to more than three hundred, the learned adopt in preference the one that places this great event in the year of the world 4004." *His probe constitutist dicimus, inter tot varias de natali Christi anno sententias, quas ad centum et triginta duas numerat Michael Moestlinus, mathematicus et chronologus non incelebris, eam placere magis sententiam eruditis viris, quae statuit Christum natum esse anno quater millesimo ab orbe condito* (Benedict XIV, n. 42, 3, 4, p. 409). See on this question the celebrated work of Père Magnan, of the Order of Minors, *Problema de anno nativitatis Christi*, Romae, 1772, especially p. 265, 267, and 328.

577 Cf. Chrysostom, *Sermon 31. Quem (censum) testem fidelissimum Dominicae Nativitatis Romana archivia custodiunt* (Tertullian, *Against Marcion*, Bk. 4, Ch. 7).

578 *Propter excellentiam festi*, says Pope Honorius III.

579 Cf. Augustine, *Epistle 119*, Ch. 1-2

580 *Circumcisio instituta erat ad remedium originalis peccati. In circumcisione conferebatur gratia non ex virtute circumcisionis, sed ex virtute fidei passionis Christi, cujus signum erat circumcisio: ita scilicet quod homo, qui acci piebat circumcisionem, profitebatur se suscipere talem fidem vel adultus pro se, vel alius pro parvulis* (*Summa Theologiae*, III, q. 38, a. 3, rep. 3; q. 70, a. 4, c.). Eugenius IV is of the same mind (Cf. *In decret. ad Arm.*). Pope Innocent III expresses himself thus: *Quoniam et si originalis culpa remittebatur per circumcisionis mysterium, et damnationis periculum vitabatur, non tamen perveniebatur ad regnum coelorum, quod usque ad mortem Christi fuit omnibus observatum* (*In decretales majores*).

Valde probabile est quod docet Sebastianus episcopus Oxoniensis, et ex eo Suarez, Pt. III, q. 70, d. 29, sect. 11: *scilicet circumcisionem, quatenus ipsa fuit remedium, quo remittebatur peccatum originale, et professio fidei de Christo venturo, potuisse esse in usu omnium gentium; potuerunt enim ipsae hoc signum eligere inter alia, quod sine dubio validum erat ad talem effectum si ea intentione fieret, quamvis non fieret cum intentione profitendi Judaismum, seque illi populo adjungendi. Itaque tales circumcisione expiabantur a peccato originali, non vero obligabantur ad legem Mosaicam* (Cornelius a Lapide, *On Genesis*, Ch. 17, v. 10). See also St. Bernard, *de Baptismo.*

581 Cf. Gn 17:10; Ex 4:25; 1 Mc 1:63-64

582 *Natus est in Bethleem, circumcisus in spelunca, oblatus in Jerusalem, in ulnas acceptus a Simeone* (Epiphanius, *Adversus Haeresus*, n. 20). It will not be ill taken if we here insert the history of our Lord's early years, as it is related by St. Epiphanius: it will help to remove several difficulties that embarrass commentators.

Anno Herodis XXXIII (seu VIII ante aeram vulgarem) Bethleemi in Judaea Salvator nascitur, atque in specu circumcisus, Hierosolymis oblatus est; ibique a Simeone inter brachia susceptus, et ab Anna, Phanuelis filia, prophetissa praedicatus, Nazaretum deportatus est. Tum anno sequenti Hierosolymis se coram Deo repraesentavit; atque inde Bethleemum propter generis propinquitatem a matre delatus est. Sed rursus Nazaretum rediens anno altero vertente (VI nempe ante aeram vulgarem) Hierosolymam Bethleemumque, gestante matre, perductus est.

Bethleemi porro cum ad aedes quasdam cum matre ei Josepho divertisset, qui jam grandis natu cum Maria degebat, secundo ab nativitatis anno a Magis adorandi causa conventus, ac donis ornatus est. Eadem vero nocte, cum Josephus per somnium ab angelo esset admonitus, in Aegyptum transfertur, Herodis anno XXXV. Unde rursus post biennium mortuo jam Herode, ac succedente Archelao, revertitur.

Quare necesse est XXXVII Herodis anno quartum aetatis suae puerulum egisse, cum Herodes, inquam, septem ac triginta confectis annis vivendi finem habuit. Post hunc Archelaus novem annis imperavit; quo regnum ineunte Josephus ex Aegypto cum Maria et puero digressus, ubi Archelaum imperare didicit, in Galilaeam secessit, ac tum Nazareti consedit (Epiphanius, *Adversus Haeresus*, n. 20, 51).

583 Cf. Lk 1:31

584 Cf. Mt 1:21

585 Cf. Phil 2:10

586 Absconditur in praesepio, sed proditur radiante stella de coelo; sic et circumcisio veritatem susceptae probat humanitatis, et nomen quod est super omne nomen gloriam indicat majestatis (Bernard, *Sermon, in Circ.*, n. 2).

587 In hoc salus mundi tota consistit (Odo of Cluny, *Opusc.*, Bk. 2, Ch. 28; Alphonsus Liguori, *Selv.*, t. 1, p. 255).

588 Cf. Tertullian, *Apology*, Ch. 23

589 Cf. Phil 2:10

590 Cf. *Hist. des indulg.*, In-12, Paris

591 Ad calcandam gentilium consuetudinem patres nostri statuerunt, privatas in kalendis januaris fieri litanias, ut in Ecclesiis psallatur, et hora octava in ipsis kalendis circumcisionis Deo propitio celebretur (Council of Tours, Anno 567, Can. 17, *apud. Labb.*; Thomassin, *Des Fêtes*, Bk. 2, Ch. 8).

592 Cf. Benedict XIV, p. 18, n. 25

593 *Per istos autem dies ad hoc jejunamus, ut quando ipsi laetantur, nos pro ipsis gemamus* (Augustine, *On Psalm 38; Sermon 7*). Elsewhere, the same father employs all his eloquence to turn Christians aside from these abuses: *Acturus es celebrationem strenarum sicut paganus, lusurus alea, et inebriaturus te? Quomodo aliud credis, aliud speras, aliud amas? Dant illi strenas, date vos eleemosynas; avocantur illi cantionibus luxurarium, avocate vos sermonibus scripturarum: currunt illi ad theatrum, vos ad ecclesiam; inebriantur illi, vos jejunate...*(Augustine, *Sermon 198*, 2nd January). *Jam vero illud quale et quam turpe est, quod viri nati tunicis muliebribus vestiuntur et turpissima demum demutatione puellaribus figuris virile robur effeminant: non erubescentes tunicis muliebribus inserere militares lacertos; barbatas facies praeferunt, et videri feminae volunt* (Augustine, *in Appendice*).

594 Cf. Isidore, *De Ecclesiasticis Officiis*, Bk. 2, Ch. 40; Alcuin, *De Div. Offic.*; Cf. also Augustine, *Sermon, in kalend. jan.*

595 See Jauffret, *du Culte public*, p. 199.

596 Mt 3:17

597 See Benedict XIV, *De Festis Dom.*, Ch. 2, p. 17, 59. Yet this is not certain. See Baronius, Anno 31, n. 34. *Illud "hodie" non refertur ad tempus rei gestae, quasi sensus sit, eo die tria illa mysteria esse facta; sed fertur ad commemorationem et celebrationem eorum trium mysteriorum eo die fieri solitam, ut sit eorum verborum hic sensus: hodie colitur et celebratur commemoratio istorum trium mysteriorum* (Severius, *On John*, Ch. 1, disp. 2, n. 3).

598 Cf. Le Vicomte Walsh, *Tableau poétique des fêtes Chrétiennes*, p. 79

599 Editor's note: See Volume XI of the Tradivox series.

600 Lesson 2.

601 Cum Magi reversi fuissent, manserunt colentes et glorificantes Deum, studiosius magis quam primum, et praedicarunt omnibus in genere suo et multos erudierunt. Denique cum post resurrectionem Domini Thomas apostolus isset in provinciam illam, adjuncti sunt ei, et baptizati ab eo, facti sunt adjutores praedicationis illius (*Auct. oper. imperf., Homily 2 on Matthew*; Sandini, p. 49).

602 Cf. Caesarius, *Sermon 139*; Leo, *Sermon 1*; *Sermon 4*; *Sermon 5*, et passim.

603 Cf. Casaub., in Baron, et Bolland., Mai, t. 1, p. 7, 8, et Benedict XIV: *Tres illo fuisse docet recepta in Ecclesia sententia* (Epiph., p. 22, n. 7, 8; Sandini, *Hist. famil. sacr.*, p. 30ff.)—*Magorum memoria variis diebus celebratur. Gasparis, die primo januarii; Melchioris, die sexto; Balthasaris, die undecimo* (Bolland., t. 1, Jan., p. 8).

604 Benedict XIV supports and establishes the opinion of their royalty (Cf. n. 11).

605 Cf. *Redemption du genre humain*, p. 80; Bible de Vence, t. 20.—If you asked me what was the star that guided the Magi to the place where the Savior was born, I should answer you that this is one of those questions on which the learned waste their time and lose their trouble, for they can never attain to a fully satisfactory solution of it. However, as all things connected with the mysteries of the holy infancy are deserving of our interest, it will not be useless to acquaint you with various conjectures that have been made regarding the appearance of this miraculous star. No person, to my knowledge, has asserted that it was one of the fixed stars, or one of the planets whose positions and revolutions in the firmament are well known to us. Some have thought that God created it for this occasion; others that an angel, clad in a body as bright as a star, preceded the Magi, to direct their steps; others, in fine, and they are far the greatest number, that this heavenly sign was a very luminous meteor, to which an angel had given the shape of a star, and which, floating in the middle regions of the air, was directed by him from east to west, as formerly the pillar of fire advanced before the children of Israel, to lead them through the desert. There is nothing certain on the matter.

606 Cf. Benedect XIV, n. 21-22

607 Cf. Ammianus Marcellinus, *Res Gestae*, Bk. 21

608 Cf. Gregory Nazianzen, *Oration 20*

609 The following history may well inspire us with a great zeal for the work of the Propagation of the Faith.

On the 31st of August, nineteen young persons, French, German, Italian, and English, took the religious habit in the Community of the Good Shepherd, Angers. Among them you might have recognized, by her copper tint, a young African, of whose life we have been kindly furnished with many interesting particulars. We regret that we can only give a hasty and imperfect sketch of it.

In 1839, Father Suchet, vicar-general of Algeria, accompanied the expedition against Constantine. After the glorious journey that secured Djidjelli as a prize to France, the general of the troops invited the abbé to sup with him in his tent. After ten o'clock at night, Father Suchet wished to go to the ambulance, whither his ministry called him. The general strove in vain to detain him, representing to him how imprudent it would be to pass through an unknown town on a dark night, when he might meet with some fugitives or ill-disposed Arabs. These remarks could not stay the priest, who, some time afterward was to go alone, amid incredible dangers, to seek Abd-el-Kader in the heart of the desert, and to treat with him about an exchange of prisoners. The intrepid missionary only asked an escort of four men, and immediately set out for his post.

While going along one of the streets, his foot struck against something, from which there escaped a heartrending cry. Stooping down, he found in a Bedouin's cloak a poor little infant, bathed in its own blood and tears: it stretched out its hands toward him. Its father, when rushing to battle, had wrapped it up in his burnoose, and doubtless committed it to the keeping of God, embracing it for the last time; for he disappeared in the fight, and the poor infant was left alone, abandoned! No, not abandoned: providence was watching over it, and a new Vincent de Paul took it in his arms, and carried it away to the ambulance of the army.

The superintendent and his wife were called by the abbé Suchet, who entrusted it to them, begging of them to lavish on it all the care that its state required. He also made them show it to a doctor. The doctor found that the poor child had received a deep wound from a ball in the shoulder. Judging that there was no hope for it, he was of opinion that it should be left to die without any attempt at relief; but the superintendent's wife preferred, at the request of Father Suchet, to take on herself the care of the child. As it had been given up by the doctor, the apostle of charity baptized it the same night under the name of Zoa, which was that of the saint of the day, and recommended it once more to the superintendent's wife. Next day, his first care was to go and see little Zoa, who appeared to be returning to life. He was greatly affected at all the tenderness shown her by the warm-hearted mother whom providence had secured for her. He begged the good woman to continue her kindness and engaged himself to defray all expenses. Some time afterward, he set out on a new expedition, and did not return to Djidjella for fourteen months. Intending to take away little Zoa and bring her to Algiers, he acquainted the superintendent with his purpose a few days previously. This news caused the poor man such grief that he fell sick. His wife went to Father Suchet with a sad and downcast look.

At the sight of her, the missionary thought that his dear little Zoa was either sick or dead; but he was soon undeceived, by learning that her deep sorrow came only from the prospect of parting with the young orphan, who had become as dear to her as her own daughter: she had one of six years old. Zoa is immediately brought to him. The good missionary, in order to win her to himself, gives her some money. The little Bedouine takes it with a wild delight and runs away. Father Suchet follows her, and is agreeably surprised when he sees that his little Zoa has borne the piece of money to her foster-father. As a reward, he gives her twice as much, saying: "Hold, here are two douros more to buy you a dress!" Father Suchet at length declares to the superintendent that he wishes to remove Zoa. An affecting conflict now begins; the argument goes on for some moments: but the soldier at last comes to understand that she belongs by right to him who saved her, and who was her declared protector. During this charitable battle, the dear child had slipped the two douros softly under the good superintendent's pillow, saying: "They are for you, papa."

Father Suchet, seeing the affliction that Zoa's departure was about to cause in this family, told them that he would agree to leave her with them for some time longer, since they felt so much pain in losing her; and that, on his arrival at Algiers, he would beg the general to transfer them to another battalion, stationed at Algiers itself, where they might always be able to see Zoa, and to send their own daughter to the same school with her. The proposal was accepted with many demonstrations of joy. Father Suchet went to Algiers. Obstacles of every kind stood in the way of his desires. The general was absent. Later on, the superintendent, having been seriously wounded in the course of a new expedition, obtained leave to go and till a few acres of land. Father Suchet, notwithstanding many searches and long journeys, was unable to find out the place of his retreat. He was sorely grieved at all these disappointments, imagining that he should never again see his interesting child. Moreover, he soon found himself obliged to accompany an expedition that took him away some six hundred miles. On his return, he made new efforts to discover the district where the superintendent had settled down, but always in vain.

At length, he one day learned that cholera was raging at Fondouk. He went there with Monsignor Dupuch. What was his surprise when one of the first persons that he met was his little Bedouine, whom he knew quite well by her looks, and by a mark that she had on her forehead! All the world can understand the joy of the holy priest and the happiness of this good child, who had always shown herself full of the liveliest gratitude. They quickly turned their steps toward the abode of the old soldier, whom they found very ill, as well as his wife and child. Zoa was the only one in the house not attacked by the disease. Hence, in spite of the earnest wish that Father Suchet had to take her to Algiers and obtain a suitable education for her, it was impossible for him to make any proposal of the kind at present to the family of which she was the only support, the only comfort. He should therefore yield to circumstances another time, and leave her to tend her generous benefactors. Monsignor Dupuch was then pleased to supply the ceremonies of baptism, which could not be observed on the night that she was found nearly dead. Her old friend recommended her to the governor of the town, hoping that he might yet be able to bring her to Algiers.

It was only in 1850 that Father Suchet, going into the hospital of Algiers to bring the succors of religion to the victims of the cholera, was informed by Sister Amelia, a daughter of St. Vincent, that a Frenchman, laboring under a very severe attack of the disease, wished to confess, and that he seemed very well disposed, because a young Bedouine, who called herself a Christian, had instructed him. The zealous missionary went at once. He found the man at the point of death, and, near him, his wife and the young girl that he had been told of. What was his joy when, after looking at her for a while, he recognized his little Zoa, who, wholly concerned with the dreadful sufferings of her godfather, had not taken particular notice of Father Suchet! He had no sooner addressed a few questions to her than she fell at his feet and burst into tears, saying: "I am Zoa, the little one that you saved! Yes, you are truly the good Christian marabout, who, after rescuing me from death, baptized me, and loaded me with favors! Oh, yes, it is you!" The man of God burst into tears. Then Zoa told him that her adopted father had sent her from Fondouk to Algiers in order to be near her sick godfather, who expired a few hours afterward in the arms of the holy priest.

The abbé Suchet, judging that it was at last time to use his rights, went to the episcopal residence, and it was decided between Monsignor Pavy and him that she should no more return to her adopted father in Fondouk, but should be placed in the establishment of the Good Shepherd, at Elbiar, near Algiers, conducted by nuns from Angers. Father Suchet sent to the convent for an attendant, and entrusted the child to her for introduction to the community. Before their departure, he handed ten francs to Zoa, telling the attendant to let her buy whatever she liked. The young Kabyle asked the good sister to take her to a milliner's shop. She, though astonished, went with her. The child asked for some wreaths of immortelles and then hastened to the cemetery, where she laid this last pledge of gratitude on the grave of her adopted mother, who had died a short time previously in the hospital of Algiers, and to whom she thus bade her last farewell. "I have nothing more now to hold me back," she said to the attendant, "take me wherever you please." Having entered the convent, the young Kabyle was very soon remarked for her wisdom, and all her companions awarded her the prize of honor. The bishop and Father Suchet, having to be absent for a couple of months, recommended her mistress to prepare her for first Communion.

Father Suchet, on his return, finding her sufficiently instructed, admitted her to this great act. Zoa prepared for it with angelic fervor, and, on the festival of St. Aloysius Gonzaga, had the happiness of sitting for the first time at the holy table. But just at this time, she asked Father Suchet's leave to make a vow of becoming a nun. The prudent missionary having refused it, she contented herself with offering up her wishes to God. Henceforth she continued to be the edification of her companions.

Before Father Suchet's departure for France, the superioress of the convent at Elbiar told him there was no doubt but his young protégée had still the desire of becoming a nun. He sent for her, expressed to her his amazement how such a thought could ever have come into the mind of a young Bedouine, and, to prove her, left her in this state of uncertainty. He said to himself that it would be better to wait for some time in order to see whether her vocation was true or not. Meantime, Zoa continued to make rapid progress in piety. Such happy dispositions and so natural an inclination for well-doing made Father Suchet decide on promising to grant her request. This crowned all her desires.

The superioress at Elbiar, having to set out shortly for the motherhouse at Angers, was thinking of taking young Zoa along with her, when her foster-father, who had heard of her resolution, came from Fondouk to the convent, begging his dear Zoa to return to him, and offering her even half of his little wealth. But the young Kabyle was immovable, refusing every proposal that would turn her aside from her vocation, notwithstanding her heartfelt gratitude for all the kindness that he had bestowed upon her. She accordingly left for Angers with her superioress. Here, as at Elbiar, she edified all her sisters by her rare virtues, and received the holy habit of religion, with the name of Mary Ferdinand, on the 24th of last August.

In a few years, doubtless, Sister Ferdinand will return to her native land, there to teach poor Mussulman girls that they can recover their dignity and happiness only by observing the sacred laws of evangelical modesty. The young negresses, brought up with so much care in the house of the Good Shepherd, will also give the same sublime lesson to the women of Africa.

610 See Durandus, *Rationale divinorum officiorum*, Bk. 6, Ch. 16; Thomassin, Bk. 2, Ch. 6; Council of Orleans in 541 and Auxerre in 578.

611 Cf. Lv 12

612 Cf. Ibid.

613 Sicut Christus, licet non esset legi obnoxius, voluit tamen circumcisionem, et alia legis onera subire ad demonstrandum humilitatis et obedientiae exemplum, et ut approbaret legem, et ut calumniae occasionem Judaeis tolleret; propter easdem rationes voluit et matrem suam implere legis observantias, quibus tamen non erat obnoxia (*Summa Theologiae*, III, q. 37, a. 4, c.).

614 Cf. Le Vicomte Walsh, *Tableau poétique des fêtes Chrétiennes*, p. 92

615 Chapter, *unic. de Purif. post partum.*—The *Roman Ritual* declares that it is a pious and laudable custom thus to visit the church: *Si qua puerpera post partum, juxta piam ac laudabilem consuetudinem, ad ecclesiam venire voluerit pro incolumitate sua Deo gratias actura, petieritque a sacerdote benedictionem, etc.* (*De benedict, mulieris post partum*).

616 Cf. Ex 13

617 Hilary, *On Matthew*, Ch. 17, n. 11

618 Cf. Butler, Feb. 2

619 Jn 13:15

620 Lk 2:29-32

621 Lk 2:34-35

622 Cf. Baronius, Anno 496

623 Cf. Baronius, *Not. ad Martyrol.*, Feb. 2

624 Cf. Procop., *de Bell. Persic.*, Bk. 2

625 See Benedict XIV, *De Festis*, p. 442, n. 13

626 Ambire urbem.

627 Quam lustrandi consuetudinem congrue et religiose Christiana mutavit religio; cum eodem mense, hoc est hodierna die, in honore S. Genetricis et perpetuae Virginia Mariae non solum clerus, sed omnis plebs ecclesiarum loca cum cereis et diversis hymnis lustrantibus circumeant (Ildefonsus, vii, *Saecul. Script.*, t. 12; Bibl. PP., p. 589).

628 Le Vicomte Walsh, *Tableau poétique des fêtes Chrétiennes*, p. 78

629 Mt 18:3

630 See Jauffret, *Du culte catholique*, p. 204.

631 Cf. Rupert, *De Div. Offic.*, Bk. 4, Ch. 3-4

632 Jn 16:20

633 Lk 6:25

634 Cf. Ferraris, art. *Eucharist.*, n. 67, 71

635 Cf. Thiers, *Exposit. du Saint-Sacrament*, Bk. 4, Ch. 17-18

636 Cardinal Bona, *Rerum liturgicarum*, Bk. 2, n. 7, 16

637 Cf. Godescard, *Fêtes mob.*, t. 1, p. 360; Mi 1; Jdt 4; Est 4; Lam 4; Jon 3; and our treatise *On Holy Water*.

638 The imposition of public penance was generally preceded by a public confession. It is well known that, in the early ages, there were two kinds of confession: public, and private or auricular. In public confession, one accused himself not only of public sins, but also, on some occasions, of the most secret sins. This was done in presence of the bishop and the priests forming his council, and sometimes even in presence of all the people. It was in consequence of this confession that the public penance was imposed. The Church took the wisest precautions that the public confession of hidden sins should not prove prejudicial to those who made it. Hence, she did not oblige murderers or robbers to accuse themselves publicly of their crimes. Yet more: a public declaration of secret crimes was not made, at least generally, without the advice of the priest to whom they had been already told in private.

An authentic proof of the discipline to which we refer is found in a celebrated passage of Origen's. After praising confession, and showing its usefulness, this father adds: "It remains for you to consider attentively what sort of a man you should trust with your sins. Be sure, first of all, about the physician to whom you are going to discover the cause of your disease. Let him know how to be weak with the weak, how to weep with those that weep...and, if he give you any advice, follow it exactly. If he judge your disease to be of such a nature that it requires to be laid open and treated in presence of the whole Church, as well to edify others as to procure a certain cure for yourself, follow the advice of your wise physician" (Origen, *Homily 2 on Psalm 36*). This quotation from Origen, to which it would be easy to add many others, proves that auricular confession was already practiced in the second century, and that it was sometimes joined with public confession. We shall find the same case occurring three centuries later on.

St. Leo, having mounted the chair of Peter, learned that some confessors obliged penitents to accuse themselves publicly of their secret faults. The illustrious pontiff, wishing to moderate this imprudent zeal, wrote to the bishops of Campania a letter, which dates from the middle of the fifth century: "I command," he says, "that the presumption of certain persons should by all means be suppressed, who, contrary to the apostolic rule and to all law, oblige the faithful to write out lists and publicly to recite all kinds of sins, since it is enough to discover to a single priest in a secret confession the sins of which one feels himself guilty. For, though the faith of those who, out of the fear of God, are quite willing to undertake a public confession of their faults, seems praiseworthy, yet the sins of all are not such that those who ask penance should have nothing to fear in making them public. Let this evil custom therefore cease, lest many should be deterred from employing the remedy of penance, either through shame, or through fear of publishing before their enemies deeds for which they might be punished by the civil law. It is enough to make a confession first to God, and then to a priest, who intercedes for the sins of the penitent" (Leo the Great, *Epistle 136, to the Bishops of Campania*).

These two passages, and many others that we might cite,* show clearly the discipline of the primitive Church in regard to confession.

If a sinner desired to return to the friendship of God, he addressed himself to a bishop or a priest, and made to him a sincere and humble avowal of all the evils with which he had to reproach himself. The director, after hearing this tale, weighed in his mind the advice that he should give, the conduct that he should prescribe. If, among the sins, there were any grave and notorious, he ordered them to be confessed aloud, so as to repair scandal. If, among the secret faults, he found some whose publication, without injuring a third party, would turn to the advantage of all or even of only one, he prescribed it.

If the director had to cure a haughty, disdainful soul, and failed in his efforts with mild remedies, he ended by reducing it to the humiliating mortification of accusing itself publicly, thus to subdue a pride previously unsubduable. And if the safety or reputation of persons were likely to be compromised by a public declaration, a wise minister would take great care not to command it: the Church herself forbade it. St. Leo's letter, cited above, is an incontestable proof on this point.

Thus did the faithful spouse of Jesus Christ, the tender mother of Christians, know how to reconcile the interests of heaven with those of earth, the honor and security of individuals with progress in virtue, the severity of principles with indulgence toward persons. Thus did she know how to repair scandal without ever causing it, to turn the confusion of sinners to their profit in the way of salvation, and to draw from evil itself the edification of all her children.

Under this beautiful and admirable discipline, everything takes place decently, everything goes forward well. Sacramental confession, instituted by Jesus Christ, always leads the way; public confession established by Jesus Christ, comes sometimes in its train, always after it: the indispensable regulates what is only auxiliary. The former, of divine origin, has existed, and will exist, in all times; the latter, of ecclesiastical origin, was, after being observed for several ages, discontinued by the same canonical authority that had instituted it (Cf. *Discussion amicale*, t. 2, p. 167).

Now, the wisdom of the Church shines forth no less in the abolition of public confession than in its establishment. The fervor of Christians diminishing, this watchful mother feared that the obligation of confessing publicly would keep penitents away from sacramental confession, necessary to salvation, and public confession was suppressed. At the close of the fourth century, it had ceased to be in vigor in Greek Churches; it was preserved a much longer time in the Latin Church.

* Cf. Tertullian, *De Paenitentia*; Irenaeus, *Against Heresies*, Bk. 1, Ch. 9, 42; Cyprian, *On the Lapsed*; Basil, *ep. Amphiloch.*, Ch. 34; Origen, *Contra Celsum*, Bk. 3; Pacian, *Paraen ad Poenitentes*, etc.

639 Flentes, audientes, prostrati, consistentes.

640 Cf. Jerome, *Epistle 77, to Oceanus on the Death of Fabiola.*

There is a custom still existing among us that proves the fidelity with which our ancestors submitted to the humiliations of fasting and penance during Lent. This custom—who would believe it?—is that of leading about a fat ox. In former days, everybody observed the quadragesimal abstinence religiously. Only one butcher in each town had leave to sell meat for the sick. This privilege was granted to him who, in the opinion of experienced and specially appointed judges, showed the finest piece of cattle. Judgment having been pronounced, the butcher, as if to give his address, led the crowned ox about through the streets of the town. Hence the custom still observed among through most people are unaware of its origin or meaning.

641 Ws 13:1

642 Is 45:22

643 Jejunium quod animabus corporibusque curandis salubriter institutum est (*Office of the Saturday before the First Sunday of Lent*).

644 See in particular those authors who have written on diet, as Junker, Arbuthnot, Hecquet, Lemerry, and Lorry (*Traité des Aliments*). Considering from a hygienic point of view the good works prescribed by the Church, a celebrated physician of our days expresses himself thus:

"Christianity is not content with seeing us observe its precepts only through fear of the pains of another life. It requires that the motive of all our actions should be the love of God and of the neighbor in God: a law of love, whose accomplishment ennobles the heart, enlightens the mind, and makes man truly free by regulating all his wants.

"Besides the sacraments, which purify the soul, while they lessen the sufferings of the body, religion prescribes the daily use of prayer as a powerful rampart against the continually renewed attacks of the passions. There is, in effect, no better means to scatter those dangerous enemies of our repose than this frequent communication of man with his Creator.

"With the sacraments and prayer, religion also joins fasting and abstinence, hygienic means very proper to deaden the passions; and, in her profound wisdom, she prescribes their longest and most severe exercises just at that period of the year when all nature is on the point of entering into a state of fermentation. Do the rigors of the season, poverty, a constitution weakened by age, sickness, or labor, stand in the way of anyone's following the precept? She easily dispenses with it; but she wishes that all should supply for it by alms proportioned to their means. It is thus that, by combating two vices, unfortunately so common, intemperance and avarice, she checks the transports of love and the impetuosity of anger, while she pours the superfluous goods of the rich into the hands of the poor. Admirable institution! which puts an end to blasphemy against providence on the lips of the needy, and changes into blessings the curses inspired by jealousy. Have human institutions ever given proof of so much solicitude, prudence, and charity?" (M. Descuret, *Médecine des Passions*).

645 Translator's note: It should not be forgotten that millions of the human family live almost entirely on vegetable diet, and enjoy robust health. A single fact of this kind is better than many long arguments. People should not think that because animal food is more stimulating, it is therefore more nutritious. It really seems to contain nothing but what may be found, at a much lower price and in a much purer state, in vegetable productions. A reference to tables of chemical analysis will show this. Hence, man's wants in this life, as regards food, are after all but few, if we set aside those artificial wants which self-indulgence has created. It is said that brown bread alone, with an occasional drink of good water, is quite sufficient to maintain the human system in health and vigor. The brown bread here alluded to is that made from wheatmeal, or unsifted ground wheat, not that made from a mixture of flour and bran. The latter kind of bread is often very inferior.

The following extract from a letter which appeared in the *Times* on the 24th December, 1878, and excited much attention at the time, may still be considered interesting:

"Lentils are to be bought in quantities at a very low price. There was lately a large cargo in Gloucester Docks, selling at less than five shillings a bushel—say a penny a pound. A penny so expended affords more nutriment than 3s. expended in lean beef. Beef contains from 70 to 80 percent of dirty water. Lentils contain only 9 to 11 percent of clean water. At once there is more than a threefold advantage in favor of lentils over beef. Lentils (*Ervum lens*, order *Legumionsae*) contain, according to Payen—nitrogenous matter 25:2; starch, etc. 56; cellulose, 2:4; fatty matter, 2:6; mineral matter, 2:3; water, 11:5—100. Thus it is at once perceived that the nutrition is of the best possible description. Everything that a human being requires as food is there. Indeed, the value of lentil soup was well known in the days of Jacob and Esau, though there is now a sad ignorance of the best human food. Small quantities of lentils (a peck is sufficient for a small family for a winter, i.e., for soup) can be purchased at most corn dealers in London. I am writing with a full practical knowledge of the subject, having for thirty years lived on seeds, vegetables, and fruits, to the total exclusion of alcohol, flesh, and fish. Yet not one man in a thousand would compete with me in strength of lungs, and few in strength of limb, under equal conditions. Infants fed indirectly on such food are free from ailments and full of strength and vitality."

In some further correspondence with the *Times*, the writer of the above, Mr. W. G. Ward, F. R. H. S., says, "Your publication of my letter on lentil soup has produced extraordinary effects. It has tied me to the desk for eight days, replying to some 200 letters, and still they come. It has startled Mark Lane with the number of inquiries for Egyptian lentils." Referring to some other articles of food, he says, "I will not enumerate the marvelous cures I have made with celery, for fear the medical men should, like the corn dealers, attempt to worry me. Let me fearlessly say that rheumatism is impossible on such diet...Cold or damp never produces rheumatism, but simply develops it. The acid blood is the primary cause and the sustaining power of the evil. While the blood is alkaline there can be no rheumatism...Haricot beans are very nourishing indeed. Simply boiled soft, and eaten with parsley sauce and potatoes, you have a dish at a fourth the cost of flesh meat, yet giving fourfold its nutriment...The sample of London split peas is about as good as it is possible to get them. No one surely requires to be told what good soup they make. We use with them the pulp of fully-ripe vegetable marrows. They are usually kept hung up in country houses for that purpose and to preserve the seeds that they contain. Of course, the usual flavoring herbs are added. Split peas are sold wholesale at 44s. per quarter of 504 lb., or 4½ cwt.—only a fraction over a penny per pound. Generally, the price retail should not be more than 2d. per pound. How trifling is the cost of human food, if what is necessary only is sought!—4d. to 6d. per day is sufficient to provide a strong man with food and to keep him in health and strength."

What a consolation for the poor, that wholesome food need not be expensive food!

646 See this important point further developed in Volume II of the catechism, Lesson 55 [i.e., Volume XI of the Tradivox series, p. 432-437].

647 Sir Edwin Sands, *Europae Speculum*

648 As regards the mysterious reasons for Lent, St. Thomas explains them thus: *Ratio autem numeri, quantum ad quadragesimale jejunium, est triplex secundum Gregorium* (*Homily 16 on the Gospels*): "*Primo quidem, quia virtus decalogi per libros quatuor sancti evangelii impletur: denarius enim quater ductus in quadragenarium surgit. Vel, quia in hoc mortali corpore ex quatuor elementis subsistimus, per cujus voluptates praeceptis dominicis contraximus, quae per decalogum sunt accepta; unde dignuin est ut eamdem carnem quater decies affligamus. Vel, quia, sicut in lege offerri jubebantur decimae rerum, ita offerre contendimus Deo decimas dierum: dum enim per trecentos et sexaginta et sex dies annus dicitur, nos autem per triginta et sex dies affligimur (qui sunt jejunabiles in sex septimanis quadragesimae) quasi anni nostri decimas Deo damus*" (*Summa Theologiae*, II-II, q. 147, a. 5, c.).

649 Cf. Jerome, *On the Fast of Lent*, Bk. 3, Ch. 7; Leo the Great, *Sermon 4 on Lent*; *Sermon 5 on Lent*; *Sermon 9 on Lent*; Peter Chrysologous, *Sermon 11*; *Sermon* 66, etc.

650 Basil, *Homily on Fasting*; Cf. Bernard, *Sermon 7 on Lent*; *Sermon 3*

651 *Act.*, St. Fructuosus

652 Cf. *Rule of St. Benedict*, Ch. 40. See the excellent developments in *Biblioth, vetus Serm. et Homil. priscor. Eccl. Pair.*, 4 vol. in-folio, t. 1.

653 Anast. Biblioth., *Hist. Eccl.*—In our history of France, the celebrated "herring day" is also known.

654 Cf. *Mémoires de Trévoux*, Anno 1741, p. 780

655 Cf. Jerome, *Epistle 52 to Nepotian*, n. 12

656 Translator's note: It may be well to remark here that those who are bound to fast are allowed eight ounces of bread, salad, or other such food, at collation, even though they do not usually take so much at breakfast. To exceed this quantity by an ounce or two is not considered more than a venial sin. Drinks such as tea or coffee, which contain little or no nutriment, may be taken without any restriction—that is to say, they do not break the fast. As regards the hour of collation, it varies in different countries. The Rev. Patk. Power, P. P., in his very instructive *Catechism*, so well-known in Ireland, remarks: "In this country, custom has authorized us to take the collation in the morning, and also something at night. What is thus taken at night must be but a little—one ounce, or, at most, two ounces."

657 Conventus Aquisgran., t. 12; Conc., t. 7, 1508

658 Cf. Thomassin, *Treatise on Fasting*

659 In pueris maxime est evidens causa non jejunandi: tum propter debilitatem naturae, ex qua provenit quod indigent frequenti cibo, et non multo simul assumpto; tum etiam quia indigent multo nutrimento propter necessitatem augmenti, quod fit de residuo alimenti. Et ideo quandiu sunt in statu augmenti quod est ut in pluribus usque ad finem tertii septennii, non tenentur ad ecclesiastica jejunia observanda. Conveniens tamen est ut etiam in hoc tempore se ad jejunium exerceant...Quandoque tamen, magna tribulatione imminente, in signum poenitentiae arctioris etiam pueris jejunia indicuntur: sicut etiam de jumentis legitur Jonae, 3:7: "Homines et jumenta non gustant quidquam, nec aquam bibant" (*Summa Theologiae*, II-II, q. 147, a. 4).

660 Cf. Chrysostom, *Homily 6, de Poenit.*; Charles Borromeo, *Acts of the Church of Milan*, Pt. 3

661 Cf. Photius, *Noinocan.*, tit. 7, Ch. 1

662 Chrysostom, *Homily 15 on Genesis*

663 Jn 13:15

664 Le Vicomte Walsh, *Tableau poétique des fêtes Chrétiennes*, p. 106

665 Cf. *Gloss.*, t. 1, p. 610; Labb., *Chron.*, Anno 1322

666 Jer 26:14-15

667 Jn 7:37; 33-34

668 Lk 7:47

669 See the discussion by Benedict XIV, *De Festo Dolor. B. Virg.*, n. 5-7.

670 During all Lent, and especially on the day of the Compassion, it is very appropriate to recite the hymn of Mary's dolors, the inimitable *Stabat Mater*. Some think that this hymn was composed by the great pope Innocent III. (See Benedict XIV, *De Festis*, Bk. 4, p. 400, n. 5.) Others attribute it to James de Benedictus, better known under the name of Jacopone, who died in 1306. He became a religious after the death of his wife, crushed by the falling of a bathroom floor.

671 Cf. Benedict XIV, *De Dom. Palm.*, p. 80, n. 24

672 Cf. Le Vicomte Walsh, *Tableau poétique des fêtes Chrétiennes*, p. 112

673 Chrysostom, *Homily 30 on Genesis*

674 Cf. *Codex Theodosianus*, Bk. 2, tit. 8, leg. 2

675 Gothofredi, noted in *Codex Theodosianus*, p. 114

676 Chrysostom, *Homily 40 on the Great Week*

677 Leo the Great, *Sermon 39, de Quadrag.*

678 Ibid.

679 Cf. Augustin, *Sermon 19*

680 Cf. Thomassin, *Des Fêtes*, Bk. 3, Ch. 11

681 Credibile est Christum Dominum, asino perpetuo insedisse, et asinam vacasse. Quamobrem Ecclesia, in quadam ex orationibus quas adhibet in distributione et processione palmarum, ait: "Omnipotens sempiterne Deus, qui Dominum nostrum Jesum Christum super pullum asinae seders fecisti" (Benedict XIV, p. 70, n. 6).

682 Animadvertendum est probe, turbas iisdem gaudii signis Christum Dominum excepisse, quibus tabernaculorum festum celebrare consueverant, quibus...venturi Messiae contineri praesagium arbitrabantur (Benedict XIV, p. 73, n. 12).

683 Cf. Lk 19:41-44

684 Few persons know that it is to the name *Pascha Floridum*, "Flowery Pasch" that a large country in America owes its name. The Spaniards gave the name *Florida* to this country, not far from Mexico, because they discovered it on the Flowery Pasch, or Palm Sunday, in the year 1513 (Garcil. de le Vega, *Discovery of Florida*).

685 Cf. Benedict XIV, p. 78, n. 20

686 Ps 23:7, 9

687 Cf. *Rational liturgique*

688 Cf. Alcuin, *De div. Offic.*, p. 45

689 Cf. Durandus, *Rationale divinorum officiorum*, Bk. 6, Ch. 67

690 Palestrina added a fourth voice, that of the people. See on this matter the *Trois Rome—Dimanche des Rameaux*. In France, all the faithful and the priest himself fall prostrate, and kiss the ground at the words, "He yielded up the ghost." At Rome, it is thought enough to pause a little during a genuflection.

691 Cf. Durandus, *Rationale divinorum officiorum*, Bk. 6, Ch. 72

692 Cf. Mabillon, *Musoeum ital.*, t. 2, p. 22

693 Mt 26:31

694 *Docuimus per hos dies intermitti campanarum sonum, et ligna quaedam adhiberi fragoris in modum obstrepentia, ut extet momoria illius consuetudinis convocandi per illorum lignorum strepitum, primis Ecclesiae saeculis, fideles ad divina officia; in veteribus ritualibus praescribi ut campanae per hos dies sileant, quae cum Christi praedicatores significent, ideo earum sonum intermitti, quod apostoli Christum in maximis cruciatibus passionis, arrepta fuga, deseruerint* (Benedict XIV, p. 125, n. 48). When relating the Savior's life, we noted the circumstance that he returned thanks after his repast, *hymno dicto*. St. Chrysostom is very severe on those who fail in the duty of prayer before and after meals: *Audiant omnes qui quasi porci cum jam comederint, eversa calcibus mensa, temulenti, consurgunt, cum agere gratias debeant, et in hymnum a mensa devenire* (*Homily on Matthew*, n. 83).

695 Cf. Thomassin, *Fest.*, Bk. 2, Ch. 13

696 Benedicimus autem et aquam baptismatis et oleum unctionis, imo ipsum etiam qui baptismum accipit. Ex quibus scriptis? Nonne a tacita secretaque traditione? (Basil, *De Spiritu Sancto*, Ch. 27; Cf. Benedict XIV, p. 134, n. 61).

697 We should read the details in the *Pontifical*. Everything there is interesting: the words, the chant, the ceremonies. See also Durandus, *Rationale divinorum officiorum*, Bk. 7, Ch. 74.

698 Cf. Le Vicomte Walsh, *Tableau poétique des fêtes Chrétiennes*, p. 135

699 Cf. Durandus, *Rationale divinorum officiorum*, Bk. 6, Ch. 76

700 Jn 13:13-15; Cf. Benedict XIV, p. 126, n. 49

701 Mt 5:23-24

702 Le Pére de Géramb, *Pèlerinage à Jerusalem*, t. 2

703 Cf. Eusebius, *Ecclesiastical History*, Bk. 2, Ch. 17

704 Cf. Leo the Great, t. 2, p. 77

705 Cf. Durandus, *Rationale divinorum officiorum*, Bk. 6, *De die Parasceve*

706 Here is the portrait of our Lord as preserved for us by antiquity:

He had a most beautiful countenance, full of life. He was above the middle height. His hair was a little yellow, not very thick, and gently curling. His eyebrows were black and slightly arched. From his clear olive eyes, there beamed something most admirable. His nose was long. His beard resembled his hair, and was of moderate size. His hair was pretty long; for no razor had ever passed over his head, nor any person's hand save his Mother's during his infancy. His neck bent forward a little, so that there was nothing at all stiff or formal in his carriage. His complexion inclined toward the color of gold or wheat. His face was neither round nor sharp, but like his Mother's, a little long and a little ruddy: gravity, prudence, mildness, and peace shone wonderfully in it. To conclude, he was in all respects exceedingly like his divine and immaculate Mother.

Egregio is vividoque vultu fuit. Corporis statura ad palmos prorsus septem. Caesariem habuit subflavam et non admodum densam, leniter quodammodo ad crispos declinantem: supercilia nigra, non perinde inflexa. Ex oculis subflavescentibus mirifica prominebat gratia. Acres ii erant et nasus longior. Barbae capillus flavus, nec admodum dimissus. Capitis porro capillos tulit prolixiores. Novacula enim in caput ejus non ascendit, neque manus aliqua nominis, praeterquam matris in tenera duntaxat aetate ejus. Collum fuit sensim declive, ita ut non arduo et extento nimium corporis statu esset. Porro tritici referres colorem; non rotundam aut acutam habuit faciem: sed qualis matris ejus erat, paullum deorsum versus vergentem ac modice rubicundam: gravitatem atque prudentiam cum lenitate conjunctam, placabilitatemque iracundiae expertem prae se ferentem. Persimilis denique per omnia fuit divinae et immaculatae suae Genetrici (Nicephorus Callistus, *Historia Ecclesiastica*, Bk. 1, Ch. 40). On the proofs of the authenticity of this portrait, see Sandini, *Hist. Famil. sacr.*, Ch. 17, p. 287.

707 Cf. Durandus, *Rationale divinorum officiorum*, Bk. 6, *De die Parasceve*

708 Cf. Leo the Great, *Epist.*, t. 2, p. 77

709 Lk 23:34

710 It is almost needless to say that Catholics do not adore the cross, but the God who died on the cross.

711 Moreover, according to Benedict XIV, she makes allusion to an event related in the Menology of the Greeks. It is there said that, under the reign of Theodosius, an earthquake brought Constantinople to the brink of ruin; that the emperor and the patriarch prostrated themselves, imploring mercy by repeating the *Kyrie eleison*; and that a child was lifted up into the air—fell, crying out to the people to sing the trisagion, *Sanctus Deus, sanctus fortis, sanctus immortails*—and then died. This prayer became very general in the Eastern Church. The Latin Church adopted it.—*Ea vero hac die praesertim utitur latine, ut propriam suam linguam adhibeat. Graece vero etiam, ut alludet illi divinae voci quam puerum illum diximus Constantinopoli edidisse* (*De Festis*, p. 251, n. 136).

712 Cf. Le Vicomte Walsh, *Tableau poétique des fêtes Chrétiennes*, p. 150. See, on all the ceremonies of Holy Week, the *Trois Rome*.

713 Translator's note: To know how much may be done by prayer for the salvation of souls, see *Apostleship of Prayer*, by Father Ramiere, S.J.

714 See Bellarmine's work, *De septem verbis*, etc., and St. Liguori's *Passion according to the Four Evangelists*.

715 On half-festivals, the obligation of ceasing from servile work did not begin till noon.

716 See Thomassin.

717 Cf. Père Menard, *Catechis.*, p. 91

718 The reason why ancient authors call this office *lucernarium* (Mabil., *Musae ital.*, t. 2, p. 101).

719 Cf. Durandus, *Rationale divinorum officiorum*, Bk. 6, Ch. 80

720 We know that *canon* means "rule." This pillar was the canon or rule for celebrating Easter and the movable festivals connected therewith.

721 Zozimus papa decrevit cereum Sabbato Sancto Paschae, per ecclesias benedici (Sigebertus, Anno 417).

722 Cf. Ennod, p. 453

723 Cf. Benedict XIV, p. 292, n. 59

724 Cf. Durandus, *Rationale divinorum officiorum*, Bk. 6, Ch. 80

725 Cf. Père Menard, *Catechis.*, p. 98; Ennod., p. 73; Ferraris, *Biblioth.*, art. *Agnus Dei*; *Trois Rome*

726 Cf. Cyril of Jerusalem, *Catechetical Lecture 3*, n. 3; Cyprian, *Epistle 69 to Januarius*, n. 1

727 Cf. Gregorian Sacramentary; Roman Ordo

728 In regard to all these ceremonies, see our treatise on *L'eau bénite.*

729 Ps 116

730 Translator's note: The French word for Easter is *Pâques*. The opening remarks of this lesson come more naturally therefore in French than in English.

731 Cf. Rom 6:4

732 Cf. Benedict XIV, p. 302, n. 7

733 Gregory the Great, *Homily 22 on the Gospels*

734 Jn 13:35

735 Cf. Rupert, *De Div. Offic.*, Bk. 7, Ch. 20, 24, 25; Durandus, *Rationale divinorum officiorum*, Bk. 6, Ch. 86

736 Editor's note: See Volume XI of the Tradivox series, p. 69-74.

737 Cf. Durandus, *Rationale divinorum officiorum*, Bk. 6, Ch. 89

738 Ex 15:1

739 Mt 28:6

740 Chrysostom, *Homily, de Resurrect.*

741 Quia quidquid in Ecclesia prima die, praesertim quod ad neophytos attinet, fieri solebat, idem per reliquos hebdomadae dies factitabatur (Martène, *De antiq. Eccles. discipl. in celebr. div. offic.*, Ch. 25, n. 25).

742 Cf. Durandus, *Rationale divinorum officiorum*, Bk. 6, Ch. 89; Thomassin, *Célébration des Fêtes*, Bk. 2, Ch. 16

743 Optime advertit Suarez, si haec festivitas in se consideretur, magnae eam esse dignitatis inter solemnitates quae ad Christi humanitatem pertinent. Sed quoniam non prius perfecte illius modi collatum est donum, quam B. Virgo peperit, inde includit, Natalis Christi diem festum praecipue ad Jesum, Annuntiationem ad B. Virginem attinere, cui Ecclesia hujus diei officium ecclesiasticum dirigit (Benedict XIV, *De Festis*, p. 444, n. 1).

744 "The belief of a Virgin Mother of God was general among the nations of antiquity." (See *Harmonie de l'Eglise et de la Synagogue*, t. 2, by M. Drach. On account of certain details regarding morals, this learned work must be read with caution.)

745 Lk 1:30-32

746 Responde jam, Virgo Sacra, vitam quid tardas mundo? (Augustine, *Sermon 21, de Temp.*).

747 Lk 1:38

748 Jn 4:10

749 In Galilaeae civitate Nazareth annuntiatio sanctae Mariae de Conceptione, quando ab angelo est salutata (Benedict XIV, p. 456, n. 18).

750 Sicut a majoribus traditum, suscipiens Ecclesiae custodit auctoritas, octavo kalendas Apriles conceptus creditur (Augustine, *On the Trinity*, Bk. 4, Ch. 5).

751 *Marie, étoile de la mer*, p. 61, 96.

752 See what we said when explaining the *Ave Maria*, Volume II, Lesson 31 [i.e., Volume XI of the Tradivox series, p. 210-215]. Also Baronius, Anno 431.

753 Si quis veniat ad Matrem Domini, dicens: *Ave Maria*, numquid poterit ei gratiam denegare? (Ricard., art. *Virt.*).

754 There is an indulgence of a hundred days each time that the *Angelus* is recited, and a plenary indulgence once a month for those who recite the *Angelus* daily. Persons who live in community and, on account of

the occupations prescribed by their rule, cannot recite the *Angelus* at the sound of the bell, gain the indulgence by reciting the *Angelus* as soon as they have ended their occupations. It is the same with such of the faithful as, not hearing the bell, recite the *Angelus* about the usual time when the bell rings.—During the jubilee, the indulgences of the *Angelus* are not suspended (*Raccolta*, etc., p. 259ff., edit. 1841).

We shall here add a few details that will not be uninteresting.

During the jubilee or the holy year, all indulgences, plenary as well as partial, and even perpetual, are suspended at Rome and everywhere else, with the following exceptions:

1. Indulgences granted at the point of death.

2. Those of seven years and seven quarantines granted to persons who visit the Blessed Sacrament in a church where it is exposed during the Forty Hours.

3. Those granted to persons who accompany the holy viaticum or supply candles for accompanying it.

4. Those of privileged altars for the dead.

5. Those granted directly for the dead.

6. Those granted to the living, with the express faculty of applying them to the dead, but available only for the dead.

7. Those granted to the living, even without the express faculty of applying them to the dead, but available only for the dead.

(Ferraris, art. *Jubil.*, art. 3).

755 *Suttee* is the name given to an Indian woman who is burnt alive on a pile with the corpse of her husband. For some years, the English government has severely prohibited this cruel sacrifice; but it has not succeeded in totally abolishing the custom. In 1868 and 1869, the suttee was still mentioned, not far from Benares. It would seem that there are no longer any widows burnt but such as ask it.

756 For other details, see *Histoire de la Société Domestique*, t. 1, and Volume II of the catechism [i.e., Volume XI of the Tradivox series].

757 *Raccolta*, etc., p. 3ff

758 M. de Sambucy, *Manuel du Scapulaire*, p. 28

759 M. de Sambucy, *Manuel du Scapulaire*, p. 20

760 Hoc erit tibi et cunctis Carmelitis privilegium; in hoc moriens aeternum non patietur incendium (Theophil. Reynaud, t. 7).

761 Arbitramur enim hominem justificari per fidem (Rom 3:28). Spe enim salvi facti sumus (Rom 8:24).—Eleemosyna a morte liberat (Tb 12:9).—Saepe numero scriptura divina tribuit vim justificandi aut etiam salvandi diversis rebus, non quod solae illae justificari aut salvare possint, sed quod illae vim suam habeant ad justificationem aut salutem, et ad eum finem perducant, si tamen caetera non desint (Bellarmine, *Controv.*, t. 4, Bk. 2, *de Poenit.*, Ch. 7).

762 Fratres, conservando verbum istud in cordibus vestris, satagite electionem vestram certam facere per bona opera et nunquam deficere (Apud Benedict XIV, p. 447, n. 8).

763 Ego Mater gloriosa descendam sabbato post eorum mortem, et quos invenero in purgatorio, liberabo, et eos in montem sanctum vitae aeternae reducam (Bull of John XXII, apud Benedict XIV, n. 7).

764 Omnipotentia supplex.

765 Cf. Benedict XIV, p. 479. One of the most learned popes that ever ruled the Church, Benedict XIV, supports and establishes the truth of the apparition of the Blessed Virgin to the blessed Simon. (See *De Canonis. Sanct.*, t. 4, Pt. 2, p. 74.) And in his treatise *De Festis*, p. 446, n. 8, he expresses himself thus: *Visionem quidem veram credimus, veramque habendam ab omnibus arbitramur*. For the authenticity of the bull, see *De Festis*, p. 478, n. 9-10.

766 For others see *Manuel du Scapulaire* by M. de Sambucy, p. 100 et suiv. This excellent work has supplied us with many of the details that we give here regarding the scapular.—*Cum denique, Beata Virgine intercedente, plura Deus miracula ediderit in eorum utilitatem, qui huic devoto cultui sunt addicti*, says Benedict XIV (p. 479).

767 M. de Sambucy, *Manuel du Scapulaire*, p. 105 et suiv.

768 Besides the two great privileges of which we have spoken, there are many rich indulgences attached to the devotion of the scapular, so much have sovereign pontiffs had at heart the favoring of it. Here are some of them: a plenary indulgence on the day of reception, on the festival of Our Lady of Mount Carmel, on one Sunday each month, and at the hour of death. To gain these indulgences, it is necessary to pray for the intentions of the sovereign pontiff: with this view, one may say five *Paters* and *Aves* (M. de Sambucy, *Manuel du Scapulaire*, p. 197).

769 It is forbidden to carry the scapular sewed in a pocket or elsewhere in the clothes.

770 Persons who are bound to recite the office of the Church by reason of a benefice, a state, a vow, or a penance imposed, satisfy the obligation of the scapular at the same time, without being bound to recite it a second time.

771 The priest who has power to give the scapular has not therefore power to commute its obligations. The Congregation of Indulgences has decided a) that it is necessary to ask and to have a special power in order to commute the commutable obligations of the holy scapular, and b) that, as regards the past, the Holy See ratifies whatever French priests, with power to bless and to give the holy scapular, have done by commuting in good faith the obligations of those whom they clothed with this holy habit.

"*Beatissime Pater, Ludovicus de Sambucy, canonicus Parisiensis et vicarious generalis San-Briocensis, Sanctitatis Vestrae orator humillimus, suppliciter expostulat responsum ad dubia gravis momenti. In Gallia, nullus adest conventus hominum ordinis Carmeli, et apparent rari hujus religionis patres: tres tantum noti adsunt in parte meridionali vastissimi regni. Inde molestissima exorta est controversia, quae magnam animis perturbationem affert paucis abhinc mensibus.*

"*Usque adhuc omnes persuasum habuerant sacerdotem, cui Sanctitas Vestra dederat benedicendi et fidelibus parva scapularia imponendi facultatem, eo ipso inclusam obtinuisse facultatem commutandi unicuique aliquas hujus confraternitatis obligationes commutabiles vice confessarii Carmelitani omnino deficientis, quidam nunc negant et huic opinioni palam obsistunt et adversantur; quapropter a Paternitate Vestra quaeritur:*

"*1. An sacerdos, qui obtinet, ut supra, facultatem benedicendi ac imponendi scapularia, habeat eo ipsos facultatem commutandi obligationes commutabiles confratrum, quando opus est, scilicet cum recursus ad alterum sit impossibilis, ut hoc commodo fideles non priventur;*

"*2. Si vero sacerdotes Galliae, falsae innixi suppositioni, commutaverunt, absque facultatibus opportunis, obligationes confratrum, supplices nunc adeunt S. V., ut dignetur sanare, ut dicitur, in radice, omnes commutationes, et unicuique impertiri facultatem specialem commutandi, si opus sit, obligationes confratrum scapularis. Et Deus, etc.*

Sacra Congregatio indulgentiis sacrisque reliquiis praeposita ad praefata dubia respondit:

"*1. Ad primum (negative); vigore enim obtentae facultatis benedicendi ac imponendi scapularia, non sequitur quod sacerdos ea quoque gaudeat potestate commutandi obligationes injunctas, nisi expresse enuntietur in rescripto concessionis pro benedictione et impositione scapularium; at vero in una Bisuntina, sub die 12 augusti, 1840, ab haec S. Congregatione responsum fuit: 'Accedente gravi impedimento, non teneri Confratres neque ad jejunia, neque ad recitationem horarum canonicarum aut officii B. M. V., neque ad abstinentiam diebus mercurii et sabbati. Consulendi tamen fideles, hoc in casu se subjiciant judicio docti et prudentis confessarii pro aliqua commutatione im petranda.'*

"*2. Ad secundum, jam provisum fuit in primo: et quatenus opus sit, sanctissimus Dominus noster Gregorius papa XVI, sanabit quemcumque defectum huc usque incursum circa obligationum commutationem; dummodo tamen sacerdotes bona gesserint fide. In quorum fidem, etc.*

"*Datum Romae ex secretaria ejusdem S. Congregationis, die 22 junii 1842.*

"*Signatum: C. Card. Castracane, praefectus;*

"*A. Canonicus Prinzivalli, substitutus.*"

772 We also recommend most earnestly the blue scapular, or that of the Immaculate Conception, the richest in indulgences, when one, wearing it, recites daily six *Paters*, *Aves*, and *Glorias*.

773 *Ex quo tempore pius hic orandi modus mirabiliter per S. Dominicum promulgari augerique coepit, quem ejusdem institutorem auctoremque fuisse summi pontifices apostolicis litteris affirmarunt. Sunt autem Leo X, S. Pius V, Greg. XIII, Sixtus V, Alexand. VII, Innocent. XI, Clem. XI, etc.* (Benedict XIV, p. 523, n. 3).—As regards beads, they were in use long before St. Dominic's time: they are already to be found with the solitaries in the first ages of the Church (Cf. Benedict XIV, p. 524, n. 8).

774 Eodem die commemoratio S. Mariae de Victoria, quam Pius V pontifex maximus, ob insignem victoriam a Christianis bello navali, ejusdem Dei Genetricis auxilio, hac ipsa die de Turcis reportatam, quotannis fieri instituit (*Martyrol. Rom.*, 1 Oct.).

775 See *Manuel du Rosaire*, by M. de Sambucy, p. 73, and Benedict XIV, p. 528, n. 17.

776 It is a pleasure to us here to point out a new devotion to Mary, namely, the Archconfraternity of the Immaculate Heart of the Holy Virgin for the Conversion of Sinners. It was founded in Paris in 1836, by M. Desgenettes, curé of Notre-Dame des Victoires. A miraculous thing; it already counts more than a million members! *A Domino factum est istud.* No, no: France, the kingdom of Mary, will not perish!

777 Chateaubriand, *Génie du Christianisme, Rogations*, t. 3, p. 157

778 Ibid.

779 Cf. 1 Cor 3:6

780 This pious custom exists in a good many dioceses.

781 Cf. M. Thirat, *Esprit des Cérémonies de l'Eglise*, p. 215

782 The procession of St. Mark's day, which occurs in spring, was, like those of the Rogation days, established to draw down the blessings of heaven on the fruits of the earth.

783 Prayer is all-powerful on earth, because it is all-powerful in heaven. Such is the belief of all peoples, manifested by their invariable conduct. God, who unceasingly directs the movements of nature, says to the sun, "March!" Josue, on the contrary, cries out to it, "Halt!" Josue triumphs over the command received from the immortal throne, and the deity, whose goodness is beyond all comprehension, yields, and obeys the word of faith, which ascends to it from the heart of man: *Obediente Deo voci hominis.*

784 Pluviam voluntariam segregabis, Deus, haereditati tuae (Ps 67:10).

785 See *Soirées de Saint-Petersbourg*, t. 1. iv *entretien.*

786 See *Histoire des Fêtes Chrétiennes.*—In many dioceses, the abstinence itself no longer exists. To avoid too many prevarications, the bishops thought it necessary to ask a dispensation regarding these days from the sovereign pontiff. Such is the religious progress of our period!

787 On this matter, see Baronius, Annal., Anno 590, p. 4.

788 Cf. *Traité des Fêtes mobiles*, t. 2, p. 99

789 Cf. Acts 10:38

790 Le Vicomte Walsh, *Tableau poétique des fêtes Chrétiennes*, p. 220

791 Cf. Cornelius a Lapide, *On Luke*, Ch. 24

792 Mt 28:18-20

793 Cf. Lk 24:48-49

794 Jn 16:7

795 Cf. Thomassin, *Célébrat. des fêtes*

796 Cf. *Apostolic Constitutions*, Bk. 5, Ch. 19

797 Acts 1:11

798 Cf. Jerome, t. 3, p. 295; Sulpicius Severus, *Historia Sacra*, Bk. 2, Ch. 48; Paulinus of Nola, *Epistle 30 to Severus*; Optatus of Milevis, Bk. 6, p. 55

799 Ibi sunt vestigia ejus, modo adorantur, ubi novissime stetit, unde ascendit in coelum (Augustine, *Tractate 47 on John*, n. 4; Cf. Benedict XIV, p. 332, n. 53).

800 Jerome, t. 3, p. 295

801 Cf. Adamnan., *in Act. SS. Benedict., lib. de locis sanctis.*

802 Bernard, *Sermon 2, On the Ascension*, n. 3. Regarding the saints who ascended, body and soul, into heaven with our Lord, see our *Histoire du Bon Larron.*

803 St. Augustine says positively that the festival of the Ascension comes from the apostles (Cf. *Epistle 54*, Ch. 1).

804 Bernard, *Sermon 3, On the Ascension*

805 Jn 16:7

806 Ps 103:30

807 1 Jn 2:1-2

808 Apud Thomassin, Bk. 2, n. 10

809 Cf. Apud Thomassin, Bk. 2, n. 10-11

810 Illa autem quae non scripta, sed tradita custodimus, quae quidem toto terrarum orbe servantur, dantur intelligi vel ab ipsis Apostolis, vel plenariis conciliis, quorum est in Ecclesia saluberrima auctoritas, commendata atque statuta retineri, sicut quod Domini Passio, Resurrectio et Ascensio in coelum et adventus Spiritus sancti anniversaria solemnitate celebrantur, et si quid occurrit, quod observatur ab universa, quacumque se diffundit, Ecclesia (Augustine, *Epistle 54*, Ch. 1).

811 Consummatio et adimpletio est reliquarum solemnitatum, et felix clausula totius itinerarii Filii Dei (Bernard, *Sermon 2, On the Ascension*).

812 Eusebius, *Life of Constantine*, Bk. 4, Ch. 44

813 Ibid.

814 Cf. Durandus, *Rationale divinorum officiorum*, Bk. 6, Ch. 206

815 *Sermon 60, sub Ambros. nomine inter Ambrosiana.*—Nullum antiquitus inter Pascha et Pentecostem fuisse jejunium; sed consequuta sunt tempora, cum laudabilis invecta est jejunandi consuetudo in pervigilio Pentecostes (Benedict XIV, p. 334, n. 38).

816 Cf. Dn 6:10

817 Cf. Acts 1:13; 12:12. The empress Helena built a magnificent church at the very place where the Holy Ghost had descended on them (Cf. Quaresmus, Bk. 4, *Elucid. Terrae Sanctae*, Ch. 5).

818 Cf. Acts 2:2

819 According to a very general belief, it was on the day of Pentecost, immediately after the miracle of the descent of the Holy Ghost, who, by giving birth to the Church, abolished the synagogue, that St. Peter celebrated the first Mass, as a solemn inauguration of Christianity. *Verisimilior Cardinalis Bonae sententia est* (*Rer. Liturg.*, Bk. 1, Ch. 5), *qui dicit et existimat ab apostolis primae missae celebrationem fuisse protractam usque ad Pentecostem, cum divino Sancti Spiritus haustu sunt repleti; vetus enim viguit lex usque ad Pentecostem: nam nova lex ante Pentecostem nondum satis promulgata habebatur: quamobrem, sacerdotio nondum translato, non decebat novum sacrificium offerri, ut nos etiam docuimus* (*Instit.*, n. 21; Benedict 14, p. 356, n. 42).

820 Cf. Ps 112:3

821 On all the circumstances of the festival of Pentecost, see our *Traite Saint-Esprit*, t. 2.

822 Chrysostom, *Homily 4 on Acts*

823 Here is a proof of it: a fact related by a missionary, who for several years past has been evangelizing the prisons of France:

There was one man, the remembrance of whom is so deeply imprinted on my soul that I can never forget him; a man whom I place above all missionaries, above all religious: it is a saint that I venerate. And this man, this saint is a convict.

One evening he came to me in the confessional, and, after his confession, I put a few questions to him, as I do very often to these poor people. However, a more special motive induced me to question this man. I had been struck by the calm expression of his countenance. I did not at first pay very much attention thereto, for I had already had occasion to remark the same thing in many of his class. But the precision with which he spoke, and the laconic character of his answers, excited my curiosity more and more.

He answered me unaffectedly, never employing a useless word or going beyond what I had asked him. Thus it was only by urging my questions that I came to know, in a few simple words, his interesting history.

"How old are you?" I said first.

"Forty-five years, Father."

"How long have you been here?"

"Ten years."

"Are you to remain long yet?"

"All my life, Father."

"What were you condemned for?"

"The crime of arson."

"No doubt, my poor friend, you are very sorry for having committed such a crime."

"I offended God much, Father; but I never committed that crime. However, I was justly condemned; but it was God who condemned me."

This answer exciting my curiosity very much, I went on: "What then have you to say for yourself, my friend? Explain yourself."

He answered me: "I offended the good God much, Father. I was very guilty, but never against society. After many wanderings, the good God touched my heart.

"I resolved to be converted, and to repair the past; but after my conversion, there remained an uneasiness with me, a dreadful weight on my heart. I had offended the good God so much! Could I expect that he had forgotten all? And, then, I met with nothing of a nature to atone for the wretched iniquities of my youth, and I felt a great need of reparation! Meanwhile, a fire occurred near the place where I lived. All suspicions fell on me. I was arrested and tried. During the trial, I was much calmer than I had ever been before. I clearly foresaw that I should be condemned; but I was ready for all. At length, the day of passing sentence on me came. The jury left the court to consult on my fate; and, at the same moment, I seemed to hear a voice within me, saying: "If I condemn thee, I will also take thy happiness upon me, and I will give thee peace." Thereupon, I really began to feel a delicious peace in my soul.

"The jury soon returned, bringing in their verdict, which declared me guilty, with extenuating circumstances. I was sentenced for life. I could hardly refrain from weeping, which, without a doubt, would have had no other motive than the happiness that I then experienced. I was led away to my cell, and here, falling on the straw that served me as a bed, I poured out such a flood of sweet tears that the most luxurious man in the world would have been glad to purchase at the cost of all his enjoyments the happiness of shedding them. An ineffable peace filled my soul. It did not leave me all along the road I traveled to reach the galleys, and has never left me since.

"Since that time, I have endeavored to fulfill all my duties well, to obey everyone in everything. In those who command me, from the governor to the ganger, I see God alone. Wherever I go, I pray—at work, at the oar; I pray always, and time passes so quickly that I scarcely notice it: hours glide away like minutes. Nobody knows me; I am supposed to have been condemned justly, and that is true.

"Neither do you know me, Father. I have not told you my name nor my number. Only pray for me, Father, that I may do the will of God to the end."

Thus did the man speak. I saw him only once, the evening that he came like the others to receive absolution. I have since endeavored to find him out again, but in vain; he escapes my search. He likewise escapes the search of the chaplain, to whom I have related these interesting details. I have returned twice to the prison, and it is always in failure that my efforts to see the man again end. He is invisible for me; but I feel myself inwardly united to him, and the remembrance of him is deeply engraven on my soul.

824 Cf. *Catéchisme de Couturier*, t, 1.—Pope Innocent III, who died in 1216, is generally supposed to have been the author of this prose. Others claim the honor for B. Hermann Contractus, a monk of Merrow, who died in 1054. See Benedict XIV, *De Festis*, p. 355, n. 41.

825 Scilicet hic amor est proprios effusus in ignes.
Placido qui fulminat ictu.

826 Jn 16:7

827 Prv 16:4

828 Mt 28:19

829 Cf. Thomassin, *Fêtes*, Bk. 2, Ch. 18

830 Proprio Filio suo non pepercit: per Spiritum Sanctum semetipsum obtulit immaculatum Deo (Rom 8:32; Heb 9:14).

831 Quem suscitavit a mortuis, qui praedestinatus est Filius Dei in virtute suâ secundum Spiritum sanctificationis ex resurrectione mortuorum Jesu Christi (1 Thes 1:10; Rom 1:4).

832 Praeterea festivitas sanctissimae Trinitatis secundum consuetudines diversarum regionum a quibusdam consuevit in octavis Pentecostes, ab aliis in dominica prima ante Adventum Domini celebrari. Ecclesia siquidem Romana in usu non habet, quod in aliquo tempore hujusmodi celebret specialiter festivitatem, cum singulis diebus gloria Patri et Filio et Spiritui Sancto, et caetera similia dicantur ad laudem pertinentia Trinitatis (*Decretal. Quoniam Tit. de Feriis*).

833 Bk. 2, Div. Offic.

834 Cf. Durandus, *Rationale divinorum officiorum*, Bk. 6, Ch. 86

835 Cf. Mabillon, *Musoeum ital.*, t. 2, p. 103

836 Cf. Thomassin, Bk. 2, Ch. 18

837 Sermonem in capitulo propter materiae difficultatem fieri non oportet.

838 Cf. Gn 1:26; 3:22; 11:7; 19:24; Ps 2:2; 109:1; Heb 10:5; M. Drach, *Harmonie de l'Eglise et de la Synag.*, t. 1

839 On images of the Blessed Trinity in creatures, see St. Augustine's magnificent treatise *On the Trinity*.

840 Lv 11:44

841 Mt 5:48; Cf. Mt 5:44-45

842 Jn 17:21; 13:35

843 Cf. Eph 4:5

844 This prayer is of apostolic tradition (Cf. Benedict XIV, p. 358, n. 6).

845 Cf. *Raccolta d'indulg.*, p. 5, Roma, 1841

846 See M. de Maistre, *Eclaircissements sur les sacrifices*.

847 Cf. 1 Cor 1:27

848 Cf. 1 Tm 1:17

849 Cf. Benedict XIV, p. 362, n. 6

850 Rainauld, Ch. 26

851 *Proprium ejusdem solemnitatis officium per B. Thomam de Aquino tunc in ipsa Curia existentem compositum edidit* (Bull. Sixtus IV. Apud Benedict XIV, p. 366, n. 2). See the miracle with which St. Thomas was favored after composing the office of the Blessed Sacrament, in the *Trois Rome*, t. 2. Here is an anecdote on the subject, which it would grieve us to pass over in silence.

When Urban IV had decided on the establishment of the festival of Corpus Christi, he wished that its office should be composed by the most learned and pious men. He sent for two of the most admirable characters of the age: the angelic Thomas and the seraphic Bonaventure. "Brethren," he says to them, "I want to establish, throughout the whole Church, the greatest and most touching solemnity: I want to celebrate the sacrament of love and mercy." He immediately informs the two religious of his plan, and orders them to set to work. These men of God, full of humility, are astonished at the pontiff's choice. They resist; but in vain. At an appointed time, they are to submit their work to him who, better than any other, is able to judge of it.

On the day fixed by Urban IV, Thomas and Bonaventure make their appearance, with modesty in their looks and distrust of themselves in their hearts.

"Begin, Brother Thomas," says the pope.

The holy religious reads the antiphons of the various parts of the office, the lessons, and the responses: all were taken from the holy scripture and with marvelous judgment. Urban observes silence. Bonaventure cannot refrain from a gesture of approbation, but soon represses his feelings out of respect.

Thomas passes on to the hymn at matins, *Sacris solemniis*. He reaches this admirable strophe:

Panis angelicus fit panis hominum,
Dat panis coelicus figuris terminum.
O res mirabilis! manducat Dominum
Pauper, servus et humilis.

Tears flow from Bonaventure's eyes. Paper is heard rustling under his robe, and its fragments fall to the ground.

At the hymn for lauds, how majestic is the opening!

Verbum supernum prodiens
Nec Patris linquens dexteram
Ad opus suum exiens,
Venit ad vitae vesperam.

What faith and sweetness in the following strophe!

O salutaris hostia
Quae coeli pandis ostium,
Bella premunt hostilia;
Da robur, fer auxilium.
* * * *
Qui vitam sine termino
Nobis donet in patriâ.

Brother Bonaventure's delight can hardly contain itself: new pieces of paper fall at the holy monk's feet.

The reading of the prose seems to engage the special attention of Urban. A learned theologian, he finds in the *Lauda Sion* a whole treatise of the most sublime theology on the mystery of the day.

Thomas ends with the *Pange lingua*, whose fourth and fifth strophes are a summary of doctrine on the sacrament of the Eucharist. He ceases to speak, and there is listening again. At length the pope says, "It is now your turn, Brother Bonaventure!" The religious falls at the pontiff's feet and exclaims: "Most Holy Father, when I heard Brother Thomas, it seemed to me as if I heard the Holy Ghost. He alone can have inspired such beautiful thoughts: they have been revealed to my brother Thomas by a special grace of the Most High. Shall I dare to acknowledge it to you, most Holy Father?—I would have thought it a sacrilege to let my poor work exist by the side of such wonderful beauties. Here, most Holy Father, are the remains of it." And the monk showed the pope the pieces of paper that covered the floor.

The pontiff admired the modesty of Bonaventure as much as the genius of Thomas. Such were the noble figures of those Middle Ages which are so often decried; such were the saints of that divine Church which civilized the world, by letting the truth shine on men.

Behold what occurred in the thirteenth century! Nearly six hundred years have since rolled by, and the admirable work of St. Thomas is still the ornament of the Roman Breviary. Permanence belongs only to the works of God.

852 On the festival of Corpus Christi, see *Histoire de la Fête-Dieu* by Père Bertholet and that by Père Fisen; St. Antoninus, *Summa*; and Thomassin, t. 2, Ch. 19.

853 Cf. Council of Trent, Session 13, "Decree concerning the Most Holy Sacrament of the Eucharist," Ch. 5. This procession seems to have taken its rise from that which was made in bringing the miraculous

corporal from Bolsena to Orvieto. *Attonitus pontifex ad se ab episcopo loci cum processione Urbemveterem (corporale) transferri voluit, et illud, solemnitate instituta, in Ecclesia Urbevetere recondidit. Probabilissima est eorum sententia qui e re ipsa putant hanc processionem esse profectam* (Benedict XIV, p. 366, n. 10).

854 Lk 9:54

855 Lk 23:34

856 Quam charitatem Christi patientis...ut fideles sub sanctissimi Cordis symbolo devotius et ferventius recolant ejusdemque fructus uberius percipiant, Clemens XIII P. M. ejusdem sanctissimi Cordis festum quibusdam petentibus ecclesiis celebrare permisit (*Lec.* 3, *secundi noct.*).

857 Cor Jesu, charitatis victimam, venite, adoremus. (See Muzarelli.)

858 Cf. Aquinas, *Opusculum, On the Motion of the Heart*

859 1 Kgs 2:35

860 See *Devotion and Worship of the Sacred Heart*, by Muzarelli. We have followed this learned theologian in the explanations just given.

861 Cf. *Mois du Sacré-Coeur*, p. 51

862 Cf. 1 Cor 1:27

863 Mgr. Languet, archbishop of Sens, *Vie de la B. Marg.-Marie*, Bk. 4, n. 57

864 Cf. Mgr. Languet, *Vie de la B. Marg.-Marie*, Bk. 6, n. 90; Bk. 7, n. 93

865 Acts 4:20

866 See his letter to the bishop of Pistoja.

867 Cf. Nouet. See also the sermons of M. Legris-Duval.

868 See *Dévotion pratique au Sacré-Coeur.*

869 Cf. *Raccolta d'indulg.*, p. 210

870 We may use for this purpose an excellent little work entitled *Month of the Sacred Heart of Jesus.*

871 See Thomassin, Bk. 2, Ch. 20.

872 Cf. Council of Bale, Session 43. See Spond., Anno 1389, n. 1, et Anno 1141, n. 3; Benedict IV, p. 740, n. 9.

873 Lk 1:39-40.—Numquid forte dubiam adhuc et incredulam oraculo, recentiore voluit confirmare miraculo? absit. Sedi deo sterilis cognatae conceptus Virgini nuntiatur, ut dum miraculum miraculo additur, gaudium gaudio cumuletur (Bernard, *Homily 4, Sup. missus*; Ambrose, *On Luke*, Bk. 2).

874 Cf. Baronius, *Apparat.* ad *Annal. eccles.*, n. 77-78

875 Cf. *Spect.*, Ch. 54

876 Lk 1:39

877 Lk 1:56

878 Bonaventure, *In Prolog. Cant. B. V.*, Ch. 1

879 Lk 1:42

880 Lk 1:43

881 Lk 1:44-45

882 Velocior est nonnunquam salus nostra, invocato nomine Mariae quam invocato nomine Jesu (*De excell., Virg.*, Ch. 6).

883 Cf. Bk. 1, Ch. 5

884 Lk 1:46, 48. See a justificatory explanation of Mary's canticle in Canisius, *De Maria V. Deipara*, Bk. 4, Ch. 7-8.

885 Cf. Benedict XIV, p. 493, 495

886 Sanctissimum corpus clarissimo praestantissimoque tumulo imponitur, unde triduo post in coelum attollitur...Sicuti sanctum incorruptumque illud corpus, quod Deus ex ea personae suae copulaverat, tertia die e monomento surrexit, sic etiam hanc e tumulo abripi, matremque ad filium migrare par erat (John Damascene, *Oration 2, De Dormit. Mariae*, n. 14).—Dominus susceptum Virginis corpus sacratissimum in paradisum deferri jussit, ubi nunc, resumpta anima cum electis ejus exultans, aeternitatis bonis nullo occasuris fine perfruitur (Gregory of Tours, *De Miracul.*, Ch. 4).—Sententiam assumptionis Virginis in corpore et anima in coelum non esse de fide; quia neque eat ab Ecclesia definita, neque est testimonium

Scripturae, aut sufficiens traditio, quae infallibilem faciat fidem; tamen summae temeritatis reus crederetur, qui tam piam religiosamque sententiam hodie impugnaret (Suarez, Pt. 3, q. 37, art. 4, disp. 25, sect. 11.—Bened. XIV, p. 491, n. 5).

887 Cf. Cedrenus; *Compt. Hist.*, Nicephorus, Bk. 2, Ch. 21; Metaphrases, *de Dormit. Mar.*

888 Cf. Metaphrastes and Gregory of Tours

889 Cf. Le Vicomte Walsh, *Tableau poétique des fêtes Chrétiennes*, p. 339

890 Cf. Benedict XIV, p. 505, n. 27, 29

891 Cf. Council of Mainz, in 813, Can. 3, 6

892 Cf. Benedict XIV, p. 501, n. 23

893 Ascendit Salvator in coelum potestativae virtutis imperio, sicut Dominus et Creator angelorum comitatus obsequio, non auxilio fultus. Assumpta est Maria in coelum, sed gratiae sublevantis indicio, comitantibus et auxiliantibus angelis, quam sublevabat gratia non natura (Peter Damian, *Sermon on the Assumption*).

894 Ps 131:8

895 Cf. Cant 2:10-11; 4:8

896 See Alphonsus Liguori, *Glories of Mary, The Assumption*

897 Omnipotentia supplex.

898 Quidquid minimum, dummodo sit constans.

899 Idem ergo mensis, secundam nobis Evam mulierum omnium et pulcherrimam et dignissimam non temere dedit, quae singulari sui conditoris beneficio sic formata et exornata prodiit, ut si humano more loquendum sit laetioribus quidem oculis vivum in terris hominem nunquam aspexerit Deus, in quo post Christum nihil maculae, et plus gratiae veraeque pulchritudinis et amabilitatis deprehenderit (Canisius, *De Maria V. Deipara*, Bk. 1, Ch. 11, p. 75).

900 Cf. Benedict XIV, p. 513, n. 8; Baronius, *Not. ad Martyrol.*, Sept. 8

901 Nullius igitur nativitas celebratur in mundo nisi Christi, et ejus (scilicet B. Mariae), atque B. Joannis, etc. (Ildefonsus, Biblioth. PP., t. 12, p. 566; Walterius, episcop. Aurelian. 118, de Ordinib.; Benedict XIV, p. 513, n. 8).

902 Even to this day, the Fair of the Nativity is called in Brittany the "Fair of Angevine."

903 Cf. Baillet, *Hist de la Nativ.*

904 Cf. Augustine, *in Nativ. B. Joannis Bapt.*—Dicuntur quidem sanctorum festivitates natalitia, et merito; quomodo enim consuete nasci dicitur, cum quis de utero matris procedens in lucem egreditur; ita rectissime potest natus dici, qui a vinculis carnis solutus ad lucem sublimatur aeternam. Et inde mos obtinuit ecclesiasticus, ut dies beatorum martyrum, sive confessorum Christi, quibus de seculo transierunt, natales vocitemus, eorumque solemnia non funebria, sed natalitia dicamus (Rabanus Maurus, *De Institutione Clericorum*, Ch. 43.)—Propterea post celebritatem nativitatis Joannis Baptistae sacratissimam et jucundam, quia sine peccato natus est per sanctificationem, instituit Ecclesia nativitatem beatae et gloriosae semperque Virginis Mariae celebriter fieri, admonita prius miraculo (Gerson, *Sermon, De Nativ. B. Virg.*).

905 Cf. *Summa Theologiae*, III, q. 27, a. 4-5

906 Ambrose, *Concerning Virginity*, Bk. 2, Ch. 2

907 Die quo nata est (B. Virgo) impositum est ei nomen Maria a parentibus secundum angelicam revelationem (Antoninus, Pt. 4, t. 15, Ch. 14).

908 Benedict XIV, p. 519, n. 3

909 St. Gregory of Nyssa, St. John Damascene, St. Germanus of Constantinople, St. Andrew of Crete, and St. Gregory of Nicomedia say that this was at the age of three years. See Benedict XIV, *De Festis*, p. 532, and Canisius, *De Maria V. Deipara*, Bk. 1, Ch. 12.

910 Cf. Bernard. de Busto, *Marian.*, p. 4, Sermon 1

911 Cant 2:16

912 Erat Maria in rebus omnibus honesta et gravis, pauca admodum eaque necessaria loquens, ad audiendum facilis et perquam affabilis, honorem suum et venerationem omnibus exhibens; statura mediocri, quamvis sint qui eam aliquantulum mediocrem longitudinem excessisse dicant. Colore fuit triticum referente, capillo flavo, oculis acribus: subflavas et tanquam olivae colore pupillas in eis habens. Supercilia ei erant inflexa et decenter nigra: nasus longior, labia florida et verborum suavitate plena: facies non rotunda et acuta, sed aliquanto longior, manus simul et digiti longiores. Erat denique fastus omnis expers,

simplex, minimeque vultum fingens, nihil mollitiei secum trahens, sed humilitatem praecellentem colens. Vestimentis quae ipsa gestavit coloris nativi contenta fuit: id quod etiamnum sanctum capitis, ejus velamen ostendit, et ut paucis dicam in rebus ejus omnibus multa divinitus inerat gratia (Epiphanius, *Orat. de Mar.*, apud Canis., Bk. 1, Ch. 13, p. 95).

913 *De Hist. Vit. Mar.*; Canisius, *De Maria V. Deipara*, Bk. 1, Ch. 12

914 Thomassin, Bk. 2, Ch. 20

915 Cf. Benedict XIV, p. 535, n. 8

916 Considerantes in timore castam conversationem vestram (1 Pt 3:2).

917 Salvabitur autem per filiorum generationem, si permanserit in fide, et dilectione et sanctificatione cum sobrietate (1 Tm 2:15).

918 Le Vicomte Walsh, *Tableau poétique des fêtes Chrétiennes*, p. 64

919 M. de Falloux, *Life of St. Pius V*

920 Servorum, latronum, sicariorum seditiosorum supplicium crux erat, cui illae affigebantur, et in ea pendebant, donec fame, siti, doloribus, enecarentur, post mortem suam canum et corvorum relicti cibus. Itaque supplicio illo non aliud apud Romanus infame magis, et acerbum magis (Lamy, *Dissert, de Cruce*, § 1, p. 573; Cf. Lipsius, *de Cruce*, Bk. 1, Ch. 12-13).

921 On the discovery of the cross, see our *Histoire du bon Larron*.

922 Translator's note: Butler's *Lives of the Saints*, St. Helen, Aug. 18.

923 See Godescard. The title of the true cross is in the Church of the Holy Cross of Jerusalem, Rome. See the *Trois Rome*, t. 1.

924 Hujus festivitatis meminit qui paulo post Constantinum vixit Chrysostomus (*Homily 51*, t. 1), quam habuit quarto nonas octobris: "Nondum elapsi sunt dies viginti, ex quo memoriam crucis celebravimus, et ecce martyrum memoriam celebramus" (Benedict XIV, p. 389, n. 10).

925 See St. Ephrem, *Sermon, in Pretios. et Vivif. Crucem Domini*, circa medium.

926 On these never-ending pilgrimages, see *St. Jerome's Letters to Eustochium*, and the *History of Our Lady of Loretto*, by M. Caillau, Ch. 1-2.

927 Cf. Brief *Cum tanta*, August 30th, 1741

928 Cf. *Via Crucis*, p. 118

929 See Bergier, *Dictionnaire de théologie*, art. *Anges*.

930 Their testimonies may be seen in Volume I of the catechism [i.e., Volume X of the Tradivox series, p. 146-164; see also, Volume XI, p. 367-369].

931 Cf. Hilar., *On Psalm 129*; *On Psalm 137*

932 Cf. Baronius, Anno 493

933 See Godescard.

934 1 Cor 12:26

935 See what St. Peter Damian says: *Ita est omnis apostolici culminis beatitudo conjuncta, et tot gratiarum compage vel glutino probatur unita, ut eum unius festivitas colitur, protinus omnium apostolorum non diversa sublimitas interioribus obtutibus ingerator. Una scilicet inter eos excellentia judiciariae potestatis, eadem dignitas ordinis, nec diversa in ligando sive solvendo virtutis habeatur auctoritas* (*Sermon on St. Bartholomew*).

936 Rom 13:7

937 Cf. *Heterot. Spirit.*, p. 4

938 Bernard, *Sermon 12, on Psalm 90*

939 Tb 12:3

940 Ex 23:20-23. See Thomassin, *Des Fêtes*, and Godescard, 2nd October.

941 Mt 5:1-10

942 See a detailed explanation of the beatitudes in our *Traité du Saint-Esprit*, t. 2.

943 Sacrificia pro eis, ut meministis, semper offerimus, quoties martyrum passiones et dies anniversaria commemoratione celebramus (Cyprian, *Epistle 34*).

944 *Jovi ultori.* See, on this building, the *Trois Rome*.

945 Legi in ejus Ecclesiae codice manuscripto, templum illud dicatum imprimis in honorem Genitricis Mariae, omnium sanctorum martyrum et confessorum illataque illuc esse reperi duodetriginta curribus ossa sanctorum martyrum e diversis urbis coemeteriis effosa, solemniterque comportata, ac decentissime collocata (Baronius, *in Not. ad Martyrol.*, 13th May).

946 Tunc monente Gregorio papa et omnibus episcopis assentientibus, Ludovicus imperator statuit ut in Gallia et Germania festivitas omnium sanctorum in Kalendis novembribus celebraretur, quam Romani ex institutione Bonifacii celebrant (Mabillon, *De re diplom.*, p. 537; Reinald, n. 29).

947 Cf. Jas 5:17

948 Cf. Godescard, *Toussaint*

949 Haec sunt vestigia quae Sancti quique in patriam revertentes nobis reliquerunt (Bede, *Sermon 18, de Sanctis*).

950 Qui moritur cum fama sanctitatis (Benedict XIV, *De Beat. et Canon. SS.*, Bk. 1).

951 Cujus sanctitatis fama judiciali fore probata est (ibid.).

952 In quorum Beatificationis et Canonizationis causis commissio introductionis signata est; non signatur enim commissio, nisi judiciale more constiterit, ex processu auctoritate ordinaria confecto, de fama sanctitatis et miraculorum (ibid.).

953 *Beatificatio est alicujus in beatos relatio,* or, as Benedict XIV says, *Beatificationem esse actum quo S. R. Pontifex indulgendo permittit aliquem Dei servorum coli posse in aliqua provincia, dioecesi, civitate, aut religiosa familia, cultu quodam determinato, ac beatorum proprio, usquequo ad solemnem canonizationem deveniatur* (*De Beat. Et Canon. SS.*, Bk. 1, Ch. 39).

The expenses occasioned by beatifications are not very considerable. Alexander VII, when prescribing that beatifications should take place in the Vatican Basilica, fixed the amount of an indemnity to be given to the Chapter of St. Peter's for ornamenting the basilica. We read in Benedict XIV's treatise that this is a most reasonable thing in the eyes of every person acquainted with the financial affairs of the chapter. One can hardly form an idea, adds Benedict XIV, of the consumption of ornaments that takes place, as well on account of the intemperature of the air at the Vatican, as of the great number of Masses that are daily celebrated in the basilica: the supply of these ornaments is charged to the chapter, and not to the building, which is not very rich itself and which has a good many debts.

This offering to the basilica apart, the expenses of beatification are reduced to a little. The tax for the brief is very small: he who reads it is entitled to a reward of fifteen paoli, and no more. The masters of ceremonies and the sacristans of the basilica receive only a very slight reward. The notary of the Congregation of Rites receives three crowns, and no more; the deputy and his companion receive five. Then come, in the scale established by Benedict XIV, a few trifling sums for the Swiss Guard, and the artillerymen who discharge cannon during the beatification.

Benedict XIV proves, with the aid of many facts, that the popes have at all times endeavored to keep down the expenses in cases of canonization: *Romanos Pontifices earum moderationi studuisse ac studere.* They took away most of the excessive and useless expenses that had been gradually and imperceptibly introduced: *Plerasque immodicas ac superfluas, quae paulatim irrepserant, sublatas fuisse.* Nothing was left but what was absolutely necessary to bring beatifications and canonizations to a close: *Expensas utique esse necessarias ad exitum perducendas beatificationum et canonizationum causas.* And these necessary expenses were regulated on scales that should be inviolably observed. He repeats in another place that the charges existing are strictly necessary: *Stricte dicimus necessarias profecto esse in pertractandis atque ad exitum perducendis beatificationum et canonizationum causis expensas.* We see in his work the total amount that certain cases of canonization cost.

There is however one matter on which the Congregation of Rites has made no statute—the fees of postulators: *Nulla porro quoad posse postulatores merces a sacra Congregatione statuta est.* Benedict XIV seems but slightly to approve of the maintaining, at great cost, of a distinguished personage, some canon, to fill the office of postulator, for it is a useless and very considerable expense: *Superfluum...ac magnum sumptum... si viri nobilis, si canonici opera hac in re adhibeatur.* He had occasion, when acting as promoter, to admire the conduct of those who, instead of employing anyone of distinction for this purpose, confided the postulation quite simply to some religious: *Dum promotoris munere fungebar, satis providam quorumdam suspexi oeconomiam, qui aliquem religiosum vel ad Urbem missum, vel in Urbe commorantem negotio praeficientes, subministrata coenobio eleemosyna pro alimoniis, et tenui quadam summa religioso ipsi pro regularibus indigentiis, superfluum hoc pacto, et magnum sumptum evitarunt alioquin necessarium, ut puta, si viri nobilis, si canonici opera hac in re adhibeatur.* There are cases in which the maintenance of postulators ends by forming a very large item in the total of expenses.

954 *Canonizatio est alicujus beati in numerum sanctorum relatio,* or, as Benedict XIV says: *Canonizationem esse S. Pontificis sententiam definitivam, qua decernit aliquem antea inter beatos, recensitum in sanctorum catalogum esse referendum, et coli debere in toto orbe catholico, atque in universa Ecclesia, cultu illo qui caeteris canonizatis praestatur* (Benedict XIV, *De Beat. Et Canon. SS.*, Bk. 1).

955 See Castellinus, Lezana, and Duranti.

956 Cf. Benedict XIV, t. 5, Bk. 1, Ch. 24 and 39, as well as our *Histoire des Catacombes*, in which will be found all details relating to canonization.

957 Cf. *Acta SS. Bened.*, n. 38. See also Ferraris, art. *Cultus Sanctorum*.

958 Ab utilitate sanctos in nostris necessitatibus invocandi, potestas canonizandi causam habet et fundamentum. Unde Banes, in *Summa Theologiae*, II-II, q. 1, a. 10, sic ait: "Haereticum est negare auctoritatem in Ecclesia et Pontifice ad sanctos canonizandos," haereticum enim est dicere sanctos non esse invocandos; ergo auctoritas est in Ecclesia ad sanctos canonizandos (Benedict XIV, Bk. 1, Ch. 3).—Papa errare non potest in canonizatione sanctorum, est de fide; attamen, concludit Benedict XIV (t. 1, Ch. 45), qui contrarium sentiunt, licet non sint formaliter haeretici, ex quo id nondum sit ab apostolica sede expresse definitum, tamen sunt temerarii, impii, scandalosi, in sanctos injuriosi, faventes haereticis, sapientes haeresim, assertores erroneae propositionis et gravissimis poenis obnoxii (Ferraris, art. *Papa*, n. 49).

959 Cf. Benedict XIV, Bk. 1, Ch. 3

960 Cf. Benedict XIV, Bk. 1, Ch. 6. See details and proofs in *l'Histoire des Catacombes*, p. 365 et suiv.

961 See Benedict XIV, Bk. 1, Ch. 3; Ferraris, art. *Cultus Sanctorum*, n. 18.

962 De fama sanctitatis et miraculorum.

963 Cf. Benedict XIV, Bk. 1, Ch. 7

964 Cf. Benedict XIV, Bk. 1, Ch. 24, and *Appendix ad* Ch. 24

965 Cf. Benedict XIV, Bk. 1, Ch. 39

966 Cf. Ibid.

967 Cf. Ibid.

968 On All Saints' day, one may read, with as much pleasure as profit, the 48th chapter of the third book of the *Imitation*; or the 35th chapter of the *Soliloquies of St. Augustine, De desiderio et siti animae ad Deum*.

969 Nevers, in particular.

970 Pro natalitiis annua die facimus (Tertullian, *De Corona Militis*, Ch. 3).

971 Ex majorum traditione pro defunctis annua die facimus (Cf. Tertullian, *De Corona Militis*).

972 Cf. Cyprian, Bk. 1, Epistle 9; Gregory Nazianzen, *Oration 10*

973 Cf. Tertullian, *Exhort. ad Cast.*; Augustine, *Confessions*, Bk. 9, Ch. 13

974 Non sunt praetermittendae supplicationes pro spiritibus mortuorum; quas faciendas pro omnibus in Christiana et catholica societate defunctis, etiam tacitis nominibus quorumcumque sub generali commemoratione suscepit Ecclesia; ut quibus ad ista desunt parentes, aut filii, aut quicumque cognati, vel amici, ab una eis exhibeantur pia matre communi (Augustine, *On the Care of the Dead*, Ch. 4).

975 Augustine, *Sermon 32, De Verbis Apostoli*

976 Cf. Thomassin, *Des Fêtes*

977 We say *institution*, that is, a public and permanent establishment; for, nearly two centuries before the time of Blessed Berno, Amalarius Fortunatus, bishop of Trèves, had composed an office for the dead, which was said in his diocese at the conclusion of the office of All Saints.

978 Venerabilis pater Odilo per omnia monasteria sua constituit generate decretum, ut sicut primo die mensis novembris, juxta universalis Ecclesiae regulam, omnium Sanctorum solemnitas agitur; ita sequenti die in psalmis et eleemosynis et praecipue Missarum solemniis, omnium in Christo quiescentium memoria celebretur, etc. (Peter Damian, *in Vita B, Odil.*; Baronius, Anno 1048, n. 6; *Not. ad Martyrol.*, 2 Nov.; Hélyot, t. 5, etc.).

979 See Volume II, Lesson 20 [i.e., Volume XI of the Tradivox series, p. 119-125].

980 Cf. Jn 5:7

981 *Roman Ritual*

982 See M. Thirat, *Esprit des Cérémonies de l'Eglise*, p. 125.

983 Eusebius, *Ecclesiastical History*, Bk. 10, Ch. 3

984 Eusebius, *Ecclesiastical History*, Bk. 10, Ch. 4

985 X.

986 To mark the perfidy of the Jews, the Hebrew characters are not employed, though Hebrew is one of the three sacred languages.

987 See our *Traité de l'eau bénite*.

988 Apoc 6:9-10

989 Cf. 1 Thes 5

990 See *Roman Pontifical* and *Spirit of Ceremonies.*

991 Cf. Butler, *Dedication*

992 Vidit Deus cuncta quae fecerat, et erant valde bona (Gn 1:31).

993 Cf. Hermias, *Irrisio philosoph.*, p. 15

994 Cicero, *De Divinatione*, Bk. 2, Ch. 58, n. 119

995 Remark of J. J. Rousseau.

996 J. J. Rousseau

997 Condorcet

998 Augustine, *Of the Morals of the Catholic Church*, Ch. 30

999 Cf. Rom 8:18

1000 Mt 6:10

1001 1 Cor 15:28

1002 Cf. Rom 8:19-23.—Creaturae hic sunt coeli, elementa, omniaque creata. Omnes creaturae avidissime naturali appetitu exspectant tempus quo filii Dei gloria donabuntur, ut cum eis quibus servierunt, quasi dominis, ipsae quoque suam gloriam, renovationem ac perfectionem, tanquam famuli accipiant. Sic arbor per appetitum, non rationalem, nec animalem, sed naturalem, dicitur exspectare suum fructum, et semen suam messem. Atque hoc magnum est argumentum, gloriam illam nobis praeparatam, ingentem esse et inaestimabilem; quod omnes creaturae etiam insensibiles totae ad illam anhaelant…Sicut enim nutrix pueri regii, cum puer coronatur, et ipsa propter ipsum de bonis regiis participat: ita pariter, cum homo gloria donabitur, hanc ejus gloriam ceterae creaturae quae homini servierunt, participabunt, inquit Chrysost. in hunc loc…ita ut similem quamdam libertatem, stabilitatem creaturae aliae accipiant (Cornelius a Lapide, *On Romans*, Ch. 8, v. 19).

1003 The opinion that the world will not be annihilated, but changed, bettered, and perfected, is that which is most authorized by fathers and theologians. The scripture itself is most favorable to this view. It says, for example, that "the Lord will make new heavens and a new earth."[a] It does not say "other heavens and another earth"—in order to mark their renovation.[b] When a boy becomes a young man, and from a young man becomes a full-grown man, and from a full-grown man becomes an old man, we do not say that he perishes at these different periods of life: he is always the same man. It is the same when an architect changes an old house into a new one, or a laborer changes a wild heath into a smiling garden.

When the psalmist speaks of the destruction of the heavens, he uses the comparison of a garment that is worn out and changed; but this is very different from being reduced to nothingness.[c] Isaias, describing the state of the world after the resurrection, says that the sun and the moon shall not shine as previously, but with far greater brightness. "The light of the moon," he says, "shall be as the light of the sun, and the light of the sun shall be sevenfold what it is today."[d]

The Savior tells us in the gospel that "heaven and earth shall pass away,"[e] and the apostle tells us that "the fashion" or the appearance "of this world passeth away."[f] They do not tell us that the world, as regards its substance, shall perish, nor that the heavens and the earth shall return into nothingness, but simply that they shall pass from the state in which we now behold them to another more beautiful and more perfect. St. Peter, in the most formal text that we have on this subject, says simply that "the day of the Lord shall come as a thief"; that "the heavens shall pass away with great noise and speed"; that "the elements shall be melted by intense heat"; and that "the earth, with everything in it, shall be burnt."[g] Now, there is nothing here to prove annihilation.

God has revealed the creation of the universe to us, but he has not declared in any place that he will reduce his work to nothingness. We acknowledge that, as he did the one, he could do the other; but we do not see in his scriptures that such is his design. Annihilation itself is a thing that we do not understand.

Solomon assures us that he learned that whatever the Lord had made should remain forever.[h] This is explained very well by St. Gregory the Great, in reconciling the scripture with itself, when he says that on the one hand the earth shall remain forever, and on the other, the heavens and the earth shall pass away: they shall pass away as regards their appearance, but not as regards their essence.[i] And when the scripture speaks of new heavens and a new earth, it does not mean that God will create new ones, but that he will renew the old ones.[j] The same St. Gregory compares this change to what we see occurring every year in the succession of the seasons. Winter follows autumn, and spring follows winter. The earth changes its face at each of these seasons, but it is always the same in its substance.

But no person has expressed himself more clearly on this matter than St. Augustine. The fire that will burn the world at the last day, says this great doctor, will change the qualities of corruptible elements, and those qualities which suit our bodies subject to corruption will be changed into other qualities which will suit our incorruptible bodies: so that the world thus renewed will be in keeping with the nature of risen man.[k] In another place, he says that heaven and earth will be renewed after the judgment; that they will pass away but will not perish.[l] Then, comparing the fire that is to consume the world at the end of time with the waters of the deluge, he draws a parallel between the expressions that the scripture uses in the description of these two great events. In the first, it is said that the world perished; in the second, that the world shall perish. But as we know that by the word *perish* the scripture meant only "an extraordinary change," so when it says that at the close of time the world shall *perish*, it means only that the world shall be changed as regard its qualities, but shall subsist as regards its substance.

St. Epiphanius,[m] Proclus, Methodius, and Oecumenius[n] maintain and prove the same thing. "The earth and the elements," says the last mentioned, "will not be destroyed. In the same manner as we pass metals through fire without intending to destroy them, God will pass the world through fire, but he will not destroy it. He will destroy things that are useful only for this mortal and perishable life, and whatever has no relation to a state of immortality and incorruption, wherein we shall exist after the resurrection of the body; but he will preserve all the rest in a happier and more perfect state, for the ornamentation of that new heaven and that new earth which are promised us, and to contribute to the bliss of the just." As he who builds a house does not build it of nothing, so, after the judgment, God will form new heavens and a new earth out of the matter of the heavens and the earth which exist today, but which he will change into a more perfect state.[o]

[a] Both the old and the new testament say so. See Is 65:17; 66:22; Apoc 21:1.

[b] *Non dixit: Alios coelos et aliam terram videbimus,* says St. Jerome, *sed veteres et antiquos in melius commutatos* (*On Isaias*, Ch. 51, 54).

[c] Ipsi peribunt,...et omnes sicut vestimentum veterascent. Et sicut opertorium mutabis eos (Ps 101:27).

[d] Is 30:26

[e] Mt 24:35; Cf. Mt 5:18

[f] Praeterit figura hujus mundi (1 Cor 7:31).

[g] 2 Pt 3:10

[h] Didici quod omnia opera quae fecit Dominus perseverent in perpetuum (Eccles 3:14).

[i] Per eam quam nunc habent imaginem transeunt, sed tamen per essentiam sine fine subsistunt (Gregory the Great, *Moralia in Job*, Bk. 17, Ch. 9).

[j] Non alia condenda sunt, sed haec ipsa renovantur (ibid.).

[k] Ut scilicet mundus in melius innovatus, apte accommodetur hominibus etiam carne in melius innovatis (Augustine, *City of God*, Bk. 20, Ch. 16).

[l] Mutatione namque rerum, non omni modo interitu, transibit hic mundus...Figura ergo praeterit, non natura (Augustine, *City of God*, Bk. 20, Ch. 14).

[m] Cf. Epiphanius, *Adversus Haeresus*, n. 64

[n] Cf. Oecumenius, *On Second Peter*, Ch. 3

[o] Cyril, *On Isaias*, Bk. 6, Ch. 51

1004 *Innovatio mundi ordinatur ad hoc quod homo etiam sensu in corporibus quodammodo per manifesta indicia divinitatem videat. Inter sensus autem nostros spiritualior est visus et subtilior. Et ideo quantum ad qualitates visivas, quarum principium est lux, oportet omnia corpora inferiora meliorari...Unde omnia elementa claritate quadam vestientur; non tamen aequaliter, sed secundum suum modum...Aer non erit clarus, sicut radios projiciens, sed sicut diaphanum, illuminatum...Terra erit in superficie exteriori pervia sicut vitrum, aqua sicut cristallus, ignis ut luminarii coeli* (*Summa Theologiae*, III-Sup., q. 91, a. 4). The heavens and all the heavenly bodies will experience a like amelioration, and become a thousand times brighter than they are today (Cf. *Summa Theologiae*, III-Sup., q. 91, a. 3).

1005 Cf. Jerome, *On Habacuc*, Ch. 3

1006 What has just been said on the state of the world after the resurrection is not a dogma of faith: it is the opinion most in conformity with holy scripture and most approved by fathers and theologians (Bible de Vence, t. 22).

1007 Ps 16:15

1008 Cf. Apoc 21:10ff. To give us an idea of the reality, St. John makes use of everything most precious with which we are acquainted. Not that we believe the heavenly Jerusalem to be built or adorned with stones and metals of which there is great account made in this world; but the Holy Ghost, to accommodate himself to our dull and gross ideas, does not speak to us of anything else, because we see nothing here more splendid or beautiful (Bellarmine, p. 61).

1009 Oculi, aures, nares, os, manus, guttur, jecur, pulmo, ossa, medullae, etc. beatorum mirabili delectationis et dulcedinis sensu replentur (Anselm, *De Similitudinibus*, Ch. 57).

1010 Cf. Phil 3:21

1011 Mt 13:43

1012 See the History of St. Dorothea in our *Traité du Saint-Esprit*, t. 2 and our work *La vie n, est pas vie.*

1013 Cf. 1 Cor 2:9

1014 Ps 88:2

1015 Ps 45:5

1016 The description of heaven just read is an analysis of the work by the pious and learned cardinal Bellarmine.

1017 Valde mirabilis es, Domino; facies tua plena gratiarum (Père d'Argentan).

1018 Bellarmine, *The Eternal Happiness of the Saints*

1019 Jn 17:23; 1 Jn 3:2

1020 Clarâ cum laude notitiâ.

1021 Cf. *Summa Theologiae*, III-Sup., q. 96

1022 Est 5:3

1023 Mk 6:23

1024 Cf. Dn 2:44; Lk 1:33

1025 Ibi erunt bona corporis et animae, qualia nec oculus vidit, nec auris audivit, nec cor hominis cogitavit. Cur ergo per multa vagaris, homuncio, quaerendo bona animae tuae et corporis tui? Ama unum bonum in quo sunt omnia bona, et sufficit. Quid enim amas, caro mea? Quid desideras, anima mea? Ibi est quidquid amatis, quidquid desideratis. Si delectat pulchritudo fulgebunt justi sicut sol. Si velocitas, aut fortitudo, aut libertas corporis cui nihil obsistere possit, erunt similes angeli Dei; quia seminatur corpus animale, et surget corpus spirituale, potestate utique non natura. Si longa et salubris, vita, ibi sana est aeternitas, et aeterna sanitas; quia justi in perpetuum vivent, et salus justorum a Domino. Si satietas, satiabuntur cum apparuerit gloria Dei. Si ebrietas, inebriabuntur ab ubertate domus Dei. Si melodia, ibi angelorum chori concinunt sine fine Deo. Si quaelibet non immunda, sed munda voluptas, torrente voluptatis suae potabit eos Deus. Si sapientia, ipsa Dei sapientia ostendet eis seipsam. Si amicitia, diligent Deum plus quam seipsos, et invicem tanquam seipsos, et Deus illos plus quam seipsos; quia illi illum, et se, et invicem per illum, et ille se et illos per seipsum. Si concordia, omnibus illis erit una voluntas: quia nulla illis erit nisi sola Dei voluntas. Si potestas, omnipotentes erunt sum voluntatis, ut Deus suae. Nam sicut poterit Deus quod volet per seipsum, ita poterunt illi quod volent per illum; quia sicut illi non aliud volent quam quod ille, ita ille volet quidquid illi volent, et quod ille volet non poterit non esse. Si honor et divitiae, Deus servos suos bonos et fideles supra multa constituet, imo Filii Dei et Dei vocabuntur; et ubi erit Filius, ibi erunt et illi, haeredes quidem Dei, cohaeredes autem Christi. Si vera securitas certa, ita certi erunt numquam et nullatenus ista, vel potius istud bonum sibi defuturum, sicut certi erunt se non sua sponte illud amissuros, nec dilectorem Deum illud dilectoribus suis invitis ablaturum, nec aliquid Deo potentius invitos Deum et illos separaturum. Gaudium vero quale, aut quantum est, ubi tale aut tantum bonum est! Cor humanum, cor indigens, cor expertum aerumnas, imo obrutum aerumnis, quantum gauderes, si his omnibus abundares! (Anselm, *Proslogion*, Ch. 25; Cf. Cornelius a Lapide, *On Apocalypse*, Ch. 22).

1026 1) *Horloge de la Passion*, in-18, 1832; 2) *Du Catholicisme dans l'éducation*, in-8, 1835; 3) *Le grand jour approche*, ou *Lettres sur la première Communion*, in-18, 1835; 4) *Le Seigneur est mon partage*, ou *Lettres sur la persévérance après la première Communion*, in-18,1835; 5) *Manuel des Confesseurs*, 2 vol. in-12, 1836; 6) *Selva, instructions pour les prêtres*, 3 vol. in-18, 1837; 7) *Marie, Etoile de la mer*, in-18, 1837; 8) *Itinéraire de la terre au Ciel*, 2 vol. in-18, 1838; 9) *Catéchisme de persévérance*, 8 vol. in-8,1839; 10) *Abregé du catéchism de persévérance*, in-18, 1839; 11) *Où allons-nous*, in-8, 1844; 12) *Histoire de la société domestique*, ou *Influence du Christianisme sur la famille*, 2 vol. in-8,1844; 13) *l'Europe en 1848*, ou *Considération sur le Christianisme, le Communisme et le Socialisme*, in-8, 1848; 14) le *Ver rongeur des sociétés modernes*, in-8,1851; 15) *Lettre à Mgr. Dupanloup sur le paganisme dans l'éducation*, in-8, 1852; 16) la *Question des Classiques ramenée à sa plus simple expression*, in-12, 1852; 17) *Catholicisme ou Barbarie*, in-8, 1856; 18) *Bibliothèque des Classiques Chrétiens, latins et grecs*, 30 vol. in-12,1852-1856; 19) *Classiques païens expurgés, Poëtes et Prosateurs*, 2 vol. in-12, 1857; 20) la *Révolution, Recherches historiques sur l'origine et la propagation du mal dans l'Europe moderne*, 12 vol. in 8, 1854-1856; 21) *Petit abrégé du Catéchisme de perseverance*, in-18, 1854; 22) *Catéchisme des mères*, in-32, 1855; 23) *Bethléem ou l'Ecole de l'Enfant Jésus*, in-18, 1860; 24) *La Situation, dangers, devoirs, etc., des Catholiques*, in-18, 1860; 25) *Traité du Saint-Esprit*, 2 vol. in-8, 1862; 26) Le *Signe de la Croix au* xixe *siècle*, in-18, 1864; 27) *L'eau bénite au* xixe *siécle*, in-18, 1865; 28) *Credo*, ou *Refuge du Chrétien dans les temps actuels*, in-8, 1867; 29) *Histoire du bon larron*, in-12, 1868; 30) *La Vie n'est pas la vie*, in-18,1869.

1027 Habere jam non potest Deum patrem, qui Ecclesiam non habet matrem (Cyprian, *On the Unity of the Church*, n. 6).

ABOUT THIS SERIES

Tradivox was first conceived as an international research endeavor to recover lost and otherwise little-known Catholic catechetical texts. As the research progressed over several years, the vision began to grow, along with the number of project contributors and a general desire to share these works with a broader audience.

Legally incorporated in 2019, Tradivox has begun the work of carefully remastering and republishing dozens of these catechisms which were once in common and official use in the Church around the world. That effort is embodied in this *Tradivox Catholic Catechism Index*, a multi-volume series restoring artifacts of traditional faith and praxis for a contemporary readership. More about this series and the work of Tradivox can be learned at www.Tradivox.com.

SOPHIA INSTITUTE

Sophia Institute is a nonprofit institution that seeks to nurture the spiritual, moral, and cultural life of souls and to spread the Gospel of Christ in conformity with the authentic teachings of the Roman Catholic Church.

Sophia Institute Press fulfills this mission by offering translations, reprints, and new publications that afford readers a rich source of the enduring wisdom of mankind.

Sophia Institute also operates the popular online resource CatholicExchange.com. *Catholic Exchange* provides world news from a Catholic perspective as well as daily devotionals and articles that will help readers to grow in holiness and live a life consistent with the teachings of the Church.

In 2013, Sophia Institute launched Sophia Institute for Teachers to renew and rebuild Catholic culture through service to Catholic education. With the goal of nurturing the spiritual, moral, and cultural life of souls, and an abiding respect for the role and work of teachers, we strive to provide materials and programs that are at once enlightening to the mind and ennobling to the heart; faithful and complete, as well as useful and practical.

Sophia Institute gratefully recognizes the Solidarity Association for preserving and encouraging the growth of our apostolate over the course of many years. Without their generous and timely support, this book would not be in your hands.

www.SophiaInstitute.com
www.CatholicExchange.com
www.SophiaInstituteforTeachers.org

Sophia Institute Press® is a registered trademark of Sophia Institute.
Sophia Institute is a tax-exempt institution as defined by the
Internal Revenue Code, Section 501(c)(3). Tax ID 22-2548708.